Covering American Politics in the 21st Century

Covering American Politics in the 21st Century

An Encyclopedia of News Media Titans, Trends, and Controversies

VOLUME 1: A–M

LEE BANVILLE

ABC-CLIO™

An Imprint of ABC-CLIO, LLC

Santa Barbara, California • Denver, Colorado

Library of Congress Cataloging-in-Publication Data

Names: Banville, Lee, author.
Title: Covering American politics in the 21st century : an encyclopedia of news media
    titans, trends, and controversies / Lee Banville.
Description: Santa Barbara, California : ABC-CLIO, 2017. | Includes
    bibliographical references.
Identifiers: LCCN 2016020318 (print) | LCCN 2016032715 (ebook) |
    ISBN 9781440835520 (hardback) | ISBN 9781440846472 (vol. 1 : acid-free paper) |
    ISBN 9781440846489 (vol. 2 : acid-free paper) | ISBN 9781440835537 (ebook (set))
Subjects: LCSH: Press and politics—United States—Encyclopedias. | Mass media—
    Political aspects—United States—Encyclopedias.
Classification: LCC PN4888.P6 B36 2017 (print) | LCC PN4888.P6 (ebook) |
    DDC 070.4/49320973—dc23
LC record available at https://lccn.loc.gov/2016020318

ISBN: 978-1-4408-3552-0 (set)
ISBN: 978-1-4408-4647-2 (vol. 1)
ISBN: 978-1-4408-4648-9 (vol. 2)
EISBN: 978-1-4408-3553-7 (set)

21 20 19 18 17   1 2 3 4 5

This book is also available as an eBook.

ABC-CLIO
An Imprint of ABC-CLIO, LLC

ABC-CLIO, LLC
130 Cremona Drive, P.O. Box 1911
Santa Barbara, California 93116-1911
www.abc-clio.com

This book is printed on acid-free paper ∞

Manufactured in the United States of America

To the Big Room,
May you always have snacks.

Contents

CONTENTS   xiii

Guide to Related Topics

BIOGRAPHIES

Ailes, Roger
Beck, Glenn
Block, Herbert (Herblock)
Breitbart, Andrew
Brock, David
Broder, David
Hannity, Sean
Huffington, Arianna
Ifill, Gwen
Jamieson, Kathleen Hall
Koch Brothers: Koch, Charles and
  Koch, David
Krauthammer, Charles
Lehrer, Jim
Limbaugh, Rush
Lippmann, Walter
Maddow, Rachel
Murrow, Edward
Oliver, John
O'Reilly, Bill
Palin, Sarah
Rove, Karl
Russert, Tim
Stone, I.F.
Steffens, Lincoln
Stewart, Jon
Sullivan, Andrew
Tarbell, Ida
White, Theodore
Winchell, Walter
Woodward and Bernstein: Woodward, Bob
  and Bernstein, Carl

CAMPAIGN ORGANIZATION AND STRUCTURE

Advance Teams
Commission on Presidential Debates
Direct Mail Campaigning
Federal Election Commission
Get Out the Vote (GOTV)
News Conferences
Opposition Research
Political Consultants
Rapid Response Teams
Surrogates
Trackers

INTEREST GROUPS AND POLITICAL ORGANIZATIONS

American Enterprise Institute (AEI)
Brookings Institution
Cato Institute
Center for American Progress (CAP)
Center for Public Integrity (CPI)
Congressional and Senate Campaign
  Committees
Conservative Blogosphere
Conservative Think Tanks
Dark Money Groups
Democratic Leadership Council
  (DLC)
Emily's List
Family Research Council
527 Organizations
Heritage Foundation
Leadership PACs
Liberal Blogosphere

MEDIA TRENDS

Aggregation
Anonymous Sources
Audience Fragmentation
Campaign Narratives and Dramatization
Campaign Strategy Coverage
Comedy, Satire, and Politics
Corporate Media Ownership
Data Journalism
Diversity in the Media
Echo Chamber Effect
Fact Checking
Fairness Doctrine
Feeding Frenzy
Horse-Race Journalism
Infotainment
Internet Advertising

Native Advertising
Newspaper Industry
Pack Journalism
Paywalls and the Free Flow of Information
Personalization and the Internet
Political Polarization and the Media
Primary Coverage
Public Interest Obligation
Public Opinion
Trust in Journalism
24-Hour News Cycle
Watchdog Journalism
White House Correspondents' Dinner
White House Press Corps
Women and the News Media

MEDIA TYPES

Alternative Newsmedia
Broadcast Television News
Cable News Networks
Daily Newspapers
Documentary Films

Newsmagazines
Non-Profit Journalism
Political Cartoons
Talk Radio

POLITICAL TRENDS

Access to Candidates
Ballot Access
Ballot Measures
Book Tours
Campaign Finance Reform
Campaign Narratives and Dramatization
Campaign Strategy Coverage
Citizens United
Comedy, Satire, and Politics
Cultural Conservatives
Damage Control
Disclosure
Early Voting
Grassroots Campaigns
Invisible Primary
Issue-Advocacy Advertising
Microtargeting

Negative Advertising
Photo Ops and Optics
Political Parties
Post-Truth Politics
Presidential Debates
Presidential Nominating Conventions
Primary Coverage
Red State-Blue State
Single-Issue Politics
Social Media and Politics
Sound-Bite Politics
Spin
Staging
Tea Party Movement
Television Advertising
Third Party Marginalization

Preface

Trying to explain the changing nature and scope of the shifting intersection between the media and American politics feels a bit like trying to carefully dissect and explain a jet plane in mid-flight. By its very nature, politics and the journalism that surrounds and informs that process are in the midst of the most significant transformation in the modern era, one that is still playing out during the 2016 campaign, when this work was written. To try and capture a sense of the change, I felt it was important to contextualize the issues and players shaping the modern political process by offering a look at the new developments fueled by technology and where they fit into the more than 200-year history of the republic.

To do this, *Covering American Politics in the 21st Century: An Encyclopedia of News Media Titans, Trends, and Controversies* offers more than 200 entries in two volumes. Each entry concludes with "See also" cross-references to other related entries and a bibliography of additional print and electronic information resources. Written for high school students, college undergraduates, and other interested nonspecialist readers, the entries in these volumes are loosely organized around the broad categories identified in the Guide to Related Topics, which will help readers easily and quickly trace related themes and topics across the entries.

Some entries cover the major trends that affect politics and the media. Some of these trends weigh more heavily on one sector than the other, but in some way they influence both. Whole works could be written about changes in the way we communicate and how they have separately affected journalism or the modern political campaign, but the goal of this work is to examine the trends that affect both in some way. These entries can be found listed under "Media Trends" and "Political Trends" in the Guide to Related Topics. An additional series of entries explores the ethical and legal issues within journalism and specifically political reporting and can be found under the "Journalism Ethics and Issues" category in the Guide to Related Topics.

Other elements of the book needed a deeper dive into specific types of organizations, be they think tanks that inform policy, forms of media, or elements of how campaigns are run. The goal here is to examine a specific kind of actor that influences politics and the media and explore how that type of organization functions and how it has changed over time. These categories of entries in the Guide to Related Topics include, on the political side, "Interest Groups and Political Organizations" and "Campaign Organization and Structure," and, on the media side, "Media Types."

Finally, political reporting and the modern world of campaigns are deeply affected by the major organizations that cover politics and supply the information the public consumes on political news, as well as the individuals who have come to play such a major role in the public conversations. Some of these organizations are polling firms, some traditional news outlets, and still others new forms of media and political persuasion. The groups can be found in the "Media Organizations" category of the Guide to Related Topics. For individuals, I sought to capture the people who helped create the modern form of political reporting and campaigning as well as the major voices in the public sphere. These are listed in the "Biographies" category.

Covering American Politics in the 21st Century also contains an Introduction that puts the topic into broad historical context, a Selected Bibliography of quickly accessed important general works in both print and electronic formats, and a detailed subject index to further help access information in the entries. Finally, all entries, except for those carrying a contributing byline, were written by me.

Lee Banville, February 25, 2016

Acknowledgments

Any project this large and this exhaustive (and exhausting) has a lot of people behind it who deserve the credit and to whom I owe much.

First, I need to start with the handful of contributors who helped write this work and who each brought a specialty and skill to their pieces. Michael Wright is a journalist with a fine sense of the narrative and a keen ability to craft a compelling story. I assume in the coming editions he is the kind of reporter for whom I will end up having to write a biography, but was happy to have him help me tackle everything from political cartooning to network news madness. Jule Banville brought her experience as a deputy managing editor of the *Washington City Paper* as well as her own background covering the alternative newsmedia for the Association of Alternative Newsweeklies to her exploration of the role of often-overlooked alt-weeklies to the political reporting landscape. And Jason Begay used his work as a reporter and editor as well as his experience as president of the Native American Journalist Association to help illustrate how the news media has often failed ethnic and racial minorities.

Of course the editors at ABC-CLIO deserve endless praise for working with me to help shape the prose and improve the collection. A special thanks needs to be said to Kevin Hillstrom who approached me with this project and helped me develop the entries (and come up with new ones as late as the end of 2015), and John Wagner for working on the tone and approach of the whole work.

There were also some critical institutions that helped with time and resources. On the time front, I owe a debt to the University of Montana School of Journalism. The school, especially Dennis Swibold and Larry Abramson, supported me through this project and scaled my teaching back a bit so I could tackle the scope of this project. As for resources, I had had wild visions of writing this work at the breweries and coffee shops of Missoula, Montana (of which there are quite a few of both), and nothing even close to that ever occurred. Instead, this book was written in the bowels of the Mike and Maureen Mansfield Library on the campus of the University of Montana. It seems wholly appropriate that I would be down here in a library named after the longest serving Senate majority leader in U.S. history and the man fabled political reporter David Broder once declared the politician he admired the most. I cannot tell you how invaluable the resources of a library are as you try to tell the wide variety of stories contained in this volume, and when I came across something I needed and they did not have, the staff of the library was always ready to go to any length to find it. I cannot ignore the contribution of the good folks at the UC Market who never judged just how much caffeine and how many bagels I purchased and consumed through the writing of this work.

I also need to thank the place that made me a political reporter and helped me become a professor: The *PBS NewsHour* (or *The NewsHour with Jim Lehrer* when I was there). They took a chance on a 22-year-old kid to help start their first digital news effort and for some 14 years I had the pleasure of getting up every day and trying to come up with the most compelling and relevant news I could. They let me launch podcasts and make video players, create Twitter feeds, and cook up crazy Election Day video projects with YouTube.

Finally, I have to thank my family who put up with my moodiness and crankiness while writing. Jule bore the brunt and still speaks to me. And my girls, Kate and Maggie, may be too young to know it, but they helped me step away from the book every day by insisting I play some elaborate pretend game with them.

To all of you and many more, thanks.

Introduction

It was a hell of a party.

That was what I remember of my first political convention. I was 23 and a newly minted member of the venerable PBS program that itself had just been re-minted—the *NewsHour with Jim Lehrer*. Upon joining the staff of the new digital version of the program, the Online NewsHour, I had set out to come up with some sort of project that would justify my attending one or both of the political conventions in 1996. I came up with one, a mix of website user-driven interviews with campaign officials in each location as well as a series of delegate-generated reports about the internal politics of the convention.

I had scored an invite to the biggest political story of the year and it was, literally, a party.

The sun was setting on another frighteningly perfect San Diego day as thousands of journalists strolled along the pedestrian paths of the Embarcadero. There were dozens of restaurants serving free food and beer. There was the Brian Setzer Orchestra playing as dusk settled in. This was just the media party. Sponsored by the still-thriving *San Diego Union-Tribune*, it was a testament to how a political convention was both a huge event and a source of civic and institutional pride. The major paper in the city of the convention always hosted such an event, and much of the real jockeying was to score invites to the best parties to be held that week.

But as great as the party was, it was just about over—or at least on the cusp of major changes.

The changes were everywhere. First of all, I was a reporter for the website of a television program. A website. That alone was a new phenomenon that year. Digital news was just at its beginning with a few large news organizations running their own sites, but they were still largely experimental. That year, the *New York Times* launched its first website. CNN was dominant and MSNBC was a month old. Fox News didn't exist, but it was coming. Still, the web was already rising in prominence. New digital-only publications were popping up—not Gawker or Buzzfeed, but sites like Suck and Salon and search engines like Web Crawler with its happy-looking spider that helped visitors find things on the web. The prototype of Google was still two years off. Looking back two decades later, Slate described the Internet this way: "It's 1996, and you're bored. What do you do? If you're one of the lucky people with an AOL account, you probably do the same thing you'd do in 2009: Go online. Crank up your modem, wait 20 seconds as you log in, and there you are—'Welcome.' You check your mail, then spend a few minutes chatting with your

AOL buddies about which of you has the funniest screen name (you win, pimpodayear94)" (Manjoo 2009).

The typical American with Internet access in 1996 averaged 30 minutes of web surfing a month. It truly was the dawn of the connected age, and most people were still living in the caves. But it was not just the Internet that was still in its infancy. Cell phones were still a luxury, not the norm, and those who had cell phones used them to really just make phone calls. There was no easy way to capture video or photos other than cameras, and broadcasters were still lugging U.S. Postal Service bins filled to overflowing with wide-mouth Betamax tapes. Still, that is not to say that things were not happening fast. While journalists lined the harbor to see Republican nominee Senator Bob Dole arrive with his vice presidential nominee, Internet gossip columnist Matt Drudge had already told us it would be former congressman Jack Kemp. That leak was only the beginning of a profound change in the way people communicate. Digital publishing and the explosion of mobile technology in the early 2000s would alter the news media and the world of political campaigns. Both fields are built on the idea of communicating with audiences—campaigns in hopes of inspiring voters and rallying support and journalists for attracting audiences and informing the public.

What would happen over the next 20 years is nothing short of a revolution. That year the three major campaigns—Ross Perot was running again and received federal matching funds—totaled $239.9 million. That is everyone running in the primary and the general election campaign. The presidential race in 2012 topped $2.14 billion, and that is not even counting the outside money. The average webpage took 30 seconds to load in 1996 and only 14 percent of Americans had Internet access. Now, near-ubiquitous Internet access is in most people's pockets.

You get the point. Things changed and they changed fast.

The political system is still in the middle of transitioning from what it was that night in San Diego in August 1996 to what it will be in a money-soaked, continuously connected world. The American political system has been in constant evolution, but the fundamental changes to communication have affected both that system and the media through which most of us see and understand that system. The bulk of my political reporting career has followed along with those changes, as I struggled to keep up and stay relevant in a digital media world adding new tools and possibilities all the time.

Covering American Politics in the 21st Century is an effort to document the things that appear to be shaping that transition of both journalism and politics and where the two meet. It is really the culmination of 20 years of political reporting, guiding digital news operations, and now teaching media history and modern reporting. Although the pages that follow have a lot (and I mean a lot) of information about the state of the media and politics, there is far more out there than can be captured in one piece of research and writing. Even as I wrote, venerable journals like the *New Republic* struggled to survive and apparently well-funded startups like Al Jazeera America suddenly evaporated. As I worked, a campaign unlike any other unfolded each day, with Donald Trump's 2016 White House run defying many of the long-held assumptions about momentum and negative media coverage. Still, as much as has changed, the American system remains surprisingly resilient in many ways, and so the idea of laying out the key players, the big questions, and the major controversies turned out to be more doable than it felt when I hunkered down to start writing.

You'll notice a lot of suggested readings for this book and that is on purpose. Each of these entries could be a book unto itself, so to the degree possible I have tried to identify sources and starting points for your own exploration of these topics.

As I said, a lot has changed in 20 years. I am no longer a giddy 23-year-old watching Brian Setzer on a balmy August evening as I got ready to head into my first convention, but for all the changes, the excitement of how the system works remains and I hope you'll find it on the pages that follow.

Further Reading

Manjoo, Farhad. 2009. "Jurassic Web." Slate. February 24. Accessed January 14, 2016. http://www.slate.com/articles/technology/technology/2009/02/jurassic_web.html.

ABC NEWS

For decades ABC News was the also-ran of broadcast journalism. Lacking the size and history of NBC and the Edward R. Murrow mystique of CBS, the American Broadcast Company seldom played a major role in covering politics until the late 1970s.

This may be related to its very inception. ABC did not bloom from audience demand or technological innovation. It was born from a government requirement. NBC had been operating two networks—the Blue and the Red. Fearing having only two broadcasters dominate the airwaves, the Federal Communications Commission ordered NBC to shed one. NBC decided to sell off Blue, "traditionally the weaker of the two in programming, audience, and income" (Young and Young 2010). The new broadcast company went on the air in 1943 with fewer affiliates and less big-name talent than its larger colleagues. It was an inferiority complex that would last for more than 30 years. Tom Rosenstiel noted in his book on the political reporting of ABC, "The third of America's two-and-a-half networks, went the line about ABC News. In 1963, when CBS and NBC boasted news budgets of $30 million each, ABC's was $3.5 million" (Rosenstiel 1994, p. 25).

Then came the era of Roone Arledge.

Arledge was tapped in 1977 to take the helm of ABC News. He had already built ABC into a sports powerhouse behind *Monday Night Football* and *Wide World of Sports*, two programs that both tested the technology of television and had built huge audiences for the third broadcast network. Journalists saw the hiring of Arledge as a move to cheapen the editorial content in the quest for ratings. "Our reaction when Roone came in was hostility, suspicion," ABC's Ted Koppel later said. "We saw Roone as something of an interloper" (Carter 2002). But that feeling would melt away as Arledge turned the network's news division around, convincing his bosses to invest more in their reporting and creating new programs that would raise the network to an equal among its peers.

Arledge saw talent as the way to attract the viewer. He wooed Diane Sawyer away from CBS, and scored a coup when he convinced former NBC anchor David Brinkley to jump to ABC to host a weekly political news program, *This Week with David Brinkley*.

Arledge saw opportunities where few others did. He put sports in primetime when no one else would, and it succeeded. While NBC and CBS were focused on comedy and chat shows late in the evening, Arledge saw another opening. When Islamic radicals stormed the American embassy in Iran in 1979, Arledge jumped at the chance to implement the kind of news reporting he wanted by fighting for something he needed—more airtime. As Ted Koppel, the man who would come to anchor the effort, wrote later, "Roone Arledge wanted air. There was no way he could begin to build a first-class news operation without more airtime. ABC wanted him to do for the news division what he'd done for sports, but it wasn't that simple. All the imaginative sports programming for which Arledge was legend—shows like *Wide Worlds of Sports* and *Monday Night Football*—would still be ideas instead of institutions if the network hadn't provided more airtime" (Koppel and Gibson 1996, p. 4). He found that airtime late in the weekday evening and built a program called *America Held Hostage*, which later morphed into *Nightline*. With *Nightline*, *This Week*, and *ABC World News with Peter Jennings*, the network grew to be the most popular broadcast outlet by the late 1980s.

The network would spar with NBC for highest nightly news viewership, ABC often taking strong stands in its political reporting. Ted Koppel and his *Nightline* crew left the 1996 Republican National Convention, saying that "they were bored and had better things to do." Koppel himself remarked that the media had managed until that point not to notice what the conventions had become. "Somehow we have very little trouble the rest of the year seeing through this kind of thing, when Hollywood tries to do it with a movie, or a factory with some new product" (Karabell 1998). Criticized by some as journalistically arrogant, Koppel was unapologetic, saying he would not use limited resources to cover an "infomercial."

ABC News also took a leading role in the emerging DC-centric approach to new media reporting about politics. Before Politico or Twitter, ABC News launched "The Note," a daily political briefing crafted by the political team for the network. "The Note" had a breezy and inside-baseball tone and soon became a must-read for political reporters in the U.S. Capitol.

It became so popular that it came to symbolize a Washington media corps that was growing out of touch with common Americans and was too interested in its own gossip and status. A piece in *Washington Monthly* blasted the service: "Cutesy, creepy, and relentlessly effusive towards the media elite, The Note confirms the old adage that life really is like high school, with The Note filling the role of cheerleader-meets-yearbook editor, keeping tabs on where the cool kids are eating lunch, what they're wearing, and who's having the big party this weekend" (Boehlert 2006). Nevertheless, "The Note" helped ensure that ABC News would continue to play a significant role in political coverage even as the viewership of the broadcast entities continued to dwindle.

See also: Broadcast Television Networks; CBS News; NBC News

Further Reading

Boehlert, Eric. 2006. "Shill Wind." *Washington Monthly*. July/August. Accessed November 25, 2014. http://www.washingtonmonthly.com/features/2006/0607.boehlert.html.

Carter, Bill. 2002. "Roone Arledge, 71, a Force in TV Sports and News, Dies." *New York Times*. December 6. Accessed November 28, 2014. http://www.nytimes.com/2002/12/06/business/roone-arledge-71-a-force-in-tv-sports-and-news-dies.html.

Karabell, Zachary. 1998. "The Rise and Fall of the Televised Political Convention." The Joan Shorenstein Center for Press, Politics and Public Policy. Accessed November 28, 2014. http://shorensteincenter.org/wp-content/uploads/2012/03/d33_karabell.pdf.

Koppel, Ted, and Kyle Gibson. 1996. *Nightline: History in the Making and the Making of Television*. New York: Times Books.

Rosenstiel, Tom. 1994. *Strange Bedfellows: How Television and the Presidential Candidates Changed American Politics, 1992*. New York: Hyperion Books.

Young, William, and Nancy Young. 2010. *World War II and the Postwar Years in America: A Historical and Cultural Encyclopedia*. Santa Barbara, CA: ABC-CLIO.

ACCESS TO CANDIDATES

As professional campaign staffs sought to control more closely the messaging and coverage of their candidates and the number of media covering political campaigns swelled, reporters covering candidates saw the amount of times they could interview and even interact with candidates slowly dwindle. This effort to control access and limit potentially damaging unplanned questions or answers makes sense from a campaign perspective, where any slip by a candidate or unplanned outburst can cause real damage to their electoral chances. Critics argue that the current highly controlled access to candidates and campaign workers stunts the amount and quality of information voters receive about candidates and their positions. They also claim that reporters' frustration over access contributes to the combativeness between the press and campaigns.

As political power in this country shifted from local and state party officials directly to voters, the importance of the media in how campaigns communicated to supporters became increasingly important. No longer was it enough to get certain internal factions within party leadership to support your candidate; campaign officials now needed to mobilize and inspire large swaths of voters in diverse geographic areas to donate money, volunteer time and, most importantly, get out and vote in a primary or on election day. This newfound importance of the media to the candidate was coupled with journalists' interest in covering the election and more specifically, the internal workings of the campaign. Campaigns and parties soon began working with the press to curry favor and win more positive coverage. This included supplying reporters with press releases that summarized key developments in the campaign and granting reporters interviews with the candidate or senior party official. This strategy amounted to the beginning of "news management," whereby press relations personnel would seek to control the message and tone of stories coming out of news organizations. By crafting statements and prepping candidates to stick to constructed messages, campaign staff strove to ensure that press coverage would reflect the story the agency or campaign wished to send out. This system is built on the idea that controlling the media message will in turn control public opinion on a matter—a contention that is hardly universally accepted. From its outset, it fostered tension between the public relations teams and the press that they sought to manage. The two sides are often portrayed in this arrangement as locked in battle. One tome on political communications contends that in this setup, "Journalists argue that they do not fight political communicators, they simply fight to get at the truth on behalf of the public. Politicians often offer the rebuttal that, without the gatekeepers, agenda-setters and media biases, they would be able to present their case to the public in the way the public would want. It is because of this that some talk of a vicious circle existing, in which media, politics and the public are all unwittingly embroiled" (Lilleker 2006). This tension has existed in the American system dating back at least a century. Consider Theodore Roosevelt's efforts to foster relationships with reform-minded journalists like Lincoln Steffens and David Graham Phillips. Roosevelt sought these reporters' support for his efforts to spur Progressive reforms, but their reporting did not always adhere to his efforts. Phillips even wrote a scathing series called "The Treason of the Senate" that highlighted the corruption of senators including friends of TR. The president then lashed out at the same reporters, labeling them muckrakers who were more interested in reporting on the filth than in improving the country. Although the term "muckraker" became a badge of honor for many journalists, its actual use highlights how even by the dawn of the twentieth century the efforts to court and influence the press could lead to deep divisions between politicians and the press.

This divide, between those that seek to influence the public through the media and a media that chafes at attempts to be managed, would become more complicated and nuanced as the interests of the press expanded from simply covering a campaign's events and speeches to exploring the tactics and strategy of the campaign itself. If pressed to decide on a moment at which the press developed this interest in tactics and strategy, a good one would be the publication of *The Making of the President* in 1961. Theodore White's seminal work on presidential politics put readers inside the campaign, allowing them to watch political drama unfold between Senator John F. Kennedy and Vice President Richard Nixon. The book offered compelling insights into how campaigns worked and allowed people to be there with Kennedy while he stumped for votes in hostile parts of Wisconsin ahead of the Democratic Party primary in the state. White recounted one day spent with Kennedy, writing:

> At noon he stood at the head of the street in the one-street village of Phillips and looked down its length and saw no one; he entered its hardboard factory and spoke to the workers on the line, who grunted and let him pass; he visited the local newspaper, which was totally indifferent to the fact that a Presidential candidate was pausing with them; he circulated the cafes of Phillips' main street, courteously saying, 'My name is John Kennedy, I'm running for President in the primary'; and they went right on eating. He left town shortly after noon and the town was as careless of his presence as of a cold wind passing through. (White 1961)

White's work, a bestseller among the public, had an even more profound effect on political reporters, many of whose sense of storytelling was drawn to a more narrative and nuanced tale of personal drama and political strategy. White would turn his tales of campaigns into regular public fodder, and political reporters were soon emulating the style and the focus on an insider's view of the campaign. This style of reporting required something new of political reporters. It was no longer enough simply to attend the day's campaign events, and write an effective synopsis of what was said and how big the crowds were and how much they reacted. Now, an effective campaign reporter needed to have access to the inner workings of the campaign. They should get leaked the latest poll numbers. They should have spent time with the candidate on the stump. They should know what ads are in the works before they appear on local television. At a minimum, they should be able to take a day's speech and be able to explain to readers or viewers what was said and how it is a part of the campaign's strategy to reach out to this group, or address this claim by their opponent, or bolster this policy weak spot.

This form of reporting pressed journalists to gain access to more than just campaign press releases. Over the next decades, the relationship between the press and campaigns evolved. Campaigns would actively choose to bring certain reporters into the fold to know about critical developments. These reporters would be trusted with embargoed information or background information that would only be quoted anonymously. The campaigns needed these key press people to get their message out, and they used the insider access they gave to the reporter as leverage. If the reporter went too far outside the information the campaign wanted out, he or she could lose that hallowed place. Rarely stated overtly, this threat hung in the air as a sort of Sword of Damocles that reporters knew could fall at any time.

In recent years, as the press became only one of many ways government officials and candidates could reach the public, the relationship began to change again. Social media allowed candidates suddenly to reach millions of likely supporters with 140 characters at any time. Media operations became more numerous and often more partisan as cable networks and blogs sought narrowly construed audiences that may inherently support or oppose a politician or policy. These outlets were more safely predictable and therefore preferable to investigative news outlets or journalists who sought to remain politically neutral. This inability by the press to demand access to the halls of power is probably best illustrated by President Barack Obama and his relationship with the White House press corps. Obama came into office promising the most transparent administration in modern history, but little of that transparency focuses on communicating with the press. A 2015 survey of the credentialed White House correspondents found that 80 percent of the reporters had never interviewed the president one-on-one or in a small group just from the journalist's news organization. In the same survey, 58 percent of the correspondents said they had interviewed no one who did not work in the press office in the past week—even off the record or on background (Politico 2015).

Many in the political establishment say this reality is the result not of a shift in the power of the press, but in the behavior and interests of the journalists themselves. Politicians accuse the press of being more interested in scandal and fights than in facts and governing. They argue that the press will seek to cast every political story in a partisan light, highlighting negative comments over positive ones and focusing on divisive issues rather than those that cross party lines. For these politicians, journalists' demands for access is ridiculous as giving them access will not help get the message out, or even govern effectively. Former presidential candidate and Democratic Party Chairman Howard Dean told Politico, "The inside-the-Beltway press is just the worst. There's too much reliance on unnamed sources, which are unreliable and can't be evaluated by the reader. And the willingness to engage in pack journalism is just appalling. My advice to the press is to remember that you're an important part of government and democracy, and act like it. You can't blame Hillary or Obama for going into the foxhole or managing the press—which drives them crazy. The reason they have a bad relationship with the press is that the press asks for it" (Ralph and Slattery 2015). Many campaigns and political communications professionals have deprioritized granting access to candidates and surrogates, with the result being a press increasingly frustrated with their inability to get anyone to talk about policy or political decisions.

A few candidates have sought to change this contentious and heavily controlled dynamic. These candidates often are mounting insurgency campaigns, attempting to unsettle a party favorite who is dominating the campaign headlines. Consider the 2000 campaign of Senator John McCain. McCain was seen as a maverick Republican. A solidly conservative candidate, he was known for bucking the political establishment when he felt they were unwilling to address real problems or playing partisan politics. McCain had built a name for himself by being aggressive in calls for campaign finance reform and working with Democrats to craft moderate solutions to some problems. When he ran in 1999 and 2000 the Republican front-runner was former Texas governor George W. Bush. McCain launched a low-key (and inexpensive) bus tour to try and build momentum for his candidacy. Central to his strategy was to bring the journalists onto his campaign bus and to answer whatever questions they may have about his campaign or certain issues. He paired this strategy with dozens of town hall meetings, especially in the critical early state of New Hampshire. But the bus—the "Straight Talk Express"—captured the imagination of the press. Friend and long-time Republican senator Warren Rudman said, "I've traveled on that bus. Several of the people here have traveled on that bus. It's remarkable—unprecedented access—not mealy-mouthed campaign bite answers. Ask a question, get an answer. But most of all, the press has watched him at 114 town meetings in New Hampshire answer every question and they've respected this guy and they like him . . . This goes beyond politics. This goes back to the Kennedy era of the American people suddenly having their minds and hearts captured by an insurgent candidacy, almost like Ronald Reagan did to Gerry Ford in 1976. So that's the reason, nothing to do with liberal-conservative. It has to do with access. It has to do with openness, it has to do with the candidate himself" (Smith 2000).

McCain would go on to win the New Hampshire primary and then lose the nomination. However, the idea of the insurgent candidate willing to embrace access, when so many campaigns are closing the door, speaks to one of the key things to remember about the relationship of the press and politicians: saying yes to an interview or calling a reporter back quickly can have a profound impact on the final piece. Consider the high-pressure world of the modern journalist who must not just craft the story, research the facts, and check for additional sources, but must also tweet out the latest discoveries or do a quick interview for cable news or their publication's website. They must constantly feed the social media outlets while drafting their reporting under tight deadlines. Into this reality, the question of who will grant reporter access by answering a question or responding to a development takes on increased importance. In a lengthy essay about the real biases of journalists, culture writer and reporter Chuck Klosterman aimed to explain the power of access. Klosterman noted that many people fear the political biases of the media and agreed that the corporations that run the media are largely conservative and the reporters that work for the media are largely liberal, but this does not really manifest itself in the reporting. Access, on the other hand, is a powerful component of what ends up on the air or in the newspaper. Klosterman notes, "Since journalism is founded on the premise that reality can only be shown through other people's statements, reporters are constantly placing phone calls to multiple sources with the hope that all of them (or at least one of them) will give the obligatory quotes the writer can turn into a narrative. That's why the first person who happens to return a reporter's phone message dictates whatever becomes the 'final truth' of any story . . . even when everyone else does call back before deadline, the template has already been set by whoever got there first; from now on, every question the reporter asks will be colored by whatever was learned from the initial source. Is it bad? Yes . . . But it's not an agenda. It's timing" (Klosterman 2003).

This element of access is important for both sources and the public to understand. Journalists depend on sources to tell them what is going on and to offer context. Who those sources are and how open people are to being those sources is a critical, if apparently mundane, aspect of how effective and accurate the reporting will be. As access becomes more highly managed and information more scripted, the public is potentially the victim of political communicators more focused on controlling the message than its accuracy and a press more bent on proving their freedom from that control than the usefulness of the information.

An important, but somewhat different, question of access has to do with whether voters have access to the reporting that is generated by this contentious process. Counterintuitively in a world of widespread WiFi, information, and ubiquitous social media, scholars and journalists worry that the continued decline of newspaper readership and the shaky quality of local television news could be harming people's understanding of issues at both the national and local levels. One study out of Princeton University noted that a person's understanding of local political information took a serious hit when they no longer subscribed to the local newspaper. The same study noted that Internet access helped improve a person's score somewhat, but the underlying troubles of local newspapers could make that improvement moot, writing, "As these newspapers falter and perhaps even fail, it is realistic to wonder where citizens will get LPI [local political information]. Without such information, they will certainly struggle to be knowledgeable about their communities . . . the problem wrought by increasing media access is not limited to only citizens who opt for non-local content: their choices lead to a spiral that may result in a decline in local choices for all citizens" (Shaker 2009).

A desire and need for access to informed sources, mixed with a press's interest in fostering an insider view of campaigns, means that more reporters covering a debate or a campaign may not lead to more or better information—especially considering the mixed picture regarding the public's ability to access truth and informative information about political issues at all levels. Combat between source and reporter, both jockeying for more control over the story and its component parts, seems to be an innate part of the modern political reporting process.

See also: Campaign Strategy Coverage; News Conferences; Photo Ops and Optics; Political Bias and the Media; Spin; Staging; White, Theodore

Further Reading
Klosterman, Chuck. 2003. *Sex, Drugs, and Cocoa Puffs*. New York: Scribner.
Lilleker, Darren. 2006. *Key Concepts in Political Communication*. London: Sage Publications.
Ralph, Elizabeth, and Margaret Slattery. 2015. "Why Politicians Hate the Press." *Politico Magazine*. May/June. Accessed September 21, 2015. http://www.politico.com/magazine/story/2015/04/why-politicians-hate-the-press-117142.
Shaker, Lee. 2009. "Citizens' Local Political Knowledge and the Role of Media Access." *Journalism & Mass Communication Quarterly* 86 (4).
Smith, Terence. 2000. "John McCain: Media Darling?" PBS NewsHour. February 14. Accessed September 21, 2015. http://www.pbs.org/newshour/bb/media-jan-june00-mccain_2-14.
"The Truth about Covering Obama." Politico. April 22, 2015. Accessed September 20, 2015. http://www.politico.com/magazine/story/2015/04/white-house-correspondents-survey-117140#.VTqSeSFVhBc.
White, Theodore. 1961. *Making of the President 1960*. New York: Atheneum Publishers.

ADVANCE TEAMS

Advance teams are campaign staff devoted to organizing events and their coverage in the media. These political professionals are charged with everything from the logistics of venues and transportation to the prepping of media and planning for the photos and video the event will generate. The work includes designing the look and feel of the event for those who will attend it, but more importantly, the advance team spends much of its time focusing on how the final speech or voter interaction will look on television or in photos.

The idea of pre-organization and planning is not particularly new in campaigns. As long as candidates have gone out and made appearances on the campaign trail, candidates have sent staffers ahead to gauge the effectiveness of an appearance, and to ensure the critical local officials were there and the right talking points made it back to the candidate. As early as the 1968 campaign, the "advance man" had become a fixture of presidential campaigns. That year *Time* magazine profiled Kingsley Hopkins Murphy, who had spent that year working for beleaguered vice president Hubert Humphrey as the Democrat waged his losing campaign against Richard Nixon. In starting the profile, the magazine wanted its readers to know, "There is no such thing as a spontaneous campaign appearance. Every candidate has his advance men, the harried unsung experts who go from town to town to make as sure as humanly possible that the crowds will be out, the schedule smooth, the publicity favorable" (Danforth 1968). Murphy called it "running the traps" so that the campaign and the candidate knew what lay ahead of a campaign trip. The goal of these early advance teams was to ensure that nothing surprised the candidate when they appeared in the town.

The advance team would meet with local officials, organize the location and decide on the timing of an event, and then pitch it to the media. As the campaigns became more sophisticated and the audience of these events shifted more to the media and away from the actual local voters, the advance team's responsibilities grew into framing the venue and shaping the talking points the campaign wanted on the news that night. As one scholar of the modern campaign put it, the advance team's "responsibility is to ensure that the event happens without a hitch and that the candidate's message is presented to an adequately prepared press corps, ready to include the day's sound bite in their story or on the evening news" (Polsby 2012). This effort involves multiple elements, including staging the event at a location that helps contextualize the message visually (say, holding a jobs speech on a factory assembly line), finding and vetting local supporters who may be allowed to ask questions or provide a human face to some element of the candidate's speech, and briefing the media about the campaign's talking points ahead of time to hopefully influence the direction of the reporting. Each of these elements reflects the way in which the media has infiltrated and changed the way candidates actually campaign. No longer is stumping for votes outside a diner simply about meeting an individual voter and convincing him or her to back the candidate. Instead these meetings are intended to be captured and distributed by the media to a far larger audience. Even in early states like Iowa and New Hampshire where voters often expect to meet and talk personally with candidates, campaign events are staged to provide the television cameras and photographers with the backdrop the campaign seeks to project. Hay bales are trucked in and set up to convey a rural aesthetic. Factory workers are dressed appropriately and positioned on the podium to be in the frame. Local officials are invited and prepped with how they will introduce the candidate. Especially on well-funded presidential campaigns, little to nothing is left to chance.

Advance teams are not limited to presidential races. Statewide campaigns and most congressional contests will usually have organized advance teams to work to create events. As they have become fixtures of campaigns of assorted sizes, advance man or woman has become one of the first jobs new political professionals will land on a campaign. The advance team members have to be highly organized and detail-oriented, and understand the goals of the campaign, but they don't deal with more sensitive jobs such as shaping the message, dealing with crises, or directing the campaign. As one guide to landing a first job on a campaign explained, "Advance work involves lots of travel; you could be on the road twenty days out of the month on a national or statewide campaign. This work is less sensitive and is more likely to go to campaign novices who exhibit independence, self-confidence, imagination, and good judgment" (Kelly and Levitt 2007). These hires are intended to execute the message and plan someone else developed.

Despite this entry-level quality to the job, on larger campaigns the advance team approaches military-style precision and organizing. Take, for example, the description of what the campaign of Republican candidate Mitt Romney did simply to choose the time for a rally to start. The *New York Times*, which spent a day and a half with the advance team as they planned an Ohio rally during the 2012 presidential campaign, described how "nearly two dozen lights were set, illuminating banners, flags and the square itself for the rally on Oct. 12. The day before, aides had taken photos of the site every 15 minutes as day dwindled to night, ensuring that Mr. Romney would take the stage—and cameras would click—at the proverbial golden hour" (Parker 2012). This focus on the visual speaks to the power of the media to shape what a campaign does. The advance team still must "run the traps" that Murphy discussed in 1968 to avoid a logistical error or candidate misstep, but the larger job now focuses on the way most people will ever see the event—through the lens of the evening news video camera or in a photo captured, ideally, during the golden hour.

Campaigns take this work seriously, and those who advise campaigns on strategy and tactics are quick to stress the importance of these staffers. Finding the right group who can plan the event to the minute and still be able to respond to events on the ground or schedule problems is seen as a critical element of a campaign of just about any size. The trade magazine of the political professional, *Campaigns & Elections*, stressed that campaign senior staff should "think of your advance staff and volunteers as special forces sent to conduct reconnaissance before a military operation. They are on the scene early, and are able to convey key information about the event to the candidate and traveling staff, such as any unexpected VIP arrivals or other candidates in attendance, issues with the venue, or changes to the format" (Chassé 2011).

See also: Campaign Strategy Coverage; Photo Ops and Optics; Staging

Further Reading

Chassé, Amelia. 2011. "Winning the Advance Game." *Campaigns & Elections*. October 16. Accessed July 14, 2015. http://www.campaignsandelections.com/campaign-insider/799/winning-the-advance-game.

Danforth, Ken. 1968. "The Campaign: Dodging the Dragon's Tail: The Advance Man's Work." *Time Magazine*. October 25. Accessed July 15, 2015. http://content.time.com/time/magazine/article/0,9171,900380,00.html.

Kelly, Sharon, and Justin Levitt. 2007. "One State, Two State, Red State, Blue State: A Quick Guide to Working on Political Campaigns." Harvard Law School. Accessed July 15, 2015. http://www.law.harvard.edu/current/careers/opia/toolkit/guides/documents/guide-campaign.pdf.

Parker, Ashley. 2012. "Romney Advance Team Works Every Angle in Pursuit of Visual Perfection." *New York Times*. November 1. Accessed July 14, 2015. http://www.nytimes.com/2012/11/02/us/politics/romneys-advance-team-tirelessly-pursues-perfection.html?_r=0.

Polsby, Nelson. 2012. *Presidential Elections: Strategies and Structures of American Politics*. Lanham, MD: Rowman & Littlefield Publishers.

ADVOCACY JOURNALISM

Often mixed with the idea of bias and cast against the ideal of journalistic objectivity, advocacy journalism has usually received a bad rap as mixing partisan or policy goals with the journalistic form. Although historically used in a derogatory way to describe reporting and editorializing that argues for a specific policy or party, advocacy journalism has a long history in the United States. It has become more a part of the mainstream media as audience fragmentation has helped spur increasingly partisan news outlets and greater diversity in news organizations.

Advocacy journalism intersects with political reporting in innumerable ways, from injecting issues into the public sphere for debate by politicians and voters to serving as a de facto organizer and promoter for political causes. This process has been part and parcel of the American media's relationship with politics since before there was a United States. Samuel Adams, who had become a vocal critic of the British presence in the American colonies, saw the newspaper as one of his most powerful weapons against the British. To use it he developed one of the first pieces of advocacy journalism in the New World, launching the *Journal of Occurrences* in the 1768 as British troop levels increased. The *Journal* was not so much a newspaper, but rather what one would call today a syndicated column that ran in established newspapers in New York and elsewhere. The column was one of the first editorial features to chronicle daily events, and it did so with salacious detail while dripping with anti-British venom. A historian of the time emphasized how Adams and others used this new journalistic tool to subtly argue larger political points, noting, "Adams and the other 'Journal' authors used it to illustrate a theme Samuel emphasized in other essays: standing armies threatened a people's basic liberties . . . Many soldiers lacked morals; many were criminals. The theme of criminality, buttressed by examples from New York as well as Boston, highlighted the soldiers' depravity. Accounts of rapes and attempted rapes appeared with regularity" (Alexander 2004). Later evidence indicated many of Adams's most explosive accusations were either exaggerated or completely fabricated, but the core message that the British military presence was evil caught fire in many future revolutionaries through these writings. Because of its effectiveness, the *Journal of Occurrences* highlights a persistent fear that has pervaded advocacy journalism: How can the writer be taken seriously if it is known at the end of the report their goal is not simply to inform but to persuade? Adams highlights the danger that in the name of the larger cause the advocacy journalist may be tempted to exaggerate for effect, to make a stronger point.

Early American newspapers did not worry about questions of impartiality or objectivity, instead embracing their role of political advocacy. Most media in America were expressly connected to either the Federalist or Anti-federalist parties and took to their pages to advocate for specific policies. None of the newspapers at this time employed reporters to go out and document the day's events, cover the new Congress, or convey the public a sense of the critical developments in the world. Instead, these newspapers served as political newsletters, publishing op-ed columns about political debates of the day and generally reaching only those active in the party or politics in a given community. In this construction of journalism, advocacy wasn't simply an extension of its mission, it was the whole mission.

As the newspaper industry moved from being a tool of political parties and elites to an advertising platform that sought the widest possible audience, its role shifted toward a more objective form of journalism. Newspapers found that downplaying explicit political advocacy in favor of a more basic "what happened today" approach to the news could attract more readers by not alienating those who had one partisan view or another. This development, mainly in the 1830s and 1840s, created the modern newspaper; most stories on the front page sought to attract the most readers, and expressed advocacy moved into a new section of editorials and opinion columns. These newspapers and their publishers still conducted bouts of advocacy reporting—such as William Randolph Hearst's anti-Spain reporting that helped spur the Spanish-American War—but by the emergence of the *New York Times* and other more balanced newspapers, that form of advocacy appeared to be waning. In its place grew a focus on objectivity and impartiality.

This newfound focus on objectivity became a sort of religion of modern journalism, espoused by an increasingly professional class of reporters and editors who saw their role as serving the public good. Journalists and thinkers like Walter Lippmann argued that objectivity would help supply the public with the facts that they need to make informed decisions about their world and their governments. To be sure, Lippmann did not argue that journalists needed to forego having their own opinions, but argued that those opinions should not shape the news. He preferred that the reporting process itself should be objective, seeking information from all sides of a debate. Lippmann described the process as ensuring reporters would have "victories over superstitions of the mind" (Berry 2005).

But the goal of objectivity and impartiality became more about the reporters themselves and less about the reporting process. Reporters increasingly sought to maintain a public position of neutrality on political issues. Some like broadcast's Jim Lehrer pointedly did not vote, for fear that this act would compromise their ability to report objectively on those elected officials later on. But others pushed back against this form of impartiality, claiming that it was unnecessary and could actually impair the news organization's ability to document the truth. One of those was perhaps the most influential magazine publisher in American history—*Time's* Henry Luce. Luce, who dubbed the twentieth century "The American Century," was an active member of the Republican Party and at one time is said to have held ambitions to be U.S. Secretary of State. Luce rejected this concept of objectivity, once telling his magazine's sales staff, "[*Time*] is attacked with equal or slightly varying bitterness for being pro and con the same thing. What is most of all amazing about this reputation is that never, at least to my knowledge and consent, did *Time* ever claim impartiality. *Time's* character is that *Time* will tell—will tell the truth about what happened, the truth as it sees it. Impartiality is often an impediment to the truth. *Time* will not allow the stuffed dummy of impartiality to stand in the way of telling the truth as it sees it" (Galison 2015).

Luce's argument is repeated by many inside and outside of journalism as the main problem with the objective approach to reporting. If journalists are too interested in maintaining the label of "objective," they may seek comments and sources from multiple sides of an argument even if those sides do not possess equal merit. (For example, for years news organizations made the source and legitimacy of global warming a political debate, offering each side—one maintaining mankind is contributing to worldwide increases in temperature and one arguing they do not—equal access to the media. Those scientists who have studied the matter almost exclusively line up on the side of those who connect human activity to the warming trend, and yet the insistence on objective reporting has allowed global warming deniers, politicians included, to continue to make their case.)

Environmental concerns, the Watergate scandal, and the Vietnam War brought a series of challenges to the country and to journalism in the 1960s and 1970s that helped spark a new wave of advocacy journalism. Widespread corruption that led to the resignation of President Nixon, and the disparity between official statements and the reported reality in Vietnam, inspired some journalists to move away from the objective ideal to a more overt skepticism. Some, like famous investigative reporter I.F. Stone, started from a basic idea—"All governments lie." This was sometimes reinterpreted to be all institutions—government, business, even the mainstream media—and therefore pretending to be impartial about this and allowing them to lie was unacceptable. Advocacy journalism itself started to fracture. To some, advocacy journalism means arguing for a specific policy or candidate. Others argue that investigative reporting that concludes the government is failing to address an issue is an act of advocacy.

Perhaps the most recent and crystallizing incident involving advocacy journalism erupted on the pages of the *Guardian* in 2013. That year, the British newspaper and international news site published a story detailing the massive high tech surveillance operation run by the National Security Agency. The reporting was based on documents leaked by former NSA contractor Edward Snowden. Snowden chose to work with two advocacy journalists—writer Glenn Greenwald and filmmaker Laura Poitras—who both had a track record of arguing against government surveillance and skepticism about the behavior of the government. Snowden approached these two because he knew they were sympathetic, as opposed to approaching a more "objective" journalist. Greenwald was not quiet in his thoughts about the implications of the reporting he and others would start doing based on the Snowden documents, writing a week after the first disclosures, "How can anyone think that it's remotely healthy in a democracy to have the NSA building a massive spying apparatus about which even members of Congress, including Senators on the Homeland Security Committee, are totally ignorant and find 'astounding' when they learn of them? . . . Put another way, how can anyone contest the value and justifiability of the stories that we were able to publish as a result of Edward Snowden's whistleblowing: stories that informed the American public—including even the US Congress—about these incredibly consequential programs? What kind of person would think that it would be preferable to remain in the dark—totally ignorant—about them?" (Greenwald 2013). The answer, it turned out, was some fellow journalists as well as many members of the public questioned the disclosure of the programs Greenwald documented and others questioned the concept that these programs ought to be overseen by Congress. Some, like the *New York Times*'s Aaron Sorkin, went so far as to say Greenwald should be jailed for working with Snowden and being a clear opponent of the program. Sorkin apologized, saying he had strayed into hyperbole, but the underlying gulf between reporters who see themselves as documenting the world and those who see themselves as agents of changing it remains deeply felt. Some, like journalist Matt Taibbi, reject the whole idea of objectivity, using the Snowden story to make a larger point about the practice of journalism. Taibbi wrote simply that "*all* journalism is advocacy journalism. No matter how it's presented, every report by every reporter advances someone's point of view. The advocacy can be hidden, as it is in the monotone narration of a news anchor for a big network like CBS or NBC (where the biases of advertisers and corporate backers like GE are disguised in a thousand subtle ways), or it can be out in the open, as it proudly is with Greenwald" (Taibbi 2013).

Viewed through this lens, all reporters and all news organizations have an agenda, and news organizations that claim they approach stories with an open mind are simply fooling themselves or their readers. However, many journalists still claim they can approach a story objectively. They do not claim to hold no opinions on the story, but rather that they do not possess the clarity of knowing they are right. A persistent criticism heard about Greenwald is not that his reporting is flawed, but rather that he resisted considering evidence on the other side. One investigative reporter took to the British *Telegraph* to note that Greenwald is "an unabashed polemicist—absolutely open about the fact he's going to show you his side, and will pour scorn on any reasonable explanations the other side offers. That's fine if you're a trial lawyer, or an opinion writer—you want them to put forward a challenging opinion, a slanted version of the facts. However, I often feel when reading a Greenwald article there are valid explanations for some of the things he's reporting on, but that's often hidden behind his apparent loathing of the West in general, and the U.S. in particular" (Foxton 2013).

This concern that some advocacy journalists are unwilling to consider alternative versions of their reality can begin to weigh on their reporting. For example, before the *Guardian* would run his original reporting back in 2013 they dispatched a second, more seasoned editor to meet with Snowden and confirm the story Greenwald had. Greenwald even later said that the *Guardian's* demands to confirm information and seek official comment were slowing things too much, telling *The New Yorker*, "I was getting really frustrated . . . I was putting a lot of pressure on them and insinuating that I was going to go publish elsewhere" (Auletta 2013). Greenwald, who was employed as a blogger, eventually left the *Guardian* at the end of that historic year and launched his own enterprise—The Intercept. The digital news source is built around investigative reporting on surveillance and government abuses and advocates on behalf of whistleblowers. In many ways, The Intercept is in the tradition of I.F. Stone's newsletter of the 1950s and 1960s, aiming to investigate without the institutional constraints that major news organizations place on traditional journalists.

Even as Greenwald's new venture reports on NSA and other high tech privacy matters, the debate rages within journalism about objectivity versus advocacy. Some have sought a new approach to reporting that tries to take advantage of the impartiality of traditional reporting while cutting through the he said-she said of shallow objectivity. The Associated Press has sought to recast its reporting as "accountability" journalism, aiming skepticism toward official actions of governments and institutions but not proposing solutions or advocating specific policies. As opinionated journalists, columnists, and bloggers take to their own news outlets or websites, the AP and others are trying to move away from reporting that involves debates about the basic premise of a story or the possible implications of a news development. Instead, the model seeks out experts who have facts to contribute to a story, treating them differently than just another source to be thrown into the mix and countered with another quote. In this still-emerging model of reporting, policies are for debating, but facts are for stating.

See also: Balance; Lippmann, Walter; Objectivity; Political Bias and the Media; Stone, I.F.; Watchdog Journalism

Further Reading

Alexander, John. 2004. *Samuel Adams: America's Revolutionary Politician.* Lanham, MD: Rowman & Littlefield.

Auletta, Ken. 2013. "Freedom of Information." *New Yorker.* October 7. Accessed November 24, 2015. http://www.newyorker.com/magazine/2013/10/07/freedom-of-information.

Berry, Stephen. 2005. "Why Objectivity Still Matters." Nieman Reports. June 15. Accessed June 1, 2016. http://niemanreports.org/articles/why-objectivity-still-matters/.

Foxton, Willard. 2013. "The Problem with Glenn Greenwald and the Creepy Cult That Surrounds Him." *The Telegraph* (UK). June 11. Accessed November 24, 2015. http://blogs.telegraph.co.uk/technology/willardfoxton2/100009225/the-problem-with-glenn-greenwald-and-the-creepy-cult-that-surrounds-him.

Galison, Peter. 2015. "The Journalist, the Scientist, and Objectivity." In *Objectivity in Science: New Perspectives from Science and Technology Studies*. Edited by Flavia Padovani, Alan Richardson, and Jonathan Y. Tsou. New York: Springer Publishing.

Greenwald, Glenn. 2013. "On Prism, Partisanship and Propaganda." *Guardian*. June 14. Accessed November 15, 2015. http://www.theguardian.com/commentisfree/2013/jun/14/nsa-partisanship-propaganda-prism.

Taibbi, Matt. 2013. "Hey, MSM: All Journalism is Advocacy Journalism." *Rolling Stone*. June 25. Accessed November 23, 2015. http://www.rollingstone.com/politics/news/hey-msm-all-journalism-is-advocacy-journalism-20130627.

AGGREGATION

Aggregation is a general term for reporting and writing that combines excerpts, quotes, and sections of other writers' works into a new piece that, ideally, adds context, analysis, or additional reporting. It is the concept that drives some of the largest news sites—from the *Washington Post* to Huffington Post—and has a history in political news that pre-dates the Internet. Still, aggregation is a controversial practice. Many accuse aggregators of being essentially journalistic parasites who make content and money by harvesting other peoples' reporting. Aggregators counter that their work helps connect the dots of individual pieces of journalism, linking stories, commenting on developments, and introducing the reporting to new audiences who otherwise would not read the original article.

Aggregation can take on many different forms but includes a few general elements: copying, attribution, and linking. A writer composing an aggregation piece takes verbatim some element of another writer's work. It may be only a headline that then links to the original story, which is what Matt Drudge does at his Drudge Report. It could be a list of articles that include headlines, the first paragraph, and a photo, which is how Google News assembles its array of news material. It could be the use of a paragraph within a story that offers another take on a piece; this is common practice on blogs. Huffington Post, an aggressive aggregator, has harvested as many as nine complete paragraphs from another piece.

Attribution is a critical element of aggregation and is what legally separates it from plagiarism. Attribution can be as subtle as a highlighted word that links to the original piece, or as explicit as naming the author, the source publication, and a date it was posted. Aggregation also usually includes a link to the original source. This fulfills several functions. It allows the reader to dive deeper into a story and explore the sources the aggregator collected to tell his or her story. It is usually the first argument aggregators will put forward to defend their work, saying it actually may drive more people to the original work than who would have seen it otherwise. Finally, it offers the aggregator a level of transparency to the reader that allows them to see how the new piece was researched.

Many journalists feel these three elements, in the wrong hands, do little to prevent the essential theft of original work. Some who endorse aggregation are careful to add other elements to the to-do list for aggregators that better justify the practice of aggregating. Steve Buttry, a veteran journalist who has worked for a variety of digital news operations, encourages reporters who are aggregating to ensure that they are adding explicit value to the original reporting they are aggregating. Buttry's core idea is to build additional reporting on top of the aggregation. He said this can include aggregators doing their own interviews, analyzing data connected to the piece, or adding commentary about the core ideas in the original piece. Creating a new piece of reporting, rather than a series of highlights of others' work, is essential.

Despite these cautions, many journalists and writers find the practice of aggregating ethically bankrupt and financially dangerous to the fundamental work of journalists. They see aggregators as creating entire information sources that are built on a business model of vampirism and doing little to benefit the original reporters and the news organizations they work for. As one freelancer put it, "Aggregators are parasites, only slightly more benign than plagiarists—and sooner or later, parasites kill the host. Someone has to actually create words for other people to steal. It's just that actually paying for people to be creative is expensive" (Foxton 2013). Ironically, this criticism itself is an aggregation of his argument, as is much academic work that builds on previous research or publications and attributes its sources. In fact, many defend aggregation as a natural offshoot of journalism. Andy Carvin made a name for himself while at NPR as a social media natural. There he began aggregating social media information coming out of the Arab Spring movement in 2010 and 2011. Carvin, from NPR's headquarters in Washington, D.C., began collecting and monitoring the Twitter feeds of activists, journalists, and officials in the countries in the midst of popular uprising against long-standing governments. Carvin created a single feed of commentary, eyewitness reports, and journalism. He engaged these sources, asking questions, trying to confirm information and discuss the news. He called what he was doing curation and when asked about it, he said, "I think curation has always been a part of journalism; we just didn't call it that. Think of the word 'media.' It's about being in the middle, between the story and the public. The job of a reporter is to capture the most important elements to tell a story, and then go ahead and tell it. Watch any breaking news story on TV and you'll see curation going on. They'll quote sources, pull up clips from wherever, pass along info from pundits, etc. So curation itself isn't new; it's just the way that some of us are doing it online that's fairly new" (Connelly 2011).

Still, these new tools raise questions about the legality of some forms of aggregation. Surprisingly, for the amount of debate and online commentary about aggregation, precious few actual legal cases have considered what limits aggregators may face in how they do their work. Of the substantive legal battles over aggregation, none have gone to trial, with the parties striking deals often on the eve of trial to avoid a costly lawsuit that could have unintended results based on the decisions. This leaves the laws connected to aggregation murky and forces those considering where to draw lines to focus on existing, and largely dated, legal concepts. Central to these is so-called fair use. Fair use allows for the use of a section of original work for the purposes of informing the public about a matter in the public interest. The laws around fair use establish a very broad set of guidelines that reporters live under whenever they use any copyrighted work. These boil down to the following: (1) the purpose and character of the use, including whether the use is of a commercial nature or is for nonprofit educational purposes; (2) the nature of the copyrighted work; (3) the amount and substantiality of the portion used in relation to the copyrighted work as a whole; and (4) the effect of the use upon the potential market for or value of the copyrighted work. Under these ideas, much of the aggregation that initially concerned media companies and reporters seems benign compared to the later sites like Huffington Post.

The general concept of fair use cleared the work of the Drudge Report and, most media lawyers agree, the work of Google News and other pure aggregators that gather and reproduce only relatively small portions of the news pieces to create a site that offers users a variety of sources, formats, and content. But elements of fair use continue to be debated when considering the actions of some aggregators. In particular the last two points—the amount of the original work used and the economic impact of that use—are still hotly debated online, but thus far not in court. One case of aggregation that raised many of these questions, but answered few, blew up in 2011. A columnist for the magazine *Ad Age* wrote a piece that analyzed the competing Twitter traffic on a day where Apple launched its iCloud storage service and ethically embattled congressman Anthony Weiner resigned from Congress. Multiple aggregators picked up the *Ad Age* story. One, Techmeme, drove almost 750 people to the original story. Another, Huffington Post—a far larger news organization than Techmeme—drove only 57 page views to the piece. The author of the original *Ad Age* story said the reason was that Techmeme is "an aggregator that takes a minimalistic approach (usually just presenting a headline and a one- or two-sentence snippet)" and Huffington Post "consisted of basically a short but thorough paraphrasing/rewriting of the *Ad Age* post—using the same set-up (i.e., pointing out that Apple had the misfortune of presenting its latest round of big announcements on the same day Weiner resigned from Congress) and the bulk of the data presented in the original *Ad Age* piece" (Dumenco 2011).

The public spat, especially one with the data to back it up, triggered a wave of commentary about aggregation generally and Huffington Post in particular. Huffington Post added to the furor when they indefinitely suspended the young blogger who had written the piece for violating its largely unstated rules around over-aggregating. One angry former employee told Gawker, "That is what we were taught and told to do at HuffPost. Arianna and the higher ups made a decision to stop linking out directly as much and rewrite stories 'the way the AP does.' They even hired people specifically to rewrite other people's work. Whenever they get caught they just blame an underling. These poor kids right out of school who have no experience get told to do XY and Z and then get punished for doing it" (Tate 2011). The Huffington Post writer returned to work a week after the incident and Huffington Post did little publicly to clarify its standards for aggregating.

The incident highlights the uneasy, largely rule-free world of aggregation that reporting—including political reporting—has faced for some time. Aggregation of political reporting has been a business since before there was a commercial World Wide Web. In 1987, a pair of political consultants launched an information service out of suburban Washington, D.C. called The Presidential Campaign Hotline (eventually shortened to The Hotline). The Hotline collected, read, and literally clipped scores of newspapers daily to produce a succinctly written summary that mixed analysis, news, and, importantly, humor to create the must-read of political reporting generated each morning around 11 a.m. Even before there was a Web, its former editor said, "The Hotline was the first political Web site. It was the first place that aggregated political news from outside the Beltway" (Schudel 2013). Once the Web arrived, the idea of creating one-stop-shops for different elements became a wildly popular way to build a news service with a devoted following—The Hotline had shown there already was an audience (and one that would pay $4,000 a year for that service). Services such as RealClearPolitics emerged to aggregate polling data and later political news. Huffington Post launched as a way of aggregating all lefty political blogs, but then made aggregation a central rationale for its existence. Newser, Pulse News, Zite, and countless others created politics sections that allowed users to organize, curate, and personalize their political news.

But more than just adding an array of new news services to the mix and making the political junkie's bookmarks longer, aggregators had other effects on political reporting. One, which has been hard to measure specifically, could be called the echo-chamber effect. Aggregation allows for the swift adoption of a story or fact by having it be repeated across the Internet. One of the elements that is often unspoken in the world of aggregation is that when people copy and paste a quote from one news source, then attribute it and link back to the original story, they almost never actually check if it is true. This contributes to stories and rumors often running like a wildfire across blogs, aggregators, and even into reported pieces. Tidbits of information can move from a blog to Twitter to reporting with stunning speed; correcting this information or even contextualizing can trail far behind (if it is even done at all). For example, in the wake of Eric Holder's resignation as Attorney General, a story in the *St. Paul Pioneer Press* reported Minnesota U.S. senator Amy Klobuchar was being considered for the position. This prompted a reporter at Minnesota Public Radio to dig a bit into it, writing:

> Here we go, again: Sen. Amy Klobuchar's name is being mentioned as a possible attorney general now that Eric Holder is calling it quits.
> Behold! The passive voice. In today's *Pioneer Press* story, it's revealed who exactly is floating Klobuchar's name. Twitter users were circulating Klobuchar's name.
> Ah.
> And who on Twitter is floating her name? Journalists. And a few Republicans who wouldn't mind getting her out of a Senate seat that's about as safe as they come.
> Twitter is also already planning the special election to fill her seat. Twitter can be insane. (Collins 2014)

The *Pioneer Press* story was picked up by some national outlets, including Huffington Post and others, citing the newspaper as the source, but as MPR reports the *Pioneer Press* itself was not the source, but rather the source was Twitter users, including Republican activists who would love for the U.S. Senate seat to come open. In an aggregation world, one activist's proposition on social media can lead to a newspaper story, which can be picked up by a political aggregator or national blog with stunning speed and little fact checking. This is a clear modern reality of political reporting. Many consultants and politicians, aware of this trend, can and do float ideas, rumors, and scenarios into the social media sphere to see how they play in a rush of aggregation. Even if aggregators follow Buttry's admonition that they should supply context, the idea for the story itself could still be founded in loosely (or barely) sourced social media rumors that have been aggregated into news stories.

Of course, this is not fundamentally different from the pre-Internet age. One reporter produces a story and others may pick that story up as fact and then add their reporting on top of it without checking the original piece. Television news for decades has had a strong connection to newspaper reporting, basing many of their nightly stories on the morning newspaper, but few think of this as aggregating. In fact, one reporter made a splash when he made the argument in the *Washington Post* that almost all journalism is essentially aggregation, writing, "But now I'm wondering if what I consider 'reporting' is just a form of aggregating, of skimming, of lifting the best parts of a scientist's work and repurposing it for my own interests. These scientists have spent many, many years doing research, much of it at the very edge of the knowable, where finding a new piece of solid data is a laborious process that may require long nights at the computer or the laboratory bench, or mulling a bust of Galileo, and this work has to be slotted among other obligations, including grant applications, peer-reviewing papers, teaching, advising graduate students, holding office hours, serving on faculty committees and schmoozing at the faculty club. And here I am calling up and saying: 'Give me the fruit of your mental labors'" (Achenbach 2014). This reality has some truth in it. Journalists' jobs are to connect the expert views, historical insights, and background of the story of the day and then turn that quickly into a more easily consumed package. The question is, how effective is the practitioner at using the tool? Do they help the reader understand the context of the story—keep in mind that the Minnesota Public Radio story about Klobuchar was aggregation, as well—or are they simply repeating another person's work or rumor? The burden lies on the reader to click the link and check the source.

See also: "The Hotline"; Huffington, Arianna; Huffington Post; Personalization and the Internet

Further Reading

Achenbach, Joel. 2014. "Journalism Is Aggregation." *Washington Post*. April 9. Accessed July 25, 2015. http://www.washingtonpost.com/blogs/achenblog/wp/2014/04/09/journalism-is-aggregation.

Collins, Bob. 2014. "Inside the Klobuchar Rumor Mill." Minnesota Public Radio. September 24. Accessed July 25, 2015. http://blogs.mprnews.org/newscut/2014/09/inside-the-klobuchar-rumor-mill.

Connelly, Phoebe. 2011. "Curating the Revolution: Building a Real-Time News Feed about Egypt." *The Atlantic*. April 10. Accessed July 24, 2015. http://www.theatlantic.com /technology/archive/2011/02/curating-the-revolution-building-a-real-time-news-feed -about-egypt/71041.

Dumenco, Simon. 2011. "What It's Like to Get Used and Abused by The Huffington Post." *Ad Age*. July 11. Accessed July 25, 2015. http://adage.com/article/the-media-guy/abused -huffington-post/228607.

Foxton, Willard. 2013. "Parasite Journalism: Is Aggregation as Bad as Plagiarism?" *New Statesman*. July 11. Accessed July 25, 2015. http://www.newstatesman.com/newspapers /2013/07/parasite-journalism-aggregation-bad-plagiarism.

Schudel, Matt. 2013. "Douglas L. Bailey, Founder of Political News Digest, Dies at 79." *Washington Post*. June 11. Accessed July 22, 2015. http://www.washingtonpost.com/politics /douglas-l-bailey-founder-of-political-news-digest-dies-at-79/2013/06/11/36c34d06 -d2b0-11e2-a73e-826d299ff459_story.html.

Tate, Ryan. 2011. "HuffPo Suspends Writer for Doing 'What We Were Taught and Told to Do.'" *Gawker*. July 11. Accessed July 24, 2015. http://gawker.com/5820099/huffpo -suspends-writer-for-doing-what-we-were-taught-and-told-to-do.

AILES, ROGER (1940–)

Roger Ailes told a reporter in 2011 that he already knew what the reporter was going to write about the Fox News founder. "I can pretty much pick the words for you. Paranoid, right-wing, fat. I love that. I'm the only guy in America who's fat," he told *Esquire* (Junod 2011).

Ailes has advised presidents, filmed wildlife in Africa, and produced Broadway shows, but is best known and most often vilified for his role as chairman and CEO of Fox News, the conservative network that has become the most successful cable news channel on American television. He has moved seamlessly between media and political consulting, and has, at times, used his power to crush his enemies or anyone who went after his friends. In that same *Esquire* profile, Tom Junod wrote, "For forty years, he has stood astride the intertwined worlds of media and politics like a veritable colossus, making sure the worlds of media and politics *stay* intertwined, to better control them. He has used his considerable powers of persuasion to persuade us to elect presidents, and, if they're not following the 'Ailes Agenda,' to turn against them" (Junod 2011).

Though he stands at the helm of the prime time leader in cable news, he likes to think of himself as a simple man from flyover country. Born in Warren, Ohio, he was the middle child of Bob and Donna Ailes. He was diagnosed with hemophilia meaning that even minor injuries could set off uncontrollable bleeding. In *Off Camera*, Zev Chafets writes about one instance when a young Ailes bit his tongue. Ailes's brother Rob told Chafets, "Blood was dripping out of his mouth like icicles." (Chafets 2013). The family rushed young Roger to a hospital in Cleveland, about 60 miles away, and doctors there stopped the bleeding. Episodes like that weren't terribly uncommon in his childhood. This was not Ailes's only burden growing up, though. His father was abusive and Ailes would later recall being beaten often. His father also kicked him out of the house when he was 18. He headed to Ohio University where he studied radio and television and was station manager at the college radio station.

After college, he took a job with *The Mike Douglas Show*, a nationally syndicated variety show, where he came up with segment ideas for the show. No idea was too farfetched—at separate times, he had a regulation size bowling lane and a tank of piranhas brought on set (Chafets 2013). He was good at producing entertaining television, and became executive producer of the show in 1967, not long before the show booked a guest that would change the trajectory of his future.

Early in 1968, Richard Nixon was scheduled to appear on the show. Before he went on, he complained to Ailes that he couldn't win the election without using television, something he considered a "gimmick." According to Chafets, "Ailes assured him that the medium was here to stay. If Nixon didn't grasp that, and figure out how to turn it to his advantage, he would never get to the White House" (Chafets 2013). That conversation got him a job offer. Ailes became a media consultant for the Nixon campaign and helped the former vice president win the 1968 presidential election. The work thrust him into the realm of Republican politics, though he never truly left television behind. He worked as a political consultant, advising Ronald Reagan and George H. W. Bush, and spent time working for Joseph Coors on a short-lived conservative news outlet called Television News, Inc.

In the early 1990s, he returned to television as the head of CNBC. In 1996, he teamed up with Rupert Murdoch to create Fox News. They had a vision of a cable news network that could beat Ted Turner's CNN—which it ultimately did.

The channel leans heavily on openly conservative commentators and talk shows and has been often dismissed as a GOP propaganda machine. Presidential candidates have hosted shows and appear on the channel frequently. Its anchors have sparred with left-leaning late night hosts. But it has also built a loyal audience and is a major force in setting the tastes of the modern Republican Party.

Fox News illustrates Roger Ailes's ability to manipulate the medium. As Tom Dickinson wrote for *Rolling Stone*, "During his days as an overt political consultant, Roger Ailes reshaped Republican politics for the era of network television. Now, as chairman of Fox News, he has reshaped a television network as a force for Republican politics" (Dickinson 2011). All of this changed suddenly in 2016 when anchor Gretchen Carlson filed a sexual harassment lawsuit against Ailes and Fox News. Within two weeks, stories of inappropriate behavior and intimidation soon led Ailes to step down after some 20 years of running the network.

Michael Wright

See also: Fox News

Further Reading

Bercovici, Jeff. 2013. "Eight Things You Didn't Know about Fox News' Roger Ailes," *Forbes.* March 19. Accessed: December 6, 2015. http://www.forbes.com/sites/jeffbercovici/2013 /03/19/eight-things-you-didnt-know-about-fox-news-chief-roger-ailes.

Chafets, Zev. 2013. *Roger Ailes: Off Camera*. New York: Sentinel.

Dickinson, Tim. 2011. "How Roger Ailes Built the Fox News Fear Factory." *Rolling Stone*. May 25. Accessed December 6, 2015. http://www.rollingstone.com/politics/news/how -roger-ailes-built-the-fox-news-fear-factory-20110525.

Junod, Tom. 2011. "Why Does Roger Ailes Hate America?," *Esquire*. January 18. Accessed December 6, 2015. http://www.esquire.com/news-politics/a9248/roger-ailes-0211.

Sherman, Gabriel. 2014. *The Loudest Voice in the Room: How the Brilliant, Bombastic Roger Ailes Built Fox News—and Divided a Country*. New York: Random House.

AIR AMERICA

"I am not a radio professional" may not be what you expect to hear from someone during their first high-profile radio program, but that is how comedian (and now U.S. senator) Al Franken kicked off his radio program. The cheekily named *The O'Franken Factor* debuted on April 1, 2004, as one of the cornerstones of the new radio network Air America.

Air America was an effort by a few wealthy liberal investors and broadcasters to create a counterbalance to the far more significant conservative talk radio business. Following a flurry of fundraising and interest from established names like Franken, who had made a name for himself on *Saturday Night Live* and later as the author of *Rush Limbaugh Is a Big Fat Idiot*, and comedian Janeane Garofolo, the network was ready to launch in early 2004.

Some observers were deeply skeptical of the new service, which launched in six cities where it purchased airtime on low performing AM stations. At this time, Limbaugh, the most popular figure on talk radio, was airing on 600 stations and garnering some 15 million listeners a day. In one blistering reaction, dubbed "Err America," *New York* magazine's Robert Kolker opined, "The new national talk-radio network, airing on stations in six cities so far, seems designed on the scale of the New Deal or the War on Poverty—a proudly massive response to a mammoth social problem. The banks have failed and the markets have crashed? Plug the leaks with inventive social programs. People are hungry and homeless? Step up and feed and house them. The airwaves are clogged with right-wing fire-breathers who set the tone of presidential campaigns? Create a new radio network to tip the balance of power" (Kolker 2004). Critics saw the new network as more of a knee-jerk response than a way to meet the needs of a liberal audience lacking an alternative on the radio.

But those joining the network were confident that the new network would soon attract an audience and a profit. Randi Rhodes, a well-established liberal talk show host from Florida, rejected the idea that the network would flounder, saying, "I got news for you, it doesn't fail. It's a lie on top of all the other lies. I've been making a ton of money doing this for a really long time" (Sullivan 2004). The network announced quickly it would expand into other markets, including San Francisco.

In addition to potential money, the network also offered liberal activists a platform to reach listeners and build a following. Franken, who had always been a political comedian, developed a sharper political voice. For three hours a day, he was able to market his work, which helped prepare him for his Senate run. The network also raised the profile of Rachel Maddow, whose program was simulcast on MSNBC. Over the next couple of years, her television presence would eclipse the radio program that brought her prominence.

Rhodes, who continued her radio career until 2014, would later say that many of these notable personalities from Air America were more interested in self-promotion than creating a compelling programming. In her farewell program, she remembered the tumultuous time, saying, "When Air America came I said, oh my God, and the opportunity is amazing, to be the advocate of even more people and to tell people even more about, you know, how you get through this life and what's important . . . But other people were not there for that. Some people saw, you know, a chance to be in a Cabinet and other people saw it as a chance to go to the Senate and other people saw it as a chance to national television" (Lifson 2014).

In addition to internal disagreements about mission, and the network's sporadic early growth, it faced internal struggles over leadership and control. The day after the network launched, its CEO left. Four weeks later its director of programming followed. Still, the network began to develop an audience, albeit far smaller than its conservative competition. Within a year it was reportedly garnering more than two million weekly listeners, and coverage of the network began to offer hopes for its future. *Time* magazine would announce in 2005 that progressive talk radio was "the fastest growing format in radio history" (Corliss 2005). Despite this optimism, the network continued to face a series of financial and management problems. During its first year, the network admitted it lost $9.1 million. It shed another $19.6 million in 2005, and had lost $13 million in 2006 when it finally filed for bankruptcy. It was eventually sold, and drifted off more and more affiliates.

By 2010 the network, having lost its major stars and struggling to attract and retain affiliates, announced it would close. On January 21, Air America chairman Charles Kireker issued a memo that announced the immediate end of the network, although it broadcast reruns for another four days to help its 100 affiliates fill airtime. Kireker said the network had fallen victim to the same "perfect storm" that swamped the newspaper industry that year, writing in a memo to his staff, "Those companies that remain are facing audience fragmentation as a result of new media technologies, are often saddled with crushing debt, and have generally found it difficult to obtain operating or investment capital from traditional sources of funding" (Ernest 2010).

Some advocates for the network blamed the ultimate demise on demographic factors, coupled with competition from a far more established public radio alternative or, to put it in an equation: "Radio trends older. Liberals trend younger. X and Y plus NPR=The Death of Air America" (Harden 2010).

See also: Limbaugh, Rush; Maddow, Rachel; Talk Radio

Further Reading

Corliss, Richard. 2005. "Radio: America Still on the Air." *Time*. April 5. Accessed January 12, 2015. http://content.time.com/time/arts/article/0,8599,1045633,00.html.

Ernest, Amanda. 2010. "Air America Stops Live Programming, Heads Towards Bankruptcy." FishbowlNY.com. January 21. Accessed January 12, 2015. http://www.mediabistro.com /fishbowlny/air-america-stops-live-programming-heads-towards-bankruptcy_b13584.

Harden, Nathan. 2010. "The Death of Air America: Why Liberals Fail at Talk Radio." *Huffington Post*. March 24. Accessed January 12, 2015. http://www.huffingtonpost.com /nathan-harden/the-death-of-air-america_b_433208.html.

Kolker, Robert. 2004. "Err America." *New York*. Accessed January 12, 2015. http://nymag .com/nymetro/news/trends/columns/cityside/n_10147.

Lifson, Thomas. 2014. "Randi Rhodes Leaving Talk Radio, Blasts Al Franken and Rachel Maddow." *American Thinker*. April 27. Accessed January 12, 2015. http://www .americanthinker.com/blog/2014/04/randi_rhodes_leaving_talk_radio_blasts_al _franken_and_rachel_maddow.html.

Sullivan, James. 2004. "A Voice for Unabashed Liberals/Air America Radio Debuts to Do Battle with Conservative Talk Shows." SFGate.com. April 1. Accessed January 12, 2015. http://www.sfgate.com/news/article/A-voice-for-unabashed-liberals-Air-America -2800476.php.

AL JAZEERA AMERICA

In 2013 Al Jazeera, a television network once decried as the "mouthpiece of Osama bin Laden," would launch one of the newest and most interesting cable news outlets in the United States. But brutal financial realities would see that network, funded by an oil-rich emirate, fail within three years. Al Jazeera America was a primarily domestic news outlet that focused on American news reported by an array of talented journalists poached from commercial and public television. The network aired more news reports, thanks to overnight updates, than CNN, Fox News, and MSNBC. But despite its focus on hard news, the channel struggled to attract and maintain viewers. It never reached more than about half of the American public and remained somewhat controversial due to its connection with the international Al Jazeera network.

Al Jazeera America represented a major expansion of Al Jazeera's English-language reporting, but far from its first foray. In 2003 the international network hired its first English-language correspondents and created an English-language website. By 2006, the cable broadcasting giant launched an International edition of Al Jazeera, broadcasting its coverage in English through satellite and Internet streaming.

The Al Jazeera Media Network launched in 1996 as a satellite news channel for the Arab-speaking world. Its founding was made possible by a $137 million loan from the emir of Qatar. Although the network has made quite a bit of money from advertising over the years, the emir has also stepped in to make several bailout loans to the tune of tens of millions of American dollars. In his history of the network, Hugh Miles noted that "exactly how many of these millions are government money and how many are his personal millions is not clear. At least two of his relatives are on the board of directors. This kind of money is small change to a man as rich as the Emir and for the impact it has had on Qatar's stature in the region, the network is cheap at the price" (Miles 2005). The new network attracted swift attention because, even though it operated thanks to a grant from the Qatar royal family, it was not an official organ of the state. Al Jazeera soon was reporting to Arab-speaking audiences about what the leaders of their nations and other countries were doing without the veil of censorship.

In the wake of the 9/11 attacks, American officials denounced the network for broadcasting statements from al-Qaeda leader Osama bin Laden. American officials also angrily rejected the network's coverage of the Iraq invasion of 2003. Later it would be leaders of Muslim nations who denounced the network, as its unfiltered reporting of the 2009–2010 Arab Spring uprisings helped spread protests throughout the region. The network added a C-SPAN–style public affairs channel in 2005 and in 2006 launched Al Jazeera English, an English-language channel that was soon carried in some 100 countries thanks to cable and satellite deals.

Al Jazeera America burst audaciously onto the scene in August 2013. The international network had expressed its intent to launch an American channel that year and soon cut a deal to purchase the remnants of Current TV, an experimental cable channel that had hoped to capitalize on user-submitted news but never found the content or audience to sustain it. What Current TV did have was agreements with several major cable operators; when Al Jazeera purchased the station and absorbed most of its employees, it retained those deals and the network was born.

Unlike the cash-strapped channels it would compete against, Al Jazeera came to the new network ready to spend money. Just before the network launched, it announced that Kate O'Brian, a veteran news executive from ABC, would take on the role of president and be wholly in charge of the editorial coverage decisions of the channel. Other senior executives from CNN, CBS, and MSNBC soon joined the team, and O'Brian boldly declared by the end of 2013 that the new network would be the "envy of the industry." The response by the media was something between awe and jealousy. Many wrote about the amount of money being spent, others the resources being devoted to reporting. One article in *Variety* gushed, "AJA is investing time and money in deep-dive and investigative reporting about meaty and undeniably significant issues ranging from homelessness and urban ills to political corruption to health and environmental concerns. Think *MacNeil/Lehrer NewsHour* in its glory days, except that AJA is round the clock. It's also endowed with international resources through the rest of the Al Jazeera Media Network—which makes a difference in covering stories like the conflict in Syria, the typhoon in the Philippines and the death of Nelson Mandela" (Littleton 2013).

Initially the new network planned to produce about 60 percent of its own programming and then run the remaining content from the older, more internationally focused Al Jazeera English. But as the network gelled and the reception improved, O'Brian and her team expanded their domestic reporting. The network added respected veterans like PBS's Ray Suarez, and CBS's Sheila MacVicar and Joie Chen. It also included an investigation team co-produced with Al Jazeera English.

Throughout its early years the network sought to differentiate itself from the trends that pushed other cable networks toward more opinionated commentary programs. In outlining its planned coverage of the 2016 presidential campaign, O'Brian stressed that her network would not lean too heavily on political pundits and horserace analysts, instead turning to subject matter experts for interviews. Amjad Atallah, the network's Executive Vice President for Content, went even further, saying in a statement, "The nature of presidential politics is to polarize the issues so much that it's difficult to get at the truth. But we'll break down the spin for our audiences so they can form their own opinions on the issues and evaluate the candidates objectively. With reporters embedded inside the Beltway and across the country, we can bring the resources and expert perspectives that no other American network can match." The plan also included partnering with respected nonprofit news outfit the Center for Public Integrity to focus on dark money organizations working to affect the election, in a series entitled "The Buying of the President 2016."

The network's reporting was generally well received, garnering numerous nominations and awards, such as the prestigious Alfred I. duPont Award from Columbia University for a six-part series on the working poor. In announcing the win for Al Jazeera America, the judges noted, "The production's gritty approach is coupled with its subjects' steely determination to portray their lives honestly. They spring to full, three dimensional life, instead of cookie-cutter stereotypes. In the strong tradition of duPont Award–winning work, this series gives voice to the voiceless." But there was major trouble on the business side, as audiences sometimes hovered around 10,000 and few advertisers signed up.

By the turn of 2016, as oil prices plunged and Al Jazeera looked to reduce its overall costs, the massive experiment in American cable television came under close scrutiny. The previous year had seen an ugly ousting of the first CEO and a series of lawsuits that alleged sexist and anti-Semitic behavior by some within the Al Jazeera networks. Still, staff felt the network was turning a corner and expressed optimism headed into their first presidential election year, hoping it would help fuel ratings. Then, the hammer dropped. The international network decided in January 2016 to shut the network down, catching many workers by surprise.

Although the failure of Al Jazeera America can be connected to many things—residual skepticism of American viewers toward a network based indirectly in the Middle East, the slumping oil economy, and the difficulty of building a cable news audience in today's fragmented media world—at least one long-time employee of the system saw it as a failure to think outside of the traditional news box. "We could have been Vice," the anchor told CNN Money. "But we blended in instead of standing out" (Stelter and Kludt 2016).

See also: Audience Fragmentation; Cable News Networks

Further Reading

Littleton, Cynthia. 2013. "Al Jazeera America Will Be 'Envy of the Industry,' Chief Says." *Variety*. December 31. Accessed January 4, 2016. http://variety.com/2013/tv/news/al-jazeera-america-will-be-envy-of-the-industry-chief-says-1201015965.

Miles, Hugh. 2005. *Al Jazeera: The Inside Story of the Arab News Channel That Is Challenging the West*. New York: Grove Press.

Stelter, Brian, and Tom Kludt. 2016. "The Final Days of Al Jazeera America." CNN Money. January 22. Accessed February 1, 2016. http://money.cnn.com/2016/01/22/media/al -jazeera-america-what-went-wrong/index.html?sr=limoney012316ajam0830story.

ALTERNATIVE NEWSMEDIA

For as long as publishable political news has existed, so-called alternative news-media has been its sidecar. Once seen as dissident, radical, "underground" press, published by muckrakers and provocateurs, the popular view of alternative news-media changed during the counter-culture movement of the 1960s and 1970s. The movement's reaction against everything mainstream, ironically, helped create the foundation for a fairly stable journalistic institution, one that even occasionally wins Pulitzer Prizes.

"Movement papers"—from radical pamphlets teaching how to make bombs to less-extreme calls for peaceful revolution—had "newsrooms" where writers were activists first and journalists a distant second. During the 1960s the number of such publications exploded, from about six such papers registered with the Underground Press Syndicate in 1965 to more than 500 by 1969 (Menand 2009). The total audience for these papers was in the collective millions (McMillian 2012). Most died out after the Vietnam draft ended, but many journalistically inclined writers—either directly involved in the movement or sympathetic to it—saw that the left hungered for its own, perhaps more established and mature, political voice.

Once the movement grew up some and perhaps smoked a little less dope, the papers that sprouted out of the underground press were more mainstream, at least if one considers mainstream as the liberal wing of the Democratic party, which most altweekly founders in the 1970s and 1980s did. One of the earliest, and one that survived the turmoil of the 1960s, was the altweekly, the *Village Voice*. The *Voice*, founded in 1955 by Norman Mailer and a few other less-marquee names, started by covering local politics, as local as Greenwich Village in Manhattan. It followed bigger political news, too, involving mayors and corruption in the NYPD. The *Voice* also played a role as an early home to New Journalism, the style of feature-writing modeled after novels with characters and plot, scenes and arcs and, often, the re-porter in the middle—think Hunter S. Thompson and *Fear and Loathing on the Campaign Trail '72*. Clay Felker, who'd written—with Mailer's encouragement—the *Esquire* classic "Superman Comes to the Supermarket" about the 1960 Democratic Convention, took over at the *Voice* and ran it in the late '70s with this kind of long-form feature at its core.

The *Village Voice* also helped establish three key aspects of the brand of altweek-lies that emerged in the '70s, '80s, and '90s and generally remain true for the genre, both as a traditional free paper and online: they're liberal, they're local, and they've wavered only a little from their long-form bread-and-butter cover stories. But where left-of-left politics gave them a foundation, a lot of alternative newsmedia have focused less on politics and more on "lifestyle"—where to find the best soup dumpling and bands only cool people know.

That's not to say alts haven't had major impacts on politics and political journalism. The clearest example of that comes from the *Willamette Week* in Portland, Oregon, founded in 1974. Three decades later, it published a story exposing former governor Neil Goldschmidt's sexual abuse of a 14-year-old girl in the 1970s, during the time he served as mayor of Portland. The reporter, Nigel Jaquiss, won the Pulitzer Prize for investigative reporting in 2005, the first Pulitzer awarded for a story initially published online. The paper hadn't planned to go online with the story exactly when it did, but had given Goldschmidt and his lawyer time to fully respond to what Jaquiss had uncovered. During the response time, the governor called the rival mainstream daily, the *Oregonian*, and the *Willamette Week* rushed to publish a portion of what it was planning to put in the paper so as to avoid getting scooped. The story resulted in Goldschmidt's public confession—to the *Oregonian*—and led to an explanation on why the popular governor hadn't sought a second term in 1990. At the time of the story's publication, he served on the Oregon Board of Higher Education and resigned.

Jaquiss stayed on at the *Willamette Week* and went on to become, as *USA Today's* media editor Rem Rieder pegged him, "the reporter who took down Oregon's governor," although Rieder referred to a different former governor this time: John Kitzhaber (Rieder 2015). Kitzhaber resigned just after beginning his fourth term after the *Willamette Week* and others reported ethical lapses connected to his fiancée's income and policy influence and the ways they directly benefited from her relationship with Kitzhaber.

In an altweekly political trifecta, Jaquiss also broke a story connecting a popular Portland mayor, Sam Adams (who has had a recurring role as a mayoral assistant on television's *Portlandia*), to a sexual relationship with a legislative intern. Adams was cleared of any criminal wrongdoing in that matter, though he admitted lying about it, and later declined to seek a second term.

The work of the *Willamette Week* is a good example of where altmedia have traditionally had the most influence in political journalism—the local and, sometimes, state levels. Most altmedia have political columnists who parse all things local, typically from a pro-liberal stance. As one example, *Washington City Paper*, which covers D.C., the city (rather than D.C., the seat of the federal government, or D.C., the catch-all term for sprawling suburbs in neighboring states), produces one of the more storied political columns, "Loose Lips." Various writers have embodied LL since it began in 1983, and it remains a space where news on local government is dissected and where stories regularly break regarding the city's politicians. It has evolved from a weekly column in the newspaper to a blog updated several times a day, but its mission remains the same.

Alts have also gained influence when it comes to elections. The Seattle blog "Crosscut" reported in 2015 that the city's leading altweekly, *The Stranger*, had comparable influence regarding its endorsements to the only daily in town, *The Seattle Times*, and that the influence of *The Stranger* was far more powerful when it came to backing long-shot or fringe candidates. Campaigns and political watchers in that city even have a proper name for it, the Stranger Effect, and watch it closely in select races.

Dailies and altmedia are not strictly competitors based on several factors (size, resources, publication schedules, obvious political bents), but the differences are smaller than they used to be. Most alts picked up the pace of their content through lively websites and figured out blogging and how to convey an online voice sooner than the big dailies in their towns and cities.

Their relationship is further defined by what's traditionally seen as the alts' watchdog role when it comes to mainstream media. To return again to Portland, the *Willamette Week* is one of the more well-known and well-documented barkers. It's broken many stories about changes to the content, finances, and staffing as the daily *Oregonian* struggles to adjust to the "digital-first" approach of chain management under owners Advance Publications (formerly Newhouse). And while alt-weeklies have reported on the reporters in their towns and their struggles to stay employed for the big dailies, alts have suffered, too, in both circulation and revenue. According to the Pew Research Center's "State of the News Media 2015," "many alternative weekly newspapers faced outright closure in 2014. The storied *San Francisco Bay Guardian* closed in October 2014 after nearly 50 years in business. Knoxville's *Metro Pulse* was shut down by E.W. Scripps in the same month, and *Real Detroit Weekly* merged with the *Detroit Metro Times* in May. Only three of the top 20 newsweeklies saw an increase in circulation in the last year," the report stated.

Altmedia's funding model as a free paper, which in 2015 was still largely bankrolled by ads in the print publications, continues to take hits. The size of a lot of the survivors—and their newsrooms—have become noticeably smaller. But solid journalism continues. In 2012, for the first time in 31 years, an altweekly won a prized Pulitzer for feature writing with *The Stranger*'s "Bravest Woman in Seattle" by Eli Sanders.

Jule Banville

See also: Daily Newspapers; Muckraking

Further Reading

Banville, Jule. 2014. "Picking Up the Pieces: What Alts Can and Should Do When Daily Papers Explode." Altweeklies.com. August 12. Accessed February 4, 2016. http://www.altweeklies.com/aan/picking-up-the-pieces-what-alts-can-and-should-do-when-daily-papers-explode/Article?oid=7800407.

Guendelsberger, Emily, and Jerry Iannelli. 2015. "City Paper Ponders Its Fate at Oscar's Tavern: A Play." October 8. *Philadelphia City Paper*. Accessed February 4, 2016. http://citypaper.net/news/city-paper-ponders-its-fate-at-oscars-tavern-a-play.

McMillian, John. 2011. *Smoking Typewriters: The Sixties Underground Press and the Rise of Alternative Media in America*. New York: Oxford University Press.

Menand, Louis. 2009. "It Took a Village." *The New Yorker*. January 5. Accessed February 4, 2016. http://www.newyorker.com/magazine/2009/01/05/it-took-a-village.

Rieder, Rem. 2015. "Rieder: Reporter who took down Oregon's governor." *USA Today*. February 19, 2015. http://www.usatoday.com/story/money/columnist/rieder/2015/02/18/nigel-jaquiss-investigative-reporter-willamette-week/23611237/.

Sanders, Eli. 2011. "The Bravest Woman in Seattle." *The Stranger*. June 15. Accessed February 4, 2016. http://www.thestranger.com/seattle/the-bravest-woman-in-seattle/Content?oid=8640991.

AMERICAN COMMUNITIES PROJECT

Political reporters are always trying to better understand the American electorate and what drives them politically; in doing so, they often seek to categorize Americans by place. The idea of "Red States" and "Blue States" is a well-known example—and in the opinion of American Communities Project founder Dante Chinni, a lousy one.

Chinni, a veteran political reporter, has made coming up with a better way to understand the different types of place a centerpiece of his reporting for the past decade, seeking to use the growing sophistication of data journalism to create a more useful way to categorize communities and understand their behavior. Chinni also represents a growing trend—one that includes Nate Silver and Ezra Klein—of moving between working independently and creating partnerships with existing news organizations.

The latest iteration of the American Communities Project includes partnerships with the *Wall Street Journal* and NBC's *Meet the Press* and has allowed Chinni to write regularly for both outlets and inform the commentaries of NBC host Chuck Todd. Chinni and his team did this by coming up with a way to analyze and categorize each county in the country. The project "used a wide range of different factors—everything from income to race and ethnicity to education to religious affiliation—and a clustering technique to identify 15 types of counties, everything from Big Cities to Aging Farmlands. It has mapped those types to show where the country's political, socio-economic and cultural fissures are" (ACP). The project uses this unique county breakdown to sift polling data and economic reports to understand what is happening in different types of places in the United States.

Chinni first explored this revolutionary idea in a book called *Our Patchwork Nation* in 2010. Chinni had developed the Patchwork Nation project, which partnered with the *Christian Science Monitor* and the *PBS NewsHour* to report on different types of place, hoping to move beyond the red state/blue state dichotomy. Chinni found the red and blue election map "in so many ways represents a lie," writing, "It's not that the red and blue map is itself misleading. It's useful as a political scorecard, especially on that one all-important evening every four years. The problem is what it has become. We have invested it with a power it doesn't deserve, as a quick identifier for places and people and what they think and do" (Chinni 2010).

By creating community types, he hoped to illustrate how two places that may appear both blue or both red are often very different and motivated by different realities. Orange County, California, and rural Wallace County, Kansas, are both solidly Republican yet similar in almost no other way. Patchwork Nation, and later the ACP, sought to understand that and have become important tools for helping print and television reporters discern what is happening in the country. So, when a county clerk in Kentucky refuses to grant marriage licenses to gay couples despite a Supreme Court ruling that she must, Chinni can explore why the fight is happening in this one place and what it says about communities like it around the country. As he wrote in the *Wall Street Journal*, "Rowan County is classified as a College Town in the American Communities Project, a data analysis project based at American University. It was one of only eight counties in Kentucky that voted for Barack Obama in 2008 . . . But the counties around it are mostly classified as Working Class Country counties, places that are marked by strong socially conservative attitudes and values. The mix of the two county types can produce tensions . . . That makes Rowan County—and communities like it—prime places for the fight now unfolding there. Both sides of the issue are represented there: Gay couples seeking marriage licenses and an official unwilling to grant them" (Chinni 2015).

For reporters like Chinni, data helps move political reporting away from the more anecdotal reporting or self-reported information. For example, when discussing the fallout from the 2012 election, Chinni stressed that he saw the Republican Party losing voters from more moderate areas of the country. He used his community type analysis to explore how Romney had lost ground in moderate communities even though self-described "independents" had gone for the Republican. Chinni told NBC's Chuck Todd, "The way I like to think of the middle is not just 'independents.' Independents are self-described. I like talking about places because places are what they are. They can't describe themselves, the numbers describe them to you and these places are moderate." He went on to point out that Romney had lost votes in many of these critical exurb counties (Finkler 2012).

The American Communities Project represents an important step in the continued evolution of how reporters consider data and place in political reporting. It aims to move beyond red and blue America, and seeks to inject more of a sense of place into sterile demographic types like "soccer moms" and "NASCAR dads." As Chinni explained at a TedX Talk in 2011, the idea of finding common beliefs and similar traits across places is increasingly important, telling the audience, "I think that we really misunderstand community in America in a couple ways that lead us off on some bad tracks when we make policy decisions and try to decide what to do as a country. And I think I have a better way of dealing with the issue of community, of understanding the idea of community that really captures the nuances and subtleties of really what makes an American place part of a cohesive whole" (Chinni 2011). By merging the demographic understanding with a geographic grouping, the work of the American Communities Project represents how political reporting seeks to move beyond horse race journalism and poll-driven who's-up and who's-down to a more sophisticated understanding of how communities differ and how they are similar, a marked difference from the us-and-them reporting that has become more of a hallmark of partisan outlets.

See also: Data Journalism; FiveThirtyEight (538)

Further Reading

Chinni, Dante. 2010. *Our Patchwork Nation: The Surprising Truth about the "Real" America*. New York: Gotham Books.

Chinni, Dante. 2011. "TEDxMidAtlantic 2011—Dante Chinni—Our Patchwork Nation." TedX. December 6. Accessed January 19, 2016. https://www.youtube.com/watch?v=6sqAkLiUlm0.

Chinni, Dante. 2015. "Rowan County, Ground Zero in Gay Marriage License Fight." *Wall Street Journal*. September 3. Accessed January 19, 2016. http://blogs.wsj.com/washwire/2015/09/03/rowan-county-ground-zero-in-gay-marriage-license-fight.

Finkler, Cathy. 2012. "America: No longer Just Red and Blue." MSNBC. December 5. Accessed January 16, 2016. http://www.msnbc.com/the-daily-rundown/america-no-longer-just-red-and-blue.

"What Is the ACP?" American Communities Project. Accessed January 18, 2016. http://americancommunities.org/about.

AMERICAN ENTERPRISE INSTITUTE (AEI)

One of the leading think tanks in Washington, D.C., the American Enterprise Institute has built a reputation for fostering and promoting some of the most influential public policy experts in the last half-century. Although these experts usually have conservative leanings and work for Republican administrations, the institute itself stresses it is an independent organization and not wedded to any one view or one party. AEI now boasts some 200 people working at its D.C. offices and an array of scholars and fellows at institutions around the country.

AEI grew out of an effort started in 1938 by asbestos manufacturer Lewis Brown. Brown launched the American Enterprise Association as a business organization that aimed to ensure the government controls that were developed in the Depression and later during World War II would not continue after the war. The AEA's "spirit was libertarian and conservative rather than simply 'probusiness.' Its founding mission statement would still serve well: to promote 'greater public knowledge and understanding of the social and economic advantages accruing to the American people through the maintenance of the system of free, competitive enterprise'" (American Enterprise Institute 2009). In 1943, the organization moved from New York to Washington, D.C. and re-established itself as AEI, with a major focus on implementing classically liberal ideas of limited government and economic freedom. The AEI board is still heavily tilted toward key business leaders, with the heads of Molson Coors, International Paper, BNSF Railways, and State Farm Insurance serving on its board alongside notable conservatives like former vice president Dick Cheney and school choice advocate Betsy DeVos.

Despite its clear intellectual bias toward business, AEI aimed at establishing a high bar for its research work from its outset. It would not simply advocate for specific policies, but would seriously examine differing policy options across a spectrum of political perspectives and on a wide array of topics—from foreign policy to education proposals. A year after being established in D.C., AEI created an economic advisory board made up of highly respected economists and political scientists that represented a mix of disciplines and views. This focus on ensuring their work be seen as independent remains a major staple of the institute. Even in its mission statement, its executives say they recognize that "AEI operates at the intersection of scholarship and politics, aiming to elevate political debate and improve the substance of government policy. Many of the subjects of AEI research and publications are controversial, and many are the focus of political contention and intense interest-group advocacy. Many AEI scholars and fellows are or have been directly engaged in practical politics and policymaking as government officials, advisers or members of official commissions" (American Enterprise Institute 2015). Because of these facts, AEI maintains clear parameters on advocating for policies and express political work, and it will not do work for hire.

Like most institutions in Washington, D.C., AEI has gone through cycles where it is highly respected and deeply influential and other periods where it was eclipsed by other groups, especially among conservatives. By the 1980s, some were wondering if the era of the post-World War II think tanks was coming to an end, supplanted by the rise of the advocacy think tanks that worked as much to get policies passed through Congress as to inform the debate on public policies. A 1986 examination of the conservative think tank movement concluded, "A.E.I., once Washington's most influential citadel of mainstream conservative policy research, has perhaps been the most seriously injured by the rise of the advocacy tanks. In 1980 it looked as though A.E.I. would be the darling of the Reagan Administration. But as the advocacy tanks sprang up, it became clear that the thoughtful, stodgy institute was not at the cutting edge of influence" (Wilentz 1986). Instead, many Republicans looked toward the Heritage Foundation for policy advice and advocacy.

Still, the research and work done by AEI continued to hold sway and the scholars the institute nurtured emerged as critical leaders of Republican policies. The institute helped shape and advocate for the Reagan era support for anti-Communist rebels in Nicaragua and Honduras. Some 20 AEI scholars or staff joined the administration of President George W. Bush after the 2000 election. AEI folks also became closely associated with the neoconservative movement that advocated for an aggressive post-9/11 foreign policy, which included the eventual invasion of Iraq.

After flourishing during the early 2000s, support for the institute appeared to sag in the post-Bush years. The recession of 2008–9 taxed the organization even as new leadership took the helm. But in 2013, conservative rival the Heritage Foundation brought on former U.S. senator and Tea Party favorite Jim DeMint to be its new president. Under DeMint's leadership Heritage has become more a political organization, allowing AEI to re-emerge as a major force among conservative-leaning think tanks. As *Newsweek* reported in 2014, "AEI is on the rise. Its influence is growing on Capitol Hill, where [AEI president Arthur] Brooks, a former musician and college professor, is now a sought-after counsel to Republicans like House Budget Committee chairman and presidential hopeful Paul Ryan, R-Wis., and House Majority Leader Eric Cantor, R-Va. Earlier this year, Brooks delivered the keynote address at both House and Senate GOP retreats" (Levy 2014). Under Brooks's leadership, the institute weathered the financial troubles of the recession and has attracted major new funding, including a $20 million donation from the chairman of the private equity group, the Carlyle Group.

AEI's influence is not limited just to influencing Republican leaders or staffing GOP administrations. The organization is also a major source for journalists seeking experts on matters from tax policy to relations with China. The institute, with its mix of intellectual influence, policy development, social media followers, and media references ranked as the best at garnering public attention, and this public role "can indicate subtler influence behind the scenes, as when reporters quote researchers known to hold the most sway" (Clark and Roodman 2013).

See also: Conservative Think Tanks; Heritage Foundation

Further Reading

American Enterprise Institute. 2001. "History of AEI." July 8. Accessed July 9, 2015. http://web.archive.org/web/20090708195505/http://www.aei.org/history.

Clark, Julia, and David Roodman. 2013. "Measuring Think Tank Performance An Index of Public Profile." Center for Global Development. June. Accessed July 10, 2015. http://www.cgdev.org/sites/default/files/think-tank-index_0_0.pdf.

Levy, Pema. 2014. "Arthur Brooks's Push to Make the American Enterprise Institute—and Republicans—Relevant Again." *Newsweek*. April 1. Accessed July 15, 2015. http://www.newsweek.com/2014/04/11/arthur-brookss-push-make-american-enterprise-institute-and-republicans-relevant-248065.

Wilentz, Amy. 1986. "On the Intellectual Ramparts: New Think Tanks Are Advocating as Well as Incubating Ideas." *Time*. September 1. Accessed July 10, 2015. http://www.cnn.com/ALLPOLITICS/1997/09/01/back.time.

ANONYMOUS SOURCES

The use of anonymous sources, a long-standing element of investigative reporting, has increased in all forms of reporting, including coverage of politics. The use of these sources raises ethical and legal questions for reporters and, according to public advocates and press critics, deepens reader skepticism about the trustworthiness of what they read or see. Despite these concerns, political reporting has come to rely heavily on loosely sourced stories that try to offer insider knowledge of what is happening on a campaign—despite the risks of manipulation by politicians or operatives seeking to make information public without their name being associated with it.

Anonymity as a tool of political speech has a long and controversial history in the United States. One of the most important early court decisions in what would become the United States stemmed from an anonymous source decrying public misdeeds. John Peter Zenger, a New York printer, was imprisoned by the colonial authorities in 1734 and charged with seditious libel. His crime was publishing a newspaper—the *New York Weekly Journal*—filled with attacks on the colonial governor and other corrupt authorities. The attacks were penned by some of the governor's sharpest critics, but ran in the paper printed by Zenger under pen names like Cato. The reason for the anonymity was to avoid economic or legal retribution from the authorities. The lawyer for Zenger argued that despite his apparent guilt under the British laws of the time, the jurors should consider a larger question: "The question before the Court and you, Gentlemen of the jury, is not of small or private concern . . . And I make no doubt but your upright conduct this day will not only entitle you to the love and esteem of your fellow citizens, but every man who prefers freedom to a life of slavery will bless and honor you as men who have baffled the attempt of tyranny, and by an impartial and uncorrupt verdict have laid a noble foundation for securing to ourselves, our posterity, and our neighbors, that to which nature and the laws of our country have given us a right to liberty of both exposing and opposing arbitrary power (in these parts of the world at least) by speaking and writing truth" (Linder 2001). The jury's decision to free Zenger established a critical separation between the laws of England and the emerging laws of America, but it also established that journalism could embrace anonymity and use it when confronting power and combating corruption.

Despite its long history, modern use of anonymous sources is more often traced back to the Watergate scandal of the 1970s. During the reporting of the break-in of the Democratic National Party headquarters in the Watergate building in downtown Washington, D.C., *Washington Post* reporter Bob Woodward reached out to someone he simply referred to as "a friend of mine," who worked in the Justice Department. Woodward's friend was then Deputy Director of the Federal Bureau of Investigations, W. Mark Felt. Felt refused to be a source for Woodward's reporting, but he did offer advice about where to focus the reporting and helped keep the paper on the trail of the story. Woodward's work with colleague Carl Bernstein reporting connected the break-in to an entire campaign of so-called dirty tricks waged by a team of Republicans and aimed at discrediting and weakening the opponents of President Richard Nixon. The group's efforts were funded by a slush fund controlled by the senior members of the campaign. In the wake of this disclosure, the Nixon administration sought to cover up the dirty tricks work. They used government agencies and intimidation to obstruct the investigation and make it nearly impossible for Woodward and Bernstein to find sources willing to go on the record. Felt, who was given the nickname "Deep Throat"—a reference to a porn movie at the time—was one of the anonymous sources the pair used in their reporting. The stories the *Post* and others reported about the cover-up, almost by their nature, required anonymity as those who knew information faced real and perceived threats from some of the most powerful intelligence agencies and political figures in the country. That, combined with the famous portrayal of Woodward's late-night meetings and cloak-and-dagger communications with Felt in the book and movie *All the President's Men*, created a mystique around anonymous sources that fueled much of their use in the later 1970s and early 1980s.

Anonymous sources emerged in the 1970s as not just a necessary evil in journalism, but a useful instrument. Even the head of the ethics program and the journalism think tank the Poynter Institute said, "I don't think we can function without it (anonymity) . . . It's an essential tool to use at the right time and in the right place" (Goodwin and Smith 1984). That ethical decision of how and when to use them led news organizations, followed by many outlets, to develop an informal set of rules about when to allow the use of these sources. First, a journalist should always weigh the importance of the story he or she is reporting: is it about a matter of such public interest that the information the source has is worth the protection of anonymity the journalist can grant? Second, the journalist must consider the motivation of the source: do they benefit from the story getting out without their taking responsibility for their part in releasing the information? Would they face some sort of retribution that makes protecting their identity clearly important? Third, the journalist must determine how much direct knowledge the source has about the matter: are they conveying first-hand information or passing on rumors?

Even with these ethical check-ins, many news organizations refused to use unnamed sources and their use was often a matter of heated debate. For example, in 1992 the *Seattle Times* was debating whether to report a story about U.S. Senator Brock Adams. Eight women were accusing him of sexual harassment, assault, and in at least one case, rape. But despite repeated attempts to have them go on the record with their accusations, they refused. The journalists continued reporting the story and the paper came up with a novel way of ensuring the sources were at least partially responsible for the information the paper was about to report. Each of the eight women signed a statement, never publicly released, that said if the paper were sued for libel they would testify as to what they told the reporters. The executive editor at the time, Michael Fancher, said without those statements the paper would have never run the story. When they did run it, the story included in the third paragraph this explanation, "The women, fearful of being thrust into the public spotlight, all spoke to the *Times* on the condition their names not be published. Seven have signed statements attesting to the truth of their stories and another has said she will. They all acknowledged they could be required to testify in court should Adams sue the *Times*, as his lawyer has threatened" (Gilmore, Nalder, Pryne, and Boardman 1992). Senator Adams denied the incidents but never sued. He announced that same day he would not seek reelection.

Despite its history and critical role in major investigations like Watergate and the Adams affair, journalists have long debated the use and overuse of anonymous sources. There are two major arguments against their use—one that sounds important and the other that actually gets reporters' hackles up. First the high-minded

argument: At a time when the public questions the techniques and honesty of reporters, using unnamed officials to report on matters of relatively little importance
deepens the reader's cynicism about the reporter. The Society of Professional Journalists, not surprisingly, leads with this criticism of anonymous sources, urging reporters, "Identify sources whenever feasible. The public is entitled to as much
information as possible on sources' reliability." The SPJ white paper on anonymous
sources goes on to explain, "The most important professional possession of journalists is credibility. If the news consumers don't have faith that the stories they are
reading or watching are accurate and fair, if they suspect information attributed to
an anonymous source has been made up, then the journalists are as useful as a parka
at the equator" (Society of Professional Journalists).

The other criticism of the use of anonymous sources is the fact that it puts the
reporter on the hook for conveying the information the source wants conveyed,
while the source him- or herself does not need to take any responsibility for the
information. It, in a very real way, shifts the power in the relationship between source
and reporter to the source. Many within Washington realize and have made use of
this shift. One particularly illuminating article, from a former member of the U.S.
Army and an official who has worked with NATO and other multinational groups,
argued that many officials in Washington incorporate anonymous sources into
media strategies. The way he explained it, "When you read a news account which
cites 'unnamed sources' and 'a senior defense official' and 'a senior military leader'
and other such anonymous sources, you are often (though not always) being fed a
line. A polite lie on the journalist's part, but the problem is, you have not been let
in on the lie. It is a well-defined pirouette between journalists, political public affairs officers in all of the federal agencies, and the professional civil servants and
military officers who serve at the direction of our political leaders" (Bateman 2013).
The idea is, political communication specialists will plan on what information they
will put into the public arena with a name and title attached to it, and then they
will put out a second wave of information with no name attributed to it and only
a general description of what kind of job the person holds.

By using this information and following the rules established by the officials,
journalists agree to protect the source so as to access the information. It is a deal
many reporters don't like making, but the idea of not having the briefing or the
quote is also unappetizing. It is an ethical challenge reporters face on almost a daily
basis, especially when covering politics. Their desire to know what is going on and
where things stand in the campaign runs into the campaign's efforts to control the
message and set the agenda. To try and combat campaign-speak and empty photo
ops of life on the campaign trail, reporters will offer a source the option to "go on
background," being identified only as something like "a source familiar with the
candidate's thinking" or "a senior campaign official." To Bateman's point, if the reporter knows the source and feels they are going to get the real story of what is going
on, it can be a worthy investment of the reporter's credibility. But if there is no relationship, the source may just be using the reporter to get out another version of

the campaign's message. There is almost no way for a reader to know, and increasingly it is hard for the reporter to know as well. The result is stories like the one that frustrated the *New York Times* public editor in 2014. Margaret Sullivan reported that a March 14, 2014, article in the paper had carried the following section, "One Democratic lawmaker, who asked not to be identified, said Mr. Obama was becoming 'poisonous' to the party's candidates. At the same time, Democrats are pressing senior aides to Mr. Obama for help from the political network." She went on to say the quote wasn't "a personal smear, it is harsh. I think it runs up against the *Times'* own admonition: 'The vivid language of direct quotation confers an unfair advantage on a speaker or writer who hides behind the newspaper'" (Sullivan 2014). Sullivan's worry, and that echoed across many editors' critiques of anonymous sources, is that the granting of anonymity happens too quickly and too often—that stories that use anonymous sources are almost never of the seriousness of a Watergate.

The use of anonymous sources creates more than just an ethical tension within the newsroom. It also can have very real and difficult legal ramifications for the reporter and the source. Although a patchwork of state laws and state judicial rulings have created a so-called reporter's privilege, by which a reporter may not be required to testify and reveal the identity of an anonymous source, at the federal level no such protection exists. This means if a reporter offers anonymity to a source and a federal court or grand jury wants to know their name, a reporter must tell them or face a contempt of court ruling and possible jail time. Reporters have been sentenced to months in jail for not divulging sources in federal leak investigations, so the offer of anonymity carries with it very legal ramifications for the reporter. Additionally, the federal government has become much more aggressive about pursuing those who cough up information to journalists, seeking indictments and jail time. A 2013 report from the Committee to Protect Journalists found that the government had pursued felony convictions under the Espionage Act of 1917 against six government officials and two contractors during the Obama presidency. Before the Obama administration there had been a total of three such prosecutions. The result, the report argues, is that "government officials are increasingly afraid to talk to the press. Those suspected of discussing with reporters anything that the government has classified as secret are subject to investigation, including lie-detector tests and scrutiny of their telephone and e-mail records" (Downie 2013).

This combination of more use of anonymous sources and a clamping down on leaks leads to an interesting result—the information these sources are leaking is less sensitive government secrets and whistleblowing, and more political positioning. Stories in local and national media now routinely carry statements that seem fairly benign, yet are anonymously sourced. A story from a July 2015 edition of *Politico* gets at this new reality. In a story about a trip to Wisconsin by President Obama, *Politico* reported that the president would seek to bash state governor Scott Walker, a possible Republican candidate in 2016. The site reported Walker "is the governor the president's aides always hold up as an example of exactly what's wrong with politics—and he would be the Democrats' nightmare scenario, if he were to win the presidency in 2016. 'The contrast between our approach on economic issues and the governor's is emblematic of the contrast between the president and the Republican Party at large,' a White House aide said Wednesday, looking ahead to the speech" (Dovere 2015). The White House aide faces little chance of being punished for such a comment and the story has other officials, like the U.S. Secretary of Labor named in the piece. Yet this kind of anonymous sourcing of officials, without a clear reason, has become a basic approach to political reporting. It is expected by officials, and usually offered by reporters.

See also: Trust in Journalism

Further Reading

Bateman, Robert. 2013. "Who Are the Anonymous Sources in DC Journalism?" *Esquire*. October 23. Accessed July 2, 2015. http://www.esquire.com/news-politics/news/a25367/anonymous-sources-in-dc-journalism-102413.

Dovere, Edward-Isaac. 2015. "Obama Will Badger Scott Walker in Wisconsin." *Politico*. July 2. Accessed July 2, 2015. http://www.politico.com/story/2015/07/barack-obama-scott-walker-overtime-wisconsin-119670.html.

Gilmore, Susan, Eric Nalder, Eric Pryne, and David Boardman. 1992. "8 More Women Accuse Adams—Allegations of Two Decades of Sexual Harassment, Abuse—And a Rape." *Seattle Times*. March 1. Accessed July 2, 2015. http://community.seattletimes.nwsource.com/archive/?date=19920301&slug=1478550.

Goodwin, Gene, and Ron Smith. 1984. *Groping for Ethics in Journalism*. Ames: Iowa State University Press.

Linder, Doug. 2001. "The Trial of John Peter Zenger: An Account." University of Kentucky Law School. Accessed June 30, 2015. http://law2.umkc.edu/faculty/projects/ftrials/zenger/zengeraccount.html.

Society of Professional Journalists. "SPJ Ethics Committee Position Papers: Anonymous Sources." Accessed July 1, 2015. http://www.spj.org/ethics-papers-anonymity.asp.

Sullivan, Margaret. 2014. "AnonyWatch, Chapter 2: A 'Poisonous' President and a Banker's Secret Yogurt." *New York Times*. March 28. Accessed July 2, 2015. http://publiceditor.blogs.nytimes.com/2014/03/28/anonywatch-chapter-2-a-poisonous-president-and-a-bankers-secret-yogurt/?_php=true&_type=blogs&_php=true&_type=blogs&smid=tw-share&_r=1.

THE *ATLANTIC*

If you want to be taken seriously as a volume of American arts and culture it helps to have the pedigree of the *Atlantic*.

Started as the *Atlantic Monthly* in 1857, the magazine was built by New Englanders of high ideals and equally high reputation to combat the evils of slavery as well as develop a more distinctive American voice on culture, literature, and the arts. It has remained a voice of educated moderation, even after moving to Washington, D.C. and reinventing itself as a digital-first publication with widely read blogs and long-form reporting.

The *Atlantic's* managing editor would later say it was a desire to combat slavery, but also to develop a more distinctive and literate perspective, that "brought a handful of men together, at about three in the afternoon on a bright April day, at Boston's Parker House Hotel. At a moment in our history when New England was America's literary Olympus, the men gathered that afternoon could be said to occupy the summit. They included Ralph Waldo Emerson, Henry Wadsworth Longfellow, James Russell Lowell, Oliver Wendell Holmes, and several other gentlemen with three names and impeccable Brahmin breeding . . . By the time these gentlemen had supped their fill, plans for a new magazine were well in hand" (Murphy 1994). The magazine also had an editor, ardent abolitionist and Romantic poet James Russell Lowell (1819–1891).

Throughout its first 150 years the *Atlantic Monthly* sought to live up to its erudite and literary founding, as Oliver Wendell Holmes once quipped, "The Atlantic is an ocean; *The Atlantic* a notion" (Goodman 2011, p. ix). That notion for decades offered writers from Mark Twain and Henry James to *Deliverance* author James Dickey their first real publication and national attention.

But the magazine was always an active participant in the political fray. From its anti-slavery beginnings, it contributed serious essays on the state of race relations, politics, war, and peace. In 1963 as thousands prepared to head for Washington for a historic civil rights march, the magazine published Martin Luther King Jr.'s "Letter from a Birmingham Jail," under a different headline—"The Negro is Your Brother." The magazine's decision to print the civil rights leader's non-violent manifesto under that title "was virtually a command that blurred the boundaries between King's viewpoint and the rising consensus of enlightened opinion" (Rieder 2014, p. 137). The magazine would for decades continue to position itself as the conscience of the country, giving space to its political leaders and conducting investigations into controversies.

Its readership was never particularly large, remaining the influential elites of Washington, New York, and Boston, but the underlying magazine industry and the sweeping changes to the media landscape would test the *Atlantic's* ability to survive. Always respected for its intellectual cache and noted contributors, the magazine was nevertheless losing money by the turn of the twenty-first century. As advertising revenue dropped, the red ink began to threaten its future viability. In 2001, the magazine stopped publishing every month and dropped to 11 issues to save money. Two years later, it went to 10 issues a year and then in 2004 it dropped "Monthly" from its name. Despite these moves, by 2005 it was losing $7 million a year and more dramatic steps were needed.

In that year the owner decided to move the magazine from its intellectual home in Boston to Washington, D.C. This was more than just a shift in locations. Most of the staff didn't leave Boston; instead, a 150-year-old media institution set about reinventing itself. The president of the Atlantic Media Group, who joined the team in 2007, said the owners and editorial team "imagined ourselves as a venture-capital-backed start-up in Silicon Valley whose mission was to attack and disrupt the *Atlantic*. In essence, we brainstormed the question, 'What would we do if the goal was to aggressively cannibalize ourselves?'" (Peters 2010). The new team became an assertive digital news company. It hired away Andrew Sullivan from Time.com, whose blog The Daily Dish would soon attract more than a million unique visitors a month. Around this time it launch the AtlanticWire, an aggregation service that culled together the best of broadcast and digital media. It also leveraged its respected brand to launch a series of popular and influential conferences that attracted thought-leaders from across the globe and brought in a healthy profit.

The magazine that had built its reputation by not just promoting new artists and thinkers but finding contributors at the peak of their influence now applied this same approach to the digital age. "From the beginnings, the *Atlantic's* authority rested on its contributors: the poets, novelists, essayists, political figures, scientists, geologists, explorers, social scientists, and their fellow writers in multiple fields, new or old" (Goodman 2011, p. xi). In this new model of media, it relied on its strength. A visit to the site now is a mix of video, news, and blogs, along with a bold list of writers along the left column. The site continues to feature and promote specific contributors like long-time writer James Fallows and new contributors.

The magazine, which still boasts a readership of some 400,000 readers and 4.2 million unique visitors a month, is owned by Atlantic Media, D.C.-native David Bradley's publishing empire that also runs the *National Journal* publications and runs a strategic messaging group called Atlantic Media Strategies that has worked with clients like C-SPAN and General Electric.

See also: C-SPAN; *National Journal*

Further Reading

Goodman, Susan. 2011. *Republic of Words: The Atlantic Monthly and Its Writers, 1857–1925.* Lebanon, NH: University Press of New England.

Murphy, Cullen. 1994. "A History of The Atlantic Monthly." *Atlantic.* Accessed January 27, 2015. https://www.theatlantic.com/past/docs/about/atlhistf.htm.

Peters, Jeremy. 2010. "Web Focus Helps Revitalize The Atlantic." *New York Times.* December 12. Accessed January 28, 2015. http://www.nytimes.com/2010/12/13/business/media/13atlantic.html?pagewanted=all.

Rieder, Jonathan. 2014. *Gospel of Freedom: Martin Luther King, Jr.'s Letter from Birmingham Jail and the Struggle That Changed a Nation.* New York: Bloomsbury Publishing USA.

AUDIENCE FRAGMENTATION

The key to mass media's business model has always been its ability to attract and maintain large audiences, which can then be monetized through advertising. With the revolution in digital production and distribution triggered by the development of the Internet, media companies have had difficulty keeping hold of their audiences. Websites, social media, and aggregators create new ways for people to find and consume content. This fragmentation across an increasingly large number of platforms and outlets has profoundly affected both the media and political communications businesses and has raised concerns that consumers can now consciously or unconsciously filter their news to align with their own political biases and to affirm their own preconceptions of political matters. It has made it difficult for media companies to attract and maintain an audience they can sell to advertisers, and it has shifted the gatekeeping function of deciding what is important away from editors and into the hands of the viewing public and their social networks.

Mass media's role in society and its entire business structure is built on the idea of appealing to a large audience. This audience has always been made up by people who come to the given news outlet based on a personal preference or geographic reality or some combination of the two. In early American media, media choices were limited by the distribution of newspapers and the affordability of directly delivered content like magazines. In most communities multiple newspapers competed for readers; by the nineteenth century there were more than a dozen newspapers in New York City alone. These papers fought one another for readers, a circulation war that literally came to blows and shots being fired during an ugly period known as the Newspaper Wars. These battles and the less bloody competition for readers were just the first of an ongoing struggle media outlets would face for the next 200 years, as media outlets sought to combat competition that would take away their market—essentially fragmenting it between competing local newspapers.

So, in essence, audience fragmentation is nothing new. Still, the changes wrought by the Internet represent a far more significant development given how media had evolved throughout the twentieth century. After the development of radio, and later television, media outlets entered an era of uneasy peace with one another. The growth of television put many papers out of business throughout the 1960s, '70s, and into the '80s, but in each of these communities at least one paper survived, often inheriting a local monopoly of newspaper readers and reaping a whirlwind of profits. Television seemed to be a limitless well of advertising revenue, so many communities could easily support multiple channels without eating into each other's profits too much. Media business plans relied on one thing: a knowable ceiling on the number of choices available to the viewer or the reader. The economics of the era made media companies a lot of money, but also did little to prepare them from the coming earthquake of cable and the later tsunami of the Internet.

Cable came first, offering an increasing number of options to viewers as more and more Americans turned away from antennas. Cable channels offered more specific programming—entire networks devoted to kids programming or sports or news or public meetings. No longer were viewers stuck waiting until the morning cartoons to entertain the kids, or hoping CBS aired the right football game. Now viewers could spread out from a handful of channels to dozens, and soon even hundreds. This first wave of fragmentation swept broadcasting throughout the 1980s and 1990s. But it was offset by two critical things: first, many people stayed with the channels they knew or never switched to cable; second, many of those that did add cable just watched more and more television, meaning there were more hours of viewership to fight over. Still, the economics of fragmentation were afoot and network viewership numbers began their inexorable slide. It is no accident that of the top 30 television series finales in the history of American television only three of them occurred after 2000—and this is to say nothing of the actual percentage of homes that tuned in, this is just raw viewership. However, all the changes that came from cable seem almost quaint compared to the fundamental shift brought by the rise of digital and mobile technologies in the 2000s.

Much has been made of the way that the Internet altered the media landscape, with good reason. Even more than cable, the Internet ended the role geography played in the creation and consumption of content. Now, a person with access to the Internet could instantly connect with information from anywhere on the globe, usually for only the cost of their Internet connection. Local newspapers, whose whole business model was based on geography, saw themselves initially freed from the limits of circulation. But soon editors realized they were competing not with one other newspaper, but every newspaper in the world—as well as television stations, radio outlets, and often even the sources they interviewed in their stories. Now the competition entered a period where consumers were far less wedded to their own local newspaper's take on a story and more driven by a desire to find "the story" or the angle on a story. This disruption to the traditional media model would be significant enough on its own, but with it came the democratization of publishing. With blogs and later social media, every individual with an Internet connection now could easily create their own content. So in addition to competing with all the other established media companies in the world that may be covering a given story, now news organizations had to compete with their own consumers to catch the attention of people. Moreover, news aggregators and commenters soon also had their own competing "news" outlets that used the original stories of newspapers and television to craft their own takes on the news.

One thorough take on how significant a development this was concluded, "Over time . . . three great technology platforms for the dissemination of news have emerged. The first to come was printing, which made the mass distribution of news possible. The second was broadcasting, which made news more readily available to large audiences more quickly and in a dramatically different format. The third great platform for the distribution of news is emerging now with the Internet and different technologies for the production and consumption of information and content that the Internet supports" (King 2010). This development has fundamentally challenged newspapers and other news outlets at the same time it has given rise to new voices less constrained and often more overtly political than the mainstream media that sought the broadest possible audience. Audience fragmentation has now become a reality of media in a way it never had before, offering nearly unlimited access to potential viewers or readers while at the same time making it incredibly difficult to maintain that audience from one story to the next. This reality marks the post-Internet media landscape and has altered everything from the economics of advertising to the ability of news organizations to claim a regular and sustainable readership.

Although the development of countless news outlets for people to receive their news from has had a clear and profound impact on the media business, the impact audience fragmentation has had on the political process itself is a source more of endless debate than of clear cause and effect. Few social scientists have mapped out a clear vision of mass media's former ability to influence elections, or how far that ability has fallen. Conventional wisdom into the 1990s went that, since most people learned about campaigns and candidates through the media, the media therefore had the ability to move large swaths of public opinion through what and whom they covered and how they chose to contextualize issues. But the quest to prove a causal relationship pushed researchers to study smaller and smaller aspects of coverage and their effects and, some argue, ended up minimizing the potential to move large numbers of voters. In fact, by the mid-1990s the prevailing perception of political scientists was that the media's power was largely an unsupported myth, perpetuated by the media itself.

Finally, a 1996 researcher pushed back and conducted research into the effects of media coverage on the independent presidential campaign of H. Ross Perot in 1992 and the coverage of the unsuccessful campaign of former senator Gary Hart. In analyzing his conclusions UCLA professor John Zaller took dead aim at the current "consensus [that] sees the media as relatively incapable of pushing citizens around, as if people are either too savvy, or too insulated from mass communication, to let that happen. I see the media as extremely capable of pushing citizens around, and I maintain that the effects of the pushing around are hard to see only because the media often push in opposite directions" (Zaller 1996).

Even if social science struggled to connect the media directly to views of the American voting public, the potential for media coverage to influence those views seemed well established when the Internet revolution overwhelmed traditional media, gave rise to a new form of peer to peer communication, and changed the entire ecosystem of how people access and process news. When Zaller planted his research flag to defend the role of the media, most Americans received political coverage from television and a large percentage turned to their local newspapers. Coverage was still heavily dependent on where you lived, and if you consumed any news you would receive a dose of political coverage whether you wanted it or not. Television, in particular, served as a political leveler, generating easy-to-understand (and some would say too shallow) political news and then delivering it to a nearly captive audience sandwiched between weather and sports. Those who wanted more information could subscribe to higher-end publications or tune into higher-brow programming on public television or a handful of cable programs, but most people had access to a similar level of local political reporting.

Into this system came the Internet, empowering citizens to access resources formerly only received through pricey subscriptions or only indirectly through local coverage. Now, with a click of a mouse a person could access the highest quality news from national and international outlets, almost always for free. The idea that information would be ubiquitously available changed the ecosystem in which voters now operated. Audience fragmentation meant that no longer would a person be told what to read or what the most important thing was to know about what happened in Washington or their state capital. One analysis of the shift sought to explain its significance: "In a media environment that is no longer constrained by a sophistication requirement or the lack of choice, people's individual choices become more important. Political information in the current media environment comes mostly to those who want it. In the starkest terms, broadcast television reduced the importance of individual content preference, while cable and Internet raises them to a level of importance not seen before" (Prior 2007).

In this era of fragmentation the individual shifted from passive recipient of the morning newspaper or evening news to an active seeker of information. Now a person could find news sources that spoke to their specific interests, skipping over those news topics that held little interest, even if those topics were the election or a war. Proponents of the new reality explained that those who really wanted to understand the dynamics of a given issue could now explore it fully from many perspectives, seeking out news sources that offered different perspectives and blogs and political information directly from leaders or activists. This notion of a fully formed opinion speaks to the democratic ideal of the empowered American voter. However, it neglects that only a relatively small percentage of people want to seek that out. The weakening of local media establishments means that more voters have potentially much less information about these same issues, unless they choose to seek it out actively. This system puts much more onus on the individual to seek, judge, find, and consume good information from reputable sources.

Instead, individuals may be more likely to seek out sources that confirm their pre-existing views, or simply unplug from political issues altogether. Now with Facebook and Twitter, even when a person is not seeking political news, the information that reaches them through their social media feeds is directly influenced by whom they have decided to follow and, especially in Facebook's case, what they have clicked on in the past. When political debates erupt into the news, people's social media feeds become inundated with news and opinion from people they have affiliated with in the past. This often means that the news being pushed to people through social media is often heavily filtered by their own preferences. After a school shooting, those pre-disposed to support gun control will be flooded by stories of the failure of policies and calls for new laws. Those who are friends with gun rights advocates or have clicked on links from those folks will see a very different line of stories and comments.

Those who seek to inform the political process worry that these tools and the fragmenting of information could damage the democratic process. Those who seek to influence and win elections have hailed many of the same developments for giving them more tools and opportunities to communicate with and energize supporters. Fragmentation can also be directly connected to the idea of microtargeting messages to specific voters for specific candidates or causes. By getting a person to follow a Twitter feed or Google the right term, a campaign can directly communicate with a voter. Through Facebook and other social media, supporters can promote a campaign's ideas and issues directly to friends and colleagues. This is, of course, fraught with potential problems for candidates. It can empower the more extreme parts of the political parties to organize and demand changes not wanted (or less fiercely wanted) by the rest of the party. For example, more ideological groups like the Tea Party on the right and celebrity politicians like Senator Elizabeth Warren on the left can become more powerful by activating social media-fueled activists to demand changes.

Despite widespread concern about its impact in fueling political polarization and weakening voters' general pool of information, many observers say it is far too soon to decry the development of more media outlets and the rise of social media. One take on the entire situation stressed the need for "caution and even disinterest. Democracies have proven to be resilient in the face of changes in the relationship between information and citizenship. The intermediaries between government and the governed may change, but many of the core institutions and social practices that underlie democratic systems appear resistant to change. As usual, whether their resilience is good or bad depends on one's perspectives. And time" (Tewksbury and Rittenberg 2012).

See also: Microtargeting; Political Polarization and the Media; Post-Truth Politics; Social Media and Politics; Trust in Journalism

Further Reading

King, Elliot. 2010. *Free For All: The Internet's Transformation of Journalism*. Evanston, IL: Northwestern University Press.

Prior, Markus. 2007. *Post-Broadcast Democracy: How Media Choice Increases Inequality in Political Involvement and Polarizes Elections*. New York: Cambridge University Press.

Tewksbury, David, and Jason Rittenberg. 2012. *News on the Internet: Information and Citizenship in the 21st Century*. Oxford: Oxford University Press.

Zaller, John. 1996. "The Myth of Massive Media Impact Revived." In *Political Persuasion and Attitude Change*. Edited by Diana Mutz, Paul Sniderman, and Richard Brody. Ann Arbor: The University of Michigan Press.

B

BALANCE

To cover a story fully, journalists often seek to ensure their reporting is balanced—that it accurately represents the multiple sides of an issue or debate. Balance has often been a goal of reporters who seek to objectively examine an issue, but as questions of trust and bias have increasingly plagued news organizations balance has become a problematic concept. Critics point out ways in which adherence to "balance" keeps reporters from offering deep insight in their reporting, and in which journalists inaccurately equate two sides of a debate.

Balance as a concept makes sense for a reporter seeking to explain a given issue. The quest for balance comes from a twentieth century focus on achieving objectivity in reporting. In the objective approach, the journalist should explore all sides of an issue and then offer up the most accurate portrayal of what they found for the reader. Although this process can take on many forms, the most traditional is for the reporter to interview different sides of a debate and then write or produce a story that reflects the debate. If a community is considering a tax plan that would benefit the major employer in a town, then the reporter ought to seek out those who support the idea and those opposed. This is a basic premise of reporting. But once you outline such a "balanced" way of reporting a story, the questions really start. What groups really benefit from the proposal and who may be harmed? Does the benefit outweigh the harm? Who decides what is a fair trade-off? Do you interview all the groups on both sides and do those groups reflect all the constituencies affected? Do you interview the same number of supporters and opponents? Are there only two sides in the debate or could there be more? Do you reflect those in the story, as well? A reporter out covering a story on deadline must grapple with all of these and may be further challenged by not knowing the subject matter intimately enough to answer many of these questions.

In the pantheon of stories where balance failed to offer readers effective and informed coverage, few stories can approach the global warming debate. As a scientific matter, human behavior impacting the atmosphere had been a discussion for decades. President Lyndon Johnson's science advisers had briefed him on early work in 1965. By the 1980s, the vast majority of science research had concluded that the earth was warming and that oil and coal use was contributing the so-called greenhouse effect. In 1988, the director of NASA's Goddard Institute for Space Studies told the U.S. Senate that human activity was fueling the problem and projections indicated it would worsen. The drumbeat of warnings would continue and by 1998 some 27 percent of Americans felt the threat of global warming was generally underestimated, 34 percent thought it correctly estimated, and about

31 percent thought it was being hyped too much according to Gallup. Since then, stories, documentaries, and political debates about the subject have continued. But more information has not created consensus on the issue. That same Gallup survey found that by 2014 the number of people who felt the global warming threat was being exaggerated had jumped 11 points to 42 percent. Not only that, but the partisan divide on the issue had deepened significantly, with 68 percent of Republicans seeing the threat as over-hyped and only 18 percent of Democrats. Global warming had, as of 2014, become a partisan issue. The underlying science had moved from being a neutral source of information to a partisan debate, subject to reporters balancing pro-global warming scientists against others who rejected the science.

When reporters started covering the story in earnest in the late 1980s and early 1990s, they turned to scientists to explain its causes and likely effects. Bill McKibben, who wrote a 1998 book on the environmental issue, watched as what had been a science story morphed into something new. He told the *Columbia Journalism Review*, "Journalists talked to scientists and just reported it. It hadn't occurred to them that it should be treated as a political issue as opposed to a scientific one . . . It wasn't long before the fossil fuel industry did a good job of turning it into a political issue, a partisan thing they could exploit, when they started rolling out all the tools that we now understand as an effort to overcome the science. And their main target was the media" (Eshelman 2014). McKibben and others who have studied what happened to the global warming debate point out that energy companies and a handful of scientists who studied climate change differed from the bulk of the scientists working in this field, arguing that climate change could be the result of other factors, including natural cycles, or may not be happening at all.

What happened next has been widely seen as a failure of balanced reporting. As journalists reported on the scientific research that noted the growing impact on climate of human activity, they sought out reaction from critics who argued there is another side. Scientific stories rarely have 100 percent agreement on the science and few reporters possess the scientific knowledge to examine the research itself for its relative strength. So many journalists reverted to the "balanced" approach of interviewing one side and then a representative of the side that disagreed. Teya Ryan, one broadcast editor who has covered story a lot, noted that "journalists have felt compelled to seek out the contrary points of view, in some cases calling on experts with doubtful expertise and motive . . . Who is right? . . . With a balanced report the audience is left with more questions than answers" (Wildavsky 1997).

One of the most striking examples of how to represent the debate came not from a journalist but from comedian John Oliver who took to his HBO program in 2014 to critique the issue and the media's coverage of it. Oliver noted that a meta analysis of climate research found that 97 percent of research papers about climate change took the position that human activity was contributing significantly to global warming. He then added, "I think I know why some people are still open to debate because on TV it is, and it is always one person for and one person against . . . more often than not it is Bill Nye the Science Guy versus some dude and when you look at the screen it is 50/50, which is inherently misleading" (Oliver 2014). Oliver then had on Nye and a purported skeptic, then brought out 96 additional scientists and two supposed deniers to debate. While creating on-screen chaos, the skit was meant to highlight the problem with balance when the groups being represented are so imbalanced.

But the quest for balance—and the problems it creates—is not limited to science. Political reporting has strained to address the increasingly partisan and shrill debates in Washington, especially as the Republican Party has moved further right. The generic idea of balance has struggled as extreme factions on the right and, to a lesser degree, on the left have pushed their parties to reject political compromises. News organizations have often simply allowed extreme partisan A to debate extreme partisan B, and the result has been called "balanced." But two long-time political observers, think tank veterans Thomas Mann and Norman Ornstein, took to the *Washington Post* to plead with reporters not to treat the derailing of America's political institutions as a process story that can rely on presenting two points of view. The authors argue, "We understand the values of mainstream journalists, including the effort to report both sides of a story. But a balanced treatment of an unbalanced phenomenon distorts reality. If the political dynamics of Washington are unlikely to change anytime soon, at least we should change the way that reality is portrayed to the public. Our advice to the press: Don't seek professional safety through the even-handed, unfiltered presentation of opposing views. Which politician is telling the truth? Who is taking hostages, at what risks and to what ends?" (Mann and Ornstein 2012).

Balance tends to become a problem when stories are driven by quoted sources. Report what source A says and then get a response from source B. Some have sought to respond to Mann and Ornstein's challenge by, at times, relying on data to tell the story and moving away from quoted sources. For example, former blogger and Washingtonpost.com writer Christopher Ingraham used a political science data analysis of voting records to examine the ideological makeup of Congress and produced a potent analysis that noted, "in the most recent Congress nearly 90 percent of Republican House members are *not* politically moderate. By contrast, 90 percent of Democratic members *are* moderates. It's quite difficult to square a chart like this with a claim that Democrats are abandoning the center faster than Republicans. As the chart shows, there are plenty of centrist Democrats left in the House—but hardly any centrist Republicans" (Ingraham 2015). Ingraham's report on the partisanship of the House Republicans involved no interview of the Republicans in question and relied solely on a statistical analysis. While this story does not answer the questions of why it is happening, it deftly avoids dismissing the changing nature of Republican politics by quoting one person who said the party is more extreme and another person who rejects that.

As has been highlighted in the global warming coverage, industries and politicians often seek to exploit the quest for balance to influence coverage of a topic.

Lobbying groups, political parties, and bloggers have all taken advantage of the media's need for balance by offering themselves up to comment on a specific topic. This reality has caused frustration for many who see political reporting as an impediment to accomplishing anything in the already fractured political system. For example, as the presidential campaign heated up in 2012, the New York Times reported on one politician who no longer saw the press as helpful to the political process: President Barack Obama. The article noted, "Privately and publicly, Mr. Obama has articulated what he sees as two overarching problems: coverage that focuses on political winners and losers rather than substance; and a 'false balance,' in which two opposing sides are given equal weight regardless of the facts" (Chozick 2012). But that very same article later carried two quotes—one from the liberal blog Talking Points Memo and one from the conservative Power Line. Each offered little additional insight on the issue and were included to offer balance about the kind of media environment the president operates within, which highlights how difficult it is to escape the quest for balance.

Yet for all the criticism, balance remains a critical idea within journalism. Balance ensures that the media offers the reader or viewer multiple perspectives on critical issues. It can help create more informed policy discussions. After all, Congress holds hearings into subjects it is considering and invites multiple representatives from different groups to offer their opposing views of proposed legislation. No one thinks this is a bad idea and applying the concept to the media is something that few, at least in principle, are opposed to encouraging. In fact, much of the history of the government's regulation of broadcasting has to do with ensuring multiple views were heard. As historian of communication policy, Robert Horwitz notes, "The public interest in broadcasting was translated to mean the preservation of diverse viewpoints, some degree of local control and local program orientation, the provision of news and information, a general balance of programming . . . and equitable treatment of political candidates" (Horwitz 2005). This has manifested itself in congressional legislation that mandates the Corporation for Public Broadcasting ensure that PBS and NPR adhere to "objectivity and balance" in their programming and reporting. It is also the idea that prompted the Federal Communication Commission to impose the Fairness Doctrine on broadcasters to ensure multiple perspectives are heard.

Despite this legislative interest in the idea of balance, the concept remains fuzzy at best. Some news organizations, most notably Fox News, have sought to embrace balance as a marketing strategy, using it as a way to differentiate itself from competitors. For journalists, on a daily basis it continues to manifest itself as a technique in reporting. But for journalism advocates it remains more a platitude or ideal to be aspired to rather than a model for reporting. In their book, The Elements of Journalism: What Newspeople Should Know and the Public Should Expect, journalists Bill Kovach and Tom Rosenstiel chose not to list balance as one of their nine principles of journalism's compact with the public. The two note, "after synthesizing what we have learned, it became clear that a number of familiar and even useful ideas—including fairness and balance—are too vague to rise to the level of essential elements of the profession" (Kovach and Rosenstiel 2001). And that may be the most critical thing about balance in news coverage. Individual stories and entire news organizations seek to ensure that their stories reflect the multitude of opinions and positions on a given story, but often the way that diversity manifests itself is severely limiting. One cannot interview every person with an opinion on a given topic. The journalist must select opinions to focus on, and balance can become a he said/she said equation that reduces complex and multifaceted issues to a simple dichotomy that does not serve the reader well. As with almost any journalistic issue, the challenge is in how the ideal moves into reality and when it comes to balance, often the reality is too simplistic to help the reader or viewer understand the facts.

See also: Objectivity; Political Bias and the Media; Post-Truth Politics; Trust in Journalism

Further Reading
Chozick, Amy. 2012. "Obama Is an Avid Reader, and Critic, of the News." *New York Times*. August 7. Accessed December 21, 2015. http://www.nytimes.com/2012/08/08/us/politics/obama-is-an-avid-reader-and-critic-of-news-media-coverage.html?_r=1&ref=politics.
Eshelman, Robert. 2014. "The Danger of Fair and Balanced." *Columbia Journalism Review*. May 1. Accessed December 21, 2015. http://www.cjr.org/essay/the_danger_of_fair_and_balance.php.
Horwitz, Robert. 2005. "Communication Regulation in Protecting the Public Interest." In *The Press*. Edited by Geneva Overholser and Kathleen Hall Jamieson. New York: Oxford University Press.
Ingraham, Christopher. 2015. "This Astonishing Chart Shows How Moderate Republicans Are an Endangered Species." *Washington Post*. June 2. Accessed December 21, 2015. https://www.washingtonpost.com/news/wonk/wp/2015/06/02/this-astonishing-chart-shows-how-republicans-are-an-endangered-species.
Kovach, Bill, and Tom Rosenstiel. 2001. *The Elements of Journalism: What Newspeople Should Know and the Public Should Expect*. New York: Crown Books.
Mann, Thomas, and Norman Ornstein. 2012. "Let's Just Say It: The Republicans Are the Problem." *Washington Post*. April 27. Accessed December 21, 2015. https://www.washingtonpost.com/opinions/lets-just-say-it-the-republicans-are-the-problem/2012/04/27/gIQAxCVUlT_story.html.
Oliver, John. 2014. "Last Week Tonight with John Oliver: Climate Change Debate." *HBO*. May 11. Accessed December 21, 2015. https://www.youtube.com/watch?v=cjuGCJJ-UGsg.
Wildavsky, Aaron. 1997. *But Is It True?: A Citizen's Guide to Environmental Health and Safety Issues*. Cambridge, MA: Harvard University Press.

BALLOT ACCESS
Supporters of third parties point to the patchwork of laws that govern whose name and what parties will appear on a given state election ballot as one of the most significant structural impediments to greater diversity in the nation's politics. These same laws also play a significant role in shaping the coverage of campaigns because many news

groups and debate organizers use access to the ballot, along with polling and campaign finance performance, to decide what amount of coverage or participation a given candidate should receive.

Ballot access laws are passed by state legislatures and vary wildly from state to state. This lack of uniformity can result in dramatically different slates of candidates. For example, in 2008 Colorado listed 16 candidates for president while neighboring Oklahoma only listed President Barack Obama and Republican challenger Senator John McCain. The reason? Colorado will place a name on the ballot if 5,000 signatures from registered voters are submitted or if the candidate pays $1,000. Oklahoma requires independents or third-party candidates to gather the signatures of the equivalent of 3 percent of voters in the previous presidential election—meaning a candidate would need to gather more than 40,000 signatures in a state with 1.5 million fewer people than Colorado. And even this requirement is not the most stringent. Georgia and North Carolina appear to be the strictest states. Georgia automatically places the name of Republican and Democratic candidates on the ballot, but any other candidate needs to get signatures from 5 percent of the registered voters in the district. North Carolina has the same setup, but only requires signatures from 4 percent of registered voters. These rules make it difficult to impossible for an independent—or even many third-party candidates—with limited funds to gather enough signatures to qualify for the ballot.

Some political leaders have sought to ease this burden. U.S. Representative Ron Paul, the Texas Republican who once ran as the Libertarian Party presidential candidate, has pushed for national reforms, including proposing the Voter Freedom Act to set more reasonable national standards for presidential ballot access. Paul said of the current system, "supporters of the two-party monopoly regularly use ballot-access laws to keep third-party and independent candidates off ballots. Even candidates able to comply with onerous ballot-access rules must devote so many resources to simply getting on the ballot that their ability to communicate their ideas to the general public is severely limited."

This stranglehold on ballot access stems from, in many cases, an effort to give the voter more anonymity in their election preferences and a post–World War II effort to battle the Communist Party. In the early days of the United States, voting was not a private affair. Political parties printed their tickets, literally a list of the party's candidates for different offices that the voter would turn in. Many of these tickets were printed on colored paper or in specific shapes so that party officials could monitor which party vote was being dropped off. Party workers could pressure voters to cast their ballot for the right party or face losing a political job or the support of the party.

By the mid-nineteenth century concerns about intimidation and vote buying prompted governments around the world to seek solutions. The UK started using secret ballots in some elections, and Australia soon followed suit, prompting the United States also to adopt what it called, incorrectly, the "Australian ballot." Several things marked this new form of voting, including a single ballot of all approved candidates that could be marked, in private, at a polling place. 1888 marked the last time that some states allowed public voting. Kentucky that year allowed verbal voting where voters cast their votes out loud to the election official. Another part of the electoral reform that became more controversial over the years was the idea that the government ought to organize and print the ballot at public expense. Those who advocate for the rights of third parties saw this aspect of the Australian ballot as a disaster, with one bemoaning, "With the arrival of the Australian ballot on these shores, the provision of ballots—and the determination of who was and who was not to be included on those ballots—would, if not in the blink of an eye then in the turn of an election cycle, become the province of the state governments. What had, theretofore, been a privately furnished good—ballots—was now monopolized by government. Mischief, to put it mildly, ensued. And democracy did not flourish" (Bennett 2009).

The move to have the state regulate and print ballots handed the decision-making for determining qualified candidates to the state legislatures. These legislatures passed a myriad of different laws, for different reasons. Many cited fear of the rise of Communism in a wave of ballot access laws passed in the 1930s and 1940s. Like many other government actions, these prompted a slew of lawsuits by candidates denied access to run for office. An array of court decisions offered some guidance over the years, permitting regulation of ballot access to "prevent clogging" and "avoid frivolous and fraudulent candidacies." Courts also said states had a valid interest in ensuring elections were legitimate and in preventing "splintered parties and unrestrained factionalism."

On the flipside, the court limited the ways in which states could try and regulate the ballot. For example, a 1974 California Supreme Court decision ruled states could not require someone to be forced to pay filing fees to get listed, writing "a State may not, consistent with constitutional standards, require from an indigent candidate filing fees that he cannot pay; denying a person the right to file as a candidate solely because of an inability to pay a fixed fee, without providing any alternative means, is not reasonably necessary to the accomplishment of the State's legitimate interest of maintaining the integrity of elections." Many states instead decided to set benchmarks of signatures as a constitutionally safe way for a candidate to demonstrate interest in and legitimacy of their candidacy. However, the signature question triggered its own wave of state regulations that sought some clarity on this issue. The result, according to experts who have studied parties, hit independent candidates and third parties hard, with one writing, "The diversity in laws among the 50 states and the District of Columbia is an expensive logistical nightmare for any third party trying to obtain access to the ballot across the nation" (Shock 2008). The effects of these laws on third-party organizing can be seen in the fact that only three minor parties are registered in more than 10 states—the liberal Green Party, the Libertarian Party, and the conservative Constitution Party.

Ballot access also has a powerful influence on media coverage of a campaign. Similar to states' interest in weeding out "unserious" candidates, the media seeks to focus its attention on candidates that will inform the voters' decisions in a way that helps them make a rational choice. This is, obviously, a fundamentally subjective decision, but a popular one. If, as happened in 2012, 412 declared candidates run for president, the media must have a way to decide which candidates to focus on. The basic test, used by almost all debate organizers and editors, is "Can the person win?" This may be subjective, or it may involve basic mathematics—does the person appear on the ballot in enough districts to win the election? If the answer is no, it is easier to discount the candidate. And here is where ballot access laws can directly affect coverage. Obtaining signatures from 4 percent of the registered voters in a given state is an enormous challenge, one made more difficult by the fact that the media will decide not to cover them until they qualify, thus creating a chick-and-egg situation.

Some impartial observers believe ballot access laws may actually be a useful way to vet candidates and develop more electable third parties. One political scientist found that these requirements force candidates to organize and to develop a base of support, so that those who did qualify had a better chance of doing well in the election (Lee 2012).

The cautionary tale of ballot access and third parties may be told in the story of Americans Elect. Americans Elect was a 2012 effort that aimed to address the ballot access issues that had dogged previous independent and third-party operations. They would do it differently, by raising money and doing the legwork to ensure access to the ballot in states for a new centrist candidate that could compete face-to-face with Democrat Barack Obama and Republican Mitt Romney. The group started out with some real momentum. Former Cabinet secretary and New Jersey Gov. Christine Todd Whitman and Manhattan private equity tycoon Peter Ackerman signed on to the effort. Soon the effort could boast some $35 million in funding, and it launched a snazzy website that encouraged people to sign up as a party delegate and "Pick a President Not a Party." Americans Elect would leave the process of selecting a candidate open to all who cared to participate and fill out an extensive questionnaire. The organization threw itself into getting ballot access and soon had 29 states lined up—putting it only behind the Libertarian Party for total states with access by a third party. Then to some fanfare, the organization opened its nominating convention to the 360,000 registered delegates. Within hours users had nominated Michael Bloomberg, Jon Huntsman, Buddy Roemer, Warren Buffett, Rahm Emanuel, and Condoleezza Rice. If any of the candidates could line up 10,000 supporters—ideally, 1,000 supporters in 10 states—they would be offered the nomination, so long as they then chose a running mate from the other major party to ensure balance.

Sadly the initial excitement soon faded, and by a self-appointed deadline of May 15 the group had no candidate meet the 10,000 vote mark. Former Louisiana governor Buddy Roemer came the closest gathering 6,000 votes. After its failure, one columnist blasted the entire effort, writing "These guys, like so many compassless folks in politics, seriously misread the American electorate and recent third party history. Third parties do not work without a guiding ideology, be it left, right, libertarian, statist, whatever. These guys stood for something a thousand times worse than the bitter hyperpartisanship they whined about: a wish-washy just do something attitude towards governance rooted in the pipe dreams of 'radical centrists'" (Quinn 2012).

Americans Elect spotlights the twin difficulties ballot access creates for upstart politicians and parties. Although it cracked the ballot access challenge by pouring resources into getting people to sign petitions in states across the country, its lack of a clear philosophy and political standing created no excitement or unity among its supporters. Other third parties may find exciting candidates, but they're usually candidates who only excite small groups that lack the numbers to generate the money and support needed to gain ballot access. Ballot access, for all its downsides, seems to be one of the more accurate bellwethers in judging whether support for a political party or candidate is widespread, or just not that deep.

See also: Political Parties; Third-Party Marginalization

Further Reading

Bennett, James. 2009. *Stifling Political Competition: How Government Has Rigged the System to Benefit Demopublicans and Exclude Third Parties.* New York: Springer Publishers.

Lee, Daniel. 2012. "Take the Good with the Bad: Cross-Cutting Effects of Ballot Access Requirements on Third-Party Electoral Success." *American Politics Research* 40 (2).

Quinn, Garrett. 2012. "Americans Elect Failed, and That's a Good Thing." Boston.com. May 17. Accessed October 19, 2015. http://www.boston.com/community/blogs/less_is _more/2012/05/americans_elect_failed_and_we.html.

Shock, David. 2008. "Securing a Line on the Ballot: Measuring and Explaining the Restrictiveness of Ballot Access Laws for Non-Major Party Candidates in the United States." *The Social Science Journal* 45 (1).

BALLOT MEASURES

The idea of citizens casting a collective vote to make major decisions about what rules they live under or how they are governed is the most democratic of concepts. It was from this desire that the citizen ballot measure movement sprang. As states have embraced the concept of voters deciding policy issues in elections, they have also had to deal with the difficulty of turning an idea into practice. Politicians in those states have at times found that referenda and initiative elections can often make it politically dangerous to make important, but unpopular, decisions. Ballot measures have also been used by interest groups whose ability to mobilize voters may put within reach political goals unachievable in a legislature. Finally, some partisan groups have worked to put initiatives that may be very popular for their party members on ballots in close elections, in hopes of driving up voter interest and turnout.

These acts of direct democracy come from a progressive history in the United States that sought to move power closer to the individual and away from interest groups and established political parties. The concept of direct democracy was pioneered by the Swiss, whose 1848 constitution sought to put certain government actions to a vote to ensure they reflected the will of the people. By the turn of the twentieth century, the work of muckraking journalists, who exposed the corruption of the political system and the lack of fairness in the economy, and a growing organization among farmers and other laborers brought the referendum idea to the United States. South Dakota became the first state to allow statewide referenda on the ballot. The idea soon faltered, though, and for decades was left to political reformers and philosophers to consider and debate.

These advocates, in America and beyond, saw referendum as almost a philosophical end to the democratic means. As one liberal Briton proudly stated in a manifesto on behalf of referenda, "whether right or wrong, I am a democrat, and not by necessity or on a point of convenience, but by conviction. I not only believe that the majority of the citizens in any civilized, educated, homogenous community must rule, and will rule, but that they ought to rule" (Strachey 1924). But even as democrats thundered for more power to be handed to the average voter, other equally eloquent orators, concerned with the theory of direct democracy, cautioned against creating a government too subservient to the will of the majority. One writer, seeking to defend the representative system, in 1911 argued that statesmen needed some separation from the fickle public, writing that leaders like Lincoln and Washington "were not the products of any political system in which bodies of mediocre men with hobbies robbed the legislature of its dignities and authority, and subjected executive, legislative and judicial officers to the fear of recall when they pursued a course distasteful to some fraction of the electorate. Only timid, shambling, ineffective men came out of a system which strips public office of character and authority and makes it directly subservient to popular whim" (Oberholtzer 1911). In these two brief but sweeping observations are contained the core arguments both for and against the referenda. On the one hand, how could we claim to be democratic in a system where political bosses ran the major cities and most elected officials were insulated from real voters? On the other, would the tyranny of any electoral majority recalling an elected representative turn our system of government into a slightly more acceptable version of mob rule?

Following South Dakota's lead, throughout the early twentieth century a handful of states enacted rules that allowed citizens to propose and adopt state constitutional amendments. Nebraska used this power in 1934 to vote to combine the state legislature into one single, nonpartisan chamber—a move that was approved in over 90 percent of the state's counties and won by a 60 to 40 percent margin. Still, direct action by the citizens remained a fairly rare occurrence.

As the system matured and legislatures, politicians, and voters came to consider how best to use this popular electoral power, three core types of ballot measures developed: initiative, referendum, and referred measures. Using an initiative, a new law or state constitutional amendment can be placed on a ballot if it receives a certain number of signatures. The rules around these signatures vary from state to state and can mandate a specific number and/or a distribution of signatures across counties or voting districts. Sixteen states allow voters to place proposed constitutional amendments on the ballot and two allow voters to force the legislature to vote on an amendment, a so-called indirect imitative. Fewer states allow the same maneuver to propose new laws, with eleven allowing direct voting, seven indirect, and two states allowing both. Referendum, often called popular referendum, is technically used to repeal laws passed by the state legislature. Twenty-four states allow for these popular vetoes, but in reality far fewer of these efforts take place and in many of the same states voters have the ability to propose initiatives and usually choose that route. Referred measures are placed on the ballot by the state legislature. These measures can reflect a desire to circumvent a gubernatorial veto or demonstrate popular support for a policy and are allowed in all states.

The political turmoil of the 1960s and 1970s inspired more direct action by the voters; state tax policies, which the public had come to see as unfair, became one of the most popular targets of these efforts. If one moment crystalizes the birth of the modern direct referendum movement, it would most likely be the taxpayer revolt in California in 1978. A succession of liberal spending policies had forced the state to implement steep property taxes to pay for government programs. For nearly a decade, voters had become increasingly frustrated at state and local government missteps in assessing the value of their homes and the moves to increase property taxes to pay for schools and other government efforts. The anger reached a breaking point in 1978 as groups organized to put to a vote a constitutional amendment to rein in government's freedom to set tax rates. The result was a petition movement called the People's Initiative to Limit Property Taxation. The idea was that the annual real estate tax on a parcel of property would be limited to 1 percent of its assessed value and that that "assessed value" could only be increased by a maximum of 2 percent per year, until and unless the property has a change of ownership. Conservative groups quickly organized signing petitions and pushed for adoption of what became known as Proposition 13. That year, some 70 percent of eligible voters cast ballots in the election, and 65 percent of them backed Prop 13. The victory helped spark a wave of anti-tax referenda around the country, where 13 states soon adopted similar laws.

These ballot measures have triggered waves of lawsuits and deep debate over whether they reflect an improvement or undermining of the representative government system enshrined in the U.S. Constitution. Advocates see the ballot measure as the way for the citizens to assert themselves in a dysfunctional political process. For those states where the legislature has been unable or unwilling to tackle certain issues, these initiatives and referenda reflect a sort of last resort step to ensure the voice of the people is heard. But opponents worry that the ballot measure can turn every legislative decision into another campaign, with political organizations waging the same mudslinging and grassroots lobbying that elected the dysfunctional legislature in the first place. Other critics contend the popular vote can repress groups that have been disadvantaged historically or are in the minority. And still more worry that the divisive issues and shrill and contentious language that surround each ballot measure may actually serve to make compromise more difficult as the political process seeks to address the issue.

Regardless of the debate, states often serve as the battleground for these electoral questions. A major question that has dogged the ballot measure movement is how well prepared the average voter is to address these complex legislative questions. For example, in 2004 voters in the state of Montana placed the issue of medical marijuana on the ballot. The voters overwhelmingly endorsed the idea of allowing those very ill patients to access the drug, but given that it was an initiative, many of the questions of how the will of the voters would be implemented were left unaddressed. Finally, another popular vote ordered the state department of health to implement a new policy. The result was a system in which suddenly caravans of mobile marijuana registration systems were signing up hundreds of people in hotel ballrooms and storefronts selling a variety of marijuana strains opened all over the state. Within a couple years 30,000 people were legally obtaining marijuana. Voters recoiled, and now pushed the legislature to rein in the industry. The pendulum swung, and the legislature ended up severely limiting people's access to the drug and causing most growers to leave the business. Many who advocated for the patients who could demonstrate medical need expressed frustration with a system that allowed such wild swings in policy. It turns out, drafting initiatives that actually spell out implementable laws that avoid unintended consequences is much harder than voicing general policy aspirations. And even if the laws are clear, many worry about how well equipped the voter is to understand what they are voting for in given initiative or referendum.

This public understanding of ballot measures is where the role of media comes in, and where the debate over whether the media does a good job starts. First, those who have studied the issue conclude that the media is critical to how the voting public comes to see the ballot measure in question. One exploration of direct democracy found that "Initiative elections usually involve extensive media campaigns . . . to persuade voters to approve or reject a proposed policy change. The more costly an initiative campaign, the more information is provided to voters at a lower cost" (Smith and Tolbert 2009). This battle to ensure the voter is informed is one where how the media cover certain issues can become fodder for the debate itself. Conservatives who support the referendum concept say the media can either propel or inhibit the effort based on whether the popular proposal aligns with journalists' beliefs. One report from the conservative Hoover Institution alleges there is a reason why the media often takes a critical view of initiatives: "The answer, it seems, is that the beauty of ballot initiatives is in the eye of the beholder. If the cause is deemed worthy by the media, then it receives easy treatment. But those initiatives that offend liberal sensibilities are destined for rough treatment by a predominantly liberal fourth estate" (Whalen 2000). And how the media portrays the fight can vary wildly. For example, in 2008 California considered what became known as Prop 8. That year, the state supreme court voted in May to allow same-sex couples to marry, saying the state constitution protected this right. The decision spawned a movement by conservative groups to get a measure on that fall's ballot to add a provision to the state constitution that read "only marriage between a man and a woman is valid or recognized in California." The fight over Prop 8 was vicious, with both sides spending big money on the vote. In the end, with some 79 percent of eligible voters casting ballots, Prop 8 narrowly passed, 52–48 percent. The initiative would later be struck down by the federal court, but the pricey campaign both before and after the vote raised questions about the value and sense of putting complex legal and human rights issues in the form of an up or down vote by the general public.

Despite their controversial role, initiatives and referenda have emerged as a major tool by interest groups, parties, and issue advocates to affect policy and to override legislative gridlock. In 2014 alone, more than 125 measures appeared on ballots in 41 states. These measures addressed everything from increasing the state's minimum wage to whether to outlaw the use of dogs while bear hunting. Interestingly, initiatives and referenda only pass 40 percent of the time. So why spend all the time, money, and effort on them? Sometimes those measures are used as a way to drive up interest in the election among critical demographics. The *Washington Post's* Reid Wilson reported in 2014, "I'd point to initiatives like minimum wage measures in Arkansas and Alaska and a medical marijuana initiative in Florida. . . . All three of those are designed to bring specific voters, that is, in two cases, low-income residents, to the polls in Arkansas and Alaska, two states with important Senate races" (Rehm 2014). The ability of these initiatives actually to get people to polls who would not otherwise vote is somewhat unknown, but that has not stopped parties on both sides of the aisle from trying. For example, a 2004 initiative to ban gay marriage in Ohio is credited with helping ensure evangelical voters, who overwhelmingly backed President Bush for re-election, got to the polls.

But often these ballot measures are more an expression of frustration with the politics of a given state rather than a subtle get-out-the-vote tool. As state legislatures continue to struggle with controversial social and economic issues, these ballot measures will almost certainly continue to appear.

See also: Ballot Access; Get Out the Vote (GOTV); Single-Issue Politics

Further Reading
Oberholtzer, Ellis Paxson. 1911. *The Referendum in America*. New York: Charles Scribner's Sons.
Rehm, Diane. 2014. "Growing Use of State Ballot Initiatives for Political Change." Diane Rehm Show (WAMU). August 27. Accessed October 18, 2015. https://thedianerehmshow.org/shows/2014-08-27/growing-use-state-ballot-initiatives-political-change.
Smith, Daniel, and Caroline Tolbert. 2009. *Educated by Initiative: The Effects of Direct Democracy on Citizens and Political Organizations in the American States*. Ann Arbor, MI: University of Michigan Press.

Strachey, John St. Loe. 1924. *The Referendum: A Handbook to the Poll of the People, Referendum, or Democratic Right of Veto on Legislation.* London: T. Fisher Unwin Ltd.

Whalen, Bill. 2000. "Who's Afraid of the Big Bad Initiative?" Hoover Institution. July 30. Accessed October 16, 2015. http://www.hoover.org/research/whos-afraid-big-bad -initiative.

BECK, GLENN (1964–)

Glenn Beck has made a name for himself by mixing strongly conservative politics with a populist appeal to "the little guy." Add in a healthy dose of media entrepreneurship and a flair for the dramatic, and it is easy to see why Beck elicits profoundly divisive reactions.

Beck is most widely known for his daily radio program, which reaches some 7 million Americas, but whether he is speaking on the radio or television his rhetoric has often drawn attention for its strident, even violent overtones. For example, in discussing government moves to stabilize the economy in the wake of the 2008–2009 housing crash Beck took to his Fox News program to declare, "The government is full of vampires, and they are trying to suck the lifeblood out of the economy." He went on during his March 2009 show to specifically target certain members of the government, saying, "President Obama, Tim Geithner, Chris Dodd, Barney Frank, Nancy Pelosi, all the other lawmakers are going after the blood of our businesses, big and small. Who's next? They have their fangs in the necks of everybody, and nothing's going to quench their thirst . . . There's only two ways for this movie to end: Either the economy becomes like the walking dead, or you drive a stake through the heart of the bloodsuckers" (Media Matters 2009). But it is not just the sharpness of his rhetoric that makes Beck such an important figure in political media. It's also his ability to tap into intense feelings on issues and his business acumen to turn that audience into a series of news services that make him a truly diverse businessman.

Beck was born in suburban Seattle and by 13 was working radio. When he graduated high school he started hosting full time, becoming a Top 40 DJ and developing some self-confessed problems with addiction. Beck admits that by the time he was 30 he had become lost in drug and alcohol use, later telling the *New York Times*, "You've never met a more flawed guy than me" (Stelter and Carter 2009). He stopped drinking and smoking marijuana in late 1994 and found guidance by converting to the Mormon faith. He also began studying the growing power of talk radio, especially the work of conservative Rush Limbaugh. His first talk producer would tell Salon, "Beck was a close student of talk radio for years. Before he thought he was ready [to do it himself], Beck paid close attention to successful practitioners of the craft" (Zaitchik 2009).

By 2000 he was ready and the *Glenn Beck Program* went on the air in Tampa that year. Within a year his mix of politics, humor, and vitriol took the show from eighteenth to first in its time slot. The show went national in 2002 and soon Beck was reaching millions of listeners daily. Like many other national talk show hosts, Beck soon found himself adding television to his portfolio when CNN's Headline News channel offered him a nightly 30-minute commentary show. The program was not advertised as particularly conservative, instead it focused on Beck's "unique and often amusing perspective on top stories from world events and politics to pop culture and everyday hassles." But once he was on the air, Beck made a name for himself with controversial commentary and incendiary rhetoric. His cross-media status helped grow the radio audience, and soon Fox News tapped him for an evening program. He went on the air in January 2009 as President Obama came into the White House. Soon Beck, with his often off-the-cuff comments about the new president and his administration, was drawing ire from Democrats and wild praise from some conservatives.

Up until this point, Beck's career seemed to mirror other conservatives like Limbaugh and, in particular, Sean Hannity, who started in radio and segued into both talk radio and commentary cable programs. Except Beck is never ordinary. In 2002, he started a company called Mercury Radio Arts, a multimedia operation named after Orson Welles's theater company. The organization is Beck's book, radio, television, and content generating engine and allowed him, when his contract was up with Fox News in 2011, to walk away and into his own media empire. Mercury Radio Arts has more than 250 employees and produces Beck's radio program. In 2010 the group launched TheBlaze, a news and entertainment website. The site turned into Beck's digital hub as he launched an on-demand television service called TheBlaze TV and a series of best-selling books. Beck stresses his company is about serving the needs of a massive audience of Americans not being helped by traditional media, and implicitly includes former cable news employers in that mix. He sees himself as part of a new regime within the media, saying, "There's a huge war going on between those who currently have power—whether you're talking about the Federal Reserve, the government, the media networks, magazines, booksellers, whatever—and then this new way of, 'I can write and publish my own book' or 'I don't need the network anymore.' These two forces are fighting against each other, and the one that is holding on by their fingernails is the one that's going to lose, and that's the old system" (Hunter 2015).

Beck, even though still ranking behind Limbaugh and Hannity, stands out as one of the most interesting businesspeople among the talk radio crowd. He has used his personal brand to become a business unto himself, leveraging that power into movements like his 9/12 group, which seeks to re-energize the patriotic fervor in the days after the 2001 terror attacks, and his "Restoring Honor" rally in Washington, D.C.

See also: TheBlaze; Limbaugh, Rush; Talk Radio

Further Reading

"Beck Portrays Obama, Democrats as Vampire." 2009. Media Matters for America. March 30. Accessed January 4, 2015. http://mediamatters.org/video/2009/03/30/beck-portrays -obama-democrats-as-vampires-going/148746.

Hunter, Glenn. 2015. "How Glenn Beck Became a Master of Media." *D Magazine*. July/August. Accessed January 5, 2016. http://www.dmagazine.com/publications/d-ceo/2015/july-august/glenn-beck-ey-entrepreneur-of-the-year-2015.

Stelter, Brian, and Bill Carter. 2009. "Fox News's Mad, Apocalyptic, Tearful Rising Star." *New York Times*. March 29. Accessed December 30, 2015.

Zaitchik, Alexander. 2009. "Glenn Beck Rises Again." Salon. September 23. Accessed January 4, 2016. http://www.salon.com/2009/09/23/glenn_beck_three.

BLOCK, HERBERT (1909–2001)

The first cartoon Herbert Block remembered drawing on the sidewalk hinted at his future. "The first caricature I can recall doing was not some modest attempt at drawing a childhood schoolteacher (if I was even of school age at the time)," he wrote in his autobiography, *Herblock: A Cartoonist's Life*. "No, it portrayed the man held to be the arch-villain of the time: Kaiser Wilhelm of Germany" (Block 1993).

From depicting the leader of World War I Germany in sidewalk chalk, Block went on to a successful career drawing cartoons in newspaper editorial pages, lambasting politicians and pioneering the importance of political cartoons in the modern age. Known to readers as Herblock, the powerful feared him and his peers adored him. He won three Pulitzer Prizes and shared in a fourth. In his 2001 obituary in the *New York Times*, Marilyn Berger wrote that his "critical eye and rapier pen made him one of the leading journalists of his day" (Berger 2001).

Herbert Lawrence Block was born in Chicago on October 13, 1909, to David and Tessie Block. He was the youngest of three sons. He started drawing young and had such an aptitude for it that he landed a scholarship to the Chicago Art Institute when he was 12. By the time he arrived at Lake Forest College, he had already started drawing some cartoons for the *Evanston News-Index*. He liked the thrill of being published, so in 1929—after just two years of higher education—he took a job as a cartoonist for the Chicago *Daily News* and never went back (Block 1993).

After a few years at the *Daily News*, he went to work for the Newspaper Enterprise Association, a syndicate. He won his first Pulitzer Prize while there in 1942, shortly before beginning a brief stint in the U.S. Army from 1943 through the end of World War II. In 1946 he joined the *Washington Post*, where he would work until his death in 2001.

Herblock arrived in the nation's capital at a time when Americans began to worry about the rise of communism. U.S. Senator Joseph McCarthy would light a fire in the city when he said he had a list of 200 so-called card-carrying communists working in the United States government. Never one to fear the powerful, Block drew a cartoon depicting three Senators pushing the Republican elephant to a tower of barrels. "For want of a better term to summarize the issue, I labeled the top barrel *McCarthyism*," Block wrote. The caption read, "You mean I'm supposed to stand on that?" (Block 1993). The term on that top barrel, though, would be what was most memorable from that frame. McCarthyism became common vernacular and a common history book vocabulary term thanks to that cartoon.

It wasn't just McCarthy that felt Herblock's wrath. Nobody who occupied the Washington spotlight was safe—especially not President Richard Nixon. Nixon even canceled the delivery of the *Post* to his home at one point—he said he didn't want his young daughters to be upset—and once admitted that he "wouldn't start the day by looking at Herblock" (Dudden 1987).

In his biography, Block recalled meeting Nixon for the first time at a cocktail party during Nixon's time as Eisenhower's vice president. Block remembered a brief conversation, with Nixon joking about his "ski-jump nose," and then being whisked away to meet Mrs. Nixon. "When we were introduced, she gave a small smile and said to the others that this is the man who hates all Republicans," Block wrote in his book. "Of course, this was untrue, but it followed the Nixon line—to make out that there wasn't anything wrong with Nixon, it was the people criticizing him who must be warped" (Block 1993).

Mrs. Nixon's pleasantness aside, Block criticized the man for years, even before Nixon became president and on through the Watergate scandal. With his cartoons appearing in the same paper as the stories that exposed the president's wrong-doing, he earned a share of the *Post's* Pulitzer Prize for their coverage of the scandal that forced the president to resign.

He kept drawing his outrage right to his death in 2001, his last cartoon appearing a little less than two months before he died that October, just six days shy of his 92nd birthday.

A foundation in his name gives grants and scholarships meant to support the future of editorial cartooning. The foundation also donated Block's archive to the Library of Congress, ensuring his wit and sharp pen are preserved for posterity.

Michael Wright

See also: Comedy, Satire, and Politics; Political Cartoons

Further Reading

Berger, Marilyn. 2001. "Herblock, Washington Post Cartoonist with Wit and Bite, Is Dead at 91." *New York Times.* October 9. Accessed September 29, 2015. http://www.nytimes .com/2001/10/09/us/herblock-washington-post-cartoonist-with-wit-and-bite-is-dead -at-91.html.

Block, Herbert. 1993. *Herblock: A Cartoonist's Life.* New York: Macmillan Publishing Company.

Dudden, Arthur. 1987. *American Humor.* New York: Oxford University Press.

Herb Block Foundation. http://www.herbblockfoundation.org.

Library of Congress exhibit. http://www.loc.gov/exhibits/herblock.

BOOK TOURS

Writing a book with an aspirational, very American title and then taking off on a whirlwind tour of major cities and early primary-voting states has become a set page from the American presidential campaign playbook.

In the summer of 2014 news emerged of former secretary of state Hillary Clinton's planned tour to accompany the publication of her book *Hard Choices*. It sounded like a presidential campaign in full swing, complete with appearances in Washington, D.C., New York, Los Angeles. Political reporters were carefully tracking locations for hints of an underlying political strategy (her stop in Ohio prompted several blog posts). There was a shiny new bus paid for by the Ready for Hillary Super PAC. There were the wall-to-wall media appearances on public radio, ABC's *Primetime* with Diane Sawyer, *The Daily Show*. She was even being tracked by a Republican National Committee intern in a squirrel costume wearing a shirt that read, "Another Clinton in the White House is Nuts." This non-campaign campaign sold books, and drew crowds of media and supporters.

Books from prospective presidential candidates are nothing new. In the 1950s then–U.S. senator John F. Kennedy penned *Profiles in Courage*, biographies of eight senators who had fought for principle. The book helped raise his profile and went on to win a 1957 Pulitzer Prize for biography. As Kathleen Hall Jamieson observed, "While Nixon could and did recite the number of countries he had visited, the number of leaders he had met, the number of conferences he had attended, none of these statistics demonstrated that he had learned history's lessons. What Kennedy's books provided was the evidence he had" (Jamieson 1996). The book was a best seller and helped package his candidacy four years later.

As time went on, writing a book became a critical step for a prospective candidate, taking part in the "invisible primary" by offering themselves and their philosophies up to the media and potential financial backers. Next came the multi-city tour where the candidate gets a chance to meet voters and potential donors without having any "official" campaign expenses or setup. "Critics charge that these books are filled with vague platitudes that offer only a limited glimpse into the candidates' real positions . . . Still, no one expects these campaign tomes to go away soon, if only because they provide an excuse for candidates to embark on a book-signing tour that can serve to kick off a future presidential campaign" (Dautrich and Yalof 2011). This can be seen in the campaign of then-first-term senator Barack Obama. In October 2006, Obama published his second book, *The Audacity of Hope*, and launched a two-week, thirteen-city tour, which included an appearance on NBC's *Meet the Press*, where he admitted he had considered a run in 2008. The publicity helped fuel increased media attention and speculation that culminated in January when he announced the formation of a formal exploratory committee and filed paperwork with the Federal Election Commission.

These books and the accompanying tours help candidates in several ways as they develop and consider a formal campaign for president. First, they allow the candidate, often with the help of speechwriters and political strategists, to develop potential themes for the coming campaign—Obama would stick with the idea of Hope throughout the coming campaign. Second, it allows them to make the case to potential backers and political insiders in the party and the media. Third, the book tour usually includes dozens of interviews with local and national media, raising the profile of the prospective candidate and offering them an early test of the skills they will need in the coming years of campaigning. Lastly, it also allows the candidate to tour potential critical states and meet with important donors before ever filing any official candidacy paperwork.

The benefits have grown to such a point that many candidates release books during a campaign, allowing them to mix book tours with active campaigning. Those tasked with regulating campaign spending and activities are increasingly pressed to try and draw a line between the activities of the candidate and the author. During the 2012 Republican primaries Michele Bachmann, Newt Gingrich, and others pushed books along with the candidacy, a move that worried former Federal Election Commissioner Ken Gross who said, "It does seem like each cycle the candidates try to push the envelope a little more. In the good old days, you wrote your book before you ran. Now, they're so entwined with the campaign, it's sometimes difficult to distinguish" (O'Connor 2011).

Further Reading

Dautrich, Kennth, and David Yalof. 2011. *American Government: Historical, Popular, and Global Perspectives*. Boston: Cengage Learning.

Jamieson, Kathleen Hall. 1996. *Packaging The Presidency: A History and Criticism of Presidential Campaign Advertising*. Oxford: Oxford University Press.

O'Connor, Patrick. 2011. "Book Tours Follow Campaign Trail." December 9. Accessed January 30, 2015. http://www.wsj.com/articles/SB10001424052970203413304577086382547766306.

BREITBART, ANDREW (1969–2012)

Andrew Breitbart was a conservative commentator and new media force that developed his political opinions and web savvy while working with conservative media and Hollywood gossip extraordinaire Matt Drudge. Breitbart translated those skills into helping Arianna Huffington launch the first version of her Huffington Post and later launched his own site, Breitbart.com, which became a source for political and scandal stories. Despite his sudden death from heart failure in 2012, Breitbart's news service remains a significant online source for political reporting and commentary from the right.

He was such a controversial figure that on the day his death was announced, Slate's writer Matt Yglesias tweeted, "The world outlook is slightly improved with @AndrewBrietbart dead." It was, said libertarian editor and journalist Nick Gillespie, the kind of thing Breitbart would have loved, noting that "it meant that liberals with an uncomplicated mainstream media perspective were taking notice of him and his point of view. That such a churlish and distasteful comment reflects poorly on its author, an establishment blogger with impeccable left of center bona fides, and his *Washington Post*-owned platform, would simply be icing on the cake" (Gillespie 2012). But Gillespie and others credit Breitbart for being more than just a gadfly of the left, saying he also found new ways to use the digital platform of the Internet to foster conversation, even if it was often not the nicest conversation.

Breitbart had started down a very different path, growing up as a liberal in California. He graduated college in 1991 saying he had no sense of what to do with his life when he had a sudden political epiphany. It came as he watched the confirmation hearings of Supreme Court Justice Clarence Thomas and helped sharpen his worldview into something more like a libertarian than his more Democratic upbringing. He became a voracious consumer of online commentary and finally emailed the upstart Drudge to compliment him on his gossipy web musings. Breitbart was soon contributing the Drudge site, declaring himself "Matt Drudge's bitch." While there, Drudge introduced him to Arianna Huffington and the two were soon developing the ideas that would become Huffington Post.

He used all of these experiences to launch the eclectic series of Breitbart-branded sites, Big Government, Big Journalism, Big Hollywood, and others and was soon breaking stories that would have major implications. His site Big Government broke the story of U.S. Representative Anthony Weiner's use of social media to approach and flirt with women, including texting pictures of his genitals. But Breitbart did more than that. When Weiner scheduled a press conference, Breitbart showed up and took questions on the story before Weiner could even address the matter, telling reporters that the weekend-long public relations campaign to discredit the Breitbart story was "a continual attempt to blame the messenger."

It was pure Breitbart. It was part-publicity stunt, part-righteous indignation and helped propel his site in viewers and his own stock among conservatives. It was also not the first time Breitbart had helped drive the narrative of a news story. Two conservative activists had secretly recorded the work of a nonprofit organization Association of Community Organizations for Reform Now (ACORN) in 2009 and had supplied the video to Breitbart. The video appeared to show ACORN representatives helping advise how to hide income from prostitution. The same group had helped register thousands of voters in poor and urban areas, and so the Breitbart expose was seen as a way of silencing a group that helped expand the number of likely Democratic voters. In the end, the political firestorms led to the defunding and collapse of ACORN and the resignation of Weiner. Through it all, Breitbart seemed to revel in his role as being the provocateur.

Breitbart and his array of sites also helped spread the early word of the Tea Party movement, seeking to influence the debate from outside the political parties. A Breitbart editor explained his former boss's position about how Breitbart wanted to influence the process, writing, "To Andrew, political power lay beyond politics, in the realm of the media and popular culture. That is where the Tea Party, and the conservative movement in general, have been most successful—primarily in reshaping political debates, especially but not solely around fiscal and constitutional issues" (Pollak 2014). It was that influence that drove many crazy, but also has helped keep Breitbart a part of the political conversation even after his death.

See also: Drudge Report; Huffington Post

Further Reading

Gillespie, Nick. 2012. "How Andrew Breitbart Changed the News." CNN. March 2. Accessed November 13, 2015. http://www.cnn.com/2012/03/01/opinion/gillespie-breitbart.

Pollak, Joel. 2014. "Why Andrew Breitbart, and the Tea Party, Chose a Different Path to Power." Breitbart.com. September 28. Accessed November 13, 2015. http://www.breitbart.com/big-government/2014/09/28/why-andrew-breitbart-and-the-tea-party-chose-a-different-path-to-power.

BROADCAST TELEVISION NEWS

In the decades before cable TV arrived and grew to dominance, broadcast televised news (generated by a handful of networks) played a mixed and powerful role in the political process. Television quickly became the primary way people accessed news, with both national and local programs serving as important, if flawed, sources of information on the political process. Often criticized for its lack of depth or focus on sound bites over context, broadcast news nevertheless played a critical role in engaging less politically interested people, offering the public a sort of baseline amount of political information.

Broadcast networks were the backbone of television from its onset in the post-World War II years through the 1980s. Four networks—the big three commercial outlets of NBC, CBS, and ABC joined by the non-commercial PBS—were major sources of information about the world as well as hugely profitable media companies. In the early days of television, the federal government mandated that stations should operate in "the public interest, convenience, and necessity" of the viewing public. This idea, often shortened to PICON, was what stations needed to demonstrate to justify the government's granting of their Federal Communications Commission license. ABC's Ted Koppel would later look back fondly at this time, saying, "In the old days, the FCC still had teeth and still used them every once in a while. And there was that little paragraph, Section 315 of the FCC code, that said, 'You shall operate in the public interest, convenience and necessity.' What that meant was, you had to have a news division that told people what was important out there. And I just don't necessarily believe that showing me what my pets are doing when I'm not at home to see them falls under that category" (Frontline 2004).

Television networks provided a nightly dose of international and national events, encapsulated into 22 minutes each night. The programs reaped large audiences. As late as 1980 more than 50 million Americans—some 22 percent of the population of the country—watched one of the network news programs each night. These programs were often criticized for dumbing down complex political matters and helping spur what became known as "sound-bite journalism" where nuanced political positions were cut down to 8-second quotes from each side of the argument. But they provided, according to scholars, a sort of universal political education. Yale Professor Markus Prior would almost pine for this basic political information in his book *Post-Broadcast Democracy*, writing, "Broadcast television brought Americans closer together in their political knowledge and their involvement in the electoral process. It did so by striking a bargain with many of those Americans who had previously ignored politics because it seemed too difficult to keep up with: 'We will bring moving pictures right into your living room that you will find impossible to resist for many hours each day—but for an hour or two, the irresistible moving pictures will show you news and politics'" (Prior 2007). This "agreement" helps explain why the United States government took such keen interest in how television would be produced and what kind of content would make it into people's homes. Unlike the First Amendment-backed freedoms that had dominated the relationship between the government and the print media, broadcast networks faced far more scrutiny and regulations. Along with the PICON requirements for the license, networks also had to abide by the Fairness Doctrine, a set of FCC rules that required the broadcasters cover issues of public interest and ensure that multiple perspectives were included in that coverage. The government seemed to be aware that how politics would be covered on these four networks posed a greater opportunity and danger to the system than the disjointed and geographically limited newspapers and magazines.

As Prior notes in his book, the system appeared to work. News programs garnered large audiences. Correspondents like Edward R. Murrow and anchors like Walter Cronkite became some of the most influential and trusted men in the country. The era would take on an almost "golden age" patina as social scientists have bemoaned the rise of increasingly partisan cable news outlets. In considering this phase of television news, one academic would describe it as the time of "more serious, objective journalism, where journalisms reported the facts without taking a side" (Levendusky 2013).

But the era was more nuanced than that description might imply. True, with increased government scrutiny and the desire to appeal to literally every American with a television, these networks had fewer economic and regulatory reasons to stray into partisan advocacy, but the era was marked by moments that do not fit cleanly into those serious and objective descriptions. Sometimes networks strayed into areas that were less objective. For example, after visiting Vietnam in 1968 in the wake of a wide-ranging series of attacks by Viet Cong rebels on the Tet holiday, Cronkite took to the air upon his return to report on what he had seen. At the end of his documentary report that looked at the situation and cast a pall on the optimistic reports from the American government about the progress of U.S. efforts, Cronkite closed his program with a three-minute editorial on camera where he declared:

> To say that we are mired in stalemate seems the only realistic, if unsatisfactory conclusion. On the off chance that military and political analysts are right, in the next few months we must test the enemy's intentions, in case this is indeed his last big gasp before negotiations.
> But it is increasingly clear to this reporter that the only rational way out then will be to negotiate, not as victors, but as an honorable people who lived up to their pledge to defend democracy, and did the best they could.
> This is Walter Cronkite. Good night.

The impact of that expression of opinion was substantial. Cronkite's documentary helped inspire anti-war candidates in the 1968 election and put more pressure on President Johnson, who soon bowed out of the race.

Not all the ways in which the "golden era" failed to live up to modern mythology involved taking positions on key policy issues. Television networks were also roundly criticized for their often-simplistic way of covering news and events. Political campaigns were boiled down more and more to slogans that did little to explain complex policy positions. And networks faced accusations of being more interested in the visual element of the story than its content—pictures driving the news rather than the other way around.

But still, with only a handful of channels—this was the era when TVs had dials—the American public sometimes amounted to a captive audience for network news. Therefore, the way the networks chose to cover events like political conventions, debates, and political news generally were important points of conversation and argument. Regardless of the public's thirst—or lack thereof—for political news, it was nearly impossible to avoid. Those who have studied the period argue that this had the important impact of providing the American public the same basic understanding of the candidates and campaigns.

As the twentieth century drew to a close, a fundamental change to television viewership was underway, and network news would never recover. The captive audience reality of the "big three" networks began to falter as more and more Americans moved away from broadcast in favor of cable. Cable television allowed viewers to access dozens—and eventually hundreds—of channels. News channels that offered 24-hour coverage cropped up and networks were no long able to force viewers to watch anything. Those who wanted news all the time drifted to the 24-hour cable news offerings, and those who had never really wanted to see news now never had to. The audience for the evening news on the big three broadcast networks dropped from some 52 million in 1980 to about 24 million in 2014. In recent years that number has remained fairly stable, but it still represents a far smaller percentage of the American viewing public. Interestingly, the audience is still far larger than the more partisan (and talked about) cable news programs on at the same time.

Networks have, to a certain degree, bottomed out as those not interested in news drift to other offerings and those who want more provocative and opinion-driven content turn to cable (and now web) news offerings. For now network news still draws decent-sized audiences and has continued to play its traditional role—although to far fewer people. The next big test for broadcast news comes as younger viewers who have turned first to social media and the web for their news grow older. Can national television networks find their new niche to serve these customers? That remains an open question.

See also: ABC News; Audience Fragmentation; CBS News; Cable News Networks; Fairness Doctrine; NBC; Public Interest Obligation

Further Reading

Frontline. 2004. "News War." Accessed January 8, 2016. http://www.pbs.org/wgbh/pages/frontline/newswar/tags/entertainment.html.

Levendusky, Matthew. 2013. *How Partisan Media Polarize America*. Chicago: University of Chicago Press.

Prior, Markus. 2007. *Post-Broadcast Democracy: How Media Choice Increases Inequality in Political Involvement and Polarizes Elections*. Cambridge: Cambridge University Press.

BROCK, DAVID (1962–)

Journalist and author David Brock has never been a man in the middle. Brock exploded into the national media through a series of investigative books that took aim at the woman who accused Supreme Court Justice Clarence Thomas of sexual harassment and that accused President Bill Clinton of having Arkansas State Troopers arrange sexual liaisons with women. Brock later renounced his earlier work and, in an apparent 180-degree turn, wrote a book about the conservative network of media groups that conspired to attack the Clintons. He also founded the liberal media watchdog group Media Matters for America that often documents what it sees as Fox News's conservative bias.

Brock has demonstrated an uncanny ability to draw and hold the political spotlight, whether he was attacking Bill Clinton or in a campaign-year book on why Hillary Clinton should be the next president. It is enough to have the Daily Beast's Lloyd Grove describe him as "a modern-day Whittaker Chambers who dramatically switched allegiances in the war between right and left, although Brock by his own admission is less motivated by ideology, a subject that barely interests him, than by political calculation and personalities" (Grove 2015). However you describe him, it is an odd career trajectory for any journalist, but especially for one who seems to live and breathe partisan warfare.

Brock, who was raised in a fairly conservative family in New Jersey, ended up going to that bastion of liberalism, the University of California at Berkeley. He wrote and edited for the campus newspaper and interned at the *Wall Street Journal*, but after his graduation he struck off in a different direction, writing for the conservative magazine *Insight on the News* and other strongly partisan conservative journals. But it was his 1992 article in the conservative *American Spectator* that put Brock in the national spotlight. In the piece he sought to discredit law professor Anita Hill, who had testified that she had been sexually harassed by then-Supreme Court nominee Clarence Thomas. Brock's piece, "The Real Anita Hill," instead cast her as a political opportunist with her own checkered past. The article drew sharp criticism from many, but also landed Brock a book contract. The resulting book, released in 1993, became a bestseller. The popularity of the Anita Hill work helped land Brock his second major book, this one that sought to expose Bill Clinton as a philanderer who used his official position to have police officers set up meetings with women. The book was one of the first pieces of investigative work to raise the possibility of an affair between Clinton and a woman named Paula Jones. The case would later be absorbed into a wide-ranging investigation into the president that also included their land dealings in Arkansas. But soon the fire-breathing conservative journalist seemed to be losing his heat. In 1996 he published a book on Hillary Clinton that seemed to lack the intensity of his previous works.

His next move caught almost everyone by surprise.

In 1997, the man who during the early years of the Clinton administration had as part of his voicemail message, "I'm out trying to bring down the president," took to the pages of *Esquire* in a stunning piece titled "Confessions of a Right-wing Hitman." In the article he outlined a well-funded effort to find and publicize scandals about the Clintons, discussed his own homosexuality, and said he was ready to leave his position as a hired gun of the right. He wrote, "Now I do want out. David Brock the Road Warrior of the Right is dead. I'm not comfortable in either partisan camp, and both camps seem uncomfortable with me. My side turned out to be as dirty as theirs" (Brock 1997). Although he may not have been comfortable with the conservatives he had worked for, he was comfortable talking and writing about his experience. He turned the *Esquire* article into a full-blown book in 2002 and was soon doing more than just denouncing his former employers, instead turning his criticism of the conservative media outlets into an industry unto itself.

In 2004 he added more fuel to his new-found campaign against the conservative movement, founding a major media watchdog organization that aims to discredit the conservative media operations he said used to use him to attack liberals. Media Matters for America is a well-funded, rapid-response media machine. Staffers at Media Matters spend countless hours reviewing digitized broadcasts from Fox News and other outlets, looking for what they see as "conservative misinformation" and seeking to counter it with their own take on the matter and calling out particularly inaccurate information. Their videos have ended up on Comedy Central's *The Daily Show* and other media reports. Campaign consultant James Carville said the organization has been essential to the left's campaigns, telling the *New York Times*, "It was always kind of a dream, that we needed something like that. I wouldn't say they've become as effective as the entire conservative media backlash thing, but they're probably more effective than any single entity" (Steinberg 2008).

By the 2016 campaign, the former bane of the Clintons had fully transformed. Brock worked for some time for one of the Super PACs supporting Hillary Clinton's run, and he also published *Killing the Messenger: The Right-Wing Plot to Derail Hillary Clinton and Hijack Your Government*, which took aim at both conservative and mainstream media outlets for their coverage of Clinton. He wrote in the book, "Contrary to what my patrons expected, I found no silver bullet that would stop the Clintons. What I did find was a woman with a steadfast commitment to public service, a clear political vision, and a deep well of personal integrity. I couldn't write the book conservatives wanted, not without betraying the facts as I saw them— and betraying myself in the process" (Brock 2015). But Brock did not stop at just defending the character of Hillary Clinton, becoming one of the most ardent supporters and quickest to attack those perceived as unfair to the former First Lady and Secretary of State. He declared that the *New York Times* deserved "a special place in hell" for its coverage of Clinton. Brock remains a controversial figure, reviled by the conservative activists who see him as a political opportunist and pretender and seen uneasily as an ally by many of the left. Journalists have written dozens of pieces questioning whether anything that comes from the "hit man"–turned liberal evangelist can be trusted, but Brock himself seems unlikely to quietly leave the political media stage anytime soon.

See also: Media Matters for America

Further Reading

Brock, David. 1997. "Confessions of a Right-Wing Hit Man." *Esquire*. July.

Brock, David. 2015. *Killing the Messenger: The Right-Wing Plot to Derail Hillary and Hijack Your Government*. New York: Twelve Publishers.

Grove, Lloyd. 2015. "Can Anyone Ever Truly Trust David Brock?" The Daily Beast. September 18. Accessed November 13, 2015. http://www.thedailybeast.com/articles/2015/09/18/can-anyone-ever-truly-trust-david-brock.html.

Steinberg, Jacques. 2008. "An All-Out Attack on 'Conservative Misinformation.'" *New York Times*. October 31. Accessed November 13, 2015. http://www.nytimes.com/2008/11/01/washington/01media.html?_r=0.

BRODER, DAVID (1929–2011)

With his trademark horned rim glasses and measured but insightful questions, David Broder stood as one of the giants of political reporting for more than 40 years, from the administration of President Dwight Eisenhower until his death in 2011. Broder was often called the dean of the Washington Press Corps and enjoyed near-universal respect for his knowledge and reporting work.

A former Indiana senator would lionize Broder at his death, saying, "In his thoughtful and probing questions based on decades of scholarship and on-the-scene observations, David Broder set the modern 'gold standard' for those of us engaged in political life as we sought to persuade others, to legislate and to administer the successful progress of our country" (Bernstein 2011). The *New York Times* would describe him as "as a reporter's reporter, a shoe-leather guy who always got on one more airplane, knocked on one more door, made one more phone call. He would travel more than 100,000 miles a year to write more than a quarter-million words. In short, he composed first drafts of history for an awful lot of history" (Weber 2011).

Broder was born and raised in Illinois and began working in journalism while pursuing a master's degree in political science at the University of Chicago, serving as editor of the independent newspaper at the university. He came to Washington after landing a job at *Congressional Quarterly*, but soon was back in daily journalism working for the *Washington Star* and later the *New York Times*. While at the *Times*, he was actively recruited by *Washington Post* editor Ben Bradlee, who was working to build the reputation of the *Post*. Bradlee would later describe his efforts to land Broder in his memoir, writing that Broder was "the first top rank reporter ever to quit the *Times* for the *Post*. The traffic had all been the other way. I romanced him like he's never been romanced—in coffee shops, not fancy French restaurants, because Broder was a coffee-shop kind of man: straightforward, no frills, all business" (Bradlee 1996). Broder joined the paper as one of the top political reporters and later added a regular column to the mix. In 1973 his reporting on the Watergate scandal earned him a Pulitzer Prize.

He was always a student of politics as well as being fascinated by the process. But he also saw political reporting's shortcomings, with its focus on the internal workings of campaigns and losing sight of the importance of voters and governing. Those who cast a more critical eye on Broder's work accused him of investing too much authority in the system itself and in not doing enough to question that authority. Liberal critic Eric Altermann wrote that "Broder's position inside Washington is absolutely unique. In the mind of the Washington insider establishment, he is virtue itself. He is a sacred cow in a business of beefeater . . . He has occupied the position of 'high priest' of political journalism . . . because, not in spite, of his opinions" (Altermann 2008). Despite that criticism, he was largely able to straddle the line between reporting and commentary unlike most. He was seen as a thorough and balanced reporter, but twice a week he published his views in a syndicated column that ran in more than 300 newspapers around the country. He also was a prolific pundit, appearing on NBC's *Meet the Press* more than 400 times over the years, more than any other guest.

Broder's love of the system could be seen whenever he discussed politics. When asked what politician he had covered he most admired, Broder did not turn to the presidents or celebrity/politicians that have become a staple of Washington. Instead he told the Big Think website the political figure he was drawn to was Mike Mansfield, the Democratic Senate leader from Montana and long-time ambassador to Japan. Broder said, "He was a remarkable individual who well into his nineties was current on public affairs and invariably wise in his comments. I'd love to know what Mike Mansfield thinks we ought to do about Iraq and other issues today" (Big Think 2007). Broder was also the first one to point out his own errors in punditry, compiling an annual list of his most inaccurate predictions and observations that he would publish in its own column. In looking back at 2005, Broder would say he had published a column so wrong that it should have earned him his own special prosecutor. That year he wrote his take President Bush's response to Hurricane Katrina was "wildly off":

> Because the commander in chief is also the communicator in chief, when a crisis emerges the nation's eyes turn to him as to no other official. We cannot yet calculate the political fallout from Hurricane Katrina and its devastating human and economic consequences, but one thing seems certain: It makes the previous signs of political

weakness for Bush, measured in record-low job approval ratings, instantly irrelevant and opens new opportunities for him to regain his standing with the public.

He's still paying a price for that episode. (Broder 2005)

Perhaps because of this self-effacing tendency and his dedication to thorough reporting, even inaccurate predictions like that one did nothing to diminish the view most politicians and journalists had for Broder.

See also: Lippmann, Walter; *Washington Post*

Further Reading

Altermann, Eric. 2008. *What Liberal Media?: The Truth about Bias and the News*. New York: Basic Books.

Bernstein, Adam. 2011. "David Broder, 81, dies; set 'gold standard' for political journalism." *Washington Post*. March 10. Accessed June 1, 2016. http://www.washingtonpost.com/wp-dyn/content/article/2011/03/09/AR2011030902821.html.

Big Think. "What Is Your Question?" September 12, 2007. Accessed November 6, 2015. http://bigthink.com/videos/re-what-is-your-question-8.

Bradlee, Ben. 1996. *A Good Life: Newspapering and Other Adventures*. New York: Simon & Schuster.

Broder, David. 2005. "A look back at year's errors, misjudgments on all fronts." *Seattle Times*. December 29. Accessed November 6, 2015. http://www.seattletimes.com/opinion/a-look-back-at-years-errors-misjudgments-on-all-fronts.

Weber, Bruce. 2011. "David Broder, Political Journalist and Pundit, Dies at 81." *New York Times*. March 9. Accessed November 6, 2015. http://www.nytimes.com/2011/03/10/us/politics/10broder.html?_r=0.

BROOKINGS INSTITUTION

If there is a quintessential think tank in Washington, D.C., it may be the Brookings Institution.

The think tank is generally seen as a moderately liberal group; a 2011 survey of its scholars' political donations found that more than 97 percent of the nearly $240,000 they had donated from 2003–2010 went to Democrats (Kurtzelben 2011). But the organization has also built a record that draws support from many Republicans. Former New York City mayor Michael Bloomberg said at one of Brookings's events that the institute "has achieved a special measure of respect in Washington because it has risen above partisanship, and that is not an easy thing to do in this town which is sort of built on partisanship" (Brookings).

The numbers seem to back up Bloomberg's praise. A 2007 survey of those people familiar with powerful D.C.-based groups found Brookings among the most respected by both Democrats and Republicans. The institution was labeled the most powerful by respondents, coming in just above the American Enterprise Institute and just behind major political funding groups like the U.S. Chamber of Commerce, the AFL-CIO, and the National Rifle Association (Taylor 2007).

The think tank grew out of the work of its founder, Robert Somers Brookings. Brookings had made a fortune as a wholesaler of household goods, and by the turn of the twentieth century he turned to more charitable and philanthropic work. He played important roles in the running and expansion of Washington University in St. Louis and was among the academic leaders tapped by fellow university leader President Woodrow Wilson to assist in making sure the government efforts in World War I were efficiently run. Brookings often expressed concern about the economic efficiency of the government and worried about the influence of Wall Street on government policies.

Those who have assessed his work stress his enthusiasm as much as his knowledge with one biographer writing, "Brookings, as his contemporaries knew, was neither a profound nor an original thinker, but his writings conveyed the sentiment of a man who saw the possibilities of building a better world. Those who knew him described him as a somewhat eccentric, talkative entrepreneur" (Grimm 2002, p. 47). He also had connections and friends in critical places in the foundation and government spheres. With the support of a $200,000 grant from the Carnegie Family Foundation, in 1916 Brookings helped create and served as a founding trustee of the Institute for Government Research. The IGR merged with other efforts Brookings was helping guide into the Brookings Institution in 1927.

The institute was headed by Harold Mouton, a brilliant economist from the University of Chicago. Mouton and Brookings at times clashed, but under Mouton's leadership the institute built a record of independent research about government policies. Throughout its history, the institution has tracked many different topics and current policy debates, but at times it has been tapped in a more substantial way. In the wake of World War II, the Republican chairman of the Senate Foreign Relations Committee asked the institution to help develop a plan for the rebuilding of Europe, writing in a letter in 1947, "It would be helpful to have an objective study by an independent research agency of highest standard. The deep and universal respect which the Brookings Institution richly deserves and enjoys would make your recommendations of tremendous value" (Brookings). The institution stopped all other work and in four weeks developed an eight-point plan for American aid to Europe. The 20-page report helped pave the way to what became known as the Marshall Plan. But historians point out that the institution did more than just write a research report, it "provided a different sort of linkage—that between business leaders and their allies among professional specialists in public administration, economics, law, international relations, and other fields" (Hogan 1989, p. 99).

Although there are few times that Brookings policy reports had such a broad impact as its role helping create the Marshall Plan, the organization has played key roles throughout modern policy debates. Its scholars helped shape elements of President Lyndon Johnson's anti-poverty plans, helped develop tax policies for President Bill Clinton, and assisted in researching the needs of government reform in the wake of the September 11, 2001, attacks. Johnson, in marking the 50th anniversary of the founding of the IGR, told those scholars and D.C. leaders gathered at the event that he had turned to Brookings since the 1930s for intellectually honest research and told the Brookings team if it did not exist, "we would have to ask someone to create you" (Smith 1991, p. 2).

The organization has also served as a source for government agencies seeking independent research and reporters on a quest for topic experts. It's a role that puts the organization under its own press scrutiny to ensure it is actually providing the independent research it says is its hallmark. In 2014, a major investigation by the *New York Times* threw that independence into question when the paper reported Brookings was one of the major think tanks taking donations from foreign entities. The report documented millions of dollars in donations to the institution from the governments of Norway, Qatar, and the United Arab Emirates. Some scholars reported they were told to refrain from taking positions critical of Qatar, with one former visiting scholar saying, "If a member of Congress is using the Brookings reports, they should be aware—they are not getting the full story. They may not be getting a false story, but they are not getting the full story" (Lipton, Williams, and Confessore 2014). The report went so far as to raise the possibility that think tanks like Brookings should disclose the money as essentially lobbying on behalf of foreign powers. The institute responded strongly to the charges, with president and former State Department official Strobe Talbott saying the paper had selected one man's claims over a long history of independence. Talbott stated emphatically, "We do not sell influence to anyone, foreign or domestic. If we were for hire to advance outside interests, we would be in violation of the academic freedom of our scholars' work and our institutional mission. We summarize our values as quality, independence, and impact—which means our own impact, not anyone else's" (Brookings Institution 2014). The controversy highlights the delicate nature of Brookings's situation. It, like other think tanks in Washington, has enormous power to convene leaders, research policy, and produce influential recommendations, but that power relies on its perception of intellectual independence and political moderation.

See also: Center for American Progress; Conservative Think Tanks; Liberal Think Tanks

Further Reading

Brookings Institution. n.d. "Brookings's Role in the Marshall Plan." Accessed January 26, 2015. http://www.brookings.edu/about/history/marshallplan.

Brookings Institution. 2014. "A Message from Strobe Talbott, President of the Brookings Institution." September 7. Accessed January 18, 2015. http://www.brookings.edu/about/media-relations/news-releases/2014/0907-message-from-strobe-talbott-on-nyt-article.

Grimm, Robert. 2002. *Notable American Philanthropists: Biographies of Giving and Volunteering.* Westport, CT: Greenwood Press.

Hogan, Michael. 1989. *The Marshall Plan: America, Britain and the Reconstruction of Western Europe, 1947-1952.* Cambridge: Cambridge University Press.

Kurtzleben, Danielle. 2011. "Think Tank Employees Tend to Support Democrats." *U.S. News & World Report*. March 3. Accessed January 15, 2015. http://www.usnews.com/news/articles/2011/03/03/think-tank-employees-tend-to-support-democrats.

Lipton, Eric, Brooke Williams, and Nicholas Confessore. 2014. "Foreign Powers Buy Influence at Think Tanks." *New York Times*. September 6. Accessed January 17, 2015. http://www.nytimes.com/2014/09/07/us/politics/foreign-powers-buy-influence-at-think-tanks.html?_r=0.

Smith, James Allen. 1991. *Brookings at Seventy-Five*. Washington, DC: Brookings Institution Press.

Taylor, Humphrey. 2007. "The Harris Poll." December 11. Accessed January 26, 2015. http://www.harrisinteractive.com/vault/Harris-Interactive-Poll-Research-Beltway-Groups-2007-12.pdf.

CABLE NEWS NETWORKS

It's hard to imagine a world where news is not a constant stream of sound bites and talking heads. But that is what largely existed until the dawn of cable news in 1980 fundamentally changed the industry's landscape. Once major cable news networks became established, what people turned to for their news, both political and breaking, changed—as did the time of day they looked for it. No longer did they have to wait for the evening broadcast or the morning paper. Now, at any time of day, cable subscribers could flip on their television and turn to a channel run by a national or international news organization that fed them footage, commentary, and reporting on the biggest news events and blow-by-blow coverage of political campaigns.

Cable news invented the 24-hour news cycle and thrived on it, with no other conventional outlets having the ability to compete with the continuous hum of cable news.

By 1980 enough people had access to cable television that cable-only networks seemed financially viable. Ted Turner, already a cable television mogul, launched the Cable News Network on June 1 of that year. At that time, television news was dominated by the three major broadcasters and their regimented schedules of nightly news broadcasts. CNN changed the notion that the news had to be read at certain times of day. Charles Bierbauer, who joined the network in its first year, told the network in a 2000 interview marking his retirement that he didn't think anyone who went to work there knew what it would become. "We were all pretty much taking a chance on something new," he said (CNN 2000).

The network had the resources and the staff to beam news into homes across the country at any time of day. With live coverage as its bread and butter, it brought the biggest stories to people in real time, from the little girl stuck in a well to the uprisings in Tiananmen Square. "Every year had one or two turn-on-your-TV stories, and over time Turner's network parlayed them into distribution and advertising gains," Scott Collins wrote in his book *Crazy Like a Fox* (Collins 2004). Fueled by these made-for-live-TV moments, the network grew quickly. Before it finished its second year, CNN launched a second network, CNN2, which eventually became Headline News, or HLN. By the end of its first decade, CNN had more than 50 million subscribers in the U.S. and was raking in profits. Competitors coveted CNN's live coverage, and it didn't take long for copycats to pop up. Many of the early interlopers, however, weren't successful. Specialized channels, like the sports network ESPN or the financial-news network CNBC, found success, but it took more than a decade for any competitor to meaningfully encroach on CNN's turf.

This was partially due to CNN's partnership with large cable providers. Time Warner and Tele-Communications Inc. had helped the network survive some financially lean years in the late 1980s and had a financial stake in making sure the network succeeded. That gave CNN a large advantage. Since cable providers wanted CNN to succeed, they had no reason to let competitors get into the game. "The cable companies thus blocked any attempts by competitors to create rival services," Collins wrote. But that changed when Time Warner merged with Turner Broadcasting System. As a condition for approving the deal, the Federal Trade Commission forced the cable providers to make room for CNN rivals.

That opened the door just in time for the other two members of the cable news "Big Three." MSNBC and Fox News both arrived on the scene in 1996. MSNBC grew out of a partnership between Microsoft and NBC and launched in July, while Rupert Murdoch and Roger Ailes brought viewers Fox News Channel that October. Soon enough, they had become serious contenders for the top spot in cable news. Fox News took over the top spot in the early 2000s and hasn't loosened its grip, topping the other two in monthly overall audience for years.

While those networks are considered the "Big Three," other channels have tried to forge their way into the game. There are regionally focused cable news channels, like Northwest Cable News and New England Cable News. On the national stage, Al Jazeera America and Fusion are two of the best-known recent arrivals. Both went on the air in 2013. Fusion, a joint venture between ABC and the Spanish-language television company Univision, aims at providing news and information for a mostly Hispanic audience. Al Jazeera, the Middle Eastern broadcaster, bought out Current TV to found its American counterpart. Hoping to reject "punditry and partisanship on the one hand, and tabloid-style infotainment on the other, while focusing instead on hard-hitting national and international news that matters to Americans" (Pompeo 2013), Al Jazeera America struggled to attract viewers. It was hampered by the fact it only had agreements with certain cable providers and then also struggled to attract viewers. By the dawn of 2016 Al Jazeera America announced it would close, marking both a failure of the network to understand the American cable audience and the inability to add a fourth major cable news outlet to the mix.

The idea that Al Jazeera wanted to avoid partisanship underscores the common criticism of cable news—that it is biased toward one political party or another. Fox News is accused by liberals of being conservative, while MSNBC and CNN are often criticized for being liberal. Part of that is driven by the networks' needs to fill 24 hours a day. All three fill daytime hours with commentary from all over the political spectrum. A 2013 Pew Study found that MSNBC filled 85 percent of its hours with commentary or opinion, which far exceeded that of Fox News and CNN, both of which were closer to a half-and-half balance (Bercovici 2013).

While the 24-hour news cycle forces them to produce shows and content at all hours of the day, it also gives them a great deal of power to set the agenda for news coverage. By feeding the public's constant thirst for information and opinions on the latest developments, a cable network's decision in what to cover helps decide what issues gain traction, especially during a political campaign. Paul Farhi wrote about the "cable news effect" for the *American Journalism Review* in 2008. If one outlet reports something worth hours of television, the cable networks won't hesitate to provide those hours of television by keeping that story at the forefront of talk and commentary shows. In this way, mistakes, gaffes, and insults are often amplified. Then, other journalists cover whatever comes next, like a prominent figure's response. Farhi gives the example of the coverage of President Barack Obama's pastor, Rev. Jeremiah Wright, who became a controversial figure in Obama's campaign for some of the things Wright said during sermons or other speeches, like calling America "the number one killer in the world." Cable talk shows and news programs used Wright as fodder, and the constant coverage led to newspapers writing about the pastor. "That's where cable exerts its biggest influence on the rest of the media—as an engine of reaction and response. Cable's intense and often immediate coverage of the day's big controversy forces candidates to fire back, which then compels the rest of the media to cover the response," Farhi wrote (Farhi 2008).

That is as true now as ever, especially as the Internet allows other organizations to do battle in the round-the-clock news arena. As news consumers turn to social media and mobile devices, newspapers, digital-only news organizations, and magazines have the ability to compete with cable networks in live coverage of events. And subscription streaming services like Netflix and Hulu are replacing traditional cable subscriptions in many homes. With so many other outlets for news to compete against, cable news has suffered a decline in its viewership for years. The 2015 Pew State of the News Media report said the core cable news audience has been shrinking. By one metric, the news audience for all three of the major cable news channels (MSNBC, CNN, and Fox) dipped to 1.8 million in 2014 (Pew 2015). Nearly everyone has the ability to feed the appetite first created by CNN, and news consumers won't stop thirsting for unceasing coverage and analysis of current events. As viewers turn elsewhere, they perhaps don't even realize that only a few decades earlier, cable news changed the world.

Michael Wright

See also: Al Jazeera America; Broadcast Television News; CNN; Fox News; MSNBC; 24-Hour News Cycle

Further Reading
Bercovici, Jeff. 2013. "Pew Study Finds MSNBC the Most Opinionated Cable News Channel By Far," www.forbes.com. March 18. Accessed: December 25, 2015. http://www.forbes.com/sites/jeffbercovici/2013/03/18/pew-study-finds-msnbc-the-most-opinionated-cable-news-channel-by-far.
CNN. 2000. "Charles Bierbauer, CNN senior Washington correspondent, discusses his 19-year career at CNN." May 8. Accessed June 1, 2016. http://www.cnn.com/COMMUNITY/transcripts/2000/5/8/bierbauer/.
Collins, Scott. 2004. *Crazy Like a Fox: The Inside Story of How Fox News Beat CNN.* New York: Penguin.

Farhi, Paul. 2008. "Cable's Clout," *American Journalism Review.* August/September. Accessed: December 25, 2015. http://ajrarchive.org/Article.asp?id=4574.

Pompeo, Joe. 2013. "Al Jazeera America: A Unicorn Is Born," *www.nymag.com.* July 11. Accessed: December 25, 2015. http://nymag.com/daily/intelligencer/2013/07/al-jazeera-america-a-unicorn-is-born.html.

Sherman, Gabriel. 2014. *The Loudest Voice in the Room: How the Brilliant, Bombastic Roger Ailes Built Fox News—and Divided a Country.* New York: Random House.

"State of the News Media 2015." 2015. *Pew Research Center.* April 29. Accessed: December 25, 2015. http://www.journalism.org/2015/04/29/cable-news-fact-sheet.

Stelter, Brian. 2009. "Doctor's Killer Is Not Alone in the Blame, Some Say," *New York Times.* June 1.

CAMPAIGN FINANCE REFORM

The 41-year-old state senator rose to address his colleagues in a hushed chamber. As senators looked on, the clerk brought in a bag stuffed with $30,000 cash.

"Men of apparent respectability and good standing in this community are trafficking in the honor of members of this body as they would buy and sell cattle and sheep," thundered Fred Whiteside. "What new code of morals or of ethics has been discovered which makes bribery a virtue, and condones the crime of a man because he is rich?" (Malone et al. 1976).

The year was 1899 and Whiteside was giving testimony about how William Clark, the copper baron who ran much of the state of Montana, was now trying to purchase a seat in the U.S. Senate. At this point in U.S. history, state legislators selected senators and Clark wanted to make sure there would be no question who would represent the Treasure State in Washington.

Clark's supporters made their way around the state capital, delivering the bribes in the most brazen way, according to long-time political reporter Chuck Johnson. Johnson told PBS's *Frontline* in 2012, "They knew where it (the money) was coming from. The envelopes had his initials on it" (PBS Frontline 2012). But unlike the movies, Whiteside was not vindicated for his stand. He was stripped of his seat and thrown out of the Senate. And Clark was sent to the U.S. Capitol.

It's stories like this that helped fuel some of the first reforms aimed at limiting the sway of money on the political system. But as Congress and others tried to rein in the possible corrupting influence of cash, they also had to balance two core and competing rights—the right of one person, one vote and the right to free expression.

Those who have studied the troubled history of campaign finance reform cast it as a battle between two core principles of democracy. "Proponents of reform suggest that economic inequalities pose a serious threat to political equality, as monied interests and wealthy individuals are believed to exert a disproportionate share of influence in the political process . . . Opponents argue that the issue of campaign finance reform is, properly understood, a question of free speech and First Amendment rights" (Grant and Rudolph 2004). The success of these monied interests—like the U.S. senator from Montana William Clark—helped spark a wave of reforms aimed at limiting the corrupting influence of money and privilege on American politics.

It started even before the soiled Montana Senate election of 1899 with an effort to limit the perks elected officials could bestow on their supports. The 1883 Pendleton Civil Service Reform Act could be seen as the first modern era campaign finance reform legislation. The bill basically ended the patronage system at the federal level where civil servants of all levels were expected to support the president or party in power through election work and contributions.

A critical first step, but the civil service reforms did nothing to prevent large, unregulated donations going to candidates for federal office. As the government began to challenge large industries, many saw the reformation of campaign finance laws as essential to limit the political power of large corporations and their wealthy owners. By 1904 trust-busting president Theodore Roosevelt was calling on Congress to act, saying, "There is no enemy of free government more dangerous and none so insidious as the corruption of the electorate. No one defends or excuses corruption, and it would seem to follow that none would oppose vigorous measures to eradicate it" (Roosevelt 1904). Without these regulations, it was argued, money would flood the system to prevent the government from moving to regulate big business.

Roosevelt, aided by stories from muckraking journalists highlighting corruption at the state and federal levels, eventually pressured Congress to act and in 1907 the body voted to ban corporate donations to political campaigns. Missing was any group to enforce the new laws, so Congress created the first systems for reporting political donations in 1910 and again in 1925. The ideas behind these pieces of legislation were really two-fold. First, they sought to limit the explicit vote-buying of people like William Clark, but second they aimed to bring more people into the process. "Underlying the political reform in this century has been the assumption that if the avenues of political participation are expanded, citizen involvement will increase. Similarly, the arguments for campaign finance reform often call for expanding the contributor base of campaigns. As electoral politics shifts from party dominated campaigns to include candidate-centered organizations, PACs and public campaign financing, the expectation has been that more citizens will become involved in the funding of campaigns" (Jones 1990, p. 29). Despite these ideas, there is little evidence that the percentage of people who give to political campaigns has changed much in the wake of reform efforts.

In fact, one of the key problems cited by many experts is the fact that most reforms are enacted in response to a specific scandal, rather than addressing the core issues that reformers seek to effect. Scholars have noted, "Much of the problem with reform efforts is that they tend to develop in response to specific activities or scandals, with the resulting reforms focusing on specific activities such as vote buying, bribery, or the elimination of certain types of campaign contributions. As a result, efforts at comprehensive reform of the campaign finance system have been rare" (Goidel, Gross, and Shields 1999). This cycle of scandal and reform played out most notably in the 1970s.

While most remember Watergate for the resignation of a president and a botched break-in to the Democratic National Committee headquarters in Washington, D.C., it was the way that bungled burglary was funded that prompted some of the most sweeping campaign finance reforms in American history. The investigations into Watergate found that the Committee to Reelect the President—the ironically named CREEP—had used undocumented corporate and personal donations to fund illegal and unethical activities without disclosing the source of the money or how it was spent. The result was a series of amendments to the Federal Election Campaign Act.

The amendments included the most rigid limits on raising and spending campaign money ever enacted by Congress. The 1974 law included limits on contributions to candidates for federal office as well as limits on independent expenditures and a cap on how much candidates could spend of their own money. The new law also created the Federal Election Commission, required the disclosure of political contributions, and provided for the public financing of presidential elections. President Gerald Ford vetoed the changes, but Congress voted to override.

The new law faced legal challenges almost immediately. By early 1975 Senator James L. Buckley, a Republican from New York, and former presidential candidate and Democratic senator from Minnesota Eugene McCarthy filed suit against the Secretary of the Senate, Francis R. Valeo, who was an ex officio member of the new FEC. The result was mixed for both sides. The court found that for the government to place any restriction on political activity it needed to demonstrate a compelling state interest. In the unsigned opinion, the court then found that "the First Amendment requires the invalidation of the Act's independent expenditure ceiling, its limitation on a candidate's expenditures from his own personal funds, and its ceilings on overall campaign expenditures, since those provisions place substantial and direct restrictions on the ability of candidates, citizens, and associations to engage in protected political expression, restrictions that the First Amendment cannot tolerate." It did allow the disclosure requirements to stay on the books, arguing that while compelling disclosure could harm political involvement by some individuals and groups, "there are governmental interests sufficiently important to outweigh the possibility of infringement."

The case *Buckley v. Valeo* essentially set the parameters for campaign finance laws for the next 30 years. It said the government could take steps to limit corruption or the appearance of corruption by requiring disclosure of political donations and expenditures and by limiting the amount any one person or group could contribute. But it also set sharp limits on how far the government could go to limit spending by campaigns and the use of personal money or independent spending on political issues. For many, they saw a court more interested in protecting the rights of the wealthy to speak than in creating a fair election process. "Over the next thirty-five years, at every critical turn, the court would reverse and undermine effective curbs on the influence of the rich on the government of the United States" (Nichols and McChesney 2013, p. 68). A large part of the campaign reformers' narrative focuses on the inherent corrupting influence of money on politics. They see it as throwing the political system out of its delicate balance. If money equals speech, they argue, then those with more money have more political power. And it is hard to argue that a small community group or individual voter has as much ability to participate in the political debate as a large union or corporation.

But many see efforts to regulate speech as inherently flawed. For these people, campaign finance reforms are nothing more than a selective silencing of political voices for the convenience of certain other interests. From the civil libertarian perspective, John Samples of the Cato Institute argues that "most people support campaign finance 'reform' because they believe it will apply to people and ideas they do not like. In campaign finance matters, the illiberal feelings and political interests of public officials and many citizens are expressed in the language of high ideals and noble public purposes . . . but we should not be misled into thinking that restrictions on campaign finance primarily seek noble ideals and a pure politics" (Samples 2006). Samples and others stress that since Congress must implement the reforms, they will be created in such a way as to benefit those in power, not the general public. It is true that Congress has often moved to reform other parts of government while conveniently leaving themselves untouched. For example, the federal Freedom of Information Act covers the executive branch and exempts the legislative branch. Samples argues the same is true when it comes to campaign finances. When incumbents are protected and challengers impeded, Congress is far more likely to act.

These debates played out every time Congress considered new regulations of political action committees, independent spending, and donations to candidates. By the late 1990s, as money continued to increase in campaigns and loopholes were exploited by parties and political groups, Congress debated a new set of regulations. When Congress passed the so-called McCain-Feingold reform act, known officially at the Bipartisan Campaign Reform Act (BCRA), in 2002 reformers hoped it would stem the growth of independent expenditures by groups seeking to influence elections and the explosive growth of so-called soft money. Soft money had grown out of a loophole in the federal election laws that allowed parties and groups to raise unlimited money to be spent on non-campaign expenditures. Envisioned as efforts to organize and run the political parties, soft money had "undermined the efficacy of contribution limits by providing individuals with a way to make contributions in excess of federal limits. It . . . allowed party organizations to raise money from sources that have long been prohibited from making contributions in connection with federal elections" (Corrado 2000). Congress had debated how to address these two loopholes—as well as other issues, like making candidates explicitly endorse their ads—for some six years before it finally reached the desk of President George W. Bush. In signing the legislation, Bush said he had hoped the new law would "result in an election finance system that encourages greater individual participation, and provides the public more accurate and timely information, than does the present system" but also expressed concerns that it also presented "serious constitutional concerns" (Bush 2002). Those concerns soon found their way into court in a series of cases that would ultimately shift the legal system from supporting most congressional efforts to limit political spending to one that would strike down most limits that were not explicitly connected to concerns of corruption.

The core legal argument triggered by the BCRA focused on the work of so-called independent groups as well as the limits on individual donations to political organizations (although not political candidates or parties). The act moved to limit campaign spending by some groups, including candidates and outside groups, in the period just before a primary and two full months ahead of a general election. It also increased some donation limits, creating more direct donations to candidates and parties. These aspects of the law faced a swift legal test. In the 2003 case *Mitch McConnell v. Federal Election Commission*, the Supreme Court upheld most of the law in a 5-4 decision, with Justices Sandra Day O'Connor and John Paul Stevens writing that "money, like water, will always find an outlet" and the government had a right to attempt to regulate it.

Two results were unexpected: more political spending rather than less, and an actual easing of public anxiety about the role of money in politics. When the 2008 campaign exploded, with Barack Obama breaking all campaign fundraising records and forgoing public funds to spend freely, the public seemed unconcerned. His campaign's reliance on donations from thousands of individuals was seen as a triumph, not a failure, of the system. In fact in his assessment of the mood of the public, noted campaign finance scholar Robert Boatright described the change as a "striking paradigm shift [that] occurred in the United States in the years between the passage of BCRA and the Supreme Court's *Citizens United* decision. Americans have traditionally been skeptical of the equation between money and speech, but the unrestricted spending in the 2008 presidential election elicited few claims that the election was being 'bought' or that fund-raising raised the specter of corruption" (Boatright 2011).

But public opinion wasn't the only thing that had changed. In 2006, Sandra Day O'Connor retired from the court and was replaced by Samuel Alito, a far more conservative justice. This new court began to strike down elements of the BCRA and even older campaign finance regulations in a series of critical rulings. In 2007, the court ruled 5-4 in *Federal Election Commission v. Wisconsin Right to Life, Inc.* that Congress could not regulate so-called issue ads in the months ahead of elections. The majority wrote that only ads that expressly called for the defeat or election of a specific candidate could face any form of regulation. The next year, in *Jack Davis v. Federal Election Commission*, the court struck down elements of the BCRA that required candidates to declare how much of their own money they would use in a campaign.

The nail in the coffin of the BCRA came in 2010 when the Supreme Court issued its decision in *Citizens United v. Federal Election Commission*. It both declared limits on donations from unions and corporations to independent political campaigns unconstitutional, and declared that any black-out of advertising ahead of primary or general elections was a violation of the First Amendment. Other court rulings have concluded, for now, that the court will err on the side of more speech than less in political campaigns and regulations will be struck down if they infringe on what the current majority of the court sees as a fundamental right of expression.

From a practical perspective, the rulings have created a system where it is not unusual for more money to be spent by groups seeking to influence the election than by those candidates seeking office. Donations to candidates and parties are now the most regulated in the system, facing caps on individual donations and a required disclosure. Super PACs have emerged as places where individuals and organizations may make unlimited donations, but such groups must not coordinate its work with the candidate they support and the sources of Super PAC money must be disclosed. The last group born out of *Citizens United* is a series of nonprofits that do not need to disclose the sources of their money, but must not expressly call for the election or defeat of a given candidate and instead must focus on issues.

It has been a long and circuitous route from Senator Whiteside's plea to his colleagues to get corruption out of the Montana State Senate, but that explicit aim—to prevent corruption or the appearance of corruption—remains the core of the justification of campaign finance reforms. Any additional effort—to level the playing field for candidates, to limit the spending of outside groups aiming to influence an election, to limit the flood of cash into elections—faces difficult legal challenges for the foreseeable future.

See also: *Citizens United*; Dark Money Groups; 527 Organizations; Super PACs

Further Reading
Boatright, Robert. 2011. *Interest Groups and Campaign Finance Reform in the United States and Canada*. Ann Arbor: University of Michigan Press.
Bush, George W. 2002. "Statement on Signing the Bipartisan Campaign Reform Act of 2002." The American Presidency Project. Accessed February 3, 2015. http://www.presidency.ucsb.edu/ws/?pid=64503.
Corrado, Anthony. 2000. *Campaign Finance Reform*. New York: The Century Foundation Press.
Goidel, Robert, Donald Gross, and Tony Shields. 1999. *Money Matters: Consequences of Campaign Finance Reform in U.S. House Elections*. Lanham, MD: Rowman & Littlefield Publishers.
Grant, J. Tobin, and Thomas Rudolph. 2004. *Expression vs. Equality: The Politics of Campaign Finance Reform*. Columbus: The Ohio State University Press.
Jones, Ruth. 1990. *Money, Elections, and Democracy: Reforming Congressional Campaign Finance*. Edited by Margaret Latus Nugent and John Johannes. Boulder, CO: Westview Press.
Malone, Michael, Richard Roeder, and William Lang. 1976. *Montana: A History of Two Centuries*. Seattle: University of Washington Press.

Nichols, John, and Robert McChesney. 2013. *Dollarocracy: How the Money-and-Media Election Complex is Destroying America*. New York: Nation Books.

PBS Frontline. 2012. "Big Sky, Big Money." October 30. Accessed January 8, 2015. http://www.pbs.org/wgbh/pages/frontline/government-elections-politics/big-sky-big-money/transcript-32.

Roosevelt, Theodore. 1904. "Fourth Message to Congress." December 6. Accessed January 8, 2015. http://www.presidency.ucsb.edu/ws/?pid=29545.

Samples, John. 2006. *The Fallacy of Campaign Finance Reform*. Chicago: University of Chicago Press.

CAMPAIGN NARRATIVES AND DRAMATIZATION

The idea of a sweeping "campaign narrative" has come to dominate the way most reporters think about telling the story of American politics. And this drive has, in turn, changed the way the media and campaigns operate. On the media side, journalists now strive for illustrative moments on the campaign trail that can be used to make larger statements about the state of the election and contextualize day-to-day developments. Those moments are woven into a narrative arc that runs from the first murmurings of a candidate's interest in running to either their victory or defeat on Election Day. On the campaign side, consultants and communications officials look for ways to construct moments on the trail or carefully build up or lower expectations ahead of key moments, like fundraising reporting or debates, to try and cook the idea of a candidate surging ahead or overcoming obstacles.

The notion of a campaign narrative has deep roots—Abraham Lincoln used the idea of splitting his own fence rails to convey his everyman origins. But early efforts by campaigns were meant to be more like a symbol of one aspect of the candidate; although such symbols would often be echoed by the media, they were not constructed by journalists as the "story" of the campaign. The modern campaign narrative really began with the advent of modern political reporting in general in the 1960s. Theodore White, historian-turned-foreign correspondent-turned novelist, decided in 1959 to tackle the 1960 election for his next book. White's combination of a novelist's narrative sensibilities and a historian's approach to contextualizing the election of the most powerful person in the free world came together in a groundbreaking book, *The Making of the President 1960*. The book was unlike any piece of reporting about the campaign that came before it, and was built on what would now be considered unbelievable access to the candidates. Considering the book decades after its publication, then-Washington Bureau Chief for the *New York Times* Jill Abramson pointed out that White was also capturing a very specific moment in political history. She noted, "White was writing at a time when television was just becoming the medium through which most Americans experienced political campaigns, though in a limited way. Much of the action still took place off camera, which enabled a respected journalist like White to gain direct but unpublicized access to the candidates as well as to their families and members of their staffs, who spoke openly about their hopes and ambitions" (Abramson 2010).

The result was a book that made presidential politics a dramatic story of human characters—the politicians themselves and the people around them—strategizing, plotting, and striving to capture the Oval Office. The candidates came alive in prose that allowed people to see them not as statesmen, but men who got frustrated, who stood in the rain trying to engage voters. One scene in the climactic battle between future nominee John Kennedy and Minnesota Senator Hubert Humphrey dueling for votes in West Virginia captured the sort of moments that built White's book. Humphrey, running on four hours of sleep, learns that Kennedy's team has poured $34,000, some 36 percent more money than Humphrey, into television ads in the state. An aide comes to Humphrey saying one station is set to cancel the candidate's 30-minute presentation that night unless they pay cash ahead of time:

> "Pay it!" snarled Humphrey. "Pay it! I don't care how, don't come to me with that kind of story!" Then, realizing that his crestfallen aide was, like himself, destitute, Hubert pulled out his checkbook at the breakfast table and said, "All right, I'll pay for it myself," and scribbled a personal check of his own.
>
> Mrs. Humphrey watched him do so, with dark, sad eyes, and one had the feeling that the check was money from the family grocery fund—or the money earmarked to pay for the wedding of their daughter who was to be married the week following the primary. (White 1961)

The scene, like so many in the book, made politics a personal drama that pitted very real people against one another and even though the end result was known by all created a palpable sense of dramatic tension. The book won the 1962 Pulitzer Prize for Nonfiction and sold well. White would replicate the book again in 1964, 1968, and 1972 and in other forms in 1980 and 1984, but the impact of the work extended far beyond one author's approach and his resulting books.

White's books helped create a deep desire within the journalists and editors who would cover campaigns to tell them not as stale debates of qualifications and position white papers, but rather stories of intense drama. Born of this new form of political reporting was the idea of the campaign narrative—the sense that the entire campaign was a story and that the candidates were characters. This approach would have other powerful entries in the form of books—most notably Richard Ben Cramer's epic tome, *What It Takes: The Way to the White House*, that told the story of the 1988 campaign. Cramer's work took four years to write and came in at over 1,000 pages, divided into chapters about each of the Democratic and Republican candidates. Politico's Jonathan Martin would wax on about the work in a 2013 piece written at Cramer's death. Martin, who described himself as a Cramer "groupie," described that 1992 work, saying, "It's insufficient to say that Cramer's 1,047-page tour de force on the 1988 presidential race is the best book ever written about a campaign. It is that. But what makes it so valuable, so rewarding, just so much damn fun is that it illustrates why politics and journalism is so much damn fun" (Martin 2013). These works by Cramer and White formed a touchstone for how political reporters have come to think about campaigns and political reporting. It is now about the process and the story—which, while driving so many political writers and many who read their work, has also been seen as a misleading way to cover politics and a tool of influence campaigns can use to influence the reporting of the journalists sent to cover the campaign.

The focus on process, and the tendency to seek out dramatic illustrative vignettes, have become deeply entrenched elements of modern political reporting. Reporters are sent not simply to record the stump speech the candidate gives again and again, but to tell the story of the campaign through the attitude of the volunteers, the behavior of the consultants and, in those rare moments of unplanned access, the off-the-cuff comments of the candidate. Those rare sherds of dramatic insight fuel whole columns and countless blogs. The narrative has come to represent such a strong force within political reporting that some observers have declared it, rather than partisan belief or corporate influence, as the real bias of political reporting. The human narrative that White and Cramer tell, and the countless reporters inspired by this form of reporting, focuses on two key biases that political scientist W. Lance Bennett criticized in his contribution to the book, *News: Politics of Illusion*: personalization and dramatization. Bennett writes of the two, "If there is a single most important flaw in the American news style, it is the overwhelming tendency to downplay the big social, economic, or political picture in favor of the human trials, tragedies, and triumphs that sit at the surface of events . . . News dramas emphasize crisis over continuity, the present over the past or future, conflicts and relationship problems between the personalities at their center, and the impact of scandals on personal political careers. News dramas downplay complex policy information, the workings of government institutions, and the bases of power behind the central characters" (Bennett 2011). Bennett argues that these two biases of press coverage of politics both play out in the focus on campaign narratives. Reporters focus on the tactics and strategy of the campaign and, to the degree they can capture this information, the anecdotes of how the candidates and consultants are acting and thinking about the state of the campaign. This focus has little to do with their policy positions, the issues that could be affected by the election of one candidate versus another, or the views of voters and their desires.

Despite these concerns, campaigns have come to see the narrative as a useful tool to exploit to shape of the coverage of a candidate and the campaign. Campaign consultants start with a core idea—a story they want the entire campaign to be about—and a clear role for their candidate in that story. The liberal magazine *American Prospect* summed up the core idea of campaign narratives in one simple, three-part formula, writing, "Part one of the story describes the state of the country and its government, clearly defining what is wrong. Part two describes the place the candidate wants to take us, the better day being promised. Part three explains why the candidate is the one and only person who can deliver us from where we are to that better day" (Waldman 2007). This story structure serves as the outline of the campaign to come. Day to day, campaigns consider the trajectory of the campaign narrative, often using the language of momentum to try and capture the sense of the story. Reporters will also use the narrative theme to build dramatic tension into their stories. A series of negative stories—many of which build on themselves through a political echo chamber—can convey a campaign in trouble; weeks of bad news followed by a single act of luck or better-than-expected debate conveys a dramatic reversal of fortune. Poll numbers may be used in conjunction to offer statistical evidence for the underlying narrative.

Campaigns seek to use the narrative as a tool to change the reporting about their candidate. A campaign struggling to raise money will work for weeks ahead of time to convey the campaign is doing worse than they know they are, seeking to build an expectation that journalists should expect the fundraising total to be lower than they will end up reporting. Why? So that when the campaign reports a total that is higher than the narrative has come to expect, the story may end up being played as the campaign beating the conventional wisdom. The same "expectations game" is played ahead of campaign debates as each campaign tries to raise the expectation of the other side while simultaneously lowering their own candidate's likely performance.

This meta-narrative of the campaign is a murky concept, one without a clear source, but clear power. The overall narrative creates a framework for all of the stories that will cover the campaign; even statistical efforts to thwart the narrative story of campaign use the narrative itself as a foil to gain traction. The British-based magazine *The Economist* sought to explain the source of the uber narrative to its readers, writing, " 'The narrative' is the emergent product of an informal consensus among journalists and commentators. If each journalist is disposed to tell the story a different way, no consensus will emerge and there will be no one dominant narrative. But if, having bantered with other members of the press at the hotel bar (or on Twitter) the night before, it becomes clear how others are going to report the story, then there is really a fact of the matter about 'the narrative' which exists more or less independently of one's own opinion and reporting. Should the lone individual report an event in an idiosyncratic way, it won't change the consensus narrative, and one would actually be wrong to present an idiosyncratic interpretation of events as *the* story" (*The Economist* 2012).

Their description raises the specter of "pack journalism," creating artificial parameters of what is and isn't an acceptable take on the campaign. For example, within 30 minutes of the end of the first presidential debate of 2012 between former governor Mitt Romney and President Barack Obama, stories began conveying a narrative that Romney had changed the trajectory of his campaign, adding new life to a faltering campaign. In the following days and weeks, other stories flowed from this as Romney campaigned with more energy in front of larger crowds and financial supporters reportedly stepped up their backing. Even national polls indicated some movement toward the Republicans, as the narrative fueled countless blog posts and hours of on-air commentary. Still, in the key states that Romney would need to win, Obama maintained a large lead. It would take more than a week for the narrative to reflect that even though Romney had done well, the core dynamics of the race had not changed. Nevertheless, based on this narrative some began predicting that a surging Romney would win the popular vote and possibly the election. It of course didn't happen. Obama won the popular vote by nearly 5 million votes and scored a lopsided Electoral College win 332–206. Statistical reporters like Nate Silver had always rejected the idea of the narrative, instead relying on the core polling data to try and refute the Romney surging storyline, but he was only one voice and the narrative responded much slower than he did.

The final concern about the narrative focus on personalities and drama is that it relegates issues and voters to minor actors. Issues are either tools for the campaigns to use to activate voter bases, or to avoid as divisive demobilizers. Will this position on abortion rights do enough to close the gender gap? Which candidate's middle class tax cut position will resonate with suburban voters so important to Pennsylvania's 20 Electoral College votes? The underlying policy, its costs, and even its feasibility of passing Congress rarely play a major role in the campaign coverage. Even preeminent political reporters have expressed concern about how this reporting treats the actual voter. David Broder, who was called the "high priest" of political reporting by Timothy Crouse in the 1970s, worried before his death about the form of political reporting that Theodore White had created. In Broder's 2011 obituary, the *Washington Post* made special note of his concerns, quoting him as saying, "My generation of reporters was deeply influenced by Teddy White, the greatest political journalist of our time. He showed us how far inside a campaign you could go. We naturally emulated him, at least as far as our skills would take us. Before long, we got so far inside that we forgot the outside—that the campaign belonged not to the candidates or their consultants or their pollsters, but to the public" (Bernstein 2011). Broder's concern can even be seen as the evolution of the tell-all book about the campaign. Although White paid attention to the telling details of his time with candidates, he also spent enormous energy observing voters and how they would interact with the candidates. His 1961 work is sprinkled with moments like John Kennedy spending a miserable morning in Wisconsin trying to get anyone to talk with him before leaving a couple hours later without a single meaningful interaction with a primary voter. Cramer, for all his epic beauty and thorough reporting, spent more time off the campaign trail with the candidates than on. Voters make brief appearances on the sidelines of the book. By 2010, the campaign book *Game Change*, which featured 300 interviews and 200 on background, would imbue far more weight into the angry outbursts of candidates in private than with any interaction between the candidate and a voter.

It would seem as campaigns became more professionalized, with legions of close and not-so-close advisers to be interviewed after the fact, that time on the trail with the candidate and the interactions between voter and candidate have drifted out of the campaign narratives. Although this has done nothing to weaken the pack-like power the narrative idea holds within political reporting, it has also done nothing to put the individual voter in the epic story of the modern political campaign.

See also: Broder, David; Campaign Strategy Coverage; Pack Journalism; Political Bias and the Media; White, Theodore

Further Reading

Abramson, Jill. 2010. "The Making of the President, Then and Now." *New York Times*. March 10. Accessed November 3, 2015. http://www.nytimes.com/2010/03/21/books/review/Abramson-t.html?pagewanted=all&_r=0.

Bennett, W. Lance. 2011. *News: Politics of Illusion*. Chicago: University of Chicago Press.

Bernstein, Adam. 2011. "David Broder, 81, Dies; Set 'Gold Standard' for Political Journalism." *Washington Post*. March 10. Accessed November 9, 2015. http://www.washingtonpost.com/wp-dyn/content/article/2011/03/09/AR2011030902821.html?sid=ST2011030903008.

The Economist. 2012. "On 'the Narrative.'" March 1. Accessed November 8, 2015. http://www.economist.com/blogs/democracyinamerica/2012/03/campaign-reporting.

Martin, Jonathan. 2013. "Richard Ben Cramer's Masterpiece." Politico. January 8. Accessed November 9, 2015. http://www.politico.com/story/2013/01/richard-ben-cramers-masterpiece-085880.

Waldman, Paul. 2007. "The Power of the Campaign Narrative." *American Prospect*. July 17. Accessed November 8, 2015. http://prospect.org/article/power-campaign-narrative.

White, Theodore. 2009. *The Making of the Presidency: 1960*. New York: Harper Perennial.

CAMPAIGN STRATEGY COVERAGE

With its sports-like focus on the game within the game, political reporting spends an enormous amount of energy covering the tactics, personnel, and internal workings of the modern campaign. Stories are filed, blogs posted, and broadcast reports aired that make the latest campaign fundraising report or ad buy the central lead of the story. Even issues are framed for the reader or viewer as an element of a larger political campaign strategy that the reporter often appears more interested in understanding. Polling is added to the mix as a way of testing the effectiveness of the strategy in connecting with the voter. This approach to political reporting is based heavily on a core premise of political reporting: that organizing and executing an effective and largely error-free campaign is one of the best ways to test the fitness of a politician to run their office, be it governor, senator, or president.

The way in which a campaign is run and the tactics behind the policy positions and speeches of the candidate can become an overwhelming theme of most reporting about a campaign. For example, a 2007 survey of the so-called invisible primary period before any caucus-goers or primary voters had cast ballots in the 2008 presidential campaign found that fully 63 percent of the stories about the campaign focused on tactics. This compared with 17 percent of stories that focused on the biography of the candidate, 15 percent on his or her positions on key issues, and only 1 percent on the candidates' records or past public performances. Those are striking numbers to consider given how important scholars and other observers say this period of candidate vetting is to the current political process. The survey, conducted by the Project for Excellence in Journalism and the Joan Shorenstein Center on the Press, Politics and Public Policy at Harvard University, found that strategy stories could be useful by connecting campaign tactics to the leadership style of the candidate, but only if reporters chose to organize their story in a way that focused on issues larger than the campaign itself. Worse, researchers discovered that 86 percent of strategy stories focused solely on how the tactics affected the campaign, rather than on leadership style or other skills that might translate into how a given candidate would lead. The authors noted, "This focus on political matters varied little by media. The most citizen-oriented coverage came from newspapers (about 18 percent compared to 79 percent oriented toward politicians). The least citizen-oriented coverage was found in network TV (9 percent vs. 89 percent). Online, cable, and radio were all somewhere in the middle" (PEJ/Shorenstein Center).

Central to the concern over this approach to reporting is that it casts politics as a process that does not involve the public, but to which the public is the target audience. Political reporting too vested in this approach focuses on the professional class of political consultants and participants who seek to "motivate their base of supporters" or "soften support" for their opponent. It uses public opinion polling to test the effectiveness of the strategy, not to gauge public opinion on substance or even style. The public is reduced to a number, critics argue, to be moved but not listened to.

Before commentators like New York University professor Jay Rosen or Buzz Machine's Jeff Jarvis railed against this form of reporting, 1960s New Left activist Todd Gitlin opined on how the news media focus on strategy was alienating the voters that political reporting was supposed to serve, writing:

> Campaign coverage in 1988 reveled in this mode. Viewers were invited to be cognoscenti of their own bamboozlement . . . This campaign metacoverage, coverage of the coverage, partakes of the postmodern fascination with surfaces and the machinery that cranks them out, a fascination indistinguishable from surrender—as if once we understand that all images are concocted we have attained the only satisfaction the heart and mind are capable of. (Gitlin 2004)

Rosen, in particular, cites the critiques by Gitlin and others to condemn political reporting for being single-minded in its interest in appealing to the smarter-than-the-average voter, tuned in to the subtle, manipulative efforts of campaign operatives and unwilling to report the claims or statements of a candidate without applying the "insider" lens to it. He blasted American reporters in a 2011 speech in Australia, saying, "In politics, our journalists believe, it is better to be savvy than it is to be honest or correct on the facts. It's better to be savvy than it is to be just, good, fair, decent, strictly lawful, civilized, sincere, thoughtful or humane. Savviness is what journalists admire in others. Savvy is what they themselves dearly wish to be" (Rosen 2011).

This shift from covering the campaign as a series of speeches and policy statements to a grand game of political "Risk" did not happen suddenly, but evolved through a series of elections. If there is a starting point, it may be the simultaneous rise of public opinion polling along with the reporting focus on the "narrative" of the campaign and the personalities behind that story. Theodore White's seminal book *The Making of the President 1960* is one of the milestones in this transition. The book captured the behind-the-scenes reality of running for president, portraying the candidates as human beings who are frustrated, defeated, determined, and fascinating. The book triggered a fundamental shift in political reporting that sent campaign reporters scurrying for the telling details of what made the candidate tick and a new focus on the logistics and strategy of the campaign. As reporters focused more and more on the campaign, they began to see how the campaigns operated, where they spent their money, how messages were framed. In many ways the interest in the tactics resulted in part from the increasingly controlled way in which consultants and others wanted the campaign to run. Candidates gave the same stump speech, reiterating the same points again and again. Photo ops were carefully organized and supporters pre-screened to ensure reporters would have access only to the campaign's preferred types of voters. Reporters were herded onto campaign buses and roped off at rallies. Few received access to the candidate; most were relegated to the press spokesperson who would only supply the pre-approved talking points. For reporters stuck in this scenario and resenting it, it became more interesting to expose the strategy behind the speeches, the political maneuvering informing the latest bus tour, and the larger reality of how the campaign reflected the candidate.

As reporters shifted their focus, campaigns sought to shape the strategy story. And so on. Soon the two sides of the equation—reporter and campaign operative— were engaged in an escalating effort to frame campaign coverage. The result for those observing the coverage was profound, said political scientist Thomas Patterson, who wrote, "The change in election news from a governing schema to a game schema is so fundamental that it constitutes a quiet revolution in the campaign that Americans see through the lens of the press . . . Whereas the game was once viewed as the means, it is now the end, while policy problems, issues, and the like are merely tokens in the struggle for the presidency" (Patterson 2011).

But it is not just the competition between campaign official and reporter that has fueled this "quiet revolution." The evolving news cycle, as well as the changing information ecosystem, have fundamentally altered the political reporting world. The growth of cable news and later the Internet pressed reporters to supply reporting throughout the day, rather than synthesizing a day's news into a single package. The strategy component of the story can be easily constructed on the fly, allowing a reporter to tease the reasons a candidate is making an appearance in a certain city in front of a certain group ahead of the event via social media, and then use the same framing ideas to inform their immediate post-appearance take on the story. That frame then often heavily influences any write-through of the story later in the day. The game frame can be quickly deployed and is a powerful tool for reporters to rely on.

Added to this functional reality is the ocean of polling data that has swamped the political world. One assessment found that between 1984 and 2000 there was a 900 percent increase in the number of polls being conducted—and that was more than a decade ago. The polling flood allows reporters to put statistical context around the campaigns' moves, identifying swing states that may suddenly appear more often on the travel itinerary, highlighting issues that may be strengths or weaknesses of a candidate, and creating an independent source of information they can fold into stories about day-to-day campaign workings. But polls also play an important role in allowing reporters to assess a campaign while maintaining objectivity. One political communications scholar has noted that polls "help insulate journalists from such claims since they provide the 'objective' organizing device by which to comment and analyze news that is being reported by other outlets. For example, if a new survey indicates that a candidate is slipping in public popularity, the reporting of the poll's results provides the subsequent opening for journalists to then attribute the opinion shift to a recent negative ad, allegation, or political slip up" (Nisbet 2007). This magnification is also spurred by a desire to be different in an increasingly competitive digital news marketplace. Google News headlines on a given day of the campaign shows story after story about the same speech or same polling number. How does a reporter stand out in such a crowd? The answer is often in the analytical approach of the story. Add to this the partisan nature of many writers and websites, and the propensity of reporters to insert their analytical take on the day's photo op becomes even stronger.

The result is a form of reporting in which the default story about a given political event is to place it in the strategic context of what is happening in a campaign. This can be a useful way to view a given story. For example, as the Republican primary churned on toward the first votes in 2016, a series of stories emerged about then-frontrunner Donald Trump. Trump, who had drawn headlines and occasional outrage for statements made about Mexican immigrants, Muslims, and blacks, announced soon after Thanksgiving that some 100 black ministers would meet with the real estate mogul and endorse his candidacy. The news swept social media as a list of attendees was released. Many of the pastors denounced the statement, saying they had not agreed to support Trump; several said they had rejected the idea of even meeting with him. Soon the campaign was backtracking on its claims, calling the meeting a sit-down with religious leaders. In the end, only two of the less than 50 who attended the meeting publicly endorsed Trump, one who organized the meeting and a Republican activist from Georgia—who was not a minister. In summing up the debacle, the *New York Times* put the story in the context of the larger campaign themes, noting, "The awkward evolution of the event highlights the perils of a haphazard-seeming campaign that revolves almost entirely around a giant personality. But it also captures the degree to which Mr. Trump, both the man and the candidate, has polarized African-Americans, a group he is now courting as he tries to shake accusations of bigotry" (Barbaro and Corrales 2015). Such a story can legitimately be seen against the backdrop of a campaign that played fast and loose, at times, with facts and recklessly made promises or issued statements that needed to be corrected later. Additionally, it was a chance to talk about the degree to which Trump's campaign had become a lightning rod, pushing pastors to reject a meeting for fear of the way their congregation would view such a sit-down. Stories like this are what this focus on strategy and tactics is about, and why it has become a dominant trope of political reporting.

The focus on strategy has also created a whole industry for reporters to write for specialized publications, like Politico, that invest much in such reporting—and to write books that build on the tradition of White's *The Making of the President* series. Mark Halperin has spent a career deep in this mode of reporting, having documented the 2008 and 2012 presidential campaigns in tell-all style. He has also expressed deep concern about the very same style of reporting, noting in a 2007 op-ed, "In the face of polls and horse-race maneuvering, we can try to keep from getting sucked in by it all. We should examine a candidate's public record and full life as opposed to his or her campaign performance . . . [V]oters and journalists alike should be focused on a deeper question: Do the candidates have what it takes to fill the most difficult job in the world?" (Halperin 2007). An unexpected plea by a reporter who has made telling the insider stories (that Rosen and others deride as alienating and discouraging to the voters political reporting is said to serve) a central part of his reporting.

Perhaps campaign strategy coverage is less the legacy of Theodore White and more that of Joe McGinniss's book *The Selling of the President*. McGinniss told the story of the 1972 campaign of Richard Nixon and how it used television and advertising to help elect the former vice president. Although McGinniss approached the subject with the enthusiasm of someone discovering something new and interesting, it was the cynicism of that title that seemed to stick and help inspire a new generation of reporters who wanted people to know the behind-the-scenes manipulation that was the real political campaign. That is what observers and media critics worry is the core goal of modern political reporting. Whether it is the boogeyman they make out, or a potentially effective way for voters to learn about the campaign and the person running for office, is perhaps judged by the effectiveness of each story and less on the entire approach to reporting.

See also: Campaign Narratives and Dramatization; Invisible Primary; Spin; White, Theodore

Further Reading

Barbaro, Michael, and John Corrales. 2015. "'Love' and Disbelief Follow Donald Trump Meeting With Black Leaders." *New York Times*. November 30. Accessed December 1, 2015. http://www.nytimes.com/2015/12/01/us/politics/love-and-disbelief-followdonald-trump-meeting-with-black-leaders.html.

Gitlin, Todd. 1991. "Foreword." In *50 Years of Dissent*. Edited by Nicolaus Mills and Michael Walzer. New Haven, CT: Yale University Press.

Halperin, Mark. 2007. "How 'What It Takes' Took Me Off Course." *New York Times*. November 25. Accessed December 1, 2015. http://www.nytimes.com/2007/11/25/opinion/25halperin.html?_r=0.

"The Invisible Primary—Invisible No Longer: A First Look at Coverage of the 2008 Presidential Campaign." Project for Excellence in Journalism and the Joan Shorenstein Center on the Press, Politics and Public Policy at Harvard University. October 29, 2007. Accessed December 1, 2015. http://www.journalism.org/files/legacy/The%20Early%20Campaign%20FINAL.pdf.

Nisbet, Matthew. 2007. "Horse Race Coverage & the Political Spectacle." Science Blogs. December 31. Accessed December 1, 2015. http://bigthink.com/age-of-engagement/horse-race-coverage-the-political-spectacle.

Patterson, Thomas. 2011. *Out of Order*. New York: Knopf Doubleday Publishing Group.

Rosen, Jay. 2011. "Why Political Coverage Is Broken." Press Think. August 26. Accessed December 1, 2015. http://pressthink.org/2011/08/why-political-coverage-is-broken.

CATO INSTITUTE

The Cato Institute sits in a beautifully glass-lined building staring out on Washington, D.C., a city it has fought to rein in for nearly 40 years. The institute is a staunchly libertarian think tank that argues for limited government and a maximization of personal freedom.

Stating it adheres to the principles of the American Revolution, Cato describes itself as following a worldview that "combines an appreciation for entrepreneurship, the market process, and lower taxes with strict respect for civil liberties and skepticism about the benefits of both the welfare state and foreign military adventurism" (Cato 2015). The institute was created in 1974 by David and Charles Koch with Murray Rothbard, a libertarian economist.

With nearly fifty full-time resident scholars and another seventy adjunct researchers, the institute publishes an array of journals and books and is one of the most prolific filers of briefs to the Supreme Court. The organization often promotes limited regulations and free market solutions to social problems. It also argues against most foreign interventions. The group runs primarily through donations by individuals and several bank foundations, but businesses like Whole Foods, Google, and Facebook have also supported its work (Cato 2013). The institute does not endorse candidates and goes to great lengths to remain nonpartisan. It does not directly lobby on behalf of candidates or specific legislation, but can be counted on to participate in most debates about the role of government in the United States.

The institute is named after Cato's Letters, a series of eighteenth-century essays on liberty that were widely circulated among the Founding Fathers ahead of the American Revolution. The institute's scholars are often quoted in the media and testify before Congress. Cato's people have taken the lead in criticizing the Affordable Care Act, the government bailout of troubled banks and auto manufacturers, and U.S. involvement in overseas actions in Libya or against radical Islamic groups.

The institute has plenty of critics from both sides of the political spectrum. Some libertarians, including backers of founder Murray Rothbard, accuse the institute of being one of the arms of the "Kochtopus," the multitude of political entities funded by the Koch family. These backers of Rothbard argue the economist "thought that

Cato's primary mission should be scholarship rather than political campaigns and attempts to secure audiences with the high and mighty in Washington" (Gordon 2014). Liberals have accused the institute of being libertarian when it was convenient and losing those positions when they ran too far afoul of the Republican Party.

The institute was at the center of an intra-board fight in 2012 when two of the major board members, Charles and David Koch, filed suit to claim control of one of the "founder" seats vacated by the death of a founding member. The fight went public when Cato launched a social media campaign to "Save Cato." "The Save Cato site pleaded with the public to join the Institute in persuading the Koch brothers to drop what Cato labeled as a takeover attempt" (Craig 2014). The lawsuit was eventually dropped when the institute agreed to a change in leadership and the Koch brothers accepted a portion of a reorganized board. The agreement meant the departure of the longtime chief of the institute Ed Crane, who had developed a personal feud with Charles Koch. Crane was circumspect about the outcome, telling the *New York Times*, "I think both sides got what they wanted. I'm happy. This was the tradeoff: Cato's independence for new leadership" (Lichtblau 2012).

Despite this criticism, Cato continues to garner attention from American media and lawmakers. A 2013 quantitative assessment of think tanks found, "the Heritage Foundation and Cato Institute dominate social media and web traffic. In aggregate, Heritage has over 765,000 social media fans, more than twice that of Cato, the next highest with nearly 290,000. Cato, however, leads in social media (and overall) once the figures are adjusted for size" (Clark and Roodman 2013). And neither controversy nor the shareholder fight seems to have had any long-term effect on the organization's role in Washington. It continues to publish guides to Congress stressing the need for federal restraint and has actively participated in many of the critical Supreme Court cases around campaign finance reform and the federal health care law. The group continues the work that economist Milton Friedman hailed them for in 1993, the effort of "documenting in detail the harmful effects of government policies" and therefore creating "appropriate incentives for the people who control the government purse strings and so large a part of our lives" (Friedman 2002).

Further Reading

Cato Institute. "Cato's Mission." Accessed January 20, 2015. http://www.cato.org/mission.

Cato Institute. 2013. "Cato Institute 2013 Annual Report." Accessed January 20, 2015. http://www.cato.org/sites/cato.org/files/pubs/pdf/annual-report-2013.pdf.

Clark, Julia, and David Roodman. 2013. "Measuring Think Tank Performance: An Index of Public Profile." Center for Global Development. June. Accessed January 20, 2015. http://www.cgdev.org/sites/default/files/think-tank-index_0_0.pdf.

Craig, Brett. 2014. "Cato Institute." *Encyclopedia of Social Media and Politics*. Vol. 1. Los Angeles: Sage Publications.

Friedman, Milton. 2002. "The Real Free Lunch: Markets and Private Property." *Toward Liberty: The Idea That Is Changing the World: 25 Years of Public Policy from the Cato Institute*. Edited by David Boaz. Washington, DC: Cato Institute.

Gordon, David. 2014. "Murray and the Rothbardians versus the Koch Brothers." *Economic Policy Journal*. March 28. Accessed January 19, 2015. http://www.economicpolicyjournal.com/2014/03/murray-and-rothbardians-versus-koch.html.

Lichtblau, Eric. 2012. "Cato Institute and Koch Brothers Reach Agreement." *New York Times*. June 25. Accessed January 20, 2015. http://thecaucus.blogs.nytimes.com/2012/06/25/cato-institute-and-koch-brothers-reach-agreement/?_r=0.

CBS NEWS

CBS News in many ways built the prestige, mystique, and profitability of broadcast television news. The network, with its mix of nightly news programs and news-magazine shows, built its reputation through the work of pioneering broadcast journalists like Edward R. Murrow, Fred Friendly, Dan Rather, and Don Hewitt. This investment made it the most influential of the radio and later television news outlets for much of the first 50 years of broadcast news. Its influence has waned in recent decades as television audiences spread out over an increasing number of cable news outlets and the Internet sapped the immediacy that had empowered early broadcast.

CBS became a leader in news mainly because it was the second network. The National Broadcast Company, founded by the brilliant and supremely confident David Sarnoff, was firmly established in the new medium of radio when a fledgling new network, the Columbia Phonographic Broadcasting System, decided it needed to reorganize. Columbia—makers of the popular phonograph of the same name—wanted out of the radio business and so the new owners purchased the network and installed the son of a wealthy Philadelphia cigar magnate as the man in charge. Although only 26 at the time, William S. Paley soon purchased 51 percent of the company by investing $400,000 of his father's money. He also dumped "phonographic" from the name and the Columbia Broadcast System was born. With a handful of stations in major cities around the country, Paley understood he needed to compete with NBC, which had already signed contracts with many of the top-tier entertainers. "Faced with that situation, Paley chose to concentrate on news and public affairs. More than anything else at that point, Paley wanted to infuse CBS with an aura of class and respectability, and an emphasis on news and 'serious' programs was the quickest and surest way to accomplish that. He also reasoned, with customary shrewdness, that such prestige, once attained, could later be parlayed into power and profits" (Gates 1978). This manifested itself by Paley spending money to woo established news professionals away from other outlets, like United Press International, and prompted him to create a CBS News division that was organizationally equal to the entertainment programming unit.

One of the early journalists hired to work for the burgeoning news division was Edward R. Murrow, who had no formal training as a journalist but had been a speech major in college. Murrow went to Europe in 1937 to book newsmaker interviews for the network, but soon found himself on the air as the news unfolding in the lead up to World War II forced the network to improvise. His 30-minute, multi-point news program, created the night Nazi Germany annexed Austria, became the model for the modern broadcast news program, mixing reporters from various locations around Europe with Murrow anchoring. Murrow was empowered to build his team in Europe, with Paley and the CBS News division backing up the hiring of those who could build CBS News into a radio and later a television news powerhouse. Murrow's reporting from Europe during the war made him a household name. His signature reports that began "This is London" brought the fear of the Nazi attacks on Britain home to American listeners. He continued his work as America entered the war, and by the end of World War II he became the head of CBS News.

As television grew swiftly in popularity following the war, the radio broadcasters moved their operations in that direction, launching television networks with the same name and often the same staffs as the former audio-only outfits. Murrow went with them and helped start CBS's television news operations, including launching his own program, *See It Now*, in 1951. Just three years later this CBS program would take on the "Red Scare" of Senator Joseph McCarthy and solidify the seriousness with which television news was seen on the political stage. Murrow and Friendly built a program that was made up almost exclusively of excerpts of McCarthy's speeches and congressional testimony. The program carefully built the case that McCarthy was exploiting the fear of Communism for political gain rather than leading an honest effort to keep America safe. It would signal the beginning of the end of the anti-Communist purges of the 1950s and highlighted the real power of televised news.

Despite this success, the CBS News division often battled with the business side as news people fought for air time over entertainment programming that made far more money. Still, throughout the 1950s and 1960s CBS made a name for itself with its serious treatment of news. Murrow recruited a college dropout by the name of Walter Cronkite to join his team in 1950, and soon Cronkite was delivering the news on Sunday evenings. Cronkite moved up the ranks and in 1962 became anchor of the CBS Evening News. The next year marked a historic period of broadcasting, the unprecedented coverage of the assassination and burial of President John F. Kennedy. Cronkite delivered the news of the shooting in a voice-only broadcast that interrupted a CBS soap opera. He would be on camera by the time news had reached New York that Kennedy was dead. For the next three days, CBS, along with other broadcasters, suspended all programming to cover all the events in Dallas and the funeral back in Washington. The events again highlighted the power of television in the American society and further cemented Cronkite's and CBS's importance.

Cronkite and CBS News had become such a force in the United States that by the late 1960s many within government had come to see his reports as a gauge of what the public thought. In the wake of a series of attacks against American forces in Vietnam, Cronkite went to the war-torn nation and produced a documentary that ended with his declaration that the war was essentially unwinnable. President Lyndon Johnson reportedly (though there is some doubt) said, "If I've lost Walter

Cronkite, I've lost middle America." The admission, whether completely accurate, speaks to the influence CBS News and its anchor had over the public dialogue. CBS's influence would grow as newsmagazine program *60 Minutes*, launched in 1968, grew in popularity and profitability in the 1970s and 1980s.

But as networks generally and CBS specifically began to lose viewers to cable networks and Cronkite was replaced with CBS veteran Dan Rather, the network's influence began to slip. Yet CBS remained an important voice in the growing media chorus covering politics, offering up critical interviews and memorable moments. One such moment erupted on the nightly news in 1987 when Rather interviewed then-vice president George H.W. Bush. Bush believed he was sitting down for a general profile about his campaign for president, but when Rather pressed for answers about the vice president's role in the Iran-Contra affair the two squared off.

> *Vice President Bush:* I'm not suggesting. I'm just saying I don't remember it.
> *Dan Rather:* I don't want to be argumentative, Mr. Vice President.
> *Vice President Bush:* You do, Dan.
> *Dan Rather:* No . . . no, sir, I don't.
> *Vice President Bush:* This is not a great night, because I want to talk about why I want to be president, why those 41 percent of the people are supporting me. And I don't think it's fair . . .
> *Dan Rather:* And Mr. Vice President, if these questions are . . .
> *Vice President Bush:* . . . to judge my whole career by a rehash on Iran. How would you like it if I judged your career by those seven minutes when you walked off the set in New York? (Rather earlier that year had stormed off the set when CBS shortened the news program to air a tennis match, forcing the network to go dark for some six minutes.)
> *Dan Rather:* Well, Mister . . .
> *Vice President Bush:* . . . Would you like that?
> *Dan Rather:* Mr. Vice President . . .
> *Vice President Bush:* I have respect for you, but I don't have respect for what you're doing here tonight.

Bush's clash with Rather marked a memorable campaign moment, but it also highlighted the weakening of CBS News as a voice of the public. Bush went on to easily win election that fall, unlike Johnson's fate after Cronkite's reporting 20 years earlier.

Today, although *CBS Evening News* has been mired in third place among network news programs since the late 1990s, CBS continues to be an important voice in the coverage of politics. *60 Minutes* remains the highest rated news program, and *Face the Nation*, its Sunday news talk show anchored by Texas native Bob Schieffer, is the top rated of the array of Sunday talk shows. *Face the Nation*, founded in 1954 by CBS News president Frank Stanton, launched with a historic program where controversial Senator Joseph McCarthy faced questions from journalists around the country about his impending censure by the Senate.

But even this good news is tempered by change. In 2015, Schieffer announced his retirement, telling *USA Today*, "I always felt that I wanted to step down when I felt like I could still do the job. I've watched a lot of these politicians who couldn't bring themselves to leave. I just didn't want that. We felt like we're really doing good these days" (Yu 2015). The effects of the change in anchor at CBS's Sunday political talk show are still too early to know, but what is clear is the father of broadcast news has grown older as audience fragmentation has taken its toll.

See also: Broadcast Television News; *Face the Nation*; Murrow, Edward; *60 Minutes*

Further Reading

Gates, Gary Paul. 1978. *Air Time: The Inside Story of CBS News*. New York: Harper & Row, Publishers.

Yu, Roger. 2015. "CBS' Schieffer Takes a Chance to Go Out on Top." *USA Today*. April 10. Accessed July 21, 2015. http://www.usatoday.com/story/money/2015/04/10/cbs -schieffer-interview/25578577.

CENSORSHIP

See First Amendment and Censorship

CENTER FOR AMERICAN PROGRESS (CAP)

John Podesta had kept the Bill Clinton White House working as its calm, but highly effective chief of staff. But by 2001, the Clinton presidency was over and George W. Bush was in the White House.

Podesta, though, was not done with Washington. In 2003, he created the Center for American Progress (CAP) as a liberal think tank and policy institute. The center was soon drafting policies, convening progressive politicians, and proving highly effective. The *New Yorker* wrote in 2014 that CAP "has become an important player in the Washington power game, providing detailed analysis and policy recommendations, a forum for conversations and debates, and daily commentary on everything from the job figures to Bill Cosby" (Cassidy 2015). The center was envisioned as part-philosophical hothouse of the left and part hard-nosed political operative effort. The trick Podesta was trying to pull off was to build a "machine for finding new ideas and marketing them in hopes that all this effort will somehow coalesce into a new and compelling governing philosophy for Democrats" (Bai 2013). The organization that developed became both a research institute that generated policy briefs and draft legislation used by congressional Democrats and a full-blown campaign operation working to get liberal positions out to supporters and through the mainstream press.

The resulting think tank offers research and policy ideas across a spectrum of issues and proudly proclaims its liberal leanings, writing, "As progressives, we believe America is a land of boundless opportunity, where people can better themselves, their children, their families, and their communities through education, hard work, and the freedom to climb the ladder of economic mobility. We believe an open and effective government can champion the common good over narrow self-interest, harness the strength of our diversity, and secure the rights and safety of its people. And we believe our nation must always be a beacon of hope and strength to the rest of the world. Progressives are idealistic enough to believe change is possible and practical enough to make it happen" (Center for American Progress 2015). The mix of idealism and practicality can be seen not just in their research projects, but also in their active and central role in shaping and directing the message of liberal Democrats on critical issues in the public realm. When President Barack Obama was elected in 2008, Podesta chaired his transition team. And over the next few years about a third of CAP's staff ended up moving to the White House to work with the Democratic president.

CAP maintains the site Think Progress, a liberal news blog that promotes the center's work and liberal Democrat policies, and also serves as a platform for criticizing Republicans. It boasts an annual budget of nearly $50 million, raised from the some of the largest corporations in the United States as well as wealthy liberal individuals. But as the organization grew in influence so did questions about its interest and supporters. Like most think tanks, CAP had not released information about its donors and by 2013 stories were emerging that CAP's donors were influencing its policy approaches. A particularly damning story in *The Nation* claimed that the center sharpened its focus on alternative energy after receiving a large donation from the company First Solar (Silverstein 2013). CAP vehemently denied its funders have any direct control over its research or policy recommendations. But questions persisted as, for more than a year, CAP refused to disclose its donors.

The organization's and its founder's continued role in Democratic politics changed that in 2015. Podesta, who maintains close ties with the Center he started, left a position as counselor to President Obama to assist in a potential run by former secretary of state Hillary Clinton in early 2015. Less than a week later, the center changed its policy on publishing information on its donors, allowing the media to look into who was funding both the research wing and political advocacy efforts. The results surprised some. The center has received support from some of the largest corporations in the United States, including retail giant Wal-mart and mega bank Citigroup. CAP president Neera Tanden defended the donations and the financing of the entire organization, saying, "We're very diversified. We have a very low percentage of corporate donors. We have a wide panoply of individual and foundation supporters. Given that transparency is a progressive value, we wanted to get our list out there" (Sargent 2015).

The center has several methods for affecting policy, especially at the federal level. It produces lengthy reports on issues as varied as gender discrimination to U.S.–Egypt policy to revitalizing Appalachia. It often organizes events and stories aimed at localizing national policies stories. These pieces receive coverage on the Think Progress blog as well as in local media often in critical states for Democratic campaigns.

They also influence media coverage by making a range of liberal researchers and policy experts available to reporters seeking sources for stories. This mix of an aggressive social media and public information campaign along with their well-established role as a source for journalists has made the center one of the most effective organizations pushing progressive policies in Washington, D.C.

See also: Liberal Think Tanks

Further Reading
Bai, Matt. 2003. "Notion Building." *New York Times*. October 12. Accessed February 4, 2015. http://www.nytimes.com/2003/10/12/magazine/notion-building.html.
Cassidy, John. 2015. "John Podesta's Legacy." *New Yorker*. January 14. Accessed February 7, 2015. http://www.newyorker.com/news/john-cassidy/john-podestas-achievements.
Center for American Progress. 2015. "About the Center for American Progress." Accessed February 8, 2015. https://www.americanprogress.org/about/mission.
Sargent, Greg. 2015. "Center for American Progress, Poised to Wield Influence Over 2016, Reveals Its Top Donors." Washington Post. January 21. Accessed February 7, 2015. http://www.washingtonpost.com/blogs/plum-line/wp/2015/01/21/center-for-american-progress-poised-to-wield-influence-over-2016-reveals-its-top-donors.
Silverstein, Ken. 2013. "The Secret Donors Behind the Center for American Progress and Other Think Tanks." *The Nation*. May 21. Accessed February 7, 2015. http://www.thenation.com/article/174437/secret-donors-behind-center-american-progress-and-other-think-tanks-updated-524.

CENTER FOR PUBLIC INTEGRITY (CPI)

Although perhaps overshadowed by its more aggressively marketed non-profit sister group ProPublica, the Center for Public Integrity has a far longer history of investigating and exposing corruption in both the public and private spheres.

Formed in 1989, CPI has grown to include 50 staffers, making it the largest non-profit investigative news organization in the country. The project boldly states its mission as, "To serve democracy by revealing abuses of power, corruption and betrayal of public trust by powerful public and private institutions, using the tools of investigative journalism" (CPI 2015). The center publishes its work through its website and hosts press conferences to outline details it has discovered through its investigations. Unlike ProPublica, which partners aggressively with other news organizations, CPI partners less frequently and releases most of its work independently. Although, perhaps spurred by the more public attention ProPublica has received, the center has lately begun working more and more with traditional media outlets.

The center has won more than 50 national and international journalism awards, including a 2014 Pulitzer Prize for investigative journalism. It has, at times, been labeled liberal in its view and the liberal Fairness and Accuracy in the Media has dubbed CPI "progressive," but it still garners support from notable and mainstream foundations to back its work. One source of funds for the center's work has drawn most of the attention. Controversial liberal investor and philanthropist George Soros's Open Society Foundation has supported the center's work for years, backing CPI for sometimes hundreds of thousands of dollars a year. The Open Society support is specifically mentioned as supporting CPI's investigation into the conservative Koch brothers' political efforts as well as projects on transportation lobbying and the tobacco industry.

CPI was born of frustration. Charles Lewis was working at CBS News, having become a producer for the flagship investigative news program *60 Minutes*, when, days before he turned 35, he quit. He would later write, "I had become frustrated that investigative reporting did not seem to be particularly valued at the national level, regardless of media form. That frustration had mounted over several years and two television networks as national news organizations only reactively reported the various systemic abuses of power, trust and the law in Washington—from the Iran-Contra scandal to the HUD scandal to the Defense Department's procurement prosecutions; from the savings and loan disaster to the 'Keating Five' influence scandal to the first resignation of a House Speaker since 1800" (Lewis 2006, p. 8). Lewis set out to build what he hoped would be a journalistic "utopia" where no corporate bosses or press pack behavior would dictate what was investigated.

A profile of Lewis, published in the *Johns Hopkins Magazine*—Lewis graduated from its graduate school in international studies—later described him at this time as having become "so disenchanted that he left one of the best jobs in broadcast journalism and began working a series of 100-hour weeks as he learned how to create a non-profit organization that has gone on to produce some of the most provocative reporting on government of the last decade" (Keiger 2000). Lewis soon built and launched CPI with an eye toward challenging Washington institutions—press and political. Its first report targeted trade representatives and found that nearly half of the White House officials charged with negotiating trade agreements almost immediately became registered lobbyists for foreign governments upon leaving office.

CPI soon made a bigger name for itself by reporting on the fact that donors who gave hundreds of thousands of dollars to the Democratic cause would be rewarded by being allowed to spend the night in the Lincoln bedroom of the White House during the Bill Clinton presidency. The story, reported by Margaret Ebrahim, garnered a major award from the Society for Professional Journalists and helped cement CPI's reputation for investigations.

CPI continued to produce major books—Lewis's work *The Buying of the President* was one of the most comprehensive deep-dives into how presidential campaigns are truly funded—and hundreds of original reports. But the center has also had its rocky financial and leadership moments. Lewis departed the center in 2005 and, according to the woman hired to replace him, there was trouble at CPI. Roberta Baskin was an experienced broadcast executive. When she joined the center, she said she found the financial situation dire and the center in disarray. She publicly admitted that CPI had asked reporter Robert Moore to quit due to plagiarizing sections of a book he penned in 2002. Baskin also said she had to raise millions to right budget overruns on several projects.

Her brief tenure at CPI ended in 2006, when she was replaced by former public radio executive Bill Buzenberg. Buzenberg set about shifting the center, focusing more on its website and de-emphasizing the lengthy books and paper reports. He also scaled the center back, reining in its budget and letting the staff shrink as people left. But it was his renewed focus on the web that would change the organization the most.

The center continued its shift toward the digital in 2014 when it hired former CNN International digital chief Peter Bale to run CPI. In announcing the new director, CPI board chair Bruce Finzen stressed that Bale "has exactly the experience and passion for great journalism that is necessary to lead the Center on a continued upward path, and assure that the vital multimedia investigative reporting that the Center is known for will reach an ever expanding audience" (Center for Public Integrity 2014).

See also: Nonprofit Journalism; ProPublica

Further Reading

Center for Public Integrity. 2014. "Peter Bale named new head of the Center for Public Integrity." Accessed February 15, 2015. http://www.publicintegrity.org/2014/12/02/16342/peter-bale-named-new-head-center-public-integrity.

Center for Public Integrity. 2015. "About The Center for Public Integrity." Accessed February 16, 2015. http://www.publicintegrity.org/about.

Keiger, Dale. 2000. "An "i" Toward Tough Journalism." Johns Hopkins Magazine. November. Accessed February 15, 2015. http://pages.jh.edu/~jhumag/1100web/lewis.html.

Lewis, Charles. 2006. "The Growing Importance of Nonprofit Journalism." Joan Shorenstein Center on the Press, Politics and Public Policy. Spring. Accessed February 15, 2015. http://shorensteincenter.org/wp-content/uploads/2012/03/2007_03_lewis.pdf.

CITIZEN JOURNALISM

As technologies allowing individuals to capture and publish information have become nearly ubiquitous—especially through smart phones—the separation between professional journalist and amateur has narrowed. Nearly every major news event is now captured in a tweet or cell phone video, and many of these snippets of news are incorporated into traditional mass media coverage. Other citizens, driven by a desire to cover their community or a frustration with an often-depleted local media ignoring critical issues, have launched their own citizen journalism news outlets. Both situations—community activist and eyewitness to news—are lumped into the term "citizen journalism," although their motivations and implications for the professional media are quite different.

The role of witnesses has always been critical to reporting about breaking news events or crises. Journalists rush to the scene of a shooting or accident to document and share what they find out with the public. They often rely on public witnesses to offer their reaction to the news and any scrap of additional information they may have to add to the coverage. With the explosion in the number of cell phones and their capability to capture photos and video, the eyewitness is no longer simply a source for a muddied and confused quote telling a reporter that the tornado sounded like a train; they are now sources of documentary evidence. When gunmen stormed the satirical magazine *Charlie Hebdo* in Paris, France, shaky cell phone footage first caught the sounds of gunfire as people huddled behind windows. A later piece of cell phone video filmed the gunman approaching a wounded police officer and ruthlessly executing him in the street as he begged for his life. Other witnesses captured the ghastly bombing attacks on the London subway system in July of 2005. Not all the citizen journalism footage is about moments of horror. A foreign exchange student's footage of a lost bear wandering the halls of a Montana high school quickly went viral, as have countless other funny, poignant, and shocking moments. The expectation has shifted from the witness providing descriptions to the media to them serving as the frontline photographer.

But it is not just the click of a cell phone camera that can create the first person reporting that has become a hallmark of the most-seen citizen journalism. The power of social media to document in real time news events that will reverberate far beyond one person's Facebook posting was never more evident than on the night of May 2, 2011. That night as computer information technology expert and café manager Sohaib Athar was at home trying to sleep, he was pestered by the sound of low-flying helicopters. It got to the point where Athar took to his Twitter account and told his 700-some followers: "Helicopter hovering about Abbottabad at 1AM is rare event." Suddenly, he added another Tweet reporting, "A huge window shaking bang here in Abbottabad Cantt. I hope its not the start of something nasty:-S." Soon friends and connections were relaying information that Athar sent out into the digital ether. There was more than one helicopter. They did not seem to be Pakistani. One may have been shot down over a house in the suburban town. Half a world away and five minutes before the White House would announce an impromptu statement by President Barack Obama, a former political aide to Secretary of Defense Donald Rumsfeld took to his Twitter to send out, "So I'm told by a reputable person they have killed Osama Bin Laden. Hot damn." More than an hour later Obama confirmed what the aide had said and what Athar had been witnessing: An American assault team had found and killed the reclusive leader of al-Qaeda in Pakistan. The social media reporting by eyewitnesses and unofficial sources had captured the news as the event happened, and the officials in Washington discovered the news. This near-real time reporting through Twitter further cemented the role of social media in conveying news and raised, once again, the role of individuals contributing to that coverage.

Soon after the killing of Bin Laden, Athar's followers had grown from 750 to 86,000. Next came a debate as to whether Athar was a journalist and whether Twitter had replaced the usefulness of the mainstream media. This is the typical cycle spurred by moments like this—news happens, a non-reporter catches it, media and other people turn to this person to use their information, and then the media debates for a while whether the person is a journalist. Dan Mitchell, writing for *SF Weekly*, was done with this entire debate, writing soon after that Athar "wondered what the hell was going on when the helicopters arrived in Abbottabad. Because he wondered on Twitter, in real time, now he's a 'citizen journalist . . .' Good for him. But does having 86,000 followers make him a journalist? For that matter, did his real-time tweets of the events make him one? Maybe in a small way, and very briefly, but he didn't know what was going on any more than anyone else did until he heard about it from news sources (via Twitter). Moreover, he was really only tweeting to his friends. His feed wasn't widely known until after the fact. Now he's posting pictures and videos of the compound. That is cool, but now the place is swarming with reporters with much better equipment and access to better information" (Mitchell 2011).

Capturing newsworthy information and sharing it with even one's own network has been declared an "act of journalism" by advocates who see public involvement in newsgathering as a way to hold the mainstream media accountable for what they report and supply important information that would not otherwise be seen. Blogger and media critic Jeff Jarvis and others have argued that "journalists aren't the only ones with a license to operate journalism. Anyone can perform an act of journalism. I think it's a big mistake to define journalism by the person who does it. Anyone can do journalism. When you witness news and you can now capture [it] on your phone, you can share that with the world over the Internet, you're performing an act of journalism" (Frontline 2006). Jarvis's argument that one should not define journalism by the person doing it, but rather the intent and impact of the act, has triggered widespread debate within journalism.

But the real impact of this shift can be seen in the debate over Athar and the legal conundrums triggered by shifting the definition from a person doing a job to an act. Take, for example, the question of legal protections for journalists and their notes and sources. Many states have shield laws aimed at protecting journalists from being compelled to testify in court cases except in the direst situations—sometimes not even then depending on the state. What happens when the individual capturing that video of a key moment is not employed by a news organization? Are they protected in the same way a journalist is? The answer is unclear because both news organizations and the authorities have been slow to test the question; both appear worried by what may be the answer. A strict reading of most laws would say the citizen journalist is not protected, but that is based largely on untested assumption. Most traditional journalists have begun to move beyond the question of labels and instead have begun to see most people who capture news as sources, like the police supplying dashboard camera footage or the interview subject describing what they saw. It is the source material that journalists then craft into stories that include more than just the blurry footage of gunshots. Lorraine Branham, dean of Syracuse University's award-winning Newhouse School of Public Communications, stresses that this is the difference between citizen journalism and "real" journalism, saying, "Usually when people are out there capturing something on video, they're capturing a moment in time of what happened and they're not attempting to put it into context." She added that camera-wielding citizens may lack the ethical training about protecting the identities of innocent people and choosing how to edit the footage (Nelson 2015).

Still, regular citizens often capture critical information, like the 2015 shooting of Walter Scott, an unarmed black man whose shooting was caught on tape. The film showed Scott unarmed and running slowly away from the officer when the white police officer shot Scott. The man who filmed the shooting, Feidin Santana, has admitted to fearing repercussions from the authorities or others for filming the incident that led directly to the officer being charged with murder. He told NBC, "At some point I thought about staying anonymous and not showing my face and not talk about it. If I want to show my face, everybody over there, including the police officers, the department, knows who I am . . . I decide to show my face to the media because my life [has] changed after this. People know where I live, people know where I work, so my normal routine of just walking from my house to work [has] changed" (Yuhas 2015). Unlike journalists, who are generally not targeted by critics or the public for the material they shoot or the news they report, citizens who choose to film incidents like police violence or capture controversial statements on the campaign trail find themselves often the target of scrutiny and sometimes intimidation. Their act is seen as more activist than a journalist doing the same work and so they often have their own backgrounds scoured by those who seek to discredit their footage or them personally.

The implications of citizen journalism are not just legal or about the scrutiny those individuals may face. Some citizens have used these newfound powers of publishing to launch their own news sites or begin using their social media feed as a way to aggregate and distribute news. Chi-Town Daily News in Chicago and iBrattleboro in Brattleboro, Vermont, are examples of these types of sites that were started to inform their community in a way the sites felt traditional media was not. The sites are run by volunteers and sometimes a single part-time employee who helps maintain the website, but the idea is that citizens will step up and supply the news content. These sites and others have been accused by some traditional journalists of distracting from the real work of journalists. Former Columbia University Graduate School of Journalism dean Nicholas Lemann famously took to the pages of the venerable and exceedingly non-citizen-produced *New Yorker* to critique this new form of journalism, comparing it derisively to a church newsletter and pointing out that the citizen journalism movement has led to an explosion of commentary about the news but not much original reporting, writing, "At the highest level of journalistic achievement, the reporting that revealed the civil-liberties encroachments of the war on terror, which has upset the Bush Administration, has come from old-fashioned big-city newspapers and television networks, not Internet journalists; day by day, most independent accounts of world events have come from the same traditional sources. Even at its best and most ambitious, citizen journalism reads like a decent Op-Ed page, and not one that offers daring, brilliant, forbidden opinions that would otherwise be unavailable. Most citizen journalism reaches very small and specialized audiences and is proudly minor in its concerns" (Lemann 2006).

Lemann's criticism is perhaps the key to understanding the anger that journalists have directed toward the term citizen journalist. Many within the profession see what they do as much more than turning the camera on and pointing it at something newsworthy. They argue professional journalism adds important elements of research, corroboration, context, and history that help the viewer or reader make real sense of the event. Why is it important? What are the implications of this moment? Is this an isolated incident or part of a larger problem that society must grapple with? Journalism, at its best, must answer those questions so people can put that shocking moment of video or tweet in context. Journalists also have the burden of checking their sources and confirming the information they receive. In the age of cameras and social media bearing witness to events, that burden has increased to helping people understand an event. That is the true thing that separates citizen journalism from professional journalism.

In the realm of political reporting, the role of citizen witness to newsworthy events has historically taken on a more partisan turn. The camera pointed at the candidate is often not being aimed by a disinterested member of the public, but rather a volunteer or paid employee of the opposing camp. The concept of citizen journalism is turned on its head by political use of "trackers" who are deployed to film candidates at every available moment seeking to capture a political blunder or inflammatory statement. Such footage is the result of a specific campaign tactic and not born of a citizen's concern. Despite such efforts, political news, though fodder for many citizen blogs and social media statements, is still largely a reflection upon what journalists have reported on in established news organization. Rarely is it the product of citizens creating their own content.

Some academics and media critics have attempted to rebrand the idea as less about *who* gathers the news and more about *what* the stories are that the media as a whole chooses to cover. To these scholars, what's important isn't who captured the news or sent the tweet; what's important is combating fundamental biases within the media that turn politics into a sport or battle. Critics like sociologist Herbert Gans want journalists—whether professional or amateur—to look beyond the vested interest groups to actually cover the concerns of average citizens, a feat they understand "will not be easy to cover. Citizens and their organizations rarely have spokespersons or other functionaries to generate news coverage or help reporters. Citizen news may thus require more legwork than other political news. But since citizens are not professional politicians, beginning journalists, supervised stringers, and even experienced amateurs—the so-called citizen journalists—can probably do a goodly share of the reporting" (Gans 2012).

For now, a handful of newspapers and television news sites offer citizen reporting platforms, allowing viewers and readers to contribute story ideas as well as completely produced reports. Few of these efforts have led to the sort of democratic reporting that Gans aspires to, but he and others hope that a wider base of political reporting can start guiding the political process toward solutions and away from partisan firefights.

See also: Advocacy Journalism; Social Media and Politics; Trackers

Further Reading

Gans, Herbert. 2012. "Citizen News: A Democratic Addition to Political Journalism." Nieman Lab. November 28, 2012. Accessed October 25, 2015. http://www.niemanlab.org/2012/11/citizen-news-a-democratic-addition-to-political-journalism.

Jarvis, Jeff. 2006. "Interview for News War." Frontline. November 30. Accessed October 26, 2015. http://www.pbs.org/wgbh/pages/frontline/newswar/interviews/jarvis.html.

Lemann, Nicholas. 2006. "Amateur Hour." *New Yorker*. August 7. Accessed October 25, 2015. http://www.newyorker.com/magazine/2006/08/07/amateur-hour-4.

Mitchell, Dan. 2011. "No, Twitter Hasn't Replaced CNN." May 3. Accessed October 26, 2015. http://www.sfweekly.com/thesnitch/2011/05/03/no-twitter-hasnt-replaced-cnn.

Nelson, Keith. 2015. "The Citizen Journalist: How Ordinary People Are Taking Control of the News." Digital Trends. June 19. Accessed October 25, 2015. http://www.digitaltrends.com/features/the-citizen-journalist-how-ordinary-people-are-taking-control-of-the-news.

Yuhas, Alan. 2015. "Man Who Filmed Walter Scott Shooting: I Worry What Might Happen to Me." *Guardian*. April 9. Accessed October 25, 2015. http://www.theguardian.com/us-news/2015/apr/09/walter-scott-shooting-south-carolina-feidin-santana.

CITIZENS UNITED

Citizens United has become political short-hand for a series of Supreme Court rulings since 2006 that have limited the government's ability to regulate spending on political campaigns, especially by groups not directly connected to a given candidate or political party. The name comes from the case *Citizens United v. Federal Election Commission*, a 2010 court case that tested and ultimately declared unconstitutional major swaths of federal election law, especially critical parts of the Bipartisan Campaign Reform Act (BCRA) of 2002. But when it's used by politicians or many in the media, *Citizens United* often refers to other decisions as well that threw out state limits on independent spending and federal limits on how much individuals can donate in aggregate to political campaigns and how much can be given to independent groups.

Taken together, these rulings essentially dismissed the core arguments that donating money to independent groups or those groups spending money on campaign ads or literature have a threat of corrupting the political process. On the other hand, the rulings left in place the limits on donations to political parties or candidates to ensure there is no direct corruption. The decisions also left intact many disclosure requirements, except in the cases of so-called social good organizations that are supposed to exist for some larger purpose but are allowed to participate in the election process.

The fairly tangled legal and monetary world in the wake of *Citizens United* is primarily because rather than being a case about the BCRA, the decision became a major shift in the high court's effort to balance a First Amendment right to speak on political matters versus reformer efforts aimed at ensuring truly free and competitive elections (the idea of one man, one vote). The case developed when the conservative group *Citizens United* produced a documentary highly critical of Democratic frontrunner Senator Hillary Clinton called *Hillary: The Movie*. The group planned to air the film on Direct TV and online and bought advertising to promote it. A federal court in Washington, D.C., ruled that the film and ads that promoted it amount to "electioneering communication"—that is it aimed to influence the way the voters felt about Clinton and perhaps affect their voting decisions—and therefore could be banned from being broadcast under BCRA within 30 days of the primary election.

The case reached the Supreme Court in 2009 and initially seemed it would be decided narrowly on the question of whether the documentary and its advertising should be considered "electioneering communication" or not. But then something happened at the court.

The case that the *Citizens United* lawyer Theodore Olson had argued was narrowly focused on the provisions of the Bipartisan Campaign Reform Act that may or may not apply to this documentary and the ads supporting it. But when career government attorney and then-Solicitor General Malcolm Stewart got up to answer Olson's case, he suddenly faced Chief Justice John Roberts. Roberts started by pressing Stewart on what should fall under the rules prescribed by BCRA—essentially what constitutes so-called electioneering communication. Stewart outlined a fairly broad definition, at which point Roberts interrupted to ask: "so if Wal-Mart airs an advertisement that says we have candidate action figures for sale, come buy them, that counts as an electioneering communication?"

Stewart agreed that would be electioneering communication. Justice Samuel Alito then asked, "What's your answer to Mr. Olson's point that there isn't any constitutional difference between the distribution of this movie on video demand and providing access on the Internet, providing DVDs, either through a commercial service or maybe in a public library, providing the same thing in a book? Would the Constitution permit the restriction of all of those as well?"

Stewart, stumbling, answered yes again. What followed was essentially a legal death spiral for Stewart and his cause.

> *Chief Justice Roberts:* If it has one name, one use of the candidate's name, it would be covered, correct?
> *Mr. Stewart:* That's correct.
> *Chief Justice Roberts:* It's a 500-page book, and at the end it says, and so vote for X, the government could ban that? . . .
> *Mr. Stewart:* Yes, our position would be that the corporation could be required to use PAC funds rather than general treasury funds.

> *Chief Justice Roberts:* And if they didn't, you could ban it?
> *Mr. Stewart:* If they didn't, we could prohibit the publication of the book using the corporate treasury funds.

The conservative justices had gotten the attorney representing the government to state that in the name of fair elections, the government could ban the publication of a 500-page book with one overt political statement in it. The questions of BCRA definitions seemed far less significant than the potentially broad ramifications of the campaign finance law's impact on speech.

The court headed off to draft a decision. Chief Justice Roberts initially crafted a decision narrowly in favor of *Citizens United* as an isolated case. Justice Anthony Kennedy agreed but argued the court should have gone further in limiting any limits on independent spending because it ran counter to the First Amendment. After spirited debate the court, surprisingly and unusually, ordered another oral argument focused on the First Amendment questions that Stewart had appeared to open up. When the final decisions emerged, Kennedy's broader interpretation became law, striking down a Supreme Court decision from 1990 and parts of an earlier 2003 decision that sanctioned the government's ability to limit some forms of political spending.

The political reaction, especially from campaign finance reform advocates and many Democrats, was furious. President Barack Obama stood before the nation and six of the members of the court a week later and accused the high court of issuing a decision that "reversed a century of law to open the floodgates for special interests— including foreign corporations—to spend without limit in our elections." Justice Samuel Alito, who had voted with the majority, was shown on camera shaking his head repeatedly as the president attacked the decision and saying "simply not true." But the decision was just the first in a series of critical Supreme Court and federal appeals court rulings that would reshape the political world.

Two months later, a federal appeals court used the newly minted *Citizens United* decision in a second critical case—*SpeechNow.org v. FEC*. SpeechNow, a registered political action committee, sought to protect the identity of its donors and wanted to no longer register with the Federal Election Commission as a formal political action committee if it did not plan on donating money to candidates or parties. The ruling struck down donation limits to independent groups, meaning individuals could now donate unlimited amounts of cash to these groups, but they would need to register as a political action committee and would need to provide information on the donors.

The next year, the Montana Supreme Court ruled that although the federal government may not be concerned by the corrupting influence of money in campaigns, Montana still was. The court argued that Montana should be allowed to maintain its standards even under the *Citizens United* decision. The U.S. Supreme Court, despite the objection of the four justices who had dissented in the original decision, refused even to hear the case and threw out the Montana ruling, effectively ending state limits on independent spending.

The raft of decisions from the court fundamentally altered the government's legal position on the regulation of political spending, moving the focus on spending from candidates and parties to independent groups. But many political observers acknowledged that the decision came after there had been a change of opinion among many voters, noting, "Americans have traditionally been skeptical of the equation between money and speech, but the unrestricted spending in the 2008 presidential election elicited few claims that the election was being 'bought' or that fund-raising raised the specter of corruption" (Boatright 2011).

Whatever comfort the public may have developed with campaign spending faced a series of tests as the money flowing into politics increased dramatically. By 2014 many competitive congressional campaigns saw far more spending on advertising and other key campaigning coming from so-called independent groups, which were the big winners in *Citizens United,* than from the campaigns or political parties.

As this money flowed into politics, groups interested in good government and campaign reform reacted with horror. One book published in 2013 bemoaned the spending by former White House staffer Karl Rove's American Crossroads, writing, "Of 53 competitive House districts where Rove and his compatriots backed Republicans with 'independent' expenditures that exceeded those made on behalf of Democrats—often by more than $1 million per district, according to Public Citizen—the Republicans won 51" (Nichols and McChesney 2013). But Democratic Super PACs like the American Bridge 21st Century also dove into opposition research, feeding their findings to the same kind of dark money groups as American Crossroads and flooding many markets with attack ads against Republicans.

Although *Citizens United* is often said to be the source of Super PAC funding, actually the *SpeechNow.org* decision created these new entities. These PACs were now allowed to raise and spend unlimited amounts of money, and the prohibitions on working in any way with a candidate or a party, though clearly spelled out, are difficult to enforce. These groups may raise money from unions and corporations as well as individuals, and report their donations. Federal law allows them to report either monthly or quarterly, meaning many of these donations may not be reported to the public until after the election has occurred.

Despite the work of American Bridge and a few others, experts said *Citizens United* and other decisions primarily benefited the Republican party in the first few years. One analysis declared, "The Democratic response to the United States Supreme Court ruling in *Citizens United* was an example of a political party refusing to participate in a major change of rules in the election process" (Smith and Powell 2013). This seemed to change during the course of the 2012 elections, though, as Democratic Super PACs and independent spending flooded Senate races. By 2014, Democrats were outspending Republicans as they battled unsuccessfully to hold on to the Senate. By 2016 both parties had fully embraced the new world of independent campaign groups.

In the wake of these decisions, reforms have focused on two different fronts. Some have pushed for a constitutional amendment that would allow Congress to limit spending in new ways, but this has failed even to come to a vote in Congress and would need the states also to ratify. The other focus has been on disclosure. Three years before *Citizens United,* another Supreme Court decision in the case *Wisconsin Right to Life v. Federal Election Commission* found that nonprofit groups could participate in the election process without disclosing their donors so long as the group was constituted solely to influence elections. An array of groups cropped up that purported to be "social welfare" groups but appeared to spend most of their money and time on elections. Some states have gone after these groups, looking to force them to disclose their donors. Montana, the same state that saw its limits thrown out because of *Citizens United,* became one of the first states to require disclosure by these so-called dark money groups in 2015. Steve Bullock, who had been the state attorney general who lost before the Supreme Court, was elected governor in 2012 and helped push the law through. In signing the bill, he said, "Montana elections are about to become the most transparent in the nation, requiring those trying to influence our elections to come out of the dark money shadows. Our elections should be decided by Montanans, not shadowy dark money groups."

Such efforts by states and the federal government to require disclosure have thus far survived legal challenges. Courts have noted that disclosure may have some chilling effect on speech, but that the state interest in making sure voters have information they need to make informed decisions outweighed any negative effects. Still, in the wake of *Citizens United* and its related decisions, disclosure will likely remain a major battleground in both courts and legislatures around the country.

See also: Campaign Finance Reform; Dark Money Groups; Disclosure; Federal Election Commission (FEC); Issue-Advocacy Advertising; Super PACs

Further Reading

Boatright, Robert. 2011. *Interest Groups and Campaign Finance Reform in the United States and Canada.* Ann Arbor: University of Michigan Press.
Nichols, John, and Robert McChesney. 2013. *Dollarocracy: How the Money-and-Media Election Complex Is Destroying America.* New York: Nation Books.
Smith, Melissa, and Larry Powell. 2013. *Dark Money, Super PACs, and the 2012 Election.* Lanham, MD: Lexington Books.

CNN

The Cable News Network, or CNN, launched in 1980 as the first 24-hour news channel, reporting on breaking news and devoting special attention to political reporting. For the first 15 years, it existed as the only live cable network devoted to covering news and helped give birth to the so-called 24-hour news cycle where stories are covered on a continuous basis and reporting occurs live and on the air. With the emergence of competitors Fox News and MSNBC, as well as the growth of social media and the Internet, CNN has seen its influence and audience size wane, but it remains a major source for breaking news in the moment.

The channel was the brainchild of broadcasting pioneer Ted Turner, who saw the changing reality of cable and how it could compete with the dominant television broadcasters of the day. Turner had developed a small station in Georgia by aggressively purchasing shows that were no longer run by the larger stations and built what would become WTBS. In 1976 Turner got the OK from the Federal Communications Commission to use a satellite to broadcast programming to local cable operators around the country. This was the infrastructure he needed to create one of the first cable-only channels, the TBS SuperStation. Turned would later say even before he had started building his SuperStation, the idea for CNN had been developed in his mind. He told one chronicler of the channel's birth, "I pride myself on being able to look into the future and say, What is the future going to look like? What can we do to be at the right spot at the right time? . . . It was clear that after the SuperStation the next important service to the cable industry would be a twenty-four hour news channel" (Whittemore 1990). But Turner also recognized that only 17 percent of American homes had cable and the network would need far more subscribers to support the cost of a 24-hour news operation.

By 1980, cable subscriber numbers had grown and Turner was ready. On June 1 the network went on the air with a broadcast statement from Turner. Turner pointed to the three flags that hung in front of the podium where he introduced the network, the flag of Georgia where the new company was based, the flag of the United States, and the flag of the United Nations. He pointed out the UN flag because, "we hope that the Cable News Network, with its international coverage and great in-depth coverage, will bring, both in the country and in the world, a better understanding of how people from different nations live and work together . . . so we can perhaps, hopefully, bring together in brotherhood and kindness and friendship and in peace the people of this nation and this world." The channel soon began broadcasting breaking news and as notable events occurred, the awareness and viewership of the channel increased. The network made a name for itself by reporting on breaking news dramas like the 1986 explosion of the Space Shuttle Challenger and the 1987 rescue of baby Jessica McClure who had become trapped in a well in Texas. But it was the coverage of the first Gulf War, which saw the United States expel Iraq from Kuwait, that turned the network into more of a force within journalism. During the brief 1991 military campaign, CNN established itself as the destination for coverage of breaking news while it was happening.

The channel, even at its debut, had a special interest in political coverage and applied much of what it learned in covering breaking news to its coverage of politics. First it created a regular series of programs that emulated many of the existing Sunday morning broadcast shows. The first year, it launched *Evans and Novak*, a political talk show anchored by journalists Rowland Evans and Bob Novak. Two years later it added a program called *Crossfire* to the mix to offer up political debate. By 1993, the network added *Inside Politics*, hiring Judy Woodruff away from

PBS to anchor the serious program that mixed pundits with reported pieces from Capitol Hill and around the country. The mix of regular political reporting and its ability capture live news events created CNN into a potent new force within policymaking and political circles. Even before the Internet and social media were a force in news, former secretary of state and Republican campaign operative James Baker said in 1996, "CNN has destroyed the concept of a 'news cycle.' . . . Now officials must respond almost instantly to developments. Because miniaturized cameras and satellite dishes can go virtually anywhere, policy makers no longer have the luxury of ignoring faraway crises" (Strobel 1996). Driven by increasingly cheap and portable broadcast technology, CNN did help shrink the world even as it also shrank the amount of time policy makers had to make decisions affecting the country.

The zenith of CNN's influence may have been in 1996. That year saw two other competitors enter the 24-hour news realm. NBC partnered with Microsoft to launch MSNBC, a channel that aimed to merge the power of CNN with the emerging importance of the Internet, and Rupert Murdoch launched Fox News, promising a more conservative option for those who felt CNN was too liberal. Even with the new competition, CNN continued to play a significant role in the coverage of campaigns and breaking news, but by the September 11 attacks in 2001, Fox News had become a major competitor. And in addition to the competition, the network faced increasing scrutiny for its programming decisions. In 2004, comedian Jon Stewart famously took the *Crossfire* program to task for in a confrontational meeting on the CNN program where he accused the hosts of being "political hacks" who played into the strategy of campaigns. Stewart went on to plead with the hosts to "stop hurting America." As time went on, the network has struggled to come up with its niche in the increasingly crowded field that sees web-only news operations challenging CNN for viewers and startups like Vice News being picked up by HBO.

CNN is, as a company, more diversified than its Fox and NBC competition. CNN offers a far more influential international edition, and the company produces national programming for Turkey, India, the Philippines, and Chile. The network also has deals to air content at almost every airport in the country. But as a political force, the "CNN Effect" that scientists studied is now seen more as a result of live information and commentary rather than the power of a single channel. CNN, in many ways, is a victim of its early success. At the end of 2014, the network hailed the fact that it had beat MSNBC in daytime viewers. Missing from that press release was the fact that it also marked the thirteenth year Fox won the ratings war and that MSNBC drubbed CNN in primetime ratings.

Despite its ratings difficulties, the network continues to offer up political fare, often stretching its technology to come up with new and creative ways to cover political stories. In 2008, the network launched a highly sophisticated map that allowed correspondent John King to select results from individual counties or to pull up polling data from key states. The map became a hallmark of the network's political coverage and highlighted the growing importance of data in reporting. But for every map that moved the technology of television reporting on politics forward, the network would also try stunts that did little to help viewers understand the process. In fact, the same year that CNN unveiled the "magic map," it also conducted a bizarre interview between host Anderson Cooper and singer Will.i.am about the election of Barack Obama—using 35 high definition cameras to project a hologram of the singer onto the CNN set. Still, with millions of international viewers and a cadre of reporters covering the campaign, CNN remains a force, if not quite so potent as it once was.

See also: Cable News Networks; Fox News; MSNBC; 24-Hour News Cycle

Further Reading

"CNN Loses Its Way." 2002. TV Week. February 18. Accessed August 24, 2015. http://www .tvweek.com/in-depth/2002/02/cnn-loses-its-way.

Strobel, Warren. 1996. "The CNN Effect: How Much Influence Does the 24-Hour News Network Really Have on Foreign Policy?" *American Journalism Review*. May. Accessed August 24, 2015. http://ajrarchive.org/Article.asp?id=3572.

Whittemore, Hank. 1990. *CNN: The Inside Story*. Boston: Little, Brown and Company.

COMEDY, SATIRE, AND POLITICS

Political comedy is old. How old is it? Well, in all seriousness, it is as old as democracy itself. Satire, parody, and comically charged commentary has served as a weapon in the electoral wars since ancient Greece. In the context of modern American politics, comedy continues to serve as comment on the day's news and, increasingly, has become an important source for genuine information. Modern American politics has an uneasy relationship with the comedians who make their living mocking and satirizing those in power. Programs like *The Daily Show* and *Last Week Tonight* have joined the more veteran late-night talk shows and *Saturday Night Live* in the nightly examination of the more ridiculous elements of modern politics and the flawed media that attempts to report on it. These video compatriots are joined by countless websites that construct often cruel, crude, and hilarious memes and satirical articles in the likes of *The Onion*.

Greek playwright Aristophanes lampooned not just policies and war but also specific Athenians in his plays. Dante put some of his contemporary political leaders in his hell. William Shakespeare carefully commented on royal houses in his historical plays, and William Hogarth in the eighteenth century used his drawings to blast English leaders and society of the day. This long history of art and comedy as tools of critique and commentary was baked in to the United States. Although it existed in the colonial era, and those arguing for a United States famously used a political cartoon of a severed snake to push for more unity, the idea of humor for political impact really caught fire in the nineteenth century. Newspapers increasingly sought to appeal to a wide variety of readers in order to make money, so political cartoons and humor grew in prominence. Thomas Nast, a political cartoonist without parallel, took to the pages of major newspapers to comment on political corruption and the elites—his cartoons are what gave us the Republican elephant, but it was not meant as a compliment.

In print and early broadcast, voices like Will Rogers would gently, but firmly, poke fun at those in power. Even into the twentieth century the business of political humor remained a restrained art. Art Buchwald, whose columns served up clear yet subtle political humor, was viewed in as many as 500 papers over the years. He often threw punches, but he did so wearing thickly padded gloves, rarely appearing too angry or partisan. By the 1960s, though, "Mr. Buchwald's satire grew more biting in Washington. When President Lyndon B. Johnson sent troops to the Dominican Republic in 1965 with the stated purpose of protecting Americans there during a rebellion, Mr. Buchwald wrote a column about the last remaining one, a tourist named Sidney, who was being detained by the Dominican authorities so that the American soldiers would not pull out" (Severo 2007). On television, late-night hosts like Johnny Carson would offer one-liners on President Nixon and others news of the day. But both Buchwald and Carson, to some degree, still aimed generally not to offend.

Historian Gerald Gardner, who documented the role of comedy and politics in this era, noted that there was often an economic reason that early political comedy tended to be less sharp-edged, telling NPR, "Political humor was kind of a benign art form at that time, perhaps because Buchwald knew he would lose newspapers, and Carson knew he would lose affiliates" (Keyes 2008). In the 1970s, though, a new breed of political comedy was on the rise, fueled more by an abrasiveness and anger over a political system seen as corrupt. Frustration over policies like the war in Vietnam and the political scandal of Watergate gave rise to new humor that had sting. These comic tendencies gave rise to NBC's *Saturday Night Live*. The program, in only its fourth episode, had Chevy Chase portray President Gerald Ford as a bumbling, stumbling fool. Unlike the more benign comedy of presidential impersonators like Rich Little who frequented Carson's *Tonight Show*, *Saturday Night Live* did not worry about the impersonation; their point was more raw and angry. And it was wildly popular.

Throughouth the 1980s and '90s the business of television and comedy was increasingly drawing audiences by being more provocative. Late-night comics like David Letterman and Jay Leno made increasingly caustic jokes about political events. A new strand of comic, represented by Bill Maher, was increasingly focusing all of their comedic work on current events. When Maher's program *Politically Incorrect* left cable's Comedy Central for ABC in 1997, Comedy Central decided to launch a parody news program called *The Daily Show*. The new program was hosted by popular ESPN anchor Craig Kilborn and featured news reporters offering taped reports, much like the traditional nightly news. Co-creator Lizz Winstead would later recall the early discussions about how much focus the program should have on politics, saying, "When we first launched, we would always have constant philo-sophical debates about how political the show should be. The network wanted it to be a little more of a hybrid of entertainment and politics, and I always thought politics was the way to go, because if you're going to satirize, it's nice to have big, powerful people to satirize. Sometimes I think when people veer into satirizing entertainment figures and stuff like that, it just gets kind of mean and cruel" (Roberts 2008). By 1999, the program had a new host, Jon Stewart, and a clear political direction. Stewart and his program would spark a series of spin-offs, including the *Colbert Report* that sought to satirize Fox News's *O'Reilly Factor* and later John Oliver's HBO program *Last Week Tonight*. These programs made daily commentary about politics and media coverage of politics their primary focus.

Although *Saturday Night Live* really created modern biting political comedy, the program also has included politicians that are willing to play along. Sarah Palin, who was mercilessly portrayed by Tina Fey, came on and in so doing offered a pres-ence that simultaneously said "I get the joke" and "I am not really like that." And she was not the first. Just two days before the 2000 election, NBC put on a special edition of *Saturday Night Live* dubbed "Presidential Bash 2000." The program re-counted 25 years of political comedy on the program, dating back to Chase and Aykroyd, up through their playful portrayals of Democrat Al Gore as a boring technocrat/robot and George W. Bush as a squinting word-murderer. Both Gore and Bush taped segments for the program. Their rationales for the appearances are unclear, but one scholar who has studied the intersection of politics and comedy offered one assessment, writing, "Perhaps they thought helpful to show the candi-dates' humaneness or sense of humor. Or perhaps it was simply a more to get free prime-time airtime two days before the election. Or perhaps they realized that by embracing the comedic routines of *SNL*, they were in essence neutralizing the rou-tines from their potential negative effect. Whatever the reasons, *SNL*'s political hu-mor did not seem dangerous enough for either candidate to refuse to poke fun so close to an election" (Jones 2009). Other programs would take their political satire further than *SNL*, pushing the envelope of acceptable comedy. *Key & Peele* would introduce a character named Luther to serve as mild-mannered Barack Obama's "anger translator," poking some fun at Obama but also conveying Obama as a fiery and passionate leader who only sounds mild-mannered. Others were much more biting, like *Lil' Bush*, a cartoon that cast President George W. Bush as a destructive and dim-witted elementary school child. The program targeted all members of the president's national security team and cast them as not just silly, but dangerous and misguided. The entire program was a brutal satire about the struggles of the Bush administration during its final two years.

For politicians the question remains how to handle satire and when to be funny. Many candidates view programs like *SNL* and the late-night comedy programs as a necessary part of their campaign strategy. Some candidates have actually officially announced their campaigns while sitting in the chair of *The Daily Show* or the *Tonight Show* and many have appeared on the programs during their race for the nomination or the White House. But how and when to be a part of the joke remains a dicey proposition. Jimmy Carter famously snapped at his staff, when they tried to insert a joke, "If the American people wanted Bob Hope for their president, they should have elected him." But most modern candidates try to use humor to defuse certain issues or appeal to voters, and they use many of the late night talk shows as a way to humanize themselves. Democratic adviser Jon Mack, who wrote for Jay Leno's *Tonight Show* for more than two decades, explained the appeal for candidates to go on those shows, telling NBC, "If a candidate goes on and says, 'Let me tell you about my three-point plan, Mr. Fallon,' that's a disaster. They want to hear personal stories about who these people are . . . I believe the late-night camera lenses give people a better sense of who these candidates are than even Sunday show camera lenses can" (Rafferty 2015). So, in critical ways, these programs offer candidates a platform to connect with voters outside of the policy debates and confrontational questions that they face on traditional news programs.

One of the outstanding issues about the role of satire and comedy in politics is to what extent viewers who might otherwise not follow politics are engaged through these programs to learn more about the politicians and central issues facing the country. Some observers have pointed to programs like *The Daily Show* and *Saturday Night Live* as serving as an entryway to politics for young people and those not willing or interested in sitting through a 30-minute hard news report. By watching these entertainment programs, the argument goes, they receive a baseline level of information and may be driven to get online and seek more coverage of the issue to better get the jokes. This would explain these programs' ability to get leading political figures to appear on their shows and sit down for interviews often more quickly then the campaigns will send those same candidates to regular news programs. Going even further, the relatively new HBO program *Last Week Tonight* hosted by *The Daily Show* alum John Oliver has moved from informing public opinion to explicitly calling for action. His 13-minute, obscenity-laden rant about net neutrality ended with a call for the trolls of the Internet (and assumedly the less vile viewers at home and online) to take to the Federal Communications Commission website to comment on the proposed end of a federal policy of offering equal access to the Internet for all content and content providers. The FCC site crashed under the pressure of the commenters the next day, and over the ensuing weeks millions of comments flooded the agency. Lobbyists who had been working to protect the net neutrality rules later said that Oliver's program had done more to mobilize the public than any other action they had taken and helped push the FCC to dump the idea.

Despite, or perhaps because of, this demonstration of political power, some see the idea of viewers receiving their political information from comedy programs as dangerous. These experts view the goal of Comedy Central and other programs as entertainment and humor, and therefore people investing the same kind of issue-focused attention to Jon Stewart that they do to CBS's Scott Pelley threatens to skew their perspective of the real issues and perhaps increase their cynicism about the political process. The answer is unclear and according to much of the research in this area very much dependent on the viewer. One study of *The Daily Show* viewers explored how the program is able to engage its audience and whether that audience views it as news or comedy. The results were essentially "it depends." If the viewer believes comedy programs are trivial and entertainment, they gathered very little political information from them. But if they did see the comedy as rooted in news, they could ascertain important understanding from the programs. This prompted the researcher, Laura Feldman, to argue, "Maximize learning from entertainment-oriented political information sources, that is, by changing people's perceptions of the task or activating an informational goal. For example, if—as the present results suggest—audiences' preconceptions regarding the amount of mental effort required by news versus entertainment lead them to engage in differential information-processing strategies, educators or journalists could do more to emphasize the informational value of political comedy" (Feldman 2013).

Some traditional journalists have raised concerns about the impact of satire on the political system, worrying that the effect of the "age of irony" is a public more cynical, more isolated, and more critical of those who do not align with their political views. For these observers, the mix of *The Daily Show*'s criticizing of Republicans and talk radio hosts like Rush Limbaugh's caustic commentary about liberals only fuels the partisan polarization in the American public. In the days after September 11, 2001, some went so far as to partially blame this form of commentary for blinding Americans to the threats they faced. Essayist Roger Rosenblatt took to *Time* magazine to argue that "the ironists, seeing through everything, made it difficult for anyone to see anything. The consequence of thinking that nothing is real—apart from prancing around in an air of vain stupidity—is that one will not know the difference between a joke and a menace" (Rosenblatt 2001). And in the immediate aftermath of the terrorist attacks, satire did go quiet and only slowly returned, with *The Onion* publishing its famous article with the headline, "Hijackers Surprised To Find Selves In Hell" on September 26.

But even those early steps included some careful pokes at those in charge. The same edition of the paper had a lead story that declared, "U.S. Vows to Defeat Whoever It Is We're at War With." *SNL* returned on the 29th in almost a defiant mood, declaring it would not be bowed by the attacks. Soon the comedy programs would regain their footing and reestablish their role as commentator on the news and the newsmakers. During this time, the influence of the programs and their hosts only grew. By 2009 one survey found some 33 percent of those under 40 reported they saw Stewart and Colbert replacing the role traditionally held by the nightly news. A 2012 survey found younger millenials not only get much of their political information from comedy programs, they also trusted Stewart more than most journalists (Gottfried, Matsa, and Barthel 2015). While some worried what that might mean for politics, many saw these shows as important tools to engage apolitical people on important issues. Penn State professor Sophia McClennen summed it up, "For the first time in U.S. history a range of satirical news sources are providing the public with valuable information from which to make educated decisions. Our knowledge as voters may be coming from HBO and Comedy Central instead of Fox News, MSNBC, and CNN, but the satire news is helping us stay informed and stay productively critical. Contrary to some criticism, satire's goal is not voter apathy; its goal is to encourage voters to turn their disgust into action and their frustrations into votes" (McClennen 2014).

See also: Oliver, John; Political Cartoons; Political Polarization and the Media; Stewart, Jon

Further Reading

Feldman, Laura. 2013. "Learning about Politics from The Daily Show: The Role of Viewer Orientation and Processing Motivations." In *Mass Communication and Society* 16, Issue 4.

Gottfried, Jeffrey, Katerina Eva Matsa, and Michael Barthel. 2015. "As Jon Stewart steps down, 5 facts about The Daily Show." Pew Research Center. August 6. Accessed June 13, 2016. http://www.pewresearch.org/fact-tank/2015/08/06/5-facts-daily-show/.

Jones, Jeffrey. 2009. "With All Due Respect: Satirizing Presidents from Saturday Night Live to Lil' Bush." In *Satire TV*. Edited by Jonathan Gray, Jeffrey Jones, and Ethan Thompson. New York: NYU Press.

Keyes, Allison. 2008. "Political Humor's Hysterical History." NPR. October 5. Accessed January 16, 2016. http://www.npr.org/templates/story/story.php?storyId=95413835.

McClennen, Sophia. 2014. "Does Satire News Influence Elections?" Huffington Post. December 31. Accessed January 14, 2016. http://www.huffingtonpost.com/sophia-a-mcclennen/does-satire-news-influenc_b_6079176.html.

Rafferty, Andrew. 2015. "2016 Candidates Flock to New Class of Late-Night Show Hosts." NBC News. September 7. Accessed January 14, 2016. http://www.nbcnews.com/politics/2016-election/2016-candidates-flock-new-class-late-night-show-hosts-n422051.

Roberts, Michael. 2008. "Q&A With Daily Show Creator Lizz Winstead." *Westword*. April 23. Accessed January 14, 2016. http://www.westword.com/news/qanda-with-daily-show-creator-lizz-winstead-5892810.

Rosenblatt, Roger. 2001. "The Age of Irony Comes to an End." *Time*. September 24. Accessed January 14, 2016. http://content.time.com/time/magazine/article/0,9171,1000893,00.html#ixzz1XfB9aCeL.

Severo, Richard. 2007. "Art Buchwald, Whose Humor Poked the Powerful, Dies at 81." *New York Times*. January 19. Accessed January 14, 2016. http://mobile.nytimes.com/2007/01/19/obituaries/19buchwald.html?referer=.

COMMISSION ON PRESIDENTIAL DEBATES

The Commission on Presidential Debates exists for one reason: to organize, plan, and execute the general election debates between the presidential and vice presidential candidates. That said, the way the commission works, how it decides the format and who will moderate, and the way it selects the candidates who will take to the platform have provoked countless debates and online campaigns. Despite this pressure, it has emerged as the undisputed authority on all these questions, even as opponents argue the group works to perpetuate the two-party system.

The commission came about as both a process of reform and a moment of political crisis. The reform came from the evolving nature that the debates were playing in the political process. The first official presidential debates occurred between Vice President Richard Nixon and then-senator John F. Kennedy. The two campaigns negotiated the four debates with television broadcasters. The result was a set of highly watched and much debated affairs, where Kennedy appeared calm and collected and helped establish himself as a equal statesman to the far more experienced Nixon.

Nixon's defeat in November of 1960 signaled the risks to incumbents of such an event, and debates seemed destined to be a one-time only affair. None were held again for the next several election cycles. But by 1976 President Gerald Ford, needing to do something to boost his low popularity, agreed to bring them back. They would occur again in 1980, although President Jimmy Carter refused to participate in one that featured Independent John Anderson. By 1984, two prestigious institutions decided to investigate the debates and to consider what should change if they were to remain a part of the process. The Georgetown University Center for Strategic and International Studies and the Harvard University Institute of Politics both conducted independent studies of the debates and as the commission itself reported, "Both studies found that debates between or among the leading candidates should become a regular part of the way Americans elect their presidents. A primary concern cited in the studies was that the leading candidates had often declined to debate or resisted debates until the last minute" (CPD). With the 1988 campaign approaching, the heads of the Democratic and Republican National Committees agreed that one of the problems was a lack of central organization, so they jointly endorsed the creation of an independent entity to run the debates. And so in February 1987, the commission was incorporated as a nonprofit based in Washington, D.C.

Even though the commission was created to "organize, manage, produce, publicize and support debates for the candidates for President of the United States," they were not the entity the candidates in 1988 chose to run the clashes. The campaigns of George H.W. Bush and Michael Dukakis went to the organization that had inherited the debates from the broadcasters in 1960 and run the ensuing meetings, the League of Women Voters. The league had organized the 1976, 1980, and 1984 contests and so they were the default organizers of 1988, even with the CPD waiting in the wings. That year, debate negotiations between Vice President Bush's team and Governor Dukakis's group went badly. The format of the debate was severely stunted as the Republicans pushed to limit the interaction between the candidates, and the battle over the moderators led to the league proposing and the candidates rejecting dozens of options. Following the first debate, the Bush and Dukakis campaigns met and organized a 16-page list of demands about how the debates should run, presenting it to the League of Women Voters less than two weeks before the second debate. The league's response was unequivocal. The group's president Nancy Neuman released a statement that declared, "The League of Women Voters is withdrawing its sponsorship of the presidential debate scheduled for mid-October because the demands of the two campaign organizations would perpetrate a fraud on the American voter. It has become clear to us that the candidates' organizations aim to add debates to their list of campaign-trail charades devoid of substance, spontaneity and honest answers to tough questions." Into the void stepped the still-new Commission on Presidential Debates.

The league was an entity that also performed many other activities around voter education and engagement. The commission existed solely to run the debates, and its running of the debates would alter their structure and evolution from almost the moment they took over. Their impact can be seen in many elements of the debates themselves. No matter what university hosts the contests, since 1992 the set appears almost exactly the same from debate to debate, the bald eagle logo lording over center stage, the podiums the same from year to year. The commission also selected host locations, developed the format of the debates, and chose the dates for the meetings long before there was a nominee from either party. Executive Director Janet Brown, who has been with the commission since it was formed, said the commission's role in the debate is often misunderstood. She argues, "There is a misconception that the campaigns dictate significant aspects of the arrangements. I don't know how many more times we can explain how it works. All the important components are put in place way ahead of time" (Banville 2013).

More than just uniformity of set, the CPD also wanted to improve the flow of information from the debates, livening the format and relaxing the rigidity. The commission implemented a town hall format in 1992. It soon reduced the number of questioners and moved to a single moderator to allow more time for questions, as well as including more time for candidates to respond and interact. In 2008 and again in 2012, the moderator's role in playing timekeeper was reduced, as candidates were given more time to engage one another.

With this authority to structure the debates, choose their location, and set the criteria for acceptance into the debates comes a fair amount of criticism. One of the most controversial aspects of the commission's work is in how they select candidates. The commission has developed a series of requirements for candidates to meet. Beyond simply being qualified and appearing on enough states to have a mathematical ability to win the presidency, they must be polling at at least 15 percent of the national electorate as determined by the average of five selected national public opinion polling organizations. This has meant that only once—in 1992—has a third party candidate appeared in a CPD debate. In fact, when the commission ruled in 1996 that Ross Perot—who had participated in 1992 and had run again as a Reform Party candidate in 1996—did not qualify to appear, at least one organization was formed to object. The Open Debates group, run by George Farah, wanted more outside candidates to be heard. He argued that the decision raised a lot of questions, saying, "In 1996 Ross Perot was running for president. Three-quarters of the American people wanted to see him and I thought it would be fascinating to see him debating again. And when he was shut out, I was astonished and I thought, who is doing this? What entity is making this happen?" (Desjardins

2012). Open Debates points out that the commission, which was headed for more than a decade by the very heads of the RNC and DNC that endorsed the commission's creation in 1987, is governed by former party officials who have an interest in maintaining the two-party system. The commission is still led by the Republican official who approved the commission, Frank Farenkopf, and former Clinton spokesman Mike McCurry took over the Democratic spot following the retirement of the Paul Kirk.

The commission's other controversial job is in selecting the moderator. Brown says the commission has specific criteria it looks for: someone who has been intimately following the campaign and the issues; has extensive experience with live news broadcasting; and who will act as a facilitator with, not competitor to, the candidates (Banville 2013). Still, some have criticized the commission and the moderators for not being aggressive enough in their pressing of the candidates, allowing the debates to be more like coordinated press conferences and less like an exchange of ideas or an opportunity to press candidates on specific policies. The commission has also faced criticism for lack of diversity, relying often on veteran white men to chair the meetings.

Despite its many criticisms and pressures, the Commission on Presidential Debates still sits as the de facto organizers of some of the most viewed moments of the presidential campaign. Their decisions and the events they organize have significant influence over the final weeks of the campaign.

See also: Lehrer, Jim; Presidential Debates

Further Reading

Banville, Lee. 2013. *Debating Our Destiny: Presidential Debate Moments that Shaped History.* Arlington, VA: MacNeil/Lehrer Productions.

Desjardins, Lisa. 2012. "The Problem with Presidential Debates." CNN Radio. October 22. Accessed August 23, 2015. http://cnnradio.cnn.com/2012/10/22/the-problem-with -presidential-debates.

"Overview." Commission on Presidential Debates. Accessed August 24, 2015. http://www .debates.org/index.php?page=overview.

CONGRESSIONAL AND SENATE CAMPAIGN COMMITTEES

Congressional and Senate campaign committees are political organizations that raise money to aid in the election of one party's candidates. Each chamber of Congress and each major party maintain a committee, so there are currently the Democratic Congressional Campaign Committee (or D-triple C or just D-trip) and National Republican Congressional Committee in the U.S. House, and a National Republican Senatorial Committee and Democratic National Senatorial Committee. All four operate as traditional political action committees according to the IRS and are required to report donations they receive and how they spend their money to the Federal Elections Commission. The groups raise much of their money from grassroots party members, often by focusing on the idea that donations will help that party re-take or protect control of either the House or Senate. In addition to being an official source of financial and political support for the individual candidate running, all four organizations also serve a critical role in raising the profile of senators and representatives who run these committees.

Despite the obvious priorities of serving the larger party interests, these organizations were, in fact, founded as a way to stand up to the national party committees. The first committees organized in the House in 1866 as the divisions between President Andrew Johnson and the radical Republicans deepened. The committee aimed to protect those Republicans wishing to stand up to the Republican Party leaders who wanted them to work with the president. For the first 50 years, these "committees" barely existed as entities unto themselves. They were "hardly more than mutual aid societies for incumbent congressman who shared ideas, campaign strategies, and some money every two years" (Cotter and Hennessy 2009). They also only existed only in the House, since it was not until 1916 that passage of the Seventeenth Amendment created the popular election of U.S. senators. Afterward, a pair of campaign committees quickly developed and so through World War II, the four committees operated as fairly informal groups that worked to help candidates win re-election.

As campaign fundraising limits and reforms began to flow from Congress, these committees took on an increasingly important function, raising more money and choosing to invest in campaigns where incumbents might be in trouble or the party had hopes of picking up a seat. The rise of these committees into something more politically significant came at a time when, according to experts, power was slipping away from the local parties. "Resources were gathered increasingly at the center, and decisions eventually followed. State and local parties had become, to a large degree, subordinate to each party's national committees, just as many states increasingly played second fiddle to the federal government" (Parker 2014). Recently an array of Supreme Court decisions has created other avenues for money into politics, allowing donors to pour unlimited and often anonymous money into independent groups. In this new era, the committees have become less important in funneling national money to federal candidates and more a platform for grassroots fundraising and centralized research opportunities.

The national congressional committees now focus fundraising toward individual party members, maintaining extensive lists of individuals who have registered as party members or donated to individual candidates. The lists have become effective tools for candidates seeking to raise money from grassroots quickly. Democrats, in particular, have aggressively pursued these smaller donors, often barraging them with solicitations. Ahead of a 2014 quarterly deadline, DCCC emails carried menacing subject lines like, "Absolute meltdown"; "Kiss any hope goodbye"; and "We're done. Go home. Give up." DCCC officials said these emails merely reflected frustration from average Democrats, but experts had a different explanation. The more desperate they got the more they worked. As Robert Epstein, former editor in chief of *Psychology Today*, told the *Washington Post,* research has shown "people are far more likely to take action to avoid negative events than to produce positive ones . . . Loss is simply more impactful than gain. People know this intuitively, and so do the campaign managers and others whose job it is to manipulate the masses" (O'Keefe 2014). Doom and gloom is an effective fundraising technique. The four committees raised and spent some $864 million during the 2014 cycle, according to the Center for Responsive Politics, much of it on attack ads against opponents of their candidate, direct mailings, and opposition research. The committees are capped, like all PACs, as to how much money they can give to a candidate, but the groups have more flexibility to conduct opposition research and air ads criticizing their candidate's opponent.

The national committees tend to stay neutral during primary campaigns. "But if one candidate is believed to be visibly stronger for the general election, early intervention can help that candidate with the primary and begin an earlier focus on the general election. With party control of Congress closely divided, especially in the House, such intervention has become much more common" (*Congressional Quarterly* 2012). These committees have also intensified their efforts at recruiting the strongest possible candidates, especially in contests where an incumbent is perceived to be in trouble or has retired.

All four committees are run by an executive director and staff of party professionals, but are chaired by a current member of the chamber. This job has become a highly sought after position for those members seeking to build a base of support among fellow party members. It is seen as a way of helping members build a coalition for a possible run at a leadership position in the House or Senate. The chairmanship carries with it the burden of organizing and fronting a strategy for either building a larger majority or recapturing the majority. This means committee chairs meet with prospective candidates as well as incumbents and can offer them support in the form of advertising spending, logistical support, and even direct contributions. This puts them in the position of building relationships and good will with members from across the country and often leads to more important roles within the national party.

See also: Campaign Finance Reform; Leadership PACs; Political Action Committees (PACs); Super PACs

Further Reading

Congressional Quarterly. 2012. *How Congress Works*. Washington, DC: CQ Press, Inc.
Cotter, Cornelius, and Bernard Hennessy. 2009. *Politics without Power: The National Party Committees*. Piscataway, NJ: Transaction Publishers.
O'Keefe, Ed. 2014. "From Shaming to Semi-Stalking, Democrats Flood Inboxes for Last-Minute Campaign Cash." *Washington Post*. September 30. Accessed July 14, 2015.

http://www.washingtonpost.com/politics/from-shaming-to-semi-stalking-democrats
-flood-inboxes-for-last-minute-campaign-cash/2014/09/30/d83f5ed2-481a-11e4
-b72e-d60a9229cc10_story.html.

Parker, David. 2014. *The Power of Money in Congressional Campaigns, 1880–2006*. Norman: University of Oklahoma Press.

CONSERVATIVE BLOGOSPHERE

With the birth of modern blogging, conservative columnists and writers took to the Internet to share their views, rally supporters, and discuss their party's positions and leaders. Many of these conservatives, especially those who were outside the mainstream of the Republican Party, found the ability to connect with one another a powerful organizational tool. Conservative sites and blogs have served as rallying points for Libertarians and Tea Party activists. Others presented platforms for commentators to build reputations for themselves that segued into cable news appearances, and others still have used these publishing tools to serve as watchdogs of the traditional media.

With powerful voices on talk radio and some conservative television programs on Fox News, conservatives were somewhat slower to warm to the power of blogs and digital publishing. Early voices like Michelle Malkin and Glenn Reynolds used the new medium to build national reputations. Malkin actually turned the success of her aggressive conservative commentary into a major business by launching the site Hot Air as a "conservative Internet broadcast network" in 2006. Three lawyers from Dartmouth started the site Power Line as a blog about their views on politics. This site exploded into the national conversation after it helped raise serious questions about the accuracy of a 2004 report by CBS's *60 Minutes* that accused President George W. Bush of receiving preferential treatment to avoid service in Vietnam. Power Line helped organize a response to the report, gathering information, analyzing the documents in the CBS report, and calling into question their accuracy. In the end, CBS retracted the story, admitting the documents they had based the reporting on were faked, and veteran anchor Dan Rather was even forced to resign over the affair. The whole series of events earned Power Line the first ever "Blog of the Year" award from *Time* magazine and helped bolster the power of blogging across the political spectrum.

By 2008 many of these activists and bloggers with limited-government and libertarian leanings found themselves gravitating toward the campaign of Texas congressman Ron Paul. Paul, who himself was not tech savvy, suddenly found his campaign bolstered by thousands of volunteers and donors willing to back the small-government message. This wave of blog-fueled support resulted in $6 million flooding into the small campaign's coffers on December 16, 2007—the anniversary of the Boston Tea Party. The event was largely organized by outside activists driven by the message of less government. Unaffiliated groups sprung up online, organizing everything from meet-ups to rallies for Paul to a 200-foot blimp that toured the east coast. Charles Froman, one of those volunteers who rallied at a blimp event outside Washington, D.C., explained to the Online NewsHour how Paul was in many ways the figurehead of something far larger, saying, "This is a grassroots campaign based on the Internet and Ron Paul's campaign has very little to do with it except for the policies. It's people, through surfing on the Web, they're learning that 'Hey, we really need to learn a little bit more about all these issues'" (Bowman 2008). Paul supporters and others would go on to help spark the rise of the tea party groups in 2009 and 2010.

One central truth of the Internet is that blogs give voice particularly to groups on the outer edges of a party's spectrum. Moderate voices that argue for compromise appear far less active and far less read than those who argue more hardline positions. One survey of readers and writers of political blogs found that "partisans— conservatives as well as liberals—are more likely to read political blogs than their moderate counterparts are" (Eveland and Dylko 2012). This fact emphasizes the idea that blogs offer a political voice that the parties they generally vote for have often ignored or marginalized. This division between the views of leaders and those of the rank-and-file has become more pronounced on the Republican side of the blogosphere, as fundamental disagreements have erupted between those political figures who want to work within the system and those voices who see such work as compromising important political principles. The tea party patriots, cultural conservatives, and evangelical voters have found themselves at times battling Republican leaders in Congress and elsewhere over the policies of the party. Many of those voices find airing and support on the conservative blogs.

In recent years the worlds of blog and talk radio have moved closer together. In particular, Salem Media Group has become a sort of blending of the two. The company began in Christian radio broadcasting and has expanded to become one of the largest businesses in the conservative talk industry. It owns 106 stations across the country and has aggressively added digital sites, including Michelle Malkin's Hot Air. Nearly one-third of its profits now come from blogs and book publishing that serves politically conservative groups. Edward Atsinger, Salem's chief executive officer, said that "Salem's mission has always been to serve our two core audiences—Christian and conservative—with engaging and meaningful content. That mission brought us into radio, and it has guided our growth ever since. As more and more of our audience seeks new ways to get information and inspiration, we have added new media platforms to our traditional radio offerings." The company now owns some of the most popular conservative blogs in the country, including Crosswalk.com, TownHall.com, HotAir.com, RedState.com, and Human Events.com.

Whether merging with talk radio or offering a voice to elements of the Republican Party once felt shunned, the conservative blogosphere has offered political activists an interconnected network to work with to build audience, attention, and potential support. It has emerged as an important tool for groups seeking to pressure the Republican mainstream as well as a platform for provocative columnists looking to develop a reputation and readership. The sites are as diverse as the conservative movement, so in a way the idea of arguing about a single conservative "blogosphere" may be misguided. However, what these publishing platforms have in common is that they give those people who feel disenfranchised by the Republican Party, or seek to influence the conservative movement, a way to have their voices be heard in a party still heavily driven by senior party leaders and celebrity radio talk show hosts.

See also: Breitbart, Andrew; Liberal Blogosphere; RedState; Talk Radio; Townhall .com

Further Reading

Bowman, Quinn. 2008. "Paul Campaign Attracts Array of Supporters." Online NewsHour. January 19. Accessed January 12, 2016. https://www.youtube.com/watch?v=65FG zf8wctI.

Davis, Richard. 2009. *Typing Politics: The Role of Blogs in American Politics*. New York: Oxford University Press, USA.

Eveland, William, and Ivan Dylko. 2012. "Reading Political Blogs During the 2004 Election Campaign: Correlates and Political Consequences." In *Blogging, Citizenship, and the Future of Media*. Edited by Mark Tremayne. New York: Routledge.

Perlmutter, David. 2008. *Blogwars*. New York: Oxford University Press, USA.

CONSERVATIVE THINK TANKS

Conservative politicians who have sought to rein in the federal government or propose effective public policy have historically been intellectually outgunned by an academic world that leans decidedly to the left, supplying philosophical and tactical advice to those on the other side of the aisle. Conservative think tanks emerged in the post–World War II era and again in the late 1970s as tools to compete with the academic world. Groups like the American Enterprise Institute and later the Heritage Foundation offered conservatives expertise on everything from the federal budget to foreign policy. These groups also helped train future senior-level government officials in Republican administrations and offered those ousted by Democratic presidents a way to stay in the debate and Washington. In recent years, several of these institutions have become more activist in their approach, with Heritage in particular becoming an outspoken critic of and active campaigner against Republicans who work with Democrats.

The first wave of conservative think tanks grew up in response to the rapid growth and expansion of the federal government during the Great Depression. The American Enterprise Institute, for example, was founded by an array of businessmen concerned that President Franklin Roosevelt's policies of controlling the cost of certain manufactured goods and war needs would continue into peacetime. These early think tanks adopted a model similar to the nonpartisan research organizations like the RAND Corporation, but added a philosophical element to their research. With the government growing increasingly complex, these early think tanks served as an important repository of expertise. Partisan-leaning groups like AEI and the Hoover Institution helped draft critical, Republican-backed tax and budget plans. Although they benefited from donations from wealthy donors and foundations with an explicit interest in policy, the think tanks stressed that their research was not simply partisan fodder, but was thoroughly balanced and grounded in fact. Often researchers from AEI would cross the think tank aisle and work with people from liberal groups like the Brookings Institution to produce reports on congressional reforms and other matters. Their influence on policy could also be more indirect, contributing to the political dialogue as experts during congressional testimony or sources for journalists covering a specific topic.

As public support for the New Deal politics waned and a growing number of Americans grew more conservative in the 1960s and 1970s, a new wave of more overtly partisan think tanks came to Washington. Most notably on the conservative side was the Heritage Foundation and the Manhattan Institute for Policy Research. These new organizations wanted to more directly affect the policy debate and wanted to be far more active in the politics of the day. Heritage, for example, was created by two veteran Capitol Hill staffers, Paul Weyrich and Ed Feulner. Feulner would later recall the moment he decided that a new, more actively conservative organization was needed. It was 1971 and Congress was voting on whether to fund supersonic transport. AEI distributed a major briefing paper to members of Congress the day after they voted on the matter. Feulner remembered, "It defined the debate, but it was one day late. We immediately called up the president of [AEI] to praise him for his thorough piece of research—and ask why we didn't receive it until after the debate and the vote. His answer: they didn't want to influence the vote. That was when the idea for the Heritage Foundation was born" (Rich 2005).

Heritage and other think tanks like it wanted to pressure government to form certain kinds of policies. One of Heritage's first major successes was an exhaustive 3,000-page study of the federal government that outlined nearly 2,000 specific actions a conservative government should take. The proposal, entitled the "Mandate for Leadership," was distributed to Ronald Reagan's Cabinet the first time they met in 1981. By the end of the first year of the Reagan administration some 60 percent of the recommendations had been implemented. Unlike think tanks in the past, Heritage was a vocal advocate for their changes. In this new system, 60 percent adoption of their recommendations was not enough. By late 1981 the Heritage Foundation was publicly expressing disappointment in Reagan's first year in office. In November, the foundation published an assessment of the administration's work and in it "criticized the Administration for decisions concerning personnel that it asserted had hindered efforts to carry out many of those recommendations. In almost every Federal agency, it said, 'delayed appointments, unqualified or misqualified appointments, or the appointment of individuals who are not committed to the President's goals and policies' had delayed or thwarted policy changes" (Gailey

1981). These new conservative think tanks deployed a public campaign to advocate for changes they proposed, using tactics like direct mail appeals, advertising, and public relations efforts.

Other nonprofits with an explicit conservative bent began to flood Washington with their agendas, mixing advocacy with research and proposing widespread changes. Groups like the U.S. Chamber of Commerce moved increasingly toward political activism, arguing for pro-business spending on issues like infrastructure while also arguing for lower corporate and individual tax rates. The key difference between traditional think tanks and these more political organizations was as a nonprofit, Heritage and the Chamber of Commerce could not expressly advocate for the election of one candidate over another. Other groups like the Club for Growth, a smaller-government advocacy group, were organized as political nonprofits, disclosing their donors, but also vetting candidates and supporting their campaigns. By 2014, Politico had declared the club "the pre-eminent institution promoting Republican adherence to a free-market, free-trade, anti-regulation agenda. It has endorsed only seven candidates so far, including three who are challenging Republican incumbents, and will back each of them to the hilt. The Club's choices—and its screening process—are in essence a road map for the electoral agenda of economic conservatives" (Palmer and Burns 2014).

Groups like the club and the Koch-funded Americans for Prosperity threatened to undercut the historical influence of the conservative think tanks and so Heritage, for one, decided to reorient itself into a more explicit political organization. The foundation hired controversial tea party-backed Jim DeMint, the former U.S. senator from South Carolina, to oversee a much more aggressive strategy that pitted Heritage and its political wing Heritage Action against fellow Republicans who did not adhere to the policy positions of the think tank. Under DeMint, the foundation pushed Republicans to shut down the government and go to the ends of the legislative earth to defund health insurance reform enacted under President Obama. More than that, DeMint publically called for Republicans who did not vote for defunding to be ousted in the party primaries. Heritage has become a more activist player in the political debates, and some who were there at the beginning worry that could cause long-term harm to the conservative cause. Mickey Edwards, a former Republican congressman from Oklahoma, told the *Atlantic* that Heritage's decision to back certain Republicans during the primaries "makes it look like just another hack Tea Party kind of group," adding, "They're destroying the reputation and credibility of the Heritage Foundation. I think the respect for their [policy] work has been greatly diminished as a result" (Ball 2013).

The struggle within the Heritage Foundation over how active it should be in Republican Party politics has created an interesting debate within Republican ranks about what role conservative think tanks ought to play. Many Republicans have turned back to the traditional Republican-leaning scholars at the American Enterprise Institute, seeking the expertise and policy recommendations over the partisan positions other active think tanks have proposed. But other, more explicitly political groups like Heritage and the U.S. Chamber of Commerce continue to loom large over Republican politics. The question of the proper role remains to be determined, but with their reliance on foundations and wealthy donors to support their work, think tanks are likely to align themselves in ways that seem to wield the most influence and therefore result in more donors and more money to invest in future work.

See also: American Enterprise Institute (AEI); Heritage Foundation; Liberal Think Tanks

Further Reading

Ball, Molly. 2013. "The Fall of the Heritage Foundation and the Death of Republican Ideas." *The Atlantic*. September 25. Accessed December 28, 2015. http://www.theatlantic.com /politics/archive/2013/09/the-fall-of-the-heritage-foundation-and-the-death-of -republican-ideas/279955.

Gailey, Phil. 1981. "Heritage Foundation Disappointed by Reagan." *New York Times*. November 22. Accessed December 28, 2015. http://www.nytimes.com/1981/11/22/us /heritage-foundation-disappointed-by-reagan.html.

Palmer, Anna, and Alexander Burns. 2014. "Inside Club for Growth's Art of War." Politico. April 7. Accessed December 28, 2015. http://www.politico.com/story/2014/04/inside -the-club-for-growths-art-of-war-105415.

Rich, Andrew. 2005. *Think Tanks, Public Policy, and the Politics of Expertise*. Cambridge: Cambridge University Press.

CONVENTIONS

See Presidential Nominating Conventions

CORPORATE MEDIA OWNERSHIP

Do those who own media companies exert too much control over the diversity and quality of journalism and entertainment individuals are able to access in their local communities? Countless academic treatises and politician statements have asked this question. This concern has prompted calls to break up media companies and regulations that banned companies from owning local newspapers and broadcasting firms. Still, despite these rules and public statements, some 90 percent of media—especially broadcast and film—are controlled by six major corporations in the United States. Even at the local level deregulation has led to a sweeping consolidation in ownership.

The core concern about media ownership is often portrayed as a fundamental question of protecting individuals' rights: if corporate interests control too much of what voters read and see, this may compromise the integrity of the American system of government. In his book *Media Concentration and Democracy: Why Ownership Matters*, noted communications legal scholar C. Edwin Baker cast the argument in grave terms, writing, "In any large society, the mass media constitute probably the most crucial institutional structure of the public sphere. To be self-governing, people require the capacity to form public opinion and then to have that public opinion influence and ultimately control public 'will formation'—that is, government laws and policies" (Baker 2006). For Baker and other scholars concerned with the free flow of information, who owns the media and how much they control that marketplace of ideas is a matter as central to the proper functioning of government as ensuring elections are free and fair and that access to the ballot box is not limited.

And this is not just the concern of university academics; conservatives and liberals on the outer edges of their parties often express frustration with the mainstream media, pointing fingers at the huge corporations behind the nightly news and daily newspapers for using their control to stifle public discussion. Vermont senator and 2016 presidential candidate Bernie Sanders has said, "The consequences of media consolidation go to the heart of the democratic process. In my view, it will be very dangerous for our country and communities around America when one company is able to own a local newspaper, television station and radio station. Opposing points of view won't be heard and our democracy will suffer."

These fundamental questions of information and democracy have influenced much of government policies connected to media ownership. Throughout the early era of printed media—from books to newspapers and magazines—there was little concern about the idea of owners exerting too much control by owning more publications. This remained true even into the early twentieth century. William Randolph Hearst started the first chain newspaper, owning publications in New York, San Francisco, Chicago, and elsewhere, seeking to turn his newspaper empire into an influence engine that would make him money and potentially fuel a political career. The government took no action against Hearst's efforts, in part because it was seen that there was no limit to the number of publications that could be produced.

But broadcasting, that would be different.

As radio broadcasting began in the 1920s, the federal government established that these new entities would face more regulations. Broadcasting would utilize a public asset—the public airwaves—to reach customers with content and advertising. The public spectrum that could convey a broadcast signal was fairly narrow and so, unlike its print cousin, broadcasting had a finite number of outlets. Even in the earliest discussions of federal licenses for broadcasting, there was this idea of ensuring that the public interest would be part of the decision-making process. When the Federal Communications Commission was established in the 1930s, it was charged with issuing the broadcast licenses. Some of the largest broadcast entities at the time—including NBC and CBS—argued the government should charge high fees for the licenses as a way to dissuade new competitors from entering the industry. The FCC rejected that bid, instead issuing licenses free of charge so long as the broadcaster could demonstrate it was operating in the "public interest, convenience and necessity." The FCC interpreted its congressional mandate to mean that people would not be served by having a company receiving more than one broadcast license per market. This same concern about consolidation of media control in the local market fueled the most significant federal rule on media ownership, which came in 1975. "The purpose of the rule is to prevent any single corporate entity from becoming too powerful a single voice within a community, and thus the rule seeks to maximize diversity under the conditions dictated by the marketplace. The cross-ownership ban does not prevent a newspaper from owning a broadcast station in another market, and indeed many large newspapers— such as the *New York Times* and the *Washington Post*—own and operate broadcast stations outside their flagship cities" (Gomery 2002). Despite the regulation, media companies could own different types of outlets, just not in the same city.

These rules did not go unchallenged. Broadcasters challenged the FCC licensing system, claiming it was an infringement on their constitutionally guaranteed right to a free press. They lost. Some court challenges also focused directly on the question of government regulations of the business of journalism. Federal regulations of broadcasters were challenged under the First Amendment, and the Associated Press was sued by the government for allowing clients of the AP to block access to their services to other local news operations. In both of these cases the Supreme Court ruled that the U.S. government could impose regulations over these businesses. Interestingly in the AP case in 1945, the court not only ruled that the AP had violated the Sherman Anti-trust Act but Justice Hugo Black used the First Amendment to bolster his ruling, writing:

> That Amendment rests on the assumption that the widest possible dissemination of information from diverse and antagonistic sources is essential to the welfare of the public, that a free press is a condition of a free society. Surely a command that the government itself shall not impede the free flow of ideas does not afford nongovernmental combinations a refuge if they impose restraints upon that constitutionally guaranteed freedom. Freedom to publish means freedom for all, and not for some. Freedom to publish is guaranteed by the Constitution, but freedom to combine to keep others from publishing is not. Freedom of the press from governmental interference under the First Amendment does not sanction repression of that freedom by private interests. (*Associated Press v. United States*)

Despite this established legal idea that the government could regulate media companies and ownership at the local level, that did not mean it had to. As the government began a wide-ranging move to deregulate industries in the 1980s and 1990s, broadcasters and media companies fought to get in on the action. The 1996 Telecommunications Act triggered one of the most substantive revisions to the way media companies were regulated. The new law required that the FCC conduct a review of its media ownership rules every other year "and shall determine whether any of such rules are necessary in the public interest as the result of competition." On top of that, the FCC was ordered to "repeal or modify any regulation it determines to be no longer in the public interest."

This legal and regulatory fight was playing out at the local level; there were no rules around corporations owning more than one network at the national level. By one estimate 50 companies controlled 90 percent of the television, radio, newspaper, and film companies in the United States in 1983. By 2013 that same 90 percent was controlled by six massive multinational corporations. Companies like Disney own ABC, Pixar, and ESPN. Comcast the cable company owns NBC, Universal Studios, and a handful of cable channels. News Corp. runs Fox News, the *Wall Street Journal*, and the Fox network. These companies also are not shy about donating to political campaigns, even as their subsidiary news wings seek to cover the campaigns, often backing incumbents and Democrats. One report in Huffington Post noted in 2012, "In the case of News Corp., Time Warner, Comcast, and the Walt Disney Co., donations made to Obama were roughly ten times the amount than donations made to Republican presidential candidate Mitt Romney. For example, Comcast donated a total of $206,056 to Obama, compared to $20,500 to Mitt Romney. CBS Corp.'s PAC differed in that the committee donated to more Republicans than Democrats" (Shapiro 2012).

Some advocates of reform argue the contagion of media consolidation extends far beyond political donations. They point to the financial benefit many media companies see from uncontrolled campaign ad spending, which has come following a series of recent Supreme Court decisions limiting government's ability to regulate such spending. The group Free Press, which advocates for stricter limits on media consolidation, has noted that "the Supreme Court's *Citizens United* decision launched a new era of big-money politics. The wealthiest 1 percent now has even more power to pick and choose our nation's leaders. And they're spending the bulk of this money on televised political ads designed to mislead voters . . . So where's the broadcast media in all of this? Instead of exposing this runaway spending and separating fact from fiction in an election year, they're lining their pockets with the windfall from this massive ad buy . . . to the tune of more than $3 billion in 2012" (Free Press). For these activists, major corporations that own local networks and cable systems are increasingly invested in the campaign ad spending system, which may fundamentally compromise their ability to cover these issues objectively.

While much attention on media ownership focuses on the mega-corporate owners of the national cable networks and broadcast networks, their consolidation may pale in comparison to the changes happening at local television stations. With little fanfare, there has been a tectonic shift in the ownership of local television, creating massive corporations that run more than 100 stations and reach huge swaths of the nation. In 2013 alone, the Pew Research Center reported that nearly 300 television stations changed hands in deals that topped $8 billion. Many local stations appear to the viewer as different stations, but are operated by the same company from the same production facilities. Companies can now operate more stations with fewer staff, but can also air the same stories on multiple stations. According to the "State of the Media 2014" report, some 25 percent of stations that air local news did not actually produce that news. They are simply rebroadcasting content that was produced by another station or group of stations.

The reason for this wave of consolidation and purchases is, not surprisingly, money, but not strictly a quest to save money. An obscure but escalating war is being waged between cable and satellite operators and local broadcasters. Local stations charge a fee to cable operators to carry their content on the cable and satellite channels. That fee has been rapidly increasing in recent years, and networks like CBS have been at the forefront of pushing cable operators to fork over fees to run the network programming. It is a battle between two massive corporate interests—companies like Charter and Comcast versus CBS and Walt Disney. With advertising dollars stalled and increasing pressure from streaming services, these fees have emerged as a critical source of revenue for content producers. But this corporate war has done little to help viewers. Former officials with the Federal Communications Commission worry that the rush to buy up local stations to increase the flow of fees and reduce production costs has hurt the viewer. Former Democratic appointee to the FCC Michael Copps was quoted in the Pew report as saying, "The original deal was [broadcasters] get free use of the public airwaves, you get the opportunity to make a nice living off of that, but in return you must serve the public interest. They're public airwaves and they're supposed to be serving community interests and local markets, not one-shop news operations that span many outlets" (Potter and Matsa 2014).

Not all voices that have discussed media ownership see it as a black-and-white question of preserving local ownership and the diversity of perspectives on television and in your local paper. Many see consolidation as perhaps a necessary evil, as media organizations adjust to the post-Internet world. Remember, newsrooms at daily newspapers have shrunk by some 42 percent in the past 14 years as fundamental changes to the advertising world coupled with a continued slide in subscriptions have hit newspapers hard. Steven Waldman, who once worked for the FCC, has argued that the never-ending debate about media ownership misses the point, writing in 2012, "Instead of having a theological debate about consolidation—'good' vs. 'evil'?—is it possible to create media policy that allows mergers that are likely to help the local media ecosystems and blocks those that are not? One possibility is that the FCC allow more companies to merge—giving them 'waivers' from the ban—if they made a strong case that such a combination would have a demonstrable positive impact on the provision of local content, including (but not limited to) journalism" (Waldman 2012). So far Waldman's ideas have gained little traction, as most attention continues to focus on mega-merger discussions involving major cable companies and other issues like net neutrality.

The discussion about media ownership comes as the overall business continues to evolve rapidly in the digital world. Cable companies have reported a slow but steady drop in people signing up for service as more people shift to Internet streaming services like Netflix, HBO, and Hulu. Newspaper companies continue to plead for an end to cross-ownership rules, hoping they, too, can benefit from the cable fees flooding the coffers of many local broadcasters. The business of media continues to change at a rapid pace, and the efforts to keep these companies separate and protect the idea that drove government regulations—that people needed information from multiple and diverse sources for the government to work—remain more an aspiration than a reality.

See also: First Amendment and Censorship; Government-Subsidized Journalism; Newspaper Industry; Public Interest Obligation

Further Reading

Baker, C. Edwin. 2006. *Media Concentration and Democracy: Why Ownership Matters*. New York: Cambridge University Press.

Gomery, Douglas. 2002. "The FCC's Newspaper-Broadcast Cross-ownership Rule: An Analysis." The Economic Policy Institute. Accessed January 12, 2016. http://www.epi.org/files/page/-/old/books/cross-ownership.pdf.

"Money, Media and Elections." Free Press. Accessed January 12, 2016. http://www.freepress.net/money-media-and-elections.

Potter, Deborah, and Katerina Matsa. 2014. "A Boom in Acquisitions and Content Sharing Shapes Local TV News in 2013." Pew Research Center. March 26. Accessed January 12, 2016. http://www.journalism.org/2014/03/26/a-boom-in-acquisitions-and-content-sharing-shapes-local-tv-news-in-2013/#fn-42094-5.

Shapiro, Rebecca. 2012. "Money, Politics and the Press: Media Political Donations to Democrats." Huffington Post. September 6. Accessed January 12, 2016. http://www.huffingtonpost.com/2012/09/06/media-political-donations-democrats_n_1855502.html.

Waldman, Steven. 2012. "How to Fix the Media Ownership Debate." *Columbia Journalism Review*. December 20. Accessed January 12, 2016. http://www.cjr.org/united_states_project/how_to_fix_the_media_ownership.php.

C-SPAN

Part nation's cable access channel and part unfiltered access to the halls of Congress and the executive branch, C-SPAN, its sister channels C-SPAN 2 and 3, its satellite radio channel C-SPAN Radio, and its website housing thousands of hours of video has grown to not just a way for Americans to glimpse the workings of Washington, but also a tool for those in Washington to reach out to supporters and build a name for themselves. The channels serve as a more direct connection between government and the people, allowing many politicians to communicate with supporters and constituents without the intermediary of reporters and producers.

C-SPAN stands for Cable-Satellite Public Affairs Network, and it has been more responsible than any other entity in pressing the government to open its proceedings to public scrutiny and cameras. The nonprofit organization that runs the networks now boasts some 300 employees. Its $60 million budget comes from the largest cable companies in America, allocating 6 cents of every subscriber's annual bill to the service.

It was all the idea of one man who saw an opportunity as cable became the dominant way most people received television. Brian Lamb developed the idea and later served as chairman, but was known by most people as one of the channel's longest serving on-air hosts. "I wanted to start something that would add to the information flow in the United States. I had no money. I didn't have a sophisticated plan," Lamb told the National Press Club in 2004, adding that he eventually talked 15 cable companies into ponying up $1,000 apiece to purchase his first camera (C-SPAN 2004). But the channel took a huge step in 1979 when the U.S. House of Representatives agreed to allow cameras into the proceedings of the lower house. Then-U.S. Representative Al Gore was the first member of Congress to address the chamber on television, hailing the decision by the Democratic leadership for the move. "It is a solution for the lack of confidence in government" that plagued government in the wake of Watergate, he said, adding, "The marriage of this medium and of our open debate have the potential, Mr. Speaker, to revitalize representative democracy." In 1986, the U.S. Senate agreed to allow cameras into the chamber, and C-SPAN 2 was born because the channel could not broadcast both houses if they were in session at the same time.

The organization that grew up in the years that followed developed a clear set of principles that aimed to improve the information flow that Lamb mentioned years later. C-SPAN has pledged to provide live coverage of both houses of Congress and other venues, including agency meetings and think tank discussions that inform policy debates in Washington. But it also goes further, promising in its mission statement "to provide elected and appointed officials and others who would influence public policy a direct conduit to the audience without filtering or otherwise distorting their points of view" and "to provide the audience, through the call-in programs, direct access to elected officials, other decision makers and journalists on a frequent and open basis." This mix of a direct look in on the process of governing—particularly the legislative branch—and the airtime for both politicians and interested members of the public to comment on matters is the hallmark of the networks.

Some members of Congress saw this role of C-SPAN to provide a direct connection to viewers without the filter of the news media as a political gold mine. Especially for members of the minority Republican Party, who had little voice in legislation or the leadership at the time, the camera created an opportunity for them to speak out and be heard. The cameras in both chambers created a new platform for them to fight the powers that be (or build a campaign to be those powers). One of the first to fully grasp the opportunity was Republican congressman Newt Gingrich. Gingrich was sworn in to Congress just a few months before C-SPAN went on the air. He and a group of fellow conservatives began to take to the floor of Congress every evening during a period of so-called personal privilege when members were allowed to address any topic. Gingrich would take to the floor and rail against the Democratic leadership, blasting their foreign policy and often launching thinly veiled personal attacks. Speaker Thomas "Tip" O'Neill, during one of Gingrich's speeches, ordered the camera to pan the House chamber, showing that Gingrich was talking to an empty chamber. C-SPAN broadcast the ensuing clash on the floor between the two. A lengthy profile of Gingrich called it the Republican's coming out party on the national stage, describing the drama as, "Back and forth they went, the brash young Republican from Georgia and the indignant white-maned Democrat from Massachusetts. 'My personal opinion is this,' O'Neill roared at last, shaking his finger at Gingrich. 'You deliberately stood in that well before an empty House, and challenged these people, and challenged their patriotism, and it is the lowest thing that I've ever seen in my 32 years in Congress'" (Osbourne 1984). The House ruled O'Neill out of order for attacking Gingrich and the Republican continued his political ascent.

Other politicians learned from Gingrich, and now floor speeches have become part explanation to colleagues and part show for the television audience—and it is not equal parts as many speeches are really directed home to their district. For members of the House of Representatives this has become a necessary tool to demonstrating they are really working for the folks back home, as junior members of the minority party have few other outlets to prove their effectiveness. And so now many members take to the floor with oversized posters to prove their point. Frederica Wilson, a Democrat from Florida, explained to NPR, "When you are in the minority, you have to find ways to get your message across because there's no other way. You don't have a bill that they're going to hear. There's no committee that will receive your suggestions" (Keith 2013).

Any discussion of C-SPAN must include a brief examination of its call-in programs. Since its first call-in show in early 1980, the network has hosted thousands of hours, allowing all stripes of Americans to rally or rail. Its primary call-in show, *Washington Journal*, can feature hours of calls from the public. Although C-SPAN producers vet the calls to try and ensure a variety of perspectives are making it on the air, once on the air they can and do say just about anything. The shows have prompted at least one ongoing comedy segment on HBO's *Last Week Tonight* show called "The Most Patient Man on Television Endures the American Public," in which one of the *Washington Journal* hosts, Steve Scully, fields a variety of outlandish calls with seriousness. Such as:

> *Call from Oklahoma:* I don't know what's going on in this world right now. Obama's a Muslim and that's all I've got to say.
> *C-SPAN's Steve Scully:* Obama is not a Muslim, but thank you for making your comment.

Whether it is broadcasting a procedural vote on the Senate floor, allowing minority members of the House a chance to speak to the public and their district, or Scully fielding more of those calls, C-SPAN remains a documenter and influencer of the political process. Its constant presence allows its some 47 million weekly viewers a chance to be a fly on the wall of the halls of Congress. Although it is only a version of what actually happens in the halls of power, its unvarnished and unfiltered view remains one of the most unique voices covering politics in any media.

Further Reading

"The Beginning of Televised House Floor Debate." U.S. House. Accessed July 9, 2015. http://history.house.gov/Historical-Highlights/1951-2000/The-beginning-of-televised-House-Floor-debate.

"C-SPAN's 25th Anniversary." C-SPAN. December 6, 2004. Accessed July 9, 2015. http://www.c-span.org/video/?184689-1/cspans-25th-anniversary.

Keith, Tamara. 2013. "How Floor Charts Became Stars of Congress." NPR. July 23. Accessed July 9, 2015. http://www.npr.org/2013/07/23/204517513/how-floor-charts-became -stars-of-congress.

Osbourne, David. 1984. "The Swinging Days of Newt Gingrich." *Mother Jones*. November 1. Accessed July 9, 2015. http://www.motherjones.com/politics/1984/11/newt-gingrich -shining-knight-post-reagan-right.

CULTURAL CONSERVATIVES

Cultural conservatives is an umbrella term for politically active groups and individuals who support the role of religion in private and public life and who back government policies that limit abortion rights, support school choice, and oppose gay marriage and other generally progressive policies. Bolstered by a wave of political activism by evangelical and other Christian activists and solidified by a an array of think tanks and lobbying organizations, these conservatives have staked a major claim within the Republican Party, helping limit the once powerful moderate wing of the party and causing cleavages with libertarian-leaning and pro-business sectors of the Republican electorate. The groups have also used the media as well as in-person networks through churches and grassroots groups to spread their positions and influence public debate.

Religion and conservatism both have long histories in U.S. political life, but the cultural conservative movement is most often associated with the rise of the so-called New Right in the 1970s. After the political trauma of the Nixon administration, Republicans found themselves deeply divided on the road forward. The older wing of the party, led by President Gerald Ford and represented most starkly by moderate vice president Nelson Rockefeller, argued the party should govern from the middle, advocating policies that sought to accommodate the post-1960s' call for equal rights and an activist government. But a growing legion of young activists rejected these movements and the general counterculture attitudes of the 1960s and sought to express the views of average Americans who felt besieged by a society in the midst of change. Americans troubled by the 1973 Supreme Court decision in *Roe v. Wade* that legalized abortion or who found problems with the push to pass an Equal Rights Amendment to the U.S. Constitution began to seek a political movement that would give them voice in a government that seemed out of touch with "the common man." The cultural conservative movement was born.

Conservative populism had a strong history in the United States but was an idea the New Right leaders thought their own party had foregone. These new groups used many of the tools at their disposal to organize from the grassroots, raising funds and finding organizers through direct mail appeals and tapping into an increasingly active religious leadership. The movement found real appeal among the rank-and-file Republicans, tapping into distrust of the leadership in both parties and catching the established powerbrokers largely off guard. One of the most effective organizers of this new political movement was a political operative who had worked as a journalist and D.C. staffer, Paul Weyrich. Weyrich would declare, "We are radicals who want to change the existing power structure. We are not conservatives in the sense that conservative means accepting the status quo" (Critchlow 2007). Weyrich rejected modern liberalism and, backed by the financial support of brewing magnate Joseph Coors and others, organized new conservative groups into a political entity. Coors backed Weyrich's new Heritage Foundation that was created in 1973, and the next year the pair helped form the Committee for the Survival of a Free Congress—what would later simply be called the Free Congress Foundation. These groups served as the policy development outlet (Heritage) and a political training ground for conservatives looking to work on campaigns or run themselves (Free Congress). Other groups would spring up, like the Family Research Council to help organize religious groups, and the movement continued to pick up seats in Congress and take important positions in state parties all over the country.

Ironically it was Democratic reforms to the presidential nomination process that many said helped finish off the main competitor to this newfound political power of cultural conservatives. Throughout the 1960s and into the 1970s, liberal Republicans such as Nelson Rockefeller had found some electoral success, especially in the Northeast and Midwest. Rockefeller and a few others had strong and wealthy political organizations, funded in large part by personal wealth and empowered by a party system that still relied on the leaders to select delegates to the national political convention and other leadership positions. Party leaders tended to respond well to such well-funded operations.

However, this was quickly changing. Following the disastrous Democratic nomination fight of 1968, the party launched a reform effort to ensure that average party members would have more power in the nomination fight, shifting the selection of most delegates from the hands of state and local party leaders into the hands of primary voters. The Republican Party followed suit, and by 1976 most Republican delegates were elected by local voters. This reform, according to a scholar on the demise of the liberal Republican movement, "ended the influence of state and local party leaders over national politics, and gave a more influential role to the media, candidates' organizations, and the ideological activists of the right. By organizing an effective network of think tanks, PACs, direct-mail specialists, and campaign organizations, the right wing was far better equipped than the liberals to deliver the vote in low-turnout primary elections" (Rae 1989). This shift in power happened in areas beyond the presidential nomination process, giving activists in both parties far broader influence on the direction of the parties and the issues those parties would advocate for and organize around.

While groups like the Heritage Foundation served as an intellectual hub for the cultural conservative movement and the Free Congress Foundation helped train a new generation of activists, the cultural conservative movement still needed a major organizational jolt to move from the grassroots to positions of more authority in the party. The changes in the presidential nomination process in the 1970s helped that movement forward in the 1980s. Southern Baptist minister and television personality Pat Robertson had been helping build the conservative movement since 1980 when his Christian Broadcast Network staff gathered for a meeting and Robertson said they discussed the growing pressure to become involved in politics. The *New York Times* would later report, "What would happen, he mused, if the Government was run by 'Spirit-filled Christians,' if 'every member of the Cabinet was Spirit-filled, the President was Spirit-filled, and the Senate and the House of Representatives were Spirit-filled?'" (King 1988). Robertson's CBN soon spawned a nonprofit educational group called the Freedom Council that aimed to expand the participation of conservative Christians in the political process. The group benefited from millions of dollars from Robertson's CBN empire and quickly became a force in Republican politics. By 1987, Robertson decided to mount his own campaign for the White House, taking on veteran Republicans Vice President George H.W. Bush and U.S. Senator Bob Dole for the GOP nomination.

Robertson rode the cultural conservative movement's grassroots power to a stunning second place finish in the first-in-the-nation Iowa caucuses, beating the sitting vice president. He also did well in other caucus states, winning the majority of delegates from Washington state's caucus. In states where volunteers and activists drove the process, the televangelist performed well, demonstrating how much power these activists had within the party. Robertson ended up struggling in more moderate and larger-turnout contests, losing the New Hampshire primary badly and floundering in the large multi-state primary fights. Still, the Robertson campaign and his idea of a "spirit-filled" government caught the imagination of a new generation of cultural conservatives. The campaign did more than just inspire; it also spawned one of the most tangible groups of the conservative Christian movement. Following his failure to grab the Republican nomination, Robertson spoke at the Republican National Convention and called for a new political activism by churches and churchgoers. He then took the remainder of his campaign money and a list of millions of volunteers and supporters and in 1989 formed the Christian Coalition, an organization that sought to build on the success of his campaign and to more directly connect ministers and churches to the political process. By the mid-1990s the cultural conservatives were firmly entrenched in most parts of the Republican Party, increasingly holding leadership roles in Congress and mounting major campaigns for president.

This rise of the New Right-inspired conservatives was not the only pressure within the Republican Party. As cultural and moral issues continued to fuel many of the grassroots activists within the party, others with the Republican establishment sought to downplay the divisive issues of abortion and prayer in school, seeking instead to unify the party around a pro-business message that stressed tax cuts and limited government. This push to scale back the role of government in the lives of businesses and individuals sometimes ran counter to the cultural conservative efforts to increase government regulation of abortion or propose government policies that interfered in state government policies around marriage rights or protecting prayer. When Newt Gingrich and his fellow Republican Revolutionaries successfully wrested control of the U.S. House away from Democrats for the first time in 40 years in 1994, these two wings of the Republican Party would come to play a far more significant role in the debate over public and party policies, often with mixed results for the activists' goals. One extensive study of the 1994 Republican Revolution found all the leaders of that electoral effort came from either the pro-business "Enterpriser" side of the party of the pro-cultural conservative "Moralist" wing. Despite that reality, the same study outlined how the Moralists struggled to have their issues represented in the "Contract with America" that served as the electoral strategy and policy framework for the new Republican House. The study concluded that "Moralists had little success pushing the small subset of directly religious issues, such as prayer in schools, abortion and homosexuality, which are their characteristic concerns. While a majority of Republicans may agree with those positions, few put them at the top of a national agenda. The September 1994 House GOP 'Contract with America' carefully avoided Moralist issues to appeal to the greatest number of voters" (Koopman 1996).

The tug of war between embracing policies that would fire up an evangelical and culturally conservative base, versus appealing to a broader set of moderate voters, would be a consistent theme in Republican politics for the next two decades. Democrats had faced similar fights between its moderate, pro-business wing and more ideological, often pro-union wing. Generally this would play out by candidates' appeal to their party's extremes during the primary campaign only to distance themselves (or at least go quiet) on many of the issues the more ideological voters endorsed during the general election.

That political calculation would become substantially more difficult in the 2000s as the rise of the so-called tea party voters seemed to throw the role of cultural conservatives into sharp contrast. Like the early Christian conservative movement, the tea party effort grew out of frustration from the grassroots conservatives about the direction of their party. Many fiscal conservatives resented the free-spending habits of "big government" conservatives who doled out tax dollars to support causes like school choice or President George W. Bush's "No Child Left Behind" education reform. For these conservatives the goal was to shrink the footprint of the federal government, both the budget and the reach, which often put them in conflict with social or cultural conservatives who wanted an activist government dictating at the federal level things like religious or marriage policies.

The Republican Party faced a difficult task navigating the demands of social conservatives and small-government proponents. The way media and political analysts deconstructed the role of the voting blocs in critical elections helped to illuminate, and perhaps magnify, the tension. For example, soon after the 2004 reelection of President Bush the story was reported widely that Bush strategist Karl Rove had used the support of social conservatives, driven to the polls to vote on issues like gay marriage bans, to win re-election. One activist who wrote about the campaign said that "'values voters,' social conservatives, religious conservatives—whatever you wanted to call them—were now the real linchpin of the Republican coalition. These voters had often been ignored and treated shabbily by the Republican Party, the argument went, but now they'd proven that when the GOP caters to them on issues such as gay marriage, stem-cell research, abortion, obscenity on TV, and judicial nominations, they can deliver the vote" (Sager 2006). This scholar argued that idea was overblown, but the narrative in the media remained that social conservatives had won the day.

As the libertarian-leaning Tea Party officially emerged with the election of President Barack Obama, a new ideological wing developed within the party and pressed for more people to endorse their smaller-government goals, even if that meant foregoing the cultural policies many conservatives supported. The media played up this internal conflict, stressing how the two wings could not really meet unless one or the other compromised. Countless analytical pieces pointed out the apparent inconsistency of thought between the two camps. Many came to portray it as a sort of GOP civil war, and some of the data seems to back it up. One *Wall Street Journal* report found, "In survey data from the Pew Research Center analyzed by the American Communities Project at American University, some of the steepest drops in support for the tea party came in counties with large evangelical populations. In those 'evangelical hubs,' the percentage of people saying they agree with the tea party fell from 39% in 2010 to about 22% in 2014, the group said" (Reinhard 2014). Republican candidates, fearing that such a split could complicate their party's effort to win general election campaigns for the White House and Congress, sought to minimize the differences between the two groups, stressing campaign themes like religious freedom rather than activist questions of involving government in state or personal matters. Although this strategy has helped ease some of the tension within Republican ranks, other issues threaten to exacerbate the split.

Gay marriage, an issue that moved from only fringe support in the early 2000s to widespread acceptance by 2015, is one such wedge. Cultural conservatives have made and continue to make the protection of traditional marriage between a man and a woman a centerpiece of their fundraising and campaigning, but many within the tea party ranks have been slow to embrace the evangelical position on the matter. These leaders have either said it is something that should be left to the states or they have offered tepid support for the idea of gay marriage. But not all divisions within the GOP are based on issues. The 2016 presidential primary saw a rhetorically bloody battle for the nomination between social conservatives like Senators Ted Cruz and Marco Rubio and businessman Donald Trump. Many social conservatives viewed Trump's candidacy with deep suspicion given his past statements in support of abortion rights and financial donations to Democrats. These conservatives helped fueled the failed "Never Trump" campaign that sought to block the nomination, but Trump still rode his popularity to clear victories in the primaries leaving the social conservative movement in an unclear position moving forward.

Social and cultural conservatives helped drive the Republican Party back into power in the 1990s and 2000s. But they now are having to face the reality of a party that, to survive, must find a middle ground that welcomes moderates and small government proponents as well as assuaging their own traditional supporters among the religious conservative base.

See also: Direct Mail Campaigning; Family Research Council; Grassroots Campaigns; Heritage Foundation; Tea Party Movement

Further Reading

Critchlow, Donald. 2007. *The Conservative Ascendency: How the GOP Right Made Political History*. Cambridge, MA: Harvard University Press.

King, Wayne. 1988. "Pat Robertson: A Candidate of Contradictions." *New York Times*. February 27. Accessed September 11, 2015. http://www.nytimes.com/1988/02/27/us/pat-robertson-a-candidate-of-contradictions.html.

Koopman, Douglas. 1996. *Hostile Takeover: The House Republican Party, 1980–1995*. London: Rowman & Littlefield Publishers, Inc.

Rae, Nicol. 1989. *The Decline and Fall of the Liberal Republicans From 1952 to the Present*. New York: Oxford University Press.

Reinhard, Beth. 2014. "A Move to Unite Tea Party, Social Conservatives." *Wall Street Journal*. June 19. Accessed September 11, 2015. http://www.wsj.com/articles/a-move-to-unite-tea-party-social-conservatives-1403224636.

Sager, Ryan. 2006. *The Elephant in the Room: Evangelicals, Libertarians and the Battle to Control the Republican Party*. Hoboken, NJ: John Riley & Sons, Inc.

THE DAILY BEAST

Tina Brown wasn't going to let a few setbacks stop her. The editor had built a very public and at-times controversial name for herself as the editor who had overhauled *Vanity Fair* magazine. She then went on to guide the *New Yorker* before hitting a few bumps in the road—a failed magazine called *Talk* and a failed CNBC talk show.

But then she released the beast—The Daily Beast.

Backed by media mogul Barry Diller and his IAC media empire, the site was announced in 2008 as a new kind of news entity. It would do original reporting and mix in unique voices, but also help the savvy news consumer find what other people were reporting as well. As Brown put it, "What's been lacking for the overwhelmed but smart reader is an intelligent guide. The time is right to do a site which cuts through the noise and cuts through the clutter" (Edgecliffe-Johnson 2008). The new site, named after a fictional London paper in Evelyn Waugh's *Scoop*, launched in October 2008. The initial site made a splash because it of its focus on smart aggregation that directed readers to content across the web, as well as for its stable of high-profile contributors like Christopher Buckley, Meghan McCain, and David Frum.

Core to its mission, though, was its feature "The Cheat Sheet," a smartly written list of must-reads from other news outlets. The feature and the site's effective design earned it accolades—it won the Webby for best news site in 2012 and 2013—and a growing following. But the site also lost money. It began adding advertising in 2009 and soon developed more specific sections—Book Beast in 2009 and later Hungry Beast on food, and Sexy Beast on fashion and entertainment. The site continued to lose money, but the new sections and a round of staff cuts had somewhat stabilized it.

Throughout its run, the site has relied on a steady stream of political reporting to fuel interest. Just after its launch, the site made a splash by featuring conservative Christopher Buckley, son of the famed William F. Buckley Jr., endorsing Barack Obama for president. It continues to contribute a series of pieces that have drawn attention and readership. But the site has also drawn fire, with one article in the Harvard Political Review blasting the site for tabloid tactics, pseudo-commentary, and "amateurish standards for its opinion pieces" (Harvard Political Review 2012).

The site spent money and created content without worrying about the underlying business. In fact, a *Politico* report on the site noted, "The Beast had launched without a formal business plan, which wasn't uncommon for a lot of tech startups. While it has been reported that Diller plunked down $18 million to finance the operation for its first two years, former employees say the billionaire never set such a hard-and-fast budget and seemed willing to spend freely" (O'Brien 2014). Yet, its revenue grew.

By 2010, the Daily Beast had built enough traffic and advertising base that publishers predicted it would break even within 18 months. Then something odd happened. The site, still under the guidance of Brown, purchased *Newsweek* magazine. The magazine had been struggling for decades as specialty publications stole away topic-driven audience and the Internet undercut the concept of a general newsweekly. The last editor before the purchase had sought to create a more highbrow journal, and the circulation only nose-dived faster.

Brown had sought to merge the two entities and get the best of both worlds, a digital platform and print circulation to sell to advertisers and a mix of editorial voices that would be unique. It failed. The site eventually sold the floundering magazine for an unreported sum and post-mortems of the effort were harsh, with the *New York Times* reporting, "It was always a quixotic project to blend a buzzy, growing Web site with the most outdated of print relics, a newsweekly. But interviews with more than two dozen former and current employees . . . suggest that Ms. Brown's intensely demanding and chaotic management style, which had thrived when contained within established companies, proved a combustible combination with Newsweek's gutted and weakened editorial and sales divisions" (Kaufman and Haughney 2013). Diller would later call the purchase of *Newsweek* "a mistake" and by September of 2013 Tina Brown and the site she founded were parting ways.

The departure of Brown left many to wonder if the Daily Beast had a future. Coverage at the time had noted the troubled financial situation, dominated by the *Newsweek* merger and then divorce, but beneath was an even more troubling idea about the site's ability to survive the departure of Brown. One review of Brown's tenure concluded, "At best it bears the hallmarks of Brown's celebrated editing style: it is elegant, savvy, urbane and writerly. Less happily, it failed to break any real ground at the frontier of digital innovation, falling back on an already familiar combination of aggregation of stories and original writing" (Pilkington 2013). Still, the site continued and under new management began to develop a stronger social media presence and a stronger mix of original reporting and aggregation.

A year after Brown's departure, rather than closing shop the site reported significant growth—a ballooning Facebook following of 1.7 million and a 30 percent increase in visits to the site. The new editor, John Avalon, credited "the creative combination of tech innovation and killer journalism that's really driving our success. Millennials, Gen Xers—and frankly, anyone with a sense of perspective—can see through the predictable partisan spin and the content-farming that's too often pedaled as news today" (Byers 2014).

Further Reading

Byers, Dylan. 2014. "One Year after Tina Brown Exit, Daily Beast Traffic Surges." Politico. October 1. Accessed January 22, 2015. http://www.politico.com/blogs/media/2014/10/one-year-after-tina-brown-exit-daily-beast-traffic-196426.html.

Edgecliffe-Johnson, Andrew. 2008. "Another Scoop for Tina Brown as She Swaps Print for Web." *The Financial Times*. October 5. Accessed January 22, 2015. http://www.ft.com /intl/cms/s/0/0a157900-9304-11dd-98b5-0000779fd18c.html#axzz3PZtbAU7i.

Harvard Political Review. 2012. "Bad Beast." Accessed January 22, 2015. http://www.iop .harvard.edu/bad-beast.

Kaufman, Leslie, and Christine Haughney. 2013. "The Last Temptation of Tina Brown." *New York Times*. August 4. Accessed January 22, 2015. http://www.nytimes.com/2013/08 /05/business/media/the-last-temptation-of-tina-brown.html?pagewanted=all.

O'Brien, Luke. 2014. "How to Lose $100 Million: The Undoing of Tina Brown." *Politico Magazine*. May/June. Accessed January 22, 2015. http://www.politico.com/magazine /story/2014/05/tina-brown-how-to-lose-100-million-105907.html.

Pilkington, Ed. 2013. "Tina Brown Steps Down after Tumultuous Tenure at Daily Beast." *The Guardian*. September 11. Accessed January 22, 2015. http://www.theguardian.com /media/2013/sep/11/tina-brown-steps-down-daily-beast-editor.

DAILY CALLER

Daily Caller is a news and opinion website that has built a sizable audience by producing original reporting, mixing it with aggregated news from other outlets, and throwing in a healthy dose of titillating sensationalism to cover the worlds of politics and celebrity. The site was created by conservative commentator Tucker Carlson and a former adviser for Republican vice president Dick Cheney. Although they stress that the site aims to balance the liberal bias of the mainstream media, Carlson also said soon after its launch in 2010, "Our goal is not to get Republicans elected. Our goal is to explain what your government is doing. We're not going to suck up to people in power, the way so many have. There's been an enormous amount of throne-sniffing . . . It's disgusting" (Kurtz 2010).

The result is a site that focuses on original reporting as a way of building traffic and winning revenue, rather than serving as another platform for conservative commentary about the news. Unlike many of the conservative blogs, Carlson, who himself built a name by serving as a political pundit, has sought to create a business built on conservative-oriented reporting. It was a shift the *New York Times* noted in a 2012 profile of the company, writing, "While his currency used to be debate— at CNN he co-hosted *Crossfire*, and at MSNBC he tangled with the liberal commentator Rachel Maddow and helped make her a TV star—now it is clicks for his site. And to get those, he doesn't need to talk to the other side" (Stelter 2012). The result is one of the largest and fastest growing of the new journalistic outlets to come along in recent years, boasting 16.5 million monthly visitors and nearly 60 million pageviews.

That is not to say that the publication doesn't have opinion. The site features fiery conservative Ann Coulter as a columnist as well as Matt Lewis and Matt Labash, but the bulk of the site is either original reporting or aggregated news pieces from other news outlets. Also, the site is not solely focused on politics, reporting on celebrities, sports, and the outdoors. The site relies on advertising to make a profit—it became profitable within two years of launching—and it has aggressively marketed itself to those interested in new forms of sponsorship like "sponsored" content and native advertising. The site has been often compared to Huffington Post, with its mix of serious reported news and aggregation alongside more click-bait sounding sensational stories, like slideshows "Candice Swanepoel's Sexiest Moments" and "These Celebrities Have Piercings in Strange Places."

But despite these more salacious posts, the Daily Caller has carved out a niche for its investigative work that has a clear conservative bent. Soon after it launched, the site reported on an email group run by *Washington Post* writer and later Vox founder Ezra Klein in which journalists talked trash about politicians, many of them Republican. Daily Caller reporters scoured the archives of the listserv called Journ-oList and found comments from reporters and academics that also sought to alleviate stories about liberal politicians the reporters liked. The site launched a series about it, reporting that "according to records obtained by The Daily Caller, at several points during the 2008 presidential campaign a group of liberal journalists took radical steps to protect their favored candidate. Employees of news organizations including *Time*, Politico, Huffington Post, the *Baltimore Sun*, the *Guardian*, Salon and the *New Republic* participated in outpourings of anger over how Obama had been treated in the media, and in some cases plotted to fix the damage" (Strong 2010).

But the site has also had a series of stories blow up in its face as its quest for juicy political gossip outpaced its ability to confirm sources. This most famously happened in 2013 when the site ran an exclusive story that Democratic Senator Robert Menendez had paid to be with underage prostitutes in the Dominican Republic. ABC News had also interviewed the same women who said they had been with the senator, but chose not to run the article because the women could not confirm their identities and the producer felt they had been coached to make the allegations. The Daily Caller spoke with two of the women, then went ahead and published the story. When the story quickly began to fall apart, the Daily Caller doubled down on its coverage, disputing *Washington Post* and ABC News accounts of the same matter and following up with stories that attempted to back up its claim. It launched what Slate's David Weigel described as a "deductive, prove-this-wrong-why-don't-you theory of the scoop. The Daily Caller noted that 'one of the clues that [former U.S. Representative Anthony] Weiner wasn't telling the truth was that he was following a lot of young girls on Twitter,' and—hey!—Menendez was following 'a very young-looking Dominican girl on Twitter.' It turned out that the girl lived in New Jersey and had appeared in a Menendez campaign ad" (Weigel 2013). The senator was eventually cleared of FBI and Dominican Republic police investigations, which found the women had been paid to lie about the senator and the story had been marketed to media by a conservative political operative.

Rather than be humbled, Carlson welcomed the attention heaped on the news organization, and traffic continued to grow. The site took another hit when a testy exchange between Carlson and the spokeswoman for New York City mayor Bill de Blasio ended with an inadvertently cc'ed-to-all comment from Carlson's brother that the woman was "a self-righteous bitch" and made several crude sexual comments about her. When the emails went public, the story raised questions about Carlson and the publication being misogynistic in its coverage, which Carlson flatly rejects. Instead, he accused the *Washington Post*, whose media blogger Erik Wemple followed the story throughout, of overhyping the story to get more web traffic.

Despite its occasional publicity problems, the site has continued to thrive, finding financial success and some Washington legitimacy in its mix of gossip and politics. The site lists 27 editorial employees and participates in the White House pool reporting. It also has fulltime reporters covering Congress as well as bloggers constantly aggregating news content on everything from the investigation into the attack on the American diplomatic compound in Benghazi, Libya, to the latest news about the Kardashian family. The mix appears to be working and making money.

See also: Aggregation; Conservative Blogosphere; Huffington Post; Political Bias and the Media

Further Reading

Kurtz, Howard. 2010. "Tucker's Excellent Adventure." *Washington Post*. January 11. Accessed October 22, 2015. http://www.washingtonpost.com/wp-dyn/content/article/2010/01/11/AR2010011100892.html.

Stelter, Brian. 2012. "Still a Conservative Provocateur, Carlson Angles for Clicks, Not Fights." *New York Times*. October 7. Accessed October 22, 2015. http://www.nytimes.com/2012/10/08/business/media/tucker-carlson-angles-for-daily-caller-clicks-not-fights.html?_r=0.

Strong, Jonathan. 2010. "Documents Show Media Plotting to Kill Stories about Rev. Jeremiah Wright." Daily Caller. July 20. Accessed October 22, 2015. http://dailycaller.com/2010/07/20/documents-show-media-plotting-to-kill-stories-about-rev-jeremiah-wright.

Weigel, David. 2013. "Keep Your Pants On: The Menendez-Dominican Prostitute Story, and Why It's Teetering." Slate. March 5. Accessed October 22, 2015. http://www.slate.com/articles/news_and_politics/politics/2013/03/menendez_s_dominican_prostitute_scandal_have_the_allegations_collapsed.html.

DAILY KOS

Markos Moulitsas Zúniga has strong opinions about what the country ought to be doing and what the Democratic Party should be doing and how the Republican Party is wrong about just about everything, but he has no plans on running for Congress.

As he said, "I have a foreign last name. I exercise. I've eaten arugula. I drink orange juice. I'm liberal. I've lived in lots of places. I'm educated. I don't go to church. I'm not Anglo. I've lived overseas. I don't wear a flag pin. I like Europe. Those things make me an 'elitist' and thus disqualify me from public office" (Barr 2008). So, instead he pours these opinions and those of other progressive activists into his blog, the Daily Kos. Named after the nickname he earned while serving in the U.S. Army in the early 1990s, the Daily Kos claims to be the "largest progressive community blog in the United States" (Daily Kos 2015).

Over the years, the Daily Kos has maintained its focus on being a community organizing tool and traditional blog where the power is more decentralized and the vast majority of content is contributed by users. The site boasts more than 300,000 registered users and currently attracts 2 million unique visitors a month. The Alexa web analytics firm pegs the site as the 587th most popular site in the United States (Alexa 2015).

The influence of the Daily Kos is structured as a conversation among Democrats and progressives about their party and their view of the country. The site does not aim to speak to everyone and, although the community is open to anyone who may wish to join, Moulitsas stresses it is a community of the like-minded. In 2006, he told PBS's *Frontline*, "Anybody can create . . . an account, and it allows them to comment on the site, to respond to what other people are writing. It allows them to write diaries, which are essentially a blog within the blog . . . but it's also a Democratic site. So if Republicans want to come in and create trouble, they're not going to last very long. It's basically our little Democratic living room, and we're going to have our discussion about what we think is important to reform the Democratic Party and to fix the mess that the Republicans have made in this country" (Moulitsas 2006).

The Daily Kos represents many of the trends facing media coverage of politics in the twenty-first century. It is driven by activism rather than an unbiased effort to deliver the news. At any time, the site is promoting several of its "Actions" where it calls on members of the community to act in some way. Often these action are aimed at fellow Democrats. On one day in early 2015, the site was calling on its community to "Sign the petition denouncing the 13 Senate Democrats that voted to roll back Wall Street reform" and put their name to another document declaring "Shame on the 28 oily House Democrats who voted for Keystone XL" (Daily Kos 2015). This focus on encouraging ideological purity in the ranks of Democrats has, some say, made it difficult for more moderate members of the party to thrive, but it is part of the Daily Kos's mission.

The fact that the site sees itself less as a news organization and more as a Democratic Party organizing tool came to the fore during the 2008 primaries. Moulitsas and his supporters had through much of the primary written largely favorable coverage of upstart candidate Barack Obama and had been cooler to the initial front-runner Hillary Clinton. In fact, commenters on the site had taken several arguably sexist shots at the New York senator, but by March of 2008 Moulitsas saw Clinton's continued run for the nomination even with Obama's lock of a majority of the elected convention delegates as an effort to "sunder the [Democratic Party] in civil war." He took to the blog to deride the Clinton campaign, writing, "She is willing—nay, eager—to split the party apart in her mad pursuit of power. . . . It is Clinton, with no reasonable chance at victory, who is fomenting civil war in order to overturn the will of the Democratic electorate. As such, as far as I'm concerned, she doesn't deserve 'fairness' on this site" (Moulitsas 2008).

The site has also actively encouraged donations to candidates and expressed explicit support for often-upstart liberal candidates at the state and federal level. By 2010 political scientists were able to "demonstrate a 'Kos bump'—a statistically and substantively significant association between mentions of candidates on the Daily Kos and donations to these candidates" (Sides and Farrell 2010). Like the tea party groups on the conservative side, the Daily Kos and other activist liberal blog communities have empowered more rank-and-file members of the party and those loosely connected to the party to rally around proposals and candidates. Whether it is financially benefitting candidates through campaign donations and activist endorsements or by threatening and shaming candidates who violate their ideological orthodoxy, the Daily Kos has emerged as a new type of political player on the party stage. Relying on a small but committed audience and by mixing news and opinion, the site has built a political following that gives it sway within Democratic Party politics and can help candidates battling against the moderation of Democratic positions on key issues.

Further Reading

Alexa. "Daily Kos Report." Accessed January 12, 2015. http://www.alexa.com/siteinfo /http%3A%2F%2Fwww.dailykos.com.

Barr, Andy. 2008. "20 Questions with Markos Moulitsas Zúniga, founder of Daily Kos." *The Hill*. August 22. Accessed January 12, 2015. http://thehill.com/capital-living/20 -questions/20864-20-questions-with-markos-moulitsas-zniga-founder-of-daily-kos.

Kos, Daily. "Masthead." Accessed January 12, 2015. http://www.dailykos.com/special/about.

Moulitsas, Markos. 2006. "Interview for News War. " PBS Frontline. August 31. Accessed January 12, 2015. http://www.pbs.org/wgbh/pages/frontline/newswar/interviews /moulitsas.html.

Moulitsas, Markos. 2008. "The Clinton Civil War." The Daily Kos. March 17. Accessed January 13, 2015. http://www.dailykos.com/story/2008/03/17/478498/-The-Clinton-civil -war.

Sides, John, and Henry Farrell. 2010. "The Kos Bump: The Political Economy of Campaign Fundraising in the Internet Age." Paper presentation at the American Political Science Association. Accessed January 13, 2015. http://www.researchgate.net/publication /228129394_The_Kos_Bump_The_Political_Economy_of_Campaign_Fundraising _in_the_Internet_Age/links/0c96052d3f74a796ad000000.

DAILY NEWSPAPERS

Battered by a fundamental change in how information flows in the world and a tectonic shift in the advertising world, daily newspapers have borne the brunt of many of the revolutionary changes wrought by the Internet and mobile technology. Even as they struggle to adapt to a world where they are no longer the sole source of information on the day's events in their city, these newspapers remain the single largest source of political reporting in the nation, often providing critical information on statewide and local campaigns and ballot issues.

In many discussions of newspapers and politics much of the attention falls on the largest circulation national newspapers like the *New York Times,* the *Wall Street Journal*, and a handful of leading regional papers like the *Washington Post* and *Boston Globe*. But there are some 1,300 daily newspapers across the country, representing the largest pool of journalists covering daily news. These news organizations have seen their readership diversify as the old geographic limitations of newspapers fell away in the digital age. But as advertising has moved into more specialized marketing made possible by the Internet, these newspapers have seen the revenue decline dramatically. The economic problems of the newspaper industry can be seen directly in the number of journalists working in these newsrooms. In 2015 the American Society of Newspaper Editors reported that 32,900 journalists work for daily papers, down from 56,400 just 14 years ago.

The trials of the digital conversion of daily newspapers have been widely reported. Once-successful regional dailies like the *Rocky Mountain News* and *Seattle Post-Intelligencer* have closed and thousands of reporters have been laid off or accepted buy-outs from struggling papers. But the daily paper has gone through more than just an economic change, as the Internet's ability to connect users to any content they desire at any given moment has changed the role the paper plays in its community. Many papers have sought to maintain their role in their given community by focusing more and more on local news. A 2008 report from the Pew Research Center found that most daily newspapers had fundamentally changed their content strategies. That year, 46 percent of editors reported that they had cut coverage of foreign issues and nearly as many (41 percent) said they had slashed national coverage. Sharon Rosenhause, managing editor of the *Ft. Lauderdale Sun-Sentinel*, told researchers, "Maybe there was a spot on the front page that everyone considered was the foreign or national story of the day, but that's changed. That story is still in the paper, but it's just inside. To make the front page, it has to be a significant development or a story that we can see through Florida eyes or some kind of Florida prism" (Pew Research Center 2008).

This focus on local news reflects a realization that the role the daily papers play in its readers' lives has changed. Newspapers established themselves—and sold themselves to readers and advertisers—as the daily report about the world made available to local residents. Newspapers fashioned a front page that mixed local events with national political reporting and international diplomatic maneuvers. The editors would weave these diverse stories together into a single presentation of the day's events, delivered to the reader's front door. They operated in an era of information scarcity, where the major competition was initially other local papers but would later become local broadcasters. The Internet changed this fundamentally. Now newspapers could offer the news to anyone online, but so could every other news outlet in the world. Readers no longer needed a single, local editor to let them know of a terrorist attack in a distant land or the latest gaffe by a politician on the campaign trail. Most daily papers reacted by doubling down on their own local coverage, seeking to differentiate themselves from other news sources.

Although the Internet has had a clearly negative impact on the economic model of the modern newspaper, the story about what it has done to their audience is far more complex. On the one hand, a given newspaper is still primarily consumed by people in the community it serves and who subscribe to the print product. The Nielsen Scarborough's 2014 Newspaper Penetration Report found that 56 percent of those who consume a newspaper read it exclusively in print. Another 27 percent access it through a mix that includes the printed paper and some mobile or computer use. Only 16 percent reported using exclusively digital devices to read the paper. This would create the impression that newspapers are still essentially dead-tree products, but when one examines their full audience the numbers seem dramatically different. Most major newspaper websites report audiences that dwarf their print circulation. For example, the *New York Times* boasted a print circulation of 650,000, but had a digital user audience of some 54 million in January 2015. But it is important to understand the difference, both in terms of content use and economic impact, between the online users and the print subscribers. Newspapers continue to supply much of the content that is talked about, commented upon, and shared across social media, but this use of their content does not carry the same economic benefit of a single subscriber. As the 2015 State of the Media report from the Pew Research Center noted, "One clue lies in the time spent. The average visit to the *New York Times'* website and associated apps in January 2015 lasted only 4.6 minutes—and this was the highest of the top 25. Thus, most online newspaper visitors are 'flybys,' arriving perhaps through a link on a social networking site or sent in an email, and so may not think of this experience as 'reading a newspaper' but simply browsing an article online" (Pew Research Center 2015). This has obvious economic value, meaning despite the use of paywalls, online advertising and sponsored content, a reader who spends four minutes or less on a newspaper website is worth less than a subscriber who receives the paper delivered daily to their door.

But the shift to digital is more than just economic. As has been noted, newspapers are catering more and more to their local community and this can manifest itself through changes in its approach to reporting on politics and political campaigns. Newspapers have often played the role of public gadfly on locally controversial issues, and some worry that the increasing reliance on local support may quietly suppress that tendency. Already the idea of bias has emerged in some newspapers as they increasingly embrace, rather than combat, local political bias, according to some researchers of newspaper content. Often in history the political interests of the owner have helped shape the content of these newspapers. William Randolph Hearst famously used his newspaper chain, the first in the country, to advocate for his policies and political position. His papers helped build a case for war with Spain, a war that Hearst himself participated in by sailing his yacht to Cuba and taking more than two-dozen Spanish soldiers prisoner. He also used his paper's influence in cities like New York, Chicago, San Francisco, and elsewhere to fuel his own political ambitions for the White House.

But today's daily newspapers carry little of the agenda of their ownership. One study by the Bureau of Economic Research found, "contrary to conventional wisdom, that the ideology of the owners doesn't correlate in any significant way with the political slant of their newspapers' coverage. When a single owner owns multiple papers, the authors find that each paper's language is tailored to its own market, rather than toeing a single, corporate line. Their data also show no significant relationship between a newspaper's slant and the political contributions made by its corporate owner. What instead has a big impact on newspaper bias is readers" (Belsie 2007). This means that often a newspaper will echo the partisan leanings of its readers and this problem, especially as less and less reporting done about national and international issues makes it into the paper, may begin to alter the worldview the newspaper presents to its readers.

The modern, digital daily newspaper is still a work in progress. Its content continues to evolve and its role in the media diet of consumers who turn to more and varied sources of information is far from set. Despite this, daily newspapers remain an integral part of most communities. As *The Economist* noted back in 2006, some of the hand-wringing over the death of the newspaper is somewhat overstated. It editorialized under the somewhat sensational headline, "Who killed the newspaper?", "Nobody should relish the demise of once-great titles. But the decline of newspapers will not be as harmful to society as some fear. Democracy, remember, has already survived the huge television-led decline in circulation since the 1950s. It has survived as readers have shunned papers and papers have shunned what was in stuffier times thought of as serious news. And it will surely survive the decline to come" (*The Economist* 2006).

Nevertheless, the decline that came was more severe than many predicted. The 2008 economic crisis pushed many newspapers to the edge and newsrooms around the country continued to shrink. But even as they contracted and bought out the contracts of veteran reporters, a new wave of journalists—many more equipped to deliver news across the web, social media, and mobile—took their places, providing more content on more platforms than newspapers ever did in the "golden age." How good that content can be and how much can it help inform the public about public issues is still an open question. But the newspaper of tomorrow will continue to modify itself to serve the evolving information habits of its community and be less a catalogue of the world.

See also: *New York Times*; Newspaper Industry; *Washington Post*

Further Reading

Belsie, Laurent. 2007. "What Drives the Political Slant of Daily Newspapers?" National Bureau of Economic Research. July. Accessed December 14, 2015. http://www.nber.org/digest/jul07/w12707.html.

"The Changing Newsroom." Pew Research Center. July 21, 2008. Accessed December 14, 2015. http://www.journalism.org/2008/07/21/changing-content.

"The State of the Media: Newspapers." Pew Research Center. April 29, 2015. Accessed December 14, 2015. http://www.journalism.org/2015/04/29/newspapers-fact-sheet.

"Who Killed the Newspaper?" *The Economist*. August 24, 2006. Accessed December 14, 2015. http://www.economist.com/node/7830218.

DAMAGE CONTROL

Even the most seasoned and skilled campaigner will end up botching a point. Then-presidential candidate Barack Obama mourned the destruction of an entire Kansas town and the death of 10,000 people killed by a tornado in a speech in 2008 when the town was in Illinois and only 11 had died. Or the time the candidate to be the next Speaker of the House stated that the Republican investigation into the attacks on Americans in Benghazi, Libya, was at least in part aimed at hurting the election chances of former secretary of state Hillary Clinton. Other times, it can be far more serious, like the time five U.S. senators were accused of pressuring federal regulators to leave a major political donor alone. In all of these cases the potential political fallout has triggered a sometimes effective and sometimes bumbled attempt to control the damage. This craft of damage control has evolved over time to become a highly structured and carefully coordinated public relations campaign that aims to either shift blame or change the conversation in the media.

In all of its many uses—political and otherwise—the idea of damage control is the effort to limit the effects of a negative and potentially devastating development. This idea in political communications is often lumped into the larger concept of crisis management, and there is no shortage of examples of both it being done well and it contributing to the problem. The way in which politicians respond to a crisis is often shaped by a close cohort of advisers and clearly affected by the man or woman's personality. For example, President Richard Nixon, who was famously secretive and possessed a penchant for blaming the press for his problems, oversaw one of the most disastrous damage control efforts in American history. Faced with the story that his re-election campaign had funded a political dirty tricks operation that sought to sabotage his opponents, Nixon and his backers launched a massive campaign of deception, lying to the press and public and actively working to block internal government investigations. Nixon would later admit in one of the Oval Office recordings released as part of the investigation that "it's not the crime that gets you . . . *it's the cover up*." That cover up by the Nixon administration would lead to his resignation ahead of likely impeachment.

Despite the danger, one of the most natural reactions when faced with an unpleasant development or potentially damaging revelation is to deny it. And much of the early days of crisis management were aimed at finding a way to legally deny the facts, ideally without lying, and then hoping the story would blow over after a news cycle or two. When news came out that the supermarket tabloid *The Star* was to publish an account by a woman claiming she had had an affair with Democratic candidate Bill Clinton, the initial reaction of Clinton and his campaign was to point out she had been paid and to deny some of the specific allegations made against him. They also sought to portray it as a sleazy story in a sleazy tabloid, but when the mainstream press picked up the story and reported it more widely, the campaign was forced to respond. Here we see the evolution of the damage control model. Unlike past campaigns that may have hunkered down and waited the story out, the Clinton campaign decided to address it head on and scheduled a single interview with the popular newsmagazine program *60 Minutes* to discuss the allegations. In a joint interview with his wife, Clinton admitted he had caused "pain in his marriage," but still carefully rejected parts of the *Star* story. He would weather the scandal and win the nomination and the presidency, but his tendency to skate on the edge of the truth at times of crisis would dog him through much of his presidency and beyond.

There are full service campaign consultants and communications experts who focus on damage control. The Stanford Graduate School of Business offers an entire course in damage control taught by former Clinton political consultant Chris Lehane and filmmaker Bill Guttentag. The pair promise, "If you don't fight back effectively in the modern spin cycle, you will no longer have your brand, your image, your reputation—or your hopes of becoming the President of the United States. Our goal is to illuminate those practices that will help you survive to fight another day" (Stanford 2012). The reason why large PR firms and veteran political consultants market themselves as experts in damage control is partly due to their experience, but most because of the highly complex legal aspects of many damage control situations. Depending on the event that has happened, especially if it involves a sitting politician, the possibility that the crisis may later trigger federal investigations or local law enforcement action is very real. Perjury, the crime that got Bill Clinton later impeached, and obstruction of justice are just two of the possible crimes that can erupt from a scandal. So when Lanny Davis, another Clinton veteran who later opened his own political consulting shop, outlined his strategy for damage control he emphasized first and foremost that the first thing to do would be to establish a lawyer-client relationship between the adviser and the politician so that anything that is said between the two would be protected by the legal concept of lawyer-client privilege. Once the privilege exists, Davis notes it is critical for that one person to be fully briefed on the real facts behind the crisis, what is true, what evidence there is, and what has yet to come out. Then, Davis writes in his book on crisis communications, "once the legal crisis manager has all the facts—meaning documents, emails, and other verification that the facts are true—the next step must be to craft a simple message. The best way to approach this task is to write the message or messages as brief headlines for the story you would like to see written. Ultimately reporters are no different from members of Congress or even regulators: You have to simplify your facts into a concise, easy to understand message" (Davis 2013). And this point by Davis emphasizes the other critical element of damage control: while the legal questions surrounding the behavior and response of the political figure weigh heavily on the team organizing a response, at its core damage control is about the story that comes out of the scandal. Is it a politician abusing their public trust, a personal flaw that is frankly none of your business, or a political vendetta by a person or party? This narrative will be constructed in the early hours of a crisis and will be deployed through the media to try and defuse the scandal or at least shift its focus.

Although crisis management efforts often appear spontaneous and driven by the individual politician, almost always a team of advisers is crafting the story, then deploying a series of techniques to get that story out, leaking information to favorable media outlets, using campaign surrogates and supporters to address specific points, and relying on independent organizations to attack the source of the scandal or to overtly politicize the issue. Advisers stress it is important to coordinate all these efforts, rather than allowing the story to play out through the media or other factors, and important that it not appear highly orchestrated. Dawn Laguens, a senior vice president at Planned Parenthood and experienced political consultant on the Democratic side, stressed that "the one thing that creates additional distrust among voters is a campaign publicizing the inner machinations, the strategy to control damage. Stories about damage control teams make the candidate look insincere and fake. Keep the team small and keep the strategizing quiet" (Faucheux 2003). The resulting PR campaign feels organic and honest, yet is carefully crafted, calculated, and cultivated. If it all works. Sometimes, it doesn't.

By looking at the so-called Keating Five scandal we can see how five different politicians, all facing the same scandal, responded to the issue with varying degrees of success. The Keating scandal grew out of the banking problems that swept the savings and loan industry in the late 1980s and early 1990s. Savings and loans operated under a different set of rules than traditional banks; deregulations and rule changes had allowed them to make riskier investments. The result was a series of failures by these firms and government takeovers to protect the savings of individuals. Charles Keating ran one of these operations, Lincoln Savings and Loan Association. The federal government began investigating Lincoln for its handling of deposits and its operations. Keating, who had become a major political donor to both parties, reached out to get the help of senators to limit the investigation. Democrat Alan Cranston of California would end up being reprimanded for his role and two others—Michigan Democrat Donald Riegle and Arizona Democrat Dennis DeConcini—would also be found to have acted improperly by the Senate Ethics Committee. Two others—Republican John McCain of Arizona and Ohio Democrat John Glenn—were cleared of wrongdoing, but criticized for poor judgment.

Riegle wrote an angry letter to the *Detroit Free Press* saying what he had done was not that different than responding to that paper's request for help in establishing a joint operating agreement with the *Detroit News*. But many pointed out that the newspaper had not been a major donor to the senator. Senator DeConcini immediately began running five-minute ads on local television in Arizona, explaining his side of the Keating Five story. The ads failed to sway many and he soon announced his retirement. In the end, three of the accused senators announced that they would not run for re-election, but Glenn and McCain fought to protect their seats and minimize the political damage. McCain publicly announced that he would turn $112,000 in contributions from Mr. Keating over to the federal government. But as he acknowledged, "I'm sure that my political obituary will always have something about the Keating Five in it. I don't see how that could be avoided" (Berke 1991). McCain's decision to return the money that Keating had donated to his campaign was just the first step of his PR offensive. He admitted his culpability, but supporters also leaked stories of how McCain had been hesitant to get involved and that Keating, at one point, had referred to the Republican as a "wimp" for not doing more.

Both McCain and Glenn also tried to manage the crisis by inundating journalists and the public with swaths of information. Eleanor Clift would refer to it in *Newsweek* as the "Flood Them with Facts" approach to damage control, writing, "Senator McCain and Ohio Sen. John Glenn have been the most successful at the data-bank approach. McCain produced a 96-page white paper supporting his contention that what he did for financier Charles Keating was 'not unlike helping the little lady who didn't get her social security.' Glenn quotes from the transcript of the senators' meeting with bank regulators where he said, 'Charge them or get off their backs.' The comment helps voters understand that Glenn was trying to hurry the investigation of Keating's Lincoln Savings & Loan, not to halt it" (Clift 1990). These efforts helped the two senators respond to the scandal and for Glenn and McCain, the two to face the lightest punishment from the Senate Ethics Committee investigation, it was enough to help them win re-election. McCain, in particular, would become a champion of campaign finance reform, fighting to limit the influence of donors on the process, perhaps a final act of damage control by the veteran lawmaker.

Not all scandals are so complex. Today's tend to erupt more quickly and either catch fire in a news cycle moving at warp speed or flame out just as quickly. An example of the speed of the damage control cycle flared briefly in 2015. Having been battered by conservatives who said he was too quick to compromise with President Barack Obama, House Speaker John Boehner announced he would step down as Speaker and resign from Congress by the end of October 2015. It was a stunning development and thrust the House Republicans into a potential leadership fight. Initially it appeared that the House Majority Leader, Kevin McCarthy from California, would step up to be the Speaker and the battle would be for McCarthy's old job. That is, until he appeared on Sean Hannity's program on Fox News on September 29 and said, "Everybody thought Hillary Clinton was unbeatable, right? But we put together a Benghazi special committee, a select committee. What are her numbers today? Her numbers are dropping. Why? Because she's untrustable. But no one would have known any of that had happened, had we not fought" (Holan 2015). Democrats and many in the media jumped on those words, especially supporters of Clinton, who was getting ready to appear before that committee in

October. McCarthy initially struggled to respond. Soon a number of Republicans announced they would not support him for Speaker; less than 10 days after making that comment he announced he would not run for Speaker.

McCarthy's mangled statement on Hannity's program followed by nearly a week of backtracking mortally weakened the Republican, and actually helped Clinton. McCarthy's comment allowed Democrats to turn what could have been a difficult hearing into something they could largely, and effectively, portray and dismiss as a political witch-hunt. Benghazi, as a whole, has reinforced the idea that trying to actively shape a story may not be the only way to deal with a crisis. Crisis management consultant Eric Dezenhall writes that "privacy tends to *work* for the Clintons, as it does for many public and private figures. So they make their enemies earn their carcass, hoping that the media and public get bored or distracted in the process. And they often do: A number of Clinton scandals *have* collapsed, receded or eroded" (Dezenhall 2015). Dezenhall and others note that in the super-heated political world of social media and polarization, the less fodder critics have to use against a politician, the better for that politician. Attackers are left to create conspiracies and force sustained interest in the crisis, rather than use reams of information released in an episode of "coming clean."

This may be the most significant element of the modern damage control operation. In the era where a tweet can be turned into news in a moment, some politicians have found it is better to try and limit the information out there about a scandal and hope that the news cycle bores of the story and moves on rather than turn it into a full-blown scandal. The drip, drip, drip of the Clinton story about her email running off a personal server at her home when she was secretary of state falls clearly into this category. For months after the story broke, the State Department would release batches of emails from the collection Clinton had turned over when news of the server broke. Reporters would pore over each release and generate new articles. Analysts would offer another grim assessment of their potential impact on the Democratic nomination fight, and Clinton would issue another sort-of apology. The drumbeat of this story has been very different than the Watergate story. Perhaps the most insightful critique of the damage control efforts around the email story came not from Clinton but from her primary opponent Senator Bernie Sanders. At one primary debate, he told a cheering crowd, "the American people are sick and tired of hearing about your damn emails."

"Thank you," Clinton responded, nodding and smiling. "Me too. Me too."

See also: Feeding Frenzy; Opposition Research; Spin; 24-Hour News Cycle

Further Reading

Berke, Richard. 1991. "Aftermath of the Keating Verdicts: Damage Control, Political Glee." *New York Times*. March 1.

Clift, Eleanor. 1990. "In Search of Teflon." *Newsweek*. January 8.

Davis, Lanny. 2013. *Crisis Tales: Five Rules for Coping with Crises in Business, Politics, and Life.* New York: Simon & Schuster.

Dezenhall, Eric. 2015. "Hillary and the Virtues of Boring Damage Control." Huffington Post. April 23. Accessed November 15, 2015. http://www.huffingtonpost.com/eric-dezenhall /hillary-and-the-virtues-of-boring-damage-control_b_7117392.html.

Faucheux, Ron. 2003. *Winning Elections: Political Campaign Management, Strategy & Tactics.* Lanham, MD: Rowman & Littlefield.

Holan, Angie. 2015. "In Context: What Kevin McCarthy said about Hillary Clinton and Benghazi." Politifact. October 7. Accessed June 13, 2016. http://www.politifact.com /truth-o-meter/article/2015/oct/07/context-what-kevin-mccarthy-said-about-hillary -cli/.

Stanford GSB Staff. 2012. "Crisis Management: The Art of Damage Control." Stanford Graduate School of Business. November 1. Accessed June 13, 2016. https://www.gsb.stanford .edu/insights/crisis-management-art-damage-control.

DARK MONEY GROUPS

If there is a political Voldemort in the minds of many government transparency advocates it would be the so-called dark money groups that have begun pouring hundreds of millions of dollars into American political campaigns. Even the name evokes something sinister and hidden.

The government watchdog group the Sunlight Foundation first used the term "dark money" to describe a new wave of nonprofit organizations that sprang up in the wake of the controversial *Citizens United v. Federal Election Commission* decision by the U.S. Supreme Court in 2010.

Unlike other groups, like political action committees and Super PACs, dark money organizations register with the Internal Revenue Service and do not need to disclose who has donated to them or how much has been given. The IRS created these groups, labeled 501(c)(4)'s for the section of the tax code that covers them, more than a century ago, to promote "social welfare." They include many trade unions and associations as well as groups like the Sierra Club, the AARP, and the National Rifle Association.

No nonprofits need to disclose the source of their funds, but over the years these social welfare groups have evolved to be more political than their nonprofit brethren. Other nonprofits have to clear a series of hurdles to campaign or lobby on behalf of political positions. For example, a 501(c)(3) must alert the IRS whenever it lobbies on behalf of a political issue but 501(c)(4)'s can perform unlimited amounts of lobbying so long as their "primary" focus is a social benefit. "It can therefore be argued that the 'primary' test, as employed in section 501(c)(4), may permit an organization lawfully to participate or intervene in political campaigns on behalf of or in opposition to campaigns for public office so long as its primary activities remain the promotion of social welfare" (IRS 1981).

So the NRA or Sierra Club can enter the political fray so long as they were advocating for their issues and addressing the underlying concerns their group was founded to support. In 2010, *Citizens United* meant corporations and unions could now begin spending on political speech, and the political 501(c)(4) quickly emerged as a popular vehicle for that money.

"In the 2010 midterms, when this practice was just getting started, $161 million was spent by groups that did not disclose donations. In [the 2014] cycle it was up to at least $216 million, and 69 percent of it was spent on behalf of Republicans, according to the Center for Responsive Politics" (*New York Times* 2014). Many groups also made large donations to Super PACs, but the nonprofits had one major advantage—donations to a 501(c)(4) would be secret. "The anonymity of the donations appeared to have contributed to their success. However, the ability to hide these donations appeared to be partly due to unclear regulations on the part of the Internal Revenue Service" (Smith and Powell 2013, p. 60). As experts note, the IRS has struggled to deal with these new groups. But the agency, already facing criticism for unfairly targeting tea party organizations, chose not to stem the growth of these new largely political nonprofits. A report from the Center for Public Integrity quoted an anonymous staffer in the nonprofit division as saying, "Nobody wanted to say 'no, you're not exempt' . . . We stalled so we wouldn't have to say no" (Patel 2014). The result was an explosion in groups and spending by both Democratic- and Republican-leaning groups.

The core argument over "dark money" focuses on whether it is encouraging more political speech or simply placing elections on the auction block to go to the highest bidder. Many in states that have seen a lot of dark money spending worry it is actually shifting the focus away from the candidates running and onto faceless groups. During a particularly nasty governor's race in Arizona, the largest paper in the state editorialized the core argument against dark money groups, writing, "The net consequence of *Citizens United* has been to enable organizations whose sources of funding often are veiled to spend heavily on many of our most important elections" (Arizona Republic 2014).

But even as editorial writers and government accountability advocates have wrung their hands over dark money, some, often libertarian-leaning thinkers and activists, have welcomed the rise of these new political players. The multistate news group Watchdog.org that draws most of its financial support from conservative activists like the Koch brothers published a six-part series in late 2014 making the case for 501(c)4's, arguing efforts to regulate dark money would have a major chilling effect on the political speech of Americans. The series culminated in the clearest argument yet for why dark money is not a subversion of the system, but a freedom to be cherished. Editor Jon Cassidy argued, "May we get together and call ourselves the NAACP or the Klan or the Communist Party or the King Street Patriots and act in that name, not our own, for causes popular or despised? May we contribute to a cause in private? Do we allow for political advocacy by group, even though some of those groups are the creation of one or two wealthy people? Or should you forfeit the right to the privacy of your political conscience when you choose to act on it?" (Cassidy 2014).

States and the IRS continue to discuss new regulations aimed at limiting the ability to anonymously fund political speech, but these groups will most likely remain a major player in federal and state campaigns in the coming years.

Further Reading
Cassidy, Jon. 2014. "May the Many Choose to Be One?" Watchdog.org. December 30. Accessed on January 4, 2015. http://watchdog.org/188071/dark-money-6-many-one.
Editorial Board. 2014. "'Dark Money' Begins to Sully Campaigns." *Arizona Republic*. October 3. Accessed January 5, 2015. http://www.azcentral.com/story/opinion/editorial/2014/10/03/dark-money-hurts-campaigns/16661367.
Editorial Board. 2014. "'Dark Money Helped Win the Senate." *New York Times*. November 8. Accessed on January 4, 2015. http://www.nytimes.com/2014/11/09/opinion/sunday/dark-money-helped-win-the-senate.html?_r=0.
IRS. 1981. "Social Welfare: What Does it Mean?" Accessed on January 4, 2015. http://www.irs.gov/pub/irs-tege/eotopicg81.pdf.
Patel, Julie. 2014. "Hobbled IRS Can't Stem 'Dark Money' Flow." Center for Public Integrity. July 28. Accessed January 5, 2015. http://www.publicintegrity.org/2014/07/15/15035/hobbled-irs-cant-stem-dark-money-flow.
Smith, Melissa, and Larry Powell. 2013. *Dark Money, Super PACs, and the 2012 Election*. Lanham, MD: Lexington Books.

DATA JOURNALISM

Data journalism is reporting that finds its core story in numerical data. This data can be the crux of the piece, illuminate a development missed in the typical reporting of a story, or simply spark a reported narrative that feels like a "traditional" piece of journalism but can trace its origin to a given data set or data point. The use of data journalism has given birth to new forms of political reporting that seek to ground the reporting in hard data versus mushy anecdote. Data reporting has spawned the creation of new political sites like FiveThirtyEight.com and has also been empowered by the flood of raw information that the Internet has helped facilitate. Data journalism can be broken down into different forms of reporting, including the development of data visualizations that create graphics from the raw information to more data-informed models of reporting that use the numerical information as the source of the story.

The idea of collecting data to inform public decision is an ancient one, and even the concept of visualizing that data to explain a concept is far from new. The first statistical census that gathered data on a civilization dates back to the Babylonians in 3,800 B.C.E. and early data visualizations go back to efforts to explain geometry in 200 B.C.E. Efforts to connect the collection of data and the need to visualize for the public began in more recent eras. Maps, mathematical diagrams, and statistical charts developed along with printing as a way to convey information. One historical analysis finds that "most of the innovations in data visualization arose from concrete, often practical goals: the need or desire to see phenomena and relationships in new or different ways. It is also clear that the development of graphic methods depended fundamentally on parallel advances in technology, data collection and statistical theory" (Friendly 2006). The role of data and data visualization very much mirrors this assessment of its global history. The desire to contextualize stories in new ways and the technological evolution of the field have empowered more journalists to tackle data projects.

In many ways, this form of journalism is not new either, having grown out of the more recent computer-assisted reporting efforts of groups like the Investigative Reporters and Editors, and dates back to the 1960s. The fact that IRE was perhaps the first real organization to dive into computer-assisted reporting, which was often referred to as CAR, speaks to how most journalists viewed that type of data-driven reporting. It was the purview of those reporters with the time and the skills to cull through box after box of government report, to read thousands of pages of testimony or use the primitive computers of the day to process bulky and complex spreadsheets. Even a 1999 book from the journalistic think tank the Poynter Institute encouraging reporters to embrace what they called Computer-Assisted Journalism (CAJ) acknowledged that, "This term can be daunting because so many different aspects of the journalist's job are lumped under it. Often, people hearing the term think immediately of expensive equipment, complicated programs and sophisticated analyses, used only in long-term, long-winded project" (Paul 1999). From its earliest development up until the last decade, data reporting was seen as a deeply specialized skill only a handful of reporters at the largest daily newspapers could handle. The idea that an average reporter could load a spreadsheet on their computer, clean the data to ensure its accuracy, and then analyze the content to find a hidden fact or seed of a story was seen as far-fetched.

But as digital technologies and Internet tools made it easier for the public and reporters to use these tools, the power of data to inform and sometimes tell the story continued to grow. Alongside the technology rose new forms of telling data stories, most notably the data graphic. Once seen as an eye-catching tidbit for newspaper designs or b-roll wallpaper on television broadcasts, graphics have become powerful visual storytelling tools and most powerful graphics are created by the underlying data reporting that generate them. Much of the initial push around data visualization came out of the academic and nonprofit spheres before it really affected journalism. Statisticians like Hans Rosling, whose project Gapminder allowed visitors to see 100 years of development data mapped out in an animated timeline, helped show students and journalists alike the way data could help offer new perspectives on stories and more easily notice outliers or interesting developments.

But it was the development of newsrooms with the capacity to take the computer-assisted reporting of the 1980s and 1990s and turn it into a beat that truly fueled the data journalism movement. That innovation is most often associated with the launch of the *Guardian*'s Datablog in 2009. The British newspaper has been an ardent champion of the use of data and its journalists are some of the most recognized leaders and advocates for the use of open information to inform journalism.

Simon Rogers is often the face of the *Guardian's* data work and his take on the role of data journalism is that it is almost subversive, creating a new form of journalist that can challenge established brands. In a piece where he called data journalism the "New Punk" he argued, "Data journalism is a great leveler. Many media groups are starting with as much prior knowledge and expertise as someone hacking away from their bedroom. Many have, until very recently, no idea where to start and great groups of journalists are still nervous of the spreadsheets they increasingly are confronted with. It's rare for the news site reader to find themselves as powerful as the news site editor, but that's where we are right now—and that power is only increasing as journalists come to rely more and more on their communities for engagement and stories" (Rogers 2014).

New data journalism outlets have sprung up to challenge existing new outlets, especially in the political reporting realm. Nate Silver, whose predictive modeling has accurately predicted the winner in presidential campaigns with impressive regularity, created the FiveThirtyEight news site that imbues political and sports coverage with a healthy dose of data. Similarly, Ezra Klein has aimed to do the same at Vox.com, building an explanatory journalism website that relies heavily on data to tell its stories. The American Communities Project has sought to use data to get beyond a red-blue dichotomy in American political reporting. Interestingly, all of these journalism projects have connections to traditional outlets. Silver worked for three years with the *New York Times* and his site is now owned by ESPN. Klein built his reputation blogging for the *Washington Post*, and ACP works with both the *Wall Street Journal* and NBC News. This may be the one limit that continues to dog data journalism. Despite the array of web tools to assist reporters in finding, sorting, and even visualizing data and even as more and more data is uploaded and made public, it remains a relatively small portion of the overall journalism output. It is still a skill set possessed by fairly few journalists. One academic assessment of the spread of data journalism called the situation at smaller newsrooms "precarious," adding, "Data projects there came as the result of a lucky hire, or at the initiative of journalists who took it upon themselves to learn data skills in their free time. Meanwhile, data journalism at the larger newspapers and online-only organizations appeared to be thriving. If the gap between data journalism resources is as wide as our preliminary research suggests, this would add to an already considerable list of concerns about the future of newspapers in all but the largest metropolitan areas in the United States" (Fink and Anderson 2014). This indicates that only on specialized websites like Vox or FiveThirtyEight, or in large newsrooms like the *Guardian* and the *New York Times*, has data journalism really taken hold. But as more journalists learn the craft of collecting, cleaning, and analyzing data, that reality may start to shift. Just in 2015, a small paper in southern California scored a Pulitzer Prize for a data-reporting project that uncovered outrageous compensation for the head of a small school district. But for every paper like the *Daily Breeze* there are scores of papers that don't possess the skills or the time to develop data projects in their community.

And that may be unfortunate as data journalism does offer reporters one of the key things they have struggled with according to public opinion surveys—credibility. Inherent in the growth of data journalism is a recognition of the need for journalists to have evidence to support their work. In an era when anyone with a mobile phone can blog or tweet and reach potentially millions, data reporting offers professional journalists a unique opportunity to apply journalistic standards and analysis to that data to uncover the actual story hidden in a spreadsheet.

Data journalism also differentiates itself from other online commentary because it contributes something tangible to the conversation, namely specific facts. In a 2013 video on the *Guardian* about their data journalism efforts one designer said, "Because numbers are so strong it is not just about opinion. It's about what is really there, so I think it is a modern way of doing journalism" (*Guardian* 2013). Many digital pioneers hail this form of journalism as a truly unique and powerful role. Tim Berners-Lee developed the World Wide Web as a way to connect to computers and networks to facilitate academic study, but he has also worked to open more data up to the public. Even though the web and Berners-Lee's Open Data Institute have created access to countless reams of data, he also knows there is a translation and explanation layer that needs to be added to truly unlock the power of data. His hope is that journalists will help create that. He has said, "Data-driven journalism is the future. Journalists need to be data-savvy. It used to be that you would get stories by chatting to people in bars, and it still might be that you'll do it that way some times. But now it's also going to be about poring over data and equipping yourself with the tools to analyze it and picking out what's interesting. And keeping it in perspective, helping people out by really seeing where it all fits together, and what's going on in the country" (Gray, Chambers, and Bounegru 2012).

Even with its promise of editorial credibility and new storytelling techniques, data journalism remains a somewhat vague concept, but a series of regular types of reporting have begun to emerge, each with its own unique features and history. The first type can be considered data-driven reporting. This form of data journalism really amounts to a workflow more than a specific output at the end. This reporting begins with the data and includes the reporter cleaning the data—that is the process of checking it for gaps, ensuring it is complete and lacking in errors—and then analyzing it to find patterns or inconsistencies. This process helps the reporter develop a series of questions or potentially a theory of what is happening and perhaps directs the reporter to a specific area particularly affected or to ask questions of specific individuals. The idea is to start with the facts found in the data and then move to the more illustrative or anecdotal story that brings the data to life, rather than allowing the anecdote to drive the story. This helps ensure the characters a journalist may find in a story can be placed in a more data-driven context to clarify what aspect of the story they actually represent.

Data journalism has also come to be associated with a specific form of reporting that data-driven reporting can produce—visualizations. Data visualizations are essentially different types of data graphics that help the reader understand the story the journalists are trying to tell. These also have a long history in journalism, but the work of Edward Tufte whose 1983 book *The Visual Display of Quantitative Information* is widely credited with greatly expanding the field. *USA Today*, the daily newspaper launched by Gannett at about the same time introduced an infographic into the bottom corner of the front page of every section. This data graphic became a mainstay of the paper. As it grew in popularity and people like Tufte helped improve the artistry and accuracy of graphics, they became increasingly important tools. As the technology developed to create interactive graphics, the tools available to designers to tell stories with data also increased. One of those storytellers is David McCandless, a designer and journalist, who has given TED Talks and written books on the idea of data visualization. To hear McCandless describe his excitement over the use of data is to hear an artist describing his or her muse. He told listeners in 2010, "I would say that data is the new soil. Because for me, it feels like a fertile, creative medium. Over the years, online, we've laid down a huge amount of information and data, and we irrigate it with networks and connectivity . . . visualizations, infographics, data visualizations, they feel like flowers blooming from this medium. But if you look at it directly, it's just a lot of numbers and disconnected facts. But if you start working with it and playing with it in a certain way, interesting things can appear and different patterns can be revealed" (McCandless 2010). But in McCandless's description is the one thing that may complicate the relationship between data and the trust Rogers and others hopes it can bring to journalism. He mentioned when you start "playing" with the data you can find patterns and uncover new information. Data, in the end, is more like an expert interview than a truly different form of reporting. Data manipulated in a graphic, through its design, size, color, can be misleading.

Data journalism still has weak spots that journalists and consumers must watch out for. Data driven journalism is only as effective as the data it uses is correct. It is only as powerful as the reporters who can interpret and correctly reflect it are. Data visualizations will only tell the story as well as the designer and information analysts can do it. Still, these tools will clearly be a major part of political reporting as outlets—especially larger newsrooms and specialized data operations—mine the data rich environments of campaigns. From voter information to campaign finances, campaigns generate lots of data and fuel enormous volumes of data reporting. That will only increase as the years go by and the tools and journalists' comfort with data increases.

See also: American Communities Project; FiveThirtyEight (538); Vox

Further Reading

Fink, Katherine, and C.W. Anderson. 2014. "Data Journalism in the United States: Beyond the 'Usual Suspects.'" *Journalism Studies*.

Friendly, Michael. 2006. "A Brief History of Data Visualization." In *Handbook of Computational Statistics: Data Visualization*. Berlin, Germany: Springer.

Gray, Jonathan, Lucy Chambers, and Liliana Bounegru. 2012. *Data Journalism Handbook*. O'Reilly Media. Accessed June 25, 2015. http://datajournalismhandbook.org/1.0/en /introduction_2.html.

McCandless, David. 2010. "The Beauty of Data Visualization." July. Accessed June 25, 2015. http://www.ted.com/talks/david_mccandless_the_beauty_of_data_visualization /transcript?language=en.

Paul, Norm. 1999. *Computer-Assisted Research: A Guide to Tapping Online Information*. Chicago: Bonus Books.

Rogers, Simon. 2014. "Data Journalism Is the New Punk." *British Journalism Review*. June.

"What Is Data Journalism?" 2013. *Guardian*. April 4. Accessed June 26, 2015. http://www .theguardian.com/news/datablog/video/2013/apr/04/what-is-data-journalism-video.

DEMOCRATIC LEADERSHIP COUNCIL (DLC)

The Democratic Leadership Council represented an organized effort by moderates in the Democratic Party to combat what they saw as the increasingly liberal policies of the national party that threatened to keep the party in the minority and out of the White House. Unlike grassroots efforts like the tea party movement on the Republican side, the DLC was organized by political insiders and elected officials who saw their own influence in the party on the wane during the 1970s and 1980s. The DLC claimed President Bill Clinton, with his pledge to end the era of big government and his financial policies that balanced the federal budget, as their most successful political result.

The DLC formed in the wake of the most crushing Electoral College defeat in American history. The 1984 re-election of President Ronald Reagan saw former vice president Walter Mondale win only his home state of Minnesota and the District of Columbia. The scale of the defeat pushed many within the party to argue that the economic populism that had marked Mondale's campaign had become politically unacceptable to a majority of Americans. The DLC was formed to combat it. In announcing the council's formation in late February 1985, then-U.S. senator Sam Nunn stressed the need to reorient the national party. A *New York Times* piece about the new council reported, "'The moderate and conservative Democrats didn't make it past the first round of primaries in 1984 and we want to change that,' said Mr. Nunn, who supported Senator John Glenn of Ohio for the party's presidential nomination last year. 'There is a perception our party has moved away from mainstream America in the 1970s. Asked to be more specific, the senator declined, saying, 'The election results speak for themselves'" (Gailey 1985). The council was organized by southern governors, including Clinton, and moderate members of Congress and operated under the leadership of Al From, a political strategist who had worked with former president Jimmy Carter and in both chambers of Congress.

From and the DLC argued that the Democratic Party should develop a so-called Third Way of leadership that was not the traditional liberalism of the Democrats and not the laissez-faire deregulation of the Republican Party. This third option would focus on progressive policies that also were structured in a way to benefit business. The DLC raised significant cash from corporate donors to back its political work and policy proposals. The council promoted the type of politicians they argued could win national elections and proposed effective government reforms. The poster child of this group emerged from the small southern state of Arkansas. Bill Clinton had been one of the founding members of the DLC. His association with the group helped land him the coveted spot of keynote speaker at the 1988 Democratic National Convention. Four years later he would make a successful run for the presidency espousing politically progressive and economically moderate positions. His election in 1992 was seen as triumph of the DLC-branch of the Democratic Party as well as a rebuke of the more liberal wings of the party. Less than a year into his first term Clinton addressed a DLC meeting and outlined the moderate Democrat worldview, saying, "Because we are Democrats we believe in our party's historic values of opportunity, social justice, and an unshakable commitment to the interests of working men and women and their children. Because we are new Democrats we promote those old values in new ways. We believe in expanding opportunity, not Government. We believe in empowerment, not entitlement. We believe in leading the world, not retreating from it" (Clinton 1993).

The policies espoused by the DLC were and remain contentious among many Democratic activists. These included efforts like the controversial 1996 welfare reform, the tax policies that benefited business, and ending deficit spending. Clinton also promoted policies like national service and community policing that drew some applause from harder core Democrats, but the core argument of the DLC was that the policies that promoted a redistribution of wealth would simply lead to further electoral losses. They argued that their goal was to achieve liberal ends through market means. Their critics accused them of being pure political animals that would sell out core voting blocs of the historic Democrat Party for a win at the ballot box.

Although the DLC was in its heyday during the Clinton years, other forces were building in opposition to it, partly as a result of some of its own choices. For example, the DLC's attempt and failure to keep an active and vibrant party in the South weakened its standing. Also, electoral successes of Democrats in other parts of the country empowered activists to reassess the direction of the party. As often happens, once the DLC had successfully reoriented the party's directions, it struggled to find its new mission. By the rise of the next Democratic president after Clinton, the group had become more of a lightning rod. Barack Obama "largely avoided the Democratic Leadership Council—the centrist group that Bill Clinton once led— and, with an eye on his national political standing, has always shied away from the liberal label, too" (Martin and Lee 2009). Rising activist elements of the party— from the digital liberals that grew out of the Netroots movement to the veterans of the Clinton administration who ran the Center for American Progress—were advocating a more progressive view. In 2011, the DLC suspended its operations. Some of the more liberal elements saw this as a victory over the so-called corporatist wing of the Democratic Party. One, Progressive Congress president Darcy Burner, told Politico on the day the DLC announced its closure, "One of the things that's happening right now in Democratic politics is that progressives are winning the battle for the party. The corporate-focused DLC type of politics isn't working inside the Democratic party" (Smith 2011).

The DLC, and its descendants like the still-thriving Progressive Policy Institute, represent an ongoing tension in both political parties between the desire to appeal to enough voters to ensure an active role in government and the argument that a party must stand on principle. DLC advocates would argue that they are not just an electoral strategy but are a realignment of the national Democratic Party to a more moderate, less anti-business entity, just as its opponents argued the DLC was a threat to the real Democratic Party. The truth lies somewhere in between, but even with its closure in 2011, the efforts of moderates within the Democratic Party continue.

See also: Center for American Progress (CCAP); Liberal Think Tanks

Further Reading

Clinton, William. 1993. "Remarks to the Democratic Leadership Council." American Presidency Project. December 3. Accessed July 16, 2015. http://www.presidency.ucsb.edu/ws/?pid=46193.

Gailey, Phil. 1985. "Dissidents Defy Top Democrats; Council Formed." *New York Times*. March 1.

Martin, Jonathan, and Carol Lee. 2009. "Obama: 'I Am a New Democrat.'" Politico. March 10. Accessed July 15, 2015. http://www.politico.com/news/stories/0309/19862.html.

Smith, Ben. 2011. "The End of the Democratic Leadership Council Era." Politico. February 7. Accessed July 17, 2015. http://www.politico.com/news/stories/0211/49041.html.

DIRECT MAIL CAMPAIGNING

Begun in the late 1950s, direct mail marketing is the sending of letters, postcards, and flyers to specific voters for the purpose of raising funds, building name recognition, or attacking opponents. In many ways, it was the first technology that allowed candidates and campaigns to target specific voters with specific messages. And despite the onslaught of digital technology, email, and social networking, campaign professionals argue that direct mail remains—for state and local contests at least—a surprisingly potent tool in the campaign manager's arsenal and often operates under the radar of the traditional mainstream media.

Early efforts at using the mail to build support for political causes dates back as far as the early twentieth century when Woodrow Wilson sent letters out to encourage the public to support his proposed League of Nations. President Dwight Eisenhower was the first to use it for personal political gain, compiling a list of critical Republican backers he would need to mount a campaign for the nomination.

But from the outset, direct mail has really been the weapon of the insurgent. The critical players in the development of political mailings were outsiders seeking to influence the process or the party. A conservative who had become involved in politics in the 1950s as a member of the Young Americans for Freedom saw direct mail as a way to build support for more ideologically conservative Republicans struggling to succeed. Richard Viguerie was a quiet man from Texas, but held strong and passionate political views. Still, he was not one for oratory. Instead, he wrote letters—a lot of letters. His skill as a wordsmith allowed him to slowly build a list of like-minded conservatives. By 1964, Viguerie had a network of fellow conservatives he could use to help an insurgent Republican. That year, he helped the campaign of conservative Senator Barry Goldwater run against more mainstream moderate Republicans like Gov. Nelson Rockefeller. A Goldwater aide later recalled direct mail was really a result of a crass political reality that the Arizona senator's campaign had to face, saying, "We couldn't go to the fat cats, because they were all with either Rockefeller or [President Lyndon] Johnson, so we had to develop our own financial base . . . We had a need that had to be met, and we had some experts who knew how to do direct mail. Everybody does it now, but that was a revolution in fundraising back in '64" (Nowicki 2014). Viguerie was the brains behind that operation. He helped Goldwater win the nomination, although not the presidency. The next year he opened his own political consultancy and direct marketing company.

Viguerie would later use direct mail not just to advocate for conservatives like Goldwater and later Ronald Reagan, but also as weapon to attack his opponents. He worked tirelessly to battle President Gerald Ford, and sent thousands of letters to conservatives to undercut the policies of President Jimmy Carter. Even recently he has used direct mail to foment opposition to former Speaker John Boehner for not adhering enough to conservative principles.

But direct mail wasn't just a tool of the right. Morris Dees, while preparing to start the Southern Poverty Law Center in 1971, also backed anti-war candidate U.S. Senator George McGovern and his long-shot campaign for the Democratic nomination. Dees had already built a name for himself as a commercial direct marketer and had used many of the same techniques to raise funds for his center. He recalled how in January 1971 the McGovern campaign asked for his help in drafting a letter to go out to announce the liberal senator's campaign, saying, "They showed me a draft, one page letter that announced his candidacy and said he was opposed to the war. And it was just a nice well-written letter. And I said, well, hey fellas, how you all going to fund this campaign? And they said, well, we got, you know, some wealthy donors who are going to kick in some money throughout the country. I said, well, why don't we take this letter you're fixing to send out announcing your campaign, and let me draft a fundraising pitch in it? And they said OK" (NPR 2012). Dees came up with a seven-page, impassioned plea to rise up against the Vietnam War and support the South Dakota senator—both politically and financially. The team rejected the length of the letter, cut it back to one page and left the fundraising ask. Dees sent his original longer letter anyway, paying for it out of his own pocket. The results took everyone (except Dees) by surprise, raising hundreds of thousands for the campaign. McGovern's campaign would send some 15 million pieces of mail that year and raise almost as much money in donations from these letters.

For opposition candidates on both sides of the aisle, direct mail emerged as a critical fundraising tool and a mode of attack. Though Viguerie pioneered both, he is famous for his direct mail attacks more than his pleas for support. In a book not-so-subtly titled *America's Right Turn: How Conservatives Used New and Alternative Media to Take Power*, he described how he saw the tool, writing, "The interesting thing about direct mail is that when it's professionally done, it has a devastating impact. It's like using a water moccasin for a watchdog—very quiet and very effective" (Viguerie and Franke 2004, p. 136). And both of those elements are important to understand, in terms of why direct mail campaigns have remained a critical part of the campaign landscape in the United States. Unlike television ads, which are costly and fairly easy to track, direct mail is much more under the radar of most media coverage. Few of the mailers are ever fact-checked and little national media attention is ever paid to mailings unless their claims reach the most incendiary or offensive levels.

Many mailers are used simply raise to awareness of a candidate or issue in the minds of the voters. Direct mail offers candidates and advocacy groups one of the most inexpensive ways to get material in front of voters and to do so in a fairly targeted way. And this targeting of messages is important to note as experts argue, "Each recipient can be targeted, not only by name and address, but also by the messages to which he or she is most likely to respond. This creates a sense of personal contact" (Sherman 1999, p. 373). This targeting takes two forms, one geographic and one demographic. The geographic one can seem pretty obvious—mail every home in a given legislative district or zip code—but it actually has become far more sophisticated as those hoping to cash in on campaigns offer new tools and services. The first provider isn't a consulting firm or direct mail operation, but the U.S. Postal Service, which rakes in millions of dollars every campaign cycle. USPS has even gone so far as to produce a 10-page brochure and suite of tools campaigns can use to target mailings. One service the postal service offers is called Every Door Direct Mail, which easily allows any marketer, including campaigns, to target specific mail routes or key demographic groups based on income or age. The brochure claims, "It's like going door-to-door via the Post Office." But figuring out what routes or specific parts of a district to target can be difficult, so on top of EDDM itself, an array of companies have developed methods and lists that help campaigns use EDDM to hit the right voters at the right time.

In fact, building and perfecting these lists is what created the companies like Viguerie's and made them so powerful. The list of voters to hit with direct mail or door-to-door visits was a skill set all campaigns sought and approached an art form. Especially in the pre-Internet, social media marketing days, these firms were seen as real powerbrokers in the campaign process. Their lists of voters were actually fairly advanced databases of not just voter names but party registration, issues the voter supported or opposed, marital status, income, likelihood of voting, whether they owned or rented their home, unions or associations they belonged to, and history of political activities. These lists informed major swaths of campaign activity and have led to campaigns developing mailers that targeted different types of supporter—parents, those who support gay and lesbian rights, churchgoers, etc. The importance of this information, according to professional direct mail advisers, cannot be overstated. As long-time Richard Schlackman and Michael Hoffman wrote, "Your award-winning brochure is worthless if it isn't delivering the right message to the right people . . . persuasion direct mail is only as good as the names you choose to mail it to" (Schlackman and Hoffman 2003, p. 340).

But many political observers watched first in 2004 with the Howard Dean campaign and then in 2008 with the rise of Barack Obama as the Internet and social media became powerful organizing and fundraising tools, overshadowing the mail brochure. Campaigns invested heavily in building and maintaining their own voter databases and using those tools to direct specific information to them via email, text, or Facebook post. The era of direct mail seemed dated, a campaign dinosaur. Even early in the advent of the Internet, pollsters and political consultants were warning that the best days of direct mail were past. In 1995 Democratic pollster Mark Mellman found Baby Boomers and other younger generations were far less likely to respond to direct mail solicitations. The expectation was that direct mail would quietly transform into newer Internet-based marketing efforts, leaving "snail" mail behind.

But something funny happened—direct mail is still thriving. One analysis from Politico found that with three months left to go in the 2014 election cycle, campaigns had already spent $150 million on direct mail. One direct mail consultant for Republican candidates summed it up by saying, "In terms of moving the needle, it's very effective because people still read their mail and some even keep it around. It's got a shelf life. It's cheaper, and you can reach a more targeted audience" (Parti 2014). Analysts have pointed to a variety of reasons for this dogged role played by the physical mail—the ease with which email can be cast aside without ever opening, let alone reading it; the tangible reality of a piece of mail; and the fact that people still only have one physical mailbox.

Although direct mail continues to exist, there have been some clear changes over the years. It is hard to imagine a seven-page campaign announcement with a donation solicitation showing up at your door today. Instead most modern direct mailers are brightly colored, oversized postcards featuring smiling candidates offering very general versions of the key talking points, or the other branch of direct mail, dark attack ads featuring creepy, often black-and-white photos of the targeted candidate(s).

Direct mail is also still being used by outsiders seeking to change a party or punish those who don't adhere to certain positions. In 2008 in Montana an outside group—Western Tradition Partnership—flooded a few Republican primary campaigns with mailers in the closing days of the primary. One Republican targeted was state senator John Ward who told his story to *Frontline* in 2012. Mailers read

"John Ward voted with criminal-coddling liberal activists" and accused him of being soft on child predators and supporting policies that raised energy prices. "Are high energy prices killing you?" Ward said the mailers showed up in "within the last four days (before the primary). You have no time to respond that way . . . The impact of receiving these graphic things right before you went to the polls—it was very, very effective" (Frontline 2012). The conservative Republican lost by 24 votes.

The story of John Ward demonstrates not only the role of outside groups but also the reason why direct mail continues to affect the political process. By creating cheap and effective ways to communicate to a certain district or a certain type of voter, direct mail remains a powerful weapon for candidates and advocacy organizations. It is one that lands, literally, in the hands of voters and can be timed to appear just before a ballot is cast. By flying under journalists' radar, it can also land stronger punches that are harder to fact-check and leave more of a mark.

See also: Microtargeting

Further Reading
"Big Sky, Big Money." PBS Frontline. October 30, 2012. Accessed June 16, 2015. http://www.pbs.org/wgbh/pages/frontline/government-elections-politics/big-sky-big-money/transcript-32.
"McGovern Campaign Marked Beginning of Direct Mail." NPR. August 1, 2012. Accessed June 16, 2015. http://www.npr.org/2012/08/01/157739995/mcgovern-campaign-marked-beginning-of-direct-mail.
Nowicki, Dan. 2014. "Direct Mail Another Legacy of '64 Goldwater Campaign." Arizona Republic. April 12. Accessed June 17, 2015. http://www.azcentral.com/story/azdc/2014/04/13/direct-mail-goldwater-legacy/7622041.
Parti, Tarini. 2014. "An Unlikely Survivor in the Digital Age: Direct Mail." *Politico*. August 3. Accessed June 14, 2015. http://www.politico.com/story/2014/08/an-unlikely-survivor-in-the-digital-age-direct-mail-109673.html.
Schlackman, Richard, and Michael Hoffman. 2003. "Direct Mail." In *Winning Elections: Political Campaign Management, Strategy & Tactics*, edited by Ron Fauchaux. Lanham, MD: Rowman & Littlefield.
Sherman, Elaine. 1999. "Direct Marketing: How Does It Work for Political Campaigns?" in *Handbook of Political Marketing*. Edited by Bruce Newman. Thousand Oaks, CA: Sage Publications.
Viguerie, Richard, and David Franke. 2004. *America's Right Turn: How Conservatives Used New and Alternative Media to Take Power*. Los Angeles: Bonus Books.

DISCLOSURE

In the wake of critical Supreme Court decisions that struck down or severely curtailed government abilities to regulate or limit the amount of money flowing into elections, the idea of disclosure has become a major focus of the debate. Initially seen as the most basic defense against the possible corrupting influence of money on the political process, the idea of publicly releasing the names and professions of political donors is increasingly being challenged by those who seek to further scale back government regulations of elections and argue disclosure inhibits people's willingness to participate in the political process due to public pressure.

From the very beginning of formal campaign finance reform laws, many have advocated disclosure as one of the core concepts that government should undertake both to battle corruption and to encourage voter education. The first major bill to address this idea was the Publicity Act of 1910—later amended in 1911 to become the Federal Corrupt Practices Act. The act targeted groups that sought to influence elections in more than one state and required the group submit all spending above $10 to the clerk of the House of Representatives. The report was to be filed 10–15 days before the election. Spurred by a series of scandals connected to corporate spending aimed at affecting elections, congressional reformers argued the goal of the 1910 act was to protect the sanctity of the ballot. Democratic Representative William Rucker argued, "Each ballot should represent the untrammeled will and best judgment of a free American citizen" (Hohenstein 2007). The act was passed and became the part of the earliest efforts at political reform. It was similar to the core sentiment that most often is associated with the idea of disclosure in politics from Supreme Court Justice Louis Brandeis, who in 1914 wrote, "Publicity is justly commended as a remedy for social and industrial diseases. Sunlight is said to be the best of disinfectants; electric light the most efficient policeman."

But for all its significance, the law held a series of fatal flaws within it. First, the clerk of the House of Representatives was poorly equipped to deal with the paperwork and tracking of spending. Additionally, the office received little support or guidance on enforcement. The act included provisions for large fines or even jail on violating the law, but the clerk had no real enforcement mechanisms. Lastly, the law did nothing to promote the publication of this information, so what paperwork was turned in sat at the clerk's office in the Capitol. Only the most intrepid reporters would make their way into the office to check on filings; reporters in states across the country essentially had no way to access the information.

Despite these problems, this was essentially the law until 1971 when Congress overhauled campaign laws with the Federal Election Campaign Act (FECA). During a series of reforms in the 1970s, the federal government moved the disclosure requirements to a new agency, the Federal Election Commission, and included new goals of collecting and publicizing campaign donations and expenditures. The new agency also had more enforcement authority and as opposed to the clerk's office, which oversaw the entire functioning of the House of Representatives, the FEC had only one job, monitoring campaigns for federal office. In studying how FECA and FEC changed campaign finance, most analysts agree that "while there is substantial criticism of the commission's enforcement activities, there is also a recognition that much more is known about campaign finance practices as a result of the FECA's disclosure provisions . . . The commission has gone beyond the statutory requirements to make contribution and expenditure data available to the public in a useful format" (Magleby and Nelson 1990). The FEC worked to create a regular flow of information through scheduled deadlines that reporters and campaign officials knew. Even prior to the Internet, the FEC would make available reports on campaign spending and lobbying and other reports filed with their office within days of receiving the filings. This fed into the coverage of campaigns and served as a source for reporting after the election as well, as reporters monitored how candidates who had received money from certain groups behaved once in office.

The Internet and digital technologies made disclosed contributions and spending available with a mouse click, and fundamentally changed the world of campaign financing. Now, reports no longer need to be formally filed and mailed to the FEC; information can move from campaign to the government and the government to the public practically instantaneously. Outside groups like the Center for Responsive Politics have developed OpenSecrets.org to facilitate understanding by the public and reporters about what can be found in the thousands of FEC documents. This new digital structure has also allowed people to connect donors and their contributions to several different candidates or over multiple years. Disclosure moved from being something you could track to one campaign or for one cycle, to being able to see at the click of a mouse a decades-long history of campaign donations by an individual.

Also notable about the idea of disclosure is the apparent consistency with which the courts have agreed to its importance. Even as the Supreme Court has struck down portions of campaign finance reforms—beginning as early as 1970s and continuing to the present day—the concept of publication of this information has passed the legal tests it has faced. One of the latest endorsements of disclosure came in 2014, when the Supreme Court struck down so-called aggregate limits on the amount of money individuals could contribute to candidates and party committees in a given two-year election cycle. The decision in *McCutcheon v. Federal Election Commission* was seen by most campaign finance reform advocates as yet another blow to the government's efforts to produce a fair election system, but within it was the latest endorsement in the importance of public reporting of campaign spending and fundraising. Chief Justice John Roberts, writing for the five justices of the majority, contended that "disclosure requirements . . . may deter corruption 'by exposing large contributions and expenditures to the light of publicity.' (*Buckley*) Disclosure requirements may burden speech, but they often represent a less restrictive alternative to flat bans on certain types or quantities of speech. Particularly with modern technology, disclosure now offers more robust protections against corruption than it did when Buckley was decided."

As much solace as campaign reformers may take in the *McCutcheon* comments, some constitutional scholars have warned that the legal rationale for disclosure is not as solid as it may seem. In one recent article, constitutional expert and campaign finance veteran Anthony Johnstone contends that most of the legal protection of the importance of disclosure "remains theoretically underdeveloped." He adds, "Without a clear constitutional justification, the informational interest does less than it might to define the means and ends of disclosure policy, and to defend that policy against constitutional challenge" (Johnstone 2011).

Even though the high court has protected the idea of disclosure, it has faced repeated attacks from actors in the political arena. The attacks on disclosure come from both sides. Reformers see a focus on disclosure as not aggressive enough to solve the real problems in our political system. One critique argued the entire idea of transparency had been "vastly oversold" because the average voter can't readily "learn about the ins and outs of the numerous programs the government carries out; evaluate their effectiveness and costs; and determine which they favor or are keen to change or discontinue" (Etzioni 2014). These reformers argue that publication of information is not enough to hold back abuse of the system, and that government should rightfully have an active role in regulating campaigns.

Conservative groups, on the other hand, have launched a more serious legal and political assault on disclosure, wishing to roll it back. Many of these cases have been championed by James Bopp, a lawyer from Terra Haute, Indiana. Bopp takes a purist approach to the First Amendment rights of people to participate in politics, arguing anything that impedes participation in the political discussion should be unconstitutional. In a 2012 report on the PBS documentary series *Frontline*, Bopp said that the case for disclosure has been radically overstated because, "Truth doesn't change because of who's funding it," adding that most public disclosures contain "completely irrelevant information that only some left-wing nut jobs care about." He also made the case, often repeated in conservative circles, that any disclosure law has a chilling effect on speech, saying, "Secrecy in government is not good, and secrecy about what politicians are doing is not good, but anonymity for citizens is [a] very important concept, because otherwise people won't associate with them" (Frontline 2012). Advocates of this position point to the case of Brendan Eich to demonstrate the perils of disclosure. Eich made a $1,000 donation to promote the controversial Proposition 8 in California, a ballot initiative seeking to ban same-sex marriage in the state. The donation was made public in 2012, but few made any note of it, until he was selected to head Mozilla, the nonprofit organization that makes the popular Firefox browser. News of the donation spread, and employees and others were outraged. They launched a full public relations campaign against him, including a call by dating site OkCupid to boycott using Firefox so long as Eich ran the company. Under pressure, he stepped down. Conservative columnist Charles Krauthammer said this caused him to reevaluate his position on transparency. Two weeks after Eich was ousted, Krauthammer wrote, "I had not foreseen how donor lists would be used not to ferret out corruption but to pursue and persecute citizens with contrary views. Which corrupts the very idea of full disclosure." He went on to argue that the core idea of disclosure is to prevent corruption—you cannot buy someone's vote or a politician—but in the case of Eich it was a referendum or what he called "a pure expression of one's beliefs. Full disclosure in that context becomes a cudgel, an invitation to harassment . . . The ultimate victim here is full disclosure itself. If revealing your views opens you to the politics of personal destruction, then transparency, however valuable, must give way to the ultimate core political good, free expression" (Krauthammer 2014).

Johnstone and other backers of the idea of disclosure may well worry about running into this idea in the near future. Even as the Supreme Court has backed the idea of transparency, it also has clear precedent on the issue of groups disclosing its members. In 1956, the attorney general of Alabama went after the National Association for the Advancement of Colored People (NAACP) for violating its state laws about foreign corporations. The law required the group register and when taken to court, the Alabama court demanded documentation from the NAACP headquarters in New York that included its members. The NAACP produced all the required documents except the list, and the Alabama courts held the organization in contempt. The case went all the way to the Supreme Court and in 1958 in *NAACP v. Patterson*, a unanimous court ruled that "immunity from state scrutiny of petitioner's membership lists is here so related to the right of petitioner's members to pursue their lawful private interests privately and to associate freely with others in doing so as to come within the protection of the Fourteenth Amendment." Bopp and others are quick to point to the NAACP case as precedent that disclosure in political activities may violate this decision. So far, the court has not agreed.

The other argument put forward by conservative critics of disclosure has to do with whether the public cares. This line of reasoning finds that the public is so inundated with information that they choose to largely ignore campaign finance data. They argue, "Public opinion polls have found that respondents are largely ignorant of campaign finance laws and care little about finance reform. Given their rational ignorance about the laws and apathy about the issue, it seems unlikely that voters use the data. If they do, their concerns about a donation may be outweighed by other considerations in voting for or against a candidate" (Samples 2008). Therefore the underlying public interest should not outweigh the potential effect on political participation. One social science experiment conducted by the conservative Institute for Justice found that when readers consumed an array of articles and information brochures, they rated the information about campaign finance the least useful, which led the researcher to conclude that "viewing disclosure information had virtually no impact on participants' knowledge" (Primo 2011).

As the court settles into the new precedent around campaign finance laws established primarily by *Citizens United*, the next real battleground appears to be shaping up around this idea of transparency and disclosure. On the one hand, a majority of the Supreme Court as well as good government groups and nearly a century of laws appear on the side of encouraging the release of information about campaign donations. But with some precedent on their side and a growing army of political dark money groups raising money from undisclosed donors, critics of transparency will continue to make the argument that if spending money on politics is afforded free speech protections, the government interest in transparency may not be enough to inhibit the free flow of speech.

See also: Campaign Finance Reform; *Citizens United*

Further Reading

Etzioni, Amitai. 2014. "Transparency Is Overrated." *The Atlantic*. January 13. Accessed June 24, 2015. http://www.theatlantic.com/politics/archive/2014/01/transparency-is -overrated/282990.

Frontline. 2012. "Big Sky, Big Money." PBS. October 30. Accessed June 22, 2015. http:// www.pbs.org/wgbh/frontline/film/big-sky-big-money.

Hohenstein, Kurt. 2007. *Coining Corruption: The Making of the American Campaign Finance System*. DeKalb: Northern Illinois University Press.

Johnstone, Anthony. 2012. "A Madisonian Case for Disclosure." *George Mason Law Review*.

Krauthammer, Charles. 2014. "The Zealots Win Again." *Washington Post*. April 17. Accessed June 23, 2015. http://www.washingtonpost.com/opinions/charles-krauthammer-the -zealots-win-again/2014/04/17/ac0b6466-c654-11e3-8b9a-8e0977a24aeb_story.html.

Magleby, David, and Candice Nelson. 1990. *The Money Chase: Congressional Campaign Finance Reform*. Washington, DC: The Brookings Foundation.

Primo, David. 2011. "Full Disclosure: How Campaign Finance Disclosure Laws Fail to Inform Voters and Stifle Public Debate." Institute for Justice. Accessed June 22, 2015. http:// www.rochester.edu/College/PSC/primo/FullDisclosurePrimoIJReport.pdf.

Samples, John. 2008. *The Fallacy of Campaign Finance Reform*. Chicago: University of Chicago.

DIVERSITY IN THE NEWS MEDIA

According to voter opinion polls, the 1982 California governor race was a lock. Democratic candidate Tom Bradley, then-mayor of Los Angeles, was running well ahead of his rival, Republican attorney general George Deukmejian, by hefty margins. The *San Francisco Chronicle* went so far as to project Bradley would be the state's first black governor on the morning of November 3, 1982, based in large part on exit polls. However, in the early morning hours, with 98 percent of precincts counted, Deukmejian had edged out Bradley with a lead less than one percentage point in what the Associated Press called "the closest race for the post in state history."

The race results were puzzling, considering the decidedly overwhelming voter support for Bradley in opinion polls leading up to Election Day. Pundits were analyzing what went wrong for days. Warren Mitofsky, a CBS Network News election director, told reporters from the *Santa Ana Orange County Register* that polls are commonly reliable. "You can do these things (projections) with a fair amount of accuracy. There's a lot of professional people who do this for a living . . . Why they had problems with it, I don't know" (Churml and Taugher 1982). But some who analyzed the results saw something beneath the discrepancy between polling and election results. Another network pollster, Mervin Field, concluded that race was the leading factor in Bradley's loss, citing his exit poll findings that three percent of voters who supported Deukmejian said "that they could not vote for a black man."

The election created the oft-used and controversial term "The Bradley Effect," an observation that voters express support for candidates of color in opinion polls but cast votes for other candidates in voting booths. According to the theory, voters tend to discount race as a factor in their decision-making when questioned face-to-face about candidates of color. Statisticians and pundits have since argued against the presence of the Bradley Effect. Still, there are similar stories from other parts of the country with nearly identical factors. "The Wilder Effect," for example, is cited after a black Virginia gubernatorial candidate, Douglas Wilder, won his race by two percentage points. Before that, polls had him winning by nearly 20 points. Similar "effect" anecdotes can be found regarding the presidential election of Barack Obama and other black candidates throughout the country. The argument over racial effects as a factor in voting is just one example of the complex ways in which the media and campaign worlds are affected by the politics of race and ethnicity.

Race-based journalism has always been a sensitive area for newsrooms, in particular for election coverage. Without a keen understanding of multi-ethnic communities and people, unforeseen miscalculations and error-prone analyses are likely to occur. It is important to note that diversity in the news media—both in newsrooms and in the news product—is not a matter of being politically correct. There is a utility in gathering and disseminating voices from all pockets of society, a utility that most journalists hold in the highest regard. Diversity is a matter of accuracy, and without that, journalists run the risk of creating an unrealistic image with little to no grasp of the authentic American experience.

Despite this benefit, news companies have been struggling to address diversity in their newsrooms for decades with mixed results. According to the American Society of Newspaper Editors, which has conducted an annual national newsroom audit since 1978, the percentage of journalists of color working in American newsrooms has actually dropped since 2010. In 2015, newspaper managers reported that 12.8 percent of newsroom staff consisted of people of color. In 2010, the percentage of minorities in newsrooms was reported at 13.3—both are significantly higher than the approximately 4 percent reported in 1978 (ASNE 2015). This person-of-color ratio has remained fairly steady throughout the recent waves of job decreases in the industry.

In their book *Race, Multiculturalism, and the Media*, Wilson and Gutierrez describe the traditional newspaper business cycle, which began with publications feeding readers to advertisers, who in turn became the main revenue source for newspapers. As a result, media coverage evolved its content to attract the highest number of readers, content that informed but also reinforced the ideals and perceptions of the largest reading demographic in the country: Caucasian males. Other groups fell by the wayside as media began to appeal to a skewed definition of the mass society. "Mass society in the United States did not necessarily mean a society of the masses, but a society in which the people were amassed into an audience for the messages of the mass media of communication" (Wilson and Gutierrez 1995). And that message soon adapted the ideals of its readership, covering ethnic issues through the lens of a dominant society ignoring or stereotyping minorities. For decades, the media and the mass society functioned together, feeding each other the same images of minority groups in an endless cycle.

A concerted effort to both improve the coverage of minority issues and increase the presence of minorities as news producers didn't begin in earnest until the Civil Rights era. The media played an integral role, mostly (but not always) as advocates, in the Civil Rights demonstrations throughout the American South and eventually throughout the country. And beginning in the 1980s, the Gannett Company became a leader in diversity initiatives in the media. The company not only recruited heavily from pools of journalists of color, it also created nationally recognized programs designed specifically to train young journalists of color and place them in newsrooms. Gannett also implemented stringent goals in its newsrooms designed to increase the presence of ethnically diverse people on the news pages. Nieman Reports, a Harvard-based journal, reported in 2003 that 17.1 percent of Gannett's collective staff were journalists of color, almost five percentage points higher than the national average as reported by the ASNE census that year.

Gannett, also implemented the controversial "mainstreaming" policy in its newsrooms. Defined as "the appropriate use of minority experts in the reporting of stories" (Witosky 2003), the policy was designed to encourage reporters to find the best methods in which to include minority experts and sources into all but breaking stories. This meant expanding some stories to include minority schools or institutions, or expanding reporting to include perspectives from people of color in larger stories. As part of the policy, newsrooms maintained a list of sources consisting of people of color. Of course, the mainstreaming policy was met with controversy and some setbacks. The lists, for instance, meant that some newspapers ended up calling the same sources for multiple stories. And in 2002, following the *New York Times* scandal in which a young black reporter, Jayson Blair, was discovered to have plagiarized or outright faked a number of stories, efforts to heavily recruit people of color then fell under scrutiny. Some journalists and critics argued the policies had pushed newsrooms to promote young journalists of color before they were ready, creating unfair pressure on the employee and less qualified journalists in the field.

Gannett executives are quick to note that diversity efforts are designed as a utility, an effort to maintain credibility with the communities they cover. In other words, this is one method in which newsrooms are trying to expand and reconfigure the mass society established by the news outlets of old. But it also should be noted, many of these questions of diversity focused only on differences between whites and blacks. And while news outlets worked to improve coverage of black communities, it was still common for smaller groups to be misrepresented with stereotypical imagery. In his "Reporting in Indigenous Communities" project, Duncan McCue, a reporter with the Canadian Broadcasting Corporation in Vancouver, British Columbia, argued that North American news organizations present five common stereotypes when producing pieces on Native Americans and First Nations People. These stereotypes are summed up simply: Warrior, Drumming, Dancing, Drunk, and Dead.

Warrior: McCue harkens to Wilson and Gutierrez's assertion that minority groups were at one point only covered when threatening the greater mass society. "Why does direct action by Aboriginal groups (such as marches, blockades, or occupations) receive disproportionate attention from news media?" McCue asks. On the other end of the spectrum, McCue also notes the "Good Indian" stereotype, the feature profile about a student attending college and doing well "despite" being Native American.

Drumming: Drumming has become synonymous with Native American and First Nations People. Modern day media still commonly use stock sound tracks (often completely unrelated to a particular tribe's musical culture) to fill in the background of Native American stories.

Dancing: Much like drumming, the image of the dancing Native American is ubiquitous in mass media, often in stories taken from powwows. However, McCue asks us to look at the equivalent, using country and western dancing at bars to portray how small town America holds on to its culture. Powwows—and the dances, art, and outfits used within—represent only a sliver of modern day Native American culture.

Drunk: McCue focuses bluntly on the most common stereotype of the drunken Indian. He points out that abstinence is twice as common in the tribal community than it is in the non-tribal. Yet, alcohol and its abuse is a common thread in stories from Indian Country.

Dead: Once again, there is truth to the news content that focuses on poverty, health issues, and high mortality rates. However, it also ignores a greater story of survival, happiness, and familial strength in the face of modern American luxuries. McCue finds that the images and stories presented by mass media about Native Americans paint a consistently bleak picture, one often at odds with the larger reality of modern Native American life.

A stereotype may have roots in truth, but gross oversimplification feeds a mass media image of ethnic groups that often bears little resemblance to reality. And such a media approach pertains to all communities of color. Most times, news outlets report modern stereotypes without realizing they are making sweeping generalizations. Obviously, if a rash of alcohol-related deaths were to strike on a tribal reservation, that news should be reported. But news outlets should consciously recognize when its reporting feeds stereotypes, and when it challenges them.

American media is often viewed as a bastion of liberal ideology. Therefore, it is easy to dismiss the plight for diversity in the media as a means to be more politically correct. However, by both staffing newsrooms and supplying news content with diverse voices, news media can curtail the use of lazy stereotypes that working journalists might not even realize exist. There is also a basic truth to the benefits of diversifying the news. If a news outlet sets out to cover its community, what does that coverage look like? How often do journalists look at the census demographics of a community and use that to better reflect the population in news content? For instance, if a community has a 10 percent black population, can the average reader see that 10 percent in the news product? And if so, how are the sources and subject used? Qualitative use of sources of color is just as important as quantitative. It's not enough to meet a quota of diverse voices, but to use them in a way that accurately reflects the greater society. A major recent study found that white Americans tend to overestimate the amount of crime committed by people of color, and that media outlets reinforce this perspective by their coverage of African Americans and Latinos. "Television news programs and newspapers over-represent racial minorities as crime suspects and whites as crime victims. Black and Latino suspects are also more likely than whites to be presented in a non-individualized and threatening way—unnamed and in police custody" (Ghandnoosh 2014). Beyond such obvious and extreme examples, journalists should also be keenly aware of more subtle instances. If 90 percent of black sources are used in the sports section, then what is the media telling readers about the community's black population?

This goal of better representing the diverse communities that media report on is becoming a necessity. America is changing rapidly. The demographics are shifting. The U.S. census indicates that people who identify as an ethnicity other than white will become the majority by 2020. Journalists will have to take greater focus on how to cover not only communities of color but also politicians of color. Richard Prince, who publishes a daily column about diversity in journalism, pointed out a comment President Obama made in 2009 during a speech on race relations in America. "I've noticed that when I talk about personal responsibility in the African American community, that gets highlighted. But then the whole other half of the speech, where I talked about government's responsibility . . . that somehow doesn't make news" (Prince 2009). A *New York Times* headline, as Prince pointed out, was blunt in its mischaracterization: "Obama Tells Fellow Blacks: 'No Excuses' for Failure." Obama offered no excuses in his speech, he did describe the reality, which is that people of color have disadvantages, singling out the challenge of getting a "world-class education" in particular. The headline was accurate, but it also lacked context. Much like a racial stereotype is based, on some level, in truth. Without the proper context, the meaning is misinterpreted and the message tainted.

Faced with an ethnically changing population and stories like terrorism, policing policies, and equal rights that are inherently controversial and racially charged, the media has struggled to convey the diversity of experiences different groups in the nation face. This reporting carries over into political reporting, where reporters and candidates often focus on issues that are a concern to white middle class voters. Other issues, like a rash of police shootings of black men in 2015, have driven some coverage but these issues seldom become major topics on the campaign trail and are often contextualized as a campaign strategy to attract minority voters. This gap in reporting is just another example that the relative lack of diversity in many newsrooms continues to plague its coverage of modern American politics.

Jason Begay

See also: Women and the News Media

Further Reading

American Society of Newspaper Editors. 2015. Minority Employment in Daily Newspapers. Newsroom Census. http://asne.org/content.asp?pl=140&sl=129&contentid=129.

Churml, Steven, and Mary Taugher. 1982. "Some Election Forecasters Became Lost in the Fog." *The Register*. November 4.

Ghandnoosh, Nazgol. 2014. "Race and Punishment: Racial Perceptions of Crime and Support for Punitive Policies." The Sentencing Project. Accessed January 27, 2016. http:// sentencingproject.org/doc/publications/rd_Race_and_Punishment.pdf.

Hopkins, Daniel J. 2009. "No More Wilder Effect, Never a Whitman Effect: When and Why Polls Mislead about Black and Female Candidates." 2009. *The Journal of Politics* 71, no. 3. July. Accessed January 20, 2016. http://people.iq.harvard.edu/~dhopkins/wilder13.pdf.

Los Angeles Times Editorial Board. 2008. "The 'Bradley Effect' Myth." *Los Angeles Times*. November 4. Accessed January 20, 2016.

McCue, Duncan. 2011. "Reporting in Indigenous Communities." Developed under the John S. Knight Journalism Fellowship at Stanford. Accessed January 20, 2016. http:// www.riic.ca.

Prince, Richard. 2009. "Obama Irritated by Race Coverage." Maynard Institute. July 19. Accessed January 28, 2016. http://mije.org/richardprince/obama-irritated-race-coverage.

Wilson III, Clint C., and Felix Gutierrez. 1995. *Race, Multiculturalism and the Media*. Thousand Oaks, CA: Sage Publications.

Witosky, Tom. 2003. "Mainstreaming and Diversity Are Gannett's Core Values." Nieman Reports. September 15. Accessed January 20, 2016. http://niemanreports.org/articles /mainstreaming-and-diversity-are-gannetts-core-values.

DOCUMENTARY FILMS

Documentaries, especially those about public affairs issues or overtly political topics, have remained one of the most potent forms of media aimed at raising awareness or urgency of a topic, finding increased audiences through the growth of digital streaming services and compelling storytelling. These filmmakers often carry an overt agenda into their work, turning their filmmaking tools to making a case for why the issue at hand should be addressed by the powers that be. The films have found sizable audiences on the web and some television networks, creating a platform for advocacy and investigation that pushes against the rushed nature of the modern news cycle, spending months and years exploring a topic.

Films have often had an overt political message. The silent epic entertainment *The Birth of a Nation* chronicled, in a troublingly sympathetic light, the rise of the Ku Klux Klan. But that film was fiction; soon filmmakers were using the tools and power of the moving picture to tell factual stories. In particular, the Communist-backed Workers Film and Photo League that developed in the 1930s aimed to inspire fellow workers and industrial groups with their documentaries about an anti-hunger march that police shut down in Detroit and the communal inspired film *Hands* in 1934 produced for the Depression-era Works Progress Administration. These works all carried an overt political message and their distribution was limited. Still, the potential of motion pictures to convey powerful political messages was clear. In the years after World War II, political documentaries appeared to split, with some pursuing a more journalistic course and others diving deeper into political movements. On the journalistic side, the team at CBS News under the guidance of Fred Friendly and Edward R. Murrow offered what could be seen as perhaps the first long-form television news documentary in 1960 with its *Harvest of Shame*. Murrow, who was perhaps the most recognizable and respected journalist in the wake of his feud with anti-communist crusader Joseph McCarthy, took to the CBS airwaves on the day after Thanksgiving to report on the plight of migrant farm workers. "We present this report on Thanksgiving because, were it not for the labor of the people you are going to meet, you might not starve, but your table would not be laden with the luxuries that we have all come to regard as essentials," he said during the open of the hour-long documentary (CBS 2010). The film mixed powerful scenes of poverty and desperation among those who harvest the food for the wealthiest nation in the world with interviews with farmers, policymakers, and social activists. In tone and structure it was the clear predecessor of PBS's *Frontline* series and the best of what would become *60 Minutes* on CBS. But even this form of reporting carried with it a strong sense of agenda. Murrow did not just present the difficult lives of those who traveled the country with the harvest, seeking to make a living that would support them through the winter; he also mixed in overt calls for action, noting at the close of the documentary, "The people you have seen have the strength to harvest your fruit and vegetables. They do not have the strength to influence legislation. Maybe we do." And people did react, according to Greg Schell, an attorney with the Migrant Farmworker Justice Project, who credited Murrow with being a "crusader," telling NPR, "He came and said, 'We can change this, people, if you get aroused and demand that the government and Congress react.' And Congress did react" (Blair 2014). The documentary is credited with helping spur congressional action like funding for health services to migrant workers and education for migrants' children.

Many filmmakers wanted to push even further to impact political movements overtly, aligning their work directly with the groups advocating change and being less concerned with constructs of traditional journalism. These documentarians aimed to provoke reaction and to alter the current political environment. "For Julia Reichert, a filmmaker who has made a career out of films like *Growing Up Female* (1974) and *Union Maids* (1976)—docs about women's liberation—and *Seeing Red* (1983)—a portrait of the American Communist Party—political docs 'are not about the ego of the filmmakers or aesthetic ideals.' Political docs are instead about raising the consciousness of audiences" (Baldwin and Bahar 2004). These films sometimes struggled to find an audience, as many traditional film distributors saw only limited appeal to the genre. Still, filmmakers expanded on the effort. *Harlan County USA*, a 1976 film about a coal mining strike in Kentucky, resonated with many audiences and certainly put the coal mining debate on the national agenda in a way it had not been.

Beginning in 1942, the Academy of Motion Picture Arts and Sciences has presented an Oscar to the film selected the best documentary of the previous year, and these awards helped spur further interest from some. But perhaps one of the most important developments in history of the political documentary was the strengthening of the Public Broadcasting Service (PBS). This publicly funded network began a series of programs—*Frontline*, *POV*, and *Independent Lens*—that offered these films nationwide exposure. PBS was the first and remains the only broadcast network to devote significant airtime to documentaries, many of which focus on current events.

These films, as well as the more partisan digital documentaries that have cropped up on YouTube and cable on-demand systems, are all built around the core idea that "the news media have failed," to quote author James McEnteer. He continues, "In the twenty-four-hour news cycle, staged and scripted pseudo-events, concocted by government press offices and public relations firms, bombard the airwaves and print media. Journalists rewrite and repeat press handouts without corroborating their 'facts' . . . Americans who truly wish to be informed about current events have begun to turn elsewhere for their information, including to nonfiction films" (McEnteer 2006). McEnteer's liberal criticism is echoed by those on the right. In all of these documentaries is an inherent frustration with traditional mainstream media, although the frustration can be born out of different things. Some filmmakers express disappointment with the lack of advocacy in journalistic coverage of an issue or politician. Others see the their film as giving voice to those marginalized by society, and still others see the coverage of an issue or incident as lacking the necessary depth and context for people to truly understand what is happening.

All of this relates to documentaries about issues of public interest and policy considerations, but there is another type of political documentary that needs to be understood—campaign documentaries. As Theodore White first captured in his 1961 book *The Making of the President 1960*, the campaign itself is a human drama of impressive scale, with winners and losers, the human beings running for president. That same year, Robert Drew, a filmmaker who would later be called the father of cinéma vérité, was following the same candidates and would produce a four-part series of films that gave the feel of being on the trail with President John Kennedy. Drew, a correspondent for *Life* magazine, took a new type of camera that allowed his team to record events and sound as they were happening. The small team shot five days of the Kennedy campaign stumping for votes in Wisconsin and the resulting widely acclaimed film *Primary*, with its shaky camera work, provided a never-before-experienced sense of being on the trail.

The appeal of politics as a subject of these films made sense. As one documentarian who has produced a series of campaign films noted, "For filmmakers trying to wrangle a narrative structure out of the messiness of real life, campaigns are made to order. Usually, two candidates face off in a race that has a beginning, a middle and a dramatic end. Someone wins and someone loses on election night . . . That said, films are also subject to the rules of successful cinema. Are the characters compelling on film? Do you have real access to them?" (Steckler 2008). And this may be the real irony of the modern political documentary. Because these filmmakers almost never produce a scrap of information before the election is over—it is hard to complete your film before you know who wins—these filmmakers are often granted one of the most cherished of gifts a campaign can bestow on a journalist: access. The 2008 campaign of Senator Barack Obama allowed a team from HBO to follow the candidate from time to time, to lurk in hotel rooms with staff and to interview speechwriters and senior advisers. It is the sort of access almost no reporter from the *New York Times* or Politico would ever receive. Mitt Romney did the same thing in 2012 for a Netflix documentary *Mitt*. Another, the 2013 film *Caucus*, tracked the plight of long-shot Republican candidate Rick Santorum. David Weigel would write in Slate that these documentaries gain access to campaigns because they also almost always lionize the candidate, especially the loser, because they are not about policy but about the people running for office. He noted, "The story of *Caucus* is that the process of running for president is completely degrading, but Rick Santorum survived it. It's Rocky recast and set at a series of suburban Pizza Ranches. Are there 30 seconds of Santorum talking about the wrongness of legal gay marriage and abortion? Then they're going to be matched by 60 seconds of him driving an audience to tears with the story of his stillborn son Gabriel and his disabled daughter Bella" (Weigel 2014). These films end up humanizing the candidate, offering a glimpse of the woman or man behind the image that the campaign does so much work to control and showing a process that makes the audience almost always empathize with those going through it.

And perhaps that is the central theme of the documentary in the modern political reporting world—humanizing. Be it the candidate out shaking hands in the snow in New Hampshire, the miner fighting for their economic rights in the hills of Kentucky, or the whistleblower leaking national security files on American government agencies spying on Americans, these political documentaries focus on the individuals involved in these larger policy stories. The result is often compelling and can affect the way in which the viewing public sees the people involved in the story. In a media environment driven by drama it is powerful, but unlike the bulk of the modern media, it is also a form of storytelling that is inherently told after much of the drama has played out.

See also: Access to Candidates; Campaign Narratives and Dramatization; *Frontline*

Further Reading
Baldwin, Belinda, and Robert Bahar. 2004. "Docs That Make a Difference: The Politics of Political Documentaries." *Documentary*. April. Accessed December 14, 2015. http://www.documentary.org/magazine/docs-make-difference-politics-political-documentaries.
Blair, Elizabeth. 2014. "In Confronting Poverty, 'Harvest of Shame' Reaped Praise and Criticism." NPR. May 31. Accessed December 14, 2015. http://www.npr.org/2014/05/31/317364146/in-confronting-poverty-harvest-of-shame-reaped-praise-and-criticism.
CBS. 2010. "Harvest of Shame." November 24. Accessed June 13, 2016. https://www.youtube.com/watch?v=yJTVF_dya7E.

McEnteer, James. 2006. *Shooting the Truth: The Rise of American Political Documentaries.* West-port, CT: Praeger.

Steckler, Paul. 2008. "Reality Candidates: Documentaries on the Campaign Trail." *Documentary.* Fall. Accessed December 14, 2015. http://www.documentary.org/content/reality-candidates-documentaries-campaign-trail.

Weigel, David. 2014. "Campaign Vérité." Slate. February 14. Accessed December 14, 2015. http://www.slate.com/articles/news_and_politics/politics/2014/02/political_documentaries_lionize_candidates_it_worked_for_mitt_romney_rick.2.html.

DRUDGE REPORT

Part gossip column, part news aggregator, the Drudge Report was one of the first and remains one of the largest sources for political news on the Internet, especially for the leaked story or the unsourced rumor. The site reports with the feel of a 1950s pulp tabloid and its editor, Matt Drudge, is almost always photographed wearing a pork pie hat befitting that era. But the Drudge Report is not a throwback to an earlier era of Walter Winchell columns; it is rather a creature of new media and has made a name for itself by breaking news quickly, even while later having to correct stories it got wrong.

Drudge has built a reputation not with a national audience, but rather for being a go-to for the journalists, politicians, and celebrities. The site Matt Drudge founded has become a source for both the sleaziest of rumor and the most newsworthy of leaks. And as his influence over D.C. and political reporters has grown, so has the volume of his detractors. Glenn Greenwald, the left-of-center reporter who broke the National Security Agency wiretapping story, describes Drudge as "the center of personality-obsessed, attack-based politics. That is the content Drudge looks for. He's a right-wing hack." Former NBC anchor Brian Williams called his site "America's bulletin board, and much more than that" and former Republican presidential candidate and conservative commentator Pat Buchanan has said, "Matt Drudge is just about the most powerful journalist in America" (Weiss 2007).

The Drudge Report grew out of its founder's interest in two things that would turn into big business—technology and gossip. At the age of 18 he got his first computer as a gift from his dad who hoped it would help combat the aimlessness of his son's life. Drudge started writing an email newsletter filled with gossip he gleaned from friends in Washington and Hollywood. He got good enough stuff and built a loyal enough readership that he soon started charging $10 a year to get his insider tips. The service caught on in two towns desperate to know what was going on and terrified of being caught out of the know. Drudge attracted some 85,000 subscribers. Soon he was more focused on the website, ditching the newsletter and posting a stripped down homepage that amounted to a pile of links and a few simple pictures. His talent was in tirelessly culling through articles and television reports to cobble together an interesting array of links, and then augmenting it with stories insiders wanted to leak. This platform for anonymous leaking soon started scoring exclusive stories. In 1996, the Drudge Report was the first outlet to report that

Republican presidential candidate Bob Dole was picking former New York congressman Jack Kemp to be his running mate.

From the earliest iteration, the Drudge Report drew the attention of journalists who sought the latest gossip, and they too emerged as some of Matt Drudge's most regular sources. Reporters and editors would often let Drudge know about stories that were not going to make it to print, and Drudge would happily post an exclusive story about it. It was this reality that moved Drudge from the fringe of gossip blogging to a force within journalism, late one January night in 1998. Drudge hit the web with this blazing headline: "NEWSWEEK KILLS STORY ON WHITE HOUSE INTERN X X X X X BLOCKBUSTER REPORT: 23-YEAR OLD, FORMER WHITE HOUSE INTERN, SEX RELATIONSHIP WITH PRESIDENT." The story would break into the public and create the political story of the decade—that intern Monica Lewinsky and President Bill Clinton had had an affair while she was working in the West Wing. But Drudge didn't get wind of the affair, he heard about the media's handling of it. "The DRUDGE REPORT has learned that reporter Michael Isikoff developed the story of his career, only to have it spiked by top NEWSWEEK suits hours before publication," Drudge wrote. He then outlined the story of "a young woman, 23, sexually involved with the love of her life, the President of the United States, since she was a 21-year-old intern at the White House" (Drudge 1998). The story did not name the young woman, but did indicate that "tapes of intimate phone conversations exist." The news was soon confirmed, and Drudge would often get credit for breaking it despite the year Isikoff spent reporting it.

But for every story like the Lewinsky scandal that Drudge broke, his site also got many wrong. Few of his exclusives have anything remotely approximating an identifiable source, and therefore the site has often pushed stories that turn out to be untrue. In 2012 the site reported that Mitt Romney would tap former national security adviser Condoleezza Rice to be his vice presidential candidate—which was not true. He has repeated several unsubstantiated claims of the so-called birther community that claims President Barack Obama was not born in the United States. But the site, with its bare-bones design, continues to amplify the reporting of others, and the audience it can drive is impressive. One columnist at Forbes.com noted that his story about an unusually large ammunition purchase by the Department of Homeland Security had attracted little attention on the established media site. Then "the Drudge Report picked up that column. Subsequently over 900,000 people viewed it. Readers provided almost 1,000 comments, mostly astute (even when ungenerous to this writer). Meanwhile, DHS was excruciatingly slow to clarify" (Benko 2013). As the DHS story indicates, the site draws millions of readers who cruise the headlines for the latest politically oriented news and bit of media gossip. The site traditionally appeals more to conservatives than average liberal readers, in part reflecting Drudge's own politics.

In addition to promoting Matt Drudge as a leading voice in some journalism circles, the site was a launchpad for Andrew Breitbart, the mind behind the Breitbart News Network—the conservative counterpoint to Huffington Post. Both

Breitbart and Drudge are self-professed conservatives. Drudge told the Miami *New Times* alternative newsweekly in 2001, "I know your angle. I can see where you're going with this. 'Drudge the conservative rebel'; 'the conservative who's not really that conservative.' That's not true. I am a conservative. I'm very much pro-life. If you go down the list of what makes up a conservative, I'm there almost all the way" (Sokol 2001).

Despite its right-leaning politics, the site remains one of the most dominant referers to traditional news on the web. Outside of Facebook, Twitter, and Google searches, Drudge is often the top source for people finding news on the web. A 2015 report from Politico summed up the reality of Drudge's influence, reporting, "The bare bones conservative aggregator and agitator hasn't changed much in more than two decades and has enormous influence in conservative circles. In 2014, DrudgeReport.com was the No. 1 site of referral traffic to the *Daily Mail*, CNN, Fox News, Roll Call, Breitbart, the *New York Times*, *National Journal*, *USA Today*, Associated Press, Reuters, the *Wall Street Journal*, and Politico, Intermarkets found" (Gold 2015).

See also: Breitbart, Andrew; Conservative Blogosphere; Echo-Chamber Effect

Further Reading
Benko, Ralph. 2013. "The Power of Drudge: A Little Civics Lesson for Janet Napolitano and Barack Obama." Forbes.com. May 12. Accessed August 20, 2015. http://www .forbes.com/sites/ralphbenko/2013/05/12/the-power-of-drudge-a-little-civics-lesson -for-janet-napolitano-and-barack-obama.
Drudge, Matt. 1998. "Newsweek Kills Story on White House Intern." The Drudge Report. January 17. Accessed August 20, 2015. http://www.drudgereportarchives.com/data /2002/01/17/20020117_175502_ml.htm.
Gold, Hadas. 2015. "Drudge Report Still Dominant." Politico. April 8. Access August 20, 2015. http://www.politico.com/blogs/media/2015/04/drudge-leads-referral-traffic-for -top-news-sites-205182.html.
Sokol, Brett. 2001. "The Drudge Retort." Miami *New Times*. June 21. Accessed August 20, 2015. http://www.miaminewtimes.com/news/the-drudge-retort-6351876.
Weiss, Phillip. 2007. "Watching Matt Drudge." *New York* Magazine. August 24. Accessed August 20, 2015. http://nymag.com/news/media/36617.

EARLY VOTING

Through a series of reforms enacted over the past 20 years, it has become easier to vote absentee without a reason or to cast a ballot at a designated polling place ahead of Election Day. A few states have enacted measures to do away with polling places and conduct all elections by mail. The result is that by the time the first polling place has opened on Election Day during presidential campaign years, more than a third of the people who will vote in an election have already cast their ballots. Campaigns and journalists have had to adapt their strategies to deal with this new reality of campaigns and voting in America.

The idea of casting a ballot before Election Day is not a new one in the United States. Traditional absentee ballots have existed since the mid-nineteenth century. Early absentee voting laws focused on ensuring members of military would not be deprived of the right to vote. In 1813, Pennsylvania became the first state to do this, making it possible for members of the military stationed more than two miles from home to cast an absentee ballot. During the U.S. Civil War, the number of states expanded quickly as 19 out of the 25 Union states and 7 of the 11 Confederate states passed similar laws. Most states dumped these laws after the war, but slowly new bills were passed and by 1924 all but three states had some form of absentee law. The federal government added the Uniformed and Overseas Citizens Absentee Voting Act in 1986, which ensured that members of the military, their family members, and other citizens of the United States could register and vote in federal elections without appearing at a polling place.

From its outset and well into the 1990s the number of people who took advantage of absentee voting remained fairly small. According to a survey conducted by the U.S. Census Bureau the number hovered around 7 percent as late as 1992. But in the 1990s a series of moves by states changed the way many more people voted. A 1994 report on early voting for the Federal Election Commission acknowledged that many of the questions connected to people voting before Election Day were only half understood due to the small number of voters using such a system, but the report also found that, "while it has long been agreed that some voters must be allowed to vote early by absentee ballot if they are going to be able to vote at all, there is a roaring debate about whether it is advisable to encourage large numbers of people to vote as much as a week or month before election day" (Rosenfield 1994). Despite the "roaring debate," a series of reforms began at the state level to move beyond enabling those unable to physically vote in person to cast a ballot before Election Day. These reforms have taken three basic forms—voting by mail, casting an absentee ballot without needing to justify it, and voting early at established polling places. When enacting each of these reforms, state legislators generally argued that making it easier to vote would encourage more people to participate in the process, although there is mixed evidence as to how effective this effort is. In 1991, Texas became the first state to establish formal early voting. Texas early voting begins, on average, 17 days before the election. Residents are given a location to vote at and can cast a ballot between 7 a.m. and 7 p.m. for those two weeks. Now 33 states and the District of Columbia allow voters to either cast a ballot during a designated period or, at a minimum, cast an in-person absentee ballot.

Quite a bit of research has been done on these voters to understand who votes early and why, but one review of that social science concluded, "The voters who take advantage of early voting procedures are essentially the same voters who show up on Election Day. However, there are attitudinal differences between early voters and Election Day voters. Early voters are more likely to believe the outcome of the election is important and to take an interest in the campaign than Election Day voters and (are) more likely to be strong partisans" (Hill 2006). And this may be no accident. Campaigns see early voting as an opportunity to lock in the guaranteed supporter. If a given voter is a solid backer, getting them to cast an absentee ballot or to go to the clerk's office to vote early leaves nothing to chance on Election Day. But each form of early voting creates unique opportunities and challenges for campaigns (and the for the journalists covering those campaigns).

All-mail elections have cropped up in a handful of states as an effort to address the same goals of encouraging more voter participation while also reducing the cost of administering elections. Oregon pioneered this form of voting. As far back as 1981, the state allowed counties to decide whether to run regular polling stations for local elections or to conduct elections via mailed ballots. By 1996, the state expanded the experiment to a statewide special election to select a replacement for Republican Bob Packwood, who was forced to resign from the U.S. Senate under a cloud of sexual harassment and abuse allegations. The special election was held in January 1996 and was run completely through the mail. The Oregon Secretary of State hailed the 66 percent voter turnout in the first statewide mail-in vote, and by 1998 a citizen initiative made mail-in voting the law of the land in Oregon. For years, Oregon remained the only state to run an all-mail election system. Other states had provisions for local elections or smaller state contests to run mail voting, but statewide campaigns and federal elections still had polling places. Finally in 2011, Washington state joined its neighbor and in 2013 Colorado became the third state to go to all mailed ballots. Colorado House Majority Leader Dickey Lee Hullinghorst later told the National Council of State Legislators that when she first heard of Oregon's decision she thought it was a mistake, saying, "It was a traditional thing for me—I liked to go to my polling place on Election Day," but as she studied the issue and considered what Colorado should do she decided that vote-by-mail "is the wave of the future because it is easy and because it is so much more economical for the voting process" (Hernandez 2014). One study found that Colorado counties would likely save $4 million per election scrapping the polling places. But the mail-in election remains the exception in the United States.

The most far-reaching reform that led more and more Americans to vote early was the development of absentee voting without having to provide an excuse. For most of its 200-year history, a voter needed to supply the election clerk with a reason why they would not be able to vote in person on Election Day. The thinking was by ensuring that voters turned up at the polls on Election Day they would have had access to the same potential information about the candidates, there would be reduced dangers of voter fraud by voting in person, and the county offices running the election could budget for a specific day and a specific way of counting ballots. But as other reforms aimed at boosting voter turnout moved through legislatures, many states embraced the idea of using the existing absentee ballot system to encourage more voting. Some 27 states and the District of Columbia allow voters to cast an absentee ballot without supplying a reason, and seven of those states (along with D.C.) also allow voters to sign up to be listed as permanent absentee voters, essentially meaning they are mail-in voters. Nine more states allow certain types of voters—usually those who are physically disabled—to be permanent absentee voters.

This mix of early voting options—all-mail elections, no-excuse absentee balloting, and in-person early voting—allows voters to cast ballots as much as a month before Election Day. Most studies have found the impact of these moves do little to change the electorate, contributing perhaps a few percentage points more to the average voter turnouts in most elections. Rather, early voting seems to ensure those who would likely show up at the polls do, indeed, cast their ballots. That said, early voting has had a profound effect on the way campaigns think about organizing their so-called get-out-the-vote or GOTV operations. As Mike DuHaim, political director for John McCain in 2008, explained it, "Election Day can spread out over weeks. That means your get-out-the-vote costs are more than ever" (Johnson 2011). Campaigns now begin encouraging their most ardent supporters to sign up for absentee ballots—where possible—and to cast their ballots long before Election Day.

Campaigns describe a new plan where often the candidate's most ardent backers are pressed earlier in the campaign to sign up for, receive, and return their mail-in ballots. And there is a clear logic to it, says those who have studied campaign strategy. "Campaigns prefer to have their supporters cast mail-in ballots. First, when supporters vote by mail well in advance of Election Day, the campaign no longer needs to expend resources communicating with them. Second, campaigns like to be seen as offering a service to people who receive their mailings; this builds rapport and may be useful in subsequent fund-raising and recruitment efforts. Third, . . . it is thought that encouraging voters to vote by mail raises their probability of voting" (Green and Gerber 2008). Therefore, candidates can target their messages to voters who are more on the fence and invest less time in keeping a given voter interested and motivated to get out to the polls on Election Day.

But building a clear strategy to address the changing nature of how America votes is a more difficult task. First the speed at which voting has moved away from a one-day affair to a multi-week marathon is striking. Only about 7 percent cast early ballots in 1992, but by 2004 that number had jumped to 20 percent. By 2012 it was north of 30 percent—and that is still with some of the most populous states like New York, Pennsylvania, Michigan, and Missouri offering no real early voting and another big one, Texas, only offering the less popular in-person early voting. In some states, well over half of the ballots are cast early now, which has fundamentally altered the campaign cycle. Still, political consultants have watched as campaigns sometimes pour thousands of dollars into last-minute ad buys just before Election Day. In California, longtime political operative Paul Mitchell told the Associated Press about one campaign where they spent most of the ad dollars at the end, saying, "They were advertising basically to ghosts, voters who had already voted" (Blood 2014). But more and more campaigns are using their voter databases to track which supporters have already cast ballots and micro-target those yet to vote. A word to a canvasser in a state that you have sent your absentee ballot in and all visits and calls suddenly stop. And campaigns are becoming more aggressive about targeting voters via social media to reach those supporters who have not cast a ballot.

And it is not just the campaigns that have been affected by the shifting voting patterns of the American electorate. Reporters and journalists who hope to inform voter decisions now must grapple with when to do it to ensure voters have the information they may need before voting. Journalists in states where absentee balloting can make up 50 percent or more of how people will vote have to take into account this reality when planning their coverage of campaigns. The date the state head of elections sends out ballots has become almost as significant as Election Day for planning purposes, and events like candidate debates have been pushed earlier in the calendar as journalists work to get information into the hands of voters before they cast a ballot. Researchers who have studied how campaigns are covered in states with and without early voting have also uncovered demonstrable differences between the two kinds of contests. A 2013 study concluded that "in states with in-person early voting and where a larger proportion of the vote is cast before election day, we observe a significantly greater volume of campaign news stories per day than in states without in-person early voting (one additional news story per day) and where a lower proportion of the vote is cast before election day (about half an additional news story per day)" (Dunaway and Stein 2013).

Another major area of coverage affected by the growth of early voting is polling. Both polls in the days before the election, and the exit polls conducted after people have voted, have become more complicated. Journalists must balance between what early vote totals tell them and compare it to polls of likely voters. It forces reporters to weigh what offers more insight: actual votes or scientific polls. In 2014, journalists struggled with how to respond to a wave of reports that showed Democrats in states like Colorado, Georgia, and Iowa faring better than expected in early voting. Poll watcher Harry Enten took to FiveThirtyEight to combat the notion, writing, "There's two problems with this line of thinking [that we should trust early votes over polls]. First, early voters and Election Day voters aren't each drawn randomly from the electorate. Research shows certain groups are more likely to vote early.

Second, early voting isn't a secret; pollsters account for it" (Enten 2014). This accounting for early voting means now pollsters focus on the big picture and are largely unaffected by when people vote. This won't stop campaigns from spinning a story or two if numbers from early voting indicate their candidate is doing well. But as pollsters and campaigns become more used to the 30-day Election Day that different forms of early voting has created in many states, it will become less an unpredictable aberration and more a regular part of the election cycle.

See also: Campaign Strategy Coverage; Get Out the Vote (GOTV)

Further Reading
Blood, Michael. 2014. "Early Voting Shifts Midterm Election Campaign Strategies." Associated Press. October 25. Accessed June 30, 2015. http://www.pbs.org/newshour/rundown/early-voting-shifts-midterm-election-campaign-strategies.
Dunaway, Johanna, and Robert Stein. 2013. "Early Voting and Campaign News Coverage." *Political Communication*. New York: Routledge.
Enten, Harry. 2014. "Unskewed Polls, Early Voting Edition." FiveThirtyEight. November 3. Accessed June 30, 2015. http://fivethirtyeight.com/datalab/unskewed-polls-early-voting-edition.
Green, Donald, and Alan Gerber. 2008. *Get Out the Vote: How to Increase Voter Turnout*. Washington, DC: Brookings Institution Press.
Hernandez, Michael. 2014. "The Canvass: States and Election Reform." National Council of State Legislatures. July. Accessed June 29, 2015. http://www.ncsl.org/research/elections-and-campaigns/states-and-election-reform-the-canvass-july-2014.aspx#All-Mail%20Elections.
Hill, David. 2006. *American Voter Turnout: An Institutional Perspective*. Cambridge, MA: Westview Press.
Johnson, Dennis. 2011. *Campaigning in the Twenty-First Century: A Whole New Ballgame?* New York: Routledge.
Rosenfield, Margaret. 1994. "Early Voting." Washington, DC: National Clearinghouse on Election Administration.

ECHO CHAMBER EFFECT

Media and political observers have for decades worried that as audiences fragment, drawn apart by news and social media organizations that only present information and perspectives they agree with, people will find themselves in media environments where views other than their own are discounted or completely ignored. In such a world, experts worry, facts can become malleable and political polarization deepens. In such media environments, certain political views or even terms that are repeated over and over again take on an aura of fact, even when fiction—President Obama is a Muslim or was not born in the United States, or the September 11 attacks were faked.

Boiled down to its most basic concept, the echo chamber argues that if an inaccurate or politically motivated claim is repeated enough times and affirmed by like-minded people and blogs, it will become a fact for at least a portion of the population. So, for example, some seven years after the claims were first made a plurality of Republican voters maintain that President Barack Obama was ineligible to serve as president because he was born overseas. For this group, no proof otherwise will change their mind, and every well-researched refutation is labeled fraudulent. The evolution of the "birther" movement—the term for that portion of the public that contends Obama is foreign—can serve as an important case study in how these echo chambers develop and can keep alive conspiracy theories for decades. The claim was born out of the bitter Democratic primary campaign of 2008 when then-senator Obama faced off with Senator Hillary Clinton. Those fighting for Clinton began circulating a series of personal attacks against Obama, including one email chain that claimed Obama's mother was living in Kenya late in her pregnancy and would not have been allowed to fly back to Hawaii for the birth of her son so he must have been born there and then his mother waited to register his birth. That claim was then compounded by a more ornate, and potentially problematic reading of immigration law that contended since Obama's father was Kenyan and his mother was only 18 at the time of his birth, Obama would not qualify for automatic citizenship at the time of his birth. This was not true either, but by then the rumor was circulating that Obama was a foreigner.

Ironically, the echo chamber of the birther movement erupted only after the Obama campaign moved to disprove the rumor. A 9/11 conspiracy theorist and former Pennsylvania deputy attorney general filed a lawsuit in 2008 saying Obama was not allowed to be president, and the official world of the birthers was put on the record. A writer for the online version of the conservative magazine the *National Review* asked the campaign to supply a copy of the birth certificate. They posted one and sent a copy to the liberal site the Daily Kos. For the *National Review* writer, it was good enough, writing, "Obama himself probably has a dog-eared yellowing copy in a desk drawer somewhere; this document is what he or someone authorized by him was given by the state out of its records. Barring some vast conspiracy within the Hawaii State Department of Health, there is no reason to think his birth certificate would have any different data" (Geraghty 2008).

However, the release of the scanned copy actually triggered a wave of amateur sleuths who parsed the image, with several declaring it had been photoshopped to copy the official seal. Still, official outlets continued to come out reporting the document was real. The state of Hawaii confirmed they had an official record of Obama's birth and the fact-checking website FactCheck.org delved into the issue. An extensive examination of the records connected to the birth certificate was also expanded to a birth announcement that ran in the *Honolulu Advertiser* newspaper that was posted by Obama's grandparents. FactCheck.org said Hawaii would need to be fraudulently signing off on birth certificates and that "it's distantly possible that Obama's grandparents may have planted the announcement just in case their grandson needed to prove his U.S. citizenship to run for president someday. We suggest that those who choose to go down that path should first equip themselves with a high-quality tinfoil hat. The evidence is clear: Barack Obama was born in the U.S.A." (Hennig 2008). FactCheck.org is a nonpartisan site that reports on claims made in campaigns and has no vested interest in supporting the president's claims, but their reporting on the matter, the claims of Republican-appointed officials in Hawaii, and even the satisfaction of most Republican lawmakers has not ended the online discussions and claims that Obama is a foreigner.

The persistence of conspiracy theories is not, in itself, a new phenomenon. For years, questions have plagued the investigation into the assassination of President John F. Kennedy. Other groups have questioned the 1969 moon landing. These theories spawned books and minor industries of fellow theorists who spoke to one another, developing alternative theories of what happened through "groupthink" and coalescing into an ever-stronger belief system. Nicholas DiFonzo, a professor of psychology, has explained this group echo chamber idea by writing, "Among like-minded people, it's hard to come up with arguments that challenge the group consensus, which means group members keep hearing arguments only in one direction. When we hear a rumor denigrating someone in the opposing political party, we are far more likely to send it to friends—typically members of our own party—whom we think would enjoy hearing that rumor. Yet most people are far less likely to challenge false rumors about the opposing party, because that might be considered a social faux pas among their friends" (DiFonzo 2011).

As DiFonzo notes, partisanship is one of the key lenses through which people see and repeat claims that support their views. Remember, partisanship—this time internal partisanship within the Democratic Party—helped drive the early discussion of Obama's citizenship; it was only once he was the Democratic nominee that these claims took off among Republicans. Those who have studied politics have for decades concluded that political beliefs are the cornerstone of the echo chamber, creating the key factor necessary to perpetuate (mis)information among like-minded people. And it's not just the masses reacting this way. It would surprise few that shared political beliefs can lead to a simplification of politics; claims of the president become echoed within Congress by those members of the same party who share the same beliefs. One study of this relationship concluded, "In general, partisanship appears to act as a microphone through which presidential rhetoric is repeated and amplified. The result of this amplification varies, however. Under many, perhaps most, circumstances, partisanship is likely to exaggerate the tendency for simplistic rhetoric to drive public policy, reducing deliberation and increasing the implementation of ill-considered policies" (Mellow 2007).

The evolution of the media in the past two decades has enhanced and enabled this propensity to find communities of like-minded individuals around politics and other controversial issues, and has become a core organizing principle of modern media. As first journalistic media fragmented, and then social media rose to allow members of these fragmented groups to find one another and coalesce, the development and hardening of echo chambers was taken to another level. As elements of the media became more hyper-partisan and specialized, their ability to shape discussion and create ideological enclaves intensified. Political communications experts Kathleen Hall Jamieson and Joseph Cappella found, for example, that talk radio host Rush Limbaugh, Fox News, and the opinion pages of the *Wall Street Journal* became a sort of de facto Republican media establishment that helped vet conservatives and served as an echo chamber of political thought. The two argued, "These conservative media create a self-protective enclave hospitable to conservative beliefs. This safe haven reinforces the views of these outlets' like-minded audience members, helps them maintain ideological coherence, protects them from counter-persuasion, reinforces conservative values and dispositions, holds Republican candidates and leaders accountable to conservative ideals, tightens their audience's ties to the Republican Party, and distances listeners, readers, and viewers from 'liberals,' in general, and Democrats, in particular" (Jamieson and Cappella 2010).

What these two described in more than 300 pages was the construction of the right-wing echo chamber in the age of mass media. What they argued had happened through cable networks and talk radio took even stronger hold as the Internet and social media allowed for far more granular audience fragmentation. The growth of the Internet and blogging has been seen as central to allowing echo chambers to develop around smaller and smaller groups. Now ideas no longer needed to attract enough people to merit the publication of a book or newsletter, and people who may not otherwise know others shared their ideas could more easily find one another through Google, Facebook, and Twitter. Many news and information services online work to personalize the information they supply to people, relying on what people have clicked on before and information these services have gathered on people to deliver information it believes to be most relevant to the individual. The danger, some worry, is that this form of Internet personalization could lead to people not being exposed to new ideas or things that challenge their assumptions about a topic. Therefore if Google knows a person has spent a lot of time exploring the authenticity of Barack Obama's birth certificate, the service is more likely to supply that person with sources that other people who have done the same thing find useful and visit often. These sites are more likely to be fellow conspiracy theorists' blogs than newspaper reporting on the debunking.

This is the modern echo chamber that worries many, including progressive web developer Eli Pariser who developed these concerns more fully in a book *The Filter Bubble*. Pariser said that the quest to personalize the Internet has created "what I call a filter bubble. And your filter bubble is your own personal, unique universe of information that you live in online. And what's in your filter bubble depends on who you are, and it depends on what you do. But the thing is that you don't decide what gets in. And more importantly, you don't actually see what gets edited out" (Pariser 2011). But others have found this editing is actually something many people choose to do. A 2013 survey of members of Congress and their Twitter accounts found few members follow those of the other party. Whether this is an effort to appear ideologically pure, or simply they are not interested in what the other side of the aisle is saying, the result is that when these members access a service like

Twitter they will only see the statements and links put out by those with whom they already caucus and politically align. The fear is that Pariser's invisible filtering, along with conscious decisions to seek out only those who agree with them, fuel very different world views separated by fundamentally different views of issues in the public sphere.

Such concerns about the self-reflective nature of a hyper-personalized web and social media world have prompted social scientists—and some of the services themselves—to take a closer look at whether they are perpetuating a damaging echo chamber that fosters a "post-truth" politics where facts like a birth certificate can be subjected to endless debate. One of the first major analyses of Twitter to examine the question answered it thus: it depends. "It depends on how we analyze Twitter. If we look at Twitter as a social medium we see higher levels of homophily [a tendency to connect with like-minded individuals] and a more echo chamber-like structure of communication. But if we instead focus on Twitter as a news medium, looking at information diffusion regardless of social ties, we see lower levels of homophily and a more public sphere-like scenario" (Colleoni, Rozza, and Arvidsson 2014). This survey found that though we may follow people who think like us, we also end up seeing more information than we would if we were not on Twitter.

Facebook undertook a similar examination of itself. It analyzed the data from more than 10 million users, and the results, like the Twitter analysis, offered a more complex assessment of how social media fuels or breaks down the echo chamber. The team concluded in research that ran in the respected journal *Science* that the Facebook "News Feed surfaces content that is slightly more aligned with an individual's own ideology, however the friends you choose and the content you click on are more important factors than News Feed ranking in terms of how much content you encounter that cuts across ideological lines." The research went on to offer some interesting statistics to back up their conclusion, including that of those who claim to be liberal or conservative:

- On average 23% of people's friends claim an opposing political ideology
- Of the hard news content that people's friends share, 29.5% of it cuts across ideological lines
- When it comes to what people see in News Feed, 28.9% of the hard news encountered cuts across ideological lines, on average
- 24.9% of the hard news content that people actually clicked on cuts across ideological lines (Facebook 2015)

Observers noted that the research confirmed a bias in the Facebook feed, but that it was based more on what individuals do than in how Facebook programmed the service. This bias was also smaller than many expected. All this means that the echo chamber does exist on Facebook, like it does in the lists of who follows whom on Twitter, but that it does not prevent people from finding or being exposed to new information. What does happen is often people won't seek out the information that challenges their own views. The belief is, though evidence is still slight, that in the old days people who picked up the newspaper could not help but see information that challenged their viewpoints and now they can easily avoid it. It is true that the echo chambers are helped by the advent of technology and the fracturing of mass media audiences, but whether this propels people into them or simply allows them to choose to insulate themselves remains perhaps the most important and least understood answer.

See also: Personalization and the Internet; Political Polarization and the Media; Post-Truth Politics; Social Media and Politics

Further Reading

Colleoni, Elanor, Alessandro Rozza, and Adam Arvidsson. 2014. "Echo Chamber or Public Sphere? Predicting Political Orientation and Measuring Political Homophily in Twitter Using Big Data." *Journal of Communication*. April.

DiFonzo, Nick. 2011. "The Echo-Chamber Effect." *New York Times*. April 22. Accessed October 23, 2015. http://www.nytimes.com/roomfordebate/2011/04/21/barack-obama-and-the-psychology-of-the-birther-myth/the-echo-chamber-effect.

Facebook. 2015. "News Feed FYI: Exposure to Diverse Information on Facebook." May 7. Accessed October 22, 2015. http://newsroom.fb.com/news/2015/05/news-feed-fyi-exposure-to-diverse-information-on-facebook.

Geraghty, Jim. 2008. "Obama's Certification of Live Birth Found and Posted at Daily Kos." *National Review*. June 12. Accessed October 22, 2015. http://www.nationalreview.com/campaign-spot/9471/obamas-certification-live-birth-found-and-posted-daily-kos-jim-geraghty.

Hennig, Jess. 2008. "Born in the U.S.A." Factcheck.org. August 21. Accessed October 22, 2015. http://www.factcheck.org/2008/08/born-in-the-usa.

Jamieson, Kathleen Hall, and Joseph Cappella. 2010. *Echo Chamber: Rush Limbaugh and the Conservative Media Establishment*. New York: Oxford University Press.

Mellow, Nicole. 2007. "The Rhetorical Presidency and the Partisan Echo Chamber." *Critical Review: A Journal of Politics and Society* 19, Issue 2–3.

Pariser, Eli. 2011. "Beware online 'filter bubbles.'" TED. February. Accessed July 25, 2015. http://www.ted.com/talks/eli_pariser_beware_online_filter_bubbles/transcript?language=en.

EMILY'S LIST

Since 1985, Emily's List has raised millions of dollars and organized countless fundraisers to promote the involvement of women in the political process, primarily through the Democratic Party.

Its founder, Ellen Malcolm, began organizing meetings in her home in the mid-1980s as a "pseudo Tupperware party, but instead of apolitical housewives discussing the merits of resealable containers and trading meatloaf recipes, the organization brought together groups of politically savvy women to discuss poll numbers, campaign platforms, and voter outreach efforts" (Pimlott 2010). Women voters had always been sought after by candidates, but the group found little support for actual women candidates and so the idea of politically active women supporting the candidacy of other women took shape. Malcolm organized these groups to help spark women candidates early in their campaigns. In fact the name of the group is an acronym for Early Money Is Like Yeast (EMILY). The idea was they would seed candidates and then that early money would help the real dough rise.

That first election cycle Emily's List boosted the profile of two Democratic U.S. Senate candidates—Missouri's Harriett Woods and Maryland's Barbara Mikulski. Both women won their primary campaigns and Mikulski won the general election. In Mikulski's case, some 20 percent of the early money donated to her campaign came through Emily's List support (McLean 1995). The group expanded its focus the next cycle to include U.S. House campaigns and Emily's List was soon one of the most critical voices on women's issues in the Democratic Party.

A registered political action committee, the group does no lobbying on issues, but is purely a political organization aimed at affecting electoral politics. Even so, it was soon doing more than just donating to female candidates, becoming a major voice in pointing out the lack of women members of Congress and advocating for better representation. When the group organized there were twenty-three women in the House and two in the Senate. Then Clarence Thomas happened.

George H. W. Bush had proposed Judge Thomas fill the seat being vacated by re-nowned liberal justice Thurgood Marshall. Thomas, an avowed conservative judge, faced a challenging confirmation process, made only more difficult by accusations from lawyer Anita Hill that Thomas had harassed her. Several female members of Congress attempted to attend the hearing of the all-male Judiciary Committee, but were barred from entering. The confrontation angered many women—activists and not—and prompted more calls to elect women to Congress. The group grew from 3,000 to 6,000 during that episode. Senator Joe Biden, who chaired the com-mittee hearing on Thomas, said later that the controversy "wasn't about her or him. It was about a fundamental issue of power: the way women are treated. As many women as men didn't believe Professor Hill, but even those who didn't were out-raged by the attitudes of some men on the committee" (Lewis 1992).

That same presidential year, 1992, the CBS program *60 Minutes* did a profile of Malcolm and her group and their membership grew to more than 15,000. The group hosted a fundraiser for seven women running for the U.S. Senate and raised $750,000. It quickly became one of the largest PACs in Washington and its influ-ence on Democratic Party politics ever since then has been significant.

For example, Emily's List only endorses pro-choice female candidates. This fact helps explain the sometimes-contentious role of abortion politics in the Democratic Party. Pro-life Democrats are sometimes shunned by national party leaders, in part as a sign of respect to the importance of pro-choice groups like Emily's List. The group has also expanded beyond simply giving money to candidates, launching state-level training programs to encourage female participation in the political pro-cess. The impact can clearly be seen in its own reporting on its success. As of 2014, the organization "has helped elect 19 pro-choice Democratic women U.S. senators,

102 U.S. representatives, and ten governors. Throughout its 29-year history, the organization has recruited and trained over 9,000 women to run for office. One of the largest and most successful political action committees in the country, Emily's List has over three million members and has raised over $400 million to support Democratic women candidates" (Emily's List 2015). The group is notable, in part, because it is one of the few PACs to funnel much of its money to challengers and non-incumbents in an effort to bolster campaigns of first-time female candidates. In fact, a review of their donations found that since 1991, the group has given more money to non-incumbents every election cycle except during the 2011–2012 campaigns.

Still, Emily's List's impact reaches beyond donations to candidates and advertising. Those connected to the group have played critical roles in the Democratic Party for years. Malcolm has served on the Democratic National Committee's Executive Committee and the former executive director, Mary Beth Cahill, left the group to run former U.S. senator John Kerry's 2004 presidential campaign.

The group has sometimes made the news not for its positions or the female candidates it supports, but for its aggressive fundraising efforts. Emily's List maintains a federal fund to support congressional candidates and a non-federal fund to aid state-wide campaigns. In 2010 it accepted $250,000 from a single donor. It then shifted that money to a so-called independent expenditure group, EMILY's List Women Vote PAC, that was running ads in the Massachusetts U.S. Senate race between Martha Coakley and Republican Scott Brown. That transfer of money came less than a week after the Supreme Court had struck down the $5,000 limit on donations to federal PACs in the case *SpeechNow.org v. Federal Elections Commission*. At the forefront of campaign finance law, women's advocacy, and politics, Emily's List remains one of the more aggressive and effective fundraising and campaigning PACs in the American political system.

See also: Political Action Committees (PACs); Women and the News Media

Further Reading

Emily's List. 2015. "Ellen Malcolm." Accessed January 30, 2015. http://www.emilyslist.org/bios/entry/ellen-malcolm.

Lewis, Anthony. 1992. "Abroad at Home; Jumpers and Doers." *New York Times*. July 17. Accessed January 30, 2015. http://www.nytimes.com/1992/07/17/opinion/abroad-at-home-jumpers-and-doers.html.

McLean, Joan. 1995. *U.S. Women's Interest Groups: Institutional Profiles*. Edited by Sarah Slavin. Santa Barbara, CA: Greenwood Publishing Group.

Pimlott, Jamie Pamelia. 2010. *Women and the Democratic Party: The Evolution of Emily's List*. Amherst, NY: Cambria Press.

ENDORSEMENTS

For more than a century many newspaper editorial boards have gathered each campaign season to weigh the pros and cons of candidates and issue the consensus pick of the editors of the paper. These endorsements have, at times, been the product of a natural political affinity between the partisan tilt of the publication and the party of the same persuasion and at other times reflected the gulf between the views of a paper's publisher and those of the staff. For some papers the decision to publicly choose a side in a campaign has itself become controversial; several major publications have ended the practice in an effort to maintain the appearance of impartiality.

Despite the widespread belief in a liberal bias in the media, newspapers have historically endorsed Republicans for president more often than Democrats. In 1972, the most extreme example, 90 percent of newspaper endorsements went to President Richard Nixon. In recent years the numbers have shifted toward Democrats. Among the 100 largest circulation newspapers the 2012 elections broke, only narrowly, toward President Barack Obama, with 41 papers backing the Democrat, 35 supporting his Republican opponent Mitt Romney, and 23 issuing no endorsement.

Often early endorsements aligned with the interests of the publisher of the paper. For example, in 1860, the *New York Times* backed the candidacy of Abraham Lincoln and his recently minted Republican Party. The paper editorialized, "We have confidence in his pacific and conciliatory disposition. He seems to us much more tolerant towards his opponents, than not enough so." It also happens that the newspaper's founder, Henry Raymond, was one of the leaders in the formation of the new party and had served as a delegate to the 1860 Republican National Convention. Endorsements also often reflected the views of more conservative owners and publishers as opposed to the liberal-leaning reporters in the newsroom.

Perhaps due to the age of the medium, newspapers were the only platform to embrace endorsing candidates in a significant way. Magazines will enter the fray, from time to time, but in 2012, for example, only five magazines published official endorsements out of the thousands published in the United States. Broadcast and radio stations are actually inhibited from entering the political debate by the very laws that grant them access to the public airwaves. Somewhat fearing the potential power of broadcasters to influence the mass opinions, the federal government used the fact that broadcasters were being granted a license to use a public asset—the broadcast spectrum—to impose limits on the political speech station managers and staff can make. The Federal Communications Commission imposed these controls not so much by banning the speech outright, which may have triggered larger constitutional questions, but by adding a requirement that most stations found unpalatable. Under the FCC rules, if a station editorially expresses support for a candidate for public office, then all other legally qualified candidates for the same office must be provided air time to respond. Even more far-reaching, if a broadcaster expresses opposition to the election of a candidate, the station is responsible for both notifying the candidate and offering them time. Although not an explicit prohibition on political endorsements, the legal concerns and potential implications of the FCC laws kept broadcasters largely silent on political campaigns, a norm that has spread to cable outlets that would not face the same limits.

Recently, papers have begun bowing out of the endorsement game, citing a desire to appear more neutral as one of the primary reasons for the shift. For example, in 2012 the *Milwaukee Journal-Sentinel* announced it would no longer publicly back any candidate for public office. In explaining the decision of the paper to end its more than a century of political participation David Haynes, editorial page editor for the *Journal-Sentinel*, told NPR that "we work hard to be open-minded and approach issues that we're going to editorialize on independently. We pull good ideas from both major schools of political thought, and we're pragmatic . . . So then, we do all that for 364 days of the year and turn around and choose sides in a bitter partisan election? I think that tends to undermine this whole idea of independence, and it really undermines this idea of being an honest broker of opinion" ("Talk of the Nation" 2012). Still, hundreds of papers continue to back individual candidates and a handful, like the *Los Angeles Times*, have returned to endorsing candidates, seeing the move as a civic service of participating in the public life the paper's reporters document.

Perhaps because they offer such tangible data for study, political scientists have invested reams of research into newspaper endorsements and their potential impact. Scholars have sought to connect endorsements to voter behavior as well as bias in the coverage of candidates by the paper itself and have offered some insights into the potential power of the press to influence voter choice. One 2011 study found that "endorsements are influential in the sense that voters are more likely to support the recommended candidate after publication of the endorsement. The degree of this influence, however, depends of the credibility of the endorsement. In this way, endorsements for the Democratic candidate from left-leaning newspapers are less influential than are endorsements from neutral or right-leaning newspapers" (Chiang and Knight 2011). This sort of impact was seen in 1988 when the *Washington Post*, which had endorsed Democratic candidates back to 1972, declined to back either candidate, accusing Vice President George H. W. Bush of using rhetoric that was "divisive, unworthy and unfair" but also slamming Democratic candidate Michael Dukakis for lacking a firm grasp of American foreign policy issues. The editorial criticized both candidates, but given its history of Democratic endorsements, the paper's move was seen as a harsher rebuke of Dukakis.

Other research has focused on how endorsements can affect the vote in elections where voters know less about candidates, like primaries and more local campaigns, and the result at this level can be even more profound. Especially in municipal or local elections, newspapers may be one of the few sources of information about the candidates and therefore any coverage, including endorsements, can have a more significant effect on voters by increasing the name recognition of candidates and creating a more favorable impression of little known or nonpartisan office-seekers. The endorsements, other researchers found, can help lead to other things that may help candidates and even if the "endorsement effect is a more a result of increased media attention, campaign contributions, or other factors resulting from increased attention, the fact remains that endorsements and electoral outcomes, at least in this context, are irrevocably tied" (Summary 2010).

Endorsements remain one of the most tangible ways in which newspapers actively participate in the political process, representing a rare, overtly partisan voice from an institution often chastened for appearing too political. Although their importance or ability to sway voters may have been diminished as individuals find new sources of information online, the endorsement still remains a stamp of critical approval for candidates for statewide or federal office. For those candidates running in local elections, the approval of a newspaper can improve name recognition, increase awareness of the candidate's core strengths, and help crystalize the argument for those voters undecided late in the campaign.

See also: Corporate Media Ownership; Daily Newspapers; Fairness Doctrine

Further Reading

Chiang, Chun-Fang, and Brian Knight. 2011. "Media Bias and Influence: Evidence from Newspaper Endorsements." *The Review of Economic Studies* 78, no. 3 (July).

Summary, Bryce. 2010. "The Endorsement Effect: An Examination of Statewide Political Endorsements in the 2008 Democratic Caucus and Primary Season." *American Behavioral Scientist* 54, no. 3 (November).

Talk of the Nation. 2012. "Should Newspapers Make Political Endorsements?" NPR. November 5. Accessed November 24, 2015. http://www.npr.org/2012/11/05/164342234/should-newspapers-make-political-endorsements.

F

FACE THE NATION

It's started in pretty dramatic fashion. Senator Joseph McCarthy of Wisconsin sat in a smoke-filled studio to discuss the special session of the Senate that planned to consider a censure of the Republican legislator and anti-Communist crusader.

"I've been so busy being investigated and preparing for this lynch bee starting tomorrow—," McCarthy told a panel of reporters from across the country.

"You call a meeting of the United States Senate a lynch bee?" William H. Lawrence of the *New York Times* interrupted, adding, "I'm interested in this. The Senate is an institution of government. It's part of the Congress. You call a meeting of the Senate a lynching?" (CBS News 1954).

McCarthy would go on to claim his impending censure was a partisan affair fueled by Democrats angered at being the "party of Communists," but the new CBS News program *Face the Nation* was already helping shape the political debate in Washington within 30 minutes of its inaugural broadcast.

The weekly Sunday news discussion program was started as part technological wonder and part panel discussion program. The idea, implied in the name, was to bring in voices and questions from across the country to pose to political leaders in Washington and New York. That first broadcast in November 1954 with Senator McCarthy started with a question from Indianapolis, and with it the 30-minute program's uniqueness was established.

The program was the brainchild of CBS president Frank Stanton, who wanted to demonstrate the ability of television to reach hundreds of miles from location to location instantly, and also to give NBC's *Meet the Press* some competition. The decision, like most of those made by Stanton, was meticulously studied. As one historian of CBS put it, "Frank Stanton . . . had a clear idea of what viewers like to watch . . . The research methods he developed back in the 1930s were established to determine, in advance, how big an audience a specific program was likely to attract, and that information was used as a selling point to potential sponsors" (Gates 1978).

In the 60 years that followed, *Face the Nation* has become one of the handful of Sunday morning talk shows that serve as a platform for aspiring national political figures as well as international leaders. To watch the archives of the program is to witness an amazing array of newsmaker interviews. In January 1959, the program originated from Havana, where Fidel Castro answered questions about his support of democratic rights and the reports of executions of former Cuban officials only three days after arriving in the Cuban capital. Or in May 1964 to watch Rev. Martin Luther King, Jr. discuss his plans for a "full-scale assault on the system of segregation in Alabama" and plans for a march on Washington.

The idea of the program seems simple enough: invite newsmakers on live to face questions from the host and other reporters about the major news of the week. Since 1991, veteran political reporter Bob Schieffer has hosted the program. Schieffer himself wrote about how the program has faced near-constant concerns about its approach and structure, writing, "Keeping the format intact has not always been easy. From the first broadcast, some worried that the program was too much 'inside baseball'—Washington insiders talking to Washington insiders about topics that would be of little interest to those outside Washington. It is a concern that has continued through the years" (Schieffer 2013). CBS executives considered moving the program to Los Angeles and making it more entertainment focused, and have occasionally tinkered with the format and the guests, but in large part the program is not all that different than the one Ted Koop anchored in November 1954.

Well, that's not completely true. The program is twice as long. From its inception until 2012 *Face the Nation* clocked in at 30 minutes—or really about 22 minutes with commercials. The other Sunday programs all were an hour, but CBS was slow to make the change and only did it in 2012 as an experiment. But even in announcing they would continue the hour-long format that July, Schieffer stressed the idea of continuity, writing to his readers, "We don't intend to change much. No bells and whistles here. We'll just turn on the lights, sit the key news makers down and ask them the questions we think you would ask. And if they don't answer, we'll try to point that out" (Schieffer 2012).

And Schieffer has changed little, occasionally a panelist comes or goes, but the program feels much like it did a decade ago, a mix of political score-keeping and questions aimed at keeping politicians on their toes. Schieffer, already Washington Bureau Chief when he took the chair of *Face the Nation* in 1991, became something of an elder statesmen of the Washington political corps. He has moderated three presidential debates and often substitutes as the anchor of CBS Evening News. He has also taken to the "Commentary" section of *Face the Nation* to criticize leaders of both parties, often for not being frank with the public. For example in 2013 he took to the airwaves to blast the Obama White House for its communications policy, telling viewers, "It's reached the point that if I want to interview anyone in the administration on camera, from the lowest-level worker to a top White House official, I have to go through the White House press office. If their chosen spokesman turns out to have no direct connection to the story of the moment, as was the case when U.N. Ambassador Susan Rice was sent out to explain the Benghazi episode, then that's what we (and you, the taxpayer) get. And it usually isn't much" (Shapiro 2013). In 2015, he stepped down after nearly 25 years as the program's host. John Dickerson, a contributor to *Slate* and longtime *Time* reporter, took the helm and has maintained many of the trademark elements of *Face the Nation*.

But whether the program is assessing the state of the presidential campaign or considering the latest maneuverings in Congress, the key players will often be there Sunday morning, making their case and trying to influence events and the coverage to come.

See also: *Meet the Press*; *This Week*

Further Reading
CBS News. 1954. "Sen. Joseph McCarthy on Face the Nation." YouTube. Accessed February 18, 2015. https://www.youtube.com/watch?v=FtVJFBSMXDk.
Gates, Gary Paul. 1978. *Air Time: The Inside Story of CBS News*. New York: Harper & Row, Publishers.
Schieffer, Bob. 2012. "'Face the Nation' to Continue as Hour-Long Show." CBS News. July 29. Accessed February 19, 2015. http://www.cbsnews.com/news/face-the-nation -to-continue-as-hour-long-show.
Schieffer, Bob. 2013. *Face the Nation: My Favorite Stories from the First 50 Years of the Award-Winning News Broadcast*. New York: Simon & Schuster.
Shapiro, Rebecca. 2013. "Bob Schieffer: Obama Press Policy 'Hurting His Credibility and Shortchanging the Public.'" Huffington Post. May 27. Accessed February 22, 2015. http://www.huffingtonpost.com/2013/05/27/bob-schieffer-obama-press-policy -hurting-credibility-public_n_3342310.html.

FACT CHECKING

As political campaigns and outside groups have intensified their use of paid advertising and reporters have sought ways to move beyond simply repeating the same stump speeches and claims made by candidates on the trail, fact-checking statements made by candidates and surrogates has become a core component of most news organizations' campaign coverage.

Fact checking is the editorial vetting of claims and speeches through reporting and researching public documents. As of 2015 there were at least two-dozen newsrooms producing ongoing fact-checking reports about campaigns. Even more journalists produce fact-check pieces during the course of the election that explore the claims made by campaigns and candidates. The idea of fact checking has become ingrained in the modern campaign, with candidates often producing fact checks about their opponent's claims and increasingly supplying supporting material to back up their own assertions. Political reporting veteran Mark Stencel has concluded, "People who work on campaigns and in government say fact-checking is changing political dialogue and practices. Some have taken editorial fact checks to heart—modifying and even dropping lines of attack that journalists found unfair or untruthful. As a matter of routine, political players try to preempt editorial scoldings with a combination of caution and supporting documentation that can keep campaigns on the truthier side of the fact-checkers' rating systems" (Stencel 2015). Having felt the power of solid fact-checking, campaigns now often wield fact checks produced by the media in their own ads, seeking to add the "legitimacy" of the news organization's assessment of an opponent to their counter-attack. Still other campaigns have organized their own fact-checking organization, such as the Hillary Clinton–supporting Super PAC Correct the Record, which uses the same fact-checking approach to counter claims made against the former secretary of state.

Editorially vetting advertisements is seen as a critical element of the reporting process because the rules governing these ads actually make them potential platforms for patently false information. A company selling a product may stretch the truth or obscure some negative facts, but they cannot lie; political candidates are not required to live up to the same standard. Political ads, as a form of political speech, are given the highest First Amendment protection, meaning they are not subject to government oversight for accuracy. In addition, stations are not legally allowed to reject ads even if they know the information is false. This stems from a 1972 Georgia campaign by National States Rights Party Senate candidate J.B. Stoner. Stoner wanted to run an ad that stated, the "main reason why niggers want integration is because niggers want our white women." The NAACP and several Atlanta-area stations objected to running the ad, but the Federal Communications Commission ruled the station could not reject the ad because of freedom of speech protections. Since ads with blatant lies must be allowed to run, examining and holding campaigns accountable for their content has emerged as an important check on political speech.

Still, fact checking is a brutal and unending job. A 30-second commercial may have a dozen or more factual assertions. A 90-minute debate is likely to have hundreds of claims or counter-claims. So organizations and reporters setting out to fact check a campaign have to come up with a rationale for what they choose to check and what they will let slide. The two primary fact-checking websites, FactCheck .org and Politifact, will publish dozens of reports a week during a campaign season. Each site has similar interests and approaches in selecting what kinds of claims to examine. Politifact has published an official rundown of its process and there it outlines the kinds of claims they choose to research, noting:

In deciding which statements to check, we ask ourselves these questions:

- Is the statement rooted in a fact that is verifiable? We don't check opinions, and we recognize that in the world of speechmaking and political rhetoric, there is license for hyperbole.
- Is the statement leaving a particular impression that may be misleading?
- Is the statement significant? We avoid minor "gotchas" on claims that obviously represent a slip of the tongue.
- Is the statement likely to be passed on and repeated by others?
- Would a typical person hear or read the statement and wonder: Is that true? (Politifact 2015)

Despite Politifact and other journalists tackling these ads and seeking to combat fabrication, good fact checking has several challenges to overcome in the modern media environment. First, usually more people see or read the original claim then the fact check. As *Time* magazine noted in considering the problem of political ads specifically, "The free market of ideas doesn't always work so well. As candidates know, a far greater percentage of voters hear the original lie in a campaign ad than ever read about the fact-checked version in a local paper or website like Factcheck

.org or Politifact.com. And even if voters do hear the refutation of an ad's claims, studies show that may not alter their perceptions created by the original ad" (Sullivan 2008). Ironically, some of this challenge is often overcome by the candidate originally targeted in the claim. These campaigns often pick up and reiterate the fact-check in their advertising as well as their own statements about the ad, amplifying the work done by the reporters, but also recasting it into their own political message.

The more significant problem facing fact-checkers is the general distrust that people have toward news reporting generally. This idea of a "post-truth politics" where even basic facts can be debated forever online has complicated the work of journalists who are striving to base their work on specific facts. Take, for example, the 2015 claim by GOP candidate Donald Trump about thousands of Muslims celebrating the attacks of September 11, 2001, across the river in New Jersey. Politifact examined the allegations and published their findings, noting, "Trump said he 'watched in Jersey City, N.J., where thousands and thousands of people were cheering' as the World Trade Center collapsed. This defies basic logic. If thousands and thousands of people were celebrating the 9/11 attacks on American soil, many people beyond Trump would remember it. And in the twenty-first century, there would be video or visual evidence. Instead, all we found were a couple of news articles that described rumors of celebrations that were either debunked or unproven" (Carroll 2015). Politifact gave the claim their harshest ranking of a "Pants on fire." But it had to compete with Breitbart.com's "9 Pieces of Documentation that Vindicate Trump's Claim of 9/11 Muslim Celebrations," a post that fueled pieces on TruthRevolt and a dozen other sites seeking to support the claims of Donald Trump.

Even as the process of convincing people of the facts in a fact check has grown more difficult, the proliferation of Internet-fueled rumors have exploded. Early in the World Wide Web a site was started called Snopes.com. Its goal was to confirm or debunk the urban legends of the day. The site tackled things like does it take seven years for gum to pass through the human digestive system or had KISS chosen its name to be an acronym for Knights in Satan's Service? The answer to both is no, but soon the Snopes folks found themselves getting political claims. Around the 2000 elections, people began sending the site things they wanted checked, and during the Obama administration those requests exploded. At the end of his seventh year in office President Barack Obama could claim 169 Snopes investigations. Unlike the other fact-checkers who are based in journalistic outfits or are trained journalists, David Mikkelson simply ran a message group that debunked rumors. When he examines the fact-checking landscape he sounds decidedly sanguine about the pressure to influence the public conversation, telling the *Washington Post* in late 2015, "The political conversation is messy overall . . . you often get a sense of despair like nobody's paying any attention to what you're actually writing. They're just determined to believe what they want to believe. Or, you write this long expository article and they focus on some minor aspect of it, completely outside of the thrust of what you've written, to claim it's wrong or it should be disregarded. So, I have to say, I don't have much faith that it does any good" (Kessler and Ye He Lee 2015).

See also: Echo Chamber Effect; FactCheck.org; Negative Advertising; Post-Truth Politics

Further Reading

Carroll, Lauren. 2015. "Fact-checking Trump's Claim That Thousands in New Jersey Cheered When World Trade Center Tumbled." Politifact. November 22. Accessed December 16, 2015. http://www.politifact.com/truth-o-meter/statements/2015/nov/22/donald-trump/fact-checking-trumps-claim-thousands-new-jersey-ch.

Kessler, Glenn, and Michelle Ye He Lee. 2015. "An Interview with the Editor of Snopes: 'Technology Changes, But Human Nature Doesn't.'" *Washington Post*. December 17. Accessed December 17, 2015. https://www.washingtonpost.com/news/fact-checker/wp/2015/12/17/an-interview-with-the-editor-of-snopes-technology-changes-but-human-nature-doesnt.

"Our Process." Politifact. Accessed December 16, 2015. http://www.politifact.com/truth-o-meter/article/2013/nov/01/principles-politifact-punditfact-and-truth-o-meter.

Stencel, Mark. 2015. "How Fact-Checking Journalism Is Changing Politics." American Press Institute. May 13. Accessed December 15, 2015. http://www.americanpressinstitute.org/publications/reports/survey-research/fact-checking-journalism-changing-politics.

Sullivan, Amy. 2008. "Truth in Advertising? Not for Political Ads." *Time* magazine. September 23. Accessed December 17, 2015. http://content.time.com/time/politics/article/0,8599,1843796,00.html.

FACTCHECK.ORG

Fact-checking the claims of candidates had already emerged as a major focus of modern campaign coverage by the late 1990s, in both network news and newspapers. But widespread misinformation was still a regular problem of campaigns. FactCheck.org turned that trend into a news service that aims to unpack the claims made in political debate, checking the sources and offering critiques of claims that lack substance.

Kathleen Hall Jamieson, an expert in political rhetoric, decided her organization, the Annenberg Public Policy Center at the University of Pennsylvania, should do something to ensure that fact checking continues to police the claims made by candidates and their surrogates. In 2003 Jamieson reached out to a veteran political reporter, CNN's Brooks Jackson, who had covered politics since the 1970s and had launched a fact-check segment on CNN that had become a staple of its political coverage to head the new effort.

By the end of the year, and with the 2004 presidential campaign looming, they launched FatcCheck.org. The mission was as simple to understand, as it was difficult to do. In their own words, FactCheck.org aims to "monitor the factual accuracy of what is said by major U.S. political players in the form of TV ads, debates, speeches, interviews and news releases. Our goal is to apply the best practices of both journalism and scholarship, and to increase public knowledge and understanding" (FactCheck.org 2015). Jackson agreed to head the new project and it was up and running in time to start checking the claims of candidates during the 2004 campaign.

The small staff of researchers and writers work out of the Annenberg Public Policy Center in Philadelphia and produce detailed reports that dissect the claims of politicians during campaigns and debates. The site states it is nonpartisan and nonprofit. It stresses it does not accept donations from corporations or unions and publishes information on all its donors on its website.

Almost immediately the site emerged as a source for candidates seeking to refute attacks from the other side. FactCheck.org's servers nearly melted down during the 2004 debates when then-vice president Dick Cheney cited the site (well, he said factcheck.com, but meant FactCheck.org) to dismiss criticism from rival John Edwards over his involvement with the corporate conglomerate Halliburton.

Four years later the campaign of Arizona senator John McCain used FactCheck .org in one of its ads, claiming the site had dismissed as "completely false" and "misleading" attacks on the vice presidential nominee, Alaska governor Sarah Palin. Jackson took to the site to write, "We don't object to people reprinting our articles. In fact, our copyright policy encourages it. But we've also asked that 'the editorial integrity of the article be preserved' . . . With its latest ad, released Sept. 10, the McCain-Palin campaign has altered our message in a fashion we consider less than honest" (Jackson 2008).

By 2012, the group's efforts had become a mainstay of the political season, but for all its work, it still faced what the *Washington Post*'s Eli Saslow described as a nearly impossible task—to combat wave after wave of misleading political claim. He wrote that for FactCheck.org, "The presidential election has become a predictable cycle of ambiguity and distortion: Candidates speak in half-truths and exaggerations, which are then amplified by the media and sensationalized in attack ads. Misinformation burns a trail across the Internet. The public trust erodes" (Saslow 2012).

That same year the difficulties of being a fact-checker became even more obvious when the campaign of Senator Barack Obama took FactCheck.org to task over its take on one of Democratic senator's claims. Obama's campaign was running an ad that claimed former Massachusetts governor Mitt Romney had overseen the outsourcing of jobs while at an investment firm, Bain Capital. FactCheck.org rejected that, saying the decision to move the jobs had come after Romney had left the firm to take the helm of the troubled Salt Lake City Olympics. The Obama campaign fired back, sending a six-page letter to FactCheck.org defending its claims and demanding that the site correct its assessment. Jackson, along with two of his reporters, responded that the letter "cobble[d] together selective news snippets and irrelevant securities documents in an attempt to show that Romney was still running Bain Capital on a part-time basis while he was also running the Olympics committee . . . In a nutshell, the Obama campaign is all wet on this point" (Dwyer 2012).

That exchange highlights the difficulty FactCheck.org and other independent fact-checking efforts face. They are challenged to respond to claims that are often complex and nuanced and are pushed to either clearly discredit or support those claims, a task made deliberately difficult through obtuse wording or misleading citation.

The site has sought to combat these trends and even expand its mission in recent years. It has added features that aim to address specific types of claims made by political figures or that affect public policy. These include one area, dubbed the "Viral Spiral," that seeks to debunk misleading or completely fabricated information that is moving through the Internet or cropping up on social media. The site produced a three-minute video that aims to help visitors identify what they dubbed, "Key Characteristics of Bogusness." Those red flags include the anonymity of the author, spelling errors, excessive use of exclamation points, and any use of math (FactCheck.org 2015). Another section of the site, launched in early 2015, seeks to battle "false and misleading scientific claims that are made by partisans to influence public policy" (FactCheck.org 2015).

Although some critics, most often on the right, point to the potential biases connected to the Annenberg Foundation, FactCheck.org created a model of holding candidates and campaigns accountable for their claims in a way that was later emulated by websites like Politifact and the *Washington Post*'s Fact Checker.

See also: Fact Checking; Post-Truth Politics

Further Reading

Dwyer, Devin. 2012. "Obama Campaign Challenges Fact Checker Report on Romney Outsourcing." ABC News. July 2. Accessed February 16, 2015. http://abcnews.go.com/blogs/politics/2012/07/obama-campaign-challenges-fact-checker-report-on-romney-outsourcing.

FactCheck.org. 2015. "Don't Get Spun by Internet Rumors." Accessed February 16, 2015. http://www.factcheck.org/hot-topics.

FactCheck.org. 2015. "Our Mission." Accessed February 16, 2015. http://www.factcheck.org/about/our-mission.

FactCheck.org. 2015. "SciCheck." Accessed February 15, 2015. http://www.factcheck.org/scicheck. http://www.washingtonpost.com/national/at-factcheckorg-the-search-for-truth-in-election-year-is-neverending/2012/10/15/e28f8fd2-16ef-11e2-a55c-39408fbe6a4b_story.html.

Jackson, Brooks. 2008. "McCain-Palin Distorts Our Finding." FactCheck.org. September 10. Accessed February 14, 2015. http://www.factcheck.org/2008/09/mccain-palin-distorts-our-finding.

Saslow, Eli. 2012. "At Factcheck.org, the Search for Truth in Election Year Is Never Ending." *Washington Post.* October 15. Accessed February 14, 2015. https://www.washingtonpost.com/national/at-factcheckorg-the-search-for-truth-in-election-year-is-neverending/2012/10/15/e28f8fd2-16ef-11e2-a55c-39408fbe6a4b_story.html.

FAIRNESS DOCTRINE

The Fairness Doctrine was a policy of the Federal Communications Commission, created in 1949, that aimed to ensure the airwaves—which were quickly becoming the most potent political medium in the nation—would not become a platform for partisan attacks. The doctrine lasted for some four decades as a testament to the concern the government had over the power of television to inform or misinform the public about matters of public concern.

The doctrine, which emerged from an FCC memo to licensees about how to cover controversial issues, included two core components: first, that stations would, indeed, cover issues that were politically controversial and, second, that those stations would offer differing viewpoints on those matters. It did not mandate each individual story had to have equal time devoted to each side of a political debate, but rather that the coverage itself would be broad and generally balanced. In a 1974 report, the FCC outlined the core ideas the fairness doctrine aimed to ensure, "(1) the broadcaster must devote a reasonable percentage of time to coverage of public issues; and (2) his coverage of these issues must be fair in the sense that it provides an opportunity for the presentation of contrasting points of view" (Carter, Franklin, and Wright 1989). Much of the discussion, and angst, over the Fairness Doctrine focused on the mandate to cover multiple angles of a story, but the part of the rule that required coverage of these controversial issues is one of the elements of the FCC policy that helped create many of the broadcast news divisions in the earliest days of commercial television.

The doctrine was a clear exertion of control over content by the federal government, a power it is specifically denied under the First Amendment, but broadcast entities were seen as a legally different beast. Because radio and television broadcasters were licensed by the federal government—essentially given a regional monopoly to use and make money off of a specific frequency of the public's airwaves—the government could exert this control. Still, broadcasters chafed under what many saw as a double standard, and it was not long before one fought the government's intrusion into their business. The Fairness Doctrine was tested in court and found constitutional, but by the 1980s the deregulation efforts of the Ronald Reagan administration reached the FCC as well. Dennis Patrick, then-chairman of the FCC, said his agency would no longer enforce the doctrine, declaring, "We seek to extend to the electronic press the same First Amendment guarantees that the print media have enjoyed since our country's inception." In 2011, the FCC finally voted to formally remove the doctrine from its rules.

To understand the source and thinking behind the Fairness Doctrine, it is important to consider the thinking of those early legislators and administrators who saw the doctrine as a necessary tool to protect the common good. The rise of terrestrial broadcasting came to be seen by politicians as a powerful tool for communicating and, it was feared, manipulating public opinion. Former FCC commissioner Newton Minow would late explain that, "freedom of speech could no longer be preserved by simply preventing government restriction. The right to be heard—and the right to hear—sought protection through other guarantees during the electronic era" (Simmons 1978). These officials came to argue that simply allowing broadcasters to decide these issues on their own left the freedoms enshrined in the

Constitution under the control of the broadcaster. The government's concerns were centered both on the power of the broadcast media, but also its relative scarcity. There were only so many channels and broadcast frequencies and only a handful of networks, so ensuring that voters who were listening and watching were exposed to politically controversial issues and made aware of differing viewpoints emerged as a critical rationale for the government actions.

In this way, the Fairness Doctrine was really an extension of the thinking that pervaded even the earliest efforts to regulate broadcasters. When Congress stepped into the chaos of broadcasting in 1927 with the Radio Act, its sponsor knew he was attempting to draw a fine line between government protection of the public and government censorship of the media. He chose Greek mythology to try and make his point, telling colleagues, "We must steer the legislative ship between the Scylla of too much regulation and the Charybdis of the grasping selfishness of private monopoly" (Simmons 1978). The result of this balancing act was a largely ad hoc set of rules, like the initial Fairness Doctrine rules that grew out of a 1949 report that focused on how licensees should handle controversial public issues. The doctrine later came to include other rules covering so-called personal attacks and political editorials.

Political editorial rules ensured that if the station endorsed a candidate or broadcast an endorsement from someone else calling for the election or defeat of a candidate, the station was responsible for notifying the candidate not receiving the endorsement that the broadcast had occurred. The station also had to take reasonable steps to offer the other candidate a chance to respond. The personal attack rules stated that when a single person or a small, identifiable group of people were attacked on air, the station had to notify them within a week of the broadcast and supply them with a transcript. It also had to grant the person or group a chance to respond on-air. It was this rule that would create the most significant legal challenge to the Fairness Doctrine and eventually cement the government's rights.

In late November 1964 a radio station in rural southern Pennsylvania broadcast a talk by Reverend Billy James Hargis. The 15-minute speech was part of a larger series of Christian addresses made by the Red Lion Broadcasting Company; in this episode Hargis took issue with a book by Fred Cook about conservative U.S. senator and recent Republican presidential candidate Barry Goldwater. During his speech, Hargis accused Cook of being fired from a newspaper job for making false charges against city officials, defending communist Alger Hiss, and being too critical of FBI director J. Edgar Hoover and the Central Intelligence Agency. The station made no attempt to contact Cook in the wake of the broadcast and when the author learned of the speech, he demanded time to respond.

Red Lion Broadcasting refused. The FCC then ruled that the broadcast amounted to a personal attack and that Cook should be granted time to speak. The company sued, claiming the First Amendment should protect them. Four-and-a-half years later, in 1969 the Supreme Court ruled in favor of the FCC. In his writing for the majority, Justice White relied heavily on the technological differences between broadcast and print media, writing, "Because of the scarcity of radio frequencies, the Government is permitted to put restraints on licensees in favor of others whose views should be expressed on this unique medium. But the people as a whole retain their interest in free speech by radio and their collective right to have the medium function consistently with the ends and purposes of the First Amendment. It is the right of the viewers and listeners, not the right of the broadcasters, which is paramount." White continued, "Freedom of the press from governmental interference under the First Amendment does not sanction repression of that freedom by private interests."

Following the decision, the government settled into a policy of enforcing the Fairness Doctrine, but usually in only the most egregious cases. It would not police the stations too tightly, but should a viewer complain and not have their legitimate concern addressed, the FCC might step in as they did in the Cook case. Also, the agency pressed the stations to live up to their requirements by carefully monitoring their applications to renew their government licenses. Each station would submit lengthy reports, including documentation of its coverage of controversial issues and its reports on complaints to the station.

This new balance would occasionally come under fire from critics. Some argued that what emerged in the wake of *Red Lion* was a deal between two "power elites," according to former NBC News correspondent Ford Rowan. Rowan argued that "while broadcasters have been successful in utilizing the system to protect their economic interests and maximize profits, the politicians have been triumphant in assuring that the power of radio and television is not turned against them, that they have access to the airwaves, that stations must be neutral in selling or giving time to candidates" (Rowan 1984). The result, Rowan said, was a sort of detente between broadcasters and politicians. It should be noted that the Supreme Court took up the issue of access to print media five years later in the critical case *Miami Herald Publishing Co. v. Tornillo*. In this case, the Florida Supreme Court had upheld a state law the required the paper provide access to its editorial pages for politicians who had not been endorsed by the paper—essentially equivalent to the "political editorials" corollary of the fairness doctrine. But unlike the *Red Lion* case, the Court ruled that the Florida law was a breach of the First Amendment, citing the role of editors guaranteed by the Constitution. It is striking the difference between these two cases and speaks to the fundamentally different view of broadcasters versus newspaper publishers according to the federal government up until the early 1980s.

In 1974, the FCC clarified its intentions by putting the onus of fairness on the broadcast journalists. It wrote in a 1974 report, "We believe . . . that the public's interest in free expression through broadcasting will best be served and promoted through the continued reliance on the Fairness Doctrine which leaves questions of access and the specific handling of public issues to the licensee's journalistic discretion. This system is far from perfect. However, in our judgment, it does represent the most appropriate accommodation of the various First Amendment interests involved, and provides for maximum public enlightenment on issues of significance with a minimum of governmental intrusion into the journalistic process" (Schmidt 1976).

This meant that the Fairness Doctrine loomed more as a threat over the heads of the broadcasters and journalists than as an active government intrusion. Should the broadcaster air a negative attack on a public figure without seeking comment from the accused or endorse a candidate for office or a specific policy, the FCC may become involved and require the channel to offer time to the other side. Should a station broadcast nothing but politically slanted discussion over a broadcast (not cable) channel, then they could face FCC fines. The more important effect of the doctrine was to limit the overtly partisan broadcasts that would continually test the personal attack and fairness questions.

Debate over the political necessity of the doctrine continued throughout the 1970s and into the 1980s. Much of the criticism of the doctrine came from the right, who saw the way the FCC chose to enforce the rule as infringing on their right to speak. Publications like the conservative *National Review* quoted former FCC officials as having their staff take out stopwatches to clock the coverage of controversial issues and the political balance of the stories (Anderson 2008). This criticism increased during the 1980s as the administration of Ronald Reagan moved to deregulate many industries and broadcasters hoped they would be among those who could cut down the government requirements they faced.

When the FCC finally scuttled the Fairness Doctrine, arguing viewers could discern for themselves differing views on public matters, the result was hard to see on the broadcast channels on television. ABC, CBS, and NBC did not suddenly change the way they reported on stories or add major opinion content. Instead the real impact of the end of the Fairness Doctrine appeared on radio. With the end of required balance, radio stations could air liberal or conservative talk shows without seeking a political balance on the other side. Conservatives, fed up with their perceived bias among the mainstream press, flocked to a new era of provocative radio hosts like Rush Limbaugh. Liberal talk radio largely floundered, but conservatives found their voice in a post-Fairness Doctrine broadcast world.

This emergence of political talk fueled some rumblings of restoring a version of the Fairness Doctrine, as politicians worried that politically oriented broadcasts were fostering a widening partisan gulf. Democrats in Congress introduced bills in 2005 that would have reestablished the doctrine, but they went nowhere. Still, the threat that the government may attempt to create a new version of the rule remained an occasional boogeyman for conservative talk show hosts. A fairly feeble attempt by some in the Democratic Congress to propose a new version of the doctrine in 2008—it never gained more than 25 supporters and quickly melted away without ever coming to a vote—prompted Laura Ingraham to warn, "Make no mistake, imposing 'fairness' on America's radio waves is an end-run around competing in the battle of ideas. Their new motto is this: If you can't beat them, silence them . . . We could soon see a Democratic Congress and a Democratic President push through a new Fairness Doctrine and that could mean that you won't hear The Laura

Ingraham Show and many of your other favorite radio shows on stations across the country" (Ingraham 2008).

From its inception in the 1920s, political forces understood the power of broadcasts and worried that this new media could be used to sway or misinform millions. The government implemented policies like the Fairness Doctrine in hopes that any egregious abuses of the public airwaves would be dealt with and broadcasters who chose to use these tools for partisan ends could be taken off the air. The result was an uneasy decades-long truce between government and broadcasters where so long as the licensees behaved "reasonably" the government would leave them be. But the threat remained in a way unfelt by journalists in other media. In the wake of its repeal, the fears of some did come to pass as far more partisan media took to the airwaves. But in a world of hundreds of cable channels and millions of websites, the theory of scarcity that drove government policy no longer justifies the government's role in broadcasting it once had.

See also: Broadcast Television News; First Amendment and Censorship; Public Interest Obligation; Talk Radio

Further Reading
Anderson, Brian. 2008. *Manifesto for Media Freedom*. New York: Encounter Books.
Carter, T. Barton, Marc Franklin, and Jay Wright. 1989. *The First Amendment and the Fifth Estate: Regulation of the Electronic Mass Media*. Westbury, NY: The Foundation Press, Inc.
Ingraham, Laura. 2008. The O'Reilly Factor. Fox News. June 20. Accessed June 1, 2015. https://www.youtube.com/watch?v=uF0U6YCZ2WQ.
Rowan, Ford. 1984. *Broadcast Fairness: Doctrine, Practice, Prospects*. New York: Longman Inc.
Schmidt, Benno. 1976. *Freedom of the Press vs. Public Access*. New York: Praeger.

FAMILY RESEARCH COUNCIL

The Family Research Council is a nonprofit political organization that aims to promote evangelical beliefs in political debates at both the national and statewide levels. The group, based in Washington, D.C., is a leading voice of Christian conservatives, arguing for the widest possible religious protections while calling on government policies to protect the unborn and oppose rights for homosexuals. The group has been an active part of the so-called culture war between liberals and conservatives that have created heated debates over many social issues, from women's rights to violent music. The group boasts a $13 million annual budget and employees nearly 100 people. It also has an affiliated lobbying group that supports candidates that agree with its positions.

James Dobson, a controversial and influential conservative author, developed the idea for the council after attending a meeting on the family organized by the administration of Democratic president Jimmy Carter. The way the council describes it in their own history, Dobson, who had founded an influential evangelical nonprofit group Focus on the Family in 1977, met with a group of eight other religious leaders to pray and reflect on the colliding world of politics and religion. The idea was that cultural conservatives needed to be more active in the political arena and this new organization could serve as a sort-of evangelical think tank and policy advocacy operation. Dobson worked with one of the other pastors present, Gerald Regier, to create the new Family Research Council. Built in the likeness of other research outfits in Washington, D.C., the new council aimed to be a political force, commenting on and helping shape coverage of issues of importance to social conservatives. The group officially organized in 1981 and incorporated itself in 1983. A video on the council's website helps explain some of the thinking behind the group and their new-found political causes, saying, "As our culture is rapidly changed and molded by secular elites, as our government grows and reaches deeper into our lives, as biblical faith and values are defined as hate, these are troubling times for our nation . . . When the days are dark we are not called to wring our hands in defeat, but to clasp them in prayer, join them with others and put them to work" (Family Research Council). That work would include focusing on limiting abortion, opposing same-sex marriage, and working to ease limits on prayer in school and other public venues. By 1988 internal reorganizations brought the council back under the Focus on the Family umbrella, although the council has focused more on its role in Washington, D.C., and influencing the national political debate on cultural questions.

Dobson, although central to the creation and direction of the council, rarely played a public role in the many political fights it would become embroiled in over the next 30 years. A 2004 profile of the pastor noted that "after he created the Family Research Council, he let others act as its spokesmen. He almost never endorsed political candidates, even when Gary L. Bauer, his protégé and the former president of the council, ran in the Republican presidential primaries four years ago" (Kirkpatrick 2004). He instead allowed the council to evolve through the work of former senior Republican officials who helped guide the council throughout its history. Regier, the first president of the council, had worked to create a network of organizations interested in the intersection of religion and politics and sought to keep the FRC as one of the primary conveners of cultural conservatives. The council expanded much of its work after the 1988 merger with Focus on the Family during which Gary Bauer took the helm. Bauer, a former deputy secretary of education, had chaired President Ronald Reagan's "Special Working Group on the Family." Bauer ran the council until 1999 when he left to mount his own unsuccessful run at the White House. In 2003, former Louisiana congressman Tony Perkins took over and has run the group since then. But the connection between the council and the Republican Party is more than just who runs the FRC. The council is often at the table when the party is discussing electoral strategy, warning Republicans against becoming too moderate on issues Christian evangelicals care about. The council often warns that the Republican Party needs social conservatives to come to the polls and that those voters make up one of the most consistent blocs of support for the party.

Although the group often works behind the scenes to shape Republican positions on social and cultural matters, much of the FRC's influence is connected to their work with the media. The Family Research Council is a go-to source for media organizations seeking the views of religious conservatives, appearing as regular guests on cable programs and news reports. The group has been at the front of public debates around abortion, taking a lead in arguing for a ban on a controversial late-term abortion technique and claiming credit for helping pass by the summer of 2015 "more than 200 pro-life bills enacted in the states since 2011." The council also works within the Republican Party to shore up and protect their values, working to combat Republicans who would support abortion rights and, in the wake of the Supreme Court ruling to legalize same-sex marriage, pushing protection of what they call "natural marriage" through legislative action and the Republican Party platform.

Their strident arguments in favor of basing public policy on firmly held religious convictions has made the FRC a lightning rod for criticism. By 2010 the council's outspoken efforts to maintain the ban on homosexuals in the military, to allow same-sex marriages, and to limit any legal protections for homosexuals landed it on the Southern Poverty Law Center's list of domestic hate groups in the United States. In their "file" on the council, the SPLC said, "To make the case that the LGBT community is a threat to American society, the FRC employs a number of 'policy experts' whose 'research' has allowed the FRC to be extremely active politically in shaping public debate. Its research fellows and leaders often testify before Congress and appear in the mainstream media" (Southern Poverty Law Center 2010). Two years after the SPLC came out with its accusation that the Family Research Council had become a hate group for spreading malicious and untrue information about homosexuality, a shooting outside the council's headquarters sparked a debate over whether the so-called culture war between socially conservative and socially liberal groups had become too close to a shooting war. One conservative law professor said the SPLC's label "gave cover to those who use the 'hate speech' and 'hate group' labels to shut down political and religious speech, and now it has spiraled out of control" (Sessions 2012).

The Family Research Council operates purely on tax deductible donations from social conservatives around the country and has often used their public campaigns in the media to help drive donations to their organization.

See also: Cultural Conservatives

Further Reading

"About." Family Research Center. Accessed June 13, 12016. http://www.frc.org/about-frc.

"Family Research Center." Southern Poverty Law Center. Accessed August 5, 2015. https://www.splcenter.org/fighting-hate/extremist-files/group/family-research-council.

Kirkpatrick, David. 2004. "Warily, a Religious Leader Lifts His Voice in Politics." *New York Times*. May 13. Accessed August 5, 2015. http://www.nytimes.com/2004/05/13/us/2004-campaign-evangelical-christians-warily-religious-leader-lifts-his-voice.html.

Sessions, David. 2012. "Is the Family Research Council Really a Hate Group?" The Daily Beast. August 16. Accessed August 5, 2015. http://www.thedailybeast.com/articles/2012 /08/16/is-the-family-research-council-really-a-hate-group.html.

FEDERAL ELECTION COMMISSION (FEC)

The Federal Election Commission, or FEC, is the agency tasked with implementing and enforcing the nation's campaign finance and electioneering laws for presidential and congressional campaigns. The agency also compiles and publishes donor and expenditure reports submitted by candidates, political parties, and certain political action committees.

The agency is the point of origin for all documents related to federal campaign financing and provides reams of information that are used by reporters as well as good government organizations like the Center for Responsive Politics to allow journalists and citizens to monitor the campaign spending and fundraising. As constructed, the agency was tasked with compiling these finance reports, helping candidates and parties understand the current regulations they must adhere to, and investigating and adjudicating any violations of federal campaign laws. The FEC has faced criticism from both sides of the debate for being co-opted by the political parties and candidates they are tasked with regulating on the one hand, and on the other for being too aggressive in limiting the First Amendment freedoms of those seeking to influence the political process.

The FEC was born out of the congressional reforms to campaign finance laws enacted in the wake of the Watergate scandal. During that time, news reports emerged of the Nixon re-election campaign using secret funds of campaign donations to fund so-called dirty tricks groups that worked to sabotage opponents and spy on the Democrats. Congress sought to crack down on these abuses as well as slow the growing costs of elections by enacting the Federal Election Campaign Act of 1975. The initial law focused on presidential campaigns more than congressional and the new agency's mission read, in part, as "to disclose campaign finance information, to enforce the provisions of the law such as the limits and prohibitions on contributions, and to oversee the public funding of Presidential elections." But central to the FEC's approach to the political process was creating a system of "voluntary compliance" with the election laws. In its first annual report, the FEC noted that "voluntary compliance suggested a presumption on the part of the Commission that the participants in the political process wanted to comply with the law and would comply if properly advised of their obligations. The Commission for its part would devote its primary effort and energy to making certain that the necessary advice was given and only thereafter would it concentrate on enforcement actions." This idea that the FEC would not really be the police, but would rather serve as a legal adviser to federal campaigns frustrated reformers who wanted to see a much stronger agency built around enforcement. But this philosophy of voluntary compliance remains an underlying approach of the FEC despite countless changes to the process and the underlying laws.

Congress knew this function would be highly controversial, and that it risked suppressing the minority party, so the FEC would be overseen by a panel of six members with no one party controlling more than three seats. Also, to make any formal ruling the commission needed at least four votes. The result, especially in the last few decades, has been gridlock with the three Democrats lining up on one side and the three Republicans on the other. The setup has become so untenable that its chairwoman admitted to the *New York Times*, "The likelihood of the laws being enforced is slim. I never want to give up, but I'm not under any illusions. People think the FEC is dysfunctional. It's worse than dysfunctional" (Lichtblau 2015). The inability of the commission to respond to the new organizations known as "dark money" groups that can raise unlimited donations anonymously and then spend those funds on independent issue-advocacy ads, many of which are clearly aimed at defeating one of the candidates in that election, has frustrated Democratic members of the panel. Two of the commissioners have even petitioned their own agency to start a rulemaking process, writing, "While the Supreme Court ruled that corporations and labor organizations have a First Amendment right to engage in independent spending, the Court also resoundingly affirmed disclosure laws requiring political advertisers to provide information to the public about their spending and their funding sources . . . Anonymous campaign spending will continue to diminish public faith in the political process, unless the Commission acts" (Ravel and Weintraub 2015).

Despite the gridlock of the agency and its political inability to address the changing landscape of the political world, the FEC does get credit for pressing the idea of disclosure of campaign fundraising sources. One analysis of the campaign finance system concluded, "While there is substantial criticism of the commission's enforcement activities, there is also a recognition that much more is known about campaign finance practices as a result of the FECA's disclosure provisions . . . The commission has gone beyond the statutory requirements to make contribution and expenditure data available to the public in a useful format" (Magleby and Nelson 1990). This process has had a tremendous impact on the coverage of campaigns by creating a source of information that can indicate how a campaign is resonating with supporters and whether a candidate is mounting a serious run for office. By creating periodic reports and then making those reports quickly public, the FEC has influenced the way campaigns approach fundraising. Pitches to supporters will plead for money ahead of reporting deadlines, knowing stories will soon run outlining the amount of money raised, the current war chest of a campaign, and the number of donors the candidate or campaign has attracted. Similarly, the FEC has worked to make that information public as soon as it is received and has worked to feed its own site as well as independent campaign finance tracking organizations like opensecrets.org. This public component of the FEC's work has been repeatedly cited by Supreme Court and other legal outlets as a critical element of the underlying campaign finance laws, ensuring that any overt efforts to influence a candidate or campaign are open to public and journalistic scrutiny.

Still, even this role of the FEC has weakened in recent years as Supreme Court decisions created new political entities that have fewer or no requirements to voluntarily submit reports to the agency. For example, the 2010 federal appeals court ruling in *SpeechNow.org v. Federal Election Commission* created so-called Super PACs. These organizations can raise unlimited donations from corporations, unions, associations, and individuals and spend that money to expressly call for the election or defeat of a given candidate. These groups cannot coordinate with a given campaign they seek to help and must disclose their donors and spending to the FEC. But in line with its philosophy of voluntary compliance the FEC allows Super PACs to report their activities either monthly or quarterly, meaning that spending in the days ahead of an election may not be disclosed until months later.

The struggles of the agency have weighed not just on the political appointees running the commission, but also on the professional staff tasked with implementing the law and working to improve the functionality of the data they produce. One 2014 study by the Partnership for Public Service concluded, "Out of 30 small federal agencies ranked for employee satisfaction and commitment, the FEC placed 29th, its score particularly affected by low marks in effective leadership, innovation, strategic management and support for diversity . . . Perhaps even more troubling for the FEC: The agency's overall score has steadily slipped each year since 2009, bottoming out this year at 40.4 out of a possible 100 points" (Levinthal 2014).

See also: Campaign Finance Reform; *Citizens United;* Dark Money Groups; Disclosure; Political Action Committees (PACs); Super PACs

Further Reading

Levinthal, Dave. 2014. "New FEC Chief on 'Dark Money' Mission." Center for Public Integrity. December 17. Accessed September 22, 2015. http://www.publicintegrity.org/2014/12/17/16527/new-fec-chief-dark-money-mission.

Lichtblau, Eric. 2015. "F.E.C. Can't Curb 2016 Election Abuse, Commission Chief Says." *New York Times.* May 2. Accessed September 22, 2015. http://www.nytimes.com/2015/05/03/us/politics/fec-cant-curb-2016-election-abuse-commission-chief-says.html?_r=0.

Magleby, David and Candice Nelson. 1990. *The Money Chase: Congressional Campaign Finance Reform.* Washington, D.C.: The Brookings Foundation.

Ravel, Ann, and Ellen Weintraub. 2015. "Petition for Rulemaking." Federal Election Commission. June 8. Accessed June 13, 2016. http://www.fec.gov/members/statements/Petition_for_Rulemaking.pdf.

FEEDING FRENZY

In terms of political coverage, a feeding frenzy refers to when a significant number of members of the press jump on a scandal story, often zealously pursuing personal information about a candidate or public official. Its hallmark is the chaotic scene of videographers, photojournalists, and reporters besieging a source, treating the subject of the scandal to the kind of badgering usually reserved for Hollywood celebrities leaving a courthouse. The term refers to moments in nature when a large group of predators simultaneous attack a wounded prey and was coined by political scientist and commentator Larry Sabato for a book about what he called "attack journalism" (Sabato 2000).

The idea is related to the concept of pack journalism—both in substance and in animal reference—but in this instance deals with the intense media scrutiny connected to a political scandal. Sabato wrote the book in the wake of the 1988 campaign, which featured the meteoric rise and Shakespearean fall of Colorado senator Gary Hart. Hart, a moderate Democrat who was initially seen as the strong front-runner for his party's nomination, had pledged to be a leader of the highest ethical standards, seeking to distance himself from the Reagan administration and its Iran-Contra scandal. In introducing his candidacy in Denver, Colorado, that year Hart chided, "We've seen high standards for public officials and public ethics be eroded." Even more notably, Hart had dismissed rumors that he had anything in his background that would be a problem. He went so far as to tell reporters in one interview, "Follow me around . . . . I'm serious. If anybody wants to put a tail on me, go ahead. They'd be very bored." But then reporters at the *Miami Herald* got a call from an anonymous woman who said she had proof Hart had been acting inappropriately at a party in Miami. The call triggered an unlikely trip to Washington by reporters tailing a young blonde woman, Donna Rice, the caller said was headed to meet Hart for a weekend alone. Three reporters—Jim McGee, Tom Fiedler, and James Savage—staked out Hart's Capitol Hill townhouse. After the senator became increasingly suspicious they decided to confront Hart. McGee approached Hart, and said he wished to ask about woman staying at his house. "We've had your house under surveillance since early last evening. I was standing near the front of your house last night at 9:30 p.m. I saw you come out of your house with a blond woman" (McGee, Fiedler, and Savage 1987).

The story of course exploded. Eventually, unable to move beyond the endless questions, Hart dropped out of the race. In his parting shot to the press, he admonished, "We're all going to have to seriously question the system for selecting our national leaders, that reduces the press of this nation to hunters and the presidential candidates to being hunted, that has reporters in bushes, false and inaccurate stories printed, photographers peeking in our windows, swarms of helicopters hovering over our roof, and my very strong wife close to tears because she can't even get in her own house at night without being harassed. And then after all that, ponderous pundits wonder in mock seriousness why some of our best people in this country choose not to run for high office" (Associated Press 1987).

The Hart episode opened a new era in the media's decisions about pursuing stories about the private lives of candidates. Hart and others in the public eye argued that private lives only mattered if they directly affected the professional life they were being considered for, while reporters argued that questions of personal character mattered to the voting public. This back-and-forth would be debated every time over the coming decades when a politician's private life made news or affected a campaign. One journalist would declare the week from the disclosure of the Donna Rice affair to the collapse of the Hart campaign as seven days that fundamentally changed political journalism. Matt Bai, who wrote a book on that change, told PBS that "after Hart, the guiding ethos of political journalism really begins to shift inexorably away from the elimination of ideas and world views and agendas and more toward exposing the lie. We know there's a lie. We know there's hypocrisy. And hypocrisy is now very broadly defined. Our job is to find out what it is" (PBS News-Hour 2014).

Sabato, looking back later, would say that the similar explosion of coverage of then vice presidential candidate Dan Quayle would be his prime example of the feeding frenzy. Quayle had been a largely unknown second-term senator from Indiana when then vice president George H. W. Bush named him as his running mate. The story exploded onto the national stage. The press had dived into Quayle's past, building a story that the 41-year-old was a lightweight. A profile in *Time* magazine years later naming him one of the nation's worst vice presidents gives a sense of the way the press constructed the image. The magazine argued that Quayle "had plenty to be modest about: he had failed an undergraduate comprehensive exam at De-Pauw University; one of his former professors referred to him as 'vapid'; and he was admitted to law school at the University of Indiana under an 'equal opportunity' program for poor and minority students" (Pickert 2008). Quayle's coverage was deeply personal as reporters delved into his military record, his sexiness, his possible relationship with a former Playboy bunny.

This intensely personal examination of candidates' lives and possible relationships was being hotly debated not only in public but also the newsroom. Some journalists worried that their coverage was being driven by tabloids. Others who had covered politics for decades noted that they had never reported on the widely known or at least rumored affairs of past presidents and candidates. But after 1988, the debate shifted. By the time Bill Clinton, governor of Arkansas and candidate in the 1992 presidential election, was facing questions about an affair with former state employee Gennifer Flowers, journalists were used to the argument. But that year the story came up when Flowers sold her story—and audio tapes—to a supermarket tabloid. ABC confronted the candidate in New Hampshire and he denied telling anyone to lie about the nature of his relationship with her. Inside ABC News the debate reignited. Correspondent Jeff Greenfield made the argument that had come to fuel the media's decision to tackle these stories, saying, "If there are millions of Americans for whom adultery is a disqualifying flaw, what is the press's responsibility? If he were a deeply religious person, he said, someone who is bothered by adultery, he would want to know if this man cheats on his wife. 'This is a mortal sin. For Catholics it's the sixth commandment'" (Rosenstiel 1993). But each time the character issue was raised and the feelings of people who may oppose a candidate based on behavior was used to justify diving into private lives, many people were angered by the media's approach.

Despite this argument, a counter argument has developed that journalists' decisions to withhold information from the public amounted to a paternalistic and elitist view of the population. Michael Kinsley struck this chord when he argued that "journalists thought that marital infidelity shouldn't affect your assessment of a politician, but their motivation for not writing about it was concern that the voters might not be as enlightened. Voters could not be trusted with the information that their elected representative was sleeping around—they might wrongly hold it against him—so journalists kept it from them for their own good" (Kinsley 2012).

Although the feeding frenzy idea is most associated with personal moral failings, it can and does erupt whenever the media latches onto a story or person and feels the need to explore every aspect of their life. One recent example of this was the nomination of Sarah Palin for the vice presidency in 2008. Palin, a first-term governor of Alaska, was a political unknown when U.S. senator John McCain chose her as his running mate. Palin delivered some early, rousing speeches, stressing her outsider status and Alaskan independence. But the media also knew precious little about Palin, and many networks and news organizations poured money into efforts to find out everything they could. Quickly, they discovered her unwed daughter was pregnant, a fact that led some commentators to question how well she had been parented. Her husband's political affiliations with the libertarian Alaska Independence Party became a story. Her moose hunting from a helicopter was a story. The amount the campaign spent on her clothes was a story. NPR dubbed the coverage a full-fledged feeding frenzy and pressed CNN for a reason why the network had chosen to dig into all aspects of her life. CNN's Jon Klein told NPR, "We will try to be respectful of the governor and her entire life—but in this case the governor was put forward as a candidate precisely because her entire life was said to exemplify a certain independent spirit and an attitude that's exactly what the country needs. Well, we need to know more about her attitudes, how she lives her life, and how that influences public policy" (Folkenflik 2008). This is much the same rationale used for any feeding frenzy into a personal life. In a nutshell: character counts. Whether it is their overcoming personal loss of professional setbacks or it's their marital affairs or drug use, the expectation is that this information can and will come out and the public who will decide by voting for or against the person has the right to pass judgment on it.

But there are two other elements of the feeding frenzy to consider as well: the legal system that allows such wild media coverage and the impact this coverage has on the candidates for higher office in America. On the legal side it is important to note that relaxed libel laws in this country toward public officials feeds this intense feeding frenzy. The critical Supreme Court libel decision *New York Times v. Sullivan* in 1965 created two standards for plaintiffs to prove in libel cases—one for public officials and one for private individuals. In *Sullivan*, the court said any investigation into public figures—especially those with political power—needed to have an even higher degree of protection from libel suits. The thinking of the court was this reporting should not be punishable by local juries and courts who disagree with the reporting, but the reality of the decision was that public figures must now show that the media outlet knowingly published false information with the intent of hurting the public figure, a tall order for most cases. So journalists can conduct these investigations into public figures' private lives with little to no fear of facing legal jeopardy.

As for how all of this has affected the political system, debate rages. The assumption, stated in most analyses even back to Sabato's book, is that good people often won't run out of fear of what the press will put them through. One political scientist actually put this concept to the test and found statistical evidence that "media screening of political candidates is costly. The proliferation of frenzies and expansion of the range of personal issues subject to scrutiny raises the expected cost to good people of running for public office" (Sutter 2006). And this is the fear, that media coverage of candidates, their lives, their families, and their business dealings force out too many qualified, civic-minded officials.

But the anger at the feeding frenzy often overlooks the public in the equation. When the public rejects the importance of a specific personal matter in deciding who should win, the press has ratcheted down its coverage of that story. For example, in 1992 a feeding frenzy—one of many he triggered—erupted over then-governor Bill Clinton's use of marijuana. Clinton famously said he had tried the drug, but had not inhaled it. The frenzy that followed raised questions about the appropriateness of a public figure having tried drugs. Some 16 years later, Senator Barack Obama admitted to marijuana use in his youth and even in his autobiography to trying cocaine, and the public and press appeared unconcerned. The press attention on personal matters and the intensity of the scrutiny into personal matters will likely continue for the foreseeable future, but what prompts these frenzies and what creates strong public reaction appears to be much more in flux as attitudes and political issues change.

See also: Damage Control; Pack Journalism; Spin

Further Reading

Associated Press. 1987. "God Can Forgive Sin, But Stupid Is Forever." *Newburgh Beacon Evening News.* May 10. Accessed. July 15, 2015. https://news.google.com/newspapers?nid =1982&dat=19870510&id=MIpGAAAAIBAJ&sjid=wzMNAAAAIBAJ&pg =3464,917610&hl=en.

Bai, Matt. 2014. "How Gary Hart's Downfall Forever Changed American Politics." *New York Times Magazine.* September 16. Accessed July 14, 2015. http://www.nytimes.com/2014 /09/21/magazine/how-gary-harts-downfall-forever-changed-american-politics.html? _r=0.

Folkenflik, David. 2008. "A Full-Fledged Feeding Frenzy on Sarah Palin." NPR. September 3. Accessed July 17, 2015. http://www.npr.org/templates/story/story.php?storyId =94217634.

Kinsley, Michael. 2012. "Being Prudish about Politicians' Private Lives: Michael Kinsley." Michaelkinsley.com. February 2. Accessed July 16, 2015. http://michaelkinsley.com /being-prudish-about-politicians-private-lives-michael-kinsley.

McGee, Jim, Tom Fiedler, and James Savage. 1987. "From the Herald Archives: The Gary Hart Story: How It Happened." *Miami Herald.* May 10. Accessed July 16, 2015. http:// www.miamiherald.com/incoming/article2154781.html.

PBS NewsHour. 2014. "How a Presidential Candidate's Personal Life Changed Political Journalism." PBS NewsHour. October 2. Accessed July 15, 2015. http://www.pbs.org
/newshour/bb/presidential-candidates-personal-life-changed-political-journalism.

Pickert, Kate. 2008. "America's Worst Vice Presidents: Dan Quayle." *Time*. August 20. Accessed
July 15, 2015. http://content.time.com/time/specials/packages/article/0,28804,1834
600_1834604_1834585,00.html.

Rosenstiel, Tom. 1993. *Strange Bedfellows: How Television and the Presidential Candidates
Changed American Politics*. New York: Hyperion Books.

Sabato, Larry. 2000. *Feeding Frenzy: Attack Journalism and American Politics*. Baltimore, MD:
Lanahan Publishing.

Sutter, Daniel. 2006. "Media Scrutiny and the Quality of Public Officials." *Public Choice* 129,
no. 1/2 (October). .

FIRST AMENDMENT AND CENSORSHIP

Perhaps more than any other system in the world, the American government has
few methods for stopping the press from publishing material deemed in the public
interest. Although there are penalties in state and federal laws for misuse of the
press—libel and sedition being two of the most significant—these steps can only
be taken after the presses have rolled or the story posted. Although the government has at times exerted more control over material broadcast by radio and television stations, the core reality is that the American system defaults to protecting
the media from so-called prior restraint, or censorship. This freedom from government control has been used to expand press protections from retaliatory libel prosecutions and to establish judicial and state legislative protection of reporters' notes,
outtakes, and sources. There are limits to the freedom of the press, but compared
to most other democratic systems they are few. That said, many have worried that
the government, through prosecution of leakers and the classification of material,
have sought to stifle the flow of information to the press, but once a journalist has
the story it is usually up to his or her news organization when and if to publish.

This is not to say there are no limits on freedom or that the flow of information
is never inhibited or blocked. It is more that the American system tends to put more
weight on the freedom of expression than on other rights. Still, it is true that throughout American history, especially at times of national crisis or war, the public and
governmental forces may seek to rein in the press, either through actual governmental sanction or through less overt, but still very real, social and economic pressure. In this way, censorship in the United States should be really subdivided into
different forms. There have been limits on political and national security-related
reporting, limits on press freedoms that damage the rights of others, efforts to protect local order and standards, and moral efforts to combat obscenity and pornography. Each of these forms of censorship has a different set of triggers and important
political and legal history to understand.

The most overt form of censorship stems from governmental efforts to control the
information published about the government, its decisions, and its national security
work. This was perhaps the most direct concept captured in the First Amendment

protections that declared Congress could not pass laws that denied people the freedom of the press, but it was also one of the first concepts to be tested by the still-new American political system. As the political divisions between President John Adams's Federalists and Vice President Thomas Jefferson's Democratic-Republicans deepened, Federalists began enacting laws that came to be known as the Alien and Sedition Acts. These proposals criminalized public opposition to the president, the military, and the diplomatic positions of the administrations. The laws allowed the government to jail newspaper publishers for up to two years and fine them up to $2,000 for any incident where "any person shall write, print, utter or publish, or shall cause or procure to be written, printed, uttered or published, or shall knowingly and willingly assist or aid in writing, printing, uttering or publishing any false, scandalous and malicious writing or writings against the government of the United States, or either house of the Congress of the United States, or the President of the United States . . ." Dozens of Jefferson-friendly politicians and newspaper editors were jailed and at least 10 were convicted under the acts. The laws were particularly chilling as they were passed in 1798 with the aim of clamping down on discontent in the lead-up to the election in 1800. The laws became a major source of debate in that election and when Jefferson was elected he moved to free the imprisoned editors, returned fines that had been levied, and moved to ensure that his party would not implement similar laws to punish the Federalists.

The laws themselves expired in 1800 and never faced Supreme Court scrutiny. The concept of judicial review would not be established until 1803 and given the laws were set to expire anyway, they passed from the books with no official verdict on their constitutionality. While publishing criticism of the president and government was largely protected in the wake of the 1800 election, one major issue remained a periodic thorn in the sides of freedom of the press advocates—namely national security matters. The question remained: Could the government stop a newspaper from publishing material it declared to be damaging to the national security? Under laws enacted on the eve of World War I, the government maintained it could punish anti-government speech that undercut the national war effort or other legitimate interests. This Sedition Act remains on the books and serves as one of the main ways the government can punish leakers of information. But up until the 1970s it remained unclear if the government could stop a news organization from publishing national security information under the Sedition Act. The case of *The New York Times v. United States*, or what is widely known as the Pentagon Papers case, would serve as the determining moment in this form of censorship.

The *New York Times* received a massive, 7,000-page history of the American involvement in Vietnam and, after weeks of reporting the story, started publishing a series of articles about the report, marked "Top Secret." The Nixon administration, stung by the revelations that American involvement had gone on longer and officials had been deeply skeptical of increasing America's role, sought a court injunction to stop the publication, saying the information was in the national security. They won and the courts stopped the *New York Times*. Other papers soon received copies of the report and began publishing and the government sought to stop them as well, but then the Supreme Court came down with its decision, ruling the government does not have the ability to stop a newspaper from publishing, although several justices noted that the paper could face lawsuits under the Sedition or Espionage Acts. Still, as Hugo Black noted in his decision, "Paramount among the responsibilities of a free press is the duty to prevent any part of the government from deceiving the people and sending them off to distant lands to die of foreign fevers and foreign shot and shell." The 6-3 decision established as clear law that the government does not possess the power to stop the presses. Since the Pentagon Papers decision, the operating presumption is that news organizations make the decision of what to print. They may weigh the government's argument as to why they should not print, but that power is the publisher's, not the government's.

Not all censorship cases deal with matters as massive as war and national security. Another form of political censorship stemmed from the idea of communities seeking to maintain law and order by suppressing voices of dissent. Unlike the overtly political tone of the Alien and Sedition Acts, these efforts at censorship were based on the community good overriding the free press rights of a publisher. The argument of this form of government censorship is expressed in a dissent by Justice Robert Jackson who worried that the Supreme Court in protecting the rights of individual speakers and publishers may be damaging the stability of the nation. He wrote famously, "This Court has gone far toward accepting the doctrine that civil liberty means the removal of all restraints from these crowds and that all local attempts to maintain order are impairments of the liberty of the citizen . . . There is danger that, if the Court does not temper its doctrinaire logic with a little practical wisdom, it will convert the constitutional Bill of Rights into a suicide pact." Jackson's worry stems from a series of decisions, many of them narrowly decided, that backed the speaker over the community. Perhaps most importantly in terms of censorship of the media was the 1931 case *Near v. Minnesota*. The case involved Jay Near, a racist who published a scandal sheet in Minneapolis called *The Saturday Press*. The paper accused public officials in the city of being controlled by the mafia and Jews. The paper was highly controversial, one of its editors was shot down on the streets of Minneapolis, and the city soon sought a permanent injunction against further copies of the paper, declaring it a "public nuisance." The Supreme Court, in a 5-4 decision, ruled that the law was unconstitutional. Interestingly, the case relied on the Fourteenth Amendment because this case was the first time the First Amendment limits on government actions were applied on a state. Until this time, the First Amendment only limited Congress's ability to inhibit freedom of the press. *Near* extended that prohibition to state and local governments for the first time, making it a critical decision in limiting the ability of all levels of government to censor the press.

A third set of censorship fights centered around balancing the First Amendment right to a free press with other rights, such as a fair trial or the more amorphous claim to privacy. But the fourth set of censorship laws, focused on issues of morality and community standards for decency, has been the most persistent in modern times, attracting scores of cases and months of congressional debate. These morality debates have centered less on the press as an institution and more on entertainment and broadcast media. These cases have often stemmed from pornography prosecutions as well as decency fights over movies, music, and video games. Such censorship has sparked some of the most heated rhetoric around government limits on speech and the press because the censor seeks not to protect the public order or defend the nation's national security interests or even balance First Amendment rights with other legal protections. Instead, it stems from the individual's religious or ethical view of the content. As one historian of censorship notes, "Because this area of censorship deals with morality and sin, such people cannot be content to avoid the material themselves; the very knowledge that some other person, somewhere, may have access to such information or is contact with such speech or press is as harmful to their psyches as if they themselves were immersed in the literature" (Hurwitz 1985). These fights about the scandalous or offensive have involved famous prosecutions of pornographers like Larry Flynt, congressional fights over the legality of offensive rap music from 2 Live Crew, and Federal Communications Commission penalties over "wardrobe malfunctions" during Super Bowl half time shows. Ironically, for having the least impact on the political forms of censorship that dot American history, these forms of moral and sin-based limits of speech have drawn the lion's share of political attention in recent decades. No one debates whether the press has the right to publish leaked documents about the National Security Agency's surveillance of millions of Americans, but whether ABC can run a profanity-laden movie about World War II will spark op-eds and debates at the FCC.

In his exploration of the American internal conflict over limiting speech and the free press, law professor Patrick Garry notes this may be the most prevalent aspect of censorship's impact on the political process—it's a time-suck. Garry notes that most political debates about government and its limits on free speech or press tend to drag on, eating up time in the political process to debate subjective ideas of what is or is not acceptable. As he puts it, "The attention-absorbing power of censorship and its consequent distractive role derive from the public's tendency to take an immediate interest in censorship matters and to become quickly opinionated on those matters. Unlike complicated budget and foreign policy issues, questions on censorship can be easily understood and lend themselves to rather quick and definitive judgments" (Garry 1993). And the political process itself has done little to help close these arguments. The endless cycle of moral censorship can be, perhaps, best captured in the 1964 Supreme Court decision in *Jacobellis v. Ohio*. In concurring with the majority in a decision, Associate Justice Potter Stewart sought to explain why he did not believe the film in question rose to the standard of "hard-core" pornography, writing, "I shall not today attempt further to define the kinds of material I understand to be embraced within that shorthand description; and perhaps I could never succeed in intelligibly doing so. But I know it when I see it, and the motion picture involved in this case is not that." That oft-cited "I know it when I see it" highlights the personal and painfully subjective idea of what is or is not permissible. This endless and shifting debate over the community standards that must be violated to merit government intervention makes this one of the most persistent conversations about censorship.

But that is not to say that the government's ability to affect or impede the flow of information is a closed debate in the American system. Far from it, as questions have shifted away from policies that stop a news organization from publishing or broadcasting information to efforts to stifle journalists' ability to access information and government officials. The First Amendment guarantees a freedom to print but nowhere does it protect an ability to report. Despite this omission, the federal government and most states passed a series of laws in the 1960s and 1970s that started to offer a baseline of access to government information. The Freedom of Information Act and the Government in the Sunshine Act created an assumption that government documents and meetings should be public and available to the press and citizens unless there are certain legitimate government interests in keeping the information secret.

Additional moves by state legislatures and courts have offered journalists in many states some level of protection of being subpoenaed to testify in court or serve as a witness for the state. The argument here is that if reporters are forced to give evidence based on what they have discovered in their reporting, they will slowly come to be seen as agents of the state—the equivalent of talking to a police officer—and that will compromise their role in the process. Therefore, reporters' notes, outtakes, and sources are generally shielded by states, although there is no uniform standard. Some states offer total protection for journalists, creating a so-called absolute shield from being forced to testify. Most states offer qualified privilege that puts the decision in the hands of a judge, meaning it depends on how much the state needs the information the journalist has.

At the federal level, there is no protection for reporters, meaning if the FBI asks for information a reporter must comply or face possible jail time. In addition to this lack of protection, many have expressed concern that the government has sought to quash the flow of information by actively pursuing criminal charges in cases where important information has been leaked to the press. While Supreme Court precedent protects journalists from prosecution in most cases, no such protection exists for the source of the leak. The Obama administration has actually used the World War I–era Espionage Act to pursue prosecutions of more leakers than all other presidents in history combined and this, many worry, may serve as a form of censorship by raising the stakes on those who may want to alert the press to the actions of the government. When NSA leaker Edward Snowden decided to give documents to the media he fled the country before doing so and now lives in a legal exile in Russia.

And this may be the reality of the modern fear of censorship. Outside of the ongoing debate over obscenity and pornography, government censorship at the official level is extremely limited and usually only balances First Amendment rights with other governmental interests. The default is the government cannot punish a news organization for publishing accurate information nor can they stop them from doing it. Still government can intimidate sources of information with possible prosecution. It can stifle access to government by using legal loopholes to block access to meetings and documents, and it can help stoke public opinion against certain organizations and individuals. This is part of the reason why those who study and advocate on issues of censorship have sought to expand the definition of what that concept entails.

Since the 1970s, Project Censor has sought to publicize the information not being made public, but when the founder of the project explained how they define censorship he noted, "For the purposes of this project, censorship is defined as the suppression of information, whether purposeful or not, by any method—including bias, omission, under-reporting, or self-censorship—which prevents the public from fully knowing what is happening in the world. In the final analysis, the greatest sin of censorship may well be the act of self-censorship. For while other forms of censorship may be seen, felt, and eventually exposed that which is censored at the source is never known" (Jensen 1996). This reality that journalists themselves may be the biggest problem of modern censorship, either deliberately or inadvertently leaving the public uninformed or under-informed, is a persistent criticism of watchdogs and many within the profession. Fabled broadcaster Walter Cronkite went even further, worrying that many journalists struggle to publish information that would frustrate their colleagues and other middle and upper class professionals with whom they congregate. Cronkite noted that "there is a weakness in the fabric of freedom that is part of the make-up of journalists themselves, and their editors and publishers. It takes courage in this business—raw physical courage at times, but more often the courage to face social ostracism for reporting the unpleasant and disagreeable, for reporting the world as it is, rather than the way one's peer group might believe it to be. Freedom of press and speech is meaningless unless it is exercised, even when bravery is required to do so" (Cronkite 1996). This concern, one that has been echoed through the years and may be the most real, if intangible, censor on the information produced by reporters remains one that concerns many, partially because of its almost unconscious roots and also because of its near invisibility to the average viewer or reader.

See also: Access to Candidates; Advocacy Journalism; Political Bias and the Media; Watchdog Journalism

Further Reading

Cronkite, Walter. 1996. "Let the Chips Fall Where They May." In *Censored: The News That Didn't Make the News—and Why*. New York: Seven Stories Press.

Garry, Patrick. 1993. *An American Paradox: Censorship in a Nation of Free Speech*. Westport, CT: Praeger.

Hurwitz, Leon. 1985. *Historical Dictionary of Censorship in the United States.* Westport, CT: Greenwood Press.

Jensen, Carl, and Project Censored. 1996. *Censored: The News That Didn't Make the News— and Why.* New York: Seven Stories Press.

FIVETHIRTYEIGHT (538)

The development of sophisticated computer models and database-driven politics has fundamentally altered both the modern campaign and the way in which journalists cover it. If there is one organization that truly represents this love affair with data and models it is FiveThirtyEight.

FiveThirtyEight is the brainchild of statistician Nate Silver, whose work in both sports and political reporting focuses on using data to create likely models of outcomes. It treats politics as a probability equation and that has made him a must-read for many but, some counter, has reduced raw politics to impersonal math. Still, it is math that often cuts through the factless punditry that can make up much of modern political reporting.

Silver first started in the area of sports, developing predictive systems that assess the likely successes of pitchers and hitters, but the son of a Michigan State University political scientist always seemed to have a soft spot of the sport of politics.

By 2007 he had taken to the liberal blog Daily Kos to post about campaigns and to begin applying his model of probability assessment to politics. He was still focused professionally on baseball and so he used the pseudonym "Poblano"—a mild green chili pepper. The posts at Daily Kos drew more and more attention to the point where in March 2008 Silver launched FiveThirtyEight.com, naming the site after the number of electors in the U.S. Electoral College. A few months later he explained his thinking in an op-ed, writing, "In polling and politics, there is nearly as much data as there is for first basemen. In this year's Democratic primaries, there were statistics for every gender, race, age, occupation and geography—reasons why Clinton won older women, or Obama took college students," Silver wrote, adding he had started FiveThirtyEight.com "to try and apply the same scientific spirit that we've used in baseball to the political world" (Silver 2008).

FiveThirtyEight's work that first presidential year drew enormous attention as it helped explain the growing tidal wave of data that was pointing to a likely win by first-term U.S. senator Barack Obama. In the end, Silver's site predicted the outcome accurately in 49 of 50 states—only erring in Indiana where Obama scored a 1-point victory. Later he would downplay the significance of his 2008 work, telling the Chicago Humanities Festival in 2012, "You basically have to be a total f****** moron to not know that Barack Obama was going to win the 2008 election" (YouTube 2012). But as easy as he said Obama's victory was to call, he still marveled at the number of political analysts who thought the race would be close or even that Republican John McCain might win.

"People who are living in a bubble, and I don't want to be too anti-elitist here or anti-elite, but the idea that Michael Barone or Dick Morris or someone who is going to these Georgetown cocktail parties, that they have their finger on the pulse of America more than the polls do where the polls go and randomly call actual Americans? Those can't be trusted but their gut instincts from the cocktail parties can be? That's just totally delusional," he said, adding, "It's time to stop paying attention to these people and start getting real," to widespread applause.

It was this sometimes hostile view of political commentary and reporting that has at times led to friction between Silver's "The Numbers Never Lie" approach that informs so much of 538's work and political reporters that see intangible factors like a candidate and their campaign as being part of the story of politics. Despite this tension, the attention heaped on Silver for predicting the election in 49 of 50 states soon landed him among the political powers that be. By 2010, Silver had signed on to work for the *New York Times*. It was a bit of bumpy marriage between the data guy and a larger political reporting team that wanted to cover the campaign and saw politics as as much art as it is science.

According to Margaret Sullivan, the *New York Times'* public editor, "His entire probability-based way of looking at politics ran against the kind of political journalism that The Times specializes in: polling, the horse race, campaign coverage, analysis based on campaign-trail observation, and opinion writing, or 'punditry,' as he put it, famously describing it as 'fundamentally useless . . .' His approach was to work against the narrative of politics—the 'story'—and that made him always interesting to read" (Sullivan 2013).

He seemed to be talking to those political reporters who delved into the "narrative" of politics early in his book on predictions, writing, "We need to stop, and admit it: we have a prediction problem. We love to predict things—and we aren't very good at it" (Silver 2012, p. 13). But that focus on predictions is one of the chief criticisms of Silver's and FiveThirtyEight's approach. First, some say, the idea of reducing politics to a model is to oversimplify it. Conservative columnist David Brooks argued this, writing, "Politics isn't a game, like poker, with an artificially limited number of possible developments" (Brooks 2012). And the other problem with their focus on prediction is there is very little it explains to the reader. It answers the question of what will likely happen or who will likely win, but, some argue, it does not do much to explain why the public feels that way.

Still it's an approach that draws millions of readers and helps fuel the very narrative of the campaign Silver often disparages. It's also an approach that has attracted major support from existing media companies. At the end of the three-year gig at the *New York Times*, sports-giant ESPN moved to incorporate FiveThirtyEight into its digital and broadcast efforts in 2013. The idea, said ESPN chief John Skipper, is FiveThirtyEight will be an independent editorial division within the sports network and will offer "a fresh take on the intersection of sports, culture, technology, economics and politics that will be provocative and completely different than anything else in the marketplace today."

See also: Data Journalism; *New York Times*; Public Opinion

Further Reading
Brooks, David. 2012. "Poll Addict Confesses." *New York Times*. October 22. Accessed November 14, 2014. http://www.nytimes.com/2012/10/23/opinion/books-poll-addict-confesses.html?ref=davidbrooks.
Silver, Nate. 2012. *The Signal and the Noise*. New York: Penguin Books.
Silver, Nate. 2014. "Margins of Error." *The New York Post*. June 1. Accessed November 11, 2014. http://nypost.com/2008/06/01/margins-of-error.
Sullivan, Margaret. 2013. "Nate Silver Went Against the Grain for Some at The Times." *New York Times*. July 22. Accessed November 10, 2014. http://publiceditor.blogs.nytimes.com/2013/07/22/nate-silver-went-against-the-grain-for-some-at-the-times.
YouTube. 2012. "Nate Silver: The Numbers Don't Lie." Accessed November 23, 2014. http://www.youtube.com/watch?v=GuAZtOJqFr0.

527 ORGANIZATIONS

In the often less-than-exact world of political reporting 527 groups are often discussed in a way that is only partially correct. A 527 group is named after the section of the U.S. tax code that governs explicitly political nonprofits. So a 527 group is any political party, political action committee, or Super PAC and covers most political organizations with the exception of so-called dark money groups that operate as 501(c)(4) "social welfare" groups according to the Internal Revenue Service.

That said, when people generally discuss or write about 527 groups, they are usually referring to types of organizations that raise and spend money independent of political candidates and campaigns. Many of these groups would be considered Super PACs, although not necessarily all of them.

These organizations largely sprang from a critical 1976 Supreme Court decision that sought to balance the desire to regulate campaign spending with the First Amendment protections of freedom of speech. *Buckley v. Valeo* struck down elements of the first major campaign finance reform legislation in some 50 years, ruling that government could not limit the spending of campaigns and candidates. It did rule that the government could limit donations to candidates and political parties, but it specifically threw out any restrictions on spending that is independent of the candidate.

The court was seeking to protect speech that advocated for or against issues, saying this type of speech was protected by the Constitution and in its footnote sought to explain what kind of speech would differentiate campaign ads from issue ads. The court said that the use of words such as "vote for," "vote against," "elect," or "defeat" indicated explicit electioneering speech. Avoid those words, many 527 groups argue, and you have issue advocacy. "In this context, the *Buckley v. Valeo* express-versus-issue advocacy distinction has been used to circumvent contribution limits in what is clearly election advertising. This development, when combined with the soft-money loophole for parties, means that in competitive House and Senate races, noncandidate campaign spending does, can and will exceed candidate spending" (Magleby 2000, p. 225).

But it is not limited to just Congress. In fact, 527 groups really rose to public awareness more for their tactics in presidential politics than for any campaign in Congress. One of the most famous of 527s organized in 2004 to take on then-Democratic presidential nominee John Kerry. The Democratic Senator had highlighted his Vietnam War record as part of his campaign against President George W. Bush, who had joined the Air National Guard. A group of veterans, with the help of Republican operatives, launched a 527 group Swift Boat Veterans for Truth. The group quickly issued an angry letter to the Democrat, saying, "It is our collective judgment that, upon your return from Vietnam, you grossly and knowingly distorted the conduct of the American soldiers, marines, sailors and airmen of that war (including a betrayal of many of us, without regard for the danger your actions caused us). Further, we believe that you have withheld and/or distorted material facts as to your own conduct in this war" (National Review 2004). Kerry won three Purple Hearts, a Bronze Star, and a Silver Star for Vietnam War combat.

The group began accepting donations—raising nearly $10 million from just three prominent Republican donors (Opensecrets.org)—and running campaign ads roundly criticizing Kerry for his war stories. Kerry responded, calling the 527 group "a front for the Bush campaign and the fact that the president won't denounce what they're up to tells you everything you need to know. He wants them to do his dirty work" (Fournier 2004). The term "swiftboating" soon entered the political lexicon as a political hatchet job where a candidate's patriotism or experience is disparaged with little factual basis, but the effort did distract from much of Kerry's actual service.

Still, Swift Boat Veterans for Truth is just one type of 527 group. Groups like the liberal MoveOn.org formed on the other side of the political aisle. Still, "There were few defenders of 527 groups in 2004 or 2006. These groups were often presented as a deliberate exploitation of vagaries in the new campaign finance laws" (Boatright 2007).

As other groups, especially dark money organizations, have grown in the wake of the Supreme Court ruling in *Citizens United v. Federal Election Commission*, the power and influence of 527 committees appears somewhat on the wane. According to the Center for Responsive Politics, spending by 527 groups at the federal and state and local levels has plummeted from $590 million in the 2010 elections to $327 million in 2014, nearly a 46 percent drop (Opensecrets.org).

Further Reading

Boatright, Robert. 2007. "Situating the New 527 Organizations in Interest Group Theory." The Forum. Berkeley, CA: The Berkeley Electronic Press. Accessed January 5, 2015. http://faculty.georgetown.edu/wilcoxc/Situating%20the%20New%20Organizations%20in%20Interest%20Group%20Theory.pdf.

Fournier, Ron. 2004. "Kerry Accuses Bush of Relying on Front Groups to 'Do His Dirty Work' on Vietnam." Associated Press. August 19. Accessed January 5, 2015. http://legacy.utsandiego.com/news/politics/federal/20040819-1432-kerry-war.html.

Magleby, David. 2000. *Outside Money: Soft Money and Issue Advocacy in the 1998 Congressional Elections*. Lanham, MD: Rowman & Littlefield Publishers.

National Review. 2004. "We Know The Truth." May 4. Accessed February 22, 2015. http://www.nationalreview.com/article/210532/we-know-truth-nro-primary-document.

Opensecrets.org. "527s: Advocacy Group Spending." Accessed January 5, 2015. https://www.opensecrets.org/527s/index.php.

Opensecrets.org. "Swift Vets & POWs for Truth." Accessed January 5, 2015. http://www.opensecrets.org/527s/527cmtedetail_contribs.php?ein=201041228&cycle=2004.

FOX NEWS

Fox News has carved out a distinct place in the world of journalism and politics. The news source of choice for conservatives, it has had Republican presidential candidates on its payroll and has filled many of its slots in the 24-hour news cycle with conservative commentators. For that, it has been attacked by other outlets and those on the left as nothing more than a right-wing propaganda machine, churning out anti-Democratic commentary during both its talk shows and its straight news reporting. The Obama administration told the *New York Times* in 2009 that it considered the channel "part of the enemy," and its motto, "Fair and Balanced," earns it derision from those who believe its news coverage is obviously slanted. Many within the network and among its supporters counter that Fox News simply balances the fact that everyone else is slanted too far to the left.

That debate aside, it's also the most watched prime time cable news channel and has been for some time now and has developed a fiercely loyal viewership. The Pew Research Center reports the core cable news audience is continuing to shrink, but that most of the people who watch cable news are watching Fox. Pew's 2015 State of the News Media finds that 1.7 million people were tuning into Fox each night, which was a 1 percent decrease from 2014 but still exceeded that of their top cable competitors, CNN and MSNBC, which is what its founders always wanted.

In 1996, billionaire media tycoon Rupert Murdoch and Republican-political-operative-turned-cable-television-executive Roger Ailes founded the channel with a single goal in mind, overtaking Ted Turner's CNN. They certainly had the capital. Murdoch is the executive chairman at News Corp. On its website, the company touts itself as "the largest news and information provider in the English speaking world." The company owns media outlets in the United States, Australia, and the United Kingdom. Its other holdings include the *Wall Street Journal*, *New York Post*, Harper Collins Publishers, 21st Century Fox Film Corporation, and the Fox Broadcasting Company.

Jumping into the cable news game was something Murdoch's company had been considering for some time, but they hadn't succeeded. As Gabriel Sherman wrote in his book, *The Loudest Voice in the Room*, Murdoch was optimistic, especially at the press conference when he introduced the CEO for his new channel. "'The appetite for news—particularly news that explains to people how it affects them—is expanding enormously,' he told reporters at the press conference introducing Ailes. 'We are moving very fast for our news channel to become a worldwide platform.'" Sherman wrote further that Ailes and Murdoch sought to "lay waste to smug journalistic standards," and that Murdoch said they planned to be "the insurgents in a business of very strong incumbents" (Sherman 2014).

Before it even went on the air, people were already raising what would become the main criticism of the channel. In the *New York Times* on the day the channel opened up shop, Lawrie Mifflin posed the question people had been considering for months, since Murdoch had announced he planned to open a cable channel: "Will FNC be a vehicle for expressing Mr. Murdoch's conservative political opinions?" (Mifflin 1996). Many journalists thought so at the time, but Murdoch would rebuff their claims, saying he wanted the network to distinguish between news and opinion programming and that their news reporting would be, as the motto suggests, fair and balanced.

The goal for this new channel, primarily, was to become the leader in 24-hour cable news. NBC had CNBC for financial news, and in 1995 the company announced a partnership with Microsoft to create MSNBC. That channel launched just three months before Fox News did. ABC had been rumored to want in on the game, too. But there was an elephant in the room of cable newsmen: Ted Turner and CNN. The company had a monopoly on the medium for more than a decade, and were set to be Fox's biggest rival. Murdoch made an attempt to buy CNN from Turner, but was rebuffed. When Murdoch announced his intention to start a 24-hour news channel, Ted Turner said he looked forward to "'squishing Rupert like a bug'" (Sherman 2014).

But Rupert would prove to be a formidable bug. Fox News Channel did well. It overtook CNN in the ratings battle in 2002 and has never let up its grip on the top spot. Its coverage of the Iraq war helped it keep that spot. The BBC reported in 2003 that Fox News's profits doubled during the conflict, as its "diet of conservative commentators and unashamedly patriotic frontline reports from Iraq" attracted viewers. Some reports said the channel was averaging as many as 3.3 million viewers a day. News Corp. profits soared at the same time. In 2014, the channel marked its 150th consecutive month of beating CNN and MSNBC in terms of overall audience. Later that year, it topped all channels for prime time cable viewership—the first time it had done so since the Iraq War in 2003.

Part of the reason it did so well in ratings picture was certainly its provocative commentary shows. One of the original shows was *Hannity and Colmes*, a debate show starring Sean Hannity—a conservative—and Alan Colmes—a liberal. The show lasted 13 years, and both commentators now host radio shows for Fox News. Other anchors achieved a more lightning-rod type celebrity status, like Glenn Beck and Bill O'Reilly. But the provocation doesn't come without controversy. The network that sought to take over the realm of 24-hour cable news has consistently made news itself, with its commentators and anchors often at the center of it.

O'Reilly, whose program consistently comes in as one of the top-rated shows on cable news, took to attacking George Tiller, a doctor who performed abortions, as "Tiller the baby killer" and denounced the man. Tiller was shot and killed in 2009, and some journalists and bloggers accused O'Reilly of inspiring the killing with his repeated berating of the man, which happened more than 25 times on his show. O'Reilly dismissed the criticisms, saying the people who were attacking him were exploiting the doctor's death as a chance to go after him (Stelter 2009). For his part, Beck called President Barack Obama a racist (a comment he later said he regretted) and called progressivism a cancer, among other claims. Those two in particular led the then-*Washington Post* media writer Howard Kurtz to write that Beck had "achieved a lightning-rod status" that was unique, even for Fox News (Kurtz 2010).

Another anchor at the channel built much of her fame by sparring with the GOP's 2015 presidential frontrunner. Megyn Kelly went back and forth with presidential candidate Donald Trump during the first GOP debate. She pressed him with questions about comments the real estate tycoon had made about women, like calling them "pigs" and "slobs" at various times. In a CNN interview the day after the debate, Trump said Kelly had "blood coming out of her eyes, blood coming out of her wherever," a comment that many perceived as a reference to her menstrual cycle (Martin and Haberman 2015). Trump denied the claim but Kelly didn't back down, saying on her show that she wouldn't apologize for doing her job. The network stood by her, but didn't entirely condemn Trump. Roger Ailes called on Trump to apologize in a statement, saying no one would scare the network out of doing their job. But other Fox anchors stopped short of calling for an apology. Sean Hannity tweeted that Trump should leave Kelly alone, but that he should do so by sticking to the issues, a line that other anchors echoed on their own shows (Gold 2015).

Eventually Trump would fall back into Fox News's good graces. Gabriel Sherman wrote for *New York* magazine in fall 2015 that Trump boycotted the network for a short time, but, after some urging from Ailes himself, he agreed to appear on Fox News shows again. Sherman writes that Ailes's decision to urge Trump to come back to the network was driven by angry comments from the network's viewers and the fact that Trump's presidential candidacy has been a ratings boon for many of the networks. "Having backed down to the GOP front-runner and all but sacrificed one of his biggest stars to appease the conservative base—a.k.a. Fox viewers—Ailes has set a dangerous precedent. The message is clear: Fox reports, but the audience decides," Sherman wrote (2015). The network entered a period of transition in 2016 after Ailes was forced out of the network following a series of sexual harassment allegations from current and former female staffers.

Michael Wright

See also: Cable News Networks; CNN; MSNBC

Further Reading

British Broadcasting Company. 2003. "War Coverage Lifts News Corp." *BBC News*. August 13. Accessed December 16, 2015. http://news.bbc.co.uk/2/hi/business/3148015.stm.

Gold, Hadas. 2015. "Roger Ailes' real message to Trump." Politico. August 27. Accessed December 16, 2015. http://www.politico.com/blogs/media/2015/08/roger-ailes-real-message-to-trump-213062.

Kurtz, Howard. 2010. "A Network Divided: The Glenn Beck Factor." *Washington Post*. March 15. Accessed December 16, 2015. http://www.washingtonpost.com/wp-dyn/content/article/2010/03/15/AR2010031500923_pf.html.

Martin, Jonathan, and Maggie Haberman. 2015. "Hand-wringing in G.O.P. After Donald Trump's Remarks on Megyn Kelly." *New York Times*. August 8. Accessed June 13, 2016. http://www.nytimes.com/2015/08/09/us/politics/donald-trump-disinvited-from-conservative-event-over-remark-on-megyn-kelly.html?_r=0.

Mifflin, Lawrie. 1996. "At the New Fox News Channel, the Buzzword Is Fairness, Separating News from Bias." *New York Times*. October 7. Accessed December 16, 2015. http://www.nytimes.com/1996/10/07/business/at-the-new-fox-news-channel-the-buzzword-is-fairness-separating-news-from-bias.html.

Sherman, Gabriel. 2014. *The Loudest Voice in the Room: How the Brilliant, Bombastic Roger Ailes Built Fox News—and Divided a Country.* New York: Random House.

Sherman, Gabriel. 2015. "How Roger Ailes Picked Trump, and Fox News' Audience, Over Megyn Kelly." *nymag.com*. August 11. Accessed December 16, 2015. http://nymag.com/daily/intelligencer/2015/08/fox-news-picked-trump-over-megyn-kelly.html#.

"State of the News Media 2015." Pew Research Center. April 29, 2015.

Stelter, Brian. 2009. "Doctor's Killer Is Not Alone in the Blame, Some Say." *New York Times*. June 1. Accessed December 16, 2015. http://www.nytimes.com/2009/06/02/us/02blame.html?scp=1&sq=%22Tiller+the+baby+killer%22&st=nyt.

Stelter, Brian. 2009. "Fox's Volley with Obama Intensifying." *New York Times*. October 11. Accessed December 16, 2015. http://www.nytimes.com/2009/10/12/business/media/12fox.html?_r=0.

FOX NEWS SUNDAY

Fox News Sunday, though now 20 years old, is still the newest of the Sunday morning talk shows that air on the four broadcast networks and represents the only news programming carried by the Fox network. The program, like NBC's *Meet the Press*, CBS's *Face the Nation,* and ABC's *This Week*, features newsmaker interviews with influential political leaders as well as panel discussions with veteran journalists and columnists. The program comes in last among the four Sunday talk shows, averaging about 1.5 million viewers, but is rebroadcast on the Fox News cable channel, giving the show a full viewership of just under 2.9 million.

The program is structured in a slightly different way than its broadcast competitors. On the other channels, programs offer only a cursory hard news look at the major stories that have occurred overnight; since *Fox News Sunday* is the only national news program on Fox, host Chris Wallace starts each program with a brief synopsis of the news before turning to a single or series of one-on-one interviews. Those interviews tend to focus on the political and diplomatic news of the week.

The program then brings on a panel of journalists and partisan commentators to consider the week and what the major points made in the earlier interviews were. The program launched as a regular discussion program in 1996, a little less than six months before Rupert Murdoch would begin the Fox News Channel, and was initially hosted by Tony Snow. Snow, who had worked as a newspaper writer before joining Republican president George H. W. Bush as a speechwriter, had developed a name for himself as a conservative columnist and occasional guest host of Rush Limbaugh's radio program. When Fox launched the Sunday morning program, they tapped the journalist in hopes of building a new, more conservative counterpart to the other morning shows. At the time Snow was cautious to say that his conservative bent would not make the program simply a mouthpiece for the Republican Party, telling the *Washington Post*, "If I come off as a right-wing hack, the show will die. With my background there's going to be a natural suspicion that I might have a viewpoint, so I'm going to take special care, as the host, to give both sides of the issue. After all, I get to present my views three times a week in my column" (Carmody 1996). Snow did present an evenhanded host and the program was soon drawing in a million viewers a week, bolstered by the network's large audience that tuned in around that time to watch football pregame coverage.

Snow would leave the anchor chair in 2003, when the network brought in veteran television journalist Chris Wallace to serve as host. Wallace, the son of CBS *60 Minutes* correspondent Mike Wallace, had worked at ABC News as a host of the network's newsmagazine program and covered the Gulf War and other international hotspots for his 14 years at the network. He has said that he sees the mainstream media as biased and has said his program aims to "cover the other side." He once got in an extended debate with *The Daily Show* host Jon Stewart about bias when Stewart appeared on the program, during this exchange:

> *Stewart:* So you believe that Fox News is exactly the ideological equivalent of NBC News?
> *Wallace:* I think we're the counterweight.
> *Stewart:* You believe that—
> *Wallace:* I believe they have a liberal agenda and I think we tell the other side of the story. (Fox News Sunday 2011)

With the stated goal of balancing the perceived liberal bias in other broadcast media, the program has developed a track record of serving as a popular destination for Republicans seeking to communicate to party faithful and potential supporters. All the candidates running for the Republican nomination in 2012 made the trek to appear on the show and face questioning from Wallace. That is not to say Wallace does not press candidates hard on the issues. On his official Fox News bio Wallace makes sure to note he has "been described as an 'equal opportunity inquisitor' by the *Boston Globe*, 'an aggressive journalist,' 'sharp edged' and 'solid' by the *Washington Post* and 'an equal-opportunity ravager' by the *Miami Herald*" (Fox News). And that hard-nosed questioning is often on display on Sunday morning, where Wallace presses politicos to address specific issues, not shying away from cutting them off and demanding an answer when he feels he has not received one. For example, the program made headlines in 2015 when Wallace pushed Republican candidate Senator Marco Rubio about whether he thought the 2003 invasion of Iraq was a mistake. Wallace ran two clips where Rubio appeared to support the invasion, saying the world was a better place without former dictator Saddam Hussein, and one where he said he doubted President Bush would order the invasion if we knew what we know now about the lack of weapons of mass destruction and the instability it would trigger. Wallace then pushed Rubio on the apparent discrepancy. Rubio tried to defend the statements saying they were two different questions, but when Wallace repeatedly asked "But was it a mistake?" Rubio struggled for a clear answer. The result, wrote the *New York Times*, was "a three-minute video clip that Republican opponents could use against Mr. Rubio in the future, given that he came across as a politician used to debating fine points and nuances in the United States Senate—a problem that then-senator John Kerry faced in his presidential run in 2004—rather than as a seasoned leader used to giving clear statements" (Healy 2015). Despite the tough questioning, the program continues to draw key newsmaker interviews, including President Barack Obama discussing the potential use of poison gas by Syria, and 2016 Republican candidates like Donald Trump.

The program has an outsized influence that extends beyond the million and a half viewers it attracts in a given week. The program, rebroadcast each Sunday afternoon and evening on the Fox News cable channel, is also used heavily in Monday morning's political coverage, helping shape much of the early week's tone and message, by supplying the cable network with a regular flow of interviews it can use to fuel the more talk-oriented programming of the cable channel. Wallace himself often appears on the cable channel, discussing what he thought were the important elements of the interviews and offering his take on the fallout. But more than just amplifying the content created on Sunday morning, Wallace's connection to the cable channel helps the smallest of the weekend talk shows land big guests. Wallace has admitted that the connection and proximity of his program to Fox News and the Fox News studios just north of the Capitol has helped the program thrive. He told the *New York Times*, "My office isn't the biggest in the building, but it's the best situated since it's directly across from the makeup room. That means that any senator, congressman, government official or other guest who's appearing on a Fox News show here has to walk past my door. I've often booked guests for *Fox News Sunday* because of that" (Olsen 2015).

See also: *Face the Nation*; Fox News; *Meet the Press*; *This Week*

Further Reading

Carmody, John. 1996. "Fox Jumps into Sunday A.M. News Fray." *Washington Post*. April 4.

"Chris Wallace." Fox News. Accessed June 13, 2016. http://www.foxnews.com/person/w/chris-wallace.html.

Healy, Patrick. 2015. "Marco Rubio Struggles with Questions on Iraq War." *New York Times*.
    May 17. Accessed October 16, 2015. http://www.nytimes.com/politics/first-draft/2015
    /05/17/marco-rubio-struggles-with-question-on-iraq-war.
Olsen, Patricia. 2015. "Chris Wallace of Fox News: Not the Biggest Office, but the One That
    Gets the Guests." *New York Times*. Accessed October 16, 2015. http://www.nytimes.com
    /2015/03/15/business/chris-wallace-of-fox-news-not-the-biggest-office-but-the-one
    -that-gets-the-guests.html.

FRONTLINE

Frontline is the premier news documentary program on American broadcast television. The Public Broadcasting System program, launched dramatically with an investigation into organized crime, gambling, and professional football, has become a critical element of public affairs reporting on television.

The series airs, on average, 21 broadcasts a year and has accumulated more than 600 episodes over its more than 30 seasons. It also was one of the first broadcast programs to launch in-depth, single issue websites to accompany its programs, creating in 1995 a model for digital reporting that took years for most other long-form broadcasters to even attempt to emulate.

When the program debuted in 1983, it was already seen as counter-programming to what was happening on the commercial networks. Put simply, "It was created, in part, to fill the void left when commercial network news divisions gradually eliminated their own documentary series in the 1970s and 1980s" (Sterling 2009). Gone were the days of CBS's news documentaries like "Harvest of Shame" and other single-issue, long-form broadcast documentaries; into that void PBS moved with the help of executive producer David Fanning.

Fanning had grown up in Port Elizabeth, South Africa, in a country that had tight controls on information and had banned television until 1976 for fear of it spreading ideas in opposition to the white minority government. As a student, Fanning travelled to California, and he said he remembered being asked to participate in a discussion of South Africa's apartheid policies, but given the restrictions on the press and history, Fanning had to go and do the research in America. "I learned my own history in another country because I had not been allowed to hear it before . . . In that moment I became a journalist," Fanning later told an audience when accepting the Fred Friendly First Amendment Award in 2011 (Quinnipiac 2011). It was that desire to understand what had driven his countrymen to build the apartheid system and to understand its effects on the black South Africans that drove his interest in filmmaking.

He started working with the British Broadcasting Company creating documentaries about South Africa before leaving his homeland and eventually finding his way to America. He soon landed at public television's Boston station, WGBH, where he produced a string of 50 documentaries in just five years before developing the idea in 1982 for *Frontline*. In January 1983, the program debuted with hard-hitting documentaries that would become its hallmark.

Always focused on public affairs, the series took perhaps its most significant step in its relationship with covering campaigns in 1988 when it debuted what would become an election-year staple, "The Choice." That year the program, in partnership with *Time* magazine, produced a documentary that sought to explain the long road that had led Vice President George H. W. Bush and former Massachusetts governor Michael Dukakis to the presidential nominations. An ad that ran in the *New York Times* the day it aired promised to "pierce the façade of campaign rhetoric" and how "the road to leadership begins long before the conventions or the primaries. It lies in the paths taken from the classroom to playing field, from scout camp to boot camp" (*New York Times* 1988, C16). Since that campaign, "The Choice" has offered viewers the most complete biographies about the presidential candidates produced by any broadcast outlet. A 2008 review of the take on Senators Barack Obama and John McCain speaks to the style that has marked *Frontline's* approach, commenting, "It certainly provides a startling contrast to the rest of the news cycle. Given the minute-by-minute media frenzy over this campaign, the air of calm that presides over 'The Choice' . . . is excruciatingly poignant" (McNamara 2008).

But *Frontline* does not limit itself to exploring the biographies of candidates. Over the course of more than 30 years of documentaries, the program has tackled complex political issues, offering important insights into campaign finance laws, the overhaul of health care, and the politics of government shutdowns. At times it has drawn fire for being too liberal for advocating government regulation of the financial industry or raising questions about the work of dark money groups. One effort by the libertarian Cato Institute singled out the documentary series in its argument for defunding PBS, writing, "It seems safe to say that there has never been a 'Frontline' documentary on the burden of taxes, or the number of people who have died because federal regulations keep drugs off the market, or the way that state governments have abused the law in their pursuit of tobacco companies, or the number of people who use guns to prevent crime. Those 'hard questions' just don't occur to liberal journalists" (Boaz 2005). Despite its critics, the program has continued to deliver some of the most thoughtful public affairs reporting on television, raising difficult questions for both Democrats and Republicans to answer.

Frontline's run has always been a bit counter-intuitive. It launched when broadcasters were moving away from documentaries. It embraced in-depth, thoroughly researched websites when most media argued the Internet only wanted short and pithy content, and it has continued to argue it is a voice of moderation in an increasingly shrill and partisan media. "There has to be someplace for the honest broker. That's our real birthright as public interest broadcasters and journalists. It's becoming an old-fashioned idea and I deeply believe it will become increasingly valuable. And it's the people who value fairness and honesty who will support it financially and politically" (YouTube 2011).

See also: Documentaries

Further Reading

Boaz, David. 2005. "Defund PBS." Cato Institute. Accessed February 9, 2015. http://www
.cato.org/publications/commentary/defund-pbs.

McNamara, Mary. 2008. "A Refreshingly Clear 'Choice.'" *Los Angeles Times*. October 14.
Accessed February 8, 2015. http://articles.latimes.com/2008/oct/14/entertainment/et
-choice14.

"Two Roads to Pennsylvania Avenue." 1988. *New York Times*. October 24.

YouTube. 2011. "18th Annual Fred Friendly First Amendment Award—2011 Honoree: David
Fanning." Accessed February 9, 2015. https://www.youtube.com/watch?v=2HJAKbjHjGw.

G

GALLUP

The Gallup organization is, to many, the gold standard of public opinion research, housing more than 2,000 researchers, pollsters, and experts who help assess the views of the public.

The premier national public opinion research organization in the country, the firm boasts 30 offices around the world. The employee-owned organization runs divisions that conduct public polls, gauge leadership and other training skills, consult with businesses and other organizations, and recruit and train executives. Although in the world of politics they are known as public opinion surveyors, Gallup actually makes most of its money by focusing on helping businesses engage with their employees and customers as well as recruit and retain talent.

But for political scientists and reporters the group is most known for the Gallup Poll, a traditional public opinion survey that for some 80 years has served as a benchmark of public thought on world matters. Gallup itself claims, "No other organization captures the human need to share opinions and the breadth of the human spirit like The Gallup Poll. Since 1935, The Gallup Poll has chronicled reactions to the events that have changed our world—and in turn, those reactions have shaped who and what we are today" (Gallup 2015). And the poll has been a critical way in which social and political scientists study the electorate and public views of world events. Political scientists have used the surveys to study swing voters, voting blocs, and demographic changes over time.

For decades it was seen as the most accurate barometer of public opinion on matters ranging from the performance of the president and Congress to the role of religion in their lives and their views of civil rights. Still, the poll at times showed its age. In 2012, the firm had perhaps its most significant public failure, showing on the eve of the election that likely voters leaned toward Republican Mitt Romney over President Barack Obama 49–48. Obama won 51–47. Gallup launched a full investigation and over the course of six months identified four areas that had gone wrong—identifying likely voters, predicting black turnout in the election, weighing regions of the country incorrectly, and not accounting for unlisted landlines in their model. By 2014, the firm had implemented major changes to its techniques and, like most surveys, predicted major losses by Democrats.

Despite its rough 2012, the organization is still largely seen as the best funded, most scientific polling firm. It's the group that "does polling the right way" wrote the *National Journal*, adding, "Gallup remains among the world's most prominent and respected public-opinion organizations, and its more than 75 years of polling data comprise a large portion of the information we have about Americans' attitudes about their government and society over that time" (Shepard 2012).

The Gallup Poll and its global sister the Gallup World Poll are the products of Gallup's founder, George Gallup. Gallup started in the advertising field, working to develop ways to gauge the effectiveness of radio ads, but his interest soon was focused more on gauging public opinion and reactions to issues more generally. Gallup's family remembers the pollster constantly trying out different question construction and ideas. "We were like guinea pigs for his ideas about polling," said his son, George Gallup III. "He'd poll us. Do you like dogs or cats better? What kind of cereal?" (Blackwell 1998). By 1935 he had launched his organization, called the American Institute of Public Opinion, and he was soon to make his mark in political history.

He exploded onto the political stage a year later when he took on the most established poll in the nation—the *Literary Digest*'s presidential poll. The magazine included a card in one edition that asked people to express their preference in the election between President Franklin Roosevelt and Republican Al Landon. When the *Digest* received the responses it was overwhelming. Landon would win 56-44. Gallup disagreed. He predicted that Roosevelt would win re-election—a thing he did handily by winning all but two states. It didn't matter that his prediction was off by 7 points (Blumenthal 2010), the win by FDR threw Gallup into the national spotlight and proved his underlying idea that you could study public behavior and attitudes about politics like you could about consumer products.

When George Gallup developed his early polls during the 1930s, he saw his work as documenting and legitimizing the democratic ideal. He sought to develop a methodology that would provide an ongoing way to understand and document the opinion of the "average mankind," and in writing about it he cast it as a critical development in the formation of representative government. "Throughout the historical debate, the case against the common man has frequently proceeded on the basis of the flimsiest circumstantial evidence . . . He has not been granted a fair chance to call his key witnesses and make his own defense. Whether the final sentence has been that the People is a Great Beast, or that the Masses are Unfit to Rule, the critics of democracy frequently issue their verdict on the basis of fear rather than fact" (Gallup and Rae 1940).

Further Reading

Blackwell, Jon. "1935: The Poll That Took America's Pulse." *Trentonian*, republished at Capital Century Project. Accessed February 12, 2015. http://www.capitalcentury.com/1935.html.

Blumenthal, Mark. 2010. "Dr. George Gallup and the Literary Digest Poll." Pollster.com. March 11. Accessed February 11, 2015. http://www.pollster.com/blogs/dr_george_gallup_and_the_liter.html.

Gallup, George, and Saul Forbes Rae. 1940. *The Pulse of Democracy*. New York: Simon and Schuster.

Gallup. 2015. The Gallup Poll. Accessed February 11, 2015. http://www.gallup.com/poll/101905/Gallup-Poll.aspx.

Shepard, Steven. 2012. "Gallup Blew Its Presidential Polls, but Why?" National Journal. November 12. Accessed February 12, 2015. http://www.nationaljournal.com/politics/gallup-blew-its-presidential-polls-but-why-20121118.

GAWKER

If there is proof that political news will attract criticism but will also attract readers, the decision of the tabloid-style Gawker website to embrace political reporting as a core mission may be no better evidence. The site built a reputation and a sizable audience by giving people what they wanted and measuring success through readers to each piece of content. And after having publicly questioned the value of meaty, policy-oriented work, Gawker in 2015 announced it would dive head-first into the political reporting game.

The site made a controversial name for itself in journalism circles by placing a large electronic scoreboard in the middle of its newsroom. The board tracked to the second the stories that were getting attention and being shared on social networks. To Gawker the board represented what stories on its site were working, and the idea was to create as many of those as they could. In describing how the board worked in 2009, Gawker founder Nick Denton told the documentary *Page One*, "It's our equivalent of the front page. It's the most visible manifestation of a writer's success. We've always been very much focused on stories that our readers want. We're not trying to force-feed them. We're trying to give them what they want. I have a friend who's at the Albany bureau of the *Times*. I told him about the big board, sent him a picture of it and 'How do you like our new innovation?' He was terrified. Albany corruption stories—they may be important to cover, but no one really wants to read them" (Rossi 2010). But with its focus on tabloid news—the entire site's tagline is "Today's gossip is tomorrow's news"—the site slowly drifted further and further into the political reporting world. Gawker was the site that broke the story of Toronto mayor Rob Ford using cocaine and has often approached political news with a biting humor and leftist sensibility similar to Comedy Central's *The Daily Show* and website Wonkette.

By 2015, the site decided to stop dipping its editorial toe in the water and announced it would reorganize itself into a pure political website. Denton, in a note to staff, explained that Gawker Media Group would "ride the circus of the 2016 campaign cycle, seizing the opportunity to re-orient its editorial scope on political news, commentary and satire . . . Is there any doubt that the 2016 US presidential election campaign, a contest between reality-defying fabulists and the last representatives of two exhausted political dynasties, will provide rich new opportunities for sensation and satire?" (Bloomgarden-Smoke 2015). Gawker garners some 50 million monthly visitors and with the November 2015 memo, the site pledged to unleash a new politically focused entity. Within weeks, its new political voice was on display in an article about one of the leading Republican candidates for president under the less-than-subtle headline, "Dirtbag Ted Cruz Describes Alleged Planned Parenthood Shooter as 'Transgendered Leftist Activist'" declaring the Texas senator a "a gnarly gourd slowly depressing a fully inflated whoopee cushion" and accusing him of being one of the politicians "politicizing a tragedy, all the while delivering to their lunatic constituents a wholly manufactured persona of the perpetrator, for the sole purpose of insulating their deranged politics from their very real consequences" (Thompson 2015).

The shift to politics comes after a time of editorial turbulence inside Gawker. The summer of 2015 had Gawker in the headlines for many of the wrong reasons. A controversial story had prompted the resignation of the top two editors, who accused Denton and others from the corporate side of the operation of interfering in the editorial work of the publication. In the piece the site reported on a married male publishing executive contacting a male escort for homosexual sex. Although the executive was related to a former Cabinet member, neither he nor anyone else in the story was a household name. After several advertisers threatened to pull their business, Denton ordered the piece removed. Tommy Craggs, the executive editor of Gawker Media, and Max Read, the editor of Gawker.com, resigned in protest, accusing Gawker Media Group of ignoring the firewall between business and editorial. The result was that Denton declared he wanted the site to be "20 percent nicer." Denton told *Wired* magazine that the departures from the scandal allowed them to revisit what the site should be, saying, "The remaking of Gawker will be careful and deliberate . . . A cultural change is needed" (Greenberg 2015). All of this soul-searching came as the organization has faced a devastating lawsuit based on its publication of a sex tape of professional wrestler Hulk Hogan. Hogan filed a $100 million lawsuit against the company because they published a portion of the tape in 2012 and refused to remove it. Hogan won that suit in a Florida court and the publication now faces bankruptcy or sale or perhaps both.

This legal and editorial turmoil served as a backdrop to the site's November reorganization and may have helped inform some of those decisions to focus on politics. Gawker stressed that its decision should not be seen as a move to become like Politico or the *New York Times*. Instead, new editor Alex Pareene told the *Times*, "There is going to be a lot of campaign coverage, because this campaign is great and a dream for any writer. But we're not going to become Real Clear Politics . . . There will be a sort of satirical tone and satirical approach to reporting real news," adding he would model the new site after *Last Week Tonight*, the HBO show featuring comedian John Oliver that mixes humor with original and aggregated news (Somaiya 2015).

The reorganization also bet more of the future of the company on the family of seven content sites run by Gawker Media Group. How much the political wing of Gawker will be the one delivering profits is yet to be seen. The company still runs wildly popular niche news sites on other topics including the sports site Deadspin, the tech site Gizmodo, and the culture and celebrity site Jezebel. The site has also expanded its work in the site Lifehacker, which offers both tips to solving everyday problems and potentially revenue-rich product endorsements. The timing allows Gawker to try and capitalize on the digital campaign spending that swamps websites every four years, but whether Gawker can carve out a niche in the crowded political reporting world is yet to be seen.

See also: Comedy, Satire, and Politics; Vox; Wonkette

Further Reading

Bloomgarden-Smoke, Kara. 2015. "Gawker Lays Off Staff as Site Pivots to Politics." New York Observer. November 17. Accessed June 13, 2015. http://observer.com/2015/11/gawker-lays-off-staff-as-site-pivots-to-politics/.

Greenberg, Julia. 2015. "Gawker Reboots, But Even Nick Denton Isn't Sure What's Next." *Wired*. July 28. Accessed November 30. http://www.wired.com/2015/07/gawker-reboots-even-nick-denton-isnt-sure-whats-next.

Rossi, Andrew. 2010. *Page One: Inside the New York Times*. Magnolia Pictures.

Somaiya, Ravi. 2015. "Gawker to Retool as Politics Site." *New York Times*. November 17. Accessed November 30. http://www.nytimes.com/2015/11/18/business/media/gawker-politics-media.html.

Thompson, Chris. 2015. "Dirtbag Ted Cruz Describes Alleged Planned Parenthood Shooter as 'Transgendered Leftist Activist.'" Gawker. November 30. Accessed November 30. http://gawker.com/dirtbag-ted-cruz-describes-alleged-planned-parenthood-s-1745187009.

GET OUT THE VOTE (GOTV)

Get out the vote, or GOTV in campaign parlance, is the wide-ranging operation campaigns undertake to identify likely supporters or those who can be convinced to support their candidate, connect with those voters, and ensure on Election Day— or during early voting—those voters cast their ballots. Always a cornerstone of a political campaign, GOTV operations have become increasingly sophisticated, taking on all of the logistical elements of a military campaign and moving from an art of persuasion to a science of micro-targeting. As it has become more of a well-funded science, GOTV efforts have also become a favorite subject for strategy-focused political reporters in the closing days of campaigns.

As long as there have been campaigns there has been some variation of the get-out-the-vote effort. Many of today's handbooks for field organizers in a campaign quote an 1840 presidential campaign plan from then-Whig party organizer Abraham Lincoln, who wrote, "Organize the whole state so that every Whig can be brought to the polls . . . Divide their county into small districts and appoint in each a sub-committee, make a perfect list of all the voters and ascertain with certainty for whom they will vote, keep a constant watch on the doubtful voters and . . . have them talked to by those in whom they have the most confidence, and on Election Day see that every Whig is brought to the polls" (Lincoln 2001). The advice didn't help Whig William Henry Harrison carry Illinois—he lost it to Martin Van Buren—but it is the kind of campaign blueprint that still works 170 years later. But for as clear as Lincoln's advice may seem, how does a campaign organize the "perfect list" and what is the best way to keep them from becoming doubtful or losing faith in a candidate? That is where social science and databases have come to the fore.

Much of politics comes from past stories handed down from previous campaigns or educated hunches of what may or may not work. Few campaigns have the interest or the time or money to conduct scientific studies of what works when it comes to the fabled "ground game." The ground game—a campaign narrative that reporters focus on in the closing weeks of the campaign—is the catchphrase for the array of tactics a campaign deploys to get its supporters out to vote for a candidate. This is partly a story of database management where campaigns identify voters, communicate with them either face to face or through flyers and mailers, and then get them to polls, which can mean everything from an Election Day reminder phone call to get out and vote to actually arranging transportation for supporters to get to the polling place. Although campaigns don't have the time to conduct a randomized test of what mobilizes a voter to cast a ballot, some political scientists have tackled the issue and their work has been surprisingly potent in informing the modern campaign.

One such work is *Get Out the Vote: How to Increase Voter Turnout*, a piece of social science research that seeks to translate political science work directly into recommendations for campaigns. The authors, Donald Green and Alan Gerber, broke down the different components of identifying voters, inspiring them to support a candidate and getting them out to cast a ballot, and then tested how effective different techniques were. Surprisingly, the work found one of the most powerful tools for campaigns of various sizes was the canvass. Canvassing, when volunteers, surrogates, and the candidate get out and knock on doors in a targeted neighborhood, is one of the most basic concepts of a campaign—at least as old as Lincoln's Whig campaign of 1840. Yet after conducting a series of tests, Green and Gerber came back and said it worked. It worked really well. "Face-to-face interaction makes politics come to life and helps voters establish a personal connection with the electoral process. The canvasser's willingness to devote time and energy signals the importance of participation in the electoral process. Many nonvoters need just a nudge to motivate them to vote. A personal invitation sometimes makes all the difference" (Green and Gerber 2008).

But this is not to argue that the best way to win an election (and therefore the elements of a successful GOTV operation) is to randomly knock on doors and make the case person by person. The strategy comes from knowing what doors to knock on, how often the campaign has knocked on those doors, and how often the people behind the door have really supported the candidate or party. One of the early micro-targeting experts who worked for 2004 Democratic candidate John Kerry and other campaigns explained the targeting like this, "To target for GOTV, a campaign could combine two micro-targeting models, one giving the likelihood that an individual was a supporter and the second giving the likelihood that that individual was going to vote, to find likely supporters who are unlikely to vote if not reached. If there are sufficient IDs where voters are asked their issue priorities, models can be built giving the percent likelihood that an individual voter cares about any given issue so that the campaign can select different messages to target to different audiences" (Strasma n.d.). This is a critical step in organizing the canvassing prospects a campaign can hit.

Once a likely voter is identified and contacted, an effective GOTV effort will repeatedly communicate with the voter, ideally about issues that are particularly important to him or her over the coming weeks. This period could include ensuring the voter's registration is up to date and, if possible, that they have filled out an absentee ballot or voted early. It can also include building a strategy in the closing days of a campaign to ensure that the voter actually gets to the polls and casts the ballot. In the early work of GOTV, the Republican Party was seen as having a clearly superior organization. Reporting as late as the mid-2000s spoke of an almost magical program of voter contact and development known as the "72-Hour Program." Similar to what Green and Gerber did in testing different approaches, the 72-Hour Program was a project organized by the Republican National Committee to test different ways of connecting with voters and seeing what methods were the most effective in generating votes. The strategy was built around the final three days of the campaign, organizing a series of personal interaction with voters as well as targeted communications to encourage the voter to turn out. Partly devised by Republican strategist Karl Rove and credited in 2004 with helping re-elect President George W. Bush, by 2006 all campaign strategies were held up in comparison to this fabled system (VandeHei 2006). But the changing nature of technology and campaigns was sowing the seeds of the 72-Hour Program's destruction. Early and absentee voting meant there was no longer a final 72 hours of the campaign since voters may be casting ballots weeks ahead of Election Day. And even though the GOP effort included database work, Democratic campaigns like Howard Dean's in 2004 and Barack Obama's in 2008 were constructing far more sophisticated methods of tracking and communicating with voters.

By 2008, the ground game had become something reporters spent enormous amounts of time researching and reporting on, trying to become aware of and understand the new communication techniques of social media, and the changing landscape caused by increased early voting. GOTV efforts were now broken into two segments, the early days of early voting when you want your hard-core supporters out casting their ballots, and the last days when you work to close the deal. According to *Campaigns & Elections* magazine, "By the midway point of any given race, campaigns should be targeting new voters and have a good idea of who is on the fence. With that information in hand, the last 72 hours should focus on getting low propensity voters to the polls" (D'Aprile and Nyczepir 2012).The role of GOTV efforts is hard to overstate. The media's fascination with GOTV efforts is equally hard to overstate. One analysis found, "Of the 222 mentions of 'ground game' in newspaper articles about the 2012 presidential campaign, more than two-thirds were published after October 22, the date of the last presidential debate and the start of the final phase of the campaign" (Prevost 2014). The ground game is a hybrid of the horse race reporting that seeks to understand who is ahead in the campaign and the strategy story that aims to explain how they got ahead or why they fell behind. Campaigns have sought to use this media interest to fuel late stories that help inspire the base and give campaigns a (sometimes bogus) sense of momentum headed into the final days of a contest. An example of this comes from Arkansas where, in the final days of Democratic senator Mark Pryor's failed bid for re-election, the campaign got a newspaper to bite on the GOTV story. The Associated Press ran a story on October 15 that read, "Democrats claimed a big success after former president Bill Clinton campaigned across several college campuses in Arkansas recently, saying they signed up enough partisans to fill more than 4,000 volunteer shifts in their drive to re-elect Senator Mark Pryor. Now the concern is the 'flake rate'—the people who fail to show up" (Espo 2014). Pryor lost by 17 points.

Why does the media heap as much attention on the ground game as it does? In large part because understanding who is going to show up at the polls on Election Day is as illustrative as any political opinion poll. In fact, pollsters try and estimate likely voter turnout when constructing their models during election year polls. When voter turnout collapses for one party or explodes for another, polls can be caught off guard. For example, polling guru Nate Silver's FiveThirtyEight had trouble with some races in 2014 for overestimating Democratic turnout. In Maryland, Silver gave lieutenant governor Anthony Brown a 93 percent chance of being elected. He lost by almost four points. The main reason? A complete failure by Democrats to get their voters to go to the polls. A Democratic activist trying to make sense of the loss later said, "The Republican candidates had virtually identical totals in 2010 and 2014; the difference was in the Democratic turnout. Overall, the Republican ticket picked up 71,000 more votes, but the Democratic falloff was 274,000 . . . Sorry, but that drop-off of 274,000 votes is real, and it was fatal. Those Democrats didn't vote for the Republican; they stayed home" (Beyer 2014). Most reporting in the days leading up to the election were driven by "ground game" stories; most overlooked the bleak reality of how discouraged Democrats had become in the months leading up to Election Day. This is the danger of the "ground game" or GOTV story in media coverage. Journalists' focus on the strategy driving the media purchases and informing the canvassing are more aspirational than they are informational. Campaigns are unlikely to convey how depressed voter turnout may be, and the reality may be very different than the impression.

Getting Out the Vote, since even before the days of the Harrison/Van Buren race, is a critical component to understanding elections. It is an essential part of any campaign and its effective execution can expand the electorate, bring new voters into the system, or even elect a long-shot candidate. It is also one of the areas where political scientists have clearly contributed to the development and testing of techniques to communicate with voters and encourage them to participate in the political process. The media's focus on it is understandable given the increasing size and expense of GOTV within the campaign and how, when one or the other party is unable to inspire its voters to turn out, it can drastically affect the election. Where the media sometime falters in this coverage is by covering the tactics of the ground game at the expense of the larger issues that may be driving voter apathy or anger. An effective ground game in 2008 was not going to elect John McCain president given the frustration with former president Bush and popularity of senator Barack Obama. Similarly, breathlessly reporting on what one party hopes to achieve in voter targeting and turnout needs to be weighed against the major issues that were depressing that party's voters and inspiring the other's.

See also: Campaign Strategy Coverage; Early Voting; Horse-Race Journalism

Further Reading

Beyer, Dana. 2014. "The Political Red Tide Washes Ashore in Maryland." Huffington Post. November 7. Accessed June 30, 2015. http://www.huffingtonpost.com/dana-beyer/the -political-red-tide-wa_b_6117686.html.

D'Aprile, Shane, and Dave Nyczepir. 2012. "The Roadmap to the Final 72." Campaigns & Elections. October 14. Accessed June 30, 2015. http://www.campaignsandelections.com /magazine/1787/a-roadmap-for-the-final-72.

Espo, David. 2014. "Getting Out the Vote: Registration Is Up, But How Many Will Then Turn Out for Election Day." Associated Press. October 15. Accessed June 29, 2015. http://m.startribune.com/politics/279328142.html.

Green, Donald, and Alan Gerber. 2008. *Get Out the Vote: How to Increase Voter Turnout*. Washington, DC: Brookings Institution Press.

Lincoln, Abraham. 2001. "Campaign Circular from Whig Committee." *Collected Works of Abraham Lincoln*. Volume 1. Ann Arbor, Michigan: University of Michigan Digital Library Production Services. Accessed June 30, 2015. http://quod.lib.umich.edu/l/lincoln /lincoln1/1:214.1?rgn=div2;view=fulltext.

Prevost, Alicia Kolar. 2014. "The Ground Game: Fieldwork in Political Campaigns." In *Campaigns and Elections American Style*, edited by James Thurber and Candice Nelson. Boulder, CO: Westview Press.

Strasma, Ken. "Micro-Targeting: New Wave Political Campaigning." Winning Campaigns. Accessed June 30, 2015. http://www.winningcampaigns.org/Winning-Campaigns -Archive-Articles/Micro-Targeting-New-Wave-Political-Campaigning.html.

VandeHei, Jim. 2006. "Democrats Scrambling to Organize Voter Turnout." *Washington Post*. August 6. Accessed June 30, 2015. http://www.washingtonpost.com/wp-dyn/content /article/2006/08/01/AR2006080101332.html.

GOVERNMENT-SUBSIDIZED JOURNALISM

There is a powerful notion in America that the press and the government ought to be separate entities and that any government relationship with the press threatens the core concept of media-as-watchdog. This concern for government-run or sanctioned media has existed since the days of the colonies and has shaped everything from the complex structure of public broadcasting in the United States to the legal concepts behind shielding media sources from state agencies. What's interesting to note, though, is that there always has been a system of tax breaks and government policies that meant billions of dollars for publishers, creating a far more quiet, but no less real economic connection between state and the press.

The fierceness of the demand for a separation of press and the government has its roots in colonial America. As British subjects settled in what would become North America they brought with them books and later printing presses. These early printing facilities operated with deep connections to the Crown. Printers had to be licensed and most relied heavily on government contracts to make ends meet. Printers, who in addition to printing operated as the forerunners of the American newspaper, also printed government money, official papers, and religious material from the Church of England. The idea of the printers working independently of the state was something the government did not allow and many with positions of power deeply feared. When Governor William Berkeley filed a report with his overseers back in England in 1671 he gave voice to the British fears of these new tools, writing, "But, I thank God, we have not free schools nor printing; and I hope we shall not have these hundred years. For learning has brought disobedience and heresy and sects into the world, and printing has divulged them and libels against the government. God keep us from both." Berkeley's great fears soon began to materialize as the British government soon began to lose control of that press. A critical court case 60 years later found that the press could not be punished for printing the truth about the government. Soon the newspapers were operating under permit, but with far fewer official tools to sanction them. Printers like Samuel Adams would use those papers to spread incendiary, and often inaccurate, information about British troops in the colonies and helped foment revolt that would become the American Revolution. As the new country established itself, many in leadership saw there was an inherent value in the press that imbued the new government's work and helped lead to the First Amendment protection of the freedom of the press.

All of this is true, but it also helps create a skewed mythology about the relationship between the government and the press. The myth is that the press was free from any interference by the government and operated completely independent of any assistance from the government. But it was just not true. As two experienced media executives-turned-academics noted in a major report on the relationship between the two, "Throughout American history, the federal government has worn many hats in its relationship with the press and the news industry: watchdog of power among news business owners; consumer advocate championing the news and information needs of underserved or neglected communities; affirmative action catalyst for extending employment and ownership opportunities to minorities and women; regulator of the public airwaves; and provider of both direct and indirect subsidies that have been important pieces of the news industry's economic health" (Cowan and Westphal 2010).

Some of the very first acts of the new United States included sizable subsidies for news organizations. On February 20, 1792, President George Washington signed the Postal Act. The law created the U.S. Postal Service and granted Congress and the government the ability to set and regulate regular postal routes. It also included a critical subsidy for the press, allowing newspapers to be sent through the mail at a discounted rate. The difference between the real cost of the mailing and the amount paid by the press was covered by the new federal government, a major decision regarding spending at a time when the government had few resources available. This subsidy by the new government was conceived of as a way of keeping the sprawling territory of the new country informed about what was happening in the state capitals and in matters of national and international interest. While traveling the still-new country in 1831 Frenchman Alexis de Tocqueville would note the importance of this government-backed system, writing to a friend, "There is an astonishing circulation of letters and newspapers among these savage woods . . . I do not think that in the most enlightened rural districts of France there is intellectual movement either so rapid or on such a scale as in this wilderness" (John 2009). While there was a clear societal benefit to keep the remote outposts of Detroit informed about what was happening in Philadelphia and New York, there was also a clear economic benefit to the newspapers. They could charge less for a subscription to the service without threatening their bottom line. Interestingly, as these news organizations moved more and more to rely on advertising as well as subscriptions to cover the cost of producing the news, the government subsidy remained in place. As late as 1970, some 75 percent of the cost of mailing a newspaper or magazine was subsidized by the government. One analysis found that amounted to $2 billion in savings for news organizations. In recent years, the government has scaled back the savings, although the Postal Service still subsidizes 11 percent of the cost, saving media companies $288 million a year. The government has also offered assistance to print media by allowing companies to claim tax breaks associated with printing and distribution costs. These tax breaks mean hundreds of millions of dollars in savings for firms at the state and federal level. Also, rules at the federal and state levels require government agencies to post public notices of rule changes, meetings, and lawsuits. One estimate found that the costs by all levels of government to purchase ad space in newspapers at the community and national level may amount to $1 billion.

But government action has not just benefited the printed press. The Federal Communications Commission has adopted rules over the years that ensure that local broadcasters have access to cable subscribers in their area and that cable news channels benefit from the flood of people subscribing to cable. As cable moved from a way to receive broadcast signals in remote and mountainous areas to a primary way of receiving television content, the FCC implemented carriage requirements that meant cable operators had to offer local channels, ensuring that broadcasters would benefit and be able to sell advertising to support their local programming, much of which is local news. On the cable side, the FCC also issued rules that every cable subscriber had to pay a fee to receive CNN, MSNBC, and Fox News, whether they wanted those channels or not.

Although these tax breaks, government regulations, and direct financial subsidies amount to a major investment in news and information by all levels of the American government, one form of journalism tends to come to mind first when considering government-backed media—public broadcasting. Public broadcasting includes hundreds of local broadcasters working in every state in the country as well as national networks of radio and television producers creating content for these local stations. The structure of public broadcasting was, in many ways, a result of the desire for this entity to be a product of local communities and not be seen as government-run media. Unlike many state-owned media operations in other countries, American public media was built in such a way that the government subsidies are deliberately several steps away from funding any particular content. NPR or *PBS NewsHour* is not an official broadcast of the American government, like state television in China. And unlike the BBC in Britain where the service is supported by a direct tax, public broadcasting in the United States is supported through an appropriation authorized by Congress. The federal government spends about $300 million a year on public media. These funds go to an organization called the Corporation for Public Broadcasting, which is a nonprofit organization and not an agency of the government. CPB was created by Congress in 1967 to support educational television and radio stations in local communities. In signing the Public Broadcasting Act of 1967 into law, President Lyndon Johnson stressed that the idea behind the government's action was to encourage the use of media to enrich the spirit and not to create a new arm of the government. He declared, "The Corporation will assist stations and producers who aim for the best in broadcasting good music, in broadcasting exciting plays, and in broadcasting reports on the whole fascinating range of human activity. It will try to prove that what educates can also be exciting. It will get part of its support from our Government. But it will be carefully guarded from Government or from party control. It will be free, and it will be independent—and it will belong to all of our people."

Under the convoluted system built by Congress and implemented by CPB, the federal government appropriates money to CPB and CPB then directs a large percentage of that money directly to the 1,400 public radio and television stations scattered across the United States. So, for example, of the $298 million CPB requested for fiscal years 2016–2018, $223 million would go directly to stations. As CPB chair Patricia Harrison explained, this money only accounts for a small chunk of the overall money needed to operate the stations, telling a Senate Appropriations subcommittee in March 2015, "The federal appropriation is the essential investment that ensures your constituents will have access to public media for free and commercial free. President Ronald Reagan said, 'government should provide the spark and the private sector should do the rest.' America's local public media stations utilize the 'spark' of the federal investment—approximately 10 to 15 percent of a station's budget—and raise the rest from their viewers, listeners, donors, and contributors. The result is a uniquely entrepreneurial system with a track record of value delivered to all citizens."

Most stations in urban areas or with strong local support can operate with only a small subsidy from CPB, but for those stations in remote locations, the costs of running a station to reach all parts of Alaska or rural Wyoming require more support from the government. Local stations use the mix of government and donated money to produce local programs as well as purchase programming from a mix of national networks, including television's Public Broadcasting Service (PBS) and National Public Radio (NPR). These networks receive some money from CPB but make most of the money from member stations, meaning that these networks are actually owned by the local stations. PBS then hires producers to produce programming like *PBS NewsHour* and *Frontline*, and NPR produces much of the content itself. CPB, which was also tasked with ensuring that public television and radio featured diversity, contributes a small portion of the federal appropriation to independent and minority media producers. All of this goes into producing public television and radio content. The complex structure does two things that supporters of public broadcasting endorse—first, it ensures that the government is at least two steps removed from the content decisions of networks or journalists. Second, it requires that the stations and individual programs raise additional money from corporate sponsors, foundations, and viewers to augment the federal money.

Despite the fairly small appropriation and the complex structure of public media to ensure local value and protect against government influence, the federal funding of public media has often been a point of heated public debate. First there is the philosophical reason for opposing public funding—that it is not the government's job to create media, especially in an environment where cable offerings usually top more than 125 channels and the Internet offers near-endless content options. Why should the American public fund one or two specific channels? Second, there has been a wide perception that public media is too liberal. As Christopher Sterling, a professor of media and public affairs and public policy at George Washington University, told ABC during one of the recent funding debates, "Republicans have never been fond of public broadcasting. Republicans have always thought that public broadcasting across the board is liberal, is not particularly supportive of Republican and conservative points of view. Democrats tend not to think that, unless they're from very conservative districts" (Khan 2011). And a 2014 report on polarization in the media seems to back up Sterling's point. The Pew Research Center found that NPR was one of the most trusted news sources among liberal Americans, while among strongly conservative voters 39 percent of people distrusted NPR and only 3 percent trusted it. This division has dogged the perception of public broadcasting, fueling the general feeling on the right that the networks' political leanings make them pro-Democratic.

The focus of the frequent defense of public broadcasting tends not to be the array of news and information programming, but rather Big Bird, the iconic character from the program *Sesame Street*. While news programs like NPR's *All Things Considered* and *Morning Edition* and PBS's *Frontline* and *PBS NewsHour* are often seen as among the best broadcast news programs available in America, the debate about public funding is often won by supporters by focusing on the children's programming produced by PBS. Defenders are also quick to point out that the amount of public support is a tiny fraction of the federal budget—roughly .012 percent of the $3.8 trillion federal budget—or about $1.35 per person per year. Elsewhere in the world, Canada spends $22.48 per citizen, Japan $58.86 per citizen, the United Kingdom $80.36 per citizen, and Denmark $101 per citizen. But in making his argument against PBS in 2005, conservative columnist George Will argued Big Bird could go find a for-profit entity to distribute it and that "public television is akin to the body politic's appendix: It is vestigial, purposeless, and occasionally troublesome. Of the two arguments for it, one is impervious to refutation and the other refutes itself" (Will 2005). And now Sesame Workshop, makers of Big Bird, have done that, cutting a deal that allows cable giant HBO to air new programs exclusively for a few months before PBS begins re-airing them. How this may affect the public debate next time is too early to know.

What is clear is that while the U.S. Postal Service has slowly weaned newspapers and magazines from subsidized deliveries and state and federal governments debate ending the public notice ads that deliver hundreds of millions of dollars to newspapers, the role of the government subsidization of the public media will remain the most controversial and easily identifiable form of public support of the media in America. To what degree that support will continue will cook up from time to time, but so far it has demonstrated surprisingly resilient public support for children's programming and news and public affairs through PBS and NPR.

See also: *Frontline*; NPR; *PBS NewsHour*; Political Polarization and the Media

Further Reading

Cowan, Geoffrey, and David Westphal. 2010. "Public Policy and Funding the News." USC Annenberg School of Communication & Journalism. Accessed December 18, 2015. http://www.niemanlab.org/pdfs/USC%20Report.pdf.

John, Richard. 2009. *Spreading the News: The American Postal System from Franklin to Morse.* Boston, MA: Harvard University Press.

Khan, Huma. 2011. "As Budget Debates Begin, Republicans Put NPR, PBS on Chopping Block." ABC News. February 15. Accessed December 18, 2015. http://abcnews.go.com/Politics/budget-debates-begin-republicans-put-npr-pbs-chopping/story?id=12915626.

Will, George. 2005. "We Have No More Need for PBS." Townhall.com. March 5. Accessed December 18, 2015. http://townhall.com/columnists/georgewill/2005/03/03/we_have _no_more_need_for_pbs/page/full.

GRASSROOTS CAMPAIGNS

Political campaigns have historically relied on party members to get involved in politics, donating money, volunteering at a phone bank, or putting a sign of support in their yard. Parties could initially promise lucrative, politically appointed jobs to party activists and later the party hierarchy could offer their own career opportunities. But as political parties became less top-down and centralized, campaigns came to rely more heavily on those activists driven to be involved by their support of a single candidate or issue. Those issues and the ground-up array of volunteers and donors who support them fueled the grassroots movements in both major parties. Grassroots politics has always had an element of insurgency in its practice. It is usually driven by activists who feel the party establishment is not adequately addressing their concerns or issues or who want to ensure the party maintains its position on the issue that drives them. These groups exist across the political spectrum and often create an unpredictable element of politics. Party candidates and organizers want to engage and inspire the grassroots but also must balance these issue advocates with efforts to attract more moderate or multi-issue voters.

The origins of the term grassroots are unclear, but it is most often associated with the rise of the political progressives early in the twentieth century. One of the primary reforms of this era involved handing more political authority to individual voters, from the direct election of U.S. senators to the growth of direct political primaries. One 1903 article about the efforts of Theodore Roosevelt describe the organization as beginning at the most local level, saying, "We will begin at the grass roots" (Salt Lake Herald 1903). This speaks to the American ideal of all residents being politically engaged citizens, and that these citizens are the source of political authority. Political organizations should, it is often felt, begin with the individual voter and grow into a movement, a party, or a campaign.

Critically, it is important to understand that grassroots tend to be fundamentally different than the established leadership of the major political parties. Parties can be thought of as the professional wing of politics, centered around people who choose politics as a career, who want to win elections, govern, and win re-election. Grassroots usually come from a very different place. These groups organize out of frustration with the status quo or a desire to change society or politics. One expert in organizing grassroots described why people get involved by writing, "We complained to our friends. We got mad. We wrote letters to the editor. We called up radio stations. We complained to our boss. We threatened. Nothing seems to work . . . We find out we're not the only ones who are mad and think something should be done. There are people on the block, in the neighborhood, in the plant, in the schoolroom, who feel the same way we do . . . That's the start of organizing: recognizing that individual solutions are not working and that therefore the answer has to be working together" (Kahn 1991). This most basic explanation of where grassroots organizing begins helps inform the turbulent, yet critical role these organizations play in modern politics. Grassroots activism grows out of anger and frustration with a perceived or real inequality or problem. It does not begin from a place of compromise or understanding, but is usually a last resort for when all other techniques have failed. Still, these groups are highly motivated and active, and when a political campaign can harness them for their electoral goals, they can have powerful impacts on the electoral process.

Grassroots efforts have a long and sometimes rocky history in American politics. The progressive movement at the dawn of the twentieth century benefited from grassroots activism, much of it inspired by crusading muckrakers who exposed corporate greed and government graft. The Civil Rights movement of the 1950s and 1960s grew out of frustration with the inequalities and brutalities of the Jim Crow South. The antiwar movement during the 1960s, the environmental movement and the anti-tax efforts of the 1970s, and the conservative Christian organizations of the 1980s all stemmed from the same tradition, and each would help to reshape the nation and its politics. All of these efforts were driven by problems that needed addressing, and in every case the resulting political movements would be absorbed into the existing political parties, but even as that happened these movement changed the policies and politics of those parties.

Still the access these movements had to the positions of political authority came much later. In each case the movement began, and attracted general media attention due to a crisis or debate. The group, cast into the public eye, would then expand with members and funding, and then political organizations would seek to attract those active members of the organization to support one party or the other. Central to most of these cycles has been the role of the media in covering the issues of the group, pressing their demands on political authorities, and exposing those not familiar with the work of the organization to the issues they are trying to address. Grassroots campaigns have relied on the media to be their megaphone.

Like most other areas of modern campaigning, grassroots organizing has gone through a series of seismic shifts as a result of the changes to campaign finance laws in the 2000s. Following the adoption of the Bipartisan Campaign Finance Reform Act, the so-called McCain-Feingold Act, new organizations sprang up that were not directly run by political parties or candidates. These new organizations, known as 527 organizations due to the section of Internal Revenue Service code they fell under, could take large donations, but needed to disclose the donors and spending. These types of 527s would morph into Super PACs in the wake of the *Citizens United* decision by the Supreme Court. The important thing for these groups was that they were not officially affiliated with any political party and often stressed their nonpartisan nature.

Still, the goal of the groups like America Coming Together was to register more people to vote, and that effort had a clear partisan advantage for Democrats. One 2004 story about ACT noted how the group had hired a phalanx of canvassers to register new voters with the help of millions of dollars from a handful of Democratic donors. The goal was nonpartisan, but Democrats also know that many of their traditional supporters—poorer voters and minorities—are also less likely to be registered. And so ACT deployed its volunteers and at the time, "The canvassers use their handhelds to enter a wealth of information about voters' political leanings and concerns. Using this data, ACT then plans repeat visits (it hopes to see each person several times before the election) and targeted e-mails. In Ohio, the handhelds have 'video capacity,' so voters can be shown a neighbor discussing some issue" (*The Economist* 2004). Liberal-leaning organizations launched countless efforts on college campuses and in inner cities seeking to register more voters who were likely to support the Democratic Party. Many of these groups also encourage voters to cast ballots early or, in states where this is possible, will even help voters register and mail their absentee ballots.

Despite these efforts in 2004, President George W. Bush largely cruised to re-election and many credited the Republicans' efforts to get their voters motivated and out to the polls. Many of those liberals who study politics or considered the efforts of groups like ACT now began to question whether these new groups, with more resources but no official connection to the candidates or parties, could actually be hurting the efforts to build a grassroots organization within the Democratic Party. One post-mortem of the 2004 election declared Democrats needed to re-embrace real community engagement, with the author lamenting, "Only through meaningful membership that involves conversations and lasting connections can social capital and social networks be harnessed to bring about political change. . . . [C]reating a political infrastructure that links local groups to national political institutions takes time and commitment: it will require people at the national and grassroots levels working together to establish grassroots connections that are deep enough to bear fruit" (Fisher 2006). This idea of efforts to build political activism from the top down had already established itself firmly in political organizing. The idea of creating a false perception of a groundswell of public support has come to be known as astroturfing (named after the artificial field first used in Houston Astrodome). One of the first uses of the term came in 1985 when then-senator Lloyd Bentsen said, "A fellow from Texas can tell the difference between grass roots and AstroTurf . . . This is generated mail" (Ostler 2011). This idea of manufacturing public outrage has also evolved with technology. Now an organization can mount a public campaign to send letters to Congress at the click of a button, making it possible for people to automatically draft a letter in support or opposition in a moment. Although this isn't truly faked support, technology has made it so simple to participate in a "grassroots" campaign that little of the passion that motivated organizers in the past needs to be present. "Liking" a photo or statement on Facebook is now expressed as popular support for an idea.

Still, it would be a mistake to dismiss all modern digital grassroots as "likes" on Facebook or retweets on Twitter. Digital technologies have given spontaneous political organizations critical tools to organize real people and to demand real change. One lengthy examination of the similarities between the spread of the Reformation in Europe and the Arab Spring throughout the Middle East highlights how the technologies of Facebook and social media had created new social dynamics that could propel grassroots movements. "The dictatorships in Egypt and Tunisia, [sociologist Zeynep Tufekci] argues, survived for as long as they did because although many people deeply disliked those regimes, they could not be sure others felt the same way. Amid the outbreaks of unrest in early 2011, however, social-media websites enabled lots of people to signal their preferences en masse to their peers very quickly, in an 'informational cascade' that created momentum for further action" (*The Economist* 2011).

This power is not just limited to the most explosive political movements, as American groups have used the same ideas to promote everything from marijuana legalization to a more strict interpretation of the commerce clause of the U.S. Constitution. The digital efforts, often nicknamed "netroots," have been particularly active on the Democratic side of the spectrum, fueled by the typically younger and more liberal users of social media. These activists built websites like MoveOn.org to raise money and recruit volunteers for progressive candidates and causes and rallied around the 2004 outsider campaign of Howard Dean, who once told a rally he would represent the "Democratic wing of the Democratic Party." They launched wildly popular online communities like the Daily Kos and pressured Democrats to stand up for the more liberal issues of the party.

A similar movement has grown up within the field of journalism, as activists frustrated with the editorial choices or perceived biases of the mainstream media have taken to the digital world to create their own reporting. Loosely described as "citizen journalism," these blogs, Twitter feeds, and Tumblr accounts have allowed individuals to research, report, and comment on the day's news, be it international or local. Technologies have made put publishing work within anyone's grasp, and this has empowered people in particular who distrust or are angry with the media. The argument is that these voices will become more professional as they mature and attract audiences. As digital advocate Dan Gillmor wrote in his book *We the Media*, "We're on the verge of a time when people can bring serious [journalistic] alternatives to the public and get paid for what they do. Ultimately, the audience will make the decisions. Success will come to those operations that make themselves required reading, listening, or viewing. This is how it's always worked and how it always will" (Gillmor 2004).

The parallels between the professional journalists and the citizen journalist in many ways mirror the tensions between the grassroots voters and the political establishment. Both citizen journalism and grassroots activism are born of a frustration with the current powers that be, and both have been transformed and empowered by the digital revolution that allowed these groups to find one another and share their desire to change things. Media organizations, parties, and candidates see themselves buffeted by the demands of these groups, wanting to attract them to be readers or voters, but not wanting to alienate those who do not agree with the activists.

See also: Cultural Conservatives; Single-Issue Politics; Social Media and Politics

Further Reading
"Boom for Gen. Torrance." *Salt Lake Herald*. September 23, 1903. Accessed June 13, 2016. http://chroniclingamerica.loc.gov/lccn/sn85058130/1903-09-25/ed-1/seq-6/#words=grass+roots.

"The Ersatz Democrats." 2004. *Economist*. May 22. Accessed September 18, 2015. http://www.economist.com/node/2688277.

Fisher, Dana R. 2006. *Activism, Inc: How the Outsourcing of Grassroots Campaigns Is Strangling Progressive Politics in America*. Palo Alto, CA.: Stanford University Press.

Gillmor, Dan. 2004. *We the Media: Grassroots Journalism by the People, for the People*. Newton, MA: O'Reilly Media.

"How Luther Went Viral." 2011. *Economist*. December 17. Accessed September 17, 2015. http://www.economist.com/node/21541719.

Kahn, Si. 1991. *Organizing: A Guide for Grassroots Leaders*. Washington, DC: National Association of Social Workers Press.

Ostler, Rosemarie. 2011. *Slinging Mud: Rude Nicknames, Scurrilous Slogans, and Insulting Slang from Two Centuries of American Politics*. New York: Penguin Books.

H

HANNITY, SEAN (1961–)

Radio talk show host and Fox News Channel personality Sean Hannity has carved out a position as one of the most influential conservative commentators in the country. He has drawn millions of listeners to his nationally syndicated radio program, and has cranked out three books as well as daily diatribes against Democratic policies. In particular, Hannity has attracted viewers and listeners who align with the tea party movement and other conservative insurgents who have accused the old guard of the party of being too willing to negotiate with Democrats.

His influence among key contingents of the Republican Party could be seen throughout 2015 as libertarian and tea party-aligned candidates first went to Hannity to be interviewed. Politico's Dylan Byers noted that both Kentucky senator Rand Paul and Texas conservative Ted Cruz embargoed all their interviews with reporters about their announcement to run for the GOP nomination to 10 p.m. "Why? Because 10 p.m. is when Sean Hannity's Fox News program airs, and both Cruz and Paul had promised Hannity the rights to the first interview. The decisions by both candidates to give their first interviews to Hannity demonstrate just how much influence the conservative pundit still holds over the insurgent wing of the Republican Party" (Byers 2015). Hannity boasts more than 13 million weekly radio listeners—only conservative icon Rush Limbaugh has more—and draws some 400,000 nightly viewers to his Fox News Channel show.

It's an impressive resume for a kid from New York City who dropped out of New York University and Adelphi University before landing his first radio program at a college radio station in southern California. He has admitted his early programs were not that good and he soon bounced to stations in Huntsville, Alabama, and later Atlanta. He caught his stride and made his way back to New York where WABC gave him a drive-time show and later moved him to an afternoon slot in 1998, where he has been ever since. In fact, in 2008 he landed a five-year, $100 million contract for his radio show, making him the second highest paid radio celebrity (again, behind Limbaugh). He built his listenership with a tough, no-holds-barred style of conservative talk—carrying the same sharp-edged message of Limbaugh, but often lacking some of the more comedic elements.

His tough approach and widespread fan base helped score him his book deals and he used those to strengthen and extend his argument against Democrats. He pulls no punches, accusing lapses by the administration of Democratic president Bill Clinton of weakening the country in the years leading up to the terrorist attacks of September 2001. He wrote in his book *Let Freedom Ring: Winning the War of Liberty over Liberalism* that "liberals told us that global warming and gays in the military were top priorities, well above securing our nation. September 11 and subsequent revelations have proven them wrong" (Hannity 2004). Hannity is one of the most well-known of the branch of conservative talkers who stridently call for ideological clarity and forcefully calls a hard-line approach to political debates, blasting Republicans who do not fight for their principles. Some within the Republican Party have worried that Hannity and other strict conservatives offer the party only something to unify against and are actually making it harder to govern, pointing to the 2015 struggle to select a new Speaker of the House after the resignation of besieged representative John Boehner who was forced out by conservative activists in his own party. One party official who was unwilling to say so on the record told a researcher in February 2015, "There's not a platform in the . . . Sean Hannity wing of conservatism. There's nothing that you can take to the country and hope to win the presidency on that they believe in. I mean, anti-immigration, don't hesitate to shut down the government, repeal Obamacare, no new taxes—that's not a governing platform. That will rally 40 percent of the population" (Calmes 2015).

Despite the influence Hannity has exerted over some aspects of the Republican Party, his commentary-focused program was moved in 2013, shifting from the 9 p.m. slot back to 10 p.m., replaced by Megyn Kelly as the network moved to beef up its ratings lead over CNN and MSNBC. The network said it was an effort to tweak the lineup to attract younger viewers, but many saw it as a demotion. Nevertheless, with the nation's political temperature and partisanship up, uncompromising voices like Hannity's will likely remain popular.

See also: Fox News; *Fox News Sunday*; Limbaugh, Rush; O'Reilly, Bill; Talk Radio; Tea Party Movement

Further Reading

Byers, Dylan. 2015. "Sean Hannity Shows His Influence." Politico. April 7. Accessed October 30, 2015. http://www.politico.com/blogs/media/2015/04/sean-hannity-shows-his -influence-205142.
Calmes, Jackie. 2015. "'They Don't Give a Damn about Governing:' Conservative Media's Influence on the Republican Party." Shorenstein Center. July 27. Accessed October 30, 2015. http://shorensteincenter.org/conservative-media-influence-on-republican-party -jackie-calmes.
Hannity, Sean. 2004. *Let Freedom Ring: Winning the War of Liberty over Liberalism*. New York: Harper Collins.

HERITAGE FOUNDATION

The Heritage Foundation is an influential conservative think tank that has, since its founding in the 1970s, sought to actively influence the political debate over both domestic and international policy, mixing research with intense lobbying of Republicans to implement its recommendations. Unlike older think tanks, Heritage has publicly pushed for its policies, deploying campaign tactics like direct mail and television advertising to draw support and punish those who oppose their efforts. In recent years, some within the Republican establishment have balked at the foundation's increasingly aggressive approach, arguing that it is more a pressure group than a research institute.

The Heritage Foundation was founded at a time when the gap between the depth of policy expertise between conservatives and liberals appeared at its widest. Despite the flagging public support for the liberal New Deal-era policies of Democrats and the raging anti-tax movements in California and elsewhere, there were only a handful of Republican-leaning think tanks in Washington, D.C. The domestic policy–focused American Enterprise Institute and the foreign policy–focused Center for Strategic and International Studies at Georgetown University offered reams of reports and stacks of books, but their influence seemed frustratingly limited. Looking back a quarter-century later, research fellow Lee Edwards would describe the situation conservatives found themselves in as follows, "Envious conservatives watched the powerful liberal coalition of academics, think tank analysts, members of Congress, White House aides, interest group officials, and journalists run much of the business of the nation's capital and wondered: 'Why can't we put together an operation like that?' And wondered some more. Yet the answer was clear: there was no conservative alternative to the Brookings Institution, the catalyst for many of the legislative successes of the liberals during the 1960s and early 1970s" (Edwards 1998). Edwards's take on the situation puts the inherent frustration that the founders of Heritage felt toward the small conservative establishment in D.C.

The founders of Heritage did want a similar apparatus to what the liberal side of the debate had, but they also saw in the right-leaning organizations in Washington a lack of public advocacy. Political veterans and former Capitol Hill staffers Paul Weyrich and Ed Feulner, with the help of $200,000 from brewing magnate Joseph Coors, formed the Analysis and Research Association in 1970. Billionaire conservative activist Richard Mellon Scaife joined the board and by 1973 the organization split into a public interest law firm and a public policy organization that became the Heritage Foundation. The goal of the new foundation was to supply conservative policy makers with the information they needed during the policy debates. Feulner would later say it was this timeliness and willingness to be a part of the debate that helped spur the development of the foundation, recalling a research report from the AEI about a supersonic transport debate. The report reached congressional offices the day after the key vote and Feulner said, "It defined the debate, but it was one day late. We immediately called up the president of [AEI] to praise him for his thorough piece of research—and ask why we didn't receive it until after the debate and the vote. His answer: they didn't want to influence the vote. That was when the idea for the Heritage Foundation was born" (Rich 2005).

The new organization aimed to answer the structural challenges Edwards saw in the congressional debate and the active participation in the political debate that Feulner said was missing. To fund their work, the foundation struck out in a new direction compared to AEI. Where AEI relied on a fairly small group of donors, Heritage Foundation launched a direct mail effort to appeal to the conservative rank-and-file, growing its donor base to include middle-income conservatives and others. By the late 1970s the organization had more than $1 million annual budget and a growing number of conservative scholars. The research team began an aggressive process of considering the entirety of the U.S. federal budget, thoroughly considering thousands of programs and hundreds of different departments. The timing was ideal as 1980 also ushered into office conservative Republican Ronald Reagan. As Reagan and his team prepared to enter the White House, the team at the Heritage Foundation was ready with a massive, 20-volume assessment of what to do with the government. As Heritage Foundation writer Andrew Blasko noted, "Heritage provided the president-elect's transition team with detailed policy prescriptions on everything from taxes and regulation to trade and national defense . . . The new president used the 'Mandate' to help realize his vision of a world free of communism, an economy that didn't crush people's dreams with high taxes and regulations, and an America the world could admire once again" (Blasko 2004). By the end of the first year, the Reagan administration had implemented or tried some 60 percent of the 2,000 ideas the foundation noted in their proposal. But their "Mandate" was only the first of a series of influential proposals that would mark the connection between the two groups. Heritage scholars helped propose the space-based Strategic Defense Initiative and other foreign policy positions for the Republican White House.

Although the two worked together, the foundation was also critical of the times when the Reagan administration failed to adopt their ideas. And that tension between the organization and the politicians they sought to help would continue to play out throughout Heritage's history. Partly driven by its campaign-like communication with a wide array of conservative activists and partly due to its very political nature, Heritage existed as both a research institute and a lobbying organization. For the scholars and funders of the foundation it was not enough simply to propose certain policies. Once proposed, the organization became a full-blown political pressure group, publicly encouraging Republicans to adopt their policies and debating Democrats who opposed them. It was a fundamental issue that liberal writers like Jonathan Cohn saw as a flaw in the structure of Heritage. Cohn saw Heritage's goals as a problem from the start, noting, "The brains and money behind Heritage saw the think-tank as an antidote to the prevailing liberal consensus in Washington, as put forth by places like the Brookings Institution (and academia generally) and reinforced by the *New York Times* (and rest of the media establishment). But there was a certain irony in this mandate: Whatever the ideological sympathies of these supposedly liberal institutions, or the people within them, they were not avowedly political organizations. On the contrary, they strove to maintain—and, I would argue, succeeded in maintaining—a strict posture of non-partisanship and even non-ideology" (Cohn 2013). For liberals like Cohn, the political nature of Heritage made it intellectually suspect in all its work and that limited the potential impact of the foundation's work. Still, the foundation was seeing much of its influence carved into by other, even more overtly political organizations, like the Club for Growth and Americans for Prosperity. These groups were even less like the traditional think tanks and aggressively campaigned for political platforms put forward by the organization.

To counter the growing influence of the political organizations and dark money groups that were holding more and more sway within the Republican ranks, Heritage took on a more aggressive political posture in 2013 by hiring former South Carolina senator Jim DeMint to run the organization. DeMint made active political campaigning a central part of Heritage's mission, running ads against Republicans who voted against government shutdowns through its accompanied political action committee, Heritage Action. Many Republicans balked. "These tactics have raised Heritage's profile as a leader among ultraconservatives, but their aggressive stance has stung Republican lawmakers. 'We went into battle thinking they were on our side, and we find out they're shooting at us,' an exasperated Representative Mick Mulvaney, a conservative Republican from South Carolina, said" (Levy 2014). Heritage was seen more and more like a tea party-type organization that fought for a particular vision of the Republican Party even if that vision could damage the party's political viability at the polls. Still the foundation boasts hundreds of thousands of paying members and has become one of the most influential bulwarks of the more hard-line conservatives in Congress. The foundation actively worked to shut down the government in 2013 and has helped fuel the conservative revolts within congressional leadership.

See also: American Enterprise Institute (AEI); Conservative Think Tanks; Liberal Think Tanks

Further Reading

Blasko, Andrew. 2004. "Reagan and Heritage: A Unique Partnership." Heritage Foundation. June 7. Accessed December 28, 2015. http://www.heritage.org/research/commentary /2004/06/reagan-and-heritage-a-unique-partnership.

Cohn, Jonathan. 2013. "Liberals Have Won a Lot. Here's One Reason Why." *The New Republic*. October 23. Accessed December 28, 2015. https://newrepublic.com/article/115325 /center-american-progress-heritage-and-liberalisms-future.

Edwards, Lee. 1998. *The Power of Ideas: The Heritage Foundation at 25 Years*. Ottawa, IL: Jameson Books, Inc.

Levy, Pema. 2014. "Arthur Brooks's Push to Make the American Enterprise Institute—and Republicans—Relevant Again." *Newsweek*. April 1. Accessed July 15, 2015. http://www .newsweek.com/2014/04/11/arthur-brookss-push-make-american-enterprise -institute-and-republicans-relevant-248065.

Rich, Andrew. 2005. *Think Tanks, Public Policy, and the Politics of Expertise*. Cambridge: Cambridge University Press.

THE HILL

Demonstrate a market and media companies will attempt to fill the need. Last long enough in one and you are likely to attract some competition. That is the story of *Roll Call*, which started in the 1950s, and *The Hill*, a competitor launched in the mid-1990s.

The Hill is the upstart new newspaper serving Capitol Hill since 1994 and it has, from its outset, sought to be even more community-oriented than its older competition. The paper was started by a corporation that ran a series of newspapers in suburban New York, and this experience covering a community within a large metropolitan area served the new paper well. From the outset, the paper's first editor, former *New York Times* correspondent Martin Tolchin, credited the success of *Roll Call* with inspiring *The Hill* and setting the standard he hoped to best, saying before the first paper hit the streets, "We think we'll be more substantive, wittier and more stylish" (Glaberson 1994).

The paper that emerged appeared quite similar to *Roll Call*, covering a mix of "inside baseball" stories about negotiations and policy debates, but aimed for the younger staffers on the Hill. In a town where members of Congress hold a 96 percent re-election rate, there is not a lot of turnover, but inside those offices a constant stream of young staffers and interns move through positions, often lasting a year or less in a given job before moving to another spot. *The Hill* recognized that and developed features like the "35 Under 35" annual listing of up-and-coming staff members who had made a name for themselves to appeal to those readers. The paper also aimed at developing a good want ads section to encourage members seeking new staff to advertise in *The Hill*.

Tolchin stayed with the paper for a decade before retiring (and three years later, emerging from retirement to help launch Politico), but the paper continued to prosper, in large part thanks to its ability to clearly deliver the kind of content its readers seek. This ranges from the high brow coverage of policy and politics to a "50 Most Beautiful" Capitol Hill staffer list. The paper also recognizes its audience's needs, publishing four days a week when Congress is in session and backing down to weekly publication when the legislature is in recess.

The access the paper has to officials and its constant presence in Capitol Hill life does allow its reporters to uncover inside information and even more often get staffers to open up in moments of frustration or excitement. One example of this flared up briefly in 2010 when White House spokesman Robert Gibbs angrily lashed out at what he called the "professional left"—commentators and columnists who were criticizing the president. Gibbs was quoted in *The Hill* as saying, ""I hear these people saying he's like George Bush. Those people ought to be drug tested," adding that liberal critics "will be satisfied when we have Canadian health care and we've eliminated the Pentagon. That's not a reality" (De Nies and Hopper 2010). Gibbs spent a couple days trying to extricate the White House and himself from the comments after sparking another flurry of negative blogs and cable news comments.

The paper has also sought to embrace the Internet, launching a series of blogs covering topical areas, like lobbying and defense issues as well as more gossipy columns like the "In the Know" blog that seeks to aggregate reporting from around the web as well as overheard and leaked tidbits of news. The paper now claims it attracts 7 million monthly visitors to its website and due to its free circulation guarantees delivery to 100 percent of congressional offices. At 21,000 printed copies, it is the largest of the Capitol Hill publications. The paper is also quick to cite a 2014 Erdos & Morgan readership survey that reported *The Hill* "has the most relevant &

valuable congressional coverage, the most reliable reporting and is preferred over-all for congressional news coverage" (*The Hill* 2014).

Much of the financial success of the paper is tied to that readership and reach. The paper benefits from the countless industries that seek to influence and inform Congress. Writer Richard Reeves at one point wrote of looking for an article in *The Hill* and "flipping through full-page advertisements—billboards for interests that want an enriching word or comma in legislation—for Microsoft, Merrill Lynch, Lexis-Nexis, the American Hospital Association, the Coalition to Protect America's Health Care, the Cellular Telecommunications and Internet Association and such" (Reeves 2003). This advertising base largely shielded the small staff of *The Hill* from the financial straits that many publications have faced during the digital revolution and has helped the paper enjoy slow but steady growth. When the paper announced the hiring of its latest editor in 2014, it also unveiled a new strategy of partnering with other organizations to potentially expand the reach and impact of its report-ing while keeping its "small town" feel.

But for the most part the paper sees itself as a community newspaper for the thousands of staffers, lobbyists, and journalists who make Capitol Hill their pro-fessional homes. The paper regularly churns out "Top [fill in the blank]" lists, and promotes and breathlessly will report on the move of a spokesperson from the State Department to the White House. The community, covering only a handful of blocks in downtown Washington, D.C., eats it up.

See also: *National Journal*; *Roll Call*

Further Reading

de Nies, Yunji, and Jessica Hopper. 2010. "Gibbs Won't Take Back Criticism of 'Professional Left.'" ABC News. August 11. Accessed February 18, 2015. http://abcnews.go.com/WN /white-house-press-secretary-robert-gibbs-back-harsh/story?id=11378661.

Glaberson, William. 1994. "New Paper to Vie for Readers on Capitol Hill." *New York Times*. May 25. Accessed February 17, 2015. http://www.nytimes.com/1994/05/25/us/new -paper-to-vie-for-readers-on-capitol-hill.html.

The Hill. 2014. "The Hill Names Bob Cusack Editor in Chief." July 28. Accessed Febru-ary 16, 2015. http://thehill.com/homenews/news/213489-the-hill-names-bob-cusack -editor-in-chief.

Reeves, Richard. 2003. "The Dance of Dollars on Capitol Hill." Uexpress. January 15. Ac-cessed February 17, 2015. http://www.uexpress.com/richard-reeves/2003/1/15/the -dance-of-dollars-on-capitol.

HORSE-RACE JOURNALISM

Horse-race journalism comes down to the press's desire to answer the most basic question in an election: who's going to win? But this angle, approaching of who is up or who is down to inform what campaigns to cover and how to frame issues, has become increasingly controversial. Journalists are now accused of caring more about how an issue or gaffe may affect a candidate's standing in the polls, and therefore the trajectory of the race, rather than the substance of what is said or the context of the fumble.

In horse-race journalism, reporters and editors focus on the standing of the candidates with voters or potential voters throughout the campaign. Stories are interpreted through the context of how it may affect or has affected where they rank in the competition for the nomination or the general election, whether a development may damage their chances of winning, and whether an internal campaign reorganization will address the political difficulty plaguing a candidate. Even coverage of issues or so-called substantive matters is framed as how a certain topic may impact the electoral chances of a candidate. Much of this reporting is informed by public opinion polls that gauge voter preferences on almost a daily basis. Put another way, horse-race reporting places emphasis on the campaign's inner workings and strategy as well as a candidate's public personality and ability to respond to attacks rather than stressing candidate qualifications, policy ideas, or any issue positions.

If journalists are fascinated with who is ahead or struggling on a given day, so is the reading and viewing public. The contest for the highest office in the land has intrigued the public, and anything that the public wants to know about will drive at least some of the media coverage of that matter. Campaigns, especially for president, have been a public spectacle for more than a century. One British ambassador from the 1880s described Americans' interest in presidential politics as a quest for "excitement" that was rare in their ordinary lives, writing, "The passion which in England expresses itself in the popular eagerness over a boat race or a horse race extends itself in America to every kind of rivalry and struggle. The presidential election . . . stirs them like any other trial of strength and speed; sets them betting on the issue, disposes them to make efforts for a cause in which their deeper feelings may be little engaged. These tendencies are intensified by the vast area over which the contest extends, and the enormous multitude that bears a part in it" (Bryce 1995). Campaigns are like any other personal sport—a battle between people where the winner is champion and the loser cast aside. And as primary elections took on more and more importance a century later, they became a multi-part drama where some candidates faltered and collapsed and others battled through adversity and persevered. They are compelling narratives of competitive people. It is hard to not see them as competition because, at the end, that is what they are.

If Americans are intrinsically intrigued by a race, especially one where the winner captures the national prize, it may not be surprising that journalists seek to report the winner of an election as quickly as possible. From the days of the penny press in the early nineteenth century, editors jockeyed to be first in reporting the winner of an electoral contest. Newspapers developed complicated techniques of identifying the key precincts that could help inform a prediction of who had won on Election Day. As technology evolved, from the telegraph to the telephone to the news wire, the drive to be first to declare a winner was a regular point of pride, and meant new potential readers and ad revenues. In order to be first, journalists would push their idea of key precincts and methods of predicting the winner to before Election Day. As political reporting evolved in the twentieth century, reporters worked to better understand the state of the race so that on Election Day they knew what to look for and what issues may be the critical ones on which voting blocs hinged. Political reporters also came to view themselves as experts in the field, so their interest in the tactics and personalities driving the race increased as well. A good political reporter can tell you what counties will decide an election months before the first vote is cast.

But as coverage evolved, from reporting a winner first on Election Day to understanding who was winning at any given moment of the campaign, criticism grew that this type of coverage left voters uninformed on the real issues at stake in a given election. Many angrily see the focus on the horse race coming at the cost of substantive issue coverage that would help the public contextualize the significance of a campaign and inform voters of a full slate of issues they should be aware of. A common assessment came from long-time Gawker writer Hamilton Nolan, "Most political journalists cover political campaigns in the same way that sports reporters cover sports. Team A has a new strategy! Team B made a mistake! Team C has a new manager! . . . So why do reporters do this? Because it is easy. It is easier to cover campaigns like this, and it requires less thought, and it leaves journalists less prone to being attacked by one side or another, and it is, in general, purely speculative rubbish which cannot be truly refuted. So it is what we get" (Nolan 2015). But despite Nolan's claims, the answer of why horse-race reporting remains such a major aspect of political reporting is a bit more complicated.

First, there the focus on campaign strategy has evolved somewhat as a way to combat the increasingly orchestrated efforts of campaign staff to manage the flow of information about the candidate. As campaigns have fought to stay on message and avoid any gaffe or position statement that may alienate a voter group, the press has ramped up efforts to pierce that strategy and explain to voters the rationale behind the campaign's positions and behavior. It has led to a sort of arms race—the campaign aims to control the message, the press seeks to expose the political reasoning behind the message, and the campaign intensifies its effort to control the message. The focus on strategy and the state of the race is, in some ways, a way to cover the messaging of the campaign in a more detached way by analyzing its components and the rationale for it, rather than simply being a tool for repeating the campaign's talking points. This had several appealing aspects to a political reporter, allowing them a way to test the claims of campaigns about how they were doing and what the public was demanding.

Some political scientists agree that this coverage amounts to a rejection of campaign messaging techniques by the press. One analysis of the state of play argued, "As strategic political communication has become more professionalized, news journalists see it as their job to uncover the strategies. This is also a defense mechanism against continually being 'spun' by parties or candidates, important since most journalists want to protect their autonomy and avoid being accused of taking sides politically. By focusing on strategic aspects of the political game, political reporters maintain an apparent stance of both independence and objectivity" (Aalberg, Strömbäck, and de Vreese 2012). New public opinion polling techniques also allowed reporters to inject a less biased assessment of the campaign into the coverage of the election and allowed the reporters to better dissect the claims and efforts of a campaign. They could then use this information to help all voters better understand what a candidate or his or her surrogates were saying, adding context from those not associated with either side of the political debate.

Another key component of that formula has emerged since the 1940s—the public opinion poll. The horse race began as an effort to know who had won an election—no easy task in the days of the hand-counted ballots and sprawling electoral districts. But as the technology and scientific nature of public opinion polls improved, it became possible for journalists to answer these questions long before Election Day, by assessing the standing of candidates throughout the campaign and not simply in the final vote. Political scientists have acknowledged that their developing of political polls has been a major contributor to the growth of the dreaded horse race, one admitting, "Clearly the contemporary reportorial approach stresses the contest over substance, and positioning in the horse race is a prime ingredient in the game story angle. This frame of reference for campaign coverage would likely be less prevalent without the credible and objective markers of each contender's progress provided by frequent poll soundings" (Atkin and Gaudino 1984).

But there is an element of political polling and the horse race that many of these analyses fail to consider: Polls have created a sort of external reality check on the campaign. First, the use of polls allows journalists to better understand and reflect how the public is responding to a candidate or message. It is a way to bring voice—ideally the voice of the voting public—into the political campaign. Second, the polling of the public allows editors and reporters to better invest limited resources on the candidates and issues the public is most concerned with. Although this inhibits addressing issues that may affect small groups or voters or marginalizes the issues and positions of third party or long-shot candidates, it does help inform the editorial conversation about how to cover the campaign and where to send reporters. Editors must make difficult decisions about what campaigns to have their journalists follow and what issues to press candidates on. Without the polling information that captures the state of the race those decisions would be more open to biases, agendas, or the attempts of the campaigns to set the agenda.

There is one more, very practical, component of the growth of horse-race coverage: namely, the kind of reporters who go into political reporting. For decades, many of the nation's top political reporters—be it the *New York Times'* James "Scotty" Reston in the 1940s or '50s or the *Washington Post's* Eli Saslow in the early 2000s—started their careers as sports writers. In exploring the history of horse-race reporting, Thomas Littlewood found it important to note that "the movement between the toy department (a dismissive nickname for the sports desk in many newsrooms) and the political beat helped to establish shared attitudes about competition and journalistic standards." He adds that this cross-over affected everything from a mutual love of "the zestful, audacious writing style of Mark Twain" to "the considerable rhetorical overlap of sports jargon and the vocabulary of political journalism" (Littlewood 1998). To grow as a professional sports reporter is to grow up with a love for the strategy and the game itself. For those reporters who move into political reporting, the connections between sports and politics are obvious. The sources are the same—a coach versus a campaign manager—the questions of strategy and the opponent abound, and so to the degree that the career path Littlewood outlines exists, the group reporting on the horse race will hold a predisposition for the contest of politics.

Despite the animosity that horse-race reporting tends to evoke, many still defend the focus on who is up and who is down. These defenders often point out the unrealistic expectations of critics, with one pointing out, "A political campaign is more than a traveling debate society. Beyond the issues, voters need to know why a candidate is (or isn't) performing well in the polls, is (or isn't) raising money, is (or isn't) drawing crowds of supporters, or is (or isn't) keeping his cool. Candidates win or lose for a reason, reasons that have to do with issue papers but also with how they carry themselves and present their positions" (Shafer 2008). These defenders of the horse race note that treating the campaign as a mystery until the West Coast polls close is no more accurate or helpful a portrayal of the campaign than focusing too much on tactics and the latest polls.

There is also the defense, not appreciated by some, that people like these stories and read these stories long before the long, thoroughly researched opus on health care policy or a new program aimed at reducing poverty. In the course of a campaign, stories will be written about both policy positions and poll positions. Voters can choose the stories to consume and those to reject. And this may be where the observations of a British ambassador made more than 120 years ago may play more a role in the discussion than a conscious decision by the media. If Viscount James Bryce is right that part of the reason Americans love the presidential campaign is the competition and the sport of it, then in a media environment increasingly driven by what the consumer wants and what they have read before, the horse race is likely to be a major component of election reporting for years to come.

See also: Campaign Strategy Coverage; Political Consultants; Public Opinion

Further Reading

Aalberg, Toril, Jesper Strömbäck, and Claes de Vreese. 2012. "The Framing of Politics as Strategy and Game: A Review of Concepts, Operationalizations and Key Findings." *Journalism*. February.

Atkin, Charles, and James Gaudino. 1984. "The Impact of Polling on the Mass Media." *Annals of the American Academy of Political and Social Science*. March.

Bryce, Viscount James. 1995. *The American Commonwealth*. Vol. 2. Indianapolis: Liberty Fund. Vol. 2. Accessed June 25, 2015. http://oll.libertyfund.org/titles/bryce-the-american-commonwealth-vol-2.

Littlewood, Thomas. 1998. *Calling Elections: The History of Horse-Race Journalism.* Notre Dame, IN: University of Notre Dame Press.

Nolan, Hamilton. 2015. "The Platonic Ideal of Horse Race Journalism." Gawker. April 6. Accessed June 25, 2015. http://gawker.com/the-platonic-ideal-of-horse-race-journalism-1695939465.

Shafer, Jack. 2008. "In Praise of Horse-Race Coverage." Slate. January 24. Accessed June 25, 2015. http://www.slate.com/articles/news_and_politics/press_box/2008/01/in_praise_of_horserace_coverage.html.

"THE HOTLINE"

"The Hotline" was the first aggregation of political news ever produced in the United States, demonstrating the power to cull multiple news sources for news and insight and combine that material into an effective news summary that people found invaluable. Begun in 1987, the newsletter was initially faxed to subscribers throughout Washington and later became a daily email that politicians and political reporters relied on to get a sense of how campaigns were playing out across the country. Countless interns in congressional offices, public relations firms, and campaigns spent thousands of hours printing the newsletter out or copying it for higher ups who wanted to know the latest political news.

"The Hotline," initially called "The Presidential Campaign Hotline," allowed political professionals to read campaign coverage from all the national news outlets—including broadcast news transcripts—as well as regional and state newspapers. Reid Wilson, who edited the publication, said in 2013, " 'The Hotline' was the first political Web site. It was the first place that aggregated political news from outside the Beltway" (Schudel 2013). Except there was no World Wide Web in 1987 and so what seems natural in an era of cable news channels, publications, and countless websites that gather and distribute political news, "The Hotline" did it first.

In an analog era it was the only way to see across multiple outlets at one time and, according to Howard Mortman, who worked for "The Hotline" in 1992, it was no small feat to produce. Mortman described how "every morning at 3 or 4 in the morning we would go collect these newspapers and bring them in to 'The Hotline.' And then, get ready for this, we clipped the newspapers—scissors, highlighters, anything we could get our hands on to go chop, chop, chop, chop to these newspapers and we'd create little piles of newspapers. We'd put them on a sorting table and then pile them up: presidential race, Senate race, House race . . . We'd assemble our coverage of the coverage based on these piles of newspapers" (*National Journal* 2009). Editors would sort through the stories, finding themes in coverage, highlighting different facts and details different papers had produced around a story. The editors would then write up a single narrative of the coverage of the different campaigns with citations (and later links) to the original stories. The result was a newsletter that any political junkie in Washington or elsewhere could not live without. The fax would go out to subscribers—only about 500 of them who paid a hefty $4,000 a year to get the publication—around 11 in the morning and was soon distributed around Washington.

"The Hotline" was the brainchild of a moderate Republican who was a pioneer in the political consulting business, Doug Bailey. Bailey, along with John Deardourff, created one of the first political consulting businesses in the country. They worked for moderate Republicans like New York governor Nelson Rockefeller and President Gerald Ford, helping develop strategy, manage campaign finances, and plan advertising buys. As the 1970s and 1980s wore on, Bailey became increasingly alarmed at the shrill tone of politics and left the business, but still was an avid follower of all things political. In an effort to build a bipartisan interest in politics, he partnered with Democrat Roger Craver to start the new enterprise. They hired young, politics-crazy reporters to work those early morning shifts and many of them went on to become some of the most influential political reporters of the last generation, including Chuck Todd, Amy Walter, and Stephen Hayes. The publication also injected something that most political reporters love about politics—humor—collecting some of the funniest quotes, moments, and ads from campaigns across the country.

Despite its influence and the stated respect many had for Bailey, others worried that the publication helped foster the idea of pack journalism within the political reporting corps. It did this by making the pack aware of itself and, to some, it "helped reporters—especially younger ones—find a context, a larger meaning, in the daily rush of campaign events" (Shaw 1988). By creating a one-stop shop for political reporting, it may have inadvertently created a self-censoring mechanism by allowing the reporters to peer over the shoulders of their colleagues and allowed editors to quickly assess whether their reporter's work was aligned with what others were finding out and reporting. Despite this concern, the publication was a must-have among reporters covering politics and those who wanted to know every detail of the campaign.

The success allowed Bailey and Craver to publish "The Hotline" independently until 1996 when it was purchased by the *National Journal*. It remains a daily publication that offers a collection of the morning's political headlines with "Wake-Up Call" and compiles a digest of election and campaign news across the country with "Latest Edition." But unlike 1987, it is no longer the only game in town. It continues to market itself to political consultants and the media and is a subscriber-only product behind a paywall at *National Journal*. No longer as influential as it was in the 1980s and 1990s, the publication still proves there was not only interest in political news, but an audience for a service that could bring together these sources. Chuck Todd, who joined the publication in 1992 at the age of 20, would rise through the ranks of "The Hotline" and from 2001–2007 served as editor-in-chief of the publication. In 2012 after having left *National Journal* to work for MSNBC, Todd credited the publication with helping spur an entire industry of political coverage, saying, "There would be no Politico without 'Hotline.' There would be no place for politics on television without 'Hotline.' I'd argue there would not necessarily be three cable channels that devote itself often on politics without sort of the idea that 'Hotline' created an hourly and daily obsession with American politics that had always been there, but had never been tapped in to" (*National Journal* 2009).

See also: Aggregation; The *Atlantic*; *National Journal*; Politico

Further Reading

National Journal. 2009. "Hotline at 25 Video." Accessed July 22, 2015. http://link.brightcove .com/services/player/bcpid635367679001?bckey=AQ~~,AAAAACpvMpk~,rAvHhAS 7JOpa4tlt0CXVebDvGzQCdYY2&bctid=2589612054001.

Schudel, Matt. 2013. "Douglas L. Bailey, Founder of Political News Digest, Dies at 79." *Washington Post*. June 11. Accessed July 22, 2015. http://www.washingtonpost.com/politics /douglas-l-bailey-founder-of-political-news-digest-dies-at-79/2013/06/11/36c34d06 -d2b0-11e2-a73e-826d299ff459_story.html.

Shaw, David. 1988. "Politics and the Media: Television: Candidates' 'Mine Field.'" *Los Angeles Times*. August 15. Accessed July 23, 2015. http://articles.latimes.com/1988-08-15 /news/mn-352_1_political-campaign/4.

HUFFINGTON, ARIANNA (1950–)

Dubbed the Queen of Aggregation, Arianna Huffington has built a digital news empire that she sold to AOL for $315 million in 2011 while maintaining her position as one of the leading voices for a new social-friendly news business model.

Her remarkable rise on the public stage began in the 1980s, writing for the conservative *National Review*, and continued as a vocal supporter of Newt Gingrich's Republican Revolution in 1994. Her very public role as the wife of then-husband Michael Huffington during his unsuccessful campaign for the U.S. Senate in 1994, and her own later candidacy for governor of California, are all part of her evolution from a humble Greek upbringing to a national political force. As a 2011 profile in *Vogue* read, "The myth begins with young Greek Arianna encouraging her mother to leave her journalist father, seeing a photograph of idyllic Cambridge University, and deciding that brains are her escape. With astonishing speed she goes from Cambridge Union debating star to best-selling author at 22 . . . to conservative-commentator wife of a billionaire Texas oilman to independent gubernatorial candidate to committed liberal and bloghost and now the sudden It girl of the branding, marketing, digital-media world" (Rubin 2011). It's a story that seems too big to be captured in one of her site's many aggregated news stories.

Her transformation to media mogul began when Huffington segued from political wife to more public commentator, teaming up with former *Saturday Night Live* writer and liberal Democrat Al Franken to cover the 1996 election for Comedy Central. By 1998, the *New Yorker*'s Margaret Talbot described Huffington as a sort of ever-changing publicity seeker who reinvented herself for different roles, choosing, as of late, to "cast herself as a kind of Republican Spice Girl—an endearingly ditzy right-wing gal-about-town who is a guilty pleasure for people who know better" (Talbot 1998). She remained an outspoken Republican through 2000, but suddenly began reinventing herself as a political progressive. During the chaotic 2003 California gubernatorial recall election Huffington ran as an independent, running to the left of Republican and eventual winner Arnold Schwarzenegger. By 2004, she was endorsing Democrat John Kerry for president and hatching with former AOL executive Kenneth Lerer the idea for a celebrity-fueled megablog called Huffington Post.

Huffington, who is not known as a techie, would soon gather 250 thought leaders—from CBS's Walter Cronkite to Microsoft's Bill Gates to entertainment business magnate David Geffen—to contribute to the new site. She also soon had some of the most forward-thinking editors working for her like the conservative Andrew Breitbart and future Buzzfeed CEO Jonah Peretti. A 2012 profile of Huffington Post would report on how Peretti was struck by Huffington's ability to connect seemingly disparate worlds, describing how he "would watch with wonderment as Arianna Huffington eased herself from setting to setting, all the while making the person she was talking with feel like the most interesting and important person in the world, hanging on every word, never shifting her attention to check one of three BlackBerries . . . Peretti saw this talent through a different prism. 'Arianna,' he says, 'can make weak ties into strong ties'" (Shapiro 2012). Huffington's ability to garner the interests and abilities of so many made her an effective publisher of the new platform and turned her into an unlikely evangelist of blogging and social media.

She also brought an unforgiving work ethic to the new publication, demanding long hours and absolute dedication from her employees. She too would pour energy into it, creating a publication of almost limitless ambition. According to a 2015 report, Huffington Post publishes a stunning 1,900 pieces of content across its numerous platforms every single day. It is driven by her focus to serve people the news they want when they want it, all through Huffington Post. Even as rumors circulated her tenure as editor-in-chief could be threatened by a possible merger of AOL, owner of HuffPo, and mobile powerhouse Verizon, the *New York Times* was reporting about how her situation was not too endangered because of relentless focus on the audience, noting, "This singular focus on audience development expresses itself in different ways at different publications. At Huffington Post, it takes the shape of an editorial mandate that, much like the universe itself, is unfathomably broad and constantly expanding . . . They cover, in most cases through aggregation, everything from Federal Reserve policy to celebrity antics, from Islamic State atrocities to parenting tips, supplemented with a steady stream of uncategorizable click bait ('Can Cannibalism Fight Brain Disease? Only Sort Of')" (Segal 2015). The versatility and tireless nature of Huffington Post is in many ways directly connected to the personality and history of its publisher and co-founder. As long as one continues to attract the millions of monthly readers who flock to the site, the other will remain a force within both politics and publishing.

See also: Huffington Post; Social Media and Politics

Further Reading

Rubin, Elizabeth. 2011. "Arianna Huffington: The Connector." *Vogue.* September 19. Accessed December 7, 2015. http://www.vogue.com/865409/arianna-huffington-the -connector.

Segal, David. 2015. "Arianna Huffington's Improbable, Insatiable Content Machine." *New York Times Magazine.* June 30. Accessed December 7, 2015. http://www.nytimes.com/2015 /07/05/magazine/arianna-huffingtons-improbable-insatiable-content-machine.html.

Shapiro, Michael. 2012. "Six Degrees of Aggregation: How The Huffington Post Ate the Internet." *Columbia Journalism Review.* May/June. Accessed December 7, 2015. http:// www.cjr.org/cover_story/six_degrees_of_aggregation.php.

Talbot, Margaret. 1998. "The Politics of Fame." *The New Yorker.* April 13.

HUFFINGTON POST

If there is one entity that represents how the media and politics have changed in the past decade it would probably be Huffington Port—or HuffPost or HuffPo to its friends and frenemies. With its partisan, left-of-center voice, its heavy use of aggregation, and its occasional dash of celebrity, the site has become a force to be reckoned with in political and national reporting. By one 2015 assessment some 1,900 stories are published across Huffington Post and its array of international and local sites every day. The site, which began as a liberal alternative to the aggregator and gossip site Drudge Report, peaked at 128 million visitors in November of 2014. Since then, it has drifted downward, reporting approximately 86 million visitors to its collection of blogs and local and international editions in November 2015—making it about the same size as social media-fueled Buzzfeed.

Even now off its highs, the site remains one of the most popular destinations for political news on the Internet and has developed a complex web of content that mixes nearly all forms of digital reporting. When it started back in 2005, though, it was banking on blogging by big names to justify itself. Arianna Huffington, who had left the Republican Party and was a one-time candidate for California governor, organized the Post as a site powered by celebrity bloggers. In announcing the launch of the site, she stressed she had signed up 250 "thought leaders" to contribute entries to a single blog site—including famed CBS journalist Walter Cronkite, author Nora Ephron, and movie stars Warren Beatty and Diane Keaton. In her solicitation offer to these contributors Huffington promised the new site would allow them to reach a wider audience and promised a site experience far beyond the array of personal blogs that had taken off at the same time. She let contributors know, "You're actually already doing the hardest work of a blogger: having interesting opinions and fresh takes on the hot stories of the day. We'll just provide the megaphone" (Glaister 2005). Within a year and a half the site could boast 2.3 million monthly visitors, but by then the idea of the celebrity-driven blog was beginning to lose steam. In its place, Huffington announced in 2006 the Post would begin hiring reporters, telling the *New York Times*, "Now is the time to generate our own original content. It was always our intention, once we had the money, to hire people to do reporting" (Seelye 2006). With the hiring of reporters, the site's mix of unpaid blogs, aggregated breaking news, and originally reported pieces was in place.

Still, response from many was lukewarm to downright hostile. As Michael Shapiro would write later in the *Columbia Journalism Review*, "There remained something unseemly about the whole enterprise, especially to journalists, a sense that in making its own rules Huffington Post had violated a few too many. Its newsgathering was done by others, even if the commentary was original. The bloggers were not paid . . . [but] these unpaid contributors had joined the phenomenon Huffington talked of and celebrated above all others: the Conversation" (Shapiro 2012). For all its success, many like Shapiro criticized its techniques. When it came to reporting, the site was accused of stealing the bulk of its news from other sites. The technique, dubbed aggregation, allowed Huffington Post to take a quote or even a handful of paragraphs from another news service, giving them credit for the reporting and linking out to the original piece. Huffington Post editors said this would allow millions of people who would never have seen the piece to be exposed to the information and benefit with people clicking through to the original report. Many of those featured took little comfort in this, arguing the larger Huffington Post could monetize the same information without paying for the original reporting.

Although its aggregation policies frustrated other publishers, Huffington Post editors were from the outset especially adept at the burgeoning world of social media. The site showed a stunning ability to mix seemingly disconnected ideas and both high and low content on the same site and attract millions of visitors. One of its original editors, Jonah Peretti, demonstrated a keen knack for understanding what kind of content people wanted to share on Facebook and the emerging powerhouse Twitter. Peretti, who also defended the aggregation policies for Huffington Post in those early days, would soon launch his own project, an "internet popularity contest" he called Buzzfeed. But Peretti helped develop the strange mix of content that has somehow worked for HuffPo. So a story on the Islamic extremist group the Islamic State might sit next to a story headlined "Donkey who Nearly Died in Flood Breaks into Grin When Rescued" and "The Best Places For Women To Find Porn Online" (all these from an actual page from the site one day in December 2015). It's a model that drives many crazy. Former *New York Times* editor Bill Keller wrote in 2011 that the site represented many of the core problems with the modern media business, in particular attacking the site's aggregation policies, writing, "In Somalia this would be called piracy. In the mediasphere, it is a respected business model. The queen of aggregation is, of course, Arianna Huffington, who has discovered that if you take celebrity gossip, adorable kitten videos, posts from unpaid bloggers and news reports from other publications, array them on your Web site and add a left-wing soundtrack, millions of people will come" (Keller 2011).

Despite Keller's criticism that same year AOL, the once-mighty online company, purchased Huffington Post from Arianna and the other private investors for $315 million. Huffington remained the top editor and the site continue to invest in original reporting, including an ambitious 10-part series that ran in late 2011 and focused on what happens to soldiers wounded on the battlefield. The series, reported by David Wood, would go on to win the 2012 Pulitzer Prize for national reporting. It marked the first time in history that a digital-only publication had garnered the top journalism prize in the nation. Wood, who had worked for 40 years in journalism, spent some eight months reporting the series and Huffington hailed the award, saying, "From the beginning, one of the core pillars of HuffPost's editorial philosophy has been to use narrative and storytelling to put flesh and blood on data and statistics, and to help bear witness to the struggles faced by millions of Americans. We are very grateful to have won for this series, the culmination of David Wood's long career as a military correspondent, and an affirmation that great journalism is thriving on the Web" (Calderone 2012).

The site continues to lean to the left in its political reporting, and through its impressive traffic remains one of the most influential news sources among Democrats. A 2012 ranking of political sites based on their website ranking from the independent tracking site Alexa declared Huffington Post the most popular political site on the Internet, boasting four times the traffic of the second site, TheBlaze. Its continued popularity, even as it has struggled to maintain its high-flying monthly visitor numbers, keeps the site at the front of many conversations on the future of news. Huffington herself has been aggressive in trying to remake its original reporting efforts. In 2015, she announced the launch of a new effort, dubbed "What's Working." The effort sought to shift the entire approach of reporting to stop focusing so much on the negative stories of dysfunction and strife and instead mix in tales of effective governance and the successes of some programs. Huffington said the move represented a rejection of the kind of reporting that is captured by the old adage, "If it bleeds, it leads." She stressed, "I'm not talking about simple heartwarming stories, or aw-shucks moments, or adorable animals (although don't worry, we'll still give you plenty of those as well). What I'm talking about is consistently telling the stories of people and communities doing amazing things, overcoming great odds and coming up with solutions to the very real challenges they face. And by shining a light on these stories, we hope that we can scale up these solutions and create a positive contagion that can expand and broaden their reach and application" (Huffington 2015). In addition to this focus on broadening its reporting interests, Huffington Post has also expanded its international scope, adding more foreign editions and growing its overseas audience, even as its American readership contracts. The moves mean that HuffPo is likely to continue to garner attention for those interested in the evolving of online news and to have some influence over political reporting, especially among more liberal readers.

See also: Aggregation; Huffington, Arianna; Social Media and Politics

Further Reading

Calderone, Michael. 2012. "Huffington Post Awarded Pulitzer Prize." Huffington Post. April 16. Accessed December 7, 2015. http://www.huffingtonpost.com/2012/04/16 /huffington-post-pulitzer-prize-2012_n_1429169.html.

Glaister, Dan. 2005. "Uber-Blog Raises a Celebrity Voice." *The Guardian*. April 26. Accessed June 14, 2016. https://www.theguardian.com/technology/2005/apr/26/weblogs .newmedia.

Keller, Bill. 2011. "All the Aggregation That's Fit to Aggregate." *New York Times Magazine*. March 10. Accessed December 7, 2015. http://www.nytimes.com/2011/03/13/magazine /mag-13lede-t.html.

Seelye, Katharine. 2006. "Huffington Post Will Add Original Reporting to Its Blog." *New York Times*. November 30. Accessed December 7, 2015. http://www.nytimes.com/2006 /11/30/technology/30paper.html?_r=0.

Shapiro, Michael. 2012. "Six Degrees of Aggregation: How the Huffington Post Ate the Internet." *Columbia Journalism Review*. May/June. Accessed December 7, 2015. http://www .cjr.org/cover_story/six_degrees_of_aggregation.php.

IFILL, GWEN (1955–)

Gwen Ifill has spent decades studying politics in Washington, D.C., be it the latest presidential campaign or the sometimes-stormy internal and racial politics of the news media, and she has handled both like a pro.

A moderator of two vice presidential debates, Ifill is a fixture of political reporting on public television. She has served as managing editor of *Washington Week* on PBS since 1999 and served as a senior correspondent and later co-anchor of *PBS NewsHour*. Although in Washington for decades, she credits her upbringing for helping her resist becoming an "inside the Beltway"–style correspondent. She told *Washingtonian Magazine*, who named her Washingtonian of the year in 2016, that "The real bias is the news we don't cover, the stories we don't see if people deciding what is news all come from the same place . . . We lived for a time in public housing. My father was a minister, and we lived in parsonages" (Washingtonian 2016).

Ifill was born in New York City, the daughter of a pastor who had immigrated from Panama and a mother who had been born in Barbados. As she grew up her family moved to several communities in the Mid-Atlantic and east coast, living in church housing and, as she said, public housing in New York and Buffalo. She attended Simmons College in Boston and began working as a reporter. Although she credits her background with helping her see stories that are missed by others, it was not always a welcome change for news organizations in the 1970s and 1980s. When she interned for the *Boston Herald-American* while still in college she came across a message left for her in the photo lab that read, "N——r go home." Her employers were so troubled by the incident they offered her a job upon graduation.

Ifill built her early career in newspapers, reporting for the *Herald-American* and in 1984 joining the *Washington Post*. She became the White House correspondent for the *New York Times* in 1991, often serving as a guest on talk shows, in particular NBC's *Meet the Press* and PBS's *Washington Week in Review*. Within a few years NBC had hired her, making Ifill their chief congressional and political correspondent.

She moved to PBS in 1999 taking the helm of *Washington Week* and becoming a senior correspondent at *PBS NewsHour*. In her official bio she described the decision to come to public broadcasting as a return to what inspired her to be a reporter in the first place, saying, "I always knew I wanted to be a journalist, and my first love was newspapers. But public broadcasting provides the best of both worlds—combining the depth of newspapering with the immediate impact of broadcast television" (*PBS NewsHour*). There she established herself as a leading moderator on political debates, questioning reporters and newsmakers with equal enthusiasm and inquisitiveness. Her work earned her two gigs moderating vice presidential debates—a stormy meeting of Vice President Dick Cheney and former senator John Edwards in 2004 and the only national debate featuring Governor Sarah Palin and Senator Joe Biden in 2008.

Ifill briefly became the story herself in 2008 with news that her book on African American politicians, *The Breakthrough*, was set to come out around the possible inauguration of Barack Obama—assuming he won. Some Republicans ahead of her debate moderation accused her of a conflict of interest. In the end, reaction was overwhelmingly positive. One reviewer in the *Los Angeles Times* wrote, "What the critics who set out to pillory Ifill failed to acknowledge—because it did not suit their political aims—was that real journalists, who doubtless have biases, can and will put them aside to do their jobs" (Rainey 2008).

When Tim Russert died suddenly in 2008, NBC reportedly came back to Ifill to see if she would consider returning to the network to host *Meet the Press* but ultimately hired David Gregory. But Ifill's star has continued rising, and she became co-anchor of the first all-women nightly news team at the *PBS NewsHour* in 2013.

In that controversial best-selling work on generation of African American politicians, which included Obama and New Jersey senator Corey Booker and others, Ifill reflected on how covering race and politics had changed over time. She wrote, "A career spent watching politicians of every gender, color, and creed trying to sort their way through the abrasions of political change has taught me much. I've witnessed the uneasy transition from the civil rights struggle to direct engagement in electoral politics. As black politicians have broken through, I've documented the friction that has resulted when new realities, demographic as well as political, confront established customs and institutions" (Ifill 2009).

See also: *Meet the Press; PBS NewsHour;* Presidential Debates

Further Reading

"Gwen Ifill." PBS NewsHour. Accessed January 8, 2016. http://www.pbs.org/newshour /author/gifill.

Ifill, Gwen. 2009. *The Breakthrough: Politics and Race in the Age of Obama.* New York: Doubleday.

Rainey, James. 2008. "Impartial, Dignified, Classy: Ifill Was the Perfect Referee." *Los Angeles Times.* October 3. Accessed January 8, 2016. http://articles.latimes.com/2008/oct/03 /nation/na-onthemedia3.

"Washingtonian of the Year 2015: Gwen Ifill." 2016. *Washingtonian* magazine. January 4. Accessed January 8, 2016. http://www.washingtonian.com/blogs/capitalcomment /profiles/washingtonian-of-the-year-2016-gwen-ifill.php.

INFOTAINMENT

As television news ratings have slumped in the face of competing pressure from the Internet and other news outlets and pressure to deliver a profit to media owners has only increased, many outlets have sought to blend the worlds of entertainment and hard news reporting. The resulting style of reporting and storytelling has come to be known as infotainment. At its best, infotainment can serve as a way to engage audiences disenchanted or disinterested in the substance of the story. At its worst, it can increase the voters' sense of cynicism about the political process and the media that reports on it. Both forms of infotainment exist in the media ecosystem, but the term has come carry a negative connotation of trivializing and dumbing-down important news.

Media organizations have felt the need to attract readers and viewers since their inception. Yellow journalism of the late nineteenth century mixed sensationalized reporting on divorce, murder, and scandal with polemical editorials about social justice for workers. The British newspaper the *Daily Mail* marked its one hundredth anniversary by publishing a book about its own history, which included an anonymous poem that captured the tension inherent in journalism's mixed goal of informing the electorate and attracting enough readers to make money. The stanza went as follows:

> Tickle the public, make 'em grin,
> The more you tickle the more you'll win;
> Teach the public, you'll never get rich,
> You'll live like a beggar and die in a ditch. (Engel 1996)

From its earliest days, the popular press faced an inherently conflicted reality: To survive and to have impact on society the press must be read by the most possible people, but to attract the most readers they often must mix the broccoli of public policy with the chocolate of scandal and human interest. Although these mixed pressures existed within media for centuries, the speed with which entertainment and journalism have merged was greatly influenced by the growth of television and the increasing variety of programs that claimed a journalistic mantle.

In the early years of television reporting the idea of public service was strongly ingrained in the news divisions of major broadcasters, in part because it had to be. To justify their license from the government, broadcasters had to demonstrate that they operated in the "public interest, convenience, and necessity." From this opaque statutory requirement came the decision that each broadcaster would report on the major events of the day to their viewers. News justified the license that broadcasters used to make money showing situation comedies and movies. It was not, itself, a major profit center. In this era of television reporting the battle was often for airtime and financial backing. A network could make more money airing purely entertaining content, so news producers had to fight for support. Often it came with early attempts at what would now be called infotainment. Edward R. Murrow, the famous CBS journalist, was given resources and airtime to produce newsmagazine shows like *See It Now* and hard news documentaries like *Harvest of Shame* but that freedom came with a cost. Murrow, who was widely respected and seen by many as one of television's first celebrities, would also host an entertainment chat show called *Person to Person* where Murrow would interview celebrities about their lives.

Person to Person was a ratings hit and helped Murrow garner the support from CBS executives to do the other reporting that interested him, but even Murrow, working in the 1950s, saw that news was losing out on television to entertainment. He famously challenged television executives to staunch this drive toward pure entertainment on their networks in a speech to the Radio and Television News Directors Association in 1958, asking the handful of major companies that operated the broadcasting networks to consider setting aside time usually occupied by Ed Sullivan and *The Tonight Show* to be devoted to serious issue reporting about education or the Middle East. He ended his plea with a call to action, declaring:

> To those who say people wouldn't look; they wouldn't be interested; they're too complacent, indifferent and insulated, I can only reply: There is, in one reporter's opinion, considerable evidence against that contention. But even if they are right, what have they got to lose? Because if they are right, and this instrument is good for nothing but to entertain, amuse and insulate, then the tube is flickering now and we will soon see that the whole struggle is lost. This instrument can teach, it can illuminate; yes, and even it can inspire. But it can do so only to the extent that humans are determined to use it to those ends. Otherwise, it's nothing but wires and lights in a box. (Murrow 1958)

Murrow's proposal went nowhere, and all that remains is the "wires and lights" line. Still, it would be Murrow's CBS that would begin to answer the challenge of finding a way to entertain and inform—and, perhaps even more importantly, make money. The newsmagazine *60 Minutes* moved the storytelling form of television news forward in important ways. With its mix of investigative, in-your-face reporting, celebrity profiles and humorous commentary, the program was a ratings and financial success. News began to make money and with that came more airtime across the networks. ABC and NBC sought to emulate the *60 Minutes* model with their own news programs, and as these newsmagazines proliferated a wave of new afternoon and morning talk shows like *Donahue* and later *Oprah* drew in millions of viewers. These programs further blurred the line between hard news and so-called soft news that focused on the individual and their story rather than the underlying policies or public institutions at play.

By the 1980s, the portmanteau of entertainment and information was growing in use and taking on an increasingly negative connotation. Authors and critics worried, even as cable news and its 24-hour news cycle was still in its infancy, that Americans' expectation that they would be entertained by television and media would overwhelm culture. Neil Postman captured this modern media concern in his work *Amusing Ourselves to Death*, writing, "When a population becomes distracted by trivia, when cultural life is redefined as a perpetual round of entertainments, when serious public conversation becomes a form of baby-talk, when, in short, a people become an audience and their public business a vaudeville act, then a nation finds itself as risk; culture-death is a clear possibility" (Postman 1985). Postman's concerns would only be heightened as cable news and other programming began to cut into broadcaster audience and profits. Audience fragmentation across an increasing number of cable channels and later Internet sites pushed broadcasters to find ways to attract audiences to their news programs. Morning news shows became less and less news and more and more lifestyle programs. Even newspapers, the buttoned-up cousins of television, added new sections, color, and graphics to try and maintain audience that continued to slip away. Infotainment became one way to pursue that audience, allowing producers to incorporate the slick production values of advertising and youth-oriented networks to staid content about political campaigns and the environment. New outlets also added more celebrities to the mix. Often they would report on celebrity scandal and news and other times they would use celebrities in the "role" of reporter. Leonardo DiCaprio interviewed President Clinton about Earth Day for ABC. PBS uses celebrity voices in their historical documentaries.

While news programs were drifting further into the realm of entertainment programming in style and content, many talk shows and comedy programs were mixing in an increasing amount of current events content. Many in the political world took note of this trend early and have sought to capitalize on it for years. Late night shows like *Saturday Night Live* and *The Tonight Show* had made fun of politicians for decades, mocking gaffes and blunders and milking scandals for laughs. Programs like Comedy Central's *The Daily Show* expanded those monologue jokes from broadcast programs into a nightly commentary on politics and its coverage in the media. Politicians often sought to ignore the criticism when reporters pressed them to respond, but in the 1990s many of them began to change tactics. Bill Clinton, seeking to appeal to younger voters, famously went on the *Arsenio Hall Show* during the 1992 campaign and played the saxophone. He also took questions from young people during an MTV forum in 1994 and answered one young man's question: "Mr. President, the world's dying to know, is it boxers or briefs?" by telling America he wore briefs.

After Clinton's embrace, it soon became an expectation that candidates would appear on late-night shows and afternoon talk shows. Oprah Winfrey became a major part of then-candidate Barack Obama's appeal to women and former senator John Edwards announced his candidacy on *The Daily Show*. The late-night shows, in particular, have taken on particular importance. One group of political scientists who have studied the relationship between comedy programs and politics noted, "Ironically, the source of negative material about candidates can become a source of positive material. It's an opportunity for politicians to present themselves as ordinary people to a broad audience that is not just political junkies. These shows are another stop that you have to make on the campaign trail. That means they're institutionalized as politically relevant" (Morella 2014).

These appearances themselves generate media coverage across the Internet, quickly become viral videos and fueling tweets and social media response. What's interesting to note is the degree to which these appearances have become so mutually beneficial. For the programs, booking a high-profile presidential candidate can be a ratings win. When Stephen Colbert became the host of CBS's *The Late Show* in September of 2015 his first weeks' guest lists looked like a C-SPAN dream team:

Jeb Bush on Sept. 8, Vice President Joe Biden on Sept. 10, Justice Stephen Breyer on Sept. 14, Bernie Sanders on Sept. 18. Biden, in particular, made headlines with a deeply personal and candid conversation about the death of his son and his own conflict about whether to enter the 2016 campaign, which he ultimately did not. These guests helped fuel far more attention to the programs from the mainstream media and quickly established Colbert as a late-night host who is not afraid to tackle serious topics. *Saturday Night Live* also offers testimony to the power of the mixing of politicians and comedy. The show has seen a revival since an inspired 2008 decision to ask back former cast member Tina Fey to impersonate GOP vice presidential nominee Sarah Palin. Fey's Palin impersonation became a central point of the campaign and Palin eventually came on the show as well, to show she got the joke. Still the program has been criticized for cozying up too much to political guest stars. In 2015 the program came under fire for having controversial GOP candidate Donald Trump not only appear but host the entire program. The show and the comedians appeared deferential to Trump and the program was blasted in the media, even if it did draw some 9 million viewers.

For politicians, though, the mixing of entertainment and politics can have very real impacts on their campaigns and their post-politics lives. Campaigns have historically found the idea of putting their candidate in a chair next to a comedian or talk show host less of a threat than agreeing to long interviews with journalists. Talk shows often want to explore the personal background of the candidate and rarely take a hard line of questioning, and comedy programs want the candidate simply to be there and will often allow the candidate to come out looking like a good sport and in on the gag. And, although Clinton faced some criticism for his embracing the infotainment world, no politician has faced serious political repercussions for agreeing to appear on one of these programs. In fact, these usually softball interviews can serve as a way to officially comment on controversial issues that would be more difficult to address in a more journalistic setting. As the *Denver Post's* television critic noted in 2015, "At this point in our technological evolution the public seems to give equal weight to a comment made on *Meet the Press* and a throwaway line on Bill Maher, a quote in a newspaper or a 140-character tweet" (Ostrow 2015). And so these infotainment programs offer candidates a less fraught way to get their comments out into the public while exposing them to potential voters who may not be tuned in to the traditional political media.

More than that, some candidates have found they can turn these appearances and their ability to thrive on television and connect with viewers into lucrative careers. Mike Huckabee, for example, was a largely unknown governor from Arkansas most notable for losing 100 pounds while in office when he announced on *Meet the Press* he would run for president in 2008. Huckabee's self-effacing charm and strong religious character helped him win the Iowa caucuses that year and his ability to mix humor with provocative policy made him a hit with evangelical voters. Huckabee lost the nomination to senator John McCain but soon found himself hosting a program on Fox News and landed a prime book contract. For decades public figures had often turned celebrity into political sway. Former actor Ronald Reagan partially rode his fame to the governorship of California and later the presidency of the United States. Jesse Ventura moved from professional wrestling to the governorship of Minnesota and *Saturday Night Live* writer and cast member Al Franken won a seat in the U.S. Senate in part with his name recognition. But Huckabee represented something new where "the door between politics and entertainment has begun to sway in the opposite direction over the past two elections cycles. Now, instead of converting celebrity into votes, politicians are converting votes into celebrity . . . Consider Sarah Palin, who, before Senator John McCain plucked her from relative obscurity as governor of Alaska, was worth about $1 million. She has turned her newfound political celebrity into even bigger book deals, $100,000 speaker fees, a lucrative Fox contract, and her own reality TV show" (Carroll 2012).

Add to all of this the fact that many Americans rely on comedy programs and other pure forms of infotainment to gather at least part of their news about what is happening in the world. The merger of celebrity and politics serves both the media and the politician well. It allows the media to attract larger audiences and often expose people to issues they had not considered before. HBO's John Oliver, for example, may be a comedian, but his 13-minute takedown of the government's plan to end a complicated policy regulating content on the Internet known as "Net Neutrality" was credited for prompting millions of comments to the Federal Communications Commission's website and for helping push the FCC to abandon its plan. Even among formal journalism, there has always been an accepted policy of mixing interesting news about people or celebrities with policy and "harder" news. On the campaign side, this infotainment bias allows candidates to appear and be quoted from interviews that are structurally less confrontational than traditional journalism. Candidates are allowed to be more personal and more engaging, and the personality of a candidate can come out in a way that carefully controlled stump speeches and 30-second ads don't allow. It can help the candidate connect with potential voters less interested in the wonky side of politics and, for some, can spur post-politics careers as talk show hosts or commentators. What's clear is the trend that worried Murrow in the 1950s and Postman in the 1980s has only strengthened in the twenty-first century. Its implications on the function of government and effectiveness of campaigns remains, though, still unwritten.

See also: Comedy, Satire, and Politics; Public Interest Obligation

Further Reading

Carroll, Conn. 2012. "Welcome to the 'Infotainment Age' in Politics." *Washington Examiner*. January 15. Accessed January 4, 2015. http://www.washingtonexaminer.com/welcome -to-the-infotainment-age-in-politics/article/1064956.

Engel, Matthew. 1996. *Tickle the Public: One Hundred Years of the Popular Press*. London: Victor Gollancz.

Morella, Michael. 2014. "Playing for Laughs on the Trail." *U.S. News & World Report*. September 25. Accessed January 4, 2015. http://www.usnews.com/opinion/articles/2014/09/24/comedians-influence-voters-shape-views-of-politicians.

Murrow, Edward. 1958. "Radio and Television News Directors Association Speech." Radio Television Digital News Association. October 15. Accessed January 4, 2016. http://www.rtdna.org/content/edward_r_murrow_s_1958_wires_lights_in_a_box_speech.

Ostrow, Joanne. 2015. "Trump and Fallon, Biden and Colbert: Here Comes More Infotainment." *Denver Post*. September 2. Accessed January 4, 2016. http://www.denverpost.com/entertainment/ci_28746363/trump-and-fallon-biden-and-colbert-here-comes.

Postman, Neil. 1985. *Amusing Ourselves to Death: Public Discourse in the Age of Show Business*. New York: Penguin Books.

INTERNET ADVERTISING

Like many industries, advertising has been fundamentally altered by the emergence of the World Wide Web and smartphones. The shift has moved advertising away from a generalized effort to deliver a business's message to a vague and possibly interested audience in a geographic region to a data-driven science that targets individual consumers with messages aimed at convincing them to make a purchase or choose a candidate. This technological revolution has placed much more power in the hands of the advertiser to create their own audience and their own brand without the help of traditional media like newspapers and television.

The impact on modern political campaigns and the coverage of politics is difficult to quantify and even more difficult to overstate. The advertising changes have turned campaigns into database-empowered machines where voters are targeted in their homes with specific issues of interest to them, followed around online with ads that reinforce one campaign's message, and sometimes turned into contributors to the campaign's outreach efforts by posting material to their own social media feeds. As profound as that shift has been, the effect of Internet advertising on news organizations has been even more fundamental. Most news organizations fueled their spectacular business returns with advertising dollars, offering businesses the ability to deliver an ad to the front door or the living room of a city full of potential customers. But who that customer was and whether they actually wanted something the advertiser was offering was a mystery to both the media and the advertiser. An often-cited quote that captured the reality of advertising in the age of mass media came from John Wanamaker, a department store mogul, who is said to have declared, "I know I waste half my advertising budget; the only problem is I do not know which half" (Ad Age 1999). Advertising in the pre-digital age amounted to educated guessing. If you owned a car dealership in Lancaster, Pennsylvania, you would turn to one of the newspapers in the town to let people know what cars you had to sell. You knew that ad went out to many of the families in your town who could easily reach your business, but not whether they wanted a new car. You could place a radio ad or television spot in the same hopes of reaching people, but all the media company could offer was a geographic sense of where the ad reached, a general demographic snapshot of the types of people likely to be watching or listening at that time and, afterwards, a sense of how many people may have seen it.

As Leverholme notes, it was an imprecise and wasteful business, with few alternatives. But the emergence of the Internet in the early 1990s seemed to offer a different vision of the future, one not bound by the geography of a business location, or the media's location-based advertising business. As the World Wide Web expanded, the U.S. government saw the potential for this more consumer-friendly technology to empower businesses. Bill Clinton, who was president at the time and a self-confessed "technophobe," tasked Vice President Al Gore to develop a plan for how to structure the commercial side of the Internet. After more than 14 revisions, the "Framework for Global Electronic Commerce" was introduced in the summer of 1997 with the idea of creating a new platform for business, above all else. Clinton said at the time, "If we establish an environment in which electronic commerce can grow and flourish, then every computer will be a window open to every business, large and small, everywhere in the world. Not only will industry leaders such as IBM be able to tap in to new markets, but the smallest start-up company will have an unlimited network of sales and distribution at its fingertips. It will literally be possible to start a company tomorrow, and next week do business in Japan and Germany and Chile, all without leaving your home, something that used to take years and years and years to do. In this way, the Internet can be, and should be, a truly empowering force for large and small business people alike."

The framework was revolutionary and radically accelerated the development of the Internet as a commercial advertising venue. Under the proposal and in the years to come the Internet would not be controlled by the tax policies of a local community or state. It would deliver whatever content was published upon it at the same speed, ensuring major businesses and a new startup would be treated equally. It would reward the aggressive, small firms who moved quickly to seize an opportunity and would punish slow-moving organizations opposed to change.

The effect of this new platform on advertising evolved quickly. First, it presented the opportunity to place fairly traditional advertising strategies on a new media platform. A computer company rolling out a new product could purchase advertising in a computer magazine, a geographically based newspaper or on a national television program. Now it could also add banner ads to the list of advertising purchases, allowing people to see their message on a service like America Online or a website like Cnet. But this was only a first step. As web services matured, some outlets began to understand how much more powerful and sophisticated the Internet could be than just a billboard. One of the first businesses to identify this was Google, a search engine developed by two Stanford University students named Larry Page and Sergey Brin. Andrew McLaughlin, former director of Global Public Policy at Google from 2004–2009, said the company came to understand that "every search is in some sense an expression of intention. It's an expression of what you want to do, where you want to go, what you're looking for. And that maps very nicely with the desire of advertisers to target their messages towards people at the moment when they are intending to go buy something" (Frontline 2014). Here was the shift. No longer would an advertiser place an ad based on an educated guess. If someone searched for the price of a flight from Seattle to Chicago, a company could do more than guess that they might be interested in a cheaper flight, a possible rental care in Chicago, a hotel to stay in, or a restaurant to visit. Now companies were developing a profile of people in real time that advertisers could access and potentially use to be far more strategic in their messages. As a Massachusetts Institute of Technology review of advertising concluded, "At last, marketers delighted; the right ads could be delivered to the 'right' people, anywhere they appeared online. To do this, marketers would analyze the data to determine patterns of consumer behavior and pinpoint what products or services the user was most likely to respond to in order to influence sales" (MIT 2013).

This new world of advertising took some time to alter both the world of media and the ways campaigns run, but the shift was inevitable. On the media side, it wasn't at first certain whether this change would improve business or hurt it. Initially, newspapers looked at the Internet as a way to break out of their geographic limitations. Now they could deliver advertising to anyone in the world, a vast improvement to their logistically limited world of print. Newspapers had embraced a business concept in the nineteenth century known as the "penny press" where newspapers would make themselves as affordable as possible, then leverage their large readership into money by selling advertising to businesses seeking to reach those people. The Internet, in the views of many early newspaper website managers, could allow them to simply reach more people. The one deal they made to do it, though, was to make their content cheaper than a penny. As late as 2007, studies offered media companies "optimistic support" about the evolution of advertising. One wrote of the "double-edged sword" the Internet created for newspapers. The papers would no longer be trapped in a specific geographic location, but users expected the content to be free. He added, "The minority portion of a newspaper's revenues that traditionally comes from subscriptions and newsstand sales is absent in the online model—and may in fact be damaged by the presence of an online edition. That leaves the future of the online newspaper squarely in the court of the advertising profession" (Bentley 2007).

But the business that newspapers and other media companies banked on was a very different business than the one they had relied on for generations. Now, for an advertiser, reaching a consumer in a given community would not suffice. Also, the company could create its own website and social media presence and could reach out to customers directly through online services like Google and, later, Facebook. Traditional media still held some value for the advertising profession, but far less than it had before.

Many media companies began to reconsider their businesses, seeking to make Internet advertising only part of their overall model. The *New York Times*, for example, introduced a paywall in 2011, asking readers who view more than 10 articles a month to pay for access. Within two years, half of the company's revenues came from subscribers to their print and digital products. By 2015, the company could boast more than a million digital subscribers, far more than its 640,000 print counterparts. Compare this to its aggressive advertising push online—the paper has sponsors for content and services as well as traditional display ads—that now only generates 30 percent of its advertising revenue. Even though the digital revolution has led to the paper drawing far more money in from subscribers than it did before the change, the advertising money that once went to the paper is far, far less than the digital money that replaced it and, as CNN Money noted in early 2015, "It has to earn every penny against brutal competition, including that of ad tech giants, Google and Facebook. At the same time, the bottom is fast dropping out of print advertising, down another 9 percent in the fourth quarter [of 2014]" (Doctor 2015). The economics of Internet advertising have yet to serve as anything other than a challenge to the news media, at times appearing to threaten the stability of the business and helping fuel a 40 percent reduction in newsroom staffs in the past decade.

For the political campaign, the explosive growth and personalization of Internet advertising has been a very different story: one not of struggling to survive, but striving to keep up. As early as the mid-twentieth century political campaigns had begun to use technology to try and appeal to voters in a more targeted way, but campaigns have often trailed behind the marketing technology used by corporate America. Whether direct mail or the opportunities presented by the Internet, it took time for campaigns to respond and in most cases they responded first to the money. Early digital advertising and outreach operations, like the 2000 campaign for the presidency, focused on campaigns using these technologies to appeal to supporters for cash. But campaigns would catch on. By 2004, the Howard Dean campaign effectively used online organizing to help spur scores of meetups around the country. Four years later, Senator Barack Obama would up the ante even more. The Obama campaign built a social network with the help of one of the founders of Facebook. "My Barack Obama" boasted more than 1.5 million users and helped spur what became, experts argue, the first viral political campaign. "As with all things viral, connecting to others outside the initial cluster of supporters depends on the quality of referrals. Friends, family, and colleagues are far more credible than any advertisement a marketer could dream up. This was what drove the campaign's online strategy" (Penenberg 2009).

But the Internet did more than just fuel the way volunteers would join the campaign or even the way the campaign would communicate to potential donors. It also affected the way campaigns considered their broader advertising and communications strategies. "The Internet allows us to rethink the mass nature of persuasive political communications as campaigning becomes faster, more intimate, more personal, and more individualized. The power of the online campaign is not primarily to change minds, but in arming them with the tools and knowledge they need to take [an] active part [in] the political process" (Thorson and Watson 2007). And this communication soon involved tailored and specific advertising that tried to use the same targeting ideas businesses had been using for nearly a decade. Campaigns soon were deploying thousands of carefully tailored ads that aimed to appeal to voters based on issue interests, location, age, income, and more. And not just presidential campaigns. By 2014 digital advertising had emerged as a major component of congressional and statewide campaigns. One estimate projected that some $270 million was spent on midterm contests on just digital advertising. While still a fraction of the $4.6 billion spent on television that cycle, stories are emerging of candidates riding digital ads to electoral success—like the "castrating senator."

Joni Ernst was an Iowa state senator and lieutenant colonel in the state's Air National Guard. She was also running third in the Republican primary when she launched an online ad where she said, "I grew up castrating hogs on an Iowa farm, so when I get to Washington, I'll know how to cut pork" over the audio track of a squealing pig. The ad went viral, attracting hundreds of thousands of views. It also sparked a wave of donations that helped get the ad on television and catapulted Ernst from third to first, and eventually to the U.S. Senate. GOP consultant Wesley Donehue, who was working for the frontrunner in Iowa when the Ernst ad went viral, would later tell Politico, "Talk about a really, really good case study of how digital and traditional media can work together. Pig castration is where it's at. That's the key to success" (Samuelsohn 2014).

The Ernst ad demonstrates how low-budget campaigns can use digital ads to cheaply get their message out. By using humor or by sharpening an attack, digital ads can draw support, increase traditional media attention, and use social media to spread core messages of the campaign. That said, even the Ernst example shows that the advertising's impact is amplified when broadcast by traditional media. For campaigns, the use of digital advertising can play multiple roles—firing up the base with intensely partisan targeted messages, sparking viral success by striking the right mix of message and tone, and ensuring their traditional supporters continue to receive their message across multiple platforms.

Digital advertising continues to evolve as the platform itself changes. In just the last decade mobile use of the Internet has gone from almost nil to now the way in which most people access the web. Advertising is sprinting to keep up with those changes. The news media and campaigns will struggle to keep up, but if history is an indication, candidates will find a way to use these new developments to encourage donations, increase name recognition, and drive support. And the news media will seek ways to deliver content to these platforms even as they seek a business model that works as well as the traditional advertising model did.

See also: Native Advertising; Negative Advertising; Newspaper Industry; Social Media and Politics; Television Advertising

Further Reading

"The Advertising Century: John Wanamaker." Ad Age. March 29, 1999. Accessed June 14, 2016. http://adage.com/article/special-report-the-advertising-century/john-wanamaker/140185/.

Bentley, Clyde. 2007. "Internet Advertising in Online Newspapers." In *Internet Advertising: Theory and Research*. Edited by David Schuman and Esther Thorson. Mahwah, NJ: Lawrence Erlbaum Associates, Publishers.

Clinton, William. 1997. "Remarks by the President in Announcement of Electronic Commerce Initiative." National Archives. Accessed August 6, 1015. http://clinton4.nara.gov/WH/New/Commerce/remarks.html.

Doctor, Ken. 2015. "The New York Times and Its Big 'Zero.'" CNN Money. February 6. Accessed August 5, 2015. http://money.cnn.com/2015/02/06/media/new-york-times.

Frontline. 2014. "United States of Secrets." PBS. May 20. Accessed August 6, 2015. http://www.pbs.org/wgbh/pages/frontline/government-elections-politics/united-states-of-secrets/transcript-61.

MIT Technology Review. 2013. "The Evolution of Ad Tech." Massachusetts Institute of Technology. September 5. Accessed August 6, 2015. http://www.technologyreview.com/view/518551/the-evolution-of-ad-tech.

Penenberg, Adam. 2009. *Viral Loop*. New York: Hyperion Books.

Samuelsohn, Daniel. 2014. "The Next Big Thing in Campaigns." Politico. August 24. Accessed August 5, 2015. http://www.politico.com/story/2014/08/2014-elections-digital-advertising-110322.html.

Thorson, Kjerstin, and Brendan Watson. 2007. "The New Online Campaign: Translating Information into Action." In *Internet Advertising: Theory and Research*. Edited by David Schuman and Esther Thorson. Mahwah, NJ: Lawrence Erlbaum Associates, Publishers.

INVISIBLE PRIMARY

The invisible primary is an imprecise term for an imprecise part of the process of electing a president. In the months before any caucus-goer or primary voter casts an actual ballot, political commentators, donors, and campaign professionals weigh the viability of the different candidates, creating front-runners and sometimes scuttling campaigns. The invisible primary serves as an unofficial first vetting of candidates to gauge their ability to mount a serious campaign for the nomination of either the Republican or Democratic Party.

This period is sometimes referred to as the money primary as candidates jockey for the support of critical political action committees and, in the post-*Citizens United* decision world, Super PACs and dark money groups. But usually this period includes more than just financial standing, growing to include assessments of campaign positions, staff, and early appearances by the candidate.

The term "invisible primary" comes from a 1976 book of the same name by journalist Arthur T. Hadley. Hadley argued that power had shifted from party elites to political donors and commentators in establishing a clear frontrunner before any delegates to the convention were selected and that that frontrunner would go on to win the nomination. Unfortunately for Hadley, he made this case in a year where this did not happen. During the period of the invisible primary, nationally known politicians like Mo Udall and Henry Scoop Jackson seemed far more likely to score the Democratic nomination, but former Georgia governor Jimmy Carter's victory in the Iowa Caucuses and his surging win in New Hampshire's first-in-the-nation primary showed this little-known candidate could do well outside of his home state of Georgia. Carter effectively used the increasing importance of presidential primaries to select delegates as a way to upset the invisible primary leaders from within the Democratic ranks.

Despite the fact that Carter won the 1976 nomination, the idea of the invisible primary stuck. Even as more and more states allowed party members—and often any voter—to cast ballots for presidential nominees, the period before the voting began took on more and more importance. To understand the complexity of this mushy period between the last presidential election and the first caucuses and primaries of the next campaign, it is important to understand the degree to which campaigns for the nomination have changed. Primaries became a critical way to win the nomination only after the controversial nomination fight in 1968 among Democrats. That year, Vice President Hubert Humphrey secured the nomination even though he did not really campaign that much in the primaries. Most delegates to the national convention were selected by the party leaders in different states and so when many rank-and-file Democrats backed anti-Vietnam War candidates like Robert Kennedy and Eugene McCarthy there was intense frustration with their inability to affect the nomination.

The Democrats decided to overhaul their system after losing the election that fall, seeking to empower the party regulars. State parties could no longer choose the delegates through a party caucus or a delegate primary. Instead, each state would hold a participatory convention open to all party members or a candidate primary. State parties could still select up to 10 percent of the delegates—primarily for senior party members or elected officials—but no longer would the party elders control the process. Throughout this change candidates were careful only to participate in primaries if that was their only path to the nomination. In fact, "The rule of thumb among party tacticians was that the earlier a candidate put himself in the field, the weaker the candidacy" (Polsby 1983). But that was changing and the importance of primaries grew. That tumultuous year of 1968 only 38 percent of the delegates to convention were selected by primaries. By 1976 the number soared to 72 percent. But still the party sought to have some control of the list of potential candidates primary voters could select from, and the invisible primary became the unofficial tool to affect the process.

The invisible primary is, itself, a changing thing. Initially, the primary served as a period of time during which potential candidates could float their name among political commentators and donors to see how much support they might have in a run. Political scientists who study the nominating process would point out that potential candidates would develop and test their messages during this period, evolving key themes, central issues, and even slogans. It's also a time when candidates seek to portray themselves as legitimate candidates for the nomination, either as a dominant frontrunner or as a surging competitor. One set of scholars argues, "Even those candidates without a prayer portray themselves as generating momentum. Obviously candidates anticipate media norms and patterns of coverage and either do their best to conform to them so that they will gain some exposure in the media or design their message to manipulate the media's coverage in a manner more favorable to their own campaign. Candidates certainly benefit when their framing of the campaign takes hold in the news media and is thus conveyed to the public with a mark of credibility" (Haynes, Flowers, and Gurian 2002). More than just a race for coverage, the process is also an effort to organize a national campaign with an effective team in place in critical early states, a strong donor base, as well as support through independent groups that can purchase ads and canvass potential voters.

This process begins unbelievably early. As one pollster told public radio's "Marketplace" program in 2015, "I recalled the first conversation I had with someone from one of the campaigns—and it is one of the major campaigns now—concerning the 2016 election happened two days after Mitt Romney was defeated (in November 2012) and it was not a trivial conversation. It was an actual game-planning thing" (O'Leary 2015). An early start is no longer a sign of weakness, but a necessary reality to build the financial, political, and media support to create a real run.

The public manifestation of the invisible primary is press coverage, but journalists often struggle with how to couch and contextualize these early developments. To be fair, the audience interested in the "inside baseball" of campaign organizing and fundraising is very small. And because the invisible primary is spread out over years and has few definitive benchmarks to assess candidate viability, some note that "journalists make little attempt to report on it in detail, and when they do, they focus more on the visible indicators of support, such as fund-raising and polls, than on the players who may give or withhold that support" (Cohen, Karol, Noel, and Zaller 2009). However, these experts argue that the press, who could be surrogates for the public to ensure that party elites are not pre-selecting candidates, instead allow themselves to be manipulated by campaigns and party officials into weeding out candidates by focusing on a handful of indicators of public support—like fundraising. And examining coverage of primaries does highlight the sometimes-strange indicators of success that the media may choose to focus on.

Take, as example number one, the Iowa Straw Poll. Political analysts have found that, indeed, "National levels of candidate viability and exposure are responsive to the dynamics of these state contests . . . [so] the happenings of the Iowa and New Hampshire campaign have an important say within the national invisible primary before the votes in these states are actually tallied" (Christenson and Smidt 2012). States like these two and South Carolina receive out-sized coverage during the invisible primary as reporters gauge their support for candidates. Polls from these first states receive national coverage and often powerfully unrepresentative gauges of support can find their way into the national campaign narrative. Which brings us to the small town of Ames, Iowa, where every four years the state Republican Party hosts a rally and fundraiser. The event comes six months before the scheduled caucuses. Between 1979 and 2011 the party met six times to rally in support of different candidates. Campaigns would encourage supporters to travel to Ames to participate in the fundraiser and then cast their ballot in a non-binding referendum to support their candidate. During the early Straw Polls voters did not even need to be from Iowa, let alone Republicans, to vote in the contest and so campaigns would bus in supporters from other states to participate. Other campaigns would pay the entrance fee—usually between $25 and $35—so their backers could participate. In 1999, the state party limited it to residents of Iowa or students at Iowa universities.

Coverage of the Straw Poll often included caveats that it was not scientific, but also highlighted the poll's ability to assess the organization of different campaigns in the critical early state of Iowa. And despite these caveats and its historically poor ability to predict the winner of the Iowa Caucuses—to say nothing of predicting the winner of the nomination—the Straw Poll still played into campaign strategies as a way to draw attention to a candidate. In 2011's crowded GOP field former Minnesota governor Tim Pawlenty hoped to use the poll as a way to reinvigorate his presidential campaign that was running low on funds. Pawlenty later said, "Our theory was we needed to make a mark early if we were going to be able to get some attention and be able to stay in his wake as the credible alternative to [Mitt Romney]. And it was the wrong theory" (Roller 2015). Pawlenty finished third in the poll that summer and dropped out the next day.

By 2012, the state party and Republican officials in Iowa had decided to scrap the poll as major candidates chose to not participate, leaving journalists to seek out new ways to assess the viability and strength of early campaigns. Those critical of the current primary system often empathize with the media as they struggle to cover a field of 10 or more presidential hopefuls. Decades ago Senator Adlai Stevenson III, the son of the two-time Democratic presidential nominee, blasted the process, arguing it forces candidates through a crazed maze of regulation and fundraising. It also cripples the press's ability to truly cover the issues and size up the candidates. He has said, "Commentators gauge viability by the most superficial devices: the size of campaign bankrolls or volume of applause at a joint appearance . . . and television, the dominating medium, offers episodes and spectacles, and the citizen is hard put to fathom their significance" (Davis 1980).

The invisible primary is really a product of multiple factors. By shifting the selection of delegates from the party elites to voting by average party members and in some states the general public, the party nomination process changed from a closed effort to another popular campaign. This created a new need for media coverage so primary voters and caucus participants could make better choices. It also created new interest from the general public about the candidates running. Campaign operatives, seeking to boost their man's or woman's chances of securing the nomination, often sought to portray their candidate as having critical momentum through stories about public appearances, financial backing, and early successes. Journalists seeking to report on the nomination fight sought ways to contextualize and prioritize candidate coverage. If there are only so many stories a report can do about the different candidates, how does one choose where to focus limited resources? The answer from reporters is usually "the candidates who have the most legitimate chance of winning." And so the invisible primary emerged as a way for reporters to select how to cover the campaign and financial backers to choose where to invest their money.

The problem, according to many reporters and commentators, is this is not really what the process triggered in 1968 aimed to do. The idea was a progressive one—to move the nomination out of the hands of the party big wigs where they sat in mythical smoke-filled rooms and chose the candidates and to give more power to the public and average party members; to make the nomination as democratic as possible. The result has fallen short of those goals, though. David Broder, one of the deans of the political reporting corps for decades, expressed real frustration with the way the invisible primary had warped the process, writing, "When the candidates are forced to do most of their campaigning for the nomination in the pre-presidential year, they quickly find that the only attentive audience members are activists, donors, pollsters and the political reporters. Those four groups—none of them remotely representative of the grass roots—have acquired the power to say who is 'expected' to win—and who usually does win . . . This rush to judgment devalues the role of the party leaders and elected officials and still fails to achieve the reformers' populist goals. It comes close to being the worst way possible to pick a president" (Broder 2003).

But this process is also not always completely determinative. For example, the unlikely run of real estate mogul and reality television star Donald Trump tested the concept of the invisible primary in 2015. Trump, who had flirted with a White House run before, launched an unorthodox campaign that included incendiary claims about Mexican immigrants, offensive tweets about female reporters, and carnival-like news conferences. The liberal Huffington Post declared they would not cover Trump's campaign because it was a publicity stunt and many commentators dismissed his candidacy out of hand, but more than three months into his run, he continued to lead the field of Republican candidates. Trump had lost the invisible primary but it seemed to do little to his chances.

Still in the modern political campaign, the invisible primary remains a powerful idea and shapes much of the political reporting in the more than a year of coverage leading up to the first caucus in Iowa. It shapes the campaigns as they seek to develop messages that resonate with donors, the media, and voters and it creates real impediments for outsider or long-shot candidates to break into the campaign. The public that Broder saw as disadvantaged by the nomination process has begun to shape the invisible primary somewhat as the growth of social media have created ways for candidates to bypass the traditional media. But it is still difficult road for outside candidates to build enough financial and organizational support to survive the brutal calendar of primaries and caucuses that select the delegates. For now, the invisible primary will continue to force some candidates out of the race before a single vote is cast. Whether that is a good thing or a bad thing will continue to be debated by politicians and journalists.

See also: Primary Coverage

Further Reading

Broder, David. 2003. "No Way to Choose a President." *Washington Post*. December 31. Accessed June 22, 2015. http://www.washingtonpost.com/archive/opinions/2003/12/31/no-way-to-choose-a-president/83f70116-8bdd-43f6-af95-febdc747f2c9.

Christenson, Dino, and Corwin Smidt. 2012. "Polls and Elections: Still Part of the Conversation: Iowa and New Hampshire's Say within the Invisible Primary." *Presidential Studies Quarterly* September.

Cohen, Marty, David Karol, Hans Noel, and John Zaller. 2009. *The Party Decides: Presidential Nominations Before and After Reform*. Chicago: University of Chicago Press.

Davis, James. 1980. *Presidential Primaries: Road to the White House*. Westport, CT: Greenwood Press.

Haynes, Audrey, Julianne Flowers, and Paul-Henri Gurian. 2002. "Getting the Message Out: Candidate Communication Strategy during the Invisible Primary." *Political Research Quarterly* 55, no. 3 (September). Los Angeles: Sage Publications, Inc.

O'Leary, Lizzie. 2015. "Inside the Not-So-Invisible Primary." Marketplace. April 24. Accessed June 21, 2015. http://www.marketplace.org/topics/elections/inside-not-so-invisible-primary.

Polsby, Nelson. 1983. *Consequences of Party Reform*. Oxford: Oxford University Press.

Roller, Emma. 2015. "Tim Pawlenty on the Death of the Iowa Straw Poll: 'Good Riddance.'" *National Journal*. June 12. Accessed June 21, 2015. http://www.nationaljournal.com/2016-elections/tim-pawlenty-on-the-death-of-the-iowa-straw-poll-good-riddance-20150612.

ISSUE-ADVOCACY ADVERTISING

Driven by legal rulings that have sought to protect political speech while curbing direct influence on elections, issue-advocacy advertising has emerged as a powerful, ubiquitous, and almost completely unregulated form of campaigning. Though they cannot explicitly call for the election or defeat of a given candidate, such ads can still attack or implicitly support a candidate, and independent organizations can—and do—raise and spend unlimited amounts of money on this form of persuasion.

These ads are also the direct result of regulating campaign spending while protecting core First Amendment freedoms. On the one hand the Supreme Court has drawn a clear line around ads that are not "express advocacy," saying organizations like the Sierra Club ought to be able to spend money on ads urging people to support environmental regulations or the League of Women Voters should be permitted to publish a pamphlet urging easier voter registration rules without the interference of the government. The other idea is that having these groups run ads calling for the election of one candidate over another could unduly affect the election itself and so that form of advertising can and should be limited. Both of these ideas have a long legal history and have come to be seen as acceptable limits on campaign speech and permissible speech by independent groups. The legal concept of this express- versus issue-advocacy can be traced to one key 1970s legal decision that struck down many of the post-Watergate efforts to regulate campaign financing.

Ironically, what would come to be seen as a major loophole in the campaign finance rules was constructed by a court seeking to save a section of the Federal Election Campaign Act. The court in the critical 1976 case *Buckley v. Valeo* would strike down many of the more vague and potentially overreaching aspects of the law, but also sought to allow many of the provisions to stand. One provision dealt with the disclosure of money donated to groups seeking to influence federal elections. The justices worried that the law as written could require any group that sought to inform the electorate of key issues and candidate stances to disclose its donors and file with the newly established Federal Election Commission. This was too much of an infringement on speech in the court's view, so they aimed to more narrowly define the kind of speech that should prompt such disclosure. The result was a footnote—number 52 in the majority decision—that would give birth to the idea of express- and issue-advocacy. The court sought to clarify what types of advertising should require disclosure and wrote, "This construction would restrict the application of (FECA) to communications containing express words of advocacy of election or defeat, such as 'vote for,' 'elect,' 'support,' 'cast your ballot for,' 'Smith for Congress,' 'vote against,' 'defeat,' 'reject.'" Thus were born the "magic words" of campaign ads.

Magic words quickly came to be the only way to differentiate the express advocacy that the court ruled could be regulated and required disclosure and the independent issue advocacy speech that could take place without the same reporting to the FEC. To save disclosure rules, the court created a huge swath of advertising that could take place without disclosure. So, for example, in the intense primary battle between U.S. senator John McCain and former governor George W. Bush in 2000, an ad went on the air in Ohio that went as follows:

> Last year, John McCain voted against solar and renewable energy. That means more use of coal-burning plants that pollute our air. Ohio Republicans care about clean air. So does Governor Bush. He led one of the first states in America to clamp down on old coal-burning electric power plants. Bush's clean air laws will reduce air pollution more than a quarter million tons a year. That's like taking 5 million cars off the road. Governor Bush, leading, for each day dawns brighter. (Perez-Pena 2000)

The ad was run by a group called "Republicans for Clean Air" and ran ahead of the Ohio primary. It is clearly pro-Bush and anti-McCain, but also it did not use any of the "magic words" established by the *Buckley v. Valeo* decision and therefore was exempt from all reporting and disclosure requirements. It was seen by the FEC as an issue-advocacy ad and not expressly advocating the election of George. W. Bush. Reporters were later able to track down the source of the funds as a billionaire pair of brothers—Charles and Sam Wyly—who wanted to support the election of their long-time friend. None of this was officially disclosed because this speech, while clearly aimed at influencing primary voters in Ohio, did not run afoul of the "magic words." But this is a reality that the court in *Buckley* seemed to see coming. In their decision they noted, "[T]he distinction between discussion of issues and candidates and advocacy of election or defeat of candidates may often dissolve in practical application. Candidates, especially incumbents, are intimately tied to public issues involving legislative proposals and governmental actions. Not only do candidates campaign on the basis of their positions on various public issues, but campaigns themselves generate issues of public interest . . ." and yet the Court said this was not reason enough to allow the limits to be imposed.

In addition to helping existing groups who hoped to influence voter views of certain issues and government policies, the *Buckley* decision gave rise to many new groups organized specifically around campaigns who could solicit donations and run ads like Republicans for Clean Air did in 2000. These new organizations, so-called independent expenditure groups, often provided thinly veiled ads supporting the good work of a candidate that would encourage voters not to cast their ballot for politician A or B, but rather to call and thank them for their work. Or if the ad aimed to undercut support, would urge viewers to call and demand the targeted politician address the issue in the ad more directly. At least one study that examined how effective these ads might be in influencing voters' views of the candidates found that those who were committed to one candidate or another changed little when exposed to issue-advocacy ads in favor or opposition to their candidate. But the same study found, "Issue-advocacy ads enhanced overall attitudes toward those candidates implicitly supported in the advertisements, and they elicited more positive perceptions of these candidates' competence and character . . . If the purpose of soft-money-sponsored issue-advocacy ads is to affect the candidate preferences of potential voters, the results of this study confirm that they are successful with precisely those prospective voters who are in position to tip the balance in close elections, that is, the unaffiliated" (Pfau, Holbert, Szabo, and Kaminski 2006). Put more simply, those groups that use issue-advocacy ads to attack or support a candidate can rest assured that voters—especially those on the fence in the election—get the message.

These independent groups took on more importance as a series of federal court decisions came down in the early 2000s. Taken together, these rulings, which included the controversial *Citizens United* decision, created two new forms of political organizations that could operate independently of the campaigns. One group, usually called Super PACs, could raise and spend unlimited amounts of cash to expressly advocate for the election of a candidate. These groups could pour money into campaign ads that used the so-called magic words of *Buckley* and could raise and spend as much money as they wanted. The two rules were, though, they would have to disclose that money and spending on a quarterly or monthly basis, and they could not coordinate in any official way with the campaign they sought to help. This increased the flow of money to these groups, but still required public disclosure of where they got their money. The other group to develop more fully in the wake of *Citizens United* and other related rulings were so-called dark money groups. These organizations were supposed to operate as "social welfare" groups that would help society, but could also participate in the political process through issue-advocacy advertising. These groups, like the Super PACs, could raise unlimited amounts of money from corporate, union, and individual donors, but had a couple of key benefits that Super PACs lacked. First, the donations were anonymous, and second these groups were not required to file paperwork with the Federal Election Commission.

"Dark money" groups quickly began testing the limits of how overtly political they can be. For example in early October 2015, the Associated Press reported that one of these issue-advocacy groups had spent millions of dollars in support of Republican presidential candidate Marco Rubio. The reporter found that "every pro-Rubio television commercial so far in the early primary states of Iowa, New Hampshire and South Carolina has been paid for not by his campaign or even by a super PAC that identifies its donors, but instead by a nonprofit called Conservative Solutions Project. It's also sending Rubio-boosting mail to voters in those same states. Rubio is legally prohibited from directing the group's spending, and he has said he has nothing to do with it. But there's little doubt that Conservative Solutions Project is picking up the tab for critical expenses that the campaign itself might struggle to afford" (Bykowicz 2015).

Still, many groups argue that to try and regulate issue-advocacy ads will inherently violate cherished constitutional principles and core ideas around the First Amendment protection of freedom of speech. The libertarian Cato Institute had law professor Bradley Smith testify at one hearing in the 1990s that "what the regulators seem to have lost sight of is the fact that politics is about the discussion of issues, and candidates' positions on issues. It is the heart of the First Amendment for individuals and groups to discuss issues and criticize officials. It is all but impossible to talk politics for long in this country without mentioning the individuals holding or seeking office" (Smith 1997). This is part of the core debate still being had in terms of issue-advocacy advertising. Can a group effectively communicate about political issues without bringing up the elected officials that have implemented or are blocking a given policy? And if that kind of communication deserves the highest level of legal protection, how can the government ensure that these groups are not unduly influencing the candidate and his or her policies? This is core concern of many good government advocates, who see unlimited donations pouring into groups airing issue-advocacy ads as potentially "buying" the loyalty of an elected official, the key corrupting influence almost all forms of campaign regulations have sought to combat.

In this post-*Buckley* and post-*Citizens United* era, the legal answer to this question hinges on the independence of the issue-advocacy groups. Former FEC commissioner Trevor Potter explained in 2012, "If it's totally independent spending, then [the court says] it cannot corrupt . . . [T]he court's theory was that there is no guarantee for the candidate that the independent spending will be helpful. Instead, it may be badly done, sloppily done, emphasize issues the candidate doesn't want to emphasize, and so the candidate may not be grateful for the spending" (Frontline 2012). So long as the candidate could not control the ad spending, the theory goes, he or she may actually be harmed by independent money aimed at supporting their candidacy.

The concern of Potter and others is that these groups may not be nearly as independent as they would seem. For example, during the 2016 Republican primaries, the *New York Times* documented how campaigns like those of former Hewlett-Packard CEO Carly Fiorina communicated with technically independent Super PACs to coordinate the Super PACs' help in running events and even building ads. How can they do that? The answer in the 2016 campaign is they do it by simply doing it in public. Fiorina's campaign would make her schedule publicly available to everyone and if the Super PAC happened to see an event coming up in Iowa, they—along with anyone else—could show up. As campaign finance lawyer Kenneth Gross told the *Times*, "Essentially, it inoculates a case of coordination by making it public. As long as it's not hidden in a 'Where's Waldo' game and meets a reasonable definition of being public, it is a way to avoid running afoul of the coordination rules" (Corasaniti 2015). Although the Fiorina-affiliated Super PAC was required to disclose its spending and donations because of their express advocacy work in support of the candidate, similar unofficial coordination can take place between the campaign and independent groups seeking to support them by doing it publicly as well. This means groups seeking to do issue-advocacy work in support of a candidate can access information about their schedule and even ad purchases so long as that information is open to everyone, and then use it to plan independent ad buys and events.

At the epicenter of this debate over whether these issue-advocacy groups should be made more accountable for their political activities is the Federal Election Commission. The FEC has published guides for groups on how not to run afoul of the express advocacy rules that would trigger disclosure and reporting to the FEC. But the larger question is whether an organization established to spend the overwhelming majority of its time and resources on issue-advocacy aimed at influencing the voting public's perception of candidates is working on a "social good." Two Democratic members of the six-person commission have pushed for changes, saying that recent court decisions actually should encourage the FEC to take a harder look at the rules they have. Two of the commissioners petitioned their own agency to start a rulemaking process, writing, "The Commission has not yet fulfilled its obligation to address the fact that *Citizens United* was premised on adequate disclosure of these new sources of outside spending. Anonymous campaign spending will continue to diminish public faith in the political process, unless the Commission acts" (Ravel and Weintraub 2015). But the commission, deadlocked between three Democrats and three Republicans, has taken no action on the issue since the wave of decisions that began in 2010.

The Internal Revenue Service, tasked with monitoring the actions of nonprofits that air these ads, also says it is unequipped to establish and enforce policies that would police independent issue-advocacy advertising by political nonprofits. An investigation by the nonprofit ProPublica reported that dozens of the groups airing political ads do little or no other work and "also found that social welfare groups used a range of tactics to underreport their political activities to the IRS. . . . Some classified expenditures that clearly praised or criticized candidates for office as 'lobbying,' 'education' or 'issue advocacy' on their tax returns" (Barker 2012). With the court speaking clearly that limits on issue-advocacy advertising will have to stand up to the strictest legal scrutiny, with Congress taking no real action on the issue, and with federal enforcement agencies in disarray over how to handle such groups, issue-advocacy advertising is expected to expand as individuals and groups aiming to influence elections take advantage of the opportunity the law has afforded them.

See also: *Citizens United;* Dark Money Groups; Disclosure; Federal Election Commission (FEC); Negative Advertising; Super PACs

Further Reading

Barker, Kim. 2012. "How Nonprofits Spend Millions on Elections and Call it Public Welfare." ProPublica. August 18. Accessed October 8, 2015. http://www.propublica.org/article/how-nonprofits-spend-millions-on-elections-and-call-it-public-welfare.

Bykowicz, Julie. 2015. "Rubio's presidential bid boosted by secret-money commercials." Associated Press. October 8. Accessed October 9, 2015. http://bigstory.ap.org/article/5926406673b047a7a34f1177e01014da/anonymous-donors-send-millions-pro-rubio-group.

Corasaniti, Nick. 2015. "Carly Fiorina's 'Super PAC' Aids Her Campaign, in Plain Sight." *New York Times.* September 30. Accessed October 9, 2015. http://www.nytimes.com/2015/10/01/us/politics/as-carly-fiorina-surges-so-does-the-work-of-her-super-pac.html?smid=tw-nytimes&smtyp=cur&_r=1.

Perez-Pena, Richard. 2000. "Air of Mystery Clouds Pitch." *New York Times.* March 3. Accessed October 12, 2016. https://partners.nytimes.com/library/politics/camp/030300wh-gop-ad.html.

Pfau, Michael, Lance Holbert, Erin Szabo, and Kelly Kaminski. 2006. "Issue-Advocacy Versus Candidate Advertising: Effects on Candidate Preferences and Democratic Process." *Journal of Communication* 52, Issue 2 (June): 301–15.

Potter, Trevor. 2012. "Trevor Potter: The Political Reality of *Citizens United.*" Frontline (PBS). October 30. Accessed October 9, 2015. www.pbs.org/wgbh/pages/frontline/government-elections-politics/big-sky-big-money/trevor-potter-the-political-reality-of-citizens-united.

Ravel, Ann, and Ellen Weintraub. 2015. "Petition for Rulemaking." Federal Election Commission. June 8. Accessed June 13, 2016. http://www.fec.gov/members/statements/Petition_for_Rulemaking.pdf.

Smith, Bradley. 1997. "The First Amendment and Restrictions on Issue Advocacy." Cato Institute. September 18. Accessed June 14, 2016. http://www.cato.org/publications/congressional-testimony/first-amendment-restrictions-issue-advocacy.

J

JAMIESON, KATHLEEN HALL (1946–)

Cover political speeches or advertising long enough and there is no avoiding Kathleen Hall Jamieson. Jamieson, director of the Annenberg Public Policy Center at the University of Pennsylvania, has spent her career studying the way politicians use words and how audiences respond. Although the bulk of her professional work focuses on communications strategies and techniques, she has also been a regular television and radio guest, particularly on public broadcasting, and has often argued for a more civil approach to politics.

Jamieson came out of the Midwest, having been born in Minneapolis and earning her BA in Rhetoric and Public Address from Marquette University in 1967. She then went on to the University of Wisconsin where she earned an MA and PhD in Communication Arts. Her work has always focused on the interplay between policy and rhetoric, although her topics have stretched from criminal justice to women and leadership to her vast scholarship in politics and campaigns. She has published some 16 books on the topic of communications and politics generally, but she chose to step beyond academic publications locked away in dusty professional journals. If she was going to examine the way in which politics is talked about and communicated, she herself had to enter the arena. Through her work at the Annenberg Center, that effort has taken on two major forms. First, she helped spur the creation of FactCheck.org and the larger fact-checking movement among journalists and second, she is often a source for journalists looking for an unbiased expert to explore how campaigns are operating and what a specific ad is saying and not saying.

Jamieson was essential in creating the concepts and even vocabulary of the idea of fact-checking campaigns. As ad spending exploded and campaigns became increasingly sophisticated in how they used tools to communicate with potential supporters, Jamieson helped apply an academically thorough way of thinking about how to hold those communications up to some consistent form of scrutiny. Jamieson worked with CNN in 1988 to design what ad watches would look like and how they ought to be structured. That work resulted in a series of ad watches reported by CNN reporter Brooks Jackson that examined the claims in the presidential campaign ads. This form of ad watch was soon replicated on national and local television, serving as the model of the modern fact check. Jamieson would team up with Jackson to create FactCheck.org ahead of the 2004 campaign. A fellow scholar would observe that the effort to fact check ads and campaign claims has been fundamentally improved through Jamieson's work, writing, "If democracy is to function effectively given the cacophony of campaign messages to which we are all exposed, the role of those who seek to separate truth from falsehood is more important than ever . . . Hopefully, the work of Kathleen Hall Jamieson will resonate for years to come as voters, journalists, and fact checkers use the tools she helped create to better inform the electorate and improve our democracy" (Brydon 2012).

Although the growth of fact checking is one the hallmarks of Jamieson's work, her most lasting impact may be her ability to swiftly and clearly explain theoretical and academic concepts to a non-academic audience. Often academics are criticized for dealing in minutia and only being interested in the feedback of fellow academics, but that could never be said of Jamieson. A quick Google News search and hundreds of articles will typically appear during a campaign cycle. Jamieson is a much-sought source for political reporters examining communications strategies; PBS's Bill Moyers and the *PBS NewsHour* have interviewed Jamieson scores of times. In considering her career a fellow scholar of rhetoric marveled at the way Jamieson can speak to a general audience without dumbing the concepts down or making them too opaque to understand. Said Penn State's Jane Sutton, "She talks about rhetoric without using the word rhetoric . . . [Her] appearances on PBS coupled with her blogs offer to the public as well as to the student some good insight into the role rhetoric plays in understanding political debates and deciphering political advertisements and campaigns. Through these lessons, Jamieson, in effect, continues to keep rhetoric right in the middle of democracy" (Sutton 2012).

Part of her work has come to include some advocacy. Jamieson is part of the Research Network for the National Institute for Civil Discourse that argues for politicians and the media to foster "an open exchange of ideas and expression of values that will lead to better problem-solving and more effective government" (National Institute for Civil Discourse n.d.). In this work, as in her service as a source and an adviser to FactCheck.org, Jamieson is one of the few academics who study politics who actively seek to inform the national conversation and ideally improve the communications about politics.

See also: Fact Checking; FactCheck.org; Television Advertising

Further Reading

Brydon, Steven. 2012. "Kathleen Hall Jamieson on Political Advertising: Unspinning the Spin Doctors." Pennsylvania Scholars Series. Accessed January 5, 2016. http://esuscholar .com/wp-content/uploads/2015/08/PSS-KHJ-2012.pdf.

"Mission." National Institute for Civil Discourse. Accessed January 4, 2016. http://nicd .arizona.edu/mission.

Sutton, Jane. 2012. "Teaching Rhetoric in the Commonwealth via the Bill Moyers Journal: Kathleen Hall Jamieson." Pennsylvania Scholars Series. Accessed January 5, 2016. http://esuscholar.com/wp-content/uploads/2015/08/PSS-KHJ-2012.pdf.

KOCH BROTHERS: KOCH, CHARLES (1935–) AND KOCH, DAVID (1940–)

As the money and thinking behind some of the most influential and secretive political organizations on the modern political right, Charles Koch and his brother David have become almost mythic figures. The Kochs are members of the family that runs Koch Industries, one of the world's largest and most influential privately held corporations. In particular, Charles has used his charitable foundations to support libertarian causes and has played an active role in fomenting the tea party movement and several other conservative causes. But their array of ambiguously named foundations and nonprofits have turned the reclusive brothers into the twin brains of an impressively funded political web of companies that have been dubbed a "Kochtopus."

It is almost impossible to overstate the influence the two brothers hold over the modern American political world. With this authority and sway has come a less-than-glamorous reputation. As one academic who has studied the tea party movement put it, "The two have been portrayed as a cross between a summer blockbuster supervillain and Uncle Pennybags, the mustachioed antihero of the Monopoly board game . . . The complexity of the brothers' relationship to the Tea Party derives from many of the same ambiguities that define American politics in the 21st century. Paths of influence are obscured behind organizations with ambiguous names and few obligations to explain who funds operations" (Brown 2015).

Charles and David are two of the four sons that came into the world in Wichita, Kansas, as the children of Fred and Mary Koch. Fred Koch's empire started out in 1940 as the Wood River Oil and Refining Company and later grew into Koch Industries. The company owns major oil refining and distribution firms, fertilizer companies, and paper mills and cattle ranches. Still based in Kansas, the company employs some 100,000 people in its different divisions and earns $115 billion a year, as of 2013 numbers. In addition to making all four brothers rich, the company also served as the battleground that would permanently push them apart. In 1980, David's twin brother Bill and the eldest son Frederick led an attempted coup against Charles and David. The result tore the family apart and left David deeply affected according to a lengthy *New Yorker* profile published in 2010. That story recounted, "As David told me about his decades of estrangement with his brother William, he began to cry. By 1980, the tension that had been brewing between Charles and William since childhood became strained to the point that William, Frederick, and a group of like-minded shareholders attempted to wrest control of Koch Industries from Charles" (Goldman 2010). Legal battles would drag on until a final settlement in 2001.

Most profiles and reporting indicate that it was Charles more than David who began using his financial powers to push for political change in the country. Charles went more public in 2015 in part to promote a book he had written, but also to counter a book in the works by *New Yorker* writer Jane Mayer. He said he remained out of politics for more than 40 years although interested in the state of public affairs. According to his account it was in 2003 that he became alarmed by the expansion of government under Republican president George W. Bush. Koch has publicly blamed government policies under Bush for artificially inflating the values of homes and triggering the 2008 and 2009 housing crisis and accompanying economic slowdown. He said it was his opposition to those policies that pushed him from being an observer of politics to an active participant. That said, the Kochs had helped start the Citizens for a Sound Economy in the 1980s, a group that operated like a traditional think tank. Charles had also supported the work of traditional conservative think tanks like the Cato Institute and the Heritage Foundation. Around the time he describes, CSE split into two groups—Americans for Prosperity and FreedomWorks. FreedomWorks helped organize and sponsor the early protests of the tea party movement, and the nonprofit Americans for Prosperity has become the Koch brothers' primary political advocacy arm.

The Koch brothers have sought to distance themselves from their political work. For example, they state they have never gone to nor supported the tea party, and yet FreedomWorks has. But in her book about Charles Koch, Mayer makes the argument that he has spent some four decades working to influence the political process, usually doing so through third party organizations with little transparency about where they receive their funds. Mayer bases her argument on a 300-page unpublished history of the Koch brothers commissioned by their estranged brother, Bill, as well as an enormous amount of original research to claim that, "For his new movement, which aimed to empower ultraconservatives like himself and radically change the way the U.S. government worked, he analyzed and then copied what he saw as the strengths of the John Birch Society, the extreme, right-wing anti-communist group to which he, his brother David and their father, Fred Koch, had belonged. Charles Koch might claim that his entry into politics is new, but from its secrecy to its methods of courting donors and recruiting students, the blueprint for the vast and powerful Koch donor network that we see today was drafted four decades ago" (Mayer 2016).

According to Mayer and others, Charles Koch has a particular vision of politics that adheres to the libertarian view that government be strictly limited. This includes sacrificing many of the issues that are dear to elements of the Republican Party, including less interference in issues like gay marriage and abortion. Also, their organizations have pushed hard for the leaders of the Republican Party to be less willing to compromise on critical issues and debates. Programs like the Farm Bill and the federal highway bill that represent politically important funding for Republicans from rural and sparsely populated regions became sources of internal Republican battles as tea party and other politicians backed by Americans for Prosperity battled their own leadership. One analysis of the behavior of Koch-aligned politicians found that "much evidence shows that the Koch network is now sufficiently ramified and powerful to sustain battles even with other powerful coalitions backed by corporate and wealthy interests. Intra-GOP elite civil wars . . . are clear indicators of the independent clout of the Koch network on the ultra right—and thus give credence to our overall argument in this paper, that the Koch network is an independent and important driver of the rightward march of today's Republicans" (Skocpol and Hertel-Fernandez 2016).

Although they rarely acknowledge their role in politics, the Koch brothers have used the array of campaign finance rules to build a potent political organization that can affect Republican Party politics, influence the public debate, and affect modern campaigning while doing so usually outside of public view. This nearly guarantees that the two brothers will remain controversial and important figures in the current American political landscape.

See also: Campaign Finance Reform; Tea Party Movement

Further Reading

Brown, Heath. 2015. *The Tea Party Divided: The Hidden Diversity of a Maturing Movement.* Santa Barbara, CA: ABC-CLIO, LLC.

Goldman, Andrew. 2010. "The Billionaire's Party." *New Yorker.* July 25. Accessed January 20, 2016. http://nymag.com/news/features/67285.

Mayer, Jane. 2016. "The Secrets of Charles Koch's Political Ascent." Politico. January 18. Accessed January 19, 2016. http://www.politico.com/magazine/story/2016/01/charles-koch-political-ascent-jane-mayer-213541.

Skocpol, Theda, and Alexander Hertel-Fernandez. 2016. "The Koch Effect: The Impact of a Cadre-Led Network on American Politics." Southern Political Science Association. January 8. Accessed January 19, 2016. http://www.scholarsstrategynetwork.org/sites/default/files/the_koch_effect_for_spsa_w_apps_skocpol_and_hertel-fernandez-corrected_1-4-16_1.pdf.

KRAUTHAMMER, CHARLES (1950–)

It may be unexpected that a medically trained psychiatrist and former speechwriter for liberal vice president Walter Mondale would emerge as one of the most thoughtful and respected conservative commentators in America, but little about Charles Krauthammer could be predicted.

Krauthammer grew up in an Orthodox Jewish household in Montreal and he said his "vigorous Jewish education" helped shape his worldview, telling the *Jewish Press* that "anybody growing up in a Jewish environment dominated by Jewish culture, religion, and history as I did is immediately endowed with a tragic sense of history. You tend to veer away from utopianism. You tend to be more suspicious of people who come around promising all kinds of wonderful things. You're closer to the founders' vision of human nature as flawed and fallen" (Lehmann 2014). But despite this focus on history and his clear interest in public affairs, he never planned on pursuing a career in politics, instead entering medical school in Harvard following his graduation from Montreal's McGill University. During his first year of medical school he was paralyzed in a diving board accident, but Krauthammer continued his studies and graduated with the rest of his class.

By 1978, he was headed to D.C. but not for politics, rather to direct planning in psychiatric research. But soon he started contributing columns to the liberal magazine *New Republic*. His style impressed many and by 1980 he was a speechwriter for Mondale. Soon he was writing for *Time* magazine and as he worked he wrote with increasing strength about the new policies of the Reagan administration, embracing the anti-Communist policies of the former California governor and coining the term "the Reagan Doctrine" to describe the policy. By 1984, Krauthammer was writing his column for the *Washington Post* and three years later earned a Pulitzer Prize for "his witty and insightful columns on national issues." Krauthammer focused on foreign policy, advocating for an active and even aggressive American approach to the world. He described the post–Cold War world as "unipolar" where the United States was the only superpower, and later outlined his vision for a post-9/11 America in a highly influential speech at the American Enterprise Institute. In that address, called "Democratic Realism," Krauthammer argued for a worldwide fight against radical Islamists, saying, "In October 1962, during the Cuban Missile Crisis, we came to the edge of the abyss. Then, accompanied by our equally shaken adversary, we both deliberately drew back. On September 11, 2001, we saw the face of Armageddon again, but this time with an enemy that does not draw back. This time the enemy knows no reason. Were that the only difference between now and then, our situation would be hopeless. But there is a second difference between now and then: the uniqueness of our power, unrivaled, not just today but ever. That evens the odds" (Krauthammer 2004). His consistent support for intervention in the Middle East has at times been deeply unpopular with the American public and even with some within the Republican ranks, but the strength of his intellect has helped him weather those periods.

Although he has built a reputation around his thorough and often neoconservative assessment of the diplomatic world, Krauthammer does not shy away from taking on domestic American politics. He has been one of the sharpest critics of President Barack Obama, accusing his 2008 campaign of being "cult-like" and his policy proposals as "radical health care, energy and education reforms," central to a "social democratic agenda." But he has also expressed admiration at the political successes of Obama and the failure of Republicans to respond. Politico's Ben Smith would say that "Krauthammer has emerged in the Age of Obama as a central conservative voice, the kind of leader of the opposition that economist and *New York Times* columnist Paul Krugman represented for the left during the Bush years: a coherent, sophisticated and implacable critic of the new president" (Smith 2009).

Krauthammer claims to have little trouble finding fuel for his commentaries, saying, "Someone, somewhere will do something very stupid or very outrageous or very noteworthy. When you first start writing a column, you're afraid you won't have anything to write about, but the world turns out to be too interesting. The Lord does provide" (Bard 1996). Those columns have become must-reads for conservatives in D.C., as has his work as a contributing editor to the conservative *Weekly Standard*. But his influence does not end at the page. For decades Krauthammer has been a regular guest on many political talk shows, from PBS to the cable networks. He is a nightly panelist on Fox News's *Special Report with Bret Baier*.

See also: *Washington Post; The Weekly Standard*

Further Reading
Bard, Mitchell. 1996. "Charles Krauthammer: Prize Writer." Accessed November 6, 2015. http://www.mitchellbard.com/articles/kraut.html.
Krauthammer, Charles. 2004. "Democratic Realism." American Enterprise Institute. February 10. Accessed November 6, 2015. https://www.aei.org/publication/democratic-realism.
Lehmann, Sarah. 2014. "Charles Krauthammer: 'America Always Comes Back.'" The Jewish Press. September 10. Accessed November 6, 2015. http://www.jewishpress.com/indepth/front-page/charles-krauthammer-america-always-comes-back/2014/09/10/3.
Smith, Ben. 2009. "Obama's Biggest Critic: Krauthammer." Politico. May 20. Accessed November 6, 2015. http://www.politico.com/story/2009/05/obamas-biggest-critic-krauthammer-022743#ixzz3p7wpQFC7.

L

LEADERSHIP PACs

Leadership PACs emerged in the 1980s as a way for congressional leaders (or those hoping to be leaders) to support candidates and party efforts while also building their own network of political allies. The funds themselves are considered "nonconnected" political action committees by the Federal Election Commission. This means they can solicit money from the general public as well as businesses and other organizations. These PACs can also make donations to other PACs and to specific campaigns. Individuals can donate to these funds at the rate of $5,000 a year—compared with $2,000 per election to a specific candidate.

These funds emerged out of reforms that aimed to limit potential corruption through campaign finance reform, and a separate set of internal reforms that aimed to create a more democratic structure to party leadership in Congress by limiting the power of leaders to appoint members to certain committees and encouraging rank-and-file members to have more of a say in the party leadership. This internal reform meant that seniority no longer would equal prime positions, and soon members were jockeying for position and building alliances with other members. PACs emerged in this environment because "one way for leaders to strengthen cohesion was to assist members with their reelection efforts. By helping their colleagues raise campaign money, leaders expected that, in return, members would toe the party line. To the extent that leaders could effectively demonstrate their ability to provide assistance, they could exercise a certain amount of influence over those members who needed help" (Currinder 2003).

These PACs could funnel up to $10,000 per election cycle to other candidates and emerged as effective tools for party leaders to help embattled incumbents or those running in open seats. The numbers grew quickly to be impressive. The *New York Times* reported in 1997 about then-Senate majority leader Trent Lott's leadership PAC that in 1996 took in $1.7 million from corporate lobbyists and handed out $1.3 million to fellow Republicans. It's a fair amount of cash to receive when Lott himself was not up for reelection until 2000. One candidate who received the maximum amount was an unsuccessful Republican in New Jersey named Dick Zimmer. Zimmer's campaign chairman explained the potential impact of Lott's donation, saying, "'It serves the purpose of building support in the Senate for the majority leader. It's a pretty effective tool. Mr. Zimmer appreciated it and, if elected, he would have remembered it" (Wayne 1997).

For those politicians with an eye toward the ultimate prize—the White House— leadership PACs also emerged as an effective way to jump-start the process, allowing them to hire some staff, conduct polling, and curry favor with other politicians in states critical for the upcoming campaign. They also give "a candidate a head start on building a direct mail program and a donor network. After a few years of fundraising a leadership PAC will have developed a list of proven contributors" (Baumgartner 2000, p. 92).

Despite their obvious political purposes, leadership PACs have drawn little attention from the media, but did suddenly pop onto the public's radar in 2013 when news emerged that leadership PACs had become a source for more than just political power. Since their inception, these PACs have evolved into what critics and former Federal Election Commissioners see as pots of money members of Congress can use for everything from personal travel to jobs for spouses and friends. "Since they weren't around when the ban on personal use was put into place, they're not covered by it and they can be used for literally anything," Trevor Potter told *60 Minutes* in 2013. "It's a political slush fund. Over time, we've had them. They've been outlawed. They spring back in new guises, and this is the latest guise" (Kroft 2013).

The *60 Minutes* report relied heavily on the work of a conservative activist who had spent years researching how members used to enrich themselves and enjoy lucrative perks that earlier reforms had sought to ban, like lavish trips to play golf and dinners that ran into the tens of thousands of dollars. Peter Schweizer, a fellow at the Hoover Institution and an editor-at-large at Breitbart, documented excessive spending from these committees that included Senator Saxby Chambliss, Republican of Georgia, spending $107,752 at the Breakers resort in Palm Beach, Florida, or U.S. Representative Charles Rangel using $64,500 of his PAC money to purchase a painting of himself (Schweizer 2013).

A more social science approach (and description) of this phenomenon showed up in an analysis of the donation patterns of leadership PACs. "The data . . . show that core leaders tend to adhere to party driven contribution strategies, whereas extended leaders tend to emphasize their own individual goals over party goals" (Currinder 2003). Some, including Republican senator Rob Portman, have called for new reforms of leadership PACs. Portman, in the wake of the book and *60 Minutes* report, said, "Clearly they ought be used for one purpose, and one purpose only, and that's to help elect people who you believe are the right folks . . . You can't use campaign funds for personal purposes. The same should apply to the leadership PACs" (Heath 2013).

Despite these concerns, Congress has made no move to modify the rules surrounding leadership PACs, and during the 2014 cycle alone leadership PACs raked in a record $55 million, according to the Center for Responsible Politics (OpenSecrets 2015).

See also: Campaign Finance Reform; Political Action Committees (PACs)

Further Reading

Baumgartner, Jody. 2000. *Modern Presidential Electioneering: An Organizational and Comparative Approach.* Westport, CT: Greenwood Publishing Group.

Currinder, Marian. 2003. "Leadership PAC Contribution Strategies and House Member Ambitions." *Legislative Studies Quarterly* 28, no. 4. http://www.jstor.org/stable/3598604.

Heath, Jim. 2013. "Portman Wants Reform for Legal Campaign Slush Funds." WBNS-10TV. October 23. Accessed on December 31, 2014. http://www.10tv.com/content/stories/2013/10/23/columbus-rob-portman-talks-pacs-reform.html.

Kroft, Steve. 2013. "Washington's Open Secret: Profitable PACs." CBS News. Aired October 21. Accessed December 31, 2014. http://www.cbsnews.com/news/washingtons-open-secret-profitable-pacs.

Opensecrets.org. 2015. "Leadership PACs." Accessed on December 31, 2014. http://www.opensecrets.org/industries/totals.php?cycle=2014&ind=Q03.

Schweizer, Peter. 2013. *Extortion: How Politicians Extract Your Money, Buy Votes and Line Their Own Pockets*. New York: Houghton Mifflin Harcourt.

Wayne, Leslie. 1997. "Congress Uses Leadership PAC's to Wield Power." *New York Times*. March 13. Accessed December 31, 2014. http://www.nytimes.com/1997/03/13/us/congress-uses-leadership-pac-s-to-wield-power.html.

LEHRER, JIM (1934–)

Known for his even-keel demeanor and seriousness, Jim Lehrer will probably always be synonymous with the presidential debates. The former host of the nightly news program *PBS NewsHour*, Lehrer has participated in more debates than any other journalist, moderating 12 of the meetings over the last 30 years.

So it is perhaps not surprising that the man who CNN's Bernard Shaw called the "Dean of Moderators," has some very clear ideas about what the job of a good moderator is:

> A moderator is there to help the people understand what the candidates believe and why they believe it. It isn't there to show how cute and clever a moderator can be and embarrass somebody. That is not the job of a moderator. Anybody who thinks it is his or her job should stand aside or be pushed aside.
>
> When a debate is over and the people are talking about the moderator, even if it is good things they are saying about the moderator, the moderator has failed. (Banville 2012)

Being the center of the American political universe some dozen times is a long way from Lehrer's humble beginnings in Kansas and Texas. The son of a bank clerk and a bus station manager, Lehrer's first job was calling the bus line destinations so people knew which bus to get on—a feat he would do from memory later in many interviews and public appearances. After graduating high school in Texas, he earned an Associate's degree from Victoria College in southeast Texas and then a B.J. from the University of Missouri School of Journalism. Lehrer entered the U.S. Marines after Missouri, later saying that he had come "from a family of Marines into the family of Marines." Lehrer would speak decades later at the dedication of Marine Corps museum in Quantico, Virginia. Lehrer told the assembled audience, "My Marine experience helped shape who I am now personally and professionally, and I am grateful for that on an almost daily basis. And I often find myself wishing everyone had a similar opportunity, to learn about shared dependence, loyalty, responsibility to and for others, about mutual respect and honor, and about the power of appealing to the best that's in us as human beings, not the worst" (Lehrer 2006).

After leaving the Marines, Lehrer returned to Texas, taking a job as a reporter at the *Dallas Morning News* and later the *Dallas Times-Herald*. Its during that time that Lehrer reported on President John F. Kennedy's fateful trip to Texas, producing a report on the president's security detail that included a map of the route the president would travel. The story would later be found in the possessions of Kennedy assassin Lee Harvey Oswald. Lehrer covered the assassination and the ensuing chaos, remembering years later how the police brought Oswald out "so people could see they weren't beating him up. He had some scars from when they arrested him. They wanted to show there were no new scars . . . I stood next to Jack Ruby. I didn't even know who he was" (Clift 2013).

Lehrer would go on to work as a political columnist and city editor before that job landed him at the Dallas PBS station as executive director of public affairs, on-air host, and editor of a nightly news program. Public broadcasting was just growing at this point and so Lehrer was soon headed to D.C. to help create the news efforts at the network, working as a correspondent for the new National Public Affairs Center for Television (NPACT). NPACT produced live coverage of the Watergate hearings in 1973, and that was when Lehrer was partnered with Robert MacNeil to anchor the hearings. When PBS launched a 30-minute nightly news program with MacNeil, it was not long before Lehrer joined as the Washington, D.C., co-anchor and the *MacNeil/Lehrer Report* was born.

The program would become an hour in 1983, becoming the *MacNeil/Lehrer NewsHour*. The program was a staple of Washington reporting, offering in-depth interviews and lengthy discussions on policy at a time when broadcast news reporting was becoming more driven by short sound bites. Lehrer became a strong advocate for reporting that kept the reporter out of the spotlight and allowed the guests to answer the questions and engage with one another. The program was decidedly civil and, it was said, "dared to be boring." The MacNeil/Lehrer brand of reporting carried several edicts, which included, "Do nothing I cannot defend" and "Cover, write, and present every story with the care I would want if the story were about me." It is perhaps not surprising then, that the Commission on Presidential Debates would see the veteran television journalist as an ideal candidate to moderate one of the 1988 debates between George H. W. Bush and Michael Dukakis. In 1992, he moderated two presidential debates; in 1996, he was selected to be the sole moderator of all three debates. In 2000, in an unprecedented show of respect and confidence, he was again selected as the sole moderator of the three presidential debates, which were conducted in different formats—podium, round-table, and town hall. In 2004, he was selected to be moderator of the first presidential debate in Coral Gables, Florida. In 2008, he was selected to be moderator of the first presidential debate in Oxford, Mississippi. At the end of that contest he announced he was done moderating the high-stress, high-stakes contests. Still, in 2012, after the commission was able to get the campaigns to agree to a less rigid event where the candidates would have more back-and-forth, he came back for one more.

That contest, the first presidential debate of 2012, turned out to be a controversial affair. With its more lax rules, Lehrer was less the timekeeper and more the middleman between two candidates. President Barack Obama came out slow in that first debate, appearing more professorial and detached than the more aggressive Mitt Romney. Some, especially Democrats, groused that Lehrer did not do more to rein in Romney. In the wake of the debate, Brian Stelter reported in the *New York Times*, "The liberal media monitoring group Media Matters said Mr. Lehrer had 'lost the debate' by missing 'repeated opportunities to press Mitt Romney into offering specifics on his policy proposals.' Richard Kim, a writer for *The Nation*, concluded that Mr. Lehrer's version of moderation 'is fundamentally unequipped to deal with the era of post-truth, asymmetric polarization politics—and it should be retired'" (Stelter 2012). Still, the idea that debates ought to have a more open format remained the goal Lehrer sought to enforce, saying in a statement after that first debate, "Part of my moderator mission was to stay out of the way of the flow, and I had no problems with doing so. My only real personal frustration was discovering that 90 minutes was not enough time in that more open format to cover every issue that deserved attention."

Lehrer retired from the anchor desk in June 2011 and has focused on his writing, having already penned some 20 books and novels, including *Tension City*, a compelling account of the modern political debate told by the moderators and politicians.

See also: Government-Subsidized Journalism; *PBS NewsHour*; Presidential Debates

Further Reading

Banville, Lee. 2012. *Debating Our Destiny: Presidential Debate Moments That Shaped History*. Arlington, VA: MacNeil/Lehrer Productions.

Clift, Eleanor. 2013. "Reporting the JFK Assassination: 'No Miranda Rule, No PR People." The Daily Beast. November 7. Accessed January 15, 2016. http://www.thedailybeast .com/articles/2013/11/07/reporting-the-jfk-assassination-no-miranda-rule-no-pr -people.html.

Lehrer, Jim. 2006. "Jim Lehrer Reflects on Marines at Museum Dedication." PBS NewsHour. November 10. Accessed January 15, 2016. http://www.pbs.org/newshour/bb/military -july-dec06-marines_11-10.

Lehrer, Jim. 2011. *Tension City: Inside the Presidential Debates, from Kennedy-Nixon to Obama-McCain*. New York: Random House.

Stelter, Brian. 2012. "After a New-Look Debate, a Harsh Light Falls on the Moderator." *New York Times*. October 6. Accessed January 15, 2016. www.nytimes.com/2012/10/05/us /politics/after-debate-a-harsh-light-falls-on-jim-lehrer.html.

LIBERAL BLOGOSPHERE

The liberal blogosphere is hardly a united entity but is populated by hundreds of bloggers who to some degree endorse the politics of the Democratic Party or espouse support for progressive ideas. These blogs are not uniform in their politics or their goals. Some work expressly to motivate Democratic voters and push for adherence to liberal positions by elected officials. Others focus on a single issue like abortion rights or environmental protection, communicating specific political debates that affect only their area of interest.

This loose confederation of progressive voices first found their freedom to express themselves and speak to one another in the digital revolution that swept publishing at the dawn of the twenty-first century. Blogging, a shortened term for web logs, developed as a simplified way to publish web content and quickly became simple way for people to write about any number of things—from raising kids to cooking to politics. That last topic drew freelance writers and reporters as well as Democratic activists. Some of those writers soon attracted an audience, and as blogs linked to one another a sort of network of politically active writers developed. These activists and advocacy journalists often discussed and critiqued mainstream media coverage of politics, commenting on but seldom making political news.

Then came Trent Lott.

Lott, the Senate majority leader and senior senator from Mississippi, had agreed to come and speak at the 100th birthday of Senator Strom Thurmond. Thurmond had a long and turbulent history in American politics, having mounted a segregationist candidacy for president in 1948 and having fought civil rights legislation in the 1960s. As Lott spoke at the birthday celebration he offered these words, "When Strom Thurmond ran for president, we voted for him. We're proud of it. And if the rest of the country had followed our lead, we wouldn't have had all these problems over all these years either." The comments appeared to endorse racial segregation and opposition to civil rights. Perhaps because of the setting, the story failed to draw the attention of Washington media, but the liberal blogs did not miss it. Sites like Talking Points Memo, a blog run by Washington writer and columnist Joshua Micah Marshall, picked up the comments and pushed the story out across their networks. The news soon drew the attention of some reporters in D.C. who had missed the initial story and days after it happened, the comments sparked a firestorm of criticism. Lott would be forced to resign and progressive blogs were suddenly wielding power. In examining the relationship between the liberal blogs and the press in the aftermath of the Lott incident, Alex Jones and Esther Scott would explain that the relationship between bloggers and the media had begun to "take root," writing, "Blogs, it was argued, served a number of purposes for the press. They acted as an early warning system for traditional journalists, wrote one observer; or, as another put it, they were the trenches where the mainstream media sees the incoming artillery. They also offered reporters a forum of sorts for sifting through news stories and evaluating their importance" (Jones and Scott 2004).

This relationship with the media was only one of the multiple roles blogs would come to play in connection with politics. These sites pushed journalists to up their game and respond to liberal criticism, but they also pressed on their own Democratic Party, arguing that the party needed to take stronger positions in opposition to the Republican Party and pressuring their own party's candidates to adhere to the positions put forward by the national party and activists. Sites like the Daily Kos and MyDD carved out roles as a voice of the Democratic Party grassroots. These sites became platforms for more liberal candidates to garner support, volunteers, and momentum. One examination of the role of blogs in politics found that "through channeling support to particular candidates and prodding Democratic leaders, bloggers can help the party elect candidates and create an energetic, vocal party organization. For them, blogging is a means to influence candidates' campaign strategies and help establish the direction of the party and its campaign messages" (Davis 2009).

By 2008, Democratic candidates in particular had come to realize that they, too, must participate in the hurly burly of liberal talk happening on the Internet. In announcing her campaign for president in 2007, Senator Hillary Clinton did not take to a podium in front of thousands of adoring supporters in her hometown as so many had before her, she blogged—and she did it to address a specific problem she faced that year. As one scholar who studies the use of digital communication in campaigns noted, "The senator from New York, wife of a former president, and frontrunner for the Democratic nomination for the presidency in 2008 was often critiqued for being too measured, distant, and cautious. In evident response, she offered a countertype: Hillary as friendly, open, and even chatty: 'I'm not just starting a campaign, though. I'm beginning a conversation with you, with America . . . Let's talk about how to bring the right end to the war in Iraq, and to restore the respect of America around the world.' The Clinton campaign posted the announcement on the Web before the Senator spoke to reporters, and surely it read like a blog-post rather than a presidential address" (Perlmutter 2008).

Perhaps bolstered by the lack of other outlets like talk radio, liberal activists have found numerous blog sites—from the almost-establishment Huffington Post to the tabloid-esque Wonkette—to discuss politics, rally support, and denounce political compromises that they feel run afoul of the beliefs of the rank-and-file members. These sites offer progressives a voice less staid and controlled than the traditional media. Yet, perhaps because these sites appeal essentially to fellow progressives, they often are less hyperbolic and incendiary than their cable news show and talk radio cousins. A statistical analysis of the political content of all of political talk across different media and the political divide found that "blogs do contain outrage less often than cable news analysis and talk radio, but probably not radically less. Taking stock of this information, it is interesting to note that it is television, the most widely used medium, that is the most likely to contain outrage talk and behavior" (Sobieraj and Berry 2011).

Blogs have been described as simply people talking, and many of those digital conversations involve politics. By providing a platform for those interested in liberal and Democratic Party politics the liberal blogosphere has helped the grassroots push back against the mainstream press and the party leaders when they appear to fall short. The blogs are part media watchdog, part party enforcer. Some worry that the network of interlinked liberal blogs may help fuel the modern media echo chamber by allowing rumors and political attacks to quickly circulate without any fact checking. But the bulk of what these sites do is offer a commentary on politics and media that speak to people with similar interests and leanings.

See also: Conservative Blogosphere; Daily Kos; Huffington Post, Social Media and Politics; Talking Points Memo; Wonkette

Further Reading

Davis, Richard. 2009. *Typing Politics: The Role of Blogs in American Politics*. New York: Oxford University Press, USA.
Jones, Alex, and Esther Scott. 2004. "'Big Media' Meets the 'Bloggers': Coverage of Trent Lott's Remarks at Strom Thurmond's Birthday Party." Kennedy School of Government at Harvard University. Cambridge, MA: Harvard University. Accessed January 12, 2016. http://shorensteincenter.org/wp-content/uploads/2012/03/1731_0_scott.pdf.
Perlmutter, David. 2008. *Blogwars*. New York: Oxford University Press, USA.
Sobieraj, Sarah, and Jeffrey Berry. 2011. "From Incivility to Outrage: Political Discourse in Blogs, Talk Radio, and Cable News." *Political Communication* 28, Issue 1.

LIBERAL THINK TANKS

Think tanks grew out of a response to the growing complexity of government and a need within the halls of power to have area experts help in the crafting of policies and programs. Many of these early think tanks had deep connections to existing academic higher institutions and were bolstered by the generally liberal bent of most academics. But these groups only indirectly affected policy, offering advice and testimony that could be used or discarded by policymakers. In recent years, some liberals found this limited impact frustrating and launched a new wave of organizations that were more interested in message development and public campaigning than in research and policy development.

Think tanks generally grew out of the Progressive era ideals of government playing a more active role in overseeing the economy and offering a social safety net. They also have their basis in a view of philanthropy that aimed to "help government think" by convening scholars and conducting research. Many of these organizations had progressive or liberal policy bents but they generally conducted nonpartisan research. One example is the Brookings Institution, begun in 1916 to inform government bureaucrats about the possible government solutions to issues like the economy and foreign relations. Organizations like Brookings shaped policy by serving as a sort of hothouse of ideas. Scholars would study problems and their potential solutions and then offer advice and draft ideas to the executive or legislative branches.

Groups often undertook research at the behest of the government. For example, in the wake of World War II Brookings was tasked with developing a set of recommendations to Congress to help form a post-war development plan. The work became known as the Marshall Plan and was widely credited for rebuilding Europe into a modern economy after the devastation of war. The work of such left-leaning institutions was mirrored by other organizations that leaned to the right side of the political spectrum, like the American Enterprise Institute, and for decades these groups worked primarily within the system to promote policy goals. Scholars from Brookings, The Century Foundation, Paul H. Nitze School of Advanced International Studies, and other left-leaning groups would appear in the media as topical experts, but rarely did they expressly advocate a specific policy outcome. They informed the process among Democrats but rarely participated as an active voice in the debate.

For many partisans within the Democratic ranks, this position of quiet consultation and serious policy work was useful to governing but did little to assist the party or its candidates. Groups like the Progressive Policy Institute grew out of a new way of thinking about think tanks among politically liberal politicians. PPI was more interested in developing centrist policies that were largely out of favor with national Democrats. The organization helped develop scholars who would go on to work on campaigns as policy specialists with the idea of helping beef up more moderate Democrats. The institute worked with more expressly campaign-oriented groups like the Democratic Leadership Council to help raise the profile of southern and western Democrats who did not always adhere to the party positions put forward by northeastern liberals. Politicians like Bill Clinton benefited from PPI scholars in developing an array of economic policies, including welfare reform and deficit reduction plans. This new style of think tanks sought to affect politics within the party, not simply shape policies in a way generally aligned with the political philosophy of liberalism. They were shifting from purely policy-oriented groups to political policy organizations. Still, like their forerunners, these think tanks usually worked behind the scenes, although scholars would appear in newspaper interviews and occasionally on highbrow political discussion shows on television.

The newest wave of liberal think tanks arose from the Democratic Party's continued inability to effectively develop communications strategies around progressive positions. These groups, like the Center for American Politics and Media Matters for America, would take the think tank more aggressively into the campaign realm, developing and deploying messaging strategies aimed at influencing media coverage and directly communicating with supporters. These new groups are as much information sources aimed at Democratic activists as they are policy research organizations. Media Matters, for example, aims to combat the influence of conservatives in the media, serving as a massive right-wing media fact checker. Media Matters rarely publishes research, instead blogging out the most factually problematic or politically inflammatory quotes generated in the broadcast media. its goal is not to influence policy makers but to battle Fox News in a war of claims and counter-claims.

The Center for American Progress, born out of the devastating election losses of 2000, aimed to merge the think tanks of yore with the messaging needs of the Internet age. The organization employs as many bloggers sending out messages to Democratic activists as PPI had scholars. As one report on the changing think tanks on both sides of the political divide noted, "For these institutions, the balance between original research and public relations is clearly tipped in the direction of the latter. As [City College of New York professor Andrew] Rich puts it, these organizations often seem more interested in selling their product than in coming up with new ideas. CAP in particular seems to have turned marketing and organizing into an art form" (Troy 2012). The center is keenly aware of news cycles and less interested in policy discussions. The organization will often release information and briefing points ahead of known news events, seeking to connect their policy objectives to almost-certain news stories. So ahead of, for example, the January employment numbers, CAP released a data-rich briefing on the state of the American job market, chock full of charts on job growth, but also noting sluggish growth in wages and some long-term unemployment. The briefing paper ended with a note to policy makers and politicians, declaring, "Unfortunately, the Fed has already shown it will raise interest rates to fight nonexistent inflation . . . Historically, the Fed tends to increase rates gradually, suggesting that December's rate increase is a sign of things to come. Yet economic fundamentals suggest that policymakers should wait to increase rates for some time—just as they suggested last month" (Madowitz, Rawal, and Corley 2016). The goal of this CAP brief is not simply to inform lawmakers about policies but to advocate against a specific government action—the Federal Reserve potentially increasing interest rates. This advocacy is aimed at journalists who will diligently be looking for information to contextualize the January employment statement from the government and the impending Fed meeting. CAP is there to influence the public discussion of this effort. It has at times even become more active, pushing many of the demands of groups like the Occupy Wall Street activists and those promoting gay, lesbian, and transgender rights. Unlike the philanthropic organizations that marked the birth of think tanks, CAP and the modern era of organizations rely more on direct donations and are far more active in promoting their positions to activists and the media.

A similar trend has occurred within conservative think tanks, as well, but with more internal divisions within the Republican Party in recent years, those think tanks have become more intense battlefields of electoral politics and influence between different wings of the party. On the progressive side of the equation a similar shift toward more overtly partisan and less policy-oriented work has occurred, but these progressive groups have been more aligned against Republicans than focused on internal debate within the Democratic Party.

See also: Brookings Institution; Center for American Progress (CAP); Conservative Think Tanks

Further Reading

Madowitz, Michael, Shiv Rawal, and Danielle Corley. 2016. "The State of the U.S. Labor Market: Pre-January 2016 Jobs Release." Center for American Progress. January 7. Accessed January 11, 2016. https://www.americanprogress.org/issues/economy/news/2016/01/07/128377/the-state-of-the-u-s-labor-market-pre-january-2016-jobs-release.

Troy, Tevi. 2012. "Devaluing Think Thanks." *National Affairs*. Winter. Accessed January 11, 2016. http://www.nationalaffairs.com/publications/detail/devaluing-the-think-tank.

LIMBAUGH, RUSH (1951–)

There's no middle ground when it comes to conservative radio host Rush Limbaugh. Former president Ronald Reagan called him "the Number One voice for conservatism" in 1992. Liberal activist (and later U.S. senator) Al Franken said in his less-than-subtly titled *Rush Limbaugh is a Big Fat Idiot*, he is a "bully who can dish it out to the poor, the homeless, and 'stupid, unskilled Mexicans,' but who can't take it when he's the target himself."

Rush Hudson Limbaugh III was born on January 12, 1951, in Cape Girardeau, Missouri, and by the time he was 8 he had committed to a career on radio. He refused to listen to his parents who urged him to pursue a job in a more stable field and while still in high school took to the airwaves on a station co-owned by his father. He briefly attended college at Southeast Missouri State University, but left to pursue radio full time. He would often draw fire for his controversial on-air comments. In fact, twice it got the deejay fired from gigs in Pennsylvania and Missouri.

By 1984, he was hosting *The Rush Limbaugh Show* out of New York and then the federal government changed Limbaugh's fortunes. In 1987, the Federal Communications Commission announced that it would no longer enforce the Fairness Doctrine that required broadcasters to offer balanced coverage of controversial public policy issues. With the Fairness Doctrine gone, politically oriented shows were allowed to flourish and Limbaugh led the way. Within a year of the rule change, the show began national syndication. Limbaugh drew millions of listeners and often advocated conservative politics and politicians.

The secret to his success, Limbaugh somewhat immodestly proposed, was him—part comedian, part harsh cultural critic, and part political bomb-thrower. "I never thought about why [his show succeeded] and in truth I was afraid of finding out. My fear was the discovery would cause me to become a caricature of myself; that is, I would try to be myself rather than just be myself" (Limbaugh 1992). He championed outspoken conservatives like U.S. representative Newt Gingrich, who orchestrated the 1994 Republican Revolution that took the U.S. House back from Democrats for the first time in 50 years. "When pundits searched for a single figure to credit for the sea change in American politics and governance, they turned not to an elected official or party operative but to a man whom many observers previously had dismissed as an inconsequential blowhard," wrote Rodger Streitmatter in the wake of the '94 vote (2012).

Over the years, some have worried that Limbaugh listeners, dubbed "dittoheads," only get their news from slanted broadcasts. Research in 2008 indicated that might be true. Kathleen Hall Jamieson and Joseph Cappella argued that with the help of new media, "Rush listeners . . . are now better able to confine themselves in an insulating, protective media space filled with reassuring information and opinion" (Jamieson and Cappella 2008). Despite the concerns of a political echo chamber, the Limbaugh show was also seen as a model for making money. His "commercial success paved the way for imitators such as Sean Hannity and Michael Medved, both of whom increased their exposure as guests on Limbaugh's show. And beyond any one program, it is this preference for tried-and-true commercial successes that fueled the development of conservative outrage on the right" (Berry and Sobieraj 2014).

Still, with 15 million listeners a day Limbaugh wields enormous sway. The number represents more than three times the viewership of Fox News's Bill O'Reilly and makes him one of the most influential figures in conservative circles.

See also: Hannity, Sean; Talk Radio

Further Reading

Berry, Jeffrey, and Sarah Sobieraj. 2014. *The Outrage Industry: Political Opinion Media and the New Incivility*. Oxford: Oxford University Press.

Franken, Al. 1996. *Rush Limbaugh is a Big Fat Idiot*. New York: Dell Publishing.

Jamieson, Kathleen Hall, and Joseph Cappella. 2008. *Echo Chamber: Rush Limbaugh and the Conservative Media Establishment*. Oxford: Oxford University Press.

Limbaugh, Rush. 1992. *The Way Things Ought to Be*. New York: Pocket Books.

Streitmatter, Rodger. 2012. *Mightier Than the Sword*. Boulder, CO: Westview Press.

LIPPMANN, WALTER (1889–1974)

A part-time political philosopher and full-time newspaper columnist, Walter Lippmann sought to connect the ideals of democracy with the modern political state, arguing for a vibrant media and for that media to pay special attention to the views of the public in conveying current events to the masses. From coining now-famous concepts like "stereotyping" and the "Cold War" to his advocacy of the objective journalist, Lippmann has been widely credited with being the most influential journalist of the twentieth century.

Born to a German-Jewish family in New York City, Lippmann was able to establish himself from a very young age as a true thinker on the relationship between the press, government, and people. At 25 he landed a position as a founding editor of the progressive magazine *New Republic* and during those early years he also would consult with then-president Woodrow Wilson. It was in that role that he helped write speeches for the Democratic president and worked on seminal documents like Wilson's "Fourteen Points" for peace in the wake of World War I. It might have been enough for most people to have one of the most influential liberal magazines in the country and the ear of the president, but Lippmann also wanted to tackle the philosophical reality of the importance of an informed electorate. In fact, to re-read his *Liberty and the News* some 90 years after its original publication is to hear many of the concerns people express about the modern media and governance. He wrote in that work, "Everywhere to-day men are conscious that somehow they must deal with questions more intricate than any that church or school had prepared them to understand. Increasingly they know that they cannot understand them if the facts are not quickly and steadily available. Increasingly they are baffled because the facts are not available; and they are wondering whether government by consent can survive in a time when manufacture of consent is an unregulated private enterprise. For in an exact sense the present crisis of western democracy is a crisis in journalism" (Lippmann 1920). For Lippmann, the modern representative democratic system required an effective press to inform the electorate of the debate at hand and to ensure that those who would select our leaders have the basis to do so.

Lippmann, who flirted with the Socialist Party during the early twentieth century, saw the press as the main surrogate for the public. But more than just serving as a stand-in for the masses, Lippmann argued that the press needed to practice a specific form of reporting, supplying the public with those facts that he worried are not readily available without the professional press. He saw this as an endemic problem in 1920s reporting. The American Press Institute notes, "Journalism, Lippmann declared, was being practiced by 'untrained accidental witnesses.' Good intentions, or what some might call 'honest efforts' by journalists, were not enough. Faith in the rugged individualism of the tough reporter, what Lippmann called the 'cynicism of the trade,' was also not enough" (American Press Institute). Lippmann's solution was for journalists to approach their reporting as scientists approach their work. The individual reporter may hold certain beliefs, but the process of reporting would be objective, focusing on testing the report's thesis and the conventional wisdom of the day. Objectivity, Lippmann argued, should be something that journalists are taught and the field itself should be professionalized to a far more significant degree. He wrote in 1931, "It has never yet been a profession. It has been at times a dignified calling, at others a romantic adventure, and then again a servile trade. But a profession it could not begin to be until modern objective journalism was successfully created, and with it the need of men who consider themselves devoted, as all the professions ideally are, to the service of truth alone" (Cleghorn 1995).

Lippmann, through many of his works, argued for a professionalization of both politics and the media. Political organizations, he noted, were being changed by the end of the patronage system and the rise of a "governing class" that could and should lead by informing and inspiring the voting public. But Lippmann did not simply take to the voluminous pages of his books to argue these big pictures, he also participated in the public conversation through a syndicated newspaper column for decades. His column served as a progressive counterpoint to some of the intensely anti-Soviet rhetoric that emerged following World War II. He would coin the term the "Cold War" to describe the clash of powers and often argued that the role of Russia in Europe should be something that the American government should somewhat accept. His column remained highly influential throughout his life, garnering him the Pulitzer Prize in 1958 for "the wisdom, perception and high sense of responsibility with which he has commented for many years on national and international affairs" (Pulitzer Prizes). He was also awarded the Presidential Medal of Freedom in 1964 and continued working up until his death in 1974.

See also: *New Republic;* Objectivity; Public Opinion

Further Reading

American Press Institute. "The Lost Meaning of 'Objectivity.'" Accessed November 20 2015. http://www.americanpressinstitute.org/journalism-essentials/bias-objectivity/lost -meaning-objectivity.

Cleghorn, Reese. 1995. "Lippmann on the New Objective Journalism." *American Journalism Review.* May. Accessed November 20, 2015. http://ajrarchive.org/Article.asp?id=934.

Lippmann, Walter. 1920. *Liberty and the News.* New York: Harcourt, Brace and Howe.

"Pulitzer Prizes—1958." Pulitzer Prize Foundation. Accessed June 13, 2016. http://www .pulitzer.org/prize-winners-by-year/1958.

M

MADDOW, RACHEL (1973–)

Rachel Maddow is a liberal commentator and author who has made a name for herself by traveling a road paved by conservatives, building a decent-sized radio audience and turning that popularity into a cable news opportunity built around her view of politics.

Maddow grew up in California and attended Stanford University. She was by all accounts a stellar student of political science and was named a Rhodes Scholar that led her to Oxford. She planned a career working to help those suffering from HIV and AIDS when she decided to attend a tryout to be the sidekick and news host of a regional FM radio program. They picked her up and soon her personality and quick wit was scoring her more and more attention. She parlayed her commercial radio experience and PhD from Oxford into a gig hosting one of the inaugural radio programs on the nascent Air America radio network, which hoped to be a liberal balance to the array of conservative talk radio. In that role, she was soon tapped to appear on cable talk shows, where her youth made her stand out in the talk panels laden with old men.

Some who worked with her trying to build Air America into a viable business accused Maddow of using the network and the progressive cause as a ticket to bigger job opportunities. Randi Rhodes, a fellow Air America host, took a shot at Maddow and fellow alum U.S. senator Al Franken in her final show on the network, saying, "When Air America came I said, 'oh my God, and the opportunity is amazing, to be the advocate of even more people and to tell people even more about, you know, how you get through this life and what's important' . . . But other people were not there for that. Some people saw, you know, a chance to be in a Cabinet and other people saw it as a chance to go to the Senate and other people saw it as a chance to national television" (Lifson 2014). Whether true or not, Maddow resonated with audiences and soon cable networks were wooing her to appear more and she became somewhat a regular on CNN and MSNBC.

Finally, MSNBC signed her up to a single-year contract that said she would only appear on their network. The network tried her out as the substitute host of the top-ranked "Countdown with Keith Olbermann." Maddow took aim at the presumptive 2008 Republican nominee John McCain, who admitted that day that the American economy was slowing. "Slowing, senator?" she said. "Try grinding to a halt. But don't worry, Senator McCain says he can balance the budget by saving all sorts of money when he wins the wars in Iraq and Afghanistan" (Steinberg 2008). It was the first of many of her issue-laden commentaries that espoused Democratic policies and despite her typical liberal stance, she was known for also criticizing Democrats, especially in the area of foreign affairs.

In all of this, Maddow has carved out a unique voice in the commentary-laden cable world, offering one of the few liberal counterparts in terms of viewership and style to the array of conservative talk emanating from talk radio and the Fox News Channel. *Variety* described her approach by writing, "Maddow has made her mark by delivering extended commentary laden with dashes of humor and flashes of wonkish prose but free of righteous rant—smart snark with a smile. Although she is graduating into ever more serious interviews . . . her show is not about the guests, but her own musings on the day's events" (Johnson 2009). Her ascension to a full-time gig as an evening news host did mark a milestone in another way, as Maddow is the first openly gay news anchor to host such a show, but her sexuality has rarely played any role in her reporting or commentary.

She does not refrain from sometimes drifting into the wonky talk that seems wholly appropriate for someone holding a doctorate from Oxford. Take, for example, the night she tried to explain the latest ad from the McCain/Palin ticket in 2008 by asking her audience "Ever heard of something called Dada?" She went on to explain, "Deliberately being irrational, rejecting standard assumptions about beauty or organization or logic. It's an anti-aesthetic statement about the lameness of the status quo . . . kind of? Why am I trying to explain Dadaism on a cable news show thirteen days from this big, giant, historic, crazy, important election that we're about to have? Because that's what I found myself Googling today, in search of a way to make sense of the latest McCain-Palin campaign ad!" It was the kind of commentary that has other liberal news outlets crowing about her as a host. *New York* magazine would later describe the scene and then add, "But then again, Rachel Maddow is not like other cable news hosts. A self-described butch lesbian with short hair and black-rimmed glasses, off-camera she resembles a young Ira Glass more than the helmet-headed anchoresses and Fox fembots who populate television news" (Pressler 2008). It was a model that brought a huge jump in the ratings of MSNBC, for a while. In recent years the program has struggled to maintain its ratings. Still, Maddow is seen as hugely influential, hosting one of the handful of Democratic candidate forums in 2016 and still attracting a nightly audience of nearly 1 million.

See also: Air America; MSNBC

Further Reading

Johnson, Ted. 2009. "Maddow's Unique Style Spikes Ratings." *Variety*. March 6. Accessed November 9, 2015. http://variety.com/2009/tv/news/maddow-s-unique-style-spikes-ratings-1118000926.

Lifson, Thomas. 2014. "Randi Rhodes Leaving Talk Radio, Blasts Al Franken and Rachel Maddow." *American Thinker*. April 27. Accessed January 12, 2015. http://www.americanthinker.com/blog/2014/04/randi_rhodes_leaving_talk_radio_blasts_al_franken_and_rachel_maddow.html.

Pressler, Jessica. 2008. "The Dr. Maddow Show." *New York*. November 2. Accessed November 9, 2015. http://nymag.com/news/media/51822.

Steinberg, Jacques. 2008. "Now in Living Rooms, the Host Apparent." *New York Times*. July 17. Accessed June 13, 2016. http://www.nytimes.com/2008/07/17/arts/television/17madd.html.

McCLURE'S MAGAZINE

Born at the end of the nineteenth century, *McClure's Magazine* flourished for a brief 20-year period, helping some of the era's most notable writers by publishing their fiction in serialized form. The magazine is most memorable for creating the muckraking form of political reporting, publishing some of the most important investigative reporting pieces about major industries and government corruption and helping spur the Progressive era of political reform. But even as the magazine reached its most powerful point, it disintegrated over internal conflicts between the writers and the publisher and soon folded. Still, its history of muckraking and the form of reporting it nurtured gives it a unique role in the history of political journalism.

By the time he set up the periodical that would carry his name, Samuel McClure had already established himself as one of the pioneers of the media. In 1884, at the age of 27, McClure launched the McClure Syndicate, a service that distributed serialized fiction and comic strips to newspapers around the country. The syndicate was the first such business to provide a centralized source for newspapers and flourished as a business model, spawning dozens of competitors over the years. McClure's syndicate introduced many Americans to the writings of some of the most notable authors of the age, including Arthur Conan Doyle, Rudyard Kipling, Jack London, and Mark Twain.

But even as the business thrived, McClure had visions of a publication of his own. Kipling recalled in his autobiography how McClure showed up at his home in Vermont wanting to discuss this new venture, writing, "He had been everything from a peddler to a tintype photographer along the highways, and had held intact his genius and simplicity. He entered, alight with the notion for a new Magazine to be called 'McClure's.' I think the talk lasted some twelve—or it may have been seventeen—hours, before the notion was fully hatched out. He, like Roosevelt, was in advance of his age, for he looked rather straightly at practices and impostures which were in the course of being sanctified because they paid" (Kipling 2004). The magazine that emerged from those and many more talks had four sections: "The Edge of Future," which would document the latest technology; portraits of famous people at different ages; "The Real Conversations," where one notable person interviewed another; and then selected fiction and poetry from his syndicate. His work at the syndicate had allowed him to see what worked in many different periodicals and he intended to learn their lessons and build a new publication that would combine the strengths of other magazines in the marketplace.

Founded in 1893 by McClure and his college classmate John Phillips, *McClure's Magazine* was established in the tradition of the American literary and political journals, like the *Atlantic*. *McClure's* made an early name for itself by focusing on literature, publishing works similar to those distributed to newspapers via his syndicate, but by 1902 McClure's reformist ideas became one of the primary goals of the magazine. McClure hired Lincoln Steffens, a reporter who had made a name for himself in New York covering police and municipal government. Steffens would later describe McClure as a man of unstoppable energy, writing, "He was a flower that did not sit and wait for the bees to come and take his honey and leave their seeds. He flew forth to find and rob the bees" (Goodwin 2013). Steffens, as a senior editor, helped inspire the new direction of the magazine toward more investigative reporting. By January 1903, the true dawn of *McClure's* occurred. In one issue, the magazine published three of the most seminal investigations of the era: the first part of Ida Tarbell's investigation into the corporate behemoth Standard Oil; a piece by Steffens on graft, corruption, and cronyism entitled "The Shame of Minneapolis"; and "The Right to Work," an examination of miners who do not participate in strikes. These three pieces, this one edition of *McClure's*, is seen by most experts as the dawn of the muckraking era of journalism.

As the leading muckraking journal of the era, *McClure's* became a major engine for political change. Theodore Roosevelt, himself a reformer that was feared and at times marginalized, saw these investigative reporters as uneasy allies and he "cultivated cordial relations with the *McClure's* writers, who were at their peak influence during his presidency" (Lears 2014). At times he embraced the reporting done by reporters like Tarbell and Steffens, but at other times, he sought to distance himself from them. In fact, the term muckraking stemmed from a speech in which Roosevelt criticized the outspoken reporters. But whether praising or criticizing the reformers, Roosevelt and other political leaders were at the same time acknowledging the potent role *McClure's* and other muckraking periodicals of the period had become.

These journals, many of which aimed to be read by the middle and upper classes, sought not just to report the news, but to change society. For reformers like McClure, Tarbell, Phillips, and Steffens this was as much a calling as it was a job. And it was in this progressive fervor that the seeds of *McClure's* demise lay. Even as the magazine was reaching its heights of power the desire to be pure reformers caused the magazine to split apart. McClure had an affair with a poet and the magazine's writers feared what exposure of this news would mean to its and their reputations. "The magazine voiced the sentiments of a readership bent upon making society conform to its predominantly Protestant, middle-class conception of morality. The *McClure's* reader had little tolerance for marital infidelity, and S.S. McClure, as editor-in-chief, could ruin the magazine's reputation if he were deemed morally reprehensible" (Gross 1997). Ashamed and angered by the affair, McClure became increasingly unpredictable and by 1906, only three years after the triumph of the January 1903 edition, *McClure's Magazine* imploded. Phillips, Tarbell, Steffens, and most of the writing staff left the magazine and purchased a competitor, forming the *American* magazine. *McClure's* itself floundered on, but by 1911 McClure had to sell. The magazine shifted its focus to women readers, but published only occasionally and by 1929 closed for good.

Still the role of advocacy journalism in shaping and fueling political reform had been demonstrated, so had the power of muckraking investigative journalism to churn up issues the public must face. McClure, despite the short life and sudden demise of his magazine, is also credited with helping journalism move away from the rush of the day-to-day reporting to give reporters the time and space to delve into a subject of great importance. The role of muckraking and later investigative reporting in helping establish and inform the political process remains one of the unique elements of the relationship between the press and politics.

See also: Muckraking; Steffens, Lincoln; Tarbell, Ida

Further Reading
Goodwin, Doris Kearns. 2013. *The Bully Pulpit: Theodore Roosevelt, William Howard Taft, and the Golden Age of Journalism*. New York: Simon & Schuster.
Gross, Greg. 1997. "The Staff Breakup of *McClure's Magazine*." Published at Allegheny College. Accessed July 7, 2015. http://sites.allegheny.edu/tarbell/mcclurestaff/chapter-iii.
Kipling, Rudyard. 2004. *Something of Myself: For My Friends Known and Unknown*. Republished by the Gutenberg Australia Project. Accessed July 8, 2015. http://gutenberg.net.au/ebooks04/0400691.txt.
Lears, Jackson. 2014. "Teddy Roosevelt, Not-So-Great Reformer." *The New Republic*. March 14. Accessed July 7, 2015. http://www.newrepublic.com/article/116790/bully-pulpit-doris-kearns-goodwin-reviewed-jackson-lears.

MEDIA MATTERS FOR AMERICA

Media Matters for America is a nonprofit research and commentary group that aims to combat what it sees as a conservative bias in mainstream media, using fast-response blog items as well as larger-scale investigations to attack conservative commentators and correct factual errors and perceived misinformation put out into the political debate from political conservatives. The group is one of the newer and more digitally savvy of the media watchdog groups that seek to combat problems in the mainstream media that may misinform the public on critical issues of public concern.

The group was organized in 2004 by controversial journalist David Brock. During the 1990s, Brock had written several books and articles that attacked Bill and Hillary Clinton as well as Anita Hill, the woman who had accused aspiring Supreme Court justice Clarence Thomas of sexual harassment. Then in 1997, Brock had a fundamental change of heart. That year he published a piece in *Esquire* magazine called "Confessions of a Right-Wing Hit Man," where he admitted he had done shoddy reporting and had paid some sources. Almost overnight, he became an ardent critic of the right, launching a series of attacks against conservative columnists and writers that were once his colleagues and publications he had written for. By 2004, several wealthy liberal donors backed a new Brock project called Media

Matters for America, an organization that aimed to continue and broaden Brock's attack on the right-wing media. The result was a new nonprofit that "put in place, for the first time, the means to systematically monitor a cross section of print, broadcast, cable, radio, and Internet media outlets for conservative misinformation—news or commentary that is not accurate, reliable, or credible and that forwards the conservative agenda—every day, in real time" (Media Matters for America, n.d.). The group would work through its own website as well as traditional media and social media to respond to what it deemed inaccurate claims made by the right.

The pseudo news organization, based in Washington, D.C., spent countless hours monitoring conservative commentators on television and reading columns in national and syndicated press. The organization houses massive servers that hold hundreds of thousands of hours of television broadcasts, allowing its analysts to cull through footage that would, in a pre-digital world, be sent out into the ether. If there is one target Media Matters has more than any other it is Fox News. Widely seen as the most conservative cable news network in the nation, Fox has provoked anger from many liberal groups and Media Matters has made that one of its core raisons d'être. A 2011 profile of Brock in *New York* magazine highlighted how much of Media Matters focused on Fox. In the story he said, "What happened after the Obama election, I think, is that Fox morphed into something that isn't even recognizable as a form of media . . . It looks more like a political committee than what it looked like pre-Obama, which was essentially talk radio on television. It's more dangerous now; it's more lethal. And so as Fox has doubled down, we've doubled down" (Zengerie 2011).

This focus on Fox represents something of a return to the partisan presses of America's past. Media Matters aims to combat what it sees as misinformation produced by a partisan news organization, but then itself becomes part of the political back-and-forth as conservatives accuse it of attempting to silence any criticism of the Democrats. Outspoken conservative talk show host Rush Limbaugh has said on his website, "Media Matters is a left-wing political operation created to censor conservative media through blacklisting and intimidation of advertisers. Their model is to create and distribute untrue statements about conservative media, and then use threats of boycotts and business interference to demand that advertisers repudiate programs they target" (RushLimbaugh.com, n.d.). The danger is that this political he-said, she-said threatens to muddy the waters for those who want to understand if Media Matters has a point or not. In many ways, this group's work, along with politically motivated efforts on both sides of the aisle, helps feed the polarization of media content by allowing liberals to dismiss anything reported by Fox and allowing conservatives to see Media Matters's critiques as partisan sniping.

Many of the criticisms from conservative groups focus less on the factual claims made by Media Matters's staff and more on Brock and the groups funding the organization. The nonprofit group garners much of its budget from foundations. In 2014, the group received more than $1 million from the Tides Foundation, which supports many socially liberal causes as well as community groups, and the Open

Society Foundation of George Soros, the liberal Hungarian-born American business magnate. In announcing a 2010 donation of $1 million, Soros said in a statement, "Media Matters is one of the few groups that attempts to hold Fox News accountable for the false and misleading information they so often broadcast. I am supporting Media Matters in an effort to more widely publicize the challenge Fox News poses to civil and informed discourse in our democracy." The group's work has prompted calls for the Internal Revenue Service to revoke its status as a 501(c)3 organization. Several petitions have been filed on online sites aimed at Congress and one former White House counsel sent a pro bono letter to the IRS demanding they take action. C. Boyden Gray, who worked for President George H.W. Bush said, "I have never seen any tax-exempt organization getting into the kind of partisan activity Media Matters is now engaging in" (MacDonald 2011). The IRS has not taken any steps to change the organization's status, but it shows the degree to which the organization's criticism of conservative media has angered some elements of both activists within the party and established figures like Gray.

But the group does more than just monitor Fox. In 2006, it released a massive survey of newspapers columns that concluded, "In paper after paper, state after state, and region after region, conservative syndicated columnists get more space than their progressive counterparts" (Media Matters for America 2007). Research like that, coupled with the continued efforts to attack misinformation from Fox News, has emerged as the hallmark of Media Matters work and contributed to their perception of being a partisan fact-checker in the political reporting world.

See also: Brock, David; Fox News; Media Watchdog Groups; Political Bias and the Media; Watchdog Journalism

Further Reading

"About Us." Media Matters for America. Accessed August 5, 2015. http://mediamatters.org/about.

"Black and White and Re(a)d All Over." Media Matters for America. September 2007. Accessed August 6, 2015. http://mediamatters.org/research/oped.

MacDonald, Elizabeth. 2011. "Former White House Counsel to IRS: Pull Media Matters' Tax-Exempt Status." FoxBusiness.com. August 4. Accessed August 5, 2015. http://www.foxbusiness.com/markets/2011/08/04/former-white-house-counsel-to-irs-yank-media-matters-tax-exempt-status.

"Media Matter Facts." RushLimbaugh.com. Accessed August 5, 2015. http://www.rushlimbaugh.com/pages/static/media_matters_facts.

Zengerie, Jason. 2011. "If I Take Down Fox, Is All Forgiven?" New York. May 22. Accessed August 5, 2015. http://nymag.com/news/media/david-brock-media-matters-2011-5.

MEDIA WATCHDOG GROUPS

In the era before the Internet empowered audiences to talk back to large media corporations and social media and blogging allowed average citizens to participate in the process of talking back to the mass media, an array of activist groups, each usually inspired by a specific critique of the so-called mainstream media, developed a handful of newsletters and research groups aimed at holding the press accountable. These media watchdog groups produced reports and held press conferences hoping to use public pressure and reporting in competing outlets as a threat to keep individual news outlets and reporters from failing in their duty to inform the public.

Many of these groups emerged in the 1960s and 1970s, as divisions in the country over Vietnam and Watergate as well as the power of the press to fuel public reaction appeared to be growing. One of the first to emerge was Accuracy in the Media, which in 1969 launched as essentially a one-man crusade by economist Reed Irvine. Irvine launched his group in response to his belief that most of the reporters and editors working at the largest news organizations were too soft on Communism and Socialism. His group started work publishing a newsletter that aimed to point out the biases within the press. Hi son, who took the helm of AIM after his father's death in 2004, told the *Washington Post*, Irvine "was a die-hard anti-communist . . . There was a bulldoggedness, an incredible determination in my father. Nothing ever stopped him; he wore a shield of armor, and you couldn't hurt him" (Sullivan 2004). Reed started his project by sending letters to newspapers who ran stories Reed felt were biased. He would demand a correction and if the paper refused, he would then buy an ad in the paper to run his own correction. By 1972 he started publishing a newsletter documenting media problems. Reed's commentaries often infuriated editors who argued he was simplifying questions of bias and objectivity. But Reed himself was often vocal in his views about individual reporters and ongoing stories he felt were soft of opponents of the United States. He most often voiced these concerns via his newsletter, but often appeared on talk shows and news programs to reach a wider audience. AIM has grown from Reed's efforts into a multimillion-dollar operation based in Washington, D.C.

But as Reed's effort was growing, other groups who saw other problems within the press began to form. Fairness and Accuracy in Reporting (FAIR) launched in 1986 based on concerns that the press had become too much a tool of large corporate owners. FAIR wanted to educate viewers about the inherent biases in the media that influenced the stories the media did and the voices they represented in those stories. In an early guide to identifying bias, the group told viewers, "Media over-rely on 'official' (government, corporate and establishment think tank) sources . . . Count the number of corporate and government sources versus the number of progressive, public interest, female and minority voices. Demand mass media expand their rolodexes; better yet, give them lists of progressive and public interest experts in the community" (FAIR, n.d.). FAIR based its criticism on exhaustive studies where it would take a program like ABC's *Nightline* or PBS's *MacNeil/Lehrer NewsHour* and count the guests, clocking their time on screen to quantify official or corporate biases in the coverage. FAIR has been accused of being liberal, in large part due to its primary criticism that mainstream media is too much in the grips of large corporations. One *New York Times* piece in 1990 linked the group to AIM and that provoked an outcry from AIM's Irvine, who wrote the columnist back, saying, "FAIR reflects the views of that numerically insignificant group who used to regard Pol Pot as a hero and who wept at the defeat of Daniel Ortega. I refuse to appear on programs with Cohen and his colleagues because I don't want AIM to be perceived as in any sense equivalent to his organization. Their Marxist class interpretation of media behavior is simply kooky, and their insistence that the media are dominated by conservatives makes sense only to people who think that anyone to the right of Noam Chomsky is conservative" (Goodman 1990).

AIM and FAIR are not alone. A year after FAIR organized conservatives formed a conservative counterpart called the Media Research Center. Smaller than FAIR or AIM, the MRC grew out of the work of Leo Bozell III, a conservative activist who had worked at the Conservative Political Action Conference. At CPAC, Bozell hosted debates over liberal bias in the media, contending reporters were primarily liberal Democrats and this political reality affected their reporting on politics. The MRC formed to expand this work, creating projects like NewsBusters and an active website to document instances of liberal bias and to serve as a platform for Bozell to comment on media coverage of controversial issues. Like FAIR's efforts on the progressive side, the MRC has compiled research to document its case, building a 50-page report entitled "Media Bias 101" that concludes, "Surveys over the past 30 years have consistently found that journalists—especially those at the highest ranks of their profession—are much more liberal than rest of America. They are more likely to vote liberal, more likely to describe themselves as liberal, and more likely to agree with the liberal position on policy matters than members of the general public" (MRC).

Groups have continued to form since these big three—Media Matters for America, for example, formed in 2004 to combat perceived conservative biases in the press—and all of these groups have targeted the coverage of politics as the primary concern, arguing that inherent flaws in the mainstream media infect their coverage and in turn are spread to the American public. They have also taken to the Internet to varying levels of success; NewsBusters and Media Matters being two of the more successful efforts to embrace the digital age. And their reports, especially when they targeted a given newsroom's handling of a story or guest selection bias, did prompt discussions in those newsrooms. Ironically, the emergence of the Internet may have slowed the growth in the number of organized media watchdogs. In the pre-digital age, to combat media problems individuals could do little on their own other than, like Reed did in the late 1960s, send letters to the editor. It took an organization to have real impact. Now, anyone angry about the media can take to the comments, or start a blog. Because of this, the number of new media watchdog groups that go through the process of forming a nonprofit are fairly small, even as the amount of commentary about the media's handling of their job becomes even more common.

See also: Media Matters for America; Political Bias and the Media

Further Reading

Goodman, Walter. 1990. "TV VIEW; Let's Be Frank about Fairness and Accuracy." *New York Times*. June 17. Accessed August 5, 2015. http://www.nytimes.com/1990/06/17/arts/tv -view-let-s-be-frank-about-fairness-and-accuracy.html.

"How to Detect Bias in the Media." Fairness and Accuracy in the Media. Accessed August 5. 2015. http://fair.org/take-action-now/media-activism-kit/how-to-detect-bias-in-news -media.

"Media Bias 101." Media Research Center. Accessed August 6, 2015. http://www.mrc.org /media-bias-101/media-bias-101-what-journalists-really-think-and-what-public -thinks-about-them.

Sullivan, Patricia. 2004. "Media Watchdog Reed Irvine, 82." *Washington Post*. November 14. Accessed August 6, 2015. http://www.washingtonpost.com/wp-dyn/articles/A58852 -2004Nov17.html.

MEET THE PRESS

For years, one Sunday political talk show stood head and shoulders above the rest. As the program's late moderator Tim Russert would tell millions of viewers each week, "If it is Sunday, then it's *Meet the Press*."

The program reigned over the Sunday political talk shows, garnering the best guests and for years boasting the best ratings. Much of the credit went to the Buffalo-born Russert and his thorough, but firm interviews and affable demeanor. "Sunday's interviews do make Monday's headlines. Sometimes from unexpected sources like Yogi Berra explaining his witticisms or Michael Jordan urging young men to accept responsibility for their behavior. But the mainstay has always been the exchanges with our political leadership," Russert wrote in the foreword to a book commemorating the show's 50th anniversary (Ball 1998).

That was true almost from the show's start. Anti-communists, segregationists, civil rights leaders, presidents, and foreign diplomats have all sat on the show's set and had their positions challenged by notable journalists. It has played a significant role in the coverage of politics by putting the powerful on the airwaves once a week, every week. Politico's Mike Allen wrote in 2008 that the show has long been "the premier forum for Washington insiders to talk to the country and each other" (Allen 2008).

However, despite its storied past, the show has faltered in recent years. After Russert's unexpected death in 2008, the program struggled to find the right replacement and ratings sagged. The 2015 Pew State of the News Media Report said the show's viewership declined 6 percent in 2013 and another 4 percent in 2014. The decline has put the show behind its other network competitors: ABC's *This Week* and CBS's *Face the Nation* (Pew 2015).

Despite that, the program will always have one thing on its competitors—it's also the longest-running television program in the world, even though it actually owes its creation to radio.

In 1945, Lawrence Spivak, then editor and publisher of the *American Mercury*, sponsored a radio show meant to help promote his magazine. His idea was to dramatize articles on air in an effort to sell more subscriptions to the magazine, but that changed when he consulted with Martha Rountree. Rountree was already an accomplished radio producer, and she and Spivak agreed that a show dramatizing magazine articles wasn't all that interesting. Instead, they hatched the idea of having a "radio press conference" where a group of journalists would pose questions to an important guest. The big networks turned Spivak and Rountree down, but Mutual Broadcasting System, which already broadcast one Rountree show, took the bait. Mutual executives didn't love the idea initially, but they gave Spivak and Rountree one shot to convince them the idea was worth sticking with.

In June 1945, they broadcast the first show, featuring Edmund Stevens of the *Christian Science Monitor* as its first guest. The show was good enough for Mutual to offer Spivak and Rountree a three-month run the following fall, during which they attracted bigger names. One of the big names was secretary of commerce and former vice president Henry Wallace, who was there to push for a national wage increase (Ball 1998).

The national response to the program was positive. One magazine proclaimed that the radio show had, in its first half-year, forced other news organizations to gather their headline news from the radio. One of its most notable early interviews was with Theodore Bilbo, a Mississippi Democrat and noted racist and segregationist. During the interview, Bilbo admitted to being a member of the Ku Klux Klan, a confession that made the front page of the next day's *New York Post*. In the 1946 *New York World-Telegram* radio awards, it won "Best program dealing with current events."

In 1947, Rountree and Spivak cut a deal with NBC to put the show on television, making that the year *Meet the Press* officially began its run. On its first televised show in November of that year, the guest was James A. Farley, the former postmaster general and former chairman of the Democratic National Committee. The program ran on NBC's New York station and achieved a wider audience in its third episode, as it was broadcast by Washington's NBC station as well. The show was canceled briefly by NBC after only five episodes, but continued on the radio. When it returned to NBC September of 1948, *Meet the Press* was back for good. Its early format was different from the way it looks now. Running for a half-hour, the show featured a panel of reporters who questioned the guests during an evening time-slot. Rountree served as moderator until 1953, and to this day is the only woman to hold that position. Spivak was on the show as a permanent panelist, joined each week by a rotating cast of characters. He liked the panels to include a mixture of experts and generalists, and tried to choose journalists from "a wide geographical range" (Ball 1998).

While the show was popular and often flexed its muscle as a news-driver, it would take almost three decades before it hosted a current U.S. president. John F. Kennedy, Richard Nixon, and Lyndon Johnson had all appeared before being elected, but none appeared while in office. Gerald Ford was the first sitting U.S. president to be on the show when he came on in 1975 for a one-hour special. The program also served as a farewell for Lawrence Spivak, who was making his last appearance as host. Between then and 1991, the show went through five other moderators before the Beltway darling Tim Russert took over. Russert was a bit of a gamble as he had never served as an on-air host, but had for years served as NBC's Washington bureau chief and had worked for several prominent Democrats before that.

Russert was the ninth moderator to take the helm. Under his direction, the show expanded to a full hour and eliminated the panel of journalists posing questions. His style worked, and *Meet the Press* frequently sat atop the TV ratings charts for Sunday morning talk shows, sometimes by a margin as wide as 40 percent (Farhi 2014). Among the Washington elite and political observers across the country, Russert gained a reputation for hard-hitting questions and a style that challenged guests to defend their past positions. His 2008 death sent the Washington crowd into a spiral of mourning that dominated newspaper and broadcast coverage for several days. He was replaced by Tom Brokaw in the short-term, and later David Gregory, a White House correspondent for the network.

Gregory only lasted six years hosting the show, however, as he struggled to fill Russert's shoes and, more importantly, his ratings. During his tenure the program's ratings dipped to a 21-year low. He left in 2014, to be replaced by Chuck Todd, NBC's political director. Todd's first show took place in the White House, where he interviewed President Barack Obama. Todd's early efforts stabilized the show's ratings, but by May 2015 it still finished third among the major network Sunday talk shows (Pew 2015).

For all the ground it has lost to its competitors, *Meet the Press* will always have one thing on them—longevity. It remains the longest-running television program in the world. And although it has mostly fallen from its revered status and the competition for eyes has grown more challenging, its interviews still make headlines. Presidential candidates and powerful figures still clamor to appear on the show, and whatever barbs they throw at competitors or the other party remain newsworthy.

Michael Wright

See also: NBC; Russert, Tim

Further Reading

Allen, Mike. 2008. "Gregory to Host 'Meet the Press.'" Politico. December 2. Accessed January 3, 2016. http://www.politico.com/story/2008/12/gregory-to-host-meet-the-press-016119.

Ball, Rick. 1998. *Meet the Press: 50 Years of History in the Making.* New York: McGraw-Hill.

Farhi, Paul. 2014. "As 'Meet the Press' Struggles in the Ratings, Plenty of Questions for Host David Gregory." *Washington Post.* April 20. Accessed January 3, 2016. https://www.washingtonpost.com/lifestyle/style/as-meet-the-press-struggles-in-the-ratings-plenty-of-questions-for-host-david-gregory/2014/04/20/247ed4c0-c72f-11e3-bf7a-be01a9b69cf1_story.html.

Sherman, Gabriel. 2014. "NBC Wanted to Hire Jon Stewart to Host *Meet the Press*." *New York.* October 8. Accessed January 3, 2016. http://nymag.com/daily/intelligencer/2014/10/jon-stewart-might-have-been-meet-the-press-host.html.

"State of the News Media 2015." 2015. *Pew Research Center.* April 29. Accessed January 3, 2016. http://www.journalism.org/2015/04/29/network-news-fact-sheet.

MICROTARGETING

Campaigns have for decades sought to identify voters who were likely—or could be persuaded—to support their candidate. Microtargeting brings that aspiration into the Internet age by merging the collecting of information about voters with the predictive analytics made possible by so-called big data. This means sophisticated campaigns now employ data technicians to identify messages, personalities, and issues that are likely to influence a given voter or group of voters. This has led to more and more direct communications between voters and campaigns through direct mail, email, or social media marketing.

Microtargeting represented an evolution of a long tradition dating back to the early twentieth century. When populist William Jennings Bryan considered a 1916 run for the presidency (it would have been his fourth), he turned to his card catalogue. Not the one at the library, but an index of voters who had mailed him letters of support during his previous runs for the White House. Since his first campaign in 1896 he and his staff had taken special care to record the name, address, and a bit about what issue most moved them to support his campaign and kept them on file. Unfortunately by 1916 he still fell short of the information and support he needed to mount a campaign, but the idea of creating these lists of voters had begun.

Targeting remained fairly out of reach until technology and campaign budgets grew. If there is a true father of the modern microtargeting campaign it is the direct mail efforts begun in the 1960s and 1970s. These direct mail efforts focused on raising money or lobbing attacks against the opposition that spoke to a specific interest of the voter. These efforts were usually focused on rallying or garnering the support of the base, so campaigns aimed to identify the party faithful who may donate money or time, or who needed a helpful push to get them to the polls. It was in this political industry that the man credited with bringing the modern age of microtargeting to the fore developed his campaign chops—Republican strategist Karl Rove. Rove started working in the direct mail campaign business in Texas and early on saw the power of technology to create more efficiency in voter contact. In describing the rise of the man George W. Bush would label "the architect" of his 2004 re-election, Mark Halperin and John Harris talked with Rove about how he used technology to build his political consulting business in the 1980s, writing, "By using computer programs to organize his mailing lists . . . he might find that a planned mailing of 100,000 could be trimmed to 93,000 by identifying people who had moved out of a district or state . . . Additionally, overhauling the lists so that they included nine-digit zip codes was a worthwhile expense since it saved money later on postal rates. These were seemingly small things, hardly glamorous, but in Rove's line of work they were the difference between a profitable business and a struggling one (and often between winning an election and losing one)" (Halperin and Harris 2006).

As technology was expanding its footprint in political operations like Karl Rove's direct mail efforts, a revolution was occurring on the data side of the equation. Targeting had historically drawn from some common data pools that anyone could access, including public records and party data. Public agencies tracked voter addresses, party registration (in most states), donations to candidates (tracked by the Federal Election Commission in federal races and statewide agencies in local campaigns), and voting history. Campaigns could identify those who had donated time or money, those who had voted in caucuses or primaries, as well as basic demographics like where they lived and age. But beyond these basic political snapshots, oceans of data were developing thanks to data tracking and collection by advertising firms like Google and Facebook and pure data operations like BlueKai and Acxiom. The effect on targeting was profound. "By the 2000 election, political data firms like Aristotle had begun purchasing consumer data in bulk from companies like Acxiom. Now campaigns didn't just know you were a pro-choice teacher who once gave $40 to save the endangered Rocky Mountain swamp gnat; they also could have a data firm sort you by what type of magazines you subscribed to and where you bought your T-shirts. The fifth source, the increasingly powerful email lists, track which blasts you respond to, the links you click on, and whether you unsubscribe" (Murphy 2012). This mixing of advertising/marketing data and the political tracking that had been done for decades created a far more complete and complex snapshot of voters that campaigns could analyze to find trends and develop groups of voters at which they could aim specific messages.

Targeting and technology were merging, and the quest for the perfect list of voters became something more realistic. Like direct mail itself, this technology grew out of the marketing world for corporate America and took some time to infiltrate politics. Large retailers like Target, Amazon, and the U.S. Postal Service have invested in predictive analytics teams to analyze behavior based on data they can collect and purchase. This analysis allows them to create "market segmentations" of people who can be communicated to in a way that appeals to their habits—Target, for example, seeks to draw parents-to-be to their stores in the hopes of creating a new habit of shopping there after the children are born. This segmentation and targeted appeal moved solidly into the modern political campaign in 2004. That year, Rove, still tuned into the power of technology to improve their list of voters, had President Bush's campaign hire TargetPoint Consulting for $3 million to identify and communicate with voters in 18 states. The results were dramatic. That year the campaign specifically contacted 84 percent of the people who voted for the president in Florida, up from 33 percent in 2000. In Iowa, the campaign reached 92 percent of his eventual voters, up from 50 percent in 2000. TargetPoint describes its process as a mix of customer relationship management, advanced marketing techniques, and traditional political targeting. It gives the example, "A group of 'Health Care Concerned Moderates' might receive literature from local doctors on GOP alternatives to nationalized medicine, while 'Anti-Tax Tea Party Goers' might get an automated call from Grover Norquist and Americans for Tax Reform; while the 'Liberal Leaning Post-Graduate Singles' would get no contact at all even if they lived right next door to each other" (TargetPoint 2015).

Campaigns could now organize their approach to voters, no matter how they planned to appeal to them. Candidates could tailor a stump speech or advertising buy, but it was used more deliberately in efforts to connect specifically with a given voter. Campaigns could identify what "type" or market segment a voter likely is and then tailor the direct mail message or inform the campaign volunteer knocking on that door what message may most appeal to the person answering the door. Campaign volunteers would come to the door not looking to talk to anyone who answered, but rather a specific person in the household the campaign had identified. As good as TargetPoint was in 2004 for President Bush, the use of and effectiveness of this form of communication took another leap in 2008 during the campaign of Senator Barack Obama. The Obama campaign hired Ken Strasma, whose targeting campaign under Kerry had been bested by TargetPoint. But unlike 2004, Democrats sought to push the limits of microtargeting in 2008. Strasma "described the Obama campaign as a two-year research and development project, 'with the most aggressive testing of microtargeting models that I have ever seen' . . . The Obama campaign used telephone IDs, asking hundreds of thousands of voters who they were supporting and how they felt on particular issues. This information, combined with demographic, commercial information and some proprietary methods was used to build statistical models predicting how others would vote" (Johnson 2011). The Obama campaign had moved beyond just targeting likely voters or historically liberal voters and instead became predictive, seeking to connect the past behavior in politics AND the real world into a mathematical model of electoral behavior, complete with possible topics and personalities that may prompt political action or involvement.

Still, this staggering data campaign existed only at the highest levels of politics—fueling primarily only presidential campaigns or large-scale advertising and direct mail efforts by well-funded independent groups. At the congressional level or statewide level, microtargeting was occurring, but at a far less grandiose scale. For these campaigns, microtargeting has come to mean more coordinated use of fairly easily accessed data. They make better use of data about party registration and voting history to identify voters they feel are likely to support a candidate, but may not get out to vote. This allows them to work on getting the person to cast their ballot early or get to the voting booth on Election Day. Using these techniques, experts say, "For those people [who are likely to support you], they just need the extra push, and that's what this has mostly been about in recent election years. The question of how to target a persuadable voter is still something that campaigns know almost nothing about . . . That's kind of the Holy Grail. And the real question is whether there is any data out there from these new sources or old sources which can help a campaign figure [it] out" (PBS NewsHour 2014).

And there are other limitations to this data-driven campaign approach. Sometimes the data itself is hard for even the most sophisticated systems to understand. Consider gathering data from social media posts about the election. If a regular reader sees a young person write something like, "Donald Trump on Mexican immigrants. Stay classy, Donald"; or a traditional Republican write on Twitter, "I'm sure Hillary Clinton is not hiding anything in her email"; then most likely you would assume the user is being sarcastic. Computers struggle to make that assumption and so some data collections can actually inaccurately alter the profile of the voter the campaign is building. But scientists are already working on ways to detect and correct for such things, as everyone from presidential strategists to direct marketers are trying to crack the same codes.

One area where the impact of all this targeting is only partially understood is in the media coverage of politics, campaigns, and public issues. Mass media has historically been unaffected by the targeting of consumers or voters by candidates or advertisers. These outlets offered broad platforms for candidates to direct messages to large swaths of a district or state. Newspapers, magazines, radio, and especially television were the platforms campaigns used to advertise, and then direct mail was the primary tool of the targeted communications. The evolution of the Internet has altered this as media consumption by voters shifts from traditional mass media to a media driven by many of the same data-fueled personalization tools that campaigns use to target voters. Digital news outlets and the search engines that direct people to them have many of the same data collection and utilization goals that prompt them to tailor information to voters. Therefore, if you are a regular Facebook user, or are exposed to ads produced by Google, the microtargeting that campaigns use to send you a flyer on an issue critical to you is also being used to target the ads you see across the Internet. It is not unusual for a voter to see advertising online and across news outlets for only one candidate through the course of the campaign if the competing campaign does not see them as a likely supporter.

So campaign messaging, whether through direct mail or consumed through online campaign ads, is fundamentally different than what appears in the 30-second ad or the newspaper ad. The content may not appear that different, but the reason you are seeing it is critically different. Mass media delivers these ads to you based on your geographic location and program you are watching. Such a shotgun-approach to voter targeting aims in a general way at a bloc of voters. The online ad appearing in the same channel or newspaper's Internet site, however, is targeted to a very specific voter type that you fall into.

The final thing to note about this marketing is its effect on coverage of the campaign. Reporters covering the campaign often rely on what they see and hear to inform the stories they do. An ad will prompt a reporter to dig into the claims or counter-claims that result, or do a story about the subject or the group that paid to send it out. In the modern world of microtargeted communication, the campaign looks very different to each individual and, so reporters struggle to see the entire picture of such a microtargeted, fragmented modern campaign. This is not to say the campaign may create fundamentally different messages for different groups, but rather the reporter struggles to see the strategy and issues that the campaign may be conveying to its core supporters as opposed to what it is broadcasting to the entire public.

In many ways, modern microtargeting campaigns are the natural evolution of the digital direct marketing that has allowed for the increased personalization of many aspects of modern media consumption—like the recommendations on Amazon or

Netflix—and the political targeting that has existed since the dawn of direct mail campaigns. These tendencies have existed within both the digital media and the campaign world for some time. As the science behind predictive analytics and big data becomes more powerful, this targeting will likely become only more sophisticated. How that will affect the way reporters cover campaigns, and the way that coverage is then consumed, is an unfolding story.

See also: Direct Mail Campaigning; Personalization and the Internet; Rove, Karl

Further Reading

Dreazen, Yochi. 2006. "Democrats, Playing Catch-Up, Tap Database to Woo Potential Voters." *Wall Street Journal*. October 31.

Halperin, Mark, and Harris, John. 2006. *The Way to Win: Taking the White House in 2008*. New York: Random House.

Johnson, Dennis. 2011. *Campaigning in the Twenty-First Century*. New York: Routledge.

Murphy, Tim. 2012. "Inside the Obama Campaign's Hard Drive." *Mother Jones*. September/October. Accessed July 21, 2015. http://www.motherjones.com/politics/2012/10/harper-reed-obama-campaign-microtargeting.

PBS NewsHour. 2014. "How 'Microtargeting' Works in Political Advertising." PBS. February 18. Accessed July 21, 2015. http://www.pbs.org/newshour/bb/how-microtargeting-works-political-advertising.

TargetPoint. 2015. "Helping to Better Understand MicroTargeting." Accessed July 22, 2015. http://www.targetpointconsulting.com/system/uploads/14/original/MicroTargeting_101_8-2009.pdf?1249570076.

MOTHER JONES

Mother Jones is a magazine and website that focuses on investigative reporting that they hope will influence policy and promote a more just society. Both news outlets are run by a nonprofit foundation and the resulting mix of advocacy and investigation has made the magazine a standard for liberal reporting for some 40 years. In part because of its reliance on donations and subscribers, the magazine has famously taken a "give 'em hell" approach, targeting the influence of big business on American life and politics.

The magazine launched in the mid-1970s as liberal activists and reporters basked in the afterglow of the 1960s, and more specifically looked to the power of investigative reporting that had just forced the most powerful man in the world, President Richard Nixon, to step down from office. The magazine formed in San Francisco and launched with a loose array of editors and writers. The group aimed to be anti-hierarchical, with each editor taking a turn atop the organization. With this unique structure, the new group would use its journalism in a way unlike investigative reporting that had marked the work of those covering Vietnam and Watergate. *Mother Jones* decided it would aim its investigative reporting at a different target—large corporations. The magazine, named after a fiery organizer of the United Mine

Workers who had famously declared, "Pray for the dead, and fight like hell for the living," soon decided it would take on one of the largest companies in the world, Ford. In looking back at its history, one of the original founders would point to the magazine's investigation of the Ford Pinto as the first important test. The magazine's business manager Mark Dowie launched an investigation that concluded not only that the car had killed at least 500 people and injured hundreds more, but "even before the first Pintos came off the assembly line, company engineers had warned management that the gas tank was dangerously close to the rear of the car. Ford executives then projected that it would cost them more money to shut down and re-tool their assembly line than to pay off the damage claims from the anticipated deaths and injuries. Dowie obtained the memo where they made these cost-benefit calculations" (Hochschild 2001). Ford viciously fought back, accusing the magazine of politically motivated, trumped-up charges. But soon Ford was forced to recall 1.5 million Pintos to be repaired and *Mother Jones* had arrived.

During the 1980s the magazine took on more international stories, spending a large part of its coverage on the anti-Communist policies in Central America that led the American government to back the work of the controversial rebel group the Contras who battled the Nicaraguan government of the Sandinistas. The magazine became itself part of the story when liberal activist Michael Moore, who would become famous later for producing documentaries on topics like the auto industry and gun violence, was fired as editor of the magazine in 1986. The magazine claimed it stemmed from different management styles, but many saw the magazine's move as punishing Moore for trying to kill a story that included some criticism of the Sandinista government. Moore sued for $2 million, but ended up settling for $58,000. Still the battle damaged the magazine while it was already working to stem a slow bleed of subscribers.

Mother Jones magazine is published by the nonprofit Foundation for National Progress, which essentially exists solely to publish the magazine (and now run the website). This system allowed the journal to appeal to a series of different sources of money, including subscribers, donors, foundations, and advertisers—a mix that served the magazine fairly well but has also shaped the attitude and audience of the publication. It continues to pride itself on its original reporting, pleading with website visitors, "Reporting takes resources. We are not a content farm or aggregators; we are shoe-leather reporters working on often hard-to-reach stories, in a skilled operation that takes talent, time, and tools. The in-depth stories, data dives, and cool visuals you see in *Mother Jones* are all built by us, for you, to inform the public debate" (*Mother Jones* n.d.). But it also has built a reputation for a hard line against corporations and relies on supporters who hold many of the same views, which ensures that the magazine has a fairly predictable approach to stories involving big business. Still the skepticism has led it to do hard-hitting and effective reporting on corporate malfeasance, including corporate salaries and unsafe food.

In the political arena, the magazine and website have traditionally taken a harder look at Republicans, but *Mother Jones* has also been known to take solid punches at Democrats. Still, the magazine's biggest "get" of the past decade was a series of short 60-second-or-less videos clips that would help shape the 2012 election. The video was a blurry, secretly shot excerpt of Republican presidential candidate Mitt Romney assessing the state of his race for the White House against President Barack Obama. Romney tells attendees at a Florida fundraiser, "There are 47 percent of the people who will vote for the president no matter what. All right, there are 47 percent who are with him, who are dependent upon government, who believe that they are victims, who believe the government has a responsibility to care for them, who believe that they are entitled to health care, to food, to housing, to you-name-it. That that's an entitlement. And the government should give it to them. And they will vote for this president no matter what . . . These are people who pay no income tax. [M]y job is not to worry about those people. I'll never convince them they should take personal responsibility and care for their lives" (Corn 2013). The video and the "47 percent" comment would resonate for the rest of the election and shape the political debate for years after, becoming political shorthand for the divide between the wealthy and the poor, the liberals and the conservatives. *Mother Jones* was the source of that video. The magazine's Washington bureau chief David Corn would later describe his reaction when he received the video, writing, "I was stunned. With conviction and passion, Romney had described the election as a face-off between the strivers (people like himself and the other 1-percenters in the room) and the parasitic hordes who sought to live off the hard work of the accomplished. He acknowledged that he was writing off the former" (Corn 2012). The magazine got the video because of Corn's work looking at Romney's connections to big business. His hard stance had convinced the leaker that the magazine was the right venue to give the video to and after a series of emails and secretly mailed hard drives with the full fundraiser, *Mother Jones* had *the* scoop of 2012.

That same no-holds-barred coverage of corporations and liberal voice on political issues has helped the magazine build a fairly stable subscription base, reporting more than 200,000 subscribers and some 8 million users across it digital and print properties. Those readers are both liberal and highly engaged in politics and public affairs. *Mother Jones* reports according to its own research that 94 percent of its readers vote and almost half have donated to a political candidate and 86 percent have donated to a nonprofit or charity. The news service continues to attract this audience with its own strong voice of activism and its focus on in-depth investigative work.

See also: Advocacy Journalism; Media Matters for America; Muckraking; *New Republic*; Nonprofit Journalism

Further Reading

Corn, David. 2012. "The Story Behind the 47 Percent Video." *Mother Jones*. December 31. Accessed August 20, 2015. http://www.motherjones.com/politics/2012/12/story-behind-47-video.

Corn, David. 2013. "Mitt Romney's Incredible 47-Percent Denial: 'Actually, I Didn't Say That.'" *Mother Jones*. July 29. Accessed June 14, 2016. http://www.motherjones.com/mojo/2013/07/mitt-romney-47-percent-denial.

Hochschild, Adam. 2001. "Mother Jones: The Magazine." *Mother Jones*. May/June Edition. Accessed August 20, 2015. http://www.motherjones.com/about/what-mother-jones/our-history.

"What Is Mother Jones?" *Mother Jones*. Accessed August 20, 2015. http://www.motherjones.com/about#02.

MSNBC

MSNBC began as an experimental effort to mix television and the emerging power of the Internet. Founded through a soon-to-be-problematic partnership between NBC News and tech giant Microsoft, the network billed itself as one of the first cross-platform news organizations. But as years wore on and the network struggled to grow its audience, it adopted more of an approach pioneered by competitor Fox News, embracing increasingly partisan talk shows as its primary reporting tool. Now, MSNBC offers less reporting and more talk than any other network and with its fairly overt liberal leaning, the network has carved itself a niche as the progressive alternative to Fox.

That is not what anyone envisioned in 1996 when Microsoft and NBC conceived and launched the 24-hour cable news channel. NBC had already taken a serious dive into cable news seven years earlier when it launched its business news channel CNBC, but MSNBC was seen as something different—a direct effort to compete with the only existing all-news cable channel CNN, the Cable News Network. MSNBC would launch the same year as a third cable news competitor—Fox News—and so it aimed to differentiate itself from the beginning. For the new channel, the difference would be the Internet. In the last promo to air before the channel went live on July 15, 1996, the network billed itself as something new, intoning, "The revolution begins here. From now on, the promise of the Internet and the power of television become one, because from now on NBC News and Microsoft will revolutionize the way you get news. MSNBC—a 24-hour cable and Internet news service. The future of news from the people you know" (Garber 2012). The network offered slightly longer, more in-depth reporting than CNN and pre-dated Fox News by four months. It used its website to focus on a single story, developing a far more slick design than many of its news competitors of the day. Early programming efforts actively sought to include multiple perspectives on the news, with conservative commentators like Laura Ingraham and Ann Coulter appearing on the network's program *The Contributors*.

Despite the early embrace of the Internet and some early demonstrations of its ability to break news—the network reported the crash of TWA 800 eight minutes before CNN on only its third day on the air—the network struggled to find viewers and soon had to deal with stormy relations between its owners. In Microsoft and NBC's deal, the network would be run by NBC but would receive healthy support from the half owner Microsoft—some $500 million, plus another $30 million a year in license fees. In return Microsoft owned half the station and the website over a 99-year partnership. It was a deal the tech firm almost immediately regretted. Within a year of launching, MSNBC would be forced to lay off 20 percent of its new staff as the network struggled to make money. Viewership remained lower than CNN and the digital connection wasn't profitable. The partnership would limp on for another 8 years, finally ending in 2005. As the *New York Times* reported at the end, "The less-than-celebratory nature of the breakup seemed to be underscored by the timing of the announcement. NBC and Microsoft released the news at 8 a.m. yesterday, the Friday before Christmas, when the offices of both companies were already closed for the holiday weekend. Of the two contacts listed on the release, one, from NBC, had a message on her office phone number saying she would be gone until Tuesday, and the other, from Microsoft, was at an airport with two toddlers ready to fly home for the holiday" (Carter 2005). The two would continue to work together on the website until 2012, but the original plan of a new kind of merging between digital and cable news never materialized. Still, the website, with an enormous amount of resources compared to many of its rivals, did have some early success. Run as a separate company from the television network, MSNBC. com became the most viewed news site in 1997, 1998, and 1999.

Despite its digital prowess, the on-air programming struggled to find its legs. In 1997, it hired ESPN sports yakker Keith Olbermann and his program drew some new viewers to the channel, but its other programming often drew decidedly mixed reviews. For example, *Entertainment Weekly* offered this withering take on a midday program in 2001: "MSNBC used to fill the afternoon with *HomePage*, a high-tech grab bag aimed at females, anchored by the Powerpuff Girls of journalism, Ashleigh Banfield, Mika Brzezinski, and Gina Gaston. The show, which had the gals gabbin' 'n' gigglin' one second, then putting on their Serious News Faces to read a disaster story off their TelePrompTers, was doomed, and the Florida recount gave MSNBC an excuse to break up the Powerpuffs and scatter them throughout the network's news-day schedule" (Tucker 2001). As the network sought to define its programming, it did add more of a focus on politics. Olbermann began talking more openly about his liberal take on the news and in 1999, MSNBC took over airing *Hardball with Chris Matthews* from CNBC. It added liberal Rachel Maddow as a 2008 political analyst and later gave her a program that drew sizable viewership. As Fox News continued its dominance, MSNBC added more programs that mirrored Fox, offering liberal counterprogramming to its conservative rival. For some years it worked, carving out a sizable audience behind Maddow, Olbermann, and Matthews. By 2013, MSNBC stood apart for its reliance on partisan talk shows. That year the Pew Research Center report "The State of the News Media" found that fully 85 percent of the network's content was commentary and opinion and only 15 percent was devoted to reporting.

This devotion to talk appears to be changing as the network once again overhauls itself to try and attract viewers and advertisers. By 2014 the president of MSNBC was telling the *New York Times* that its focus on politics as well as its liberal leanings had hurt the network, saying, "You can look at the dysfunction in Washington, the wariness about politics, the low approval ratings. That's had an impact. But we've got to adjust; we've got to evolve" (Carter 2014). That evolution has included a renewed focus on daily and breaking news. Many of the mid-day talk shows once hosted by Democratic politicians or liberal commentators have been scrapped, although liberal talkers still take up a healthy hunk of the primetime schedule. The network has come under more control from NBC News and that has helped fuel the shift towards more reporting. Andrew Lack, a veteran news executive, rejoined NBC in April and heads both the broadcast and cable news efforts. He told *Variety* in 2015 that he saw MSNBC's heavy focus on opinionated talk as flawed and has infused more hard news into the mix, saying, "It's just the beginning. We are early days. These were important steps, the first few steps, but there is a lot more we are thinking about. It's a long game, as I have said, and we are just at the beginning of it" (Steinberg 2015).

So, some 20 years into its history MSNBC remains a network still seeking the mix of news and commentary that can find and hold an audience and a regular source of income, but is likely to appear more like NBC News than it has in years.

See also: Cable News Networks; CNN; Fox News; Maddow, Rachel; NBC

Further Reading
Carter, Bill. 2005. "Microsoft Quits MSNBC TV, but Web Partnership Remains." *New York Times*. December 24. Accessed January 11, 2016. http://www.nytimes.com/2005/12/24/business/media/microsoft-quits-msnbc-tv-but-web-partnership-remains.html?_r=0.
Carter, Bill. 2014. "Leaning Forward, MSNBC Loses Ground to Rival CNN." *New York Times*. October 12. Accessed January 11, 2016. http://www.nytimes.com/2014/10/13/business/media/leaning-forward-msnbc-loses-ground-to-rival-cnn-.html.
Garber, Megan. 2012. "'The Revolution Begins Here': MSNBC's First Broadcast, July 1996." *Atlantic*. July 16. Accessed June 16, 2016. http://www.theatlantic.com/technology/archive/2012/07/the-revolution-begins-here-msnbcs-first-broadcast-july-1996/259855/.
Steinberg, Brian. 2015. "MSNBC to Undergo More Changes, NBC News Chief Andrew Lack Says." *Variety*. October 5. Accessed January 11, 2016. http://variety.com/2015/tv/news/msnbc-changes-news-chief-andrew-lack-1201610162.
Tucker, Ken. 2001. "The Spin Room, Hardball." Entertainment Weekly. February 16. Accessed January 11, 2016. http://www.ew.com/article/2001/02/16/spin-room-hardball.

MUCKRAKING

Muckraking is a form of investigative journalism that emerged at the dawn of the Progressive era in the twentieth century, but has come to stand for any reform journalism that seeks to identify and offer solutions for social problems. The original muckraking, which was fueled by the rise of popular magazines, also helped spur a range of political and civic reforms that sought to rein in the power of corporation on the political process. Muckraking helped spur the growth of the Progressive movement early in the twentieth century and although less affiliated with any specific movement now, it continues to influence the political process by raising difficult and controversial issues for public discussion.

The term has come to be a badge of honor for reporters who tackle challenging stories or those that speak to issues of justice or equity. The editors of one recent collection of pioneering journalism that stood up to power or uncovered corruption explained that the examples they chose "could not merely represent good writing and good reporting. Always, they had to, in a substantial way, contribute to change, the kind of change, in the American reform tradition, that we believe makes America a better place" (Serrin and Serrin 2002). Although this is what muckraking has come to mean in the modern parlance of journalism, that's not how Theodore Roosevelt intended it when he coined the term a century ago.

The term's official birth was an angry speech by the president aimed at discrediting the very reporters he had often sought advice from and attempted to befriend. Roosevelt had grown frustrated with the strident demands of the reporters who criticized everything from the monopolies dominating corporate America to unions for squelching worker freedom to government corruption at nearly every level. As the journalists took on more and more aspects of America, their targets became more personal, including friends of TR. It was a series published in *Cosmopolitan* on the state of U.S. Senate that finally pushed Roosevelt to fire back. David Graham Phillips had just published the first of a series of searing articles that came to be known as "The Treason of the Senate." The article had blasted the corrupt practices that filled the Senate and how many of the senators had purchased their seats. At that time, state legislatures rather than voters selected senators and many of the votes had been rigged. One of those, New York senator Chauncey M. Depew, had been targeted as a tool of the railroad interests who had taken some $50,000 in bribes. The article pushed Roosevelt, Depew's friend, to lash out at all forms of the investigative reporting. At a ceremony commemorating the laying of the cornerstone of what would later become the Cannon House Office Building, Roosevelt shot back at the journalists, declaring, "There is filth on the floor, and it must be scraped up with the muck rake; and there are times and places where this service is the most needed of all the services that can be performed. But the man who never does anything else, who never thinks or speaks or writes, save of his feats with the muck rake, speedily becomes, not a help but one of the most potent forces for evil" (Roosevelt 1906). Roosevelt's term, "the muck raker," borrowed from John Bunyan's *Pilgrim's Progress*, and sought to tar the reformers with an epithet that would highlight their radicalism. But in so doing Roosevelt created a term of defiance that seemed to fit the reporters of the period and would be turned to a compliment by investigative journalists for generations.

The original muckrakers flourished for a brief time—essentially 1902–1912— and are credited with helping fuel many of the Progressive era laws that sought to protect the public from unsafe labor practices, rid government of corruption, and end the laissez faire approach of government toward business. Although the concept of journalists crusading for the less fortunate and arguing for reform was not new, this approach was. First, there was the timing. As one pair of historians of the period noted, muckrakers emerged at the right time in the evolution of the press and the public. "Early in the century muckrakers had recognized that a sense of uneasiness about the malfunctioning political, economic, and social institutions which had begun to become evident several decades earlier was troubling increasing numbers of Americans . . . An audience was there, and the means for reaching them at hand. The muckrakers availed themselves of that fortuitous combination" (Stein and Harrison 1973). The muckraking magazines of the era—*McClure's, Cosmopolitan*, and *Collier's*—represented a new form of journalism. Part yellow journalist newspaper and part New England literary journal, these new periodicals aimed to market themselves to the growing middle class and even some working class readers because of their relatively cheap cost. Also the increasingly literate American public sought the mix of exposé and entertainment that these magazines offered, so soon these publications were reaching far beyond the elites of urban America.

Although it was magazines that would serve as the primary distribution mechanism for the muckrakers, many of them started out in daily newspapers. Lincoln Steffens, a highly influential editor and writer, grew out of this tradition. A reporter based in New York who covered police and other municipal issues, Steffens was hired away to join the new magazine *McClure's*. There he was given the thing he'd never had before as a journalist—time. At the magazine, he was granted the time necessary to put together well-reported investigations into city and state corruption. In 1902, as the city of St. Louis prepared to host the World's Fair, Steffens published his account of a city wrecked by corruption. He wrote, "Go to St. Louis and you will find the habit of civic pride in them; they still boast. The visitor is told of the wealth of the residents, of the financial strength of the banks, and of the growing importance of the industries, yet he sees poorly paved, refuse-burdened streets, and dusty or mud-covered alleys; he passes a ramshackle fire-trap crowded with the sick, and learns that it is the City Hospital . . . he calls at the new City Hall, and finds half the entrance boarded with pine planks to cover up the unfinished interior. Finally, he turns a tap in the hotel, to see liquid mud flow into wash-basin or bath-tub" (Weinberg and Weinberg 1961). Steffens also served as an editor at *McClure's* and worked with many of the other muckrakers including Ida Tarbell and Ray Stannard Baker, whose 1903 piece, "The Right to Work," marked a critical piece on the state of mining and the life of those who dare cross strike lines.

The muckrakers were a diverse array of reporters and writers. Some, like Ida Tarbell, essentially were historians. Tarbell, whose 1903 report on the Standard Oil Company helped spur the United States to break the oil monopoly up, used a historical approach to inform her work. It was through the intense use of documents and interviews that Tarbell built her case against John D. Rockefeller and his huge corporation. The reporting now reads almost like a textbook about the company as Tarbell walks the reader through the early days of the American oil business and how Rockefeller's hard-nosed business practices forced competitors into his company or out of business altogether. The story was a personal one, as Tarbell's own father had been one of those businessmen to fall before the Standard Oil machine. Tarbell seemed to recognize that the issues she and other muckrakers sought to expose and change were not new and that for years before their work, "Men struggled to get at causes, to find corrections, to humanize and socialize the country, for then as now there were those who dreamed of a good world although at times it seemed to them to be going mad" (Fitzpatrick 1994). But her reporting sought to achieve what others had failed to do—change.

And that may be the one unifying idea that connects the muckrakers. The traditional journalist of the day, Steffens was connected to the document-based history writer Tarbell, and both were seen in the same light as fiction writer Upton Sinclair. Sinclair, an avowed socialist, sought to raise awareness of the plight facing workers in one of the most brutal and dangerous fields of the day—meatpacking. Sinclair told the story through the fictional story of Jurgis Rudkus, a Lithuanian immigrant struggling to support his family. To research the book Sinclair went undercover to work in a meatpacking plant in 1904. When his book was published it became a sensation and the American public had a strong reaction to it, but not the one Sinclair wanted. The book sold 1 million copies in the first year in publication, but instead of reacting to how the businesses treat their workers, Americans reacted with horror to the filth that their meat was butchered under and demanded change. His work helped prompt the government to pass the Pure Food and Drug Act in 1906. "I aimed at the public's heart," Sinclair would later admit, "and by accident I hit it in the stomach" (Schlosser 2006). But like Steffens and Tarbell, Sinclair's work aimed at producing change. These reporters wanted to do more than just document the failings of society and government. They wanted to fix them. As the historian of the muckraking movement wrote, "Muckraking achieved its place in history by bringing together an unusual corps of talented and earnest writers who persuaded readers that they were discussing not petty or personal matters, but events which affected the entire nation. In effect, readers were made aware that social crises far away affected them directly or indirectly, and were fascinating and educational in their own right" (Filler 1976).

To many, producing change meant becoming more overtly political, which differs from modern current investigative reporting. These early reformers saw their reporting as often an act of political protest. Sinclair, Steffens, and fellow muckraker Charles Edward Russell were all socialists, and so their reporting was part of the effort to build a case against capitalism, by proposing solutions. Steffens was particularly forceful in this. "Having examined 'the shame of our cities' to the satisfaction of his readers, [he] turned (as did many other muckrakers and progressives) to the problem of constructive thinking. A product of Steffens's effort was his *Upbuilders* (1909) . . . He urged reformers to avoid the liquor issue, which, he insisted, confused perspectives and broke up movements" (Filler 1976). He also outlined a political philosophy that would mix his intellectual socialism with American democracy. In that book's intro he argued, "The first rule for the political reformer is: Go to the voters. And the reason seems to be, not that the people are better than their betters, but that they are more disinterested; they are not possessed by possessions; they have not so many 'things' and 'friends.' They can afford, they are free to be fair." This philosophy fueled many of the reforms of the Progressive era. Muckrakers helped spur laws that ended child labor, and the Seventeenth Amendment that allowed the voters to choose their senators.

Muckraking remains a major component of political reporting. Many reformers who want to change the system enter politics, nonprofits, political advocacy. Some enter journalism. These journalists, should they pursue deep investigations, are the descendants of the muckrakers, using the tools of the trade to conduct wide-reaching investigations into injustice and disparities in the system and then connect these issues directly to voters. The literary editor Edwin Slosson would come to the defense of the original muckrakers in 1906, as Roosevelt and other political figures sought to discredit them. In words that still resonate today, he wrote of the work, "It has taken the tale of facts from the year books and the official reports from the statutes and the decisions, and from unwilling witnesses before investigating committees, and has wrought them into narratives that stir the blood. Its writers have seen in the dead material that which only the imaginative insight ever sees—their significance, their relation to life, their potential striking force" (Filler 1993).

This kind of reporting is still done. The magazine *Mother Jones* prides itself as a modern muckrake and sites like ProPublica sound oddly familiar for those who studied the muckrakers: A group of journalists, empowered by technological and audience shifts that allow them to publish and distribute more affordably, seize the moment and use these tools to bring what was previously hidden or un-reported to light. Stories that capture the public attention can trigger or fundamentally change political debate. Reports on deficiencies in veterans' care prompts firings and reform. Bloggers uncovering lax reporting by CBS News can lead to a retraction and the retirement of a long-time anchor. Journalism's impact on the political process comes from those who investigate—whether they have an overt agenda or simply want to tell the story—and that process is the real heir to the muckraker mantle. Although it was meant as an insult by a politician angered by the work of journalists, muckraking remains a powerful inclination in the media and when done well and accurately can be a force to help drive public opinion on an issue.

See also: Advocacy Journalism; Nonprofit Journalism

Further Reading

Roosevelt, Theodore. 1906. "The Man with the Muck Rake." PBS. Accessed July 9, 2015. http://www.pbs.org/wgbh/americanexperience/features/primary-resources/tr-muck-rake.

Schlosser, Eric. 2006. "'I Aimed For The Public's Heart, and . . . Hit It in the Stomach.'" *The Chicago Tribune*. May 21. Accessed August 31, 2015. http://articles.chicagotribune.com/2006-05-21/features/0605210414_1_upton-sinclair-trust-free.

Serrin, Judith, and William Serrin. 2002. *Muckraking!: The Journalism That Changed America*. New York: The New Press.

Stein, Harry, and John Harrison. 1973. "Muckraking Journalism in Twentieth-Century America." In *Muckraking: Past, Present and Future*. Edited by John Harrison and Harry Stein. University Park: The Pennsylvania State University Press.

Weinberg, Arthur, and Lila Shaffer Weinberg. 1961. *The Muckrakers*. Champagne, IL: University of Illinois Press.

MURROW, EDWARD R. (1908–1965)

The man who pioneered many of the reporting techniques that became the standard for radio and later television news and who stood up to the anticommunist hysteria of Senator Joseph McCarthy seemed destined for a very different life when he was born into a family that lived without electricity in rural North Carolina in 1908. But Edward R. Murrow would not stay in that impoverished home in Polecat Creek and would instead build the Columbia Broadcasting System news division in the heat of World War II, become the voice of the war to millions of Americans back home, and push television news to be more than just entertainment.

In considering the profound legacy of Murrow on broadcast news, public radio icon Bob Edwards would write, "The profession looks so bad today, in part, because Murrow set the standard so high at its birth. We see a bit of his legacy every time there is an important story and broadcast journalism functions as it's supposed to. It's important to remember that once upon a time we turned to radio and television to entertain us and nothing more. If we expect the broadcast media to inform us, educate us, and enlighten us, it's because Edward R. Murrow led us to believe that they would" (Edwards 2004).

Egbert Roscoe Murrow got his first taste of the wider world at six, when his family packed up and moved across the country to a small town in Washington State. Murrow would go to college at what would become Washington State University, while looking beyond to the national stage. In college he became active in politics and attended the National Student Federation of America. There his address urging college students to be more interested in national and world affairs led to his election as president of the federation and helped him garner attention. Soon after graduation in 1930 he landed a job at the Institute of International Education. The institute found itself at the center of efforts to get German scholars out of Nazi-controlled parts of Europe. It was this connection with those scholars and other academics, and not his desire to be an on-air celebrity, that landed Murrow at CBS.

The Columbia Broadcasting Service hired Murrow in 1937 to book lectures and interviews in Europe with key European leaders and academics. His job was to line up these figures to talk with hosts back in America before the two giants of NBC—the blue and the red network—scooped them up. But just a year later CBS asked Murrow and colleague William Shirer to put together a live news roundup about the annexation of Austria by the increasingly aggressive Germany. Murrow reported from Vienna and discussed the reaction around Europe with others in Berlin, Paris, London, and Washington, D.C. The program went nearly flawlessly and served as a sort of model for breaking news broadcasts, one that continues essentially to this day. Murrow would go on to report on the war and fly aboard dozens of bombing missions. He also broadcast rumors of the widespread killing of Jews as early as 1942 and was one of the first reporters to enter Buchenwald death camp. The *New York Times* would eulogize Murrow in 1965 by writing of how his reporting from Europe had been delivered with "compelling precision," describing his work by writing, "Had a London street just been bombed out? The young correspondent was soon there in helmet, gray flannel trousers and sport coat, quietly describing everything he saw against the urgent sound patterns of rescue operations. Or he would be in a plane on a combat mission, broadcasting live on the return leg and describing the bombing he had watched as 'orchestrated hell'" (*New York Times* 1965). His reporting on incidents as they happened and his almost innate ability to conceive of news programming that mixed reporters in multiple locations established CBS News as a leader in broadcasting and made Murrow a celebrity at home.

Upon his return he, along with his network, turned their attention to the emerging technology of television. By 1951 Murrow moved his regular program *Hear It Now* to television and changed the name to *See It Now*. In his first broadcast in November of that year he cautioned, "This is an old team, trying to learn a new trade." The team Murrow had helped recruit, which included Shirer and Eric Sevareid, Charles Collingwood, and Howard K. Smith, came to be known as "Murrow's Boys" and helped build the CBS News division on radio and this new effort on television. Murrow was intrigued by television but also deeply disturbed by its growing use to entertain rather than inform. He developed *See It Now* into a weekly news program and began sending reporters around the country to shoot film and bring it back to New York to be edited into a program. Despite his early efforts, fear of government regulations of broadcasters had somewhat suppressed radio and television's investigative spirit, as crossing the government could conceivably earn CBS and local stations large fines or even potentially cost them their license to broadcast. So when it was an act of some determination when he went on the air in March 1954 and declared:

Tonight *See it Now* devotes its entire half hour to a report on Senator Joseph R. McCarthy told mainly in his own words and pictures . . . Because a report on Senator McCarthy is by definition controversial, we want to say exactly what we mean to say, and I request your permission to read from the script whatever remarks Murrow and Friendly may make. If the Senator feels that we have done violence to his words or pictures and so desires to speak, to answer himself, an opportunity will be afforded him on this program. Our working thesis tonight is this question: If this fight against Communism is made a fight between America's two great political parties, the American people know that one of these parties will be destroyed, and the Republic cannot endure very long as a one party system. (Media Resource Center)

McCarthy's anti-Communist investigations had paralyzed many within the media and government. To be labeled a Communist or even a sympathizer could cost people their jobs and blacklist them. Murrow, along with producer Fred Friendly, constructed a devastating 30-minute documentary that used McCarthy's own statements and attacks against him. In the wake of the broadcast, President Dwight Eisenhower and others would speak out against McCarthy and he would soon be censured by the Senate. The moment clarified the power of television to affect public opinion in a way that print had failed to, as well as the power of personality to shape television. Murrow was respected and McCarthy appeared petulant and mean-spirited.

Still Murrow and Friendly had to fight for airtime on a network making enormous sums from movies and comedies. By 1958, Murrow would challenge those making the decisions at television stations to do more with the medium, saying, "This instrument can teach, it can illuminate; yes, and even it can inspire. But it can do so only to the extent that humans are determined to use it to those ends. Otherwise, it's nothing but wires and lights in a box. There is a great and perhaps decisive battle to be fought against ignorance, intolerance and indifference. This weapon of television could be useful" (Murrow 1958).

Murrow would produce a handful of television broadcasts in the late 1950s for CBS and by 1960 he was producing his last piece, a groundbreaking news documentary about farm workers in America called *Harvest of Shame*. Murrow left CBS to join the new Kennedy administration where he worked at the United States Information Agency, helping broadcast pro-democracy news and information around the world. But the real mark he left was in the people he brought to CBS and the standards he set. One of those who worked with Murrow was Mike Wallace, who would go on to fame at *60 Minutes*. Decades later, Wallace would recall advice Murrow had given him early in his career, saying, "The thing you have to remember is that just because your voice carries halfway around the world, you are no wiser than when it carried only to the end of the bar." That idea helps capture what Wallace said was Murrow's never-calmed nerves about television. Wallace would later recall, "Ed Murrow's fear when he left television was that television wasn't living up to its possibilities as he saw them. He used to marvel at the electronic wonders the scientists had dreamed up, and then despair that we, who program television, news and entertainment, were not sufficiently honoring the tool we had been given in the caliber of our broadcasts" (CBS News 2015).

See also: CBS News; Documentary Films; Infotainment

Further Reading

"Edward R. Murrow, Broadcaster and Ex-Chief of U.S.I.A., Dies." 1965. *New York Times.* April 28. Accessed January 7, 2016. http://www.nytimes.com/learning/general/onthis day/bday/0425.html.

"Edward R. Murrow's Advice." 2015. CBS News. April 27. Accessed January 7, 2016. http://www.cbsnews.com/news/edward-r-murrow-first-televised-broadcast.

Edwards, Bob. 2004. *Edward R. Murrow and the Birth of Broadcast Journalism.* Hoboken, NJ: John Wiley & Sons, Inc.

Media Resource Center. 2006. "A Report on Senator Joseph R. McCarthy." Library, University of California, Berkeley. Accessed June 14, 2016. http://www.lib.berkeley.edu/MRC/murrowmccarthy.html.

Murrow, Edward. 1958. "Radio and Television News Directors Association Speech." Radio Television Digital News Association. October 15. Accessed January 4, 2016. http://www.rtdna.org/content/edward_r_murrow_s_1958_wires_lights_in_a_box_speech.